Personality

Temperament, Social Behavior, and the Self

Arnold H. Buss
The University of Texas at Austin

Allyn and Bacon
Boston • London • Toronto • Sydney • Tokyo • Singapore

To Mimi

Executive Editor: Laura Pearson
Vice-President, Publisher: Susan Badger
Editorial Assistant: Jennifer Normandin
Marketing Manager: Joyce Nilsen
Production Coordinator: Holly Crawford
Editorial-Production Service: Connie Leavitt/Camden Type 'n Graphics
Composition Buyer: Linda Cox
Cover Administrator: Linda Knowles
Cover Designer: Suzanne Harbison
Manufacturing Buyer: Megan Cochran

This book is printed on recycled, acid-free paper.

Library of Congress Cataloging-in-Publication Data

Buss, Arnold H.
  Personality : temperament, social behavior, and the self / Arnold
H. Buss.
    p. cm.
  Includes bibliographical references and indexes.
  ISBN 0–205–14069–6
  1. Personality. 2. Personality—Social aspects. I. Title.
BF698.B877 1955
155.2—dc20   93–44703
                                                      CIP

Printed in the United States of America

10 9 8 7 6 5 4 3 2 1   99 98 97 96 95 94

Contents

Preface

Most personality texts are different from other texts in being organized around theories or approaches. The reader discovers facts about personality only in the context of a particular theoretical perspective. In other areas—social psychology, learning, and cognition, for example—texts are organized around content areas. Theory is not ignored, but it does not determine how the book is organized. Rather, the focus, appropriately, is on the various topics that make up the field of study.

This book is like texts in other areas of psychology in being organized largely around content areas. It emphasizes the methods of mainstream psychology: experiments, controlled observations, and psychometrically rigorous questionnaires. It also focuses on normal personality and offers explanations that originate in mainstream psychology. Readers are expected to have some familiarity with these determinants of personality, such as learning, motivation, cognition, and development, though detailed knowledge is not necessary.

The field of personality is too broad for any single text to encompass it. In selecting particular topics of personality, Chapters 3–11, I used three related criteria. First, knowledge about the topic is required for a full understanding of the personality of most people. Second, the behavior occurs throughout life and has been studied in children as well as adults. Third, the topic is currently being heavily researched or has endured over decades as an object of research, as reflected in the three major journals that deal with personality: *Journal of Personality and Social Psychology*, *Journal of Personality*, and *Journal of Research in Personality*.

Features to Look For

The methods used to study personality should not be presented devoid of content, for that would be like studying anatomy without a cadaver. Similarly, the origins of personality would be mere abstractions if not accompanied by the behaviors they are intended to explain. My solution to these problems is to use a single topic as the content in introducing the methods of personality (Chapter 1) and the determinants of personality (Chapter 2). The topic must have been studied with a variety of methods and have many different determinants. A topic that clearly meets these criteria is aggression. As you learn about the methods and origins of personality (including theory), you also learn about the topic of aggression.

How shall we deal with history? One way is an introductory chapter on the history of the entire field. The problem, though, is that the topics of personality have very different histories. Thus the history of research and theory on aggression is different from that of temperament or self-esteem. Therefore I present a brief history of each topic separately, at the start of the chapter on that topic.

Chapters 3–11 deal with specific topics of personality. In each, behavior is analyzed into its components or even subcomponents. There are a number of ways to analyze behavior, which will be introduced in Chapter 1. Thus aggression may be divided descriptively, using the dichotomies of physical-verbal, direct-indirect, and attack-threat. A more conceptual analysis separates aggression into instrumental, affective, and cognitive components. Other analyses employ the dichotomies of personal-social, overt-covert, and active-passive. If a man is called aggressive, does he get into fights, argue a lot, have a quick temper, display vindictive resentment, or harbor suspicions? We must specify which of these behaviors he manifests; that is, we must obtain *detailed* knowledge about him. And analytic distinctions also *deepen* our understanding of personality, as you will see. Thus we want to know if an aggressive act derives from anger (intrinsic) or a nonemotional motive (extrinsic).

As study aids, there are compare-and-contrast tables in each chapter. I have also included tables that summarize data or list the items on questionnaires so that you learn precisely what is being studied. There are also citations in parentheses, indicating literature sources that are listed alphabetically in the References near the end of the book.

At the end of each of the first three sections, a commentary integrates themes or facts that have appeared within each separate chapter. Thus we may compare the sex differences from each chapter to discover any patterns across personality dispositions. Combinations of traits may inform us beyond our knowledge of each particular trait. Thus, a high-active, sociable person behaves differently from a low-active, sociable person. And we can observe where various analytic distinctions apply.

There is only one theme common to the fourth (last) section of the book: classes and continuity. Otherwise, the three chapters are too diverse to lend themselves to integration, so there is no commentary at the end of this section.

Acknowledgments

Steve Finn read the entire manuscript, offering great advice. David Cohen was a sounding board for ideas. My wife, Ruth, had levelheaded suggestions. Two reviewers, James Johnson of Illinois State University and John W. Nichols of Tulsa Junior College, made useful comments. Finally, I received help and encouragement from Susan Badger, Laura Pearson, and Jennifer Normandin of Allyn and Bacon, and from Connie Leavitt of Camden Type 'n Graphics.

PART I   FOUNDATIONS

Chapter 1

Introduction

Chapter 1 introduces the rest of the book, so it starts with an overview of the book's structure and contents. Then I discuss the dimensions of behavior relevant to subsequent chapters, using aggression to illustrate the points I make. The chapter closes with the major methods used in research on personality, again aggression providing illustrative examples.

Organization of the Book

I. Foundations

Part I offers information that will be useful throughout the book. Chapter 1 is outlined above. Chapter 2, Origins, deals not only with the sources of personality dispositions but also with how they are maintained over years and decades. The origin of personality has been the focus of older, broader theories of personality. In Chapter 2, however, I discuss origins that most personality psychologists agree are important—for example, heredity, development, and socialization. While theories differ in the weight they give to any particular source of personality, in Chapter 2 I attempt a neutral account of the major sources. I use aggression again to put meat on conceptual bones.

Chapters 3 and 4 are on *temperament*, which is defined as inherited tendencies that first appear in infancy and continue throughout life. Thus temperament may be regarded as a foundation on which other content areas of personality are built. For example, the temperament of sociability—the preference for being with others—exerts an influence on attachment, prosocial behavior, and dominance; and the temperament of emotionality is one determinant of shyness.

II. Social Behavior

Part II starts with *attachment* (Chapter 5), first between parent and infant, and then between adults in close relationships. Children who are securely attached are more likely to empathize with others and help them, that is, they are likely to engage in *prosocial behavior* (Chapter 6). The content area *dominance* (Chapter 7) involves struggles for power and status.

III. Self

The enormous research literature on the self-concept was reviewed by Wylie (1974, 1979), who concluded that the yield was meager and ambiguous. One reason for such a poor yield may be that the self-concept refers to anything you say about yourself, from something as important as your basic worth to something as trivial as whether you like broccoli. One solution to such chaos is to decide which aspects of the self-concept are important. There would probably be a consensus on four topics.

The first is *self-esteem* (Chapter 8), or how you evaluate yourself and your confidence in various situations. These issues are linked to *identity* (Chapter 9), which is who you are. Your awareness of self-esteem and identity, and of other private and public aspects of yourself, is *self-consciousness* (Chapter 10). Self-esteem, identity, and awareness of self all play a role in the self in social interaction, which includes *shyness* (Chapter 11).

IV. General Issues

There are also broad issues in personality that cut across the individual content areas of Chapters 3 through 11. Knowing the content areas is a prerequisite for understanding the broad issues, as the content areas offer examples that pin down the more abstract conceptual issues.

Disputed Issues

In Chapter 12 I discuss issues that have been debated over the last generation or so. Psychologists who study the senses, cognition, learning, motivation, brain-and-behavior, or development, to name just a few issues, seek general laws of behavior. These psychologists are not especially concerned about variations from one person to the next. But personality by its very nature involves individuals and how they differ. Therefore, personality psychologists study the dimensions along which people differ, how their enduring dispositions are organized, and the origins of these tendencies. These distinctly different perspectives and goals help define personality and how it is studied.

The study of personality assumes that individuals are reasonably consistent in their behavior across situations and over time. Which people tend to be more consistent? Which behaviors? In which settings? If we know a person's personality, can we predict how that individual will behave in specific situations?

Classification

The last question leads directly into the topic of Chapter 13, classification in the study of personality. Most classifications strive for a few overarching categories. How and why do we classify? What are the advantages and disadvantages of classes versus dimensions in studying personality?

Personality and Abnormality

The field of personality abuts abnormal psychology. In Chapter 14 I consider the place of personality in abnormal psychology. For some abnormal conditions, personality is a major issue; for others, it is ancillary. One set of clinical problems has been designated *personality disorders*. Which areas of personality are relevant to these disorders? Some people, called *hardy*, seem to cope with the stresses of living, whereas others, called *vulnerable*, often develop clinical problems. Which aspects of personality tilt people toward hardiness? Which toward vulnerability?

Dimensions of Behavior

The behaviors relevant to personality can be analyzed into their components. There are several ways of partitioning particular behaviors, each offering its own enlightenment. Recall that the content area of aggression will be used to provide concrete examples of the various distinctions among behaviors.

Behavioral Systems

Instrumental Acts

Instrumental acts have an impact on the environment. They are so named because they are often instrumental in attaining a goal or a reward, or in avoiding punishment. Thus the instrumental component of aggression, indeed, the defining feature of the behavioral class called aggression, is the act of hurting or harming another individual, trying to do so, or threatening to do so. There are several closely related categories of instrumental aggression.

Most aggressive acts are *direct*: A person attacks a victim. A major kind of direct aggression is *physical aggression*. We can beat with fists, slap with hands, kick with feet, scratch with nails, or even bite with teeth. As tool users, we can escalate the hurt or harm with such weapons as knives, spears, axes, arrows, clubs, and a variety of guns. Physical aggression is ordinarily accompanied or preceded by facial expressions (staring or a ferocious look) and bodily preparations for attack (clenched fists or bared teeth). These accessory behaviors, through their link with aggressive acts, can come to signal forthcoming aggression. As such they constitute *threats* of physical aggression.

An alternative to physical attack is *verbal aggression*. We can curse, jeer, censure, reprove, chide, deride, mock, ridicule, and taunt others, often causing psychological distress, anxiety, or loss of self-esteem. The verbal content of the attack is often accompanied by such stylistic, paralinguistic features as yelling and screaming. And threats can be delivered verbally: a promise to deliver bodily or psychological harm. A few years ago, a television evangelist publicly rebuked another television evangelist (direct verbal aggression). The victim thereupon collected evidence of sexual indiscretions by his attacker and threatened to reveal them unless he received a public apology (threat of direct aggression). When the threat did not work, the victim made public his attacker's indiscretions, causing the latter a severe loss of reputation and income.

Another category of attack, seen mainly in humans, is *indirect aggression*, in which the victim typically is not present but is harmed in a roundabout way. The aggressor may leave behind a booby trap that explodes when the victim triggers it. The attacker may get at the victim by harming the latter's wife, husband, or child. Other options are letting air out of someone's tires, setting fire to the car, spilling garbage on the lawn, knocking down a fence, or trashing the bedroom. All these are instances of indirect physical aggression.

Examples of its counterpart, indirect verbal aggression, include malicious gossip about someone or the deliberate spread of lies (cheating, stealing, infidelity) that will ruin the victim's reputation. In political contests, such indirect aggression, especially in television advertisements, now seems as common as the more direct verbal aggression that occurs in political debates.

There is also the threat of indirect verbal aggression. This is the ploy of the blackmailer who, unless paid off, promises to publicize facts or even fabrications that would dishonor the victim's family.

In brief, there are three dichotomies of aggressive acts: direct-indirect, physical-verbal, and attack-threat. These dichotomies generate eight kinds of aggressive actions, as shown in Table 1.1.

Affect

Affect is another word for emotion, which itself has two components, as illustrated by anger, the emotion closely linked to aggressive acts. Anger involves *physiological arousal*. Heart rate and breathing accelerate, blood pressure rises, blood is directed away from the gut to the large skeletal muscles, and sugar is mobilized

TABLE 1.1   Dichotomies of Aggressive Behavior

	Physical	Verbal
Direct		
Attack	Fight	Taunt, curse
Threat	Get ready to fight	Promise harm
Indirect		
Attack	Harm victim's kin	Spread gossip
Threat	Threaten victim's kin	Blackmail victim's kin

in the blood. These are preparations for the massive muscular effort that occurs in physical aggression (Cannon, 1929), for anger is often a precursor to aggression. As an emergency reaction, physiological arousal cannot last long. It sets in motion homeostatic mechanisms that eventually restore the body to its resting state.

Anger also has an *expressive aspect*. The brows are knitted, the nose is slightly flared, the mouth is grim or the teeth are bared, and the fists are clenched. The facial characteristics of anger are recognized in all the cultures in which it has been studied, which suggests that these features are universal (Ekman & Friesen, 1971). Like their physiological counterparts, these expressions of anger are not long-lasting. Virtually no one walks around for hours with bared teeth, clenched fists, and a scowling mien.

Intrinsic and Extrinsic Aggression

Aggression often occurs when a person is angry. Such aggression was originally called *angry aggression* (Buss, 1961), but the term *intrinsic aggression* is preferred here for reasons to become apparent. Intrinsic aggression typically starts with insults, threats, or attack by others, or even with the angry person's annoyance at the nonaggressive actions of others.

The reward for intrinsic aggression is hurt or harm to the victim. The reward is intrinsic in that it derives directly from the act, and no other reward is needed for the aggressor to be satisfied. Said another way, the angry aggressor's intent is to hurt or harm the victim, which means that the aggressive act is itself pleasurable, no outside reward being necessary. This motive to hurt another person is usually transient, waning as the arousal of anger dissipates. Meanwhile, an enraged person may do considerable harm, as may be seen in statistics on homicide. A large percentage of murders in this country are committed by family members within the home. Very frequently, murder is the outcome of a verbal battle in which at least one enraged person picks up the nearest weapon, usually a knife or gun, and uses it.

Does an attack always occur in the presence of anger? Is the motive of the aggressor always a desire to hurt or harm the victim? The answer to both questions is no. Aggression can occur in the absence of anger, thus with little or no physiological arousal. The reward can be any of the incentives that are commonly sought when a person engages in nonaggressive behavior. This kind of aggression is called *extrinsic aggression* because the reward is not specific to aggression but is often the consequence of *any* instrumental behavior. The aggressor who uses attack might try nonaggressive behavior if it led to the sought-after rewards.

Some examples may help to clarify the distinction. A mugger wants his victim's money, but the victim is almost always unknown to the mugger, who therefore is unlikely to be angry at the victim. Without anger, the mugger may use threat but not hurt or harm his victim except as an incidental part of the aggressive act. Or the mugger may hurt his victim but derive no satisfaction from it, for his goal is only to steal money.

Similarly, when two politicians are contending for an electoral post, they often attack each other verbally, sometimes viciously. Again, they tend not to be angry nor wish the victim of the attack to be harmed or humiliated; they just want to win the election. There are other, nonaggressive means of winning elections, and they are sometimes employed. One way of reducing extrinsic aggression would be to ensure that nonaggressive ways of obtaining extrinsic rewards are easily available. To reduce angry aggression, however, it is necessary to diminish the intensity of anger.

Thus extrinsic aggression differs from intrinsic (angry) aggression, but this distinction does not preclude their occurring together. A mugger might become angry with a victim, and a politician might become enraged with an opponent. But each kind of aggression can and does occur in the absence of the other.

The differences between intrinsic and extrinsic aggression are summarized in Table 1.2. The terms *hurt* and *harm* have been used in both the table and the text. The difference between the terms is worth noting. One result of physical aggression, especially angry aggression, is pain to the victim however it is inflicted; this is hurt. But in the absence of injury, pain subsides and leaves no lasting physical imprint. Injury, of course, is an enduring consequence of physical aggression; it defines harm. Harm is not limited to physical injury but also includes the psychological damage that can result from physical or verbal aggression.

Cognition

Cognition includes a wide range of mental activities: thoughts, attributions, memories, fantasies, and planning. We are sometimes aware of these covert processes, and at other times, not. The cognitive component of aggression is *hostility*, which in part consists of dislike, ill will, and resentment toward others. Hostility also involves suspicion that others are lurking or that they mean harm. At first glance, it might not seem appropriate to place both resentment and suspicion under the heading of hostility, but, as we shall see, there is an empirical basis for doing so.

Hostility may accompany anger as an immediate reaction to a current situation. The negative cognitions of hostility, however, usually await later reflection. Then there is time to make sense out of previous events and to make negative attributions about others. Then there is time to mull over the harmful actions of others, either real or imagined. And if there is a belief in an eye for an eye, the hostile person can plot how to get even.

Hostility can occur even when there have been no prior attacks or slights, real or imagined. Others are disliked for no other reason than that they are different, which of course is an example of prejudice. Widespread hatred of others may occur simply because of their different nationality, religion, skin color, or sexual preference. For example, homophobia in this country is not the result of homosexuals harming

TABLE 1.2   Intrinsic versus Extrinsic Aggression

	Intrinsic aggression	Extrinsic aggression
Stimulus	Insult, attack, annoyance	Any incentive
Emotion	Anger, rage	Usually none
Reward	Hurt or harm to victim	Achievement of incentive

anyone. Most of those who harbor ill will toward homosexuals have few personal contacts with them and therefore rarely become angry with them or act aggressively toward them. Thus prejudice may be regarded as the prototype of hostility, for it often involves only negative cognitions, unaccompanied by anger or aggressive acts.

Anger and Hostility

Both anger and hostility may accompany aggressive acts or lead to them, which is perhaps why in everyday usage the concepts are interchangeable. But they *are* different. Hostility consists of dislike, ill will, and resentment toward others that can endure for years. Anger is an immediate negative reaction to a current situation, a transient reaction that involves physiological arousal and facial expressions. There is no particular bodily arousal in hostility, nor is there necessarily an expressive aspect. There is a Sicilian adage that revenge is best taken cold: no rage, just coolly getting even. Then how do we recognize hostility? By verbalizations of hatred, the avoidance of disliked persons, or, in its collective form, by prejudice.

As a temporary, arousal state, anger can be reduced by aggression, exercise, or even the passage of time. When aggression succeeds in diminishing anger, the process is called *catharsis* (see Buss, 1961, chap. 5). Hostility involves little or none of the arousal of anger and so is irrelevant to catharsis. Finally, other animals may have the emotional component, anger, but they appear to lack the higher cognitions necessary for hostility.

The various distinctions between hostility and anger are summarized in Table 1.3. The two of course are related, and they can occur together: Enduring hatred can lead to momentary rage, and temporary anger can lead to long-lasting hostility. However, a wife may become angry with her husband but not hate him. Or a bigot may dislike Jews but not be angry with them. Yet because each may occur in the absence of the other, it is important to distinguish between them.

Hostility and Aggression

Now consider the differences between hostility and aggressive behavior. A white who is prejudiced (hostility) may never become aggressive toward Blacks; a paid assassin (aggression) usually does not hate his victim. Aside from these examples, there is evidence that hostility and aggression are often independent. The aggression of children at play was observed in free play, and the children were asked

TABLE 1.3   Comparison of Anger and Hostility

	Anger	Hostility
Time	Immediate	(Usually) Subsequent
Duration	Temporary	Enduring
Autonomic arousal	High	Low
Catharsis	Sometimes	Never
Expressiveness	Yes	(Usually) No
Occurrence	Mammals	Humans

afterward whom they disliked (Shantz, 1986). Dislike (hostility) correlated $-.05$ with the frequency of physical aggression and $-.10$ with the frequency of verbal aggression. These findings represent one end of the spectrum of the relationship between hostility and aggressive behavior. Surely there are circumstances when the two are related, for sometimes we aggress against those we hate. But in other circumstances, as in children's free play, hatred and attacks may be unrelated, which is why hostility and aggression must be regarded as separate concepts.

Measures

How do we measure the instrumental, affective, and cognitive components of behavior? There are four basic kinds of measures.

The most commonly used measure is *frequency*. We can count the number of physical attacks—for example, on a playground, how often each child gets into fights, the number of arguments, or the number of temper outbursts.

We are also interested in the amplitude, or *intensity*, of behavior. Thus physical aggression can vary from a slap in the face to a punch on the jaw to stabbing with a knife, or from criticism to nasty, personal attack to cursing and screaming. Anger can be as mild as a child's pouting or as severe as a raging temper tantrum. And hostility can vary from dislike to bitter hatred.

A less commonly used but sometimes important measure is *latency*, or the time taken to initiate a response. On occasion, people may be spoiling for a fight or merely in a grouchy mood. Then the slightest remark by another person can trigger a brawl or a fierce argument. On other occasions, considerable time may elapse before an aggressive act occurs. And just as there are people who have a hair-trigger temper, there are others who are slow to anger.

The fourth measure is *duration*, or how long the behavior lasts. Sometimes a verbal attack occurs and is over in less than a minute. Other times, an argument can go on for hours. Anger is typically brief, for this heated emotion usually cools off in a matter of minutes. When anger lasts for hours, presumably it is sustained by the cognitions that occur in hostility. Most of us have had the experience of mulling over an insult or an unfair act, and the more we think about it, the more our anger is fueled. Without the support of hostile cognitions, however, anger typically dissipates. Thus the duration of behavior varies considerably, depending in part on which component is being assessed. Physically aggressive acts may be measured in minutes, and so can anger, unless it is supported by hostile cognitions and maintained for hours. Hostility may be measured in weeks, months, and even years.

Three Dichotomies

Personal-Social Dichotomy

The *personal-social dichotomy* would seem not to apply to aggression, which of course is social behavior. However, as will be seen, aggression can tilt toward either the personal side of the dichotomy or the social side.

Most instrumental aggression is direct, with the aggressor hurting or harming another person or attempting to do so; this is the personal aspect of aggression. But aggression can also be experienced vicariously, as, for example, watching others argue or seeing violence on television; this is the social aspect.

When we are angry, the negative affect is directed against the person who ostensibly gave cause for anger. Thus the anger is *other-directed*, that is, social. But sometimes we become angry with ourselves, which is *self-directed* anger. Self-directed anger represents the personal side of the dichotomy.

Aggression, by definition, is likely to hurt or harm others. The aggressor may be unconcerned about the damage that results, as in the case of a mugger who knocks down an elderly person and steals money. Such aggression may be called *egocentric* in that the attacker attends only to his own needs, to the exclusion of the harm he is causing. Such egocentricity may also occur in angry aggression, when the intent is to cause hurt or harm.

Most people, however, are socialized to regret causing harm. What may happen is that they realize that they have overreacted or that they have caused harm when they meant only to hurt. Another possibility is that the victim's reaction—crying or displaying signs of harm—may elicit regret or guilt in the attacker. Then the attacker's reaction is *sociocentric*, in that it takes into account the feelings of others.

Overt-Covert Dichotomy

Anger may be expressed (*overt*) in a variety of ways: staring, glaring, scowling, growling, bared teeth, lowered brows, clenched fists, or even screaming, such as when young children throw a temper tantrum. In older children and adults it may be inhibited (*covert*), so that it may be difficult to tell if the person is angry. There may be an intermediate mood here, in which the blatant signs of anger are suppressed and all that is observed is pouting; in older children and adults, the observed mood is more likely to be sulking.

The overt expression of anger may also indicate that an individual is aware of ongoing actions, affects, or cognitions. Thus we also have the *conscious-unconscious dichotomy*. When people bear ill will and resentment, they are often aware of it. But they may be unaware of such hostility and are surprised when they learn of it, either from a friend or a therapist. .

Active-Passive Dichotomy

The various examples of aggression offered have all been *active*—fighting and arguing, for example. But aggression may also be *passive*, when the aggressor interferes in some way with the victim. College sit-ins, which occupy the office of the college president, for example, and do not allow him to function are one form of passive aggression. The efforts of antiabortion groups to block access to abortion clinics are another. Though adults occasionally engage in passive aggression, children are more likely to exhibit such behavior, and in their case it is called *negativism*. A related immature behavior consists of deliberately acting hurt, with the implication that the other person is to blame. Not only children but also adults show this behavior, when they say, "You're killing me" or "You're making me sick." There is nothing active in such behavior, which makes it difficult to deal with.

There is a related active-passive dichotomy that might be called *push-pull*, in which people are pushed by needs or pulled by incentives. Thus an enraged man tends to be strongly motivated to aggress against the object of his anger. The anger is almost like a force that is impelling him to aggress. In the absence of anger, though, a child might want another child's desirable toy, which is tempting enough for the child to take it by force. As these examples reveal, intrinsic aggression represents push, and extrinsic aggression represents pull (temptation).

Some people seem to be in charge of their own destiny, or at least they believe they are. They control social situations by actively initiating interactions. In the area of aggression, this tendency may be seen in the behavior of bullies. The opposite tendency, being controlled by others, is exhibited by victims of bullies. The two tendencies, which occur in many areas of behavior, may be called *master versus pawn* of the environment.

For a summary of the three sets of dichotomies, see Table 1.4.

TABLE 1.4   Dichotomies of Behavior

Dichotomy	Aggressive examples
Personal-Social	
Direct	Attack
Vicarious	Observation of an attack
Other-directed	Anger at another
Self-directed	Anger at self
Egocentric	Uncaring aggression
Sociocentric	Regret after aggression
Overt-Covert	
Expressed	Temper tantrum
Inhibited	Unexpressed anger
Conscious	Aware of own hostility
Unconscious	Unaware of own hostility
Active-Passive	
Active	Attack
Passive	Negativism, acting hurt
Push	Intrinsic (angry) aggression
Pull	Extrinsic (cold) aggression
Master	Bully
Pawn	Victim

Methods

Personality may be studied by various methods, each providing information that the others may not offer, each with advantages and disadvantages. Consequently, no single method is sufficient as a means of studying personality, and the optimal strategy is to employ several different methods. When we obtain information by different methods and the findings converge, we can rely on the results.

This survey provides a sample of only the major methods of studying personality. Most of the commonly employed methods have been used to study aggression. The few that have not are useful for studying other behavior and will be mentioned in later chapters.

Laboratory

Highly Controlled Conditions

The laboratory offers controlled conditions, precision, and quantification and may allow us to infer causality. But the laboratory has its problems. The behavior being studied may be artificial, and it may be difficult to extrapolate the findings to everyday situations.

Physical aggression presents a particular challenge to researchers. There is the ethical problem of not allowing anyone to suffer hurt or harm, and the practical problem of quantifying physical aggression. And when subjects know that aggression is being investigated, they may alter their typical behavior. One solution to these various problems is an apparatus/procedure called the *aggression machine* (Buss, 1961).

The subject, let us say a man, is instructed that he will be the experimenter and will train another person (ostensibly a subject but really an experimental accomplice, hereafter called the victim) in a concept-learning task. The cover story is that we are studying the effect of the sex and personality of the experimenter on speed of learning.

The apparatus has two sides: the "experimenter's" side (the real subject) and the victim's side. The subject is shown how to present stimuli to the victim, and which responses are correct. Incorrect responses are to be followed by electric shock, the intensity chosen by the subject. There are ten shock buttons, representing increasing amperage of electric shock, which is delivered to one finger (attaching the electrode to a finger avoids any possible danger in the use of electric shock, which is well within safe levels in any event). The subject is given electric shock from buttons 1, 2, 3, and 5, so that he can feel what the victim will experience. The subject is told that the shock levels (and therefore the pain) continue to escalate from buttons 6 through 10.

The victim is brought in, surreptitiously turns off the shock, and then programs a series of correct and incorrect responses, constant for each "subject." The usual dependent variable is the average intensity of thirty-five electric shocks, a stable measure of the intensity of physical aggression. Afterward the real subject is debriefed as to the real purpose of the experiment.

One potential disadvantage of the aggression machine, indeed of any laboratory procedure, is artificiality, for no one uses electric shock as a means of aggression in everyday situations. However, the procedure does square with the definition of aggressive acts as those that hurt others or attempt to do so.

Furthermore, the facts that have emerged from this procedure are in accord with facts derived elsewhere. Thus it is known that men are more aggressive than women. In the laboratory, men aggress more than women, and male victims receive more aggression than female victims (Buss, 1966a). Frustration is believed to lead to aggression. In the laboratory, frustrated subjects aggress more intensely than control subjects, and, perhaps more interesting, verbally attacked subjects aggressed the most intensely of all (Geen, 1968). And the trait of aggressiveness, as assessed by questionnaire, correlates with aggression intensity in the laboratory (Scheier, Buss, & Buss, 1978). These various findings suggest that the laboratory procedure offers knowledge that generalizes to everyday situations.

Minimally Controlled Conditions

Behavior may also be studied in the laboratory under looser conditions, which do not constrict the subject so much. Such relaxation of control is especially useful with children, who tend to chafe when their movement is restricted.

A toy that lends itself especially well to the study of aggression is the Bobo doll. The doll is inflated to child-size and counterweighted to return to an upright position when struck. A child can pounce on the doll, punch it, kick it, toss it around, or even strike it with a mallet. Boys are observed to be more aggressive than girls, and children tend to imitate the aggressive behavior of adults with the doll (Bandura, Ross, & Ross, 1963).

Observation

Every day we see many examples of aggression, and the news on television seems to be full of violence. But aggression is rarely observed *systematically* in adults, probably because most adults object to being watched while they interact with others. Children, of course, are accustomed to being watched, and most observations of aggressive behavior are carried out in school and at camps. In a typical study, school-age children in England were monitored on the school playground during three six-week periods (Humphreys & Smith, 1987). Various categories of physical aggression were sampled: hit, kick, poke, maul, pounce, pile on, play-fight, chase, grab, push, hand wrestle, wrestle standing, sit on, and pull. If we were to observe adolescents and adults in everyday situations, it would be necessary to add a variety of aggressive acts involving such weapons as knives, clubs, chains, and guns.

Verbal aggression has also been observed in schoolchildren. One study demonstrated reasonable stability over an eight-month period for these categories: threatening to hurt others, ridiculing, teasing, ranting, shouting, and yelling (Deluty, 1985). If we were to observe adults in everyday situations, it would be necessary to add epithets, curses, sarcasm, and even irony.

This kind of research usually includes at least two observers, to counteract any bias that a single observer might have. The observers identify target behaviors or rate a particular kind of behavior, say, teasing, for intensity and frequency. A period of training smooths out differences among observers so that they can agree on how the children are actually behaving. It helps, of course, to have the permanent record that videotaping allows, but children are likely to be much more aware of a camera than of the mere presence of adult observers.

Knowledgeable Informants

It is a short step from observations to reports by parents, teachers, or schoolmates on the behavior of those whom they know well. One procedure uses a checklist of behaviors that a knowledgeable informant has observed over weeks, months, or years. Ghodsian-Carpey and Baker (1987) had mothers mark the following checklist of aggressive behaviors: destructiveness, attack, insult, verbal threat, yelling, screaming, teasing, and negativism. Identical twins were considerably more alike in these behaviors than were fraternal twins, an issue for Chapter 2.

A more popular procedure for the study of aggression is to identify those who are especially aggressive. This method is used mainly with children, and the ratings are necessarily done by those who know an entire group of children. Sometimes the informants are teachers or camp counselors, who have had contact with a group of children for weeks or months. When other children in the group are used as informants, the technique is called *peer nomination*. Eron, Walder, and Lefkowitz (1971) had schoolchildren nominate aggressive children by answering these questions:

Who does not obey the teacher?
Who gives dirty looks or sticks out their tongue at other children?
Who makes up stories and lies to get other children into trouble?
Who does things that bother others?
Who starts a fight over nothing?
Who pushes or shoves children?
Who gets what they want by fighting?
Who says mean things?

In peer nomination, children in a group compare other children in the group with their peers. The method is effective in that when children are identified as aggressive by a consensus of informants, these target children are likely to be aggressive. A drawback of the technique is that the informants are not trained, and they may confuse unpopularity with aggressiveness.

Eron and his colleagues also followed up the children in their study over a period of twenty-two years, an example of *longitudinal research* (Huesmann, Eron, Lefkowitz, & Walder, 1984). Children nominated as aggressive when they were eight years old were found twenty-two years later to be above average in aggressiveness, punishment of their children, and frequency of criminal offenses. Such research is rare because it is time-consuming and expensive, and it is difficult to track down subjects over the years. Difficult as it may be, however, it is worth the effort, because it is the only way we can discover the life course of individuals.

The Self-Report Questionnaire

Perhaps the most frequently used method of studying personality is a *self-report*, or questionnaire that is filled out by subjects about their own behavior. These questionnaires can be administered to large groups of subjects simultaneously, the questions are the same for all subjects, and the results are easily quantified. As an example of a self-report, consider a recent aggression questionnaire (Buss & Perry, 1992) that is a revised and updated version of a widely used older one (Buss & Durkee, 1957).

Construction

Like any other method, self-reports have their own problems. One problem with such questionnaires is that some people are reluctant to reveal much about themselves. This defensiveness may occur when personality is studied, but it is certain to occur when assessing aggressiveness. To minimize defensiveness and allow subjects to admit to behaviors that might be socially undesirable, we used several item-writing techniques in our aggression questionnaire. First, the items assumed that the undesirable state already existed, and the question concerned how it might be expressed: "When I get mad, I say nasty things." This kind of item minimizes value judgments about anger (everyone becomes angry sometimes) and asks merely for a report of behavior.

Second, the items offered some justification for aggressing: "People who continually pester you are asking for a punch on the nose." A rationale for aggressing should make it easier for a subject to agree with an item. Third, the items contained idioms designed to match the way most people think about and verbalize issues concerning aggression. Thus a feeling of anger is well captured by this idiom: "I often feel like a powder keg ready to explode."

We wrote a total of fifty-two items for six categories of aggressive behavior: physical aggression, verbal aggression, indirect aggression, anger, resentment, and suspicion. The items were administered to three samples of college men and women, the total being 1,253 subjects. They rated each item on a scale of 1 ("extremely *un*characteristic of me") to 5 ("extremely characteristic of me").

Factor Analysis

Each item was correlated with every other item, and the matrix of correlations was factor analyzed to yield the underlying dimensions. The results were so similar for men and women that their data were combined. Four factors were extracted for twenty-nine of the items (the other items were discarded), and these were stable over all three samples of subjects. For the total sample, the internal consistency of the factors (alpha) ranged from .72 to .85, a range adequate for short scales. The items are presented in Table 1.5.

TABLE 1.5   The Aggression Questionnaire

Physical aggression

1. Once in a while I can't control the urge to strike another person. (.66, .55, .62)
2. Given enough provocation, I may hit another person. (.79, .84, .80)
3. If somebody hits me, I hit back. (.60, .65, .60)
4. I get into fights a little more than the average person. (.44, .52, .58)
5. If I have to resort to violence to protect my rights, I will. (.63, .68, .58)
6. There are people who pushed me so far that we came to blows. (.60, .62, .65)
7. I can think of no good reason for ever hitting a person. (.47, .53, .51)
8. I have threatened people I know. (.45, .48, .65)
9. I have become so mad that I have broken things. (.47, .57, .47)

Verbal aggression

1. I tell my friends openly when I disagree with them. (.41, .41, .48)
2. I often find myself disagreeing with people. (.38, .49, .35)
3. When people annoy me, I may tell them what I think of them. (.45, .45, .40)
4. I can't help getting into arguments when people disagree with me. (.38, .41, .36)
5. My friends say that I'm somewhat argumentative. (.37, .56, .46)

Anger

1. I flare up quickly but get over it quickly. (.53, .49, .49)
2. When frustrated, I let my irritation show. (.47, .45, .37)
3. I sometimes feel like a powder keg ready to explode. (.60, .35, .35)
4. I am an even-tempered person. (.64, .62, .69)
5. Some of my friends think I'm a hothead. (.63, .51, .64)
6. Sometimes I fly off the handle for no good reason. (.75, .64, .70)
7. I have trouble controlling my temper. (.74, .66, .69)

Hostility

1. I am sometimes eaten up with jealousy. (.41, .43, .49)
2. At times I feel I have gotten a raw deal out of life. (.61, .58, .52)
3. Other people always seem to get the breaks. (.65, .65, .63)
4. I wonder why sometimes I feel so bitter about things. (.48, .45, .59)
5. I know that "friends" talk about me behind my back. (.55, .37, .47)
6. I am suspicious of overly friendly strangers. (.42, .35, .43)
7. I sometimes feel that people are laughing at me behind my back. (.66, .64, .70)
8. When people are especially nice, I wonder what they want. (.55, .50, .47)

Source: From "The Aggression Questionnaire" by A. H. Buss and M. Perry, 1992, *Journal of Personality and Social Psychology, 63,* p. 454. Copyright 1992 by the American Psychological Association. Adapted by permission of the publisher.

Note: The numbers in parentheses are the factor loadings for the three samples of subjects. All items load at least .35 on the factor to which they were assigned, and with one exception all items loaded less than .30 on the other three factors.

Three of the factors—physical aggression, verbal aggression, and anger—are no surprise, because we wrote items specifically for these components. It is one thing, however, to write items, and another to have them survive an empirical test and appear in the appropriate factors; not all the items did. The hostility factor consists of both resentment ("I am sometimes eaten up with jealousy") and suspicion ("I am suspicious of overly friendly strangers").

The items written for indirect aggression do not cohere as a factor. Inspection of the items reveals that they spread out over the other factors, especially physical and verbal aggression. The finding tells us something that is easy to see in hindsight: One can be indirectly aggressive by aggressing physically (letting air out of someone's tires) or verbally (spreading nasty gossip) or because one is angry or hostile.

These factorial results provide an empirical basis for applying the three basic components of behavior to aggression. Thus physical and verbal aggression represent the instrumental component, anger represents the *affective* component, and hostility represents the *cognitive* component: resentment and suspicion.

Correlations

The four factors correlate significantly with each other, as might be expected, for they all fall under the umbrella of aggression (see Table 1.6). Anger correlates strongly with all three of the factors, but instrumental aggression (verbal and physical) correlates only moderately with hostility. Perhaps the relationship between instrumental aggression and hostility rests on their relationship with anger. To test this idea it is necessary to control for the influence of anger by using partial correlations. These correlations reveal that anger is still significantly related to instrumental aggression and to hostility. However, when anger is partialled out, there is no relationship between instrumental aggression and hostility. Thus anger may be regarded as a psychological bridge that links physical or verbal attack with hostility: People prone to anger tend to aggress physically or verbally, and angry people tend to become hostile.

Reliability

Everyone knows that if a questionnaire were administered several times, and each time the scores of individuals bounced considerably, the questionnaire would be

TABLE 1.6   Correlations among the Four Aggression Factors

	Anger	Physical	Verbal
Physical	.48		
Verbal	.48	.45	
Hostility	.45	.28	.25

Source: From "The Aggression Questionnaire" by A. H. Buss and M. Perry, 1992, *Journal of Personality and Social Psychology, 63*, p. 454. Copyright 1992 by the American Psychological Association. Adapted by permission of the publisher.

too unreliable to be of any use. To discover the stability of this questionnaire, we administered it twice, nine weeks apart, to 372 college men and women. The test-retest correlations ranged from .72 to .80, which demonstrates reasonable stability for short scales.

Sex Differences

Men are known to be more aggressive than women, but does this sex difference hold for all four factors of aggression? Men are clearly more physically aggressive than women. Men are only just a little more verbally aggressive than women, and barely more hostile; these two differences, though statistically reliable, are so small as to be psychologically unimportant. And there is no sex difference for anger. These findings tell us that there is a sharp sex difference mainly in physical aggression.

Projective Techniques

Projective techniques were originally so named on the assumption that subjects imbue the stimuli with meaning by projecting their own needs and personal tendencies onto them. Currently, these techniques are assumed to present stimuli that elicit cognitive responses linked to personality characteristics and abnormal ways of perceiving the world. They have proved to be valuable in assessing personality. The major instruments are the Thematic Apperception Test (TAT) and the Rorschach Ink Blots.

Thematic Apperception Test (TAT)

The *Thematic Apperception Test (TAT)* consists of a series of drawings that depict various scenes, some without people and others with people in different relationships. The subjects are instructed to use the drawings to make up a story with a beginning, a middle, and an end. Presumably, the subjects' life experiences and therefore their personality will be injected into the stories they tell.

The TAT has been used to assess aggression. In one study, the stories were scored for death, physical aggression, and verbal aggression, these categories being given weights of 3, 2, and 1, respectively (Stone, 1956). The subjects were army prisoners with a history of either violent or nonviolent crime. The violent prisoners told more aggressive stories than the nonviolent prisoners.

Another study used high-school boys who were categorized by teachers as either aggressive (disruptive, defiant, surly, or destructive) or nonaggressive (Jensen, 1956). The boys were shown drawings most likely to elicit violent themes. The aggressive boys told stories that were much more violent than those told by the nonaggressive boys and in which the perpetrators were unlikely to be punished.

Would men tell more aggressive stories than women? In one study TAT stories were coded for violence: themes of death, suicide, murder, rape, or a fatal disease (Pollak & Gilligan, 1982). Half the men told at least one violent story, but only one woman in five told a violent story.

Rorschach Ink Blots

Subjects respond to the *Rorshach Ink Blots* by seeing a variety of objects, animals, and people. Some responses include aggressive interactions. Elizur (1949) developed a scoring system for aggressive content, examples of which are reproach, hatred, fighting, killing, or injury to an animal or person. Using this scoring scheme, he compared the Rorschach responses of college men with a self-report questionnaire, self-ratings, and ratings based on interviews with the men. The correlations between Rorschach aggressive responses and the other measures were as follows: questionnaire, .74; self-ratings, .45; interview, .60.

A different scoring scheme for assessing aggression in Rorschach responses was used on male and female prisoners. One study compared men who had attacked or threatened someone or who had a record of armed robbery or murder with men of comparable age whose crimes involved no aggression (Kane, 1955). The assaultive group had much higher scores for aggressive content on the Rorschach. Similar findings were reported for women prisoners (Sjostedt, 1955).

One category of Rorschach responses is human movement, and some of these responses involve aggression. The Rorschach measure was used in several studies reported in Exner (1986). The Rorschach responses of psychiatric inpatients were compared with the aggressive behavior of the same patients during occupational and recreational therapy. Patients observed to be more physically aggressive had more aggressive movement responses on the Rorschach. Next, the measure was compared with the physically aggressive behavior observed in sixth-grade children. Again, aggressive subjects had more frequent aggressive movement responses on the Rorschach.

Evidently, the Rorschach does elicit responses that reflect aggressive tendencies in subjects and is therefore a useful instrument for assessing aggression. Similarly, on the TAT, aggressive people tell more aggressive stories than nonaggressive people. These projective techniques are cumbersome to use and require elaborate scoring schemes. For most purposes, investigators may be better off using self-report questionnaires, which are efficient and can be scored objectively and quickly.

Why use projective techniques? One reason is that their stimuli are somewhat ambiguous, which makes their purpose less obvious. When subjects have reasons for concealing personal thoughts or tendencies, such as hostile cognitions or aggressive motives, projective techniques might be preferred over questionnaires, which cannot conceal the information they seek. In addition, young children cannot answer questionnaires, but projective techniques can be applied to children and offer valuable information about their personality.

Chapter *2*

Origins

As its title indicates, Chapter 2 deals with the sources of behavior relevant to personality. To consider the origins of personality we must go beyond facts and enter the realm of theory. Theory here does not mean any particular theory of personality, such as psychoanalytic theory. Rather the focus in this chapter will be the psychological and biological roots of personality that are agreed on by most psychologists. Psychologists disagree not so much about the determinants of personality but about which are crucial. Thus some psychologists believe that virtually all personality traits are inherited, and others that all personality traits are learned. A more neutral position is to inquire which determinants are essential for a particular behavioral tendency. The answer is likely to be complex but closer to the facts. The answer is also necessarily more detailed and more useful than a sweeping statement that there is a specific source for *all* behavior or traits. Again, aggressive behavior supplies concrete examples.

Learning

The several kinds of learning range from the simplest (habituation) to the most complex (cognitions). This dimension of simple to complex parallels evolutionary trends in learning (Buss, 1988).

Habituation

Habituation is regarded as the simplest form of learning because it is passive and involves no associations among stimuli, responses, or consequences of responses. There are two kinds of habituation. In the first, prior to learning, a stimulus or event evokes an orienting response, the person becoming alert and turning the senses toward the source. If the event is unimportant and merely a background stimulus, after several repetitions it is ignored. Thus country noises, which on the first night keep a visiting city dweller awake, after several nights are just ignored and do not interfere with sleep.

In the second kind of habituation a stimulus stirs an emotional reaction but otherwise has no negative impact on the observer. With successive repetitions the emotional reaction weakens, though it might not disappear entirely. This kind of habituation is especially relevant to our reaction to observed violence. In one experiment, two groups of children in elementary school were shown either a video of a police show replete with violence or an exciting volleyball game (Thomas, Horton, Lippincott, & Drabman, 1977). Then both groups watched what ostensibly was live television of two children attacking each other verbally and physically and destroying objects in a playroom. The children who saw the earlier violent video reacted with less emotion, as measured by the galvanic skin response, than the control children who saw the volleyball game. When the experiment was repeated with college students, they too manifested a diminished emotional reaction to observed violence.

This research is consistent with related studies on children (Cline, Croft, & Courrier, 1973) and on college students (Geen, 1981). Taken together, they demonstrate that we can become so accustomed to violence that it is no longer the aversive, emotional event that it was before habituation occurred. It has been suggested that the televised atrocities in Vietnam diminished the horror of viewers, preparing them for the escalation of aggression. The impact of televised violence on aggression, however, cannot be explained simply by the mechanism of habituation, for imitation also plays a role, as will be discussed shortly.

We also habituate to pleasant stimuli. When repeated over time, they lose their novelty and therefore some of their positive value. Habituation may affect the trait of sociability. After years of continuous association, two friends may know each other so well that each knows what the other will say in a given situation. The novelty or indeterminacy in conversation that makes responsivity so rewarding thus wanes or is lost, thereby weakening the tendency to seek out each other.

Failure to habituate, on the other hand, is an important issue in shyness. As we shall see in Chapter 11, social novelty often elicits shy behavior, and shy people may remain so because they do not habituate to strangers or novel contexts.

Classical Conditioning

Classical conditioning is a familiar kind of learning in which a neutral stimulus is linked to a stimulus that elicits a response. After repeated pairing of the two stimuli, the previously neutral stimulus becomes a *conditioned stimulus*—that is, it elicits the response. Certain places, through their association with aggressive behavior, can facilitate the occurrence of attacks. A particular bar, for instance, may become known among its clientele for the tendency of customers to get into fights. When people congregate in such a bar, the bar's reputation as a locus of violence may serve as a conditioned stimulus, intensifying the customers' urge to fight. In addition, alcohol, which as a pharmacological substance can inhibit proscribed behavior, can also act as a conditioned stimulus after it has been consistently coupled with aggression. To cite another example of classical conditioning, for some children the playground may become a place that is closely linked to aggression, so that entering the playground may make fighting more probable.

Classical conditioning may be more a determinant of angry aggression than of instrumental aggression. Some victims of aggression, by their behavior, can come to be conditioned stimuli for aggression. Adolescents who have been labeled *provocative victims* tend to have a hot temper, tease others, and generally serve as irritants in social interaction (Olweus, 1978). Similarly, a group of children identified as victims tended to make fun of others, pick fights, push others, and become easily angered (Perry, Kusel, & Perry, 1988). Presumably, after eliciting angry aggression from others, these provocative victims become conditioned stimuli for anger and angry aggression.

Instrumental Conditioning

Consequences

Instrumental conditioning is reward learning. The kind of reward sought by the learner may be related to personality tendencies already present. Thus a sociable person typically wants to share activities with others and have others be responsive. If such rewards are not forthcoming, however, the trait of sociability may be weakened.

When a child wants a toy possessed by another child, one means of obtaining the toy is to take it away, or if there is resistance, to hit the other child until he or she gives up the toy. In a courtroom, a defense lawyer may badger and deride a prosecution witness in an attempt to win a case. Subjects can be induced to aggress more frequently or more intensely merely by the verbal reward "Good" (Walters & Brown, 1963). In an aggression machine experiment, the accomplice (victim) "rewarded" the subject by making several successive correct responses each time the subject escalated the intensity of electric shock (Buss, 1971). The minimal reinforcement of successive correct responses was sufficient to intensify aggression—that is, the level of shock delivered by the subject.

One can also reward aggression by turning away the initial aggression of another person. Perhaps the most powerful immediate stimulant for aggressive behavior is an attack. In the laboratory, a virtually guaranteed means of eliciting aggression is to have an experimental accomplice attack the subject (Buss, 1961). When there is a counterattack, it is often rewarded by the termination of the other person's aggression.

Also to be considered are *outcome value* (how potent the reward is) and *outcome expectancy* (whether the instrumental response will lead to it) (Boldizar, Perry, & Perry, 1989). Outcome value, or the importance of the reward, is roughly equivalent to the strength of the motive to aggress. Aggressive children, however, appear to have no greater incentive for aggressing than do nonaggressive children

(Boldizar et al., 1989). Outcome expectancy, the estimate of whether aggression will succeed in obtaining the reward, is based on the past history of aggressing. Those whose aggression has previously paid off, especially children known to be aggressive, develop confidence that aggression generally does pay off. They are more likely to expect tangible rewards for aggressing than are nonaggressive children (Perry, Perry, & Rasmussen, 1986). Perhaps, then, aggressive children may not be more strongly motivated to aggress but are more likely to expect their (habitual) aggression to succeed.

Of course, an attack may not succeed in reaching its target, and any response tendency that is not rewarded tends to wane. Worse still, an attack may be met with sufficient retaliation to make the aggressor think twice about subsequent aggression. In addition, there are agents of society (police, parents) who may punish aggression. Such punishment, however, poses two problems. It induces anxiety, and it may serve as a model for future aggression.

Schedules

A response is acquired most rapidly when it is rewarded every time it is made. Once the habit has been established, it can be maintained through a *schedule of reinforcement* (Ferster & Skinner, 1957). The reward may occur after only several responses have been made or after as little as 10% of the responses. These ratio schedules, rewards after a percentage of responses, make a habit extremely resistant to extinction. Thus schedules of reinforcement offer one explanation for the stability of personality traits. For instance, a boy who learns to bully others may be rewarded intermittently for aggressing, which would be sufficient to maintain his bullying.

Some parents may inadvertently place their children on a ratio schedule that rewards aggression (Patterson, 1986). Parents may provoke the child, say, by teasing, and when the child has a verbal or physical outburst, the parents occasionally stop their provocative behavior. The child learns that at least sometimes aggression can terminate parental aversiveness.

Preparedness

Some responses are learned with surprising ease. We do not have an instinct to walk, but children learn quickly. Acquiring a new language, though difficult for most adults, is accomplished with astonishing rapidity by children in the second year of life. It has been suggested that we are especially *prepared* to learn certain behaviors—that is, we are ready to make a response, with virtually no trial-and-error, as soon as the appropriate stimulus occurs (Seligman, 1970).

Are we especially prepared to acquire aggressive behavior? Do we react with angry aggression virtually the first time an inciting stimulus occurs? Or is a more restrictive hypothesis more tenable: Are certain children predisposed by heredity to learn aggressive behavior rapidly? As we shall see shortly, one determinant of aggressiveness is heredity, so the latter hypothesis is tenable. We may also be especially prepared to learn certain fears, an issue to be discussed in Chapter 3.

Imitation

Imitation of the behavior of a model can provide a shortcut in the lengthy trial-and-error sequence of instrumental conditioning. Imitation is a significant aspect of learning to drive a car, for example; a neophyte driver might not survive if all the learning occurred through trial-and-error. Imitation also opens up response options that may not already be in a person's repertoire. When newspapers and television spread news of teenage suicides, for example, a rash of such suicides frequently follows. When the media report the details of an airplane hijacking, such piracy often increases dramatically. In one experiment, children watched an adult attack a Bobo doll by punching it and hitting it with a mallet; later, when given the opportunity, they copied these responses, which they had not previously used (Bandura, 1965).

Imitation may also cause an eventual increase in aggression even when attempts are made to suppress such behavior. When a parent punishes a child's aggressive behavior by hitting the child, the child temporarily ceases being aggressive. But the parent is serving as a model for the child's subsequent attacking behavior, especially against siblings or peers. To avoid such imitation, a parent might use physical punishment that cannot easily be copied by a child, such as spanking. Perhaps a better option is to refrain from physical punishment.

Today the media provide the most salient models for aggression. When he kills criminals in his movies the actor Clint Eastwood provides viewers with a model who uses justified aggression, and the wholesale massacres carried out by the actor Sylvester Stallone in his film role as Rambo are rationalized as patriotism or revenge on behalf of a victim. Laboratory research has demonstrated that justified aggression is more likely to be imitated than irrational aggressive acts (Berkowitz & Rawlings, 1963).

Saturday morning cartoons, watched exclusively by children, are well known for their violence. Young children who have substantial exposure to cartoons tend to imitate the violent behavior they see, as is evidenced in the increase of kicking and hitting among children in preschool playrooms (Friedrich & Stein, 1973). After reviewing many studies, Eron (1982) concluded that in Western countries, television violence makes a clear if modest contribution to children's aggressiveness.

A more serious problem is the *enduring* impact of television violence. As a longitudinal study of aggressive behavior revealed, "Early television viewing habits are also related to aggressive behavior 22 years later. For example, there is a . . . correlation of .41 when predicting a variety of aggressive behaviors at age 30 from TV violence viewing and frequency at age 8" (Eron, 1987, p. 440). We must be wary, though, of concluding that television violence is the origin of the trait of aggressiveness. It is just as likely that the children who watch a lot of television violence do so because they are already highly aggressive, which would also account for their criminal behavior later in life. In fact, the reasons for aggression among children may be even more complex: Children who are already somewhat aggressive tend to watch more television violence, which makes them still more aggressive. Perhaps the only children who imitate media violence are those who are primed to do so because they are already high in the trait of aggressiveness.

This hypothesis is supported by two sets of evidence, one focusing on children and the other on adults. The first was a three-year longitudinal study of the connection between television viewing and aggression in elementary-school children in six countries: Australia, Finland, Israel, the Netherlands, Poland, and the United States (Wiegman, Kuttschreuter, & Baarda, 1992). The frequency of watching violent television was correlated with peer nominations of aggressiveness: "A significant positive relationship was observed between aggression and television violence viewing. However, when we controlled for aggression in the first year, television violence was not found to be a significant predictor of aggression" (p. 158). Said another way, there was a relationship between television violence and aggression *only* for children who were initially aggressive.

In the second study, audiences of adults watched either a violent movie or a nonviolent one (Black & Bevan, 1992). They were administered the verbal and indirect aggression scales of an aggression questionnaire (Buss & Durkee, 1957) before and after the movie. The aggression scores rose significantly for those who had watched the violent movie but not for the viewers of the nonviolent movie. What is special about this experiment is that the subjects chose to attend one movie or the other. Those at the violent movie had significantly higher aggression scores than those at the nonviolent movie not only after the movie but before it. Presumably one of the reasons they chose the violent movie was that they already had aggressive tendencies.

This research also raises the issue of arousal. Watching a violent film may be so arousing that it *temporarily* increases aggressive tendencies. As arousal wanes, though, aggressive tendencies also diminish. The *enduring* effects of media violence may be the result of imitation, not arousal. But the bottom line is that it is aggressive individuals who are most likely to watch violence and to be affected by it.

Cognition

Imitation of aggression is not inevitable, especially imitation of media aggression. The cognitions of viewers can lessen the impact of television violence (Huesmann, Eron, Klein, Brice, & Fischer, 1983). Grade-school children were asked to prepare a speech about how television differs from real life, and they were videotaped giving the speech. Subsequently, though they continued to watch violence as much as before, their aggression toward classmates declined. The researchers had periodic meetings with the schoolchildren during which the children were taught that it is not good to imitate the aggressive behavior seen on television and that aggressive behavior is not accepted in everyday situations. The children's cognitions were used to minimize the impact of media violence.

We do not know whether aggression precedes cognitions or follows. It may do both. In any case aggression and cognitions clearly are linked. Highly aggressive children report more daydreams about attacking others and more positive attitudes about aggression (Eron, 1982). Aggressive children are confident that they have the requisite ability to aggress, that it is easy to do but hard to inhibit, and that it leads to rewarding outcomes (Perry et al., 1986). And compared to nonaggressive children, aggressive children value their control over the victim more and are less concerned with either retaliation or the victim's suffering (Boldizar et al., 1989).

Attributing intentions to others is another kind of cognition. Grade-school boys watched videotapes and were asked about the intentions of the characters on the videotapes (Dodge & Somberg, 1987). Aggressive boys thought that the intentions of the televised characters were significantly more hostile than did nonaggressive boys. Even when aggressive boys did not attribute hostile intent to the characters, the boys thought that the characters would be likely to aggress. In other words, aggressive boys tend to be hostile and believe that those around them are aggressive.

The learning of group myths and prejudice can also lead to aggression. Children may be taught from an early age to hate people who belong to certain ethnic or racial groups different from their own. These prejudices are sometimes rooted in centuries-old conflicts between groups and can be an impetus for group or individual violence. The idea of a vendetta, an eye for an eye, helps enmity between groups to persist over generations. Such cognitions may facilitate the occurrence of aggression by offering the justification "They deserve it."

In short, cognitions—fantasying, thinking about others, or attributing causality to their actions—can affect our emotions and instrumental behavior. Thus cognitive learning is one of the mechanisms by which personality tendencies are acquired, enhanced, or minimized.

Varieties of Learning

Personality is to some extent learned. Even when aspects of personality are inherited, they can be modified or enhanced by learning. The five kinds of learning just discussed are summarized in Table 2.1. Again, the examples provided are from the study of aggression.

TABLE 2.1   Varieties of Learning

Kind	Example
Habituation	Children accept aggression as commonplace
Classical conditioning	Victims become targets of aggression
Instrumental conditioning	Successful aggressors become more aggressive
Imitation	Television violence may escalate aggression
Cognitive learning	Myths about outgroups can lead to prejudice and violence

Development

Maturation

Growth and Differentiation

Newborn infants have virtually no instrumental behavior, but as time goes by, they add to their behavioral repertoire. Thus at first the movements of their hands are so uncontrolled that they appear to be random. As months pass, infants slowly become able to grasp objects, examine them, and place them in the mouth. This development represents the *growth* of motor skill.

During the first year or two, infants use either hand to manipulate objects. During the second year, however, they start using one hand more than the other, usually the right hand. Thereafter, it is clear which is the dominant hand. This development represents the *differentiation* of motor skill.

Growth and differentiation are not limited to the maturation of motor skills. There is growth as infants' entire behavioral repertoire expands with the passing months and years, and they acquire new responses that are relevant to personality. Then through the process of differentiation the various behaviors are subdivided, so that some are preferred and others neglected. As the example of handedness reveals, differentiation entails two issues. First, there is a developmental progression from the general to the particular and from the diffuse to the specific (from vague hand movements to skilled hand movements). Second, once a path has been taken, it is difficult to turn back or to take another path (from either hand being used to a dominant hand).

Growth.   During the first year of life, infants display signs of anger: screaming, red face, kicking, and thrashing. This tantrum behavior needs to be distinguished from the more generalized distress reaction, but in the second half of the first year of life, anger can be recognized as different from distress (see Chapter 3). As the months pass, infants develop sufficient motor control to engage in angry aggression. In the second year of life, anger is no longer a necessary condition for aggression, and instrumental aggression occurs. After the second birthday, children manifest stubbornness and the passive aggression called *negativism*, which results in the designation of this era as the terrible twos. As children's language capability progresses, they start using words to attack others, and many parents are horrified to discover that occasionally their child uses curse words, sometimes words copied from parents' vocabulary. Gradually, subtlety is added to children's behavioral repertoire, and they enter the realm of indirect aggression: purposely destroying others' toys and telling lies to get others in trouble. Aggressiveness can also be partially disguised in the form of teasing or ridicule. When more sophisticated language skills have been acquired, the door is open to sarcasm, irony, and aggressive humor.

During childhood, the enhanced cognitive abilities of children can lead to hostility. Children acquire intense dislikes, often of peers or siblings, and, sometimes to the surprise of parents, hatred of parents. They are capable of strong resentment about not getting their own way or about real or fancied unfair treatment. As the years pass, they may project their hostility and become suspicious that others are out to get them. Now revenge becomes possible, together with elaborate plans for hurting or harming others. Aside from specific plans, children can spin aggressive or destructive fantasies, sometimes with the justification that they are fighting evil (the Superman syndrome) or just to get even. They also acquire the prejudices of their family or subculture and become hostile to members of outgroups. The development of various kinds of aggressive behavior is shown in Table 2.2.

Differentiation.   The process of growth inevitably results in an expanded range of behavioral possibilities. The process of differentiation then places individuals into particular tracks, some persons typically using certain behaviors and not using others. Thus one child might aggress only when angry, and another might aggress only when calm and motivated to acquire another's toys or to dominate another child. One child might rely mainly on physical aggression, another on verbal aggression. Older siblings, being stronger, typically use physical aggression against younger siblings, whose only recourse may be taunts and insults. Similarly, more powerful children can easily use direct aggression, whereas less powerful children, wary of retaliation, are better off using indirect aggression, in which the aggressor may be hard to identify. Adolescents and adults, having learned social rules that proscribe serious verbal aggression, may rely on humorous aggression ("The joke is on you"). Some individuals might rarely display anger and instead coolly plot revenge.

There can be even further differentiation within any given category of aggressive behavior. There is a range of physical aggression, for instance, that includes not only hitting, kicking, and scratching but also clubbing, spearing, and stabbing. Anyone might have a preferred mode of physical aggression to the exclusion of all others. Thus there are individual differences not only in components of aggressive behavior (physical versus verbal) but also within physical aggression (hands versus weapons).

TABLE 2.2   Development of Aggressive Behavior

Earlier	Later
Anger	Angry aggression
Angry aggression	Instrumental aggression
Physical aggression	Verbal aggression
Active aggression	Passive aggression (negativism)
Direct aggression	Indirect aggression
Serious aggression	Humorous aggression
Spontaneous aggression	Planned aggression
Anger	Hatred (prejudice)
Attack	Threat

Inhibitory Control

Growth and differentiation establish such complexity of behavior as to require some kind of internal organization. Organization of differentiated behavior patterns offers a basis for self-regulation: control of one's own behavior. At birth, however, the infant is largely reflexive: "It is difficult to escape the concept of the infant as a qualitatively different organism, operating through large blocks of relatively undifferentiated, mass muscular effort, triggered by a relatively small number of stereotyped stimuli. The progressive increase of upper-echelon control over these cruder, downstream mechanisms effects (largely by inhibition) increasingly precise motor patterns, progressively more appropriate to stimuli" (Scheibel & Scheibel, 1964, p. 513).

The maturation of control over muscles is merely one aspect of a more general neural trend for higher centers of the brain to control lower centers through inhibition. Such maturation also marks the beginning of control over a variety of impulses and motives, starting with the need to eliminate and progressing through biological motives (hunger) and various psychological motives (the need to be active, as we shall see in Chapter 3).

Inhibitory control is especially relevant to the expression of anger. Infants are allowed their temper tantrums because parents know that infants lack self-control. But as children mature and gradually achieve control over their emotions, rage reactions are expected to diminish in frequency and intensity. Similarly, older children's displays of angry aggression are strongly punished, for more mature children are expected to inhibit violent outbursts.

The maturation of inhibitory control, which starts with control of muscles and proceeds developmentally through control over biological and psychological motives, is assumed to be complete by the end of adolescence. Adults who cannot exercise self-control are regarded as immature, for inhibitory capability is regarded as a hallmark of maturity.

Stability

Development over the span of life is not always smooth and continuous. There are periods of rapid movement from one era to the next, the most obvious being the brief period of rapid growth at the onset of puberty. This period in early adolescence marks the transition from childhood to adulthood, which is accompanied by the swift development of secondary sex characteristics.

Does personality change markedly during such periods of transition? Caspi and Moffitt (1991) studied girls who were either early or late maturers and found that girls who experience menarche early were likely to have behavioral problems. Specifically, the early maturers who had adjustment problems in childhood were found to have the greatest problems of adjustment in adolescence. Caspi and Moffitt observed that "stressful transition events, such as the early onset of menarche, do not generate uniform reactions among people; they appear, rather, to accentuate pretransition differences between them" (p. 166). It has also been found that differences among preschool children are enlarged by entry into elementary school (Alexander & Entwistle, 1988), as are differences among high-school students after they enter college (Feldman & Newcomb, 1969). Thus transitions do not appear to induce alterations in personality but to intensify personality traits already present.

What about the stability of personality in adulthood? A nineteen-year longitudinal study revealed high levels of stability for neuroticism, extraversion, and impulse control (Conley, 1985). These traits correspond to the temperaments of emotionality (neuroticism), sociability and activity (extraversion), and impulsivity (impulse control). There was less stability for other dispositions—for agreeableness, for example. However, McCrae and Costa (1990) reported considerable stability for agreeableness, as well as for the other three dispositions studied by Conley.

Aggression

The tendency to be aggressive is moderately stable over the life course. In Chapter 1 we saw that children above average in aggressiveness at eight years of age were inordinately aggressive twenty-two years later (Huesmann, Eron, Lefkowitz, & Walder, 1984). A large-scale study tested almost 2,000 subjects first in college and then in mid-life; the correlation for overall aggressiveness was .39 (Siegler et al., 1990). A briefer, four-year longitudinal study on middle-aged subjects found a much higher correlation, .84. Presumably, by the time people reach the fourth or fifth decades of life, their personalities tend to stabilize.

Is there is a sex difference in the stability of aggression? A small four-year longitudinal study reported a before-and-after correlation of .56 in the total sample of elementary and high-school students (Woodall & Matthews, 1993). However, while the correlation for females was .65, that for males was a nonsignificant .29. These findings should be replicated on older subjects and with a larger sample, for we need to know if the sex difference is real.

Social Behavior

Parents

Caretaker and Partner.   Newborn infants are so helpless that they will die if not for parental care, and virtually all parents respond by playing the role of *nurturer*. This role is typically filled by the mother, so she will be the focus here; and to simplify exposition, let us assume the infant is a boy. The mother feeds the infant, often with her own milk, keeps him warm, cleans him up, tries to keep him from hurting himself, and rescues him from danger. When he is upset, she calms him. In general, she provides a tranquil, secure base from which he can explore the environment, knowing that she will be available when he needs her.

Parents also take the role of *partner* with their young children. For simplicity let us focus on the father as partner with his daughter. The father initiates frisky, elementary play, tossing his daughter in the air and tickling her. He plays peek-a-boo and talks to her even though she may not understand the words. He responds to her nonverbal requests and carries her around. Beyond supplying social stimulation, he shows considerable affection. He hugs and kisses her, smiles and laughs at her, and welcomes her when she wakes from sleep or when he returns to the home.

Most parents play the nurturant and partnership roles reasonably well, but a minority neglect their children, failing to keep them well fed and secure from danger. They do not soothe their children when they are upset, and may even be the cause of upset. As partners, they do not supply the requisite stimulation, relying instead on television or just leaving the child alone. There appears to be a connection between parental neglect and aggression on the part of offspring. Cold, indifferent, and rejecting mothers, for example, are likely to have sons who are aggressive in adolescence (Olweus, 1980).

In addition, parents may actually be the opposite of affectionate—that is, physically punitive. Preschool children who are beaten by their parents tend to attack other children (George & Main, 1979). And the early home life of adult criminals has been found to be marked by parental violence toward children (McCord, 1979).

Discipline.   By the second year of life, infants have sufficient mobility and motor control to lay waste almost any object they can reach. And they become capable of hurting others. At first parents may merely keep objects out of reach or simply remove the young child to prevent harm to others. But eventually, parents must try to prevent such behavior from recurring and therefore are forced to assume the role of *disciplinarian*.

In attempting to control their children, parents represent all points on a dimension bounded by restrictiveness at one end and permissiveness at the other. Baumrind (1971) has identified clusters of behaviors displayed by parents at either end. *Authoritarian* parents are strict in their demands for obedience, adherence to absolute standards, and respect for their authority. They are likely to say, "Do it because I say so," brook no argument, and tend to use punishment. *Permissive* parents tend to exercise little control over their children, preferring to make few demands and using reason instead of punishment. In the middle of this dimension are *authoritative* parents, who reason with their children but also set firm guidelines and use punishment occasionally. Concerning aggression, Baumrind's research revealed that only boys were affected by the extremes of parental control. Authoritarian parents are more likely to have boys who are either obedient and nonaggressive or defiant and rebellious. Permissive parents are more likely to have boys who openly display anger.

There are parents who use excessive force when punishing their sons; they threaten their sons and direct violent outbursts toward them. Such parents tend to have adolescent sons who are aggressive (Olweus, 1980). It was also found, paradoxically, that the opposite kind of discipline, permissiveness and indifference, had the same effect: "A young boy who gets too little love and interest from his mother and too much freedom and lack of clear limits with regard to aggressive behavior is likely to develop into an aggressive adolescent" (p. 657). Thus there is converging evidence that parents can err in either direction, too much or too little discipline, but these extremes seem to affect boys more than girls.

Holden (1983) suggested another dichotomy of parental control over children: reactive versus proactive. He observed mothers and their young children in supermarkets. When their children grabbed merchandise or stood up in the cart, some mothers tried reasoning, diversion, or assertion of power; this is reactive control. But other mothers adopted a more tactical approach, talking to their children in advance or giving them things to eat, play with, or hold so that the child would not get into mischief; this is proactive control. When preventive, proactive control was used, the children were better behaved in the supermarket.

Socialization

Children must be prepared to become self-sufficient adults who can fit in with others and meet the requirements of society. Parents prepare their children for adulthood through discipline, modeling, and the teaching of rules and other cognitions. Other socializing agents—caretakers, teachers, older siblings, and peer groups— also help to move children closer to the adult world.

What are the goals of socialization? The normative developmental sequence in our culture, as determined by a survey of literature, has been outlined as follows by Dubin and Dubin (1963):

1. Control of elimination and of grabbing for food
2. Control of thumb-sucking and masturbation
3. Learning what and who can be touched
4. Learning how to relate to people, including control of aggression

The control of aggression is essential, for no social group can survive if its members are continually fighting. In most societies, including ours, laws govern physical aggression (assault) and verbal aggression (slander). Thus a person convicted of assault is sentenced to jail, and the more harm or potential harm, the longer the sentence. Long before jail becomes an issue, however, children are taught moral principles that deter them from hurting or harming others. Such socialization is necessary to counteract the (sometimes intense) motivation to engage in angry or instrumental aggression. Children also learn when it might be all right to aggress and which social roles or activities allow physical aggression (military, police, boxing) or verbal aggression (politics).

Another survey, which included files from fifty different countries, revealed that the period from five to seven years of age is a time of transition (Rogoff, Sellers, Perrotta, Fox, & White, 1975). Before this period, children are allowed considerable latitude in their behavior. Afterward, they are strongly inculcated with the traditions, beliefs, and values of their society. They must adhere to rules, including the rules governing aggression, and prepare for adulthood by practicing the roles that they will later assume. Although previously boys and girls played together easily, now they tend to be separated, and distinct gender roles are emphasized.

In Kenya, girls ordinarily cook, serve food, clean house, and tend to babies, but in households with no girls, boys are assigned these tasks (Ember, 1973). These boys are less aggressive than boys assigned to typically masculine tasks. Thus the female social role diminished the aggressiveness of boys. However, girls assigned to feminine tasks were the least aggressive, which suggests a residual, biological sex difference in aggression.

Socialization has been the central focus of those who believe that sex differences in personality are wholly acquired: "One possible link between a personality and a social role approach utilizes the gender-role principle that expectancies about behavior apply to people merely on the basis of their sex. To the extent that this is so, it is likely that agents of socialization, such as parents and teachers, hold these expectations and attempt to prepare children to perform the expected behaviors. In addition, socializing agents may be aware of the differing distributions of sexes into occupational and other social roles and therefore emphasize training and education that prepares boys and girls for roles that they have a fairly high probability of occupying. For these role-linked reasons, then, girls and boys may be treated differently and may develop somewhat different traits and abilities" (Eagly, 1983, p. 979).

Interaction of Person and Environment

Clearly, the environment shapes individuals through various kinds of learning, parental behavior, and socialization. Here the direction of effects is from environment to person. But this is just one direction of effects. The other is from person to environment (Bell, 1968). Recall the research of Baumrind (1971) on parents who exercised excessive control, firm control, or little control (permissiveness). She interpreted her findings as parental control having an impact on children's behavior. Lewis (1981) reinterpreted these results, suggesting that what is regarded as the impact of firm control may be merely the child's willingness to obey. As adults and parents, psychologists tend to adopt the perspective of parents. Lewis adopted the perspective of children in attempting to understand the consequences of parental discipline that respects children's decisions and uses reason. He wrote that children might think, "'My parents withdraw their demands after I convince them with my arguments' (from 'respects child's decisions'); or, 'Since we handle things by discussing them, my parents never attempt to get their way by coercing me' (from 'use of reason to obtain compliance')" (p. 561).

This perspective is needed to balance the dominant psychological approach that attributes children's behavior to the actions of parents. Most parents know that they must accommodate to their children as much as control them.

Person Affects Environment

Persons can influence environments in three ways (Buss & Plomin, 1975, 1984). Children and adults have a voice in selecting the environments that might affect them. They can also act as stimuli for others, thereby playing a major role in determining a social environment. And on entering a setting, they may decide not to conform to it but instead to alter it.

Choosing Environments

When watching television, people decide which program to watch. Recall the connection between television violence and a child's aggressiveness. One way of interpreting this relationship is that aggressive children prefer violent television programs, which tends to enhance subsequent aggressiveness. Nonaggressive children may prefer nonviolent programs.

Older children of course have a wider array of options. In school, they can join the debating team and engage in socialized verbal aggression. Sports such as football, hockey, and wrestling provide an outlet for physical aggressiveness. Notice that these and other sports that lend themselves to physical aggression appeal mainly to boys. Also, boys who participate in these sports are often provided with models who aggress. These boys are encouraged to aggress and are rewarded for aggressing, all presumably within the rules of the game. Thus self-selection of an aggressive environment may be only the first act in the sequence, which is followed by the enhancement of aggression through one or another kind of learning.

Children who are not aggressive can also choose their own environment. In school, they can join the stamp club or the band. They can engage in athletics such as swimming or track, which involve no physical violence at all. In such sports, individuals may become more competitive but not necessarily more aggressive.

Setting the Tone

An aggressive or hostile woman can make a social setting tense and negative by her demeanor. She may wear a perennial frown, scowl at others, appear grouchy, and launch immediately into a litany of complaints about her life generally or directed toward the others with her. She quickly establishes a nasty tone for social interaction that can elicit aggression or anger from others toward her.

An agreeable, companionable woman can of course set the opposite tone. She may wear a perennial half-smile, appear glad to see others, and launch immediately into compliments on their appearance or accomplishments. She establishes a pleasant and nonaggressive environment in which she will receive no aggression or anger.

Thus we play a role in constructing the very environment that shapes our behavior. Aggressive children tend to experience more turmoil and receive more aggression from others. They are not trusted, are strongly disliked, and sometimes are the object of open displays of hatred (Dodge, 1983). The way they set the tone of an interaction may enhance their original aggressiveness: "Highly aggressive individuals to a considerable degree actively select and create the kinds of situations in which they are often observed" (Olweus, 1979, p. 873).

Some children, frequently picked on, become known as easy targets for aggression. These victims can be identified as early as the preschool period, during which they reward the aggression of others by giving in and crying (Patterson, Littman, & Bricker, 1967). Their being scared has been found to derive from an infancy during which they were insecurely attached (Troy & Sroufe, 1987). In the elementary years perhaps one child in ten selectively is the target of aggression, and there are no sex differences (Perry et al., 1988).

Adolescent victims have been identified by Olweus (1978, 1984), who discovered two different kinds of what he called *whipping boys*. The passive kind were much like the preschool victims in that they were insecure and anxious, but they were also unpopular, had low self-esteem, and were physically weak. The provocative victims, mentioned earlier, were restless and quick-tempered and when attacked fought back. These two kinds of victims have also been reported at the elementary-school level (Perry et al., 1988).

Modifying the Environment

Often we are stuck in an environment that we have not chosen or set the tone for, but we can still modify it. Even infants can alter their environment. When they do not like being alone, they can elicit a social environment by smiling or babbling, which will bring parents to them. Failing that, they can cry, which usually brings immediate parental attention. Bell and Harper (1977, chap. 6) have detailed various tactics infants can use to control the behavior of parents and thus their social environment.

Environments may also be modified by aggression. An aggressive man in a bar, for instance, may insult other patrons, thereby converting an ordinary barroom conversation into a brawl. During a practice scrimmage, a football player may continue blocking or tackling after the whistle has blown, thereby inciting retribution. A baseball batter, after being hit by the pitcher, may charge the pitcher with intent to do bodily harm, which can start a riot among all the players. And a boy, bored in the classroom, may intentionally disrupt the class by starting a fight.

Aggressive individuals, it seems, sometimes convert peaceful interactions into violent ones, because they are spoiling for a fight. The cognitions of aggressive individuals also play a part. When aggressive boys were shown videotapes of social behavior, they attributed hostile intent to the characters (Dodge & Somberg, 1987). The ordinary social behavior of others might be misinterpreted as hostile by aggressive individuals, who respond with their own hostility and aggression. They can escalate a relatively quiet social interaction into a stormy one in which others retaliate. Thus hostile cognitions can become self-fulfilling prophecies.

The whipping boys mentioned earlier tend to be attacked mainly by aggressive individuals called *bullies*: "The bullies were distinguished by strong aggressive tendencies and a weak control of such tendencies, if activated. They clearly had a more positive attitude toward violence and violent means. . . . Moreover, they felt fearless, confident, tough, non-anxious, and had, on the whole, a positive attitude toward themselves" (Olweus, 1984, p. 62).

Those at the other end of the aggression dimension are likely to modify the environment in the opposite direction. They have a more benign interpretation of others' actions, responding to aggression with attempts to minimize the turmoil. Such people, the peacemakers and mediators, can alter their own environment in the direction of tranquility.

Thus the personalities of bullies and mediators are partial determinants of their own social environment. The bullies tend to convert peaceful interactions into violent ones, especially when in the company of victims. The mediators tend to convert aggressive environments into peaceful ones. The three ways in which a person can affect environment—choosing, setting the tone, and modifying—are illustrated in Table 2.3.

Match between Person and Environment

Some individuals seem to be entirely at home in their surroundings, fitting comfortably into their own particular niche. There are New Yorkers born and bred in the city who thrive on the bustle and willingly tolerate the crowds and the noise. They are matched to their environment. If circumstances forced these individuals to move to a rural, isolated community, there would be a serious mismatch between person and environment.

A different kind of mismatch can result from precocity in development. An adolescent who acquires secondary sex characteristics very early will have the physical features of an adult and may therefore be treated as an adult by strangers or casual acquaintances. A young girl who looks like a woman may be subjected to sexual overtures that she is too young to handle. There is a mismatch between her physical development and the expectations of others. Recall that early-maturing girls tended to have more problems of adjustment (Caspi & Moffitt, 1991).

A similar mismatch in development occurs for extremely intelligent children, who are placed in school grades well above those of their peers. Intellectually at the level of adolescents, they are physically and socially as immature as their age-mates. Precocity can also pose a problem for talented child actors, musicians, or athletes who may be thrust into the adult world of performance and competition but who otherwise remain children.

These examples of mismatches between person and environment are of course only half the story. The other half comprises matches between person and environment, especially the social environment.

Child and Parent
The focus in the child-parent relationship is on the traits of each. For the sake of simplicity only the extremes of a trait are considered and only when both parents are at the same extreme of the trait dimension. Within these limitations, there are four combinations: two kinds of match and two kinds of mismatch.

TABLE 2.3   Ways a Person Affects Environment

	More aggressive ways	Less aggressive ways
Choice	Watch violent TV Play hockey	Watch nonviolent TV Swim
Setting of tone	Be grouchy or surly Be a bully	Smile, be receptive Be a victim
Modification	Escalate conversation into argument	Convert argument into conversation
	Have hostile cognitions	Have peaceful cognitions

In one kind of match, both child and parent are highly aggressive and prone to anger. This combination inevitably generates a tempestuous relationship. The parent is easily angered and is likely to use punishment quickly and frequently. This punishment tends to incite the aggressive child to anger and rebellion against the parents. The child may seek victims who cannot retaliate so easily: younger siblings or children outside the family, especially the aforementioned whipping boys.

The other kind of match, between a nonaggressive parent and child, poses no particular problems. Both want to avoid turmoil, and the parent is unlikely to use physical or verbal punishment, instead using reason and withholding privileges. The child finds such parental behavior amenable, and the relationship should be peaceful.

Between these extremes of parent-child relationships are the two mismatches. If the parent is not aggressive and the child is, there will be difficulties. The parent will not understand why the child is so angry and gets into so many fights. It is up to the parent to teach the child nonaggressive ways of obtaining rewards and to delay outbursts of anger ("Count to 10"). Being nonaggressive, the parent does not use physical punishment, and so does not serve as an aggressive model for the child, nor is the child likely to become rebellious. The greatest danger in this mismatch is parental permissiveness, which would allow the child freedom to have temper tantrums and to be rewarded for instrumental aggression. The optimal kind of discipline here may be authoritative (Baumrind, 1971).

The mirror-image mismatch is an aggressive parent and a nonaggressive child. Physical punishment, expected from an aggressive parent, may anger the child, making aggression against peers more likely; and an aggressive parent can be imitated. But parental punishment can also instill fear in the child, especially a nonaggressive child, thereby diminishing the potential for the child's aggressing. The outcome, therefore, might be a frightened child who typically does not aggress but occasionally explodes with angry aggression. In addition, later in life adults who have been abused as children may abuse their own children.

Marriage

It has been reported that we are attracted to those who are similar to us (Byrne, 1972), a finding that holds for computer dating services (Byrne, Ervin, & Lamberth, 1970). What are the implications for marriage of similarity in aggressiveness? If both spouses are aggressive, there are likely to be intense arguments and perhaps physical attacks. When one partner is irritable, it annoys the other. Verbal aggression by one often results immediately in retaliation by the other, setting up a vicious cycle of attack leading to retribution, which leads to further attack.

The opposite match, both spouses being nonaggressive, results in a peaceful marriage. Each partner refrains from attacking, and if one is irritable, the other might be willing to tolerate it. There might be a potential problem, however. Inevitably, there are conflicts in marriage. Such conflicts need to be resolved, and one means is through verbal aggression. If both partners avoid being aggressive, they need to find some way of airing grievances, which otherwise might intensify and weaken the relationship.

If there is a mismatch, the husband is usually the aggressive one, men being the more aggressive sex, as we saw in Chapter 1. The wife's nonaggressiveness tends to minimize what would otherwise be virtually continual fighting. There is, however, a down side. The wife's tolerance of the husband's aggression will allow him to continue it and perhaps even be rewarded by it, which will make his habit even stronger. Other things being equal, the husband's aggression tends to be verbal if he is middle class, and physical if he is lower class, although wife-beating is certainly not unknown in middle-class marriages. Also, if the wife is the aggressor, she is likely to attack with words rather than with fists or weapons.

Meyer and Pepper (1977) gathered data on young couples who were judged to be adjusted or not adjusted. For the adjusted couples, the husband's aggressiveness correlated only .08 with the wife's aggressiveness, but for the maladjusted couples the correlation was .40. The adjusted couples got along whether there was a match or a mismatch in aggressiveness, presumably because they had other things going for them. For the maladjusted couples, however, a mismatch caused problems. The couples in Meyer and Pepper's study were young, though, and it would be interesting to discover whether the results would hold for older married and divorced couples.

Jobs

Some of the best examples of how personality can result in a fit or a misfit with a job may be found in the acting profession. Sylvester Stallone appears to have found his niche playing an inarticulate hero who blasts through all opposition with fists or weapons. Similarly, Clint Eastwood is entirely at home playing a laconic, solitary man who uses violence to best villains in the Old West or in modern cities. Can we imagine either actor playing the role of sophisticated banker or weakling husband? The public simply would not accept such bad casting (mismatch).

For simplicity, let us restrict examples of matching in aggressiveness to men, though what follows also applies to women. What would be a good match between a job and a man who is aggressive? One possibility is a football linebacker, a position that requires the player to knock down blockers, tackle ball carriers, and in general, intimidate the opposing players. Other possibilities are professional boxer and Marine drill sergeant. Obviously, a nonaggressive person would be mismatched in such positions.

Sports also provide examples of matches and mismatches between positions and angry individuals. A hair-trigger temper would cause little trouble in a professional hockey player, as some hockey players are employed for their readiness to fight as well as for their athletic skill. But such a temper would cause trouble for a professional tennis player. For an example, we need only recall tennis pro John McEnroe's outbursts on the court, which resulted in fines and loss of fans.

It would be rational to decide on a job or profession on the basis of a match between personality and job requirements, for the outcome would be satisfaction on the part of the individual and good performance on the job. But the major determinants of job placements appear to be opportunity, training, and skills. In making a living, most of us cannot consider whether our personality matches the job, so mismatches between person and job are to be expected and do occur.

Enduring Outcomes

A close match over time between person and environment is expected to intensify the relevant personality trait. Thus if a compulsive person spends many years as an accountant, a job that requires close attention to detail, that person is likely to become increasingly compulsive. After an aggressive man plays linebacker in college and professional football for a decade, he will probably be even more aggressive than when he started college. But if parents and their child are low in aggressiveness, parental reinforcement and modeling may make the child even less aggressive.

These lasting effects are examples of enduring outcomes. Mismatches have the opposite effect, that of moving persons from the extremes of a trait dimension toward the middle. Thus in a parent-child mismatch, an aggressive child is likely to become less aggressive, and an unaggressive child is likely to become slightly aggressive. Suppose the person playing the position of football linebacker started out as low in aggressiveness. After years of training and being rewarded for aggressive play, he might end up being somewhat more aggressive than when he started. However, the impact of such a violent environment is expected to be weaker for him than for the man who was already aggressive. And a minority of men might even be unaffected by such training. Thus whether an environment has an impact depends in part on the particular person exposed to that environment. Socialization agents—parents, teachers, and coaches—send messages to children about how they should behave in the adult world. Most childen receive these messages; some do not. In other words, environments interact with individuals.

Mismatches may have another enduring outcome: strain. Consider the situation of women who have been reinforced in college for being bright and interested in intellectual matters. If some of these women opt for work that is not challenging, or have a child soon after finishing college and spend most of their days caring for their child, the mismatch between the interests or abilities of these women and their daily life may become extremely frustrating and stressful.

Now consider a quick-tempered man who is stuck with a tyrannical boss. If the man desperately needs the job, he will have to grit his teeth and inhibit his tendency to explode into anger. If this situation endures, he might develop bodily complaints. Square pegs can tolerate round holes for a little while, but chronic mismatches typically produce strain.

Heredity

Research on Twins

Identical and Fraternal Twins

To discover whether some aspects of human personality have an inherited component, researchers study identical and fraternal twins for reasons familiar to most people. Identical twins are so named because they develop from a single fertilized egg (monozygote) and so their genes are identical. Fraternal twins are so named because their genes are no more alike than those of siblings born at different times.

They develop from two different fertilized eggs (dizygote). Thus there is a 100% overlap in the genes of identical twins but only a 50% overlap in the genes of fraternal twins. Being born at the same time, twins are expected to share roughly the same environment. These two different kinds of twins therefore may be regarded as one of nature's experiments.

If a trait were completely inherited, theoretically the correlation between identical twins should be perfect, but we know that errors of measurement might reduce the correlation to well below 1.00. Theoretically the correlation between fraternal twins should be .50, but errors of measurement might reduce the correlation below that figure.

When the correlation between identical twins is significantly higher than the correlation between fraternal twins, we infer that the trait is inherited. To derive a quantitative measure of inheritance, researchers compute the difference between these two correlations and double it (Falconer, 1960). For example, in one study the correlations for weight were .83 in identical twins and .43 in fraternal twins (Lykken, 1982). The difference between these correlations, .40, is doubled to yield an estimate that roughly 80% of the origin of weight is inheritance. However, such quantitative estimates assume a precision of measurement not yet attained in the study of personality, so they will not subsequently be reported.

Possible Artefacts

Identical twins look more alike than fraternal twins. It follows that identical twins might be treated more alike, and, generally, their environment might be more similar than that of fraternal twins. Parents and others, knowing that twins are identical, might treat them more alike than they would fraternal twins. Thus the higher correlations between identical twins might be the result of environment, not heredity.

Several studies have focused on these issues. Identical twins vary slightly in appearance, and these variations were correlated in one study with sixteen personality traits (Matheny, Wilson, & Dolan, 1976). The average correlation was zero, though perhaps this correlation was held down by the lack of variance in the twins' appearance. In a more telling study (Loehlin and Nichols, 1976), the *disparity* in the environments of identical twins was correlated with how different they were in eighteen personality traits. The correlation was .06. A third study addressed the issue of others knowing which twins are identical, the personality trait being extraversion (Scarr & Carter-Saltzman, 1979). Some fraternal twins are thought by themselves or others to be identical, and a comparable mistake is sometimes made in the case of identical twins. Only true zygosity predicted the greater similarity of identical twins over fraternal twins. Mistaken identification of zygosity, whether by twins or others, was unrelated to this difference in similarity.

These three studies offer evidence about the possible role of artefacts. Identical twins are more similar in personality than fraternal twins not because of variations in the physical resemblance of identical twins, disparities in their environments, or in mistaken beliefs about zygosity. Rather, identical twins are more similar because they overlap so completely in their genes.

Aggression

Research on aggression in twins has been sparse because aggression is not represented on the major personality inventories. There are, however, some relevant studies. Mothers of twins completed a checklist of aggressive behaviors observed in their children (Ghodsian-Carpey & Baker, 1987). When the various categories of aggressive behavior were summed, the correlations were .65 for identical twins and .35 for fraternal twins. Considerably lower correlations for aggressiveness were obtained from the self-reports of adults, .40 for identical twins and .04 for fraternal twins (Rushton, Fulker, Neale, Nias, & Eysenck, 1986). In an all-male sample, the correlations were .47 for identical twins and .15 for fraternal twins.

One study compared twins reared together with those reared apart (Tellegen et al., 1988). For those reared together, the correlations for aggression were .43 for identical twins and .14 for fraternal twins. For those reared apart, the correlations were .46 for identical twins and .06 for fraternal twins. There was also a scale measuring *alienation*, which includes feeling mistreated, a victim of bad luck, and betrayed, as well as believing that others wish one harm. This scale clearly measures the combination of resentment and suspicion that I call hostility. The correlations for hostility for those reared together were .55 for identical twins and .38 for fraternal twins. For those reared apart the correlations were .48 for identical twins and .18 for fraternal twins. The data from twins reared apart is especially convincing because the parents who raise the children (environment) are not the biological parents who contributed the genes.

In another study of aggression identical and fraternal twins were tested once at an average age of twenty years and again at thirty years (McGue, Bacon, & Lykken, 1993). The correlations for aggression at the first testing were .61 for identical twins and −.09 for fraternal twins. The second time the correlations were .58 for identical twins and −.14 for fraternal twins.

Other research on twins has found heritability by means of an adjective checklist of aggression (Scarr, 1966), items reflecting argumentativeness (Loehlin & Nichols, 1976), and anger and meanness (Horn, Plomin, & Rosenman, 1976). The findings were consistently positive, and most of the studies used a reasonably large sample of subjects. These results, taken together with other twin data, lead to the conclusion that aggressiveness is an inherited trait.

Multiple Genes

Most people are familiar with the action of single genes and the concepts of dominance and recessiveness. Thus blue eyes are inherited through recessive genes, and brown eyes through dominant genes. The basis of this conclusion is the distribution of these two eye colors in the population.

The inheritance of personality traits yields a normal distribution very different from that of eye color. The presence of a normal distribution leads us to infer that personality traits are inherited through the action of many different genes (*polygenic inheritance*). The multiple genes involved in any trait might work *additively*.

For example, more genes would operate for aggressive people than for people low in aggressiveness. Another possibility is that multiple genes work *configurally*. If aggressiveness, for example, were inherited configurally, the entire set of genes would have to be present for a person to be intensely aggressive. If only one gene were missing, the person might be just a little less aggressive, a lot less aggressive, or even nonaggressive.

If a trait is inherited through the configural operation of multiple genes, there should be a particular pattern of findings (Lykken, 1982; Lykken, McGue, Tellegen, & Bouchard, 1992). As a product of multiple genes, the trait should be normally distributed. Identical twins, sharing the entire configuration of genes, should be highly similar. Fraternal twins, sharing only some of the genes, not the entire configuration, should show little similarity even though the trait is inherited. In quantitative terms, the correlation for identical twins should be high except for errors of measurement or the action of the environment (an issue to be discussed shortly). The correlation for fraternal twins should be very low.

Lykken et al. (1992) mentioned one trait that matches this pattern: social potency, a composite, as he sees it, of attractiveness, self-esteem, and assertiveness. The correlations for this trait were .67 for identical twins and .07 for fraternal twins. Some of the twin data for aggressiveness also fit the pattern needed to infer genes acting configurally. Recall that Rushton et al. (1986) found that for aggression identical twins correlated .40 and fraternal twins only .04. And Tellegen et al. (1988) and McGue et al. (1993) reported a similar pattern of correlations. Perhaps, then, the inheritance of aggression occurs through a configuration of multiple genes.

Heredity and Environment

Virtually every behavior genetics study that reveals the role of heredity also demonstrates the role of environment. Genes may operate differently in different environments. Furthermore, virtually any tendency that is inherited can also be altered by everyday events. In brief, the evidence for the inheritance of personality dispositions does not deny the importance of the environment.

Some inherited traits are fixed and unchanging once they have occurred during development. For example, eye color stabilizes during the first year of life and remains the same thereafter. But other characteristics, though reasonably stable, can be modified by life experiences. For example, height, weight, muscle mass, and distribution of fat—the various components of physique—are inherited. As everyone knows, though, physique can be altered by dieting, overeating, and body-building exercise. But there are limits, determined by heredity, to how much one's basic physique can be changed. For some people these limits are stringent. Thus there are thin people who cannot seem to gain weight no matter how much they try, much to the chagrin of those who want to lose weight but cannot. Others may manifest startling changes in build during the adult years, especially men and women who seriously work at weight lifting or who inflict steroids on themselves.

Inherited personality tendencies may be regarded as analogous to physique. Heredity plays a major role in their origin, but they can be modified by the environment and individual experience. In fact, research on twins, which has informed us of the role of heredity, has also suggested how important environment is (see Plomin, DeFries, & McClearn, 1980).

When heredity and environment are invoked to explain the origins of personality, there are two extreme positions. Some behavior geneticists believe that all personality traits are inherited, just as some environmentalists believe that no personality traits are inherited. The twin data on aggressiveness, reviewed earlier, establish that this trait is inherited, and, as we shall see, there is evidence that other traits are inherited. But for a number of personality traits, there is no evidence of inheritance, which means that these traits are wholly acquired. Thus there is evidence for both extreme positions, but a categorical statement that all traits are inherited or that no traits are inherited is clearly wrong. Furthermore, it bears repeating that the very behavior genetic research that establishes the inheritance of some personality traits also demonstrates that environment is important. Perhaps, then, a better way of construing this issue is to ask these questions:

1. Which aspects of personality are inherited?
2. For those that are inherited, how important are family environment and individual experiences?
3. How do genes and environment interact?

Family and Individual Environment

Most research on the environment as a determiner of personality traits has focused on how parents treat their children. In the past, the simplest assumption has been made: that all the children in a given family share the same environment. Presumably, whatever the personalities and the child-rearing attitudes of the parents, they are the same for all their children. It follows that one source of individual differences should be the way one familial environment differs from the next.

A moment's reflection, though, suggests that children in the same family can experience different environments. The parents may prefer one child over the others, treat boys differently than girls, and learn from mistakes with an older child to act differently with a younger child. A student once reported that her parents labeled her the smart one, and her sister the pretty one. She grew up thinking that she was not physically attractive, and her sister grew up thinking that she was not very bright.

Thus it is possible that the environment *within* a family may be as different as the environment in one family is different from that in the next family. This point is underscored by research showing that differences from one family to the next account for negligible variance in personality traits (Rowe & Plomin, 1981). Scarr and Grajek (1982), after reporting low correlations in biological siblings and nearly zero correlations in adopted children, offered this example: "Upper middle class brothers who attend the same school and whose parents take them to the same plays, sporting events, music lessons, and therapists, and use similar child rearing practices on them are little more similar in personality measures than they are to working class or farm boys whose lives are totally different" (p. 361). These negative findings mean that the familial environment shared by the children of any one family contributes little or nothing to their personality. These data also are consistent with the previously mentioned hypothesis that many genes act configurally, so that siblings and fraternal twins will not be particularly similar in personality.

Concerning the environment generally, from a large-scale study of twins came this conclusion: "Thus, a consistent—though perplexing—pattern is emerging from the data (and it is not purely idiosyncratic to our study). Environment carries substantial weight in determining personality—it appears to account for at least half the variance—but that environment is one for which twin pairs are correlated close to zero. . . . In short, in the personality domain we seem to see environmental effects that operate almost randomly with respect to the sorts of variables that psychologists (and other people) have traditionally deemed important in personality development" (Loehlin & Nichols, 1976, p. 92).

If the environment is important, but the shared family environment is not, we might do better to turn our attention to the individual experiences of children. Plomin and Daniels (1987) reviewed their own and others' findings on adoptive children, twins, and siblings in the same family and concluded that "when more than one child is studied per family, it is apparent that siblings in the same family experience considerably different environments, in terms of their treatment of each other, in their peer interactions, and perhaps in terms of parental treatment" (p. 49).

A focus on individual experiences fits well with a perspective that sees persons interacting with the environment. Thus a father who prefers to be permissive with his children may do so with a nonaggressive child but be forced to be more authoritarian in attempting to control an aggressive child. And when a new baby is born, it is likely to have a greater impact on the former baby of the family than on older siblings. Of course, emphasizing individual experience means that studying the environment will be more difficult, and any theory of the development of personality will necessarily be more complex.

Heredity-Environment Relationships

Recall that the relationship between heredity and environment is a two-way street, the one affecting the other. In fact, three kinds of relationship between the two have been outlined (Plomin et al., 1977). In the passive kind of relationship, parents have the same inherited traits as their children and therefore offer an environment that matches the traits of their children. Thus aggressive parents, who are likely to use strong punishment on their children, offer an environment likely to enhance their children's (already present) tendency to aggress.

In the reactive kind of relationship, the reactions of others provide an environment that intensifies the inherited trait already present. For instance, aggressive children are often cordially disliked by their playmates, who regard them as hostile. Peers, then, may reject aggressive children or attack them, which can only make the latter more aggressive (Dodge, 1983). The opposite reaction is also possible, however. Parents and teachers may react to children's aggression by attempting to minimize or eliminate it. It has been suggested that during development there is a shift from the passive kind of heredity-environment relationship to the reactive kind (Scarr & McCartney, 1983).

In the active kind of relationship, the individual refuses to accept the current environment but changes it to make it more amenable to his or her inherited traits. Thus an aggressive person might escalate a conversation into an argument or a slight difference of opinion into a heated debate.

The three kinds of relationship apply only to inherited traits. However, each kind of relationship may be subsumed under the heading of the previously mentioned, broader concept that applies to all of personality, whether inherited or acquired. The passive kind of relationship harks back to the idea of a match between person and environment. The reactive kind may be recognized as setting the tone for social interaction. And the active kind is a special case of modifying the environment.

Sex Differences

Both heredity and environment may be expected to contribute to sex differences, and this arena has sparked the hottest debate between the two. With respect to aggression, the contest is between the contributions of biology, specifically hormones, and the contributions of socialization, specifically culturally defined sex roles.

But, first, let us consider the facts of sex differences. When preschoolers' reactions to anger were observed during play, boys reacted more often with physical aggression than girls; otherwise there was no other sex difference in aggression (Fabes & Eisenberg, 1992). On the aggression questionnaire described in Chapter 1, men were clearly and significantly higher than women mainly in physical aggression (Buss & Perry, 1992). Other questionnaires have shown that young men are higher in overall aggression than young women (Woodall & Matthews, 1993) and that men are higher than women in overall aggression throughout life (Barefoot et al., 1991).

There are other ways of studying aggression, however, and other sex differences might appear when other methods are used. In the most complete review, which included various methods, Eagly and Steffen (1986) concluded that men are generally more aggressive than women by about one-third of a standard deviation. The difference was larger for physical aggression than for verbal aggression. Men were also found to be the targets of aggression more often than women, especially when the aggression is physical and there is provocation.

Are there similar sex differences in other societies? In five out of six cultures, boys were found to be more physically and verbally aggressive than girls in the age range of three to eleven years (Whiting & Edwards, 1973). In a review of worldwide sex differences, young boys were found to be more aggressive than girls in ten cultures, and there was no sex difference in four cultures (Rohner, 1976). Among adults, the same review revealed that men were more aggressive in six cultures, women were more aggressive in five cultures, and there was no sex difference in twenty cultures.

These various findings lead to a dual conclusion: Worldwide, boys tend to be more aggressive than girls, but men are no more aggressive than women. Our society represents the minority of cultures in which males are more aggressive than females throughout life, though the sex difference is smaller for adults than for children.

Biology.   There is a basis for implicating the male sex hormone, testosterone, in the greater aggressiveness of males, for it is well known that castrated animals become less aggressive, which is why steers are herded rather than bulls. Can we extrapolate to human males, though? The findings are mixed. Two studies report no relationships between level of testosterone and frequency of aggression, as assessed by self-report (Kreuz & Rose, 1972; Meyer-Bahlburg, Nat, Sharma, & Edwards, 1974).

Several other studies, however, yielded positive results. Testosterone level was found to be higher in men who self-reported more intense or more frequent aggression in response to provocation or threat (Olweus, Mattson, Schalling, & Loow, 1980). Criminals with a history of violence were found to have higher testosterone levels than nonviolent criminals (Kreuz & Rose, 1972). Violent criminals have a higher level of testosterone than nonviolent criminals (Dabbs, Frady, Carr, & Besch, 1987). A group of women given testosterone for medical reasons reported more violence after a period of treatment (Ehlers, Rickler, & Hovey, 1980). Normal adolescent males who were reported to act out and misbehave had higher levels of the male hormone androstenedione than those who did not act out (Susman et al., 1987).

A recent experiment extended the testosterone-aggression relationship to normal college men (Berman, Gladue, & Taylor, 1993). In this paradigm, a modification of the aggression machine procedure, two opponents compete, and on each trial the one with a faster reaction time shocks the other. Both, however, know in advance how much shock they will receive on each trial. Men higher in testosterone used more intense shock than those lower in testosterone. The correlation between this male hormone and intensity of aggression was .42. Would this finding generalize to a situation in which there was not the provocation of the competition or the threat of being shocked? We need an experiment with the original aggression machine paradigm to answer this question.

In brief, there is evidence for a relationship in males between testosterone and physical aggression. We cannot assume that the effect is in one direction only: from hormones to aggression. Consider the conclusions of a recent comprehensive review: "In adults, comparisons between groups showing high or low levels of aggressiveness revealed higher testosterone levels in the more aggressive group. Correlations between testosterone and aggression were low but positive for trait measures, but considerably higher when they were based on ratings of aggressiveness by others in the person's environment. Nevertheless, such positive findings do not necessarily indicate an influence of testosterone on aggressiveness because other studies show that the outcome of aggressive and competitive encounters can increase or decrease testosterone levels" (Archer, 1991, p. 21).

Socialization.   This approach to aggression emphasizes social roles: "Like other social behaviors, aggression can be viewed as role behavior and therefore regulated by the social norms that are applied to people based on the roles they occupy.

To account for sex differences in aggression from this perspective, we must understand the ways in which aggression is sustained or inhibited by the social roles occupied mainly or exclusively by persons of each sex" (Eagly & Steffen, 1986, p. 310).

Cultures vary in the social roles assigned to each sex, so it follows that in some cultures men will be more aggressive and in other cultures women will be more aggressive. As Rohner's (1976) survey revealed, there were such variations from one culture to the next. Recall that in Kenya boys assigned to feminine tasks were found to be less aggressive than boys assigned to typical masculine tasks (Ember, 1973). In the United States, men are expected to be more aggressive (Cicone & Ruble, 1978), and men view violence on television and war more favorably than do women (T. W. Smith, 1986).

Thus there is evidence for the socialization position. It might be argued that socialization practices merely follow the dictates of biology, reflecting an innate sex difference in aggression. Given our sparse knowledge, perhaps we should adopt the more conservative position: Both biology and socialization contribute to the sex difference in physical aggression.

Chapter *3*

Temperament I

History

The history of temperament begins over two thousand years ago with the Greek physician Galen. His physiological theory assumed four types of personality, each determined by an internal substance:

1. The *sanguine* person, having an excess of blood (*sanguine* means "bloody"), tends to be lively and upbeat.
2. The *phlegmatic* person, having an excess of phlegm, tends to be slow-moving and controlled.
3. The *melancholic* person, having an excess of black bile (*melancholy* means "black bile"), tends to worry and be sad.
4. The *choleric* person, having an excess of bile, tends to be excitable and prone to anger.

Galen's theory that these body fluids determine personality long ago disappeared into the graveyard of ideas supplanted by modern knowledge. The classification of four basic personality types persists into the modern era, however.

Europe and Great Britain

In England, Hans Eysenck (1947) arranged the four types of personality in a circle with two axes: extraverted-introverted and emotionally stable-unstable. Thus the sanguine person is extraverted and emotionally stable, the melancholic person is introverted and emotionally unstable, and so on.

The Russian physiologist Ivan Pavlov (1927) also was influenced by Galen's typology. He viewed personality as reflecting three properties of the central nervous system: strength, balance, and excitation-inhibition. These properties were used to account for the four types of temperament:

1. Sanguine = strong, balanced, excited
2. Phlegmatic = strong, balanced, inhibited
3. Melancholic = weak, unbalanced, inhibited
4. Choleric = strong, unbalanced, excited

The Polish psychologist Jan Strelau (1983) has used Pavlov's theory as a springboard for his own conception, though he discards the fourfold classification of temperaments. His major concepts are energetic level and temporal characteristics. Energetic level embodies Pavlov's concepts of strength and balance of the nervous system. It consists of both activity and reactivity. Activity is manifest in the amount and range of activities engaged in by the individual. Reactivity also has two facets: threshold of stimulation and intensity of reaction. Temporal characteristics roughly match Pavlov's mobility of the nervous system. Relevant personality traits are tempo and persistence of behavior.

United States of America

Gordon Allport, a pioneer in the field of personality, wrote about temperament earlier, but his clearest statement of what temperament is can be found in his 1961 book: "Temperament refers to the characteristic phenomena of an individual's nature, including his susceptibility to emotional stimulation, his customary strength and speed of response, the quality of his prevailing mood, and all the peculiarities of fluctuation and intensity of mood, these being phenomena regarded as dependent on constitution, and therefore largely hereditary in nature" (p. 34). Though the first part of this definition is vague ("characteristic phenomena of an individual's nature"), the last part appropriately emphasizes the constitutional and hereditary origin of the traits included as temperaments.

The Pediatric Tradition

Modern research on temperament began with the work of Alexander Thomas, Stella Chess, and their colleagues (1963, 1968). They called their project the New York Longitudinal Study (NYLS). Thomas and Chess are pediatric psychiatrists who were dissatisfied with the psychoanalytic approach to children's problems that predominated after World War II. They interviewed parents who described their children's behavior, and an armchair analysis of twenty-two interviews led them to establish nine categories or dimensions of temperament:

Activity level
Rhythmicity
Approach or withdrawal
Adaptability
Intensity of reaction
Threshold of responsiveness
Quality of mood

Distractibility
Attention span and persistence

In addition, they originally categorized children as easy, difficult, or slow to warm up. This classification was replaced by the dimension of easy to difficult. Emphasizing the child's interaction with the environment, they suggested the concept of goodness of fit, that is, how well the child's temperament was adapted to the current environment.

The NYLS approach focuses on the problems in children's behavior that occupy parents and pediatricians. Thus some of the items deal with food ("The child is willing to try new foods"), and others deal with sleep ("The child falls asleep as soon as he/she is put to bed"). There are also items pertaining to personality, but many of them deal with potential difficulties ("The child is slow to adjust to changes in household routines"). Are difficulties with food, sleep, or changes in household rules likely to leave behind residual personality tendencies? No, these minor problems, like nail-biting or thumb-sucking, having no enduring consequences for personality.

There is also a pressing empirical question: Are there nine dimensions of temperament? Several factor analyses of items, reviewed by Buss and Plomin (1984), come up with a negative answer. Not only are there fewer than nine factors (dimensions), but the obtained factors match only two of the NYLS dimensions. The pediatric approach clearly is important for dealing with problems of childhood, its original purpose, but of less value as a perspective on personality.

The Personality Tradition

A little earlier, Solomon Diamond (1957) published his evolutionary approach to temperament. He described four temperaments shared by primates (including our species) and perhaps some social mammals: fearfulness, aggressiveness, affiliativeness, and impulsiveness. He conducted no human research, nor did he offer specific means of testing his hypotheses. In the 1950s, however, there was little interest in an evolutionary approach to personality, and Diamond's ideas were neglected by most psychologists.

Nevertheless, I found his ideas fascinating, and eventually Robert Plomin and I built on them to formulate our own theory (Buss & Plomin, 1975). We see temperaments as a subclass of personality traits, shared by our species and primates (see Buss, 1988), and defined as being inherited and appearing early in life. To be more precise, temperaments in our approach are *inherited personality traits that appear during the first two years of life and endure as basic components of personality.* Notice that there are three defining properties of temperaments: they are inherited, they appear early, and they endure. Then consider the following. There are personality traits that appear during infancy, but they are not inherited. There certainly are inherited personality traits that appear later in life, but they appear too late to be called temperaments. And there may be early childhood problems that leave behind no residue of any importance for personality.

Our four temperaments are emotionality, activity, sociability, and impulsivity, which are represented by the acronym EASI. These temperaments are broad personality dispositions. It is of course possible that humans possess inherited propensities that are highly specific, but most of our inherited dispositions appear to be generalized. Thus hunger is a strong, built-in motive, but it can be satisfied by a wide variety of foods. We are programmed to speak, but even that tendency is so inclusive that it encompasses hundreds of languages and a bewildering number of speech sounds. And intelligence is sufficiently broad to cover a wide array of intellectual abilities. Thus temperaments appear to be consistent with other inherited human psychological tendencies in being broad rather than narrow.

In this chapter I treat the first two temperaments, *emotionality* and *activity*. Emotionality, as will be seen, is regarded as differentiating into anger and fear. Anger was examined in Chapters 1 and 2 and will not be further mentioned except in the context of differentiation. Emotionality and its other derivative, fear, will be discussed here. The last two temperaments, sociability and impulsivity, comprise Chapter 4.

Emotionality

Emotionality refers to negative affect, specifically, being distressed or upset. In everyday usage, these terms include not only the high (physiological) arousal states of frustration, pain, or generalized discomfort, but also the low arousal states of bereavement and depression. These low arousal states are specifically excluded on the assumption that what is inherited in emotionality is the tendency to become (autonomically) aroused easily and intensely. In brief, emotionality is here defined as high-arousal, generalized negative affect, its synonym being *distress*.

The emotionality scale of the EAS Temperament Survey (Buss & Plomin, 1984) contains these items:

> I frequently get distressed.
> I often feel frustrated.
> Everyday events make me troubled and fretful.
> I get emotionally upset easily.

Heritability

Various twin studies using the emotionality scale of the EAS were combined to yield a total of 228 identical twins and 172 fraternal twins, with an average age of five years (Buss & Plomin, 1984, p. 122). Identical twins correlated .63; fraternal twins, .12. More recently, twins in the second year of life were assessed for emotionality on the Colorado Child Temperament Inventory. The correlation for identical twins was .35, and for fraternal twins −.02 (Emde et al., 1992).

In an unusual longitudinal study, twins were first tested at an average age of twenty years and again ten years later (McGue, Bacon, & Lykken, 1993). The trait was *negative emotionality*, which, as we shall see shortly, is close to the temperament of emotionality. At the first testing the correlations were .53 for identical twins and .31 for fraternal twins. At the second testing the correlations were .50 for identical twins and .28 for fraternal twins.

Twins reared apart offer especially valuable information about heritability because the twins do not experience the same family environment. The only relevant study compared the negative emotionality of twins reared apart. For identical twins, the correlation was .61; for fraternal twins, .29 (Tellegen et al., 1988). These various studies attest to the heritability of emotionality.

Development

First Appearance

Distress may be observed in an infant, say, a boy, on the first day of life. He crinkles his face as if to cry, though tears will not be available until later. His face reddens, and his breath comes in gasps. He may kick his legs, move his arms vigorously, or even arch his back. The infant obviously is uncomfortable, and his distress can usually be relieved by feeding him, warming him, or picking him up and comforting him.

The Chinese are known for their placidity, especially in comparison to Americans. The children of Chinese-American parents were compared in a San Francisco hospital on the second day of life (Freedman, 1971). American infants were observed to be more excitable, restless, and emotional than Chinese-American infants, especially in their reaction to annoyance: "In an item called *defensive movements*, the tester placed a cloth firmly over the supine baby's face for a few seconds. While the typical European-American infant immediately struggled to remove the cloth, the typical Chinese-American infant lay impassively, exhibiting few overt motor responses" (Freedman, 1971, p. 93). Parenthetically, the Chinese babies were no more sleepy than the American babies.

On the first day of life, American babies vary considerably in how much they cry (Korner, Hutchinson, Koperski, Kraemer, & Schneider, 1981), and these individual differences are stable for at least several days. There are also sharp individual differences early in life in the physiological arousal that accompanies the observable distress responses (Lipton & Steinschneider, 1964).

Differentiation

I follow Bridges (1932) in assuming that during the first year of life, primordial emotionality differentiates into fear and anger. After observing infants in a foundling home, she suggested that distress splits into fear and anger sometime during the first year, perhaps at about six months. Sroufe (1979), who updated Bridges's conception, suggested that fear or wariness first appears at four months of age, followed by anger at seven months of age.

If the differentiation hypothesis is correct, it follows that the three emotions—distress and its two derivatives, fear and anger—should be related to each other. Plomin (1974) intercorrelated them, using mothers' and fathers' ratings of their young sons' and daughters' temperaments. The correlations between emotionality (distress) and fear ranged from .39 to .52; between emotionality and anger, from .52 to .72. Thus both fear and anger are related to distress, though as might be expected, the size of the correlations suggests that they are differentiated.

In adults, however, the picture is different. The correlations between distress and fear are .52 for women and .63 for men, but the correlations between distress and anger are .37 for men and .28 for women (Buss & Plomin, 1984, p. 101). There is no obvious explanation for this shift from childhood to adulthood in the relationships between emotionality and fear and anger. Though these various correlations cannot prove the differentiation hypothesis (that would require a longitudinal study), they are consistent with it.

Differentiation does not cause distress simply to disappear. Older children or adults may become upset without being afraid or angry when confronted with frustrating situations, especially those over which they have no control: rain washing out a picnic, a flat tire on a car, or just plain hunger.

Matching

Childhood.   The following examples pair a mother with a son, but what is said also applies to other gender combinations. If the mother and son are both low in emotionality, their relationship should be tranquil, for neither becomes upset easily.

If the son is emotional and the mother is not, there will be upheavals because of the son's temperament. However, though the mother regards her child as difficult, she tends to react calmly when he becomes upset. Her ability to handle his explosiveness should in the long run minimize it.

If the son is not emotional and the mother is, she may magnify his slight tendency to become distressed. By presenting a tumultuous environment, she may intensify his reactions. She offers an emotional model that he may copy. This mismatch, like the other, modifies the son's inherited disposition.

If both mother and son are emotional, his jeopardy is multiple. It starts with his own negative affect, which is worsened by both the emotional climate and the model that the mother provides. This match amplifies the child's inherited tendency to be emotional.

Adulthood.   Analogous problems arise in marriage, though little change should be expected in adult temperament. If both husband and wife are emotional, the relationship is likely to be too stormy to endure. In a mismatch, the calm spouse is available to soothe the upset one. In such a marriage, the emotional one may come to rely on the other to keep things level. And of course, if both are unemotional, temperament poses no problems for the relationship.

Mood, Neuroticism, and Negative Affectivity

A study of self-reported daily mood found a general factor (Buss & Plomin, 1975, chap. 8). Items that overlapped temperament were eliminated ("felt tense," for example). The remaining items, pegged at the low or negative end of the dimension, were

Depressed
Felt hemmed in, constrained
Felt pessimistic, cynical
Couldn't think clearly
Touchy, easily hurt
Felt confident of self

These items were aggregated and found to correlate with emotionality .29 for men and .42 for women. Given the mixture of mood items, which included self-esteem and not thinking clearly, we may conclude that emotionality plays a significant role in mood, especially for women.

A factor analysis of adjectives describing personality yielded a factor, called neuroticism, consisting of these adjectives (McCrae & Costa, 1985):

High-strung
Envious/jealous
Insecure
Emotionally unstable
Subjective
Nervous
Emotional
Temperamental

Most of these adjectives, with the exception of *subjective*, which no approach will easily explain, fall under the heading of the temperament of emotionality, or, alternatively, negative mood. Notice that two of the adjectives (*emotionally unstable* and *nervous*) refer to abnormal affect.

A similar higher-order factor, negative emotionality, mentioned earlier, emerged from a personality questionnaire (Tellegen, 1985). Those who score high on it describe themselves as "being unpleasurably engaged, stressed and harassed, and prone to experiencing strong negative emotions such as anxiety and anger" (Tellegen et al., 1988). This description sounds like an echo of negative mood or the temperament of emotionality.

Negative emotionality has been found to correlate consistently with many of the symptoms of anxiety and depression (Watson, Clark, & Carey, 1988). These relationships make sense, for anxiety and depression involve negative mood and, by extrapolation, the temperament of emotionality. This chain of reasoning and empirical relationships leads to the conclusion that an extremely high state of emotionality is likely to be a precursor of mood-related abnormal behavior (see Chapter 14).

This account of emotionality is necessarily brief because the temperament of emotionality has received less attention than its derivatives, fear and anger. Perhaps one reason for the paucity of research is that emotionality is very broad and diffuse, while the dispositions of fear and anger are more narrowly defined and lend themselves more readily to study.

Fear

Fear is a universal emotion, not only in our species but probably in most animals and certainly in all mammals. Within each species, individuals differ greatly in the intensity and frequency of fear reactions. The fear reaction itself is not unitary but consists of several components.

Components

Feelings and Cognitions

Though animals may have feelings, they cannot verbalize them; we can, however. Frightened people report a variety of internal sensations: butterflies in the stomach, a vague feeling of unease or weakness, a tightening of the muscles as tension mounts in the neck or back, nausea, cramps, or a constricted or dry throat.

The cognitions reported in fear usually focus on imminent or distant danger: becoming hurt or sick, having an accident, failing an exam, being rejected, and so on through a list of harmful physical or psychological events. In a word, this is *apprehension*. These feelings and cognitions are what we identify as fear in everyday situations, but there are other components.

Physiological Reactions

The pioneering research of the physiologist Walter Cannon (1929) established the internal bodily reactions of fear. Sugar is released into the bloodstream; blood is shifted from the viscera to the skeletal muscles, which slows digestion; the bronchioles of the lungs expand, and breathing rate increases; and the heart beats faster. All these bodily reactions allow greater muscular exertion, which in turn produces sweating (though sometimes sweat breaks out even before muscles contract). Cannon recognized that these various physiological reactions were part of the body's preparation for massive action in the face of threat.

Instrumental Behavior

Fear typically occurs in the face of threat, real or imagined. One immediate and typical way of dealing with danger is to escape by running, climbing, or even hiding. Another way is to seek reassurance from a more powerful person who is strong enough to cope with the threat, offer soothing, or both.

Fear can paradoxically induce an inhibition of behavior, either because the frightened person freezes into immobility or because he or she becomes wary and stops all behavior unrelated to the immediate danger. When the immediate threat has dissipated, there is a residual tendency to avoid the event or the place associated with danger. Thus some people simply cannot enter an airplane even when they must travel thousands of miles, and others cannot be induced to get up and talk to an audience.

Emotional Expression

A fearful face is so easily recognized that it can be identified by people from a variety of cultures around the world (Ekman & Friesen, 1971; Ekman et al., 1987). The eyes are especially prominent: open wide to expose an unusual amount of white. The mouth is open, and the lips, tense. The brows are raised and drawn together. When the intensity of the reaction approaches terror, facial blood may drain to produce a blanching of the cheeks.

The body is tense. Neck and shoulder muscles tend to be rigid, and the hands are usually clenched tightly. There may be a spillover into random movements, as the person sits down and gets up repeatedly, paces back and forth, makes vague gestures, wrings the hands, wipes the brow, and touches the hair or face. If the fear is sufficiently intense, the person may cringe in terror, the hands and lips trembling, and the voice quivering or becoming hoarse as the throat constricts.

Patterning

The four components of fear have been described in a sequence from covert to overt. Fearful feelings and cognitions may remain completely private. Many of the physiological reactions of fear are entirely internal, though sweating and rapid breathing may be observed by others. The expressive and instrumental components are entirely overt, easily observable by others.

When people become intensely fearful, all four components are usually present, but in mild fear only one or two components might be observed or reported. Even when the fear is intense, one or two components might be most salient, the others being less intense and less important parts of the fear pattern. Thus when afraid, some people are more tense or engage in random pacing and self-touching; others have powerful physiological reactions; and others worry excessively and experience feelings of panic (Buss, 1962).

Might the components be sharply differentiated for some people but homogeneous for others? If so, would it matter? Hodgson and Rachman (1974) studied clients undergoing psychotherapy to deal with their intense fear of open places (agoraphobia). They initially assessed indicators of the cognitive, physiological, and instrumental components of fear: subjective feelings, heart rate increases, and behavioral avoidance. For some clients, called *synthesizers*, the three aspects were highly similar. For others, called *desynchronizers*, when one measure was elevated, the other two were lower—for example, higher heart rate, but less avoidance and milder feelings of fear. Psychotherapy turned out to be more beneficial for the synthesizers than for the desynchronizers.

In another study of agoraphobics undergoing psychotherapy the timing of improvement differed for two components (Mavissakian & Michelson, 1982). The first component to improve was instrumental behavior: starting to approach previously feared stimuli. Only later in treatment did the physiological component (heart rate) show similar improvement. These two studies demonstrate the importance of knowing that fear comprises several components.

Measures

Self-Reports

The questionnaires that assess fear tend to be global. A recent questionnaire has these items, which cluster together on being factor analyzed (Buss & Plomin, 1984, chap. 7):

1. I am easily frightened.
2. I have fewer fears than most people my age.
3. I often feel insecure.
4. When I get scared, I panic.
5. I tend to be nervous in new situations.

The two week test-retest correlation for this scale is .75.

Another kind of self-report inquires about a wide range of situations that might elicit fear. The fear survey of Wolpe and Lang (1964) contains sixty-three different contexts, including these examples:

Traveling on an airplane
Being alone at home
Closed places
Spiders
Dogs
Hospitals

This questionnaire complements a global self-report by specifying precisely which stimuli are frightening, for even the most fearful person is not afraid of everything.

Laboratory

Laboratory measures have been devised for specific fears, especially when these fears are so strong as to be considered phobias. Lang and Lazovik (1963) presented snake phobics and controls with a live, nonpoisonous snake in an open glass case. The subjects were instructed to walk up to the snake and, if possible, touch it. The measure was how close they would come to the snake. Some subjects stayed far away, but some were able to touch it.

Physiological Reactions

Bodily arousal in fear, as we saw earlier, involves activation of the sympathetic division of the autonomic nervous system. Most frequently cardiovascular arousal is assessed, especially heart rate and blood pressure. Thus when Ax (1953) scared subjects with the threat of strong electric shock, the male subjects' systolic blood pressure rose an average of 23 points; diastolic blood pressure, 18 points; and heart rate, 32 beats per minute. In other research on fear, the heart's output of blood rose by close to 50% (Schachter, 1957). Fear also produces sweating, which can be measured by the galvanic skin response.

Origins

Heredity

Are identical twins more similar in fear than are fraternal twins? The answer is yes, as may be seen in Table 3.1. Plomin (1974) used parental ratings of children on a fear questionnaire similar to the one mentioned earlier (Buss & Plomin, 1984): "Child is easily frightened" and so on. In three different age groups, starting at three months of age, identical twins were considerably more similar in fear than were fraternal twins.

Table 3.1 also contains twin data on specific, common fears in adults (Rose, Miller, & Cardwell, 1981). Again, identical twins are more alike than fraternal twins. Does this mean that specific fears are inherited? Probably not, though it has been argued that there is an inherited tendency to acquire certain fears rather than others, as will be seen shortly. Finally, recall that Tellegen et al. (1988) studied twins reared apart. They found that identical twins are much more similar in harm avoidance (fear) than are fraternal twins.

Learning

Habituation.   The habituation relevant to fear consists of the waning and gradual disappearance of the response to a stimulus that at first induces arousal.

TABLE 3.1   Correlations between Twins with Regard to Fear

	Identical twins	Fraternal twins
Children (Plomin, 1974)		
3–12 months	.74	.54
18–30 months	.65	.22
Almost 5 years old	.74	.38
All subjects	.70	.38
Adults (Rose et al., 1981)		
Snakes, spiders	.51	.24
Public speaking	.54	.24
Adults reared apart (Tellegen et al., 1988)		
Harm avoidance (fear)	.49	.24

Observe the behavior of squirrels new to a college campus. At first, they bound away at the approach of a student, but the squirrels slowly learn that students will not harm them, and eventually the approach of a student evokes no particular reaction.

Like squirrels, children who are at first fearful of a stimulus may learn that the stimulus is innocuous and eventually show no fear of it. Toward the end of the first year of life, many infants react to strangers with wariness or outright fear. Evidently, the social novelty is simply too arousing and therefore frightening. As the novelty wears off and the stranger becomes a familiar figure, the fear reaction typically wanes and eventually disappears. But such habituation may not occur in shy infants, who may remain fearful of social novelty for many years.

Classical Conditioning.   Many of the fears of children and some of the fears of adults are learned through classical conditioning. After children receive painful injections in a physician's office, they subsequently become scared when they enter the office. The unconditioned stimulus is the pain, and the conditioned stimulus is the office. Also, when a child is given a painful hypodermic and the medic giving the injection always wears a white coat, the child may start whimpering whenever confronted with a similar white-coated person.

Instrumental Conditioning.   Closely linked to such classical conditioning is the instrumental conditioning of fears, which has been demonstrated in laboratory research on avoidance conditioning with dogs in a shuttle box (Solomon, Kamen, & Wynne, 1953). Each dog is given a warning signal, followed by a painful electric shock. The dog quickly learns to jump from the shock compartment to the safe compartment. Subsequently, this avoidance response continues to occur even after the shock is completely turned off: The dog will not risk staying put once the warning signal is given.

Similarly, after humans have learned how to escape from pain or danger, any stimulus that signals potential pain or danger triggers a strong avoidance response (the instrumental component of fear). Frightened people tend not to discover that the danger is past—that is, they fail to extinguish the avoidance response. Many children and some adults, bitten only once by a dog, become scared if any dog is nearby. If left alone, this fear of dogs may never be extinguished.

Thus fears can be acquired and maintained through classical and instrumental conditioning. Certain fears, however, seem to occur with a high frequency—fear of snakes, for example. Seligman (1971) has suggested that we are especially *prepared* to acquire fears that may be adaptive. That is, we do not inherit specific fears, but we do inherit a tendency to learn certain fears more easily than others.

This idea has been supplemented by Ohman's (1986) hypothesis, which assumes that modern fears date back to a period in our evolutionary past when mammals were starting to evolve but reptiles predominated. It was adaptive then to fear reptiles, and this adaptation presumably continues to the modern era. This adaptation is not an instinctive reflex but a readiness (preparedness) to learn a particular fear as part of a system of defense against predators: "Thus learning is critically involved in selecting which stimuli activate the predatory defense system. But this learning is likely to be biologically primed or constrained in the sense that the responses are much more easily attached to some types of stimuli than to others" (Ohman, 1986, p. 29).

Are we especially prepared to learn certain fears or phobias? The answer from laboratory research is mixed (McNally, 1987). It has *not* been established that some human fears are easier to condition than others. But some fears, of snakes, for example, are extinguished much more slowly than others. Thus it is possible that the so-called adaptive fears may last longer, which is an issue for therapists who attempt to treat such fears.

Imitation.   Some fears are acquired merely through imitation. Casual observation reveals that children copy fears from older siblings and from parents. It would be unethical to use human subjects to demonstrate such learning, but research has been conducted on humans' close animal relatives. Monkeys who were not afraid of snakes watched monkeys who were afraid of snakes when the latter were confronted with a live snake (Mineka, Davidson, Cook, & Keir, 1984). Later the observer monkeys were tested with a live snake, and almost all became frightened and drew away. The strong fear and avoidance persisted when the same test was conducted three months later.

In everyday situations, young children often mimic the fears of their parents. Thus if a mother becomes panicky when she sees a snake in the garden, her child is likely to copy this fear. In our technologically advanced society, live fearful models are not even necessary. Television and movies can portray actors who are fearful, thereby increasing the number of frightened people who can be observed. Thus imitation is a significant and common means of acquiring fears.

Cognition.   Television and movies are also involved in cognitive learning, for they enlarge the number of potentially frightening objects and events. Most of us have never seen a live shark, but the movie *Jaws* scared millions of viewers and caused children to have nightmares for months. And after watching a woman stabbed to death in the shower in the movie *Psycho*, some adults reported tension whenever they showered.

Visual media and books can portray not only real dangers—events reported in the nightly news, for example—but the fictional threats of ghosts, returned dead people, invaders from other worlds, killer plants, and giant insects who devour people. Children and some adults have developed unrealistic fears of these fantasied stimuli.

Then there are superstitions. Some people will not stay on the thirteenth floor of a hotel; thus many hotels skip from twelve to fourteen in their numbering of floors. Bad luck is also linked to walking under a ladder, breaking a mirror (seven years' bad luck), and having a black cat cross one's path. These beliefs are the result of cognitive learning.

In brief, one kind of learning, habituation, leads to the waning of fear. And four kinds of learning are involved in the acquisition and maintenance of fear: classical conditioning, instrumental conditioning, imitation, and cognitive learning (see Table 3.2). Anyone who is exposed frequently to frightening stimuli may become an intensely fearful person. During the last decade or so, one group of youngsters has been identified as being especially at risk: abused children.

But inheritance also plays a role. As the twin research has revealed, some children are genetically disposed to be high in the trait of fear. This disposition may be regarded as the tendency to have an intensely strong unconditioned response to frightening stimuli. The intense unlearned reaction enhances the learning of a fear response to previously neutral stimuli (classical conditioning). It also leads to more frequent instances of traumatic avoidance learning (instrumental conditioning), makes imitation of others' fear responses more likely, and enhances the acquisition of superstitions. Thus those with an inherited disposition to be afraid seem to be especially prepared to learn fear responses.

Of course, if there is an inherited tendency to be afraid, it may show up even in the absence of an especially frightening childhood. When the inherited disposition combines with a high frequency of traumatic events during childhood, we should expect to see the clinical extreme of the dimension of fear: phobia, generalized anxiety, and perhaps even panic.

Development

When infants are afraid, they express it openly and loudly. As the years pass, children gradually inhibit expression of fear, as they acquire inhibitory control and become better able to cope with threats. Such inhibition is enhanced by parents and other socialization agents, who discourage panicky behavior and reward courage and stoicism. Furthermore, peers are likely to ridicule signs of fear in their playmates. The effect of these influences is a gradual waning of fearfulness in children. A minority of children, however, may be raised in a threatening environment (some of our cities, for example, are dangerous places for children); for these children fear becomes an adaptive response.

The content of children's fears varies with age. By the age of one year, many infants are sufficiently wary of social novelty for the phenomenon to have been well studied under the heading of stranger anxiety. During the preschool years, various kinds of learning introduce children to fear of snakes, spiders, insects, and other animals; fear of physicians, dentists, and hospitals; and fear of imaginary

TABLE 3.2   Effects of Kinds of Learning on Fear

Kind	Example of effect
Habituation	Stranger anxiety wanes
Classical conditioning	Dentist's office elicits anxiety
Instrumental conditioning	Dog bite causes enduring fear of dogs
Imitation	Child copies mother's fear of snakes
Cognition	Scary stories lead to fear of ghosts

or unrealistic dangers featured on television, in movies, or in fairy tales. During the school years, some children develop test anxiety, and by adolescence, many youngsters intensely fear death.

Matching

Let us start with a mother and son. When both are low in fear, the mother's relative tranquility serves as a model and enhances the son's inherited disposition to be low in fear; this is a good match. If the mother is fearful and the child is not, the mismatch can affect him in two ways: by offering a fearful model who can be imitated and a social environment that magnifies threats and danger. A likely outcome is a rise in his original disposition to be low in fear.

In the other kind of mismatch, the child is fearful and the mother is not. One problem for the mother is to try to understand and empathize with the child's tendency to become aroused and to panic easily. She may regard her child as difficult, but her relatively calm demeanor and the model she offers can offset the child's tendency to be afraid. Both kinds of mismatch tend to move the child's behavior from an extreme of the dimension of fear toward the middle, though given the fact that fear is inherited, large shifts are unlikely.

In a bad match, both mother and son are high in fear. Now the child's original disposition to be afraid is enhanced by the mother, who offers a fear model for the child to imitate and supplies a tense, emotional social environment for him. Notice that a match between mother and child, whether it has good or bad consequences, serves to move the child toward one or another extreme of the dimension of fear.

Person Affects Environment

Choice.   The issue of choice mainly concerns fearful people, who may become so frightened in some situations that they may avoid them altogether. Those who are afraid of the dark simply will not venture out unless an area is well lit. Those who fear being alone will constantly seek the company of others. A mother may worry so intensely that her children might be hurt accidentally that she will restrict them to home and school. Some people are so afraid of physicians that they avoid them at a cost to their health.

Setting the Tone.   Individuals can also affect the mood of a social occasion. Suppose students are studying together for an examination. A fearful student may voice a variety of concerns about the examination: material not adequately covered in class, material too difficult to understand, the teacher's tendency to give hard exams, or previous failures on this exam. Such talk can change a study session to an incubator for anxiety.

Modifying the Impact.   Some situations are so frightening that everyone is scared. When an airplane engine loses power, for example, there is good reason for passengers to be concerned. But people vary in their reactions to such danger. A person high in fear might become so panicky as to lose control completely and start screaming. But a person low in fear would probably remain sufficiently calm as to realize that the pilot and crew are well trained and can probably deal with the emergency. Thus when there is a threat to life and limb, the impact of the situation may be modified by the trait of fear toward intensification rather than diminution.

Similarly, when there is pressure to perform, especially in public, fear can make a difference in the performance. Fearful basketball players, for example, may be so scared of failure that they either suffer a loss of skill or play so as not to lose, thereby failing to win. Basketball players low in fear would be able to maintain their usual level of performance, and some might even rise to the occasion ("Give me the ball"), performing even better under pressure. Thus the impact of a threatening situation may be determined by whether one is fearful or not.

Sex Differences

Females are more fearful than males, but the sex difference appears only during the course of development (see the reviews by Buss & Plomin, 1975; Maccoby & Jacklin, 1974). Preschool girls are no more fearful than boys, but during the school years, a slight sex difference shows up, though the evidence is mixed. By adulthood, women score higher on fear questionnaires, report a greater variety of specific fears, and more frequently seek help for phobias than men.

The explanation may be the greater size, strength, and aggressiveness of males. Wife-beating is more common than husband-beating, and with rare exception only women are raped. So women have good reasons for being more fearful. But women may also be more fearful than men of spiders, snakes, and heights, for example. The explanation may lie in the way the sexes are socialized. Traditionally, girls are socialized to admit their fears and to avoid stimuli that frighten them, but boys are supposed to suppress their fears and act brave.

Activity

Activity is defined as *the amount of energy expended in body movements*. As such, it is the temperament most open to observation, as is clear when children are at play. They climb ropes, clamber over playground equipment, dash up a ladder to race down a slide, or pump vigorously on a swing. They ride bicycles or tricycles, roller-skate, ice-skate, leap over curbs on skateboards, jump rope, or push wagons. They play tag, chasing each other until exhausted, wrestle each other to the ground, or whirl around just to become dizzy. Infants kick, thrash, creep, or crawl, getting into things they should not, perhaps exhausting the caretaker.

Notice that the energy is physical, not the "mental energy" assumed to be involved in thinking, remembering, and imagining, which may require intense concentration. Such prolonged concentration may induce fatigue, hence the assumption that energy has been expended. But these cognitive processes are excluded from the definition of activity, which consists only of physical behavior.

As any parent or teacher knows, children vary greatly in the energy they display. Some are so active that they seem bursting with energy, whereas others are so languid that they seem to be weak or chronically ill. Most children are somewhere between these extremes, but in discussing activity, special attention will be paid to the extremes because they are easier to describe.

Components

In their movements, active adults may speak rapidly, ascend stairs quickly, and perhaps even dash for an elevator. Even their gestures may be brisk as they bustle through life. They prefer working amidst the frantic pace of a newsroom to the more leisurely rhythm of a library. Tennis is preferred over golf; basketball is preferred over bowling. In modern idiom, they like being in the fast lane of life.

At issue here is the *tempo* of behavior. One way of expending energy is through a rapid rate of responding, which means that tempo is a major component of the trait of activity. People at the low end of this trait dimension tend to speak deliberately or even drawl, stroll when they walk, take their time ascending stairs, and, in general, maintain a slow pace of life. They regard high-tempo people as excessively driven and perhaps even manic. They are regarded by people with a rapid tempo as being lethargic, sluggish, and dull.

There is of course an alternative means of expending energy: through *vigor*. Vigorous responses are of greater amplitude or intensity—for example, talking loudly, laughing heartily, pushing doors open with force, taking longer strides when walking, and making broader and more emphatic gestures. Vigorous people prefer sports that involve great strength or endurance, such as weight lifting, mountain climbing, swimming, or running a marathon.

At the other extreme are people who talk and laugh softly, tread lightly, and gesture minimally. Outdoors, they prefer croquet or picnics and being a spectator to playing strenuous sports. A person of less vigor might in fact nod in agreement to this sentiment, expressed by a friend of mine: "When I feel the urge to exercise, I lie down until it passes."

Highly active people need to expend energy, whether through tempo or vigor. Some like their schedule fully taken up with appointments, classes, specific jobs, and other responsibilities; having an empty schedule may cause boredom, for there is nothing to do. Others want a fast pace or vigorous activity at work or play and may chafe at enforced idleness or the requirement of just sitting still or waiting. In brief, there is a *motivational component* at the high end of the activity dimension; active people become frustrated if they cannot release their profligate energy. This motivational component is absent at the low end of the activity dimension, low-active people having no particular need to be up and doing something.

In summary, activity has two major components: Tempo involves fast-paced, repetitive behavior, and vigor involves responses of great amplitude. But at the upper end of the trait dimension there is also a third, minor component that cuts across tempo and vigor: the motivation to be up and around, to keep busy, and, generally, to be expending energy.

Measures

Self-Reports

Given that energy can be expended by tempo or vigor, it would be optimal to measure each when assessing the trait of activity. Typically, however, activity is measured globally, no distinction being drawn between rate of responding and amplitude of behavior. An exception is a self-report questionnaire (Buss, 1988, p. 55):

Tempo
1. I usually seem to be in a hurry.
2. My life is fast paced.
3. I do not like to dawdle.
4. My friends tell me that my speech is rapid.
5. I walk faster than most people.

Vigor
1. My voice is on the loud side.
2. My gestures tend to be emphatic.
3. When I knock on a door, I usually knock hard.
4. I like using my strength.
5. My handshake is on the firm side.

Though this questionnaire distinguishes tempo from vigor in the content of the items, it remains to be seen whether these subtraits of activity are stable over time and whether the items on each scale form a coherent entity. All other measures of the trait do not separate tempo from vigor but instead yield a global measure of activity.

A global self-report measure includes items on both tempo and energy (Buss & Plomin, 1984, chap. 7):

1. My life is fast paced.
2. I usually seem to be in a hurry.
3. I like to keep busy all the time.
4. I often feel as if I'm bursting with energy.
5. I often feel sluggish and tired.

Factor analysis revealed that the first four items formed a coherent cluster. When subjects were administered this scale on two separate occasions, the correlation was .75, suggesting moderate stability over time.

Another kind of self-report asks subjects to record their everyday acts every fifteen minutes for a period of three days (Bouchard et al., 1983). Each act is given an energy score, from the lowest at 1 to the highest at 9. Thus resting in bed is 1, walking slowly is 4, cutting wood is 7, and playing tennis is 9. Energy expenditure appears to be stable from day to day and over a period of many days, the correlations ranging from .71 to .96.

When these reports of specific physical activities were added to objective measures of body build and strength, the multiple correlation between them and the vigor scale of the EASI was .52 for women and .43 for men (Wellems, Malina, & Buss, 1990). For tempo, the multiple correlation with these measures was .40 for women and .04 for men, a sex difference that is surprising and has no obvious explanation. In general, though, these correlations make sense, for it is reasonable to expect that tempo and especially vigor are related to both body build and number of energetic activities.

Ratings by Observers or Informants

Ratings may occur in the laboratory or in the field. When observers are allowed to watch subjects (usually children), they may be asked to rate the activity level of specific body movements such as movements of the hand, arm, and leg (Goodenough, 1930). It is helpful to know whether observers agree in their ratings, and in this instance the correlation among raters of .86 suggests that they were in close agreement. Even when global activity is rated by teachers during a single day, the correlation among raters is high, .88 (Halverson & Post-Gordon, 1983).

Observers may also rate the activity of children in a variety of situations, while watching television or while at school, for example (Werry & Sprague, 1970). Alternatively, judges can watch a videotape of children at play and make a gross rating of activity.

Ratings can also be made by those who know the subjects well and have observed their behavior for days, weeks, or months under the naturalistic conditions of everyday situations. Such raters are likely to be parents, teachers, roommates, or spouses. Thus the global self-report questionnaire (Buss & Plomin, 1984) can be modified to yield a rating measure that can be used by teachers:

1. At recess, the child is always on the go.
2. When the child moves about, he or she usually moves slowly.
3. The child is full of vigor when he or she arrives in the morning.
4. The child is very energetic.
5. The child prefers quiet, inactive games.

Objective Measures

Subjects can be timed when asked to carry out specific tasks, such as finger tapping, writing, sorting cards, or turning cranks (Harrison, 1941). McGowan and Gormly (1976) measured the speed of routine movements such as walking, climbing stairs, and changing posture. They found that the pace of these movements, when aggregated, correlated .74 with ratings of activity made by peers who knew the subjects well.

More active children tend to move around more, by definition. It follows that they would traverse a larger area of any given room. Such movements can be measured by marking the room off in squares and then recording how many squares are crossed per unit of time.

Of the many measures of active behavior (see Tryon, 1984), the most popular one, used especially with children, is a modified self-winding watch that faithfully records the movements of a limb. It is called the *actometer* (Schulman & Reisman, 1959). These investigators repeated actometer measurements at intervals of one to three weeks and reported an average correlation between successive measurements of .67, which is reasonable stability.

Are actometers good measures of activity level? Two studies suggest they are. The actometer readings of nursery-school children correlated .69 with nursery-school staff rankings of the children's activity and .75 with parental ratings of children's activity at home (Eaton, 1983). Overactive children may be administered the drug methylphenidate, which is known to slow down such children. Actometer readings clearly reflected the lowered activity that occurs when this drug is given (Barkley, 1977).

Origins

These measuring instruments have revealed a fact that even a casual observer might notice: People vary markedly in the trait of activity. Starting in childhood, some individuals are bundles of energy, in contrast to those at the opposite extreme, who are quieter and apparently low in energy. Where do these individual differences originate, and how are they maintained over time? As might be guessed, there is more than one answer to each of these questions.

Heredity
One problem in studying the heritability of the temperament of activity is that until the 1970s activity was assessed in twins through self-report measures here regarded as too broad. For example, one twin study included a factor called activity that consisted of items about working and hobbies (Schoenfeldt, 1968). Subsequently, the temperament of activity was pinned down more precisely. In an early study, parents rated the activity of their twins, whose average age was fifty-five months (Buss, Plomin, & Willerman, 1973). As the correlations in Table 3.3 reveal, identical twins are much more alike in activity than are fraternal twins. Similar differences have been reported in other research, though the correlations vary from

TABLE 3.3   Correlations between Twins with Regard to Activity

	Identical twins	Fraternal twins
Buss & Plomin (1975)	.62	.09
Plomin & Rowe (1977)	.65	−.38
Matheny (1980)	.54	.14

one study to the next (see Buss & Plomin, 1984, p. 122). A more recent study assessed activity in twins in the second year of life with the Colorado Child Temperament Inventory. For identical twins the correlation was .50, and for fraternal twins −.25 (Emde et al., 1992).

Do these correlations occur merely because parents know that their identical twins are more similar than fraternal twins? One way of answering this question is not to use parents as raters. A relevant study had experimenters observe and rate behavior in the laboratory without knowing whether the twin was identical or fraternal (Matheny, 1980). This procedure, when used with two year olds, yielded correlations for activity of .58 for identical twins and .14 for fraternal twins. Thus both parental ratings and experimenters' observations yielded a low correlation for fraternal twins.

Another answer may be obtained by using the actometer, an entirely objective measure (Saudino & Eaton, 1991). Actometers were attached to each limb of infants less than a year old for a period of two days. When the actometer readings were composited, the correlations were .76 for identical twins and .56 for fraternal twins, which is clear evidence of heritability. Notice that the correlation for fraternal twins is much higher than those in Table 3.3, and, indeed, higher than the fraternal twin correlations for any of the temperaments. The explanation may lie in the age of the subjects in these studies: less than a year in age in the study by Saudino and Eaton but considerably older in the other research.

In any event, these various findings converge in revealing that for activity, identical twins are significantly more similar than fraternal twins. Clearly, one origin of the trait of activity is inheritance.

Development

Individual differences in activity appear as early as the first weeks of life, but the energy level of neonates is partly determined by the length of gestation, problems attending birth, and the amount of waking time. Perhaps because of these transient influences, the level of activity of very young infants is unstable. Instability during the early months of life is common, however. Consider, for example, that one hand does not achieve unequivocal dominance until a child is roughly two years old.

By the end of the first year, infants crawl well, start to walk, stay awake longer, and, in general, become more mobile with each passing month. Then they are sufficiently active for researchers to check on stability over time. When testers of children rated them for activity first at one year of age and then at three years, the correlation was .48, suggesting at least moderate stability (Schaefer & Bayley, 1963). In another longitudinal study, activity correlated .52 from two years to five through seven years, and .45 from four years to fourteen through sixteen years (Battle & Lacey, 1972).

There may be a ceiling on the stability of activity, caused by the potential differentiation of tempo from vigor. These two means of expending energy are undifferentiated during the first year of life, when so many of children's movements are diffuse or uncoordinated and when there are few outlets for energy expenditure. But as children acquire motor skills and greater coordination, the variety of motor acts allows them to display activity through either a rapid pace of responding or a large amplitude of response.

The assessment of activity in older children should include measures of both tempo and vigor, but most previous instruments have not. As a result, the difference between tempo and vigor falls into the error term. A larger error term inevitably lowers the stability correlation for activity in a longitudinal study.

Matching

Again, we consider only the extremes. A child's first and perhaps most important environment is social: the parents. For ease of exposition, let us again limit this discussion to a boy and his mother, though what follows applies to the various gender combinations.

In one kind of match, both mother and child are low in the trait of activity. Knowing her own level of energy expenditure, the mother easily understands her child's low activity and perhaps even reinforces it. Harmony prevails.

In the other kind of match, both mother and child are high in activity. Again, the mother understands and accepts the child's behavior. But very active children pose problems for any parent, for their exuberant energy may cause them to get into places they should not, refuse to take naps, have difficulty in sitting quietly, and generally, push the limits of the parental household. As a result, the parents of highly active children tend to intrude more when their children are performing tasks, and parent-child relations seem to be more troublesome (D. M. Buss, Block, & Block, 1980).

It is a reasonable guess that the conflict just mentioned occurs mainly in one kind of mismatch: between an active child and an inactive parent (the study, unfortunately, did not assess parental activity level). A highly active boy might soon exhaust his low-active mother, irritating her and making her wonder if he is normal. There is little harmony here. In the other kind of mismatch, a highly active mother will expect a great deal of energy from her child but be disappointed. She may regard the boy as lazy or perhaps even ill.

Aside from the issue of tranquility versus conflict, what is the impact of a match or a mismatch between parent and child? A match is likely to strengthen the child's original, inherited tendency. The inactive child will remain so; the active child may become even more active. A mismatch may move the extreme child toward the middle of the trait dimension: The inactive child becomes more active, and the active child lessens energy expenditure.

Person Affects Environment

Choosing Environments

Young children are placed in one or another context by adults. As they mature, children begin to have some choice regarding their environment and by adulthood have considerable latitude. Thus persons with a quick tempo might seek the fast lane of life that typifies urban living. They would enjoy the frantic action of the floor of a stock exchange, a daily newspaper, or broadcasting. Their preferred participant sports are likely to be squash or tennis; spectator sports, hockey or basketball. Aerobic exercise is also appealing. Those with a slow tempo would opt for the more leisurely pace of country life, seek jobs that are not rushed (as an accountant or architect, for instance), enjoy sailing or bowling, and watch a golf match.

There are also options available to persons at the extremes of the vigor dimension, though education and social class might make a difference. Thus a vigorous person might seek a job as a construction worker or dockworker and would gravitate to such athletics as weight lifting or rowing. A person low in vigor would be more likely to enjoy being a librarian or computer programmer and might prefer games such as croquet, bridge, or chess.

In a rare study involving choice, Gormly (1983) had fraternity members rate each member for energy and physical activity. Then each member was individually given a choice of watching a videotape of people either being vigorous (high-active) or engaging in fine motor behavior (low-active). The trait of activity correlated .62 with the choice of the high-active videotape.

Setting the Tone

People at the extremes of the trait dimension of activity can also influence what happens on social occasions. Someone with a rapid tempo of speech and gestures can animate a conversation, just as someone who speaks slowly with long pauses can deflate interaction. Only a few energetic people are needed to escalate the pace and noise of a party, though they may give up if the other guests are at the lethargic end of the activity dimension.

Modifying the Environment

The environment may not be passively accepted, for individuals at the extremes often modify it. A fast-tempo person who feels slowed down by stately music can replace it with driving rock music; a slow-tempo person might do the opposite. A vigorous person in need of exercise can dissipate energy by doing isometric exercises or by stretching in the absence of any equipment. A leisurely walker may be able to slow the pace of the group merely by lagging behind, forcing the others to stroll.

Then there is the more special case of overcoming obstacles in the environment placed there by one's own limitations. Consider the publicized incidents of energetic people disabled by illness or accident. Confined to a wheelchair, they enter marathons, play basketball, or lift weights. And they campaign vigorously to obtain ramps, special parking spaces, access to classes and workrooms, and generally insist on changing the physical environment that may limit their movement.

Children at the high extreme of the temperament of activity may have difficulty adjusting to an environment that requires them to sit still, as in a school classroom. Such children, under the strong push to move around, may modify the environment, behaving as though the classroom is a playground. They may leave their seats when they are not supposed to, jumping up and disturbing the other children. The teacher is likely to label them as hyperactive.

Sex Differences

Are males more active than females? Eaton and Enns (1986), after reviewing ninety studies, concluded that "males were more active than females by roughly one-half of a standard deviation, a difference that accounts for a little less than 5% of the variation in the activity level distribution" (p. 24). Clearly, there is a sex difference, though not a large one.

Perhaps males are *innately* more active than females. Rough-and-tumble play requires more energy than most other kinds of children's play, and boys engage in more of such play than girls (Maccoby & Jacklin, 1974). In this respect human children may be typical primates, for the sex difference also occurs in the higher apes, and it has been systematically observed in normal rhesus monkeys (Goy, 1978). Energetic, aggressive play in rhesus monkeys can be altered by manipulating prenatal male sex hormones (see Goy & McEwen, 1980, for a review). Though similar research obviously cannot be tried with human subjects, "nature's experiments" reveal a link in human children between rough-and-tumble play and prenatal levels of androgens. According to Ehrhardt (1985), "Girls with a history of prenatal androgenization were typically long-term tomboys, frequently involved in physically active play and sports behavior, and preferred boys to girls as playmates" (p. 45). Converging evidence has come from children who are genetic males (XY chromosomes) but are insensitive to androgens. Raised as girls, they have a low frequency of rough-and-tumble play (Ehrhardt, Epstein, & Money, 1968).

Another possibility is socialization: Boys and girls are treated differently, their play being channeled into grooves deemed appropriate for each sex. Such socialization starts early. In one study, mothers supervised the play of six-month-old infants who were not their own (Smith & Lloyd, 1978). The children were dressed as boys or girls regardless of their real sex, so that the mothers' reactions were based on *perceived sex*. Perceived boys were verbally encouraged to be more physically active than were perceived girls. Dolls were offered only to perceived girls, and hammers were offered only to perceived boys. Thus the mothers supplied six-month-old infants with sex-appropriate toys and encouraged more activity in boys, and they did so even when they knew the true sex of the infants. If the sexes are treated differently so early in life, we should not be surprised that boys subsequently are more active.

Regardless of how we attempt to explain sex differences, there is the empirical question of *when* they occur. In a longitudinal study, no sex difference in activity was found for children assessed at thirteen, twenty-nine, and forty-four months (Feiring & Lewis, 1980). This negative finding is consistent with those of Kagan (1971), whose subjects were eight, thirteen, and twenty-seven months old, Fish and Crockenberg (1981), whose subjects ranged from thirty to forty-one weeks, and Garside (1975), who used preschool children. Also, at the ages of twelve, eighteen, and twenty-four months both sexes preferred the more active toys, and there was no sex difference in activity (O'Brien & Huston, 1985).

Aside from these negative findings, there have been reports of sex differences, but the results have been equivocal. There was no sex difference among 2½-year-olds in the rate or force used in tearing down a barrier, running, tricycling, or restlessness during story time, but boys had higher actometer scores and did more walking, whereas girls spent more time on gliders and swings (Pederson & Bell, 1970).

Among 2½- to 5-year-old children, boys preferred less structured activities, which may be an indication of greater activity, but when boys and girls were compared in the same activities, there was no sex difference in energy expenditure (Carpenter & Huston-Stein, 1980). In the 4- to 5-year-old age range, physical assault, wrestling, and rough-and-tumble play are more frequent in boys, but the play of girls includes more jumping (DiPietro, 1981).

Thus below the age of 5 years, the evidence for a sex difference is neither consistent nor compelling. Beyond the age of 5 years, available studies suggest that boys are slightly but significantly more active than girls (Eaton & Enns, 1986).

Returning to explanations of sex differences, we should consider events of the past several decades in this country, especially the change in sex roles. Forty years ago, few girls and women participated in highly energetic sports. Now they freely play basketball and touch football, race in marathons, lift weights, and engage in such exhausting activities as triathlons and jazzercise. In only two generations, women have increased their participation in sports previously limited largely to men, thereby minimizing or perhaps even eliminating the sex difference in activity. This fact argues for the socialization explanation.

Thus one cause of the sex difference in activity appears to be that peer pressure, models, encouragement, and availability of toys and games all contribute to boys displaying more energy than girls in their play. But this conclusion does not deny the case for biology. There are facts consistent with the hormonal explanation of the sex differences, though the evidence deals largely with rough-and-tumble play. Thus among nonhuman primates, the play of males is more energetic than that of females, and socialization cannot be invoked to explain that. Also, androgens may well be involved in the sex difference among human children in rough-and-tumble play.

Finally, perhaps socialization practices simply mirror the biological differences already present, the small innate sex difference being magnified by socialization of the two sexes. Men typically do the heavier work, requiring larger muscles. This traditional division of labor reflects anatomical and physiological differences between the sexes, but the biological difference is enhanced by the training and expectations of society.

Temperament II

Sociability

Sociability is defined as *a preference for being with others*, as opposed to remaining alone. We evolved from ancestral primate stock, and most living primates are highly social animals; our species is no exception. It is not much of an exaggeration to say that no normal person can become a hermit. Even the least social person still likes to be with others, though his or her motivation to do so may be weak. Highly sociable persons are strongly motivated to seek out others and remain in their company.

What are the incentives that make us want to be with others? If there is a task to be performed, others can help us do it. We can barter for goods or services, and we can better defend ourselves in a group. But even when these incentives are absent or not relevant, we still want the company of others. Why?

Intrinsic Social Rewards

Even when there is no external reason for being with others, such as cooperation, exchange, or defense, we may still prefer to do so. Certain social stimuli are pleasurable in and of themselves—that is, they are intrinsically rewarding. These stimuli may be divided into two classes (Buss, 1983).

Stimulation Rewards

There are some things we like to do with others: eating, working in an office, attending a movie, singing in a group, or just watching a beautiful sunset. Somehow, just the fact that someone else is sharing an activity makes it more pleasant. Many students opt to study with others, perhaps in a library, rather than studying alone in a room, and most children would rather play in a nursery filled with children than alone at home. There may even be a social facilitation effect. Those who eat together consume more food, those who work together produce more work, and each member of an audience laughs louder at humor than does a solitary person (Zajonc, 1965). *Sharing* is one kind of *stimulation reward*.

There can be a downside to sharing activities, however. Sometimes there are too many people. In a packed movie theater, people may talk during the film, to the annoyance of others. When a cafeteria table is jammed with people, there may not be enough room to eat. If there are too many children on a playground, there will be a long wait to use the swings or slide. And excessive crowding causes invasion of personal space, that "envelope" of space that we need to maintain an adequate distance from strangers or acquaintances (Hall, 1966). Thus though sharing tends to be rewarding, crowding can make shared activities aversive.

We want not only to share an activity with others but also to receive their *attention*. No one likes to be ignored, for it spawns feelings of rejection, anger, or hurt. This general observation has been confirmed in the laboratory (Fenigstein, 1979). In a waiting room, subjects were uncomfortable and felt rejected when they were shunned by other "subjects" (experimental confederates) who were strangers. We want people to look at us and listen to us, for these sensory actions convey an interest in us. Attention is another stimulation reward. Attention of the kind described is normative; its absence implies that something is socially wrong.

As we all know from experience, however, there can be too much attention from others. Most of us do not like to be stared at as if there were something wrong with our appearance or demeanor. Close scrutiny by others is likely to reveal faults or defects that we are unaware of or wish to conceal. Imagine entering a party at which all conversation stops and everyone present stares at the newcomer. Clearly, too much attention can be just as aversive as too little.

Beyond attention, others can offer *responsivity*. When I speak, at first you listen, and then it is your turn to speak. What I say partially determines what you say, and then what you say stimulates me to respond. These back-and-forth behaviors may well represent the peak of social behavior.

Notice that responsivity, the third stimulation reward, includes the first two rewards, for in a conversation an activity is shared and each person receives attention. Added to responsivity, however, is a *dynamic indeterminacy*. Responsivity is dynamic in that the interaction flows back and forth between two people. It is indeterminate in that one person's response is not completely determined by what the other person says; it can be novel, amusing, or even tangential. If one person could predict the other's response completely, the conversation would be dull. To some extent we seek novelty in social behavior, a tendency we share with other primates. In one study, infant monkeys were raised with robot mothers that were either immovable or allowed to swing free (Mason, 1970). The infants strongly preferred even the minimal responsivity of the movable robot mother that was capable of rebound and would touch or bump back against the infants when struck. And human infants delight in giving an adult a toy, only to have it given back to them—this interaction may actually be the forerunner of the responsivity of later conversation.

Can there be too much responsivity? Perhaps. Another person's response may be too detailed: for example, offering a complete medical history when asked,

"How are you?" The reaction may be too emotional (anger, astonishment). Or the other person may reveal intimate details on very short acquaintance, causing embarrassment.

Each of the three rewards may be regarded as a dimension, whose extremes may be unpleasant, but whose middle range is pleasurable. Thus most of us do not like being alone in unshared activities, but we do not like being crowded; the middle of the dimension, shared activities without crowding, is rewarding. Similarly, receiving attention from others is pleasant, but we dislike being shunned or made to feel conspicuous. A lack of responsivity from others is dull and boring, and their overreactions may also be unpleasant, but the middle range of responsivity is entirely enjoyable.

All three rewards may be aligned on a dimension of social stimulation, hence the name of this section. Doing things in parallel is pleasant and is slightly stimulating. Receiving attention appears to heighten arousal, but the peak of social stimulation is the back-and-forth interaction that occurs when people are responsive. These points are summarized in Table 4.1.

Affective Rewards

The stimulation rewards tend to occur naturally in social situations. Requiring no particular relationship among the participants, stimulation rewards can be offered by people who are merely acquaintances or even strangers.

The other class of social stimuli, *affective rewards*, is more familiar than the first class. It consists of *praise*, *sympathy*, and *affection*. Usually offered only by friends or those in intimate relationships, these rewards tend to induce moderate to strong positive affect in the recipient, hence their name.

That these three rewards are universally sought and valued requires no elaboration. Each has its unpleasant opposite: for praise, criticism; for sympathy, disdain; and for affection, dislike. Again, each reward may be regarded as a dimension, but each dimension is bipolar: positive at one end and negative at the other. By definition, only the positive end is reinforcing, and there cannot be too much of the positive end: praise, sympathy, or love. These three rewards may be ranked in order of increasing intensity and the degree to which they enhance a relationship. The more intense the affective reward, the more likely it is to occur in a close relationship. Thus praise may be offered by friends, sympathy by very good friends, and love by family members or lovers.

TABLE 4.1   **Stimulation Rewards**
(in order of increasing stimulation)

Reward	Too little	Too much
Sharing	Isolation	Crowding
Attention	Shunning	Conspicuousness
Responsivity	Boredom	Overreaction

Relevance for Sociability

It is assumed here that only the stimulation rewards are relevant to the trait of sociability. As a sociable species, we seek out others for sharing, attention, and responsivity, and these three rewards are especially prized by highly sociable people. Beyond this general preference and other things being equal, sociable people are assumed to seek the more stimulating of these rewards. They like sharing and attention from others but are most rewarded by responsivity. Presumably, people low in sociability might be satisfied by sharing or attention and not demand the higher intensity of responsivity.

Of course, other things might not be equal, and individuals might develop a strong preference for one of the stimulation rewards over the others. Sharing of activities often occurs in an organized group, such as volunteers helping the needy, an athletic team, or even a family. As they share activities directed toward a common goal, members of such groups report a feeling of solidarity and kinship. When forced to leave the group—when it breaks up, when individual members leave, or as a result of retirement—former members say that they strongly feel the loss of comradeship, sense of purpose, and, above all, sharing of activities.

For others the crucial reward is attention from others, though a distinction must be drawn between extrinsic and intrinsic attention. Some professional people, such as teachers, politicians, and entertainers, must have the attention of others to do their job. They are trained to make others look and listen, and they must capture the attention of others to attain the expected goals of their profession. Thus the attention they attract is extrinsic.

If attention were valued for itself alone, it would be intrinsic—for example, if an entertainer or a teacher sought that same amount of attention offstage or outside of school as he or she did onstage or in the classroom. Of course, we all want at least a moderate degree of attention, but a minority of exhibitionists seek and demand excessive attention. They are willing to be seen as clowns, to engage in outrageous behavior, or even to annoy those around them as long as all eyes are on them.

In brief, only the stimulation rewards are relevant for the trait of sociability. Said another way, highly sociable persons especially desire these social rewards.

As for the affective rewards, who does not want praise, sympathy, and love? These rewards are wanted not only by sociable individuals but also by unsociable persons. But there may be individuals who especially need one of the affective rewards and therefore place a higher value on it. Those who are low in self-esteem, for instance, might be especially motivated to seek praise as a way of boosting self-esteem.

The affective rewards are also linked to the *affiliation motive*, which is assessed by the Thematic Apperception Test or TAT (Shipley & Veroff, 1952). Those high in the affiliation motive tell stories in which the characters try to start or continue a relationship and say that they want to receive praise, sympathy, or affection. These findings tell us that the affiliation motive, as assessed by the TAT, is broader than the temperament of sociability—that is, affiliative persons are highly motivated to seek not only stimulation rewards but also affective rewards.

Warmth

So far I have focused on sociability as the need to be with others, which is its defining characteristic. What about the response to others? Presumably, sociable people will reciprocate by offering precisely the stimulation rewards they seek. Sociable people are expected to share activities, so when approached to study or eat together, they will. They tend to be attentive to others, gazing at them and listening with interest to what they say. And they will be responsive, answering questions and keeping the conversation going. These various responses convey *warmth*.

However, there are other ways to convey warmth. People reveal their social interest by welcoming gestures such as a handshake, touching the other person, or even a hug. But the most common and perhaps the best indicator of warmth is a smile, especially a broad smile.

Infants display warmth by vocalizing, smiling, and social overtures. This group of behaviors was reasonably stable from 1 year to 2½ years (Clarke-Stewart, Umeh, Snow, & Pederson, 1980). Also, warmth toward mothers was related to the warmth displayed toward strangers.

In brief, warmth is the reciprocal side of sociability. Sociable people need to be with others to share activities and receive attention and responsivity. Having these needs, they are likely to feel good when the needs are satisfied, hence the smiling and other signs of warmth. This hypothesis of a strong correlation between sociability and warmth, first suggested by Buss and Plomin (1975), was subsequently confirmed by Costa and McCrae (1984).

Not all sociable people are warm, though. A minority of sociable people are also shy (Cheek & Buss, 1981). They seek out others (sociability), but when with them they are too shy to display warmth. They may be seen as cold or aloof with strangers or acquaintances, when actually they are merely socially inhibited.

Substitutes

The motive involved in sociability may be satisfied by social animals, which is why we have pets—in the United States, tens of millions of them. The most popular pets are dogs, and with good reason. They share activities, pay attention to their owners, and respond eagerly to their masters. Notice too that dogs convey social pleasure spontaneously with an analogue of the human smile: tail wagging.

Less sociable is the cat, whose tail does not indicate social pleasure. Cats sometimes share activities and attend and respond to their owners, but they do not need their owners the way dogs do. Whether it is a dog, a cat, or a bird, a pet may offer at least some of the intrinsic social rewards sought by everyone.

There is also a well-known technological substitute for people: the computer. The computer pays attention to commands even to the point of asking questions, which can become more humanlike when the computer is given a mechanical voice. It can share the play activities called computer games. And it is responsive: advanced computers, for example, compete in chess—a back-and-forth game if ever there was one—and beat everyone but grand masters. Of course, a truly sociable person would never be satisfied with a computer as a substitute for another person, though this option might be preferred at times by those low in sociability.

Measures

Self-Reports

Sociability is typically assessed as part of a self-report of a combination of traits called *extraversion*. Even when sociability is singled out as a trait, the questionnaire often contains items on shy behavior. Thus the sociability scale of the EASI Temperament Survey (Buss & Plomin, 1975) includes the item "I tend to be shy." A revision yielded the following scale, which contains only sociability items (Cheek & Buss, 1981):

1. I like to be with people.
2. I welcome the opportunity to mix socially with people.
3. I prefer working with others rather than alone.
4. I find people more stimulating than anything else.
5. I'd be unhappy if I were prevented from making many social contacts.

The two-week test-retest correlation for this scale is .85.

The intertwining of sociability and shyness in previous questionnaires may derive from the implicit assumption that shyness is the tendency to avoid being with people. As such, it would be the opposite of a preference for being with others and therefore would be represented as the low end of the trait dimension of sociability. But *shyness* can and should be defined separately as *the inhibition, awkwardness, and turmoil that may occur when one is with others.* When so defined, shyness has been found to correlate −.30 with the sociability questionnaire above (Cheek & Buss, 1981). Thus, other things being equal, low-sociable people tend to be shy, and shy people tend to be low in sociability, but the correlation is modest enough for the two traits to be separate.

Observations

When people can be observed over time, several measures of sociability become available. Researchers can simply count the frequency of attempts to initiate contacts and the subject's reaction to such attempts by others: welcoming or rejecting. Accordingly, sociable people tend to have more acquaintances and casual friends, though not necessarily more intimate relationships, and they are more likely to give parties and go to parties. They also tend to stay longer in social situations, the measure being duration of contact.

Sociable people tend to be joiners of clubs, professional organizations, and community groups, and they tend to be active in them. They may even enjoy large assemblages of people and be more willing to tolerate crowding. The measures here would be the number of social activities, the preference for large groups, and the choice of sports or hobbies.

When sociable people are prevented from being with others, how intense is their *frustration?* Are they at a loss like the child who was heard to say, "I've got nothing to do because there's no one to play with," or do they manage nicely being alone for extended periods of time? We would like to know what they do about enforced loneliness. Thus a good measure of sociability would be the intensity or frequency of responses designed to overcome obstacles to being with others.

Laboratory

As a motive to being with others, sociability is difficult to study in the laboratory, but it can be done. One way is to study the behavior of subjects who presumably are waiting for an experiment to begin. S. Schachter (1959) had subjects in a waiting room decide whether to participate in an experiment alone or with another person. Sociable persons presumably would choose to be with another person, whereas unsociable persons would prefer to be in an experiment alone.

In an experiment on the traits of sociability and shyness, subjects were asked to become acquainted in a waiting room before the experiment was supposed to begin (Cheek & Buss, 1981). They were videotaped surreptitiously, and the following behaviors were evaluated by judges who watched the videotapes: time talking, frequency of self-touching, time looking at the other person. The judges also rated the subjects for tense-relaxed, inhibited-expressive, and friendly-unfriendly behavior. Subjects who were both sociable and shy talked less, engaged in more self-touching, looked at the other less, and were judged to be more tense, inhibited, and unfriendly.

In another experiment that involved videotapes, subjects were aware of the camera, and time sampling was used, the measure being whether a subject was conversing during random time intervals (Gifford & Gallagher, 1985). A questionnaire measure of sociability correlated .31 with the frequency of talking. Thus sociability, when not accompanied by shyness, predicts social participation.

Origins

Heredity

Again, virtually all the evidence on the inheritance of this temperament derives from research on twins. Parents of young twins, whose average age was fifty-five months, rated the twins for sociability (Buss, Plomin, & Willerman, 1973). The correlations for boys were .63 for identical twins but only .25 for fraternal twins; for girls the identical twin correlation was .53, and the fraternal twin correlation was .20. Greater similarity in identical twins than in fraternal twins has also been found in research with an adjective checklist of affiliativeness and with observers' ratings of friendliness (Scarr, 1969), parental ratings of sociability (Cohen, Dibble, & Grawe, 1977), and observers' ratings of infants' friendliness (Plomin & Rowe, 1979). In a recent study, infant twins were evaluated for sociability with the Colorado Child Temperament Inventory. The correlation for identical twins was .35 and for fraternal twins .03 (Emde et al., 1992).

Sociability is a major component of extraversion, which has been found to be highly heritable. Together with earlier documentation (see Buss & Plomin, 1984, p. 122) these findings make a strong case for the inheritance of sociability.

Learning

The preference for being with others has already been linked to three stimulation rewards: sharing, attention, and responsivity. Assume for a moment that when an individual is with others, the major reward is sharing and the other two rewards occur only infrequently. The principal reinforcement for seeking out others eventually would be the sharing of activities. Such learning is instrumental conditioning. As this example suggests, instrumental conditioning can lead to differentiation among the three stimulation rewards, causing some people to prefer one of them.

Instrumental conditioning is of course reward learning, which means that any social reward can reinforce the tendency to seek out others. But the affective rewards—praise, soothing, and love—are likely to occur only in the context of a relationship. If one of these particular rewards is the crucial one being sought, the individual must first become involved with another person in friendship or love. There may be an exception for praise, however, when it is offered for physical beauty. Handsome men and beautiful women tend to be admired even by strangers, and it has been established that attractive people receive special treatment (Berscheid & Walster, 1978). Other things being equal, attractive people are likely to be more sociable than unattractive people.

Another exception is *vicarious status*. Many famous people, especially in the world of entertainment, are trailed by unknown persons who somehow share the public acclaim merely through association. These "groupies" appear to bask in reflected glory, which is a strong incentive for this specific kind of affiliation.

Cognitive learning may also play a role in enhancing sociability. When people are unsure of how to react, or when they need to check out their emotional reactions, they may engage in social comparison (Festinger, 1954). Should I be scared or angry? When children fall and are not sure whether they are hurt, they look to an adult. If the adult stays calm, children pass it off, but if the adult seems concerned, they may cry and complain of pain. When others can offer us clues as to how to behave or react, this cognitive information can serve as reward for associating with others.

Development

Infancy.   Recall that two kinds of rewards are specifically and intrinsically social: stimulation and affective rewards. These are the major social incentives sought by young children and offered to them, especially by their parents. Only the stimulation rewards are relevant to the trait of sociability. The relationship rewards, however, especially praise and affection, are also important in the broader context of social behavior. Thus, in what follows, both kinds of rewards are discussed.

Immediately after birth, infants receive a combination of soothing and affection. They are cradled and fondled and allowed to cling and to suckle. When distressed, they are held, rocked, and offered soft, soothing murmuring.

Childhood.   As the months pass from infancy into childhood, children need less contact comfort, and as the frequency of distress diminishes, they need less soothing. Now the rewards differentiate and can be observed more clearly. Affection is displayed by kissing and hugging and, eventually, by verbal manifestations of love. In traditional families, parents still hug their daughters as they mature, but their sons gradually resist such open displays of affection as unmanly.

Soothing progresses from holding the child to offering sympathy and putting on bandages. Parents no longer need to be next to their children or in direct contact but can be some distance away though still in sight. Children are not as demanding of parental attention as they were as infants. Once children acquire speech, the reward of praise is added.

There is little research on sociability in childhood, perhaps because investigators are more interested in shy and withdrawn children, who are believed to be at risk with respect to psychological problems. There is a relevant study of children in the second grade of elementary school (Asendorpf & Meier, 1993). Mothers answered questions about sociability, and their children were then classified as high or low in sociability. The children were observed during and after school. Compared to unsociable children, sociable children spent more time with friends but less time with siblings; they talked less during school but talked more after school, during free time. The authors concluded, "Unsociable children can satisfy their social needs by interaction with very few, easily available persons such as siblings. Sociable children seek out for more interaction partners and often find them outside the home" (p. 1081).

Adolescence.   As they mature, children are expected to garner information about social behavior. They gradually learn distinctions involving status and deference, how to behave with the opposite sex, and, generally, the unspoken rules that govern social behavior. By adolescence, they should have acquired complementary social skills: how to make friends, put someone at ease, make small talk, and deal with rebuff.

Highly sociable adolescents, by definition, have been strongly motivated to engage in social behavior. Other things being equal, they are likely to have acquired the social information and skills. Unsociable adolescents, by definition, have been less motivated to seek out others, and they spend less time with others.

Matching

Childhood

Again, let us start with the mother-son interaction as the prototype of matches and mismatches during infancy and later childhood. If both are highly sociable, the mother should be receptive to the infant's demand for shared activities, attention, and responsivity. Being sociable herself, she understands and expects her child to require these stimulation rewards, and later in childhood to need playmates. If both mother and son are low in sociability, she will also understand that her child has a weaker motive for sharing, stimulation, and responsivity and need not have many playmates. Thus a match in sociability offers a good mother-infant fit, which promotes harmony.

If the mother is very sociable and her son is unsociable, she is likely to be perplexed or annoyed by his behavior. She will have no intuitive basis for understanding that he is satisfied to play alone and may not be receptive to her need to share activities with him. Later in childhood, she may push the child to have more playmates and, generally, to have a higher level of social behavior. Her best course, though, is to accept the fact that the child's temperament is different from her own and let it go at that.

If the son is sociable and the mother is not, he will seek more contact and attention than she thinks is appropriate. She may regard him as excessively demanding and clinging, unable to play by himself when others are not available. Once peers become available, though, he can receive the stimulation rewards from them, and the mother-son mismatch becomes less important.

Adulthood: Marriage

If both spouses are sociable, they can seek others together. If both are unsociable, one can spend time alone without the other complaining. And, being similar in this motive, each easily understands the other. Therefore, a relationship should be helped by a match in sociability.

If there is a mismatch, however, there will have to be an accommodation. If the wife wants to spend a lot of time with her friends and the husband wants to read or watch television, they might argue. Conflict is not inevitable, though. If each understands that the other is different and each seeks different rewards, the mismatch should cause no problems.

Research on young couples reveals that in adjusted pairs the husband's sociability correlates .38 with the wife's (Meyer & Pepper, 1977). In maladjusted couples, the correlation is −.03. For sociability, matches are associated with harmony, but mismatches are not associated with conflict. Recall, though, that in Chapter 2 we saw that for adjusted couples, aggressiveness correlated .08, whereas for maladjusted couples, it was .40. Presumably, in the maladjusted couples the match was mainly between high-aggressive spouses.

Person Affects Environment

Choice

Sociable children prefer the group play of a playground to sitting alone and watching television or reading a book. Sociable adults gravitate toward professions that involve groups of people: teaching, coaching, or sales, for instance. Those high in sociability like team sports such as baseball or soccer, and they are especially motivated to seek out games involving responsivity such as tennis or chess. They are likely to join clubs or political parties and tend to be active in them.

Those who are low in sociability are more likely to choose solitary professions: astronomy or mathematics, for example. Having only a weak need to be with others, they are likely to choose as avocations long-distance running, fishing, or hunting. Indoors, they might do crossword puzzles, play solitaire, or choose to reflect and introspect.

Gormly (1983) had fraternity members rate each other for sociability. These subjects then were asked whether they preferred to watch a more socially interactive videotape or a less interactive videotape. The trait of sociability correlated .53 with choice of the more interactive tape.

When people are allowed to choose, the trait of sociability is an important determinant of how they will spend their time (Emmons, Diener, & Larsen, 1986). Over a period of several weeks, subjects recorded the situations they encountered, including how long each situation lasted and whether it was social or nonsocial. For situations the subjects were allowed to choose, the percentage of time spent in social situations correlated .36 with the trait of sociability.

Sociability is manifested not only in behavior but also in expressed interest. College students were asked if they would rather be with friends or be alone (wishes); they also responded repeatedly to an electronic pager by saying what they were doing at the moment (behavior) (Wong & Csikszentmihalyi, 1991). Both men and women who were sociable wished that they could be with friends more than did unsociable subjects. But there were sex differences in behavior. Regardless of how sociable they were, women spent more time with friends than men did. Why is there a sex difference in behavior when there is none in motivation (wishes)? Perhaps women have more opportunities to get together with friends than men do. Perhaps the greater competitiveness and aggressiveness of men precludes their interacting very closely or frequently. Perhaps women's sociable behavior is more interpersonal, and men's is more oriented toward group activities such as work or athletics—a hypothesis to be considered shortly.

Choice also occurs in preference for dating partner. Women were given descriptions of men who varied in the temperaments of sociability, activity, and emotionality and asked which of the men described they would find pleasurable and arousing (Krueger & Caspi, 1993). The women found sociable and active men to be pleasurable and arousing but not emotional men.

Setting the Tone

Each of us can also determine the course of a social interaction. Those low in sociability tend to talk less, use fewer gestures, and, in general, display less animation in their conversations. Less responsive to others, their conversations are subdued and may lag or peter out. But sociable people tend to be responsive, reinforcing the liveliness of others, and the participants seem to enjoy the interaction. Research on extraversion-introversion, a major component of which is the trait of sociability, bears on these hypotheses (Thorne, 1987). Previously unacquainted women were matched for extraversion or introversion and were videotaped while conversing for ten minutes. The talk of extraverts contained likes, dislikes, opinions, and compliments. The talk of introverts was limited to current problems, and they avoided commitment to opinions or ideas. Thorne concluded, "Extraverts promoted upbeat and expansive conversations, whereas introverts promoted more serious and focused discourse. This overall finding supports the view that the expression of a disposition creates a situation for the person who encounters it" (p. 724).

Changing the Environment

Those high in sociability, in their need to be with others, often refuse to accept being alone. Stuck in the house, they use the telephone. Isolated geographically, they may become ham radio operators and converse with people hundreds of miles away. If they must memorize material for an examination, which can easily be done alone, they may organize a study group. If their vocation is writing, they may seek out collaborators. Unsociable people do not ordinarily need to alter the environment, for if there are too many people or there is too much interaction, they can just leave.

Sex Differences

Again, sex differences must be viewed from a developmental perspective (Buss & Plomin, 1975). Preschool girls and boys do not differ in sociability, but starting in late childhood, girls are slightly but significantly more sociable, and this difference stabilizes in adulthood. Though men and women differ little in the motive to be with others, they diverge in how it is expressed in behavior. Women tend to exchange the social rewards of praise, soothing, and affection; thus their contacts are more interpersonal. Men tend to assemble more in groups in which there may be two opposing tendencies: "solidarity and peership, on the one hand, and competition for jobs, prestige, competence, and women on the other. These tendencies are governed by norms governing their appropriateness. The norms make it clear whether the goal of solidarity or competence takes precedence in a particular situation" (Holter, 1970, p. 236).

When men and women offered written descriptions of prior conversations with friends, men were found to disclose less about themselves or others and to choose less intimate topics (Reis, Senchak, & Solomon, 1985). However, this sex difference occurred only with same-sex interactions, for in mixed-sex interactions, men were no less intimate than women.

Thus men and women differ in how they interact with others of the same sex, a difference that may derive from the sex roles assigned to each gender. If socialization practices changed and sex roles started converging—women becoming more competitive and men becoming more nurturant, for example—we would expect the sex difference to attenuate or disappear.

Meanwhile, women's sociability tends to be expressed more interpersonally than men's. The sex difference has implications for help women might receive in the face of calamity. Then, women can call on close friends or others who are part of a support network. After divorce, for example, a woman's friends gather around to help her recover, whereas a man in the same situation rarely can depend on such support from other men. As a result, divorce, widowhood, and retirement tend to be more devastating to the adjustment of men than of women. Furthermore, men are less likely to seek help, say, psychotherapy, because their sociability is not expressed interpersonally.

Impulsivity

Impulsivity, or impulsiveness, is a complex personality trait, as is clear in the following definition: Impulsivity is "the tendency to respond quickly and without reflection. It is a rather coarse variable which includes: (1) short reaction time to social press, (2) quick intuitive behavior, (3) emotional drivenness, (4) lack of forethought. The subject is usually somewhat restless, quick to move, quick to make up his mind, quick to voice his opinion. He often says the first thing that comes into his head, and does not consider the future consequences of his conduct. Deliberation is easier to observe than Impulsion. It is marked by: (1) long reaction time to social press, (2) inhibition of initial impulses, (3) hesitation, caution, and reflection before action, (4) a long period of planning and organizing before beginning a piece of work. The subject may have obsessional doubts: a 'load' of considerations which he must 'lift' before beginning. He usually experiences difficulty in an emergency" (Murray, 1938, pp. 205–206).

Impulsive people tend to respond immediately to whatever stimulus impinges on them, without forethought or care for later consequences. At the other end of the dimension, deliberate people wait, reflect, and consider many possible consequences before they are ready to act. In short, impulsive people act quickly, and deliberate people act slowly.

The concept of quick action may seem familiar, overlapping the tempo component of activity, but there is a difference. Tempo refers to the rate of response once the behavior has started. Impulsivity refers to the time between a stimulus and the start of the response, which may be called the *latency of response*. For example, a man may be slow to act (deliberate), but once action is initiated, he moves rapidly (fast tempo). Another man may be quick to act (impulsive), but once action is initiated, he moves at a leisurely pace (slow tempo). Thus impulsivity and tempo are linked by the dimension of time but differ in when the issue of time comes up: before responding (impulsivity) or during responding (tempo).

The relationship between activity and impulsivity is of course an empirical issue. The correlations on the EASI I were in the thirties for both sexes, but subsequent examination of the activity items revealed one that appears to overlap impulsivity: "Cannot sit still for long" (Buss & Plomin, 1975, p. 24). When that activity item was replaced by another one on the EASI II, the correlation was not different from zero for both sexes. Despite their linkage in being related to time, the two traits are independent.

Components

The various behaviors that make up impulsivity may be divided into three major classes. In each instance, there is a dimension that extends from the impulsive extreme to the deliberate extreme.

Control

Even the least emotional person may at times become furious. Is the rage let loose on the other person, or is it kept under close rein, remaining hidden? Some people, lacking control over their *emotions*, explode quickly into temper tantrums. Others exercise superb control and keep their anger in check.

Closely allied to emotions are a variety of *motives*. When hungry, children may just grab food and stuff it in their mouths, whereas most adults wait until others are ready to eat. Some people, when sexually aroused, cannot contain themselves, but others can delay gratification.

Motives represent psychological pressure from within, a push to action. The counterpart of motives are incentives or rewards that pull one toward them: the sweet smell of baked bread or money just lying around for someone to pocket, for instance. These are *temptations* that can be withstood or may prove irresistible.

Thus the three aspects of control differ in the tendency to be controlled. The first two are emotions that can be suppressed or expressed and motives that one can act on, delay, or entirely inhibit. Both emotions and motives represent internal pressure to act. Incentives, on the other hand, can be so enticing that they may prove difficult to resist. Incentives represent an external pull on behavior.

Discipline

When a person has begun a task, does he or she stay until the task is completed, however long it takes? Does the person persist and remain steadfast even when boredom starts to set in? Is there tenacity, perseverance, and dogged, single-minded pursuit of the goal? If the answer is yes, such a person represents the deliberate end of the impulsivity dimension.

At the opposite extreme is the person who jumps from one activity to the next without completing any of them. He or she may start reading one book and quickly switch to another. A decision to study may be quickly replaced with the alternative of watching television. Motivation appears to be transient and mercurial, and the person's erratic behavior often seems capricious and whimsical. Impulsive college students often sign up for classes only to drop them, switch their major, and revise their vocational goals several times. Impulsive people tend to be the first to adopt the latest fad and the first to abandon it.

Focus is closely related to impulsivity. Impulsive people tend to be distractible, unable to concentrate on a book, a paper, or a lecture. Their attention wanders from the immediate stimulus to any event that happens to occur. When a door opens at a lecture, they immediately look away from the lecturer to see who is coming in, or they may gaze out the window at passersby. When they should be absorbed, they are easily diverted.

At the other extreme are people whose intense concentration does not wane; they are continuously engrossed in the task at hand. Such people may be so caught up in an activity as to disregard anything else occurring around them. They simply will not waver in their vigilance and can maintain it for hours at a time.

Another aspect of discipline is *impatience*. Consider the many contexts that require us to wait: a physician's office, a supermarket line, the delivery of mail, or an appointment or rendezvous with someone. Some people can endure the wait calmly, even stoically. They simply are not bothered by having to stand in line and may get in line for a popular concert or ball game the day before. Slow salespeople do not bother them nor are they disturbed by the late arrival of a friend or by a procrastinator who misses deadlines when turning in work.

At the opposite extreme are people who seem unable to cope with even the slightest delay. They fidget, pace restlessly, glance repeatedly at the clock, and complain bitterly about the passage of time. They will not stay more than a few minutes if another person is late for an appointment or remain on a long line. When a mechanic is slow to repair a car, impulsive people may become angry. Time weighs heavily on them, and they must throw off the burden.

Reflection

Many activities require preparation if they are to go off smoothly. Cooks, for example, need to lay out the appropriate utensils and raw food before they begin. Earlier, they must shop for ingredients or they will be caught short. Impulsive people somehow do not prepare adequately; they seem to lack planfulness. When cooking, they must scurry around searching for the right knife or pot, or they must hurry to the supermarket to pick up a missing spice or herb. If they are students, they do not register early, and they tend to leave required courses for their last semester. When taking a trip, they just get in the car and start driving, relying on locals to give directions if they get lost. They have little idea what they will be doing next year, next month, or even next week.

At the other extreme are those who may plan a meal weeks in advance and lay out everything needed before they start cooking. These people map out a detailed itinerary weeks or months before the start of a trip. They tend to register early for classes, buy tickets in advance for concerts, and schedule vacations months ahead of time. Their calendar is filled in carefully, and they know precisely what they will be doing next month or for their next vacation.

Making decisions is closely related to making preparations. Consider two men who need to buy a car. One drops into a showroom to look at a car, drives it, looks under the hood, likes its color and the way it performs, and buys it on the spot. The other goes through the same process but does not buy the car immediately. He needs time to think about such an expensive purchase and is cautious about making a sudden choice. He ponders whether he can afford it, whether to finance it or pay cash, whether the car is reliable. He consults consumer magazines and asks his friends about their cars. For any given make, he shops around for the best bargain. He may ruminate about these issues for weeks, being in no hurry to come to a decision.

Closely allied to decisiveness is the dichotomy between acting rashly and acting cautiously. Impulsive people, seemingly unable to look before they leap, jump headlong into situations that may prove their undoing. They may buy expensive items on credit, only to discover that they cannot make the payments. An acquaintance reported that he bought a motorcycle and rode off without reading instructions or receiving any training, learning to handle the motorcycle on the road. An impulsive person might decide to marry after only a few days' acquaintance, perhaps offering an example of the phrase "Act in haste, repent at leisure." At the other extreme are people so cautious that they never take a chance. They seek safety and stick to well-worn paths of behavior. They almost never make foolish mistakes, their lives being marked by prudence and circumspection. When opportunity knocks, however, they may not open the door, and their lives tend to lack excitement, sometimes to the point of boredom.

Three Components

The three components of impulsivity are illustrated in Table 4.2. Control refers to pressure to act, whether the pressure is internal or external. Discipline consists of one or another aspect of persistence: staying with an activity, remaining focused, or just waiting. Reflection refers to planning, deliberation, and caution, or their opposites. The three behaviors *within* each component are highly similar and may even overlap, which is why the behaviors have been grouped together.

Is there any concept that links all three components? Perhaps it is time. Lack of reflection involves time, virtually by definition. Lack of discipline may be regarded as failure to persist over time. Lack of control may be seen as failure to wait until a motive or emotion has waned or a temptation is no longer present. Time as the link among the three components is entirely consistent with Murray's (1938) defini-

TABLE 4.2   Components of Impulsivity

Lack of control	Control
Expresses emotions	Suppresses emotions
Acts on motives	Inhibits action
Gives in to temptation	Resists temptation
Lack of discipline	**Discipline**
Jumps from one activity to another	Persists in one activity
Is easily distracted	Remains focused
Cannot wait	Patiently waits
Lack of reflection	**Reflection**
Does not plan	Plans painstakingly
Decides on spur of the moment	Deliberates at length
Acts rashly	Acts cautiously

tion of impulsivity mentioned earlier: "the tendency to respond quickly and without reflection."

Measures

Self-Reports

Impulsivity has been part of questionnaires for more than half a century. Guilford's (1940) *rhathymia* scale contained these items: "act on the spur of the moment without thinking things over," "often say things on the spur of the moment and later regret them," and "plan work beforehand." These early items assess reflection, and most subsequent questionnaires have concentrated on either extreme of this component.

The control component is rarely represented on questionnaires, probably because it does not emerge as a cluster when items are factor analyzed. The root of the problem is what is being controlled: motives, emotions, and the urge to give in to temptation. If emotions are intense, for example, it may be difficult to control behavior even if one is not impulsive; and if they are weak, it may be easy to control behavior even if one is impulsive. As a result, impulsivity is linked to emotionality. On the EASI I (Buss & Plomin, 1975) the two temperaments correlate in the thirties for both men and women. In brief, any self-report measure of the control component of impulsivity must take into account individual differences in motives and emotions, and so far this has not been accomplished.

The other two components, being free of this complication, have been assessed by self-report. The factor of *broad impulsivity* (Eysenck & Eysenck, 1977) favors the behaviors of the reflection component: "Do you often buy things on impulse?" "Do you often get into a jam because you do things without thinking?" "Do you like planning things carefully well ahead of time?" "Do you usually make up your mind quickly?" "Can you make decisions quickly?" The Barratt Impulsiveness Scale-II (Barratt, 1965) contains these items: "I make up my mind quickly" (reflection) and "My interests tend to change quickly" (discipline).

The only questionnaire to tap all three components is the EASI III (Buss & Plomin, 1975), and the items were assigned to scales a priori and not empirically.

Control

1. I have trouble controlling my impulses.
2. I can tolerate frustration better than most.
3. I have trouble resisting my cravings (for food, cigarettes, etc.).

Discipline

1. I generally like to see things through to the end.
2. I tend to hop from interest to interest quickly.
3. I tend to give up easily.
4. Unfinished tasks really bother me.
5. Once I get going on something, I hate to stop.

Reflection

1. I often say the first thing that comes into my head.
2. I often have trouble making up my mind.
3. I like to plan things way ahead of time.
4. I often act on the spur of the moment.
5. I like to make detailed plans before I do something.

Laboratory

Control.   Only one aspect of control has been studied: the resistance to temptation. The subjects inevitably have been children who are still impulsive enough to give in to temptation. Adults are sufficiently self-controlled to resist temptation, at least any temptation ethical enough to be tried in the laboratory.

In one paradigm, children are told not to play with enticing toys because they are reserved for older boys (Aronfreed & Reber, 1965). Then the children are left alone with an unattractive toy (allowed) and a very attractive toy (not allowed). The experimenter surreptitiously observes whether the subjects play with the forbidden toy and if so, how soon.

In the other major paradigm, children are tested for their ability to wait for a better reward: "I would like to give you each a piece of candy but I don't have enough of these (indicating the larger, more preferred reinforcement) with me today. So you can either get this one (indicating the smaller, less preferred reinforcement) right now, today, or, if you want to wait for this one (indicating) which I will bring back next Friday (one-week delay interval)" (Mischel, 1961, p. 4). The child can either be impulsive and take the inferior reward or resist immediate temptation and take the larger, delayed reward.

Discipline.   Only the persistence aspect of discipline has been studied. Subjects have been given a dull task—copying single letters for half an hour, for example—to see how long they persist (London, Schubert, & Washburn, 1972). Of course the task need not be boring for the purposes of the study, and in one paradigm subjects were asked to make as many words as possible out of the letters *B*, *R*, *T*, *A*, *O*, and *U* (Thornton, 1939). In another paradigm, subjects read a text that became increasingly difficult as errors crept into spacing, punctuation, and capitalization (Rethlingshafer, 1942). In all these tasks, impulsive people presumably would tend to give up sooner.

Reflection.   A good measure of planning is the mazes developed by Porteus (1950). They require foresight and a delay in putting pencil to paper until a rational spatial strategy has been worked out.

Kagan's reflection-impulsivity task (Kagan, 1966; Messer, 1976) involves matching-to-sample, which was first developed by Harlow (1949) for use with primates. Children are presented with a series of drawings. A typical drawing shows a doll with various features (facial, bodily, clothes) and is to be matched to one of five other drawings of the doll. All but one vary from the original, and the subject must make a precise match. Impulsivity is measured by the time spent in making the choice.

Both the mazes and the matching-to-sample task are correlated with intelligence. So when impulsivity is assessed by such tasks, IQ needs to be controlled.

Observations

One of the scales used by Thomas, Chess, Birch, Hertzig, & Korn (1963) was distractibility: whether a child can maintain attention or loses it to extraneous stimuli. Another scale is persistence: at one year of age, a child loses interest in toys quickly; at two years, a child gives up quickly if a toy is hard to use, or asks immediately for help in dressing; at five years, a child gives up tying shoes if success is not immediate; and at ten years, a child rarely finishes a book, and gets up often from homework and may not finish it.

Dibble and Cohen (1974) suggested several categories of behavior that might be observed in children: "Persists in trying to do something, even if he has some small problems along the way. Can pay attention for a long time to something. Gives long attention to objects, toys, or books that interest him. Pays close attention when you show him something. Loses interest in what he has started doing. Goes from one thing to another. Even a slight distraction will make him forget what he was doing" (p. 806).

Origins

Heredity

A review of the twin research on impulsivity prior to 1974 summarized the literature as follows: "The heritability data are mixed. Roughly half the studies have yielded positive evidence and the other half, negative evidence. In several instances, a larger sample would have yielded a significant difference between monozygotic and dizygotic twins, thereby tipping the weight of evidence in a positive direction. But such a change would not radically alter the way we interpret the data; they are mixed" (Buss & Plomin, 1975, p. 146). Sample size assumes importance when we realize that, given errors of measurement, a large number of subjects may be needed for identical twin and fraternal twin correlations to be significantly different. Nevertheless, before 1974 the heritability of impulsivity had not been firmly established.

The twin studies since then are summarized in Table 4.3. Plomin (1974) assessed the three components of impulsivity—control, discipline, and reflection—and for all three, identical twins were more similar than fraternal twins. Plomin and Rowe (1977) showed that identical twins were more alike than fraternal twins in attention span and persistence, as did Cohen, Dibble, and Grawe (1977). Loehlin and Nichols (1976) demonstrated heritability for the self-control scale of the California Psychological Inventory, and Torgersen and Kringlen (1978) reported significant heritability in nine-month-old twins for the distractibility measure of Thomas et al. (1963).

TABLE 4.3   Twin Studies of Impulsivity since 1974

	Identical twins	Fraternal twins
Plomin (1974)		
Control	.54	.02
Discipline	.62	−.20
Reflection	.66	−.14
Eaves & Eysenck (1975)	Significant heritability*	
Dworkin et al. (1976)	Significant heritability*	
Loehlin & Nichols (1976)		
Self-control	.57	.32
Cohen et al. (1977)	.55	.12
Torgersen & Kringlen (1978)		
Distractibility	Significant heritability*	
Pedersen et al. (1988)		
Reared together	.45	.09
Reared apart	.40	.15
Tellegen et al. (1988) control		
Reared together	.41	−.06
Reared apart	.50	.03
McGue, Bacon, & Lykken (1993) control		
20 year olds	.53	.01
30 year olds	.44	.19

*Correlations for twins were not reported, but analyses of variance revealed significant heritability.

    Two studies had access to twins reared together and twins reared apart. Pedersen, Plomin, McClearn, and Friberg (1988) used a Swedish measure of the reflection component of impulsivity. Tellegen at al. (1988) used Tellegen's (1985) control scale, a measure of impulsivity. In both studies identical twins were significantly more similar than fraternal twins even when the twins were reared apart. The remaining studies showed heritability for the general trait of impulsiveness.

    When all the data are examined, two patterns emerge. Before 1974 there were both positive and negative studies, suggesting a weak case for the inheritance of impulsivity. Since then, research has yielded consistently positive findings with a variety of measures, including some of the components of impulsivity. The overall picture is one of earlier mixed findings and later consistently positive findings. When all the findings are examined, the preponderance of evidence for the inheritance of impulsivity is positive.

There is another relevant issue. The usual strategy in science is to give greater weight to recent findings, on the assumption that later investigators have an opportunity to remedy any possible errors of earlier research. Also, as more data accrue, we expect them to converge and offer more definitive answers to empirical questions. The more recent data do offer a more definitive answer to the question of the inheritance of impulsivity. It is yes.

Learning

Instrumental conditioning is important in the shaping of impulsive behavior, especially the control component. Reward training is generally preferred. Each time children suppress anger, delay acting on a strong motive, or resist temptation, they should be reinforced by parental approval or even by the delivery of a substantive reward. However, this procedure requires almost constant monitoring of children, which is impractical. As a result, most instrumental conditioning of impulsive behavior involves punishment after the proscribed behavior occurs. Such punishment needs to be carried out early in the behavioral sequence, when it is more effective than after the response has occurred and the behavior has been rewarded (Aronfreed & Reber, 1965). Unfortunately, immediate punishment of impulsive behavior also requires constant monitoring of children, which again is impractical. Therefore punishment tends to occur long after the forbidden response has occurred, and so it is not especially effective.

The importance of the timing of punishment may be seen in schools. Students who do not plan—that is, who cram at the last moment—tend to perform poorly. Their distractibility and lack of persistence occur long before the delivery of punishment—a low grade—and this delay weakens the impact of punishment on impulsive behavior. Some parents and some college fraternities and sororities monitor such behavior by setting required study hours, which virtually force students to persist. Mandatory study hours even help some to acquire the habit of spaced studying.

Another option is to train children through *imitation learning*. Recent Asian immigrants to the United States offer one example. The parents work hard and delay gratification as they work toward distant goals. These behaviors often are copied by their children, who excel in school. In addition, if parents inhibit the expression of anger and resist temptation, their children have appropriate models to follow. Most parents, however, are not paragons of virtue; they may explode with anger or fail to resist temptation. Too often parents cannot stay on a diet, drink too much, or smoke cigarettes, while instructing their children not to engage in such behaviors: "Do as I say, not as I do." Some parents are horrified to discover that their young children swear like troopers, using the same phrases as their parents.

Observational learning can also shape the other two components of impulsivity. Some parents show great persistence, remain focused on what they are doing, and wait patiently in line at the supermarket and other places. They plan carefully for trips, deliberate at length before making important choices, and generally exercise caution. Their children have models for the behaviors their parents are trying to instill. At the other extreme are parents whose lack of discipline and reflection provide models for precisely the kind of behavior they may punish in their children.

Cognitive learning also plays a role. After acquiring language, children can talk to themselves. They can say, "Wait" or "Don't do that," instructing themselves as they have been instructed by others. They can try counting to 100 before giving vent to exasperation. Using their imagination, they can envision distant, major goals to work toward, which may help them to forsake immediate, minor goals (Mischel, 1974).

As cognitive development proceeds, children become more aware of the consequences of their actions and can anticipate later rewards and punishments. This future orientation helps children to delay gratification, inhibit immediate expression of anger, and maintain persistence. It also helps them to plan and to make more deliberate choices.

Once children have acquired the requisite cognitive ability, they can be taught moral precepts and rules of behavior. Most of these precepts and rules are designed to oppose the possibility of impulsive behavior.

Development

There is nothing more impulsive than a newborn infant. He or she reacts instantaneously to noises or movement and cries when hungry or cold. The infant's lack of inhibitory control may be attributed to an immature brain and incomplete insulation of the axons of nerves. Bipedal locomotion, which freed the hands for manipulation, led to "scars of evolution," one of which is the excessive narrowing of the birth canal. One consequence of this narrowing is a strict limitation of the size of the fetus's head and therefore its brain. The development of the brain is therefore incomplete at birth; this is compensated for by a growth spurt during the first months of life. As the cerebral cortex matures, it gradually comes to inhibit other parts of the brain and the rest of the nervous system. There is a slow maturation of control, a shift from reflexive responding to delay and inhibition in behavior.

During the first year, infants react instantly to external and internal stimuli. During the second and third years of life, most children achieve control over bodily elimination and can delay eating for a while when hungry. Those who delay attaining these kinds of self-control are appropriately labeled as impulsive. Next, parents and other caretakers insist that temper tantrums and other emotional outbursts start to wane in intensity and frequency, and most children gradually accommodate.

Children three years of age still tend to grab toys from others, break toys, get into the cookie jar, throw occasional temper tantrums, and become extremely impatient when asked to wait. During the fourth and fifth years, most children start to resist temptation, stop having tantrums, cry less often, start to work toward remote goals, show some persistence, and wait more patiently.

These trends, especially in discipline and reflection, continue for the remainder of childhood. There is a gradual diminution in childish spontaneity, as children increasingly inhibit emotions and motives, are less susceptible to distraction, plan more, and act more cautiously.

Of course, there are great individual differences in the development of inhibitory control. At one extreme are precocious children who, with respect to impulsiveness, seem like little adults. At the other extreme are older children who are no less impulsive than infants. The two main causes of such individual differences, heredity and learning, have already been discussed.

Matching

Let us continue with mother and son as the pair that will illustrate matching between parent and child. When both are impulsive, the mother serves as an appropriate model, though she may punish the child for behavior that she herself displays. The conflict between the mother's impulsiveness, which can be copied, and her son's impulsivity, which may be punished, may lead to turmoil in the relationship.

When both mother and son are low in impulsivity, there is little conflict. Parental modeling and reinforcement for delay and inhibition strengthen tendencies already present in the child. The only problem that might arise is excessive parental expectations. The mother, being low in impulsivity, may not realize how impulsive children are, and therefore may expect self-control in her son that exceeds the maturity of even a low-impulsive child. But this is a minor issue, and a match in low impulsivity appears to be optimal for the parent-child relationship.

In one kind of mismatch the mother is impulsive and the son is not. She may not understand her son's deliberate ways ("He sometimes acts like a little old man") but finds him easy to live with because he quickly learns the lessons of socialization. His temper tantrums diminish early, he learns to resist temptation with little trouble, he shows persistence and patience, and he cautiously makes plans and carries them out. He does not imitate his mother's impulsive behavior because his behavioral tendencies are in the opposite direction.

The other kind of mismatch, in which the son is impulsive and the mother is not, is expected to produce the greatest conflict. The mother is confronted with a son who has trouble controlling his temper, resisting temptation, and who is lacking in persistence. He is impatient, distractible, and rash in his actions. This child is difficult to live with and to socialize with, and the mother, being at the inhibited end of the impulsivity dimension, has little empathy for his behavioral tendencies ("Why is he so childish, and when will he start growing up?").

A mismatch can also pose problems in a marriage. The patience, persistence, and planning of one spouse can be undone by the other's explosive emotions, impatience, lack of planning, and impulsive purchases. One solution is for one partner to do the planning and exercise caution, and the other to abide by this division of labor. If the arrangement succeeds, the unstable and erratic behavior of the one partner will be complemented by the other's steadfast, settling ways.

If both spouses are impulsive, there may be more severe problems. Each has a problem controlling emotions, and one's outburst can easily trigger an outburst on the part of the other. When one is late, the other is likely to become furious at the wait. One partner's impulse buying may be augmented by the other's incautious purchases, resulting in deep debt. The lack of planning by both tends to result in a chaotic household, and this lack of stability will bode ill for the marriage.

When both partners are low in impulsiveness, there is a good marital fit. There is planning, focus, steadfastness, and control of emotions. Such a marriage might seem dull and stodgy to an outsider, but it is steady and likely to be harmonious. In a marriage that is expected to endure, boring stability may be better than exciting chaos that can lead to a breakup.

Person Affects Environment

Choice

Impulsive people tend to select environments that allow at least some uninhibited behavior. They prefer informal contexts in which status is of no consequence and there are few rules to govern social behavior. They like to go to lively parties, where drinking offers an excuse for cutting loose from the everyday need for propriety. They like horse racing and gambling. The vocations they seek are marked by time pressure and spur-of-the-moment decisions (commodities trader, for example). They are likely to choose a job that requires little planning, brief encounters with others, and a quick change of pace (such as sales work that involves a quick turnover of customers).

People at the deliberate end of the impulsivity dimension tend to find quieter jobs that involve routine, demand planning and patience, and require caution (librarian). If resistance to temptation is added to the list of job characteristics, they might seek a position as bank teller or executive. Low-impulsive people prefer more formal social contexts for which they know what to wear and how to behave and which will contain few surprises. They attend quiet dinners and like to invite others for dinners that are planned well in advance. In their social life, as in their vocation, they choose activities that are routine and without risk or uninhibited behavior.

Modifying the Impact

Impulsive children tend to resist socialization practices aimed at the inhibition of behavior. They often feel put upon by being told to wait patiently, persist in boring tasks, plan for the future, and exercise caution in making choices. Parents and socialization agents send those kinds of messages to impulsive children, who may not receive them. Unable to conform to the demand for self-control, impulsive children may rebel against all authority. They are restless in school and cannot endure the lengthy time required for homework or study. They may rashly cut class or suddenly decide to run away from home. In brief, they modify the impact of socialization pressure and are likely to be labeled difficult.

Highly impulsive children may also be difficult in school, where they resist the quiet, orderly environment. If their problem is lack of discipline, they may jump from one activity to another and be highly distractible and impatient. Such children are likely to be said to have an attention deficit disorder.

When children resist socialization pressures, their impulsivity may lead them into serious trouble. The problem may lie in giving in to temptation and acting rashly. Thus when another person's property is available, they are likely to steal it; when confronted, they are likely to lie; when they should act prudently, they are likely to take bad risks. And in doing any of these things, they are likely to inflict harm on others, either directly or indirectly. Such persons used to be called psychopaths, a label that is still meaningful, but now the term for their condition and behavior is *antisocial personality disorder*.

At the opposite extreme are adults for whom the problem is excessive reflection, the third component of impulsivity. They make elaborate plans, deliberate at length, and often never get around to acting. The appropriate label for such persons is *obsessive*.

Notice that the extremes of impulsivity slide into the realm of abnormal behavior, implying continuity between personality and abnormality. Continuity is certainly true descriptively, but in some instances descriptive continuity may conceal qualitative differences between the origin of personality and the origin of abnormal behavior. This issue will be treated at greater length in Chapter 14.

Part I Commentary

Part I has dealt with two areas of personality: aggression and the four temperaments, with most attention given to temperaments. Here, then, I will comment on only temperaments alone or temperaments in relation to aggression. In what follows the phrase "other things being equal" may need to be added, and, for the most part, only the extremes of the temperaments are relevant.

Combinations of Temperaments

Aggressiveness

Three of the temperaments may be regarded as predispositions to aggressiveness. People high in activity are likely to be more intensely aggressive, mainly because of the vigor component, which amplifies any behavior. Most of their responses are delivered with more force, and when the behavior is aggressive, more force means more intense aggression.

Emotionality affects aggressiveness in two different ways, depending on which of its differentiated components is ascendant. If anger predominates, the person will display considerable angry aggression. If fear predominates, it will inhibit all aggression.

The control component of impulsivity appears to be the most potent determinant of aggressiveness. When people low in control become angry, they are likely to express this emotion in angry aggression, by definition. In addition, there may be an incentive they badly want, which can be attained by instrumental aggression. Lacking control, they are likely to aggress to achieve the reward. Thus highly impulsive persons tend to display both angry and instrumental aggression.

When these three temperaments are combined, they strongly tilt people toward or away from aggression. Those who are vigorous, easily angered, and impulsive are likely to attack others, either to ventilate anger or to achieve an incentive. Those who are not vigorous, rarely angered, and in control of their impulses tend not to aggress.

Extraversion

Extraverts, above all, want the stimulation of interacting with others—that is, they are highly sociable. And being sociable, they respond warmly to others. Extraverts tend to speak faster (tempo) and have broader gestures (vigor), which means that that they are high in activity. They are spontaneous, enjoying the excitement of doing things on the spur of the moment, which means that they are low in the reflection component of impulsivity. They are also expressive, laughing or crying easily, which means that they are low in the control component of impulsivity.

Thus extraversion appears to be a combination of the high end of the dimensions of sociability, activity, and impulsivity. These three temperaments, taken together, define animation: warmth, fast tempo of speech and gestures, broad gestures, and spontaneity of social behavior. Introversion is at the low end of these dimensions, representing the opposite of animation: quietude and staidness.

The trait of shyness is relevant here. Introverts tend to be above average in shyness, and extraverts are extremely unshy. As we shall see in Chapter 11, though, shyness itself may be regarded as a combination of high emotionality and low sociability.

Socialization of Temperaments

Some temperaments are the focus of socialization practices, and others are ignored. Society has little to say about individual differences in activity. Parents may become irritated by an overactive child or worry about a lethargic child, but otherwise this temperament receives no special attention.

Sociability does receive some attention, especially at the low end of the dimension. Children are not supposed to be off by themselves, and teachers are trained to pick out these loners. Such children are then pressured to mingle more. This pressure is particularly strong in cohesive cultures such as Japan, where the group is accorded greater importance than the individual.

Emotionality is allowed during the first year of life, but thereafter it is strongly socialized. Temper tantrums are frowned on early in childhood and punished later in childhood. Young children are allowed to express fear but gradually are expected to be more courageous. And even if they are frightened, they are expected to overcome their fears and not withdraw.

The temperament that is the central focus of socialization is impulsivity. Infants are allowed to be impulsive in some respects but not in others. Thus by the second year of life, toilet training begins. By two years of age, children are starting to be taught to control their emotions and not to give into temptation. School-age children are strongly encouraged to be disciplined about their schoolwork, to wait patiently, and to start planning. Thus there is a development sequence in the socialization of impulsivity: control, discipline, and reflection.

Consider also that the low end of the impulsivity dimension represents a metaphorical brake on the engine of psychological emotions and motives. Thus if we ask which temperaments need to be inhibited, the answer is emotionality and activity. Children high in these two temperaments are seen as immature and are subjected to strong socialization practices.

Sex Differences

Males are physically much more aggressive than females and barely more verbally aggressive and hostile. The difference in physical aggression appears to be a combination of hormones and socialization. Males have more testosterone, and females are more strongly socialized to inhibit physical aggression. Boys are encouraged to stand up and fight, and there is enough machismo in young men for them to demonstrate their manhood through fighting. The sex differences in verbal aggression and hostility are too trivial to require explanation.

There is no sex difference in fear or activity until the school years, and starting then, females are more fearful than males. There appears to be no biological explanation for the greater fearfulness of females, which means that socialization practices probably account for it.

There is a similar pattern for activity: There is no sex difference in the preschool years, but after that, males are slightly more active. We know that primate males are more active than females, so by extrapolation to our species a biological explanation is tenable. But males' games and sports tend to be more active, and vocations requiring strength generally belong to men, so the socialization explanation may also be invoked.

There is no sex difference for impulsivity. However, most of those with attention deficit disorder are males, which raises the question of whether this specific disorder has a sex-linked genetic basis.

C h a p t e r **5**

Attachment

History

The history of attachment starts at mid-century with Erik Erikson's (1950) specification that trust versus mistrust is the first stage in the development of personality: "Mothers create a sense of trust in their children by that kind of administration which in its quality combines a sensitive care of the baby's individual needs and a firm sense of personal trustworthiness" (p. 249). A trustful infant lets the mother leave without any particular fear or rage; this behavior is typical of what are called *secure* infants.

John Bowlby (1958) examined infancy using concepts from ethology (see Ainsworth & Bowlby, 1991) that he had introduced to psychoanalytic theory. Bowlby's approach starts with the fact that infants are helpless, needing an adult to supply biological necessities and the psychological requisites of social stimulation and love. On the basis of such parental behavior and the infant's response, a close parent-infant relationship develops. Bowlby (1969) called this bond attachment. He saw the infant's bond with the mother as a means of ensuring that the infant would be protected. Whenever infants feel threatened, they immediately seek contact with their mothers, who comfort them and offer security. Initial research using the concept of attachment involved mothers and infants in Uganda (Ainsworth, 1967).

Harry Harlow (Harlow & Zimmerman, 1959) isolated infant rhesus monkeys from their mothers and discovered that in adulthood these animals had abnormal play, defense, and sexual behavior. Evidently, it is crucial for an infant to have a bond of attachment to the mother (or a maternal substitute) for normal development to proceed. Harlow's work and that of his students established that attachment was not limited to humans but extended to primates and probably to all highly social mammals—dogs, for example. However, modern research on attachment derives mainly from Bowlby's writings on human attachment.

Infant Attachment

The Sequence

During the first year of life, infants' reactions to others move through several stages. The sequence has been succinctly described: "When a baby is born, he cannot tell one person from another and indeed can hardly tell person from thing. Yet by his first birthday he is likely to be a connoisseur of people. Not only does he come quickly to distinguish familiars from strangers but amongst his familiars he chooses one or more favorites. They are greeted with delight; they are followed when they depart; and they are sought when absent. Their loss causes anxiety and distress; their recovery, relief and a sense of security" (Bowlby, 1967).

Generalized and Specific Responses

Newborn infants are curious about all kinds of stimuli, both human and nonhuman. Both kinds arouse their interest, keeping them occupied and satisfied. During the first month of life infants attend as quickly to a noisy rattle as to a smiling human face. They may spend as much time looking at a checkerboard as at a human face.

It takes only a few weeks for infants to reveal their highly social nature by preferring humans to things. Beginning with the second month of life, infants increasingly spend more time looking at humans, seek them more often, appear more satisfied when they are present, and cry more when they leave. Thus starting in the second month of life, infants become progressively more attached to humans. Not coincidentally, social smiling starts at about the same time. Smiling, a purely social response, has no other function than to indicate friendly intentions to others. During the first half-year of life, infants smile not only at their parents but at other humans as well. And infants can be soothed and comforted not only by their parents but also by other humans. Thus their attachment appears to be a generalized response to humans, which is why this stage has been called the *indiscriminate-social phase* (Schaffer & Emerson, 1964).

As the months pass, infants gradually differentiate more clearly between caregivers and other persons. By about six months the attachment has become more specific, centering on the parents; this is the *specific-social phase*. Infants now smile more at their mothers than at anyone else, though they also smile at fathers and other adults. Infants may no longer smile at strangers and now start to become wary of them, and even frightened if strangers come too close.

Security and Stimulation

Infants want to be held and touched. They like to clutch soft, furry objects such as stuffed toy animals. This basic tendency of mammalian young may be seen in pet dogs and cats, and it has been demonstrated in primates. Harlow and Harlow (1962) constructed two robot mothers for their infant rhesus monkeys. One offered a nipple that would deliver milk but was made of wire mesh; the other gave no milk but was covered with a soft, furry cloth. When presented with both robot mothers, the monkeys occasionally suckled from the wire-mesh robot but spent most of their time clinging to the soft, furry robot. The same tendency may be seen in human infants who will not let go of their security blanket.

Infants tend to be startled easily, for they have not yet habituated to the sights and sounds that are familiar to older children and adults. And infants may become cold, hungry, or ill. Whatever the cause, infants regularly become fussy and need to be calmed. All parents know that the best way to soothe a fussy infant is to pick the infant up and cradle him or her, offering contact comfort, softness, and warmth.

As the months pass and infants start to crawl and eventually to walk, the need for security slowly wanes. Parents, especially mothers, remain a safe haven, sheltering them from a threatening world. Gradually, though, young children need not be in physical contact with the parents, and just being able to see the parents usually offers enough security. In addition, a security blanket, favorite teddy bear, or doll may offer a partial substitute for the security of the physical presence of a parent.

When infants are secure, they are strongly motivated to explore the environment. Long before they can crawl or walk, infants stare fixedly at novel objects and events and listen carefully to new sounds. Early on, they attempt to put anything they can grasp into their mouth. Thus through their various sensory modalities, they are seeking stimulation. Once infants can crawl or walk, they will move toward novel stimuli to investigate them. Turn infants loose in the kitchen, and they will empty every available drawer or cabinet.

Infants need both security and stimulation, but they will seek stimulation only when they are secure. This fact has been demonstrated in monkeys with a robot terry-cloth mother (Harlow & Harlow, 1962). When presented with an unfamiliar toy, the infant monkey clung in terror to the robot mother. Once secure, however, the infant gradually let go of the mother and began to explore the new toy. Similar behavior can be observed in human infants, who will move away from the mother to investigate a new toy as long as the mother is close and can be reached easily. The infants may occasionally return to the home base of mother just to be reassured by contact. Crying infants tend to ignore the environment, but, once offered the security of being held and comforted, they eagerly look around and are ready to explore.

As intensely social animals, human infants are especially interested in social stimuli, particularly novel social stimuli. Strangers fascinate them, but the social novelty may also be threatening. A fairly typical response to strangers in eight-month-old infants is to cling to the mother while staring intently at the intriguing unfamiliar person. Here the need for stimulation is opposed by the need for security. Many children of this age will let a stranger approach and touch them only if they are in contact with the mother. Thus beginning at roughly eight months of age and continuing for the next year or two, many infants have *stranger anxiety* (to be discussed fully in Chapter 12).

Attachment Types

The attachment of infants to their mothers has been investigated in the "strange situation" (Ainsworth, Bell, & Stayton, 1971). In the laboratory and at home, observers watch the infant's reaction first with the mother present, then when she leaves the infant alone, then when the infant is alone with a stranger, and, finally, when mother and infant are reunited. Subsequent studies also studied mother-infant behavior over longer periods of time (Ainsworth, Blehar, Waters, & Wall, 1978; Main & Cassidy, 1988). Infants become attached to both parents, but most of the research has been on infant-mother attachment (for a review, see Fox, Kimmerly, & Schafer, 1991), reflecting the more important role of the mother in everyday life. Researchers were seeking answers to these questions: When the infant is with the mother, does the infant seek contact and then use the mother as a base from which to explore the environment? When she leaves, does the infant protest, and if so, is it because the infant likes being with the mother and trusts her to return or is the infant anxious about being left alone because the mother is not trusted to return? When she returns, is the infant glad to see her, and if not, does the infant become angry or just shun the mother?

This research has yielded three major patterns or types of attachment (and several subgroups that need not concern us here). Infants labeled *secure* use the mother as a base from which to explore the environment. They want to touch the mother, especially on reunion, but even before she leaves, they seem to need some contact with her. If she leaves, they may temporarily be distressed, but this is because of her absence not because of being left alone. They may be friendly toward the stranger but much less so than toward the mother. They tend to be outgoing and cooperative with unfamiliar adults.

Infants labeled *anxious/ambivalent* have also been called resistant because they sometimes resist contact or interaction with the mother. For simplicity, I shall use the label *ambivalent*. Once there is contact, they fight against breaking it off, hence the term *ambivalent*. They cry more than most infants and are hard to soothe. Like avoidant infants, they display considerable separation distress. In the strange situation, they display either anger or passivity. They do not use the mother as a base from which to explore novel stimuli.

Infants labeled *avoidant* seem to need less contact with the mother, both before her leaving and on reunion. When she leaves, they are either not upset or upset only because of being left alone. At home they show considerable distress when the mother leaves. At reunion, if she approaches, they often avoid her gaze or turn the head away.

Thus there is one secure type of infant and two insecure types. The insecure types differ in how they display their distress with the mother. Avoidant infants seem to be hurt and turn away, almost as though they were playing hard to get. Ambivalent infants either protest by showing anger or give up and remain passive.

Ainsworth et al. (1978) differentiated among the three types through discriminant analysis, which yielded two dimensions. The dimension of seeking contact and maintaining it split the secure and ambivalent groups from the avoidant group. The dimension of *separation anxiety* differentiated between the ambivalent group and the other two.

The parent-infant attachment is the infant's first relationship. As such, it can become the model for subsequent relationships. To discover whether this is so, researchers have followed some of the infants and observed their social behavior later in childhood. In this vein, Sroufe, Fox, and Pancake (1983) made observations and collected teachers' evaluations of preschool children who were about four years old. The clearest distinctions were between the behavior of secure children and that of the other two types. Compared to secure children, avoidant and ambivalent children made more requests for hugging, kissing, cuddling, help, and attention; that is, they seemed extremely dependent on the teachers. There were also some differences between avoidant and ambivalent children. Avoidant children tended to withdraw from teachers when greeted or when teachers intervened in disputes; when disappointed or hurt, they retreated to a secluded spot. Ambivalent children tended to stay close to teachers during free play, and waited to be told what to do rather than taking any initiative.

This research is just one example of several short-term longitudinal studies that have revealed how important attachment is for children's later relationships (Egeland & Farber, 1984; Main & Cassidy, 1988; and Sroufe, 1985). Clearly, the attachment infants develop with their mothers is an important element in the children's personality (see below).

Culture

The early work on attachment spurred research around the world, revealing some consistency across cultures and some inconsistencies. In every culture examined, most infants are labeled secure. However, there are cultural differences in the two insecure groups. Compared to the American norms, there is a higher frequency of avoidant infants in Germany, and there is no obvious explanation for this difference (Grossman, 1990).

In Israel, there is an unusually high proportion of ambivalent infants who live in a kibbutz (Sagi, 1990). In this setting, the caregivers are mainly not the infants' mothers but women assigned to the job. Infants are with their mothers briefly at the end of the day, and the mothers may be anxious about this arrangement. The caregivers are sometimes lax, and the infants may be confused by the multiple "mothers." Any or all of these possibilities might explain the relatively high frequency of ambivalent infants in the so-called strange situation.

Oddly enough, there is also a relatively high frequency of ambivalent infants in Japan (Takahashi, 1990). Japanese infants stay with their mothers almost all the time, sleeping in the same room and being brought into the parental bed when upset. Many are carried on the mother's back. Japanese mothers were asked how often they left their infants with someone else, and the mean was two times per month. Some of the infants became so upset in the strange situation when the mother left that the episode had to be curtailed. Evidently, being left alone was so rare an event that it was traumatic for many infants.

Thus there are contrasting patterns of infant care in Japan and Israeli kibbutzim, both yielding an excess of ambivalent children. In Japan, the mother's constant presence makes separation more difficult for some children, and they become extremely upset. In a kibbutz an infant sees the mother so seldom that the separation during the strange situation is also traumatic. Are there enduring consequences of this distress? Probably not. When the Israeli infants were assessed at the age of five years, there was no relationship between the earlier attachment style and social-emotional behavior (Sagi, 1990).

One other cultural difference is intriguing: There appear to be no avoidant Japanese infants. According to Takahashi (1990), "It is simply contrary to Japanese culture to exhibit avoidant behaviors in interpersonal interaction" (p. 28). Presumably, Japanese infants have absorbed at least some of this enculturation even during the first year of life.

Origins

Mother's Behavior

Parents play three roles with their children (see Chapter 2), two of which are relevant here. Mothers are caregivers, offering food, warmth, cradling, love, and protection, which contribute to infants' sense of security. Mothers are also partners in social interaction, offering sharing, attention, and responsivity, which meet infants' need for stimulation.

Developmental psychologists believe that the mother's behavior is linked to the infant's attachment to her, and there is some evidence that this is so. When mothers are keenly aware of their infants' needs and quickly respond to these needs, the infants are likely to develop a secure attachment (Ainsworth et al., 1978). Mothers who are tense or irritable or who ignore their infants when they cry are likely to have avoidant infants (Egeland & Farber, 1984). These researchers also reported that mothers of ambivalent babies tend to be unskilled and insensitive caregivers. These are just a sample of studies demonstrating that the mother's behavior has been shown to be a major determinant of the infant's attachment to her. For a review of earlier work, see Sroufe (1985).

Some recent evidence is consistent with earlier findings: "Mothers of highly secure infants noticed their babies' signals, effectively used these signals to guide their behaviors, knew a lot about their infants, enjoyed cuddling, and spoke positively about their babies. In sharp contrast, mothers of less secure infants were less responsive and more resentful of their babies" (Pederson et al., 1990, p. 1980). Mothers of secure infants offer an optimal degree of stimulation, and they are consistent and predictable (Isabella & Belsky, 1991). Mothers of ambivalent infants tend to be underinvolved and inconsistent, and mothers of avoidant infants are intrusive and insensitive to their babies' needs.

However, there is also evidence that the mother's behavior is a weak determinant of her infant's attachment. Schneider and Rothbaum (1993) reported that this relationship was barely better than chance. Furthermore, their review of previous research reveals a bleak picture: "When the association between parenting and attachment has been examined, there are mixed results. That is, there is inconsistent support in the literature for an association between dimensions of maternal responsivity or sensitivity and attachment classifications" (p. 358). In addition, their review and their own research found that paternal behavior played no role in infants' attachment.

Why are there inconsistencies in the literature, and why is maternal behavior not a stronger determinant of infant attachment? To answer these questions, let us start by recalling the social rewards discussed in the last chapter. Mothers share activities with their infants and offer them attention. And mothers are especially responsive, playing peek-a-boo games, tickling, and smiling when the infant smiles. These are the familiar stimulation rewards that are especially prized by those high in sociability.

When an infant is frightened or distressed, the first person sought is the mother. She cradles the upset infant, stroking, rocking, and murmuring softly. These maternal behaviors fall under the heading of one of the affective rewards, soothing. Which infants especially require soothing? Those high in emotionality, who have a lower threshold for distress and become more intensely aroused.

Emotionality and sociability are of course temperaments, which may also help answer the questions above. We expect infants to vary in temperament from one study to the next, and this may account for the inconsistencies. In addition, if an infant's temperament influences attachment, that puts a ceiling on the mother's contribution.

Infant Temperament

How might temperaments lead to different kinds of attachment? Emotionality, especially the fear component of emotionality, would seem to be the crucial temperament; recall that one dimension underlying the three attachment types is separation anxiety (Ainsworth et al., 1978). Infants who are low in emotionality, by definition, do not become upset easily, tend to become distressed less frequently and less intensely, and are relatively easy to soothe. It follows that they have a relatively weak need for security and will be able to use the mother as a base from which to explore unfamiliar environments. Their attachment to the mother is likely to be secure.

Infants who are high in emotionality, by definition, tend to become distressed easily, intensely, and frequently, and so are more difficult to soothe. It follows that they have a stronger need for security than other babies, as manifested in their tendency to become upset with strangers, excessive crying, clinging to the mother, and resistance to separation. They are likely to develop an insecure attachment to the mother, of either the avoidant or the ambivalent kind.

There are data consistent with the explanation of attachment on the basis of temperament. In one study, infants' heart-rate variability was measured at three, six, and nine months (Izard et al., 1991). Heart-rate variability, which is known to indicate emotionality, predicted whether infants were secure or insecure in attachment at thirteen months.

Infants who were already known to vary in fearfulness were observed during the strange situation (Thompson, Connell, & Bridges, 1988): "Infants rated as temperamentally more fearful showed more intense distress and also displayed more proximity/contact seeking and more resistance to the mother when compared with infants lower in fear" (p. 1108). The infants were not classified according to attachment type, but the combination of distress, contact seeking, and resistance points to the ambivalent type.

In another study (Fox, Kimmerly, & Schafer, 1991), the emotionality of infants was observed at two days of age, five months, and fourteen months: "Infants who cried to mild frustration at 2 days of age were more likely to cry to novel stimuli at 5 months of age and were more likely to cry to maternal separation at 14 months of age" (p. 223). Thus emotional children will probably be classified as insecure in the strange situation.

A group of researchers combined the data of several studies that related temperament to attachment (Vaughn et al., 1992). Children were assessed as having various degrees of security-insecurity of attachment. When the various measures of temperament were factor analyzed, the first and most important factor was negative reactivity, which is conceptually similar to what is here called emotionality. When this temperament was assessed at six months of age, there was no relationship with attachment. However, when it was measured at nine months and thereafter, the correlations between negative reactivity and security of attachment varied from the twenties to the forties. Given the variety of subjects, measures, and researchers, this is unequivocal evidence of the role of emotionality in attachment.

Infants also vary greatly in their need for the presence of others, attention from others, and social responsivity—in other words, they vary greatly in sociability. Recall that the other dimension of the three attachment types is seeking contact and maintaining it (Ainsworth et al., 1978). Infants who are high in sociability, by definition, will seek out the mother more, welcome her, and display joy on reunion after separation. Being sociable, they are more willing to tolerate the arousal arising from unfamiliar but welcome strangers, though to a less extent than that from familiar figures.

Infants low in sociability, by definition, need less social stimulation and are less willing to tolerate any unpleasantness that arises from being with others. Their motivation to seek out others is weak. As a result, they are likely to resist the advances of others, including the mother, and are less willing to deal with strangers. Thus their low sociability tilts them toward an insecure attachment, just as high sociability tilts other infants toward a secure attachment.

There are relevant data from research in which infants were observed early in the first year of life, before the mother's behavior could have much impact. Then the infants were observed in the strange situation months later and were assigned to one of the attachment categories. The face-to-face behavior of mothers and infants was observed when the infants were six to fifteen weeks old (Blehar, Lieberman, & Ainsworth, 1977). Infants later classified as secure were more responsive than insecure infants, who were also more negative. Presumably, the insecure infants were less sociable and more emotional. Infants at three months of age were observed playing with toys in the presence of their mothers (Lewis & Feiring, 1989). Those who focused mainly on the toys—by inference, the less sociable infants—were later classified as avoidant.

In a rare twin study, infants were first observed early in their first year, later classified in the strange situation, and also observed playing with other infants (Vandell, Owen, Wilson, & Henderson, 1988). The twins who were later classified as securely attached spent more time, as early as six months of age, than did insecurely attached twins interacting with other infants. The authors of the study concluded, "Attachment and peer competence may both be mediated by infants' underlying dispositional characteristics that predate both attachment and peer competence. . . . Some infants may be less sociable with their mothers and peers, resulting in them receiving more avoidant attachment ratings as well as engaging in less peer interaction" (p. 176).

We might also start with attachment types and and see how they might derive from infants' temperaments. Avoidant infants are assumed to be relatively unsociable, which is why they play less with the stranger and ignore the mother on her return. Ambivalent infants are assumed to be highly emotional, which is why they become extremely upset with the mother when she leaves, and angry when she returns. Secure infants are assumed to be at least average in sociability (they play easily with the stranger and greet the mother warmly on her return) and below average in emotionality (they are not especially upset when the mother leaves).

There is evidence consistent with these assumptions. When allowed to play with other infants, secure infants are more sociable than ambivalent infants (Easterbrooks & Lamb, 1979). Infants who earlier displayed a low threshold for expressing negative affect were classified as ambivalent (Fox, 1989). During the first few months of life, infants later labeled as ambivalent cried roughly twice as much as secure infants (Ainsworth et al., 1978).

In brief, both the infant's temperament and the mother's behavior determine the infant's attachment to the mother (Mengelsdorf, Gunnar, Kestenbaum, Lang, & Andrews, 1990). A study by Crockenberg (1981) offers an example of how these determinants interact. Of the infants who were irritable early in life (temperament of emotionality), only those whose mothers were unresponsive developed an insecure attachment. The maternal and temperamental determinants of attachment are outlined in Table 5.1.

Matches and Mismatches

What determines the mother's responsivity? Her ability to care for her child and her motivation to do so have been rightly emphasized by developmental psychologists. But her personality surely is important, particularly her temperaments. Perhaps even more important than the individual temperaments of mother and child

TABLE 5.1 Maternal and Temperamental Determinants of Attachment

	Secure attachment	Insecure attachment
Mother's behavior	Attentive Responsive Cuddling Soothing	Inattentive Unresponsive Little touching Little soothing
Infant's temperament	Low-emotional High-sociable	High-emotional Low-sociable

is the match between their temperaments. For ease of exposition, consider only the interaction between a mother and her son.

Let us start with a match in emotionality in which both mother and infant are low in this temperament. He infrequently becomes upset, but when he does, he is easy to soothe. The mother tends not to become distressed easily and therefore can calm him. The outcome is a tranquil mother-infant interaction, the mother being available as a secure base.

In the opposite match, when both infant and mother are high in emotionality, there is a double jeopardy. He tends to become upset easily and is hard to soothe. When confronted with his difficult behavior, the mother becomes disturbed and cannot offer the calm haven he needs. The mother's inability to provide quiet reassurance leads to an insecure attachment for the infant.

Now consider a mismatch in emotionality. If the infant is highly emotional and tends to become aroused easily, the mother's low emotionality will moderate the intensity of his reaction. Remaining in control when he becomes anxious or angry, she can soothe him and lower the level of his arousal. Despite his high emotionality, he may be able to develop a secure attachment.

If the infant is low in emotionality and his mother is high, he presents her with few problems. However, whenever he does become fussy, her distress only magnifies his. He may learn to avoid her when he is anxious or angry, preferring solitude to his mother's excessive reaction. This mismatch, then, has the potential to produce the avoidant type of attachment.

Matches and mismatches in sociability were discussed in Chapter 4, but their relevance here warrants a brief repetition. Suppose there is a match in sociability, with both mother and infant being high in this temperament. The boy wants lots of attention and responsivity, and the mother tends to be comfortable with this high level of social stimulation. Being sociable herself, she welcomes his need to be with her and is usually available to him. Similarly, if both mother and infant are low in sociability, she will be comfortable with his low need for social contact. Both matches should lead to a secure attachment.

If she is high and he is low in sociability, however, she will not understand his weak need to interact. But, being sociable, she will respond whenever he seeks her out, the result being a secure child. The other mismatch—the infant is very sociable and the mother is not—causes problems. She cannot satisfy his need for the social rewards of sharing, attention, and responsivity, and his frustration may lead to one of two outcomes. He may react with irritation and ambivalence, or he may simply give up and become avoidant. Either way, this particular mismatch is likely to produce an insecure infant.

Development after Infancy

Once past infancy, children are less emotional and can deal better with their own distress, which means that contact comfort is less important for them. People and environments, once novel, gradually become familiar and therefore do not provoke anxiety. Young children can make their needs known through language, and their growing mobility gives them greater ability to fend for themselves. As a result, young children allow the mother to leave without protest and do quite well playing on their own. The attachment bond is still strong, but the child is no longer as dependent on the mother for security.

For the first year or two of their lives, infants have the exclusive love and attention of their parents, or so it seems to the infants. Then, or within a few years, another child may be born. Now the newborn receives most of the attention, or, at the very least, parental affection is shared between the newborn and the next older child. The typical result is *jealousy* on the part of the older child. This resentment of the new baby and anger at the parents can be handled by the parents, especially if they teach the older child that the new baby belongs to everyone in the family. But regardless of parental guidance, attachment plays a role in determining whether there is jealousy.

For children who are secure in their attachment to their parents, the new baby poses only a minimal threat. True, they must now share parental affection, but they are deeply rooted in the family and so can stand the winds of change.

Insecurely attached children are likely to become extremely jealous, however. Avoidant children tend to deal with this problem in the same way they typically confront any issue of attachment, by sulking and staying away. Ambivalent children tend to become intensely jealous, for the parental love offered to the new baby reinforces anxiety about whether they are loved. Their ambivalence is likely to spill over to the baby, leading to behavior that is superficially paradoxical: They may display excessive fondness for the baby by caressing and kissing it repeatedly, but then surreptitiously hurt the baby by pinching it, for example.

The residuals of attachment also affect peer relationships. Children who are secure in their attachment to their parents confidently expect others to be friendly. Insecure children lack this confidence and may be wary of subsequent intimate relationships. Youngblade and Belsky (1992) assessed the attachment of infants to their mothers and fathers in the strange situation at about one year of age. Then they evaluated the relationship of these children at age five with a close or best friend. Secure attachment at one year was associated with more positive friendship at five years. Insecure attachment at one year was linked to more negative friendship at five years. These relationships were not strong, reminding us that security of attachment in infancy is only one determinant of later social relationships.

Type of attachment may also have consequences for self-esteem. The infant who receives abundant affection is likely to develop a healthy sense of self-worth. The insufficiently loved infant lacks one of the bases of self-esteem, parental love.

Adult Attachment

The kind of attachment that occurs in infancy surely undergoes some change during development. Nevertheless, we can ask whether the consequences of attachment in infancy and early childhood endure into adulthood. The ultimate answer must come from longitudinal studies that follow infants through to adulthood.

Such research is difficult and can occupy much of the professional lifetime of investigators, so it is rare. Fortunately, other research offers an empirical basis for applying the attachment paradigm to adult relationships.

The initial research consisted of retrospective reports by adults about their childhood relationship with their parents (Main, Kaplan, & Cassidy, 1985). These adults could be assigned to one of the three attachment categories. The secure group had no trouble recalling the events of childhood, generally had positive memories, and valued their parents. The avoidant group (the authors of the study called them detached) reported their parents as being distant or rejecting or not being available when needed. The ambivalent group (the authors called them preoccupied) remembered being close to their parents but being annoyed at their parents' lack of support.

Using a different approach, Hazan and Shaver (1987) asked adults questions about their present relationships that specifically targeted the three attachment types. The subjects, ranging from fourteen to eighty-two years of age, responded to a newspaper questionnaire. The secure questions included ease in getting close to others, comfort in depending on others, and lack of worry about others getting too close or abandoning them. The avoidant questions included discomfort at being too close to others, distrust, and anxiety about others getting too close or wanting intimacy. The ambivalent questions included concern that others do not get close and that the partner might not offer love or might leave, and a need for closeness so strong that it might drive others away. More than half the subjects fell in the secure group, and the insecure groups split the remaining percentage.

The subjects were also asked about their parents. The secure subjects reported much warmer relationships with their parents and between both parents than did the two groups of insecure subjects. Avoidant subjects saw their mothers as more cold and rejecting than did ambivalent subjects. Ambivalent subjects saw their fathers as unfair.

These findings were repeated with college students. "Secure subjects tended to report positive early family relationships and to express trusting attitudes toward others. Anxious-ambivalent subjects were most likely to perceive a lack of paternal supportiveness; they also expressed dependence and desire for commitment in relationships. Subjects in the avoidant group were most likely to endorse items measuring mistrust of and distance from others" (Feeney & Noller, 1990, p. 286).

It should be added by way of parenthesis that the dependence of anxious-ambivalent subjects suggests a possible linkage with what is called *dependent personality disorder* (American Psychiatric Association, 1987). Those so diagnosed are described as clinging, helpless, and in need of others to direct their lives. This personality disorder sounds like an echo of anxious-ambivalence and may represent that kind of insecure attachment in its most extreme form.

There are parallels between the three types of infant attachment and the three types of adult attachment. In Table 5.2 infants' behavior is compared with adults' attitudes. Because of the difference between behavior and attitudes, however, the parallels cannot be expected to be precise. In addition, adult relationships are

TABLE 5.2   Comparison of Infant and Adult Attachment

Infant attachment (based on behavior)	Adult attachment (based on reported attitudes)
Secure	
Is close to mother, seeks contact Is friendly toward strangers	Has warm relationship with parents Has positive memories of childhood
Ambivalent	
Shows considerable distress Is clinging but angry or passive	Is close to parents but sees them as not supportive Wants more commitment in relationships Sees fathers as having been unfair
Avoidant	
Is hurt when mother leaves Keeps distance from mother	Sees mother as having been cold, rejecting Keeps distance from others Sees parents as unavailable when needed

clearly in some ways different from parent-child relationships. Nevertheless, the comparison is revealing.

It has already been noted in this chapter, in the discussion of the opposed needs for security and stimulation, that secure infants are free to explore the environment. On the assumption that adult work involves stimulation, Hazan and Shaver (1990) related attachment types to attitudes toward work. Those with a secure adult attachment enjoyed work, expected to succeed at it, and did not allow it to interfere with after-work social interaction or relationships. Ambivalent subjects were afraid that they would perform poorly at work and allowed concerns about relationships to interfere with their work. Avoidant subjects reported that work interfered with getting together with friends and having a social life, and they apparently used work to avoid social interaction. The authors suggested that the attachment bond spills over into the work situation. There is an alternative explanation, however: The individual differences that appear in both work and attachment situations are due to underlying personality differences (more on this below).

Avoidant individuals, by definition, withdraw from relationships. Mikulincer and Nachshon (1991) reasoned that avoidants would keep their psychological distance from others by revealing little about themselves. As predicted, avoidants disclosed less personal information than did those who were either secure or ambivalent. In addition, the secures and ambivalents felt better about being with another person and were more attracted to that person than were the avoidants.

How people react to danger is also related to attachment type. Consider, for instance, the missile attacks on Israelis during the Gulf War (Mikulincer, Florian, & Weller, 1993). Compared to those with a secure attachment, ambivalents reported being more distressed, and avoidants reported more bodily ills and hostility. Those with a secure attachment reacted to danger by seeking support from others. Ambivalent people were more emotional, for example, wishing they could change how they felt. And avoidant people reacted by keeping their psychological distance from the danger, trying not to think about it, for example.

Attachment and Romantic Love

Romantic Love

Infant-mother attachment is the first love relationship. Older children often develop childish infatuations, and young adolescents daydream about teachers, actors, and, generally, about those made popular by the media. Romantic love blooms in adolescence and continues thereafter.

Romantic love differs from other kinds of love and other relationships. The differences were pinpointed in a questionnaire (Rubin, 1970). The items about romantic love included ignoring the loved one's faults, being extremely altruistic and possessive, feeling lonely without the loved one, and being completely absorbed in the other one.

Subsequently, Tennov (1979) renamed the phenomenon *limerence* and defined it as obsessive thoughts about the other, acute longing to be loved by the other, imagining doing things with the other, fear of rejection, elation when the other reciprocates love, intense feeling, accentuating the other's virtues and ignoring faults, and intensification of feeling through adversity (the Romeo and Juliet effect).

These features of romantic love must seem familiar, for they overlap those of infant-mother attachment. Of course in infantile attachment there are no sexual feelings, and more social rewards flow from the mother than from the infant. These differences aside, there are parallels between infant-mother attachment and adult romantic love. The most observable parallel is intimacy. There is mutual touching, caressing, and fondling, and the partners are usually close in space or actually in body contact. There is mutual smiling, and the smiles are loving. This intimacy is accompanied by an exclusivity that advertises to others that this relationship is not to be shared. When the dyad is separated, the isolation breeds desolation; when the pair is reunited, joy abounds. In both relationships, the love is unconditional. Just as mother and infant are aware of no deficiencies in each other, so lovers can see only the virtues of each other.

Attachment Types

The first researchers to study attachment types (styles) in relation to romantic love were Hazan and Shaver (1987). Their secure subjects, compared to the other two types, saw their most important love experience as especially happy and friendly, felt that the intensity present at first could recur later in the relationship, believed that in some relationships romantic love does not wane, and were less jealous. They also reported that their relationships lasted longer than those of the other two types.

The ambivalent subjects reported more love at first sight, stronger sexual attraction, more obsessive thoughts about the other person, and a stronger desire for union. They believed that one rarely finds someone to love, and they were more jealous than the secure subjects. The behavior of individuals of this type apparently comes closest to meeting the criteria for limerence (Tennov, 1979) and represents the ideal of romantic love held by most people.

The avoidant subjects believed that the romantic love portrayed in movies is largely fictitious and that if it does occur, it does not last. They were the least accepting of their partner's faults and were also more jealous than the ambivalent subjects. In brief, each attachment type was linked to romantic love in ways that make theoretical sense.

A later study found consistent effects for the ambivalent and avoidant types (Feeney & Noller, 1990). Ambivalent subjects were most extreme in obsessive thoughts about the partner and in dependence on the partner, and they displayed the most neurotic style of romantic love. Avoidant subjects were less likely to idealize the romantic partner and more likely to avoid intimacy; they reported the lowest intensity of love experiences, and a higher frequency of avoidants said they had never been in love.

Jealousy

Jealousy has been empirically differentiated from envy. When subjects were asked to recall instances of the two emotions, "envy was characterized by feelings of inferiority, longing, resentment, and disapproval of the emotion. Jealousy was characterized by fear of loss, distrust, anxiety, and anger" (Parrott & Smith, 1993, p. 906). This description of jealousy sounds suspiciously like the feelings reported by people who are insecurely attached.

Jealousy in close relationships is as much of a problem among adults as it is among young children, but there is another source of adult jealousy: sex. Would there be more jealousy if the other person had another sexual relationship or loved another person? College students were asked to think of a serious present or past romantic relationship and to imagine that the other person became interested in someone else (D. M. Buss, Larson, Westen, & Semmelroth, 1992). Then they were asked which would distress them more, if the other person formed a deep emotional attachment to someone else or had sex with another person. Sexual jealousy bothered the majority of men, but an overwhelming majority of women were more distressed by romantic jealousy. The authors interpreted the greater sexual jealousy of men as an evolutionary-based concern with propagating their own genes.

Of immediate interest to security of attachment, however, is whether sexual or romantic jealousy would differ among the different attachment types. This issue may be moot for women because 83% of them reported romantic jealousy. Only 40% of the men reported romantic jealousy, however, so the question is relevant for them.

Our knowledge of attachment types leads to two hypotheses. Men who are securely attached are not as affected by romantic jealousy, virtually by definition.

Therefore, an overwhelming majority of them should be more distressed by their partner having sex with another person. Men who are insecurely attached are very concerned with romantic jealousy, virtually by definition. Therefore, the majority of them should be more distressed by the partner loving someone else.

There is another sex difference in jealousy that does not involve sex. With the advent of the first child, the mother spends a great deal of time with the infant, of necessity cutting back on time spent with her husband. Before, her love was directed exclusively toward him, but now it is shared with the baby. Some men become jealous. Most do not, for their delight precludes jealousy. We expect such behavior of men who are securely attached to their wives, and most men are. However, a minority are insecurely attached, and they are likely to display jealousy.

Attachment in Dating and Married Couples

There are also relationships between attachment types and the social and emotional responses of partners in intimate relationships. Romantically attached college students were asked about how they dealt with conflict and how satisfied they were with the relationship (Pistole, 1989). Secure subjects used compromise and other adaptive strategies more than insecure subjects did. And the use of adaptive strategies correlated with satisfaction in the relationship.

In another study of college dating couples, secure subjects reported higher levels of trust, commitment, and satisfaction than insecure subjects, especially the avoidants (Simpson, 1990). Most of the couples were contacted six months later. Of those who had split up, the male avoidants reported less distress after the breakup than did the other two attachment types.

Dating couples tend to idealize each other, but these perceptions vary with attachment type (Feeney & Noller, 1991). Ambivalent subjects idealized their partners the most, followed by secure subjects, and avoidant subjects idealized their partners the least. These results are consistent with other research on attachment types. Ambivalents tend to be more emotional and more caught up in close relationships, hence the greater idealization of the partner. Avoidants are psychologically more distant from their partners and so can be more rational in their perceptions of them.

Attachment type also predicts what happens in dating relationships over time. Shaver and Brennan (1992) followed up dating couples eight months after their attachment styles were determined. Ambivalent subjects tended to be in shorter relationships or not currently in a relationship. Avoidants had shorter relationships and were less satisfied and committed in their relationships.

The importance of attachment types carries over into marriage (Senchak & Leonard, 1992). There were three combinations of newlywed couples: both secure, both insecure, and one partner secure and the other insecure. Compared to the other two combinations, when both partners were secure, they evaluated each other more favorably and reported both more intimacy and a better adjustment to marriage.

Not surprisingly, when one partner can rely on the other and the other is seen as available, the marriage is more solid and happier (Kobak & Hazan, 1991). These findings with two dimensions of reliance and availability are consistent with similar findings in dating couples (Collins & Read, 1990). The various findings about adult attachment are summarized in Table 5.3.

Four Attachment Types

Virtually all researchers of adult attachment have adopted Bowlby's (1973) conception of the child's implicit model of self and other in the attachment situation: "Confidence that an attachment figure is, apart from being accessible, likely to be responsive can be seen to turn on at least two variables: (a) whether the attachment figure is judged to be the sort of person who in general responds to calls for support and protection; (b) whether or not the self is judged to be the sort of person towards whom anyone, and the attachment figure in particular, is likely to respond in a helpful way" (p. 138).

The Model

Bartholomew (1990), taking Bowlby seriously, suggested two variables: (1) whether the person feels worthy of attention, care, and affection; and (2) whether the other person is dependable, caring, and trustworthy. The first variable appears equivalent to self-esteem, and the second to trust, so these are the labels I shall use. Bartholomew dichotomized each variable into high versus low and then cross-cut them to yield four types of adult attachment (see Table 5.4).

The types in the top row of the table have high trust in others. The secure type has high self-esteem and expect those close to them to be available and caring. The ambivalent type tend to have low self-esteem, and seek out others who might offer care and affection. They hope that others will approve of them, for they desperately need approval. But they are not sure whether they are good enough to earn others' approval, hence their ambivalence and occasional resistance to others. Bartholomew calls this type preoccupied because they are continually grappling with problems in relationships.

TABLE 5.3   Adult Behavior or Feelings According to Kind of Attachment

Behavior/feelings	Secure attachment	Insecure attachment
Compromise	More	Less
Trust, commitment, and satisfaction	More	Less
Evaluation of partner	More favorably	Less favorably
Intimacy	More	Less
Couples' adjustment	Better	Worse

TABLE 5.4   Four Types of Adult Attachment

	Self-Esteem	
Trust	*High*	*Low*
High	Secure	Ambivalent
Low	Detached	Fearful

Note: Bartholomew's four types of attachment have been renamed to make them consistent with the terminology used for infant attachment types.

The types named in the bottom row of the table are low in trust. The *fearful* type are low in self-esteem and expect others to reject them, feelings that leave them with an abiding anxiety about relationships. Such people are like the rejected or ignored children described by Bowlby (1973) who come to believe that they are not worthy of attention and affection.

The other type in the bottom row combines low trust and high self-esteem. Bartholomew calls this type dismissing because they tend to dismiss close relationships as unimportant. I prefer the term *detached* because they simply are not involved in attachments. In the face of rejection, such people figuratively pull up the drawbridge and retreat into the castle of individuality, denying the importance of attachment. They are cool and detached, have little need to depend on others, and avoid intimacy.

Thus there is only one secure type, two insecure types, and one that is difficult to classify. One reason for insecurity is low self-esteem. Ambivalent and fearful people have strong dependency needs, but ambivalents hesitantly reach out for others, whereas fearful people shun close relationships, remaining lonely and unhappy. The fourth type, detached, cannot be characterized as truly secure or insecure, for its attachment needs are denied. Such people have made their peace with their avoidant tendencies and are satisfied to be coolly impersonal in everyday life.

Research

Bartholomew's (1990) classification was tested by interviewing college students, having them fill out questionnaires, and obtaining ratings from friends who knew them (Bartholomew & Horowitz, 1991). The tape-recorded interviews were rated by three judges for how close each subject came to each of the four attachment types. A discriminant analysis revealed that 92% of the subjects were correctly classified.

Next, multidimensional scaling of the interviews, self-reports, and friends' ratings yielded two dimensions that roughly matched those hypothesized by Bartholomew (1990). These were self-esteem and trust (or dependability) of others. When the ratings for subjects were plotted on these two dimensions, they fell into four quadrants that matched the four attachment types: secure, ambivalent, fearful, and detached.

A subsequent study by Brennan, Shaver, and Tobey (1991) tested the fourfold classification, and replicated it. These researchers also compared the fourfold classification with the earlier threefold classification of Hazan and Shaver (1987). As expected, subjects classified as avoidant in the threefold classification were split between the fearful and detached categories in the fourfold classification. As Bartholomew (1990) suggested, when people cannot trust others or depend on them, they tend to lack confidence and display negative emotions toward others: the fearful category. There are others, however, who cannot trust or depend on others but have excellent self-esteem; they look elsewhere to purely personal sources of self-esteem, remaining distant from others: the detached category.

The division of the earlier avoidant category into fearful and detached types also revealed sex differences that were masked by the threefold classification. More men than women were detached, and more women than men were fearful. One explanation lies in a sex difference in sources of self-esteem (see Chapter 8). Men tend to emphasize personal sources of self-esteem, such as individual accomplishments, and may therefore be more willing to give up close relationships and depend solely on personal achievements. Women are more oriented toward social sources of self-esteem—friends, family, romantic relationships—and may therefore be unable to give up on close relationships, which leads to fearful attachment.

Let us return to the study by Bartholomew and Horowitz (1991). Ambivalent and fearful subjects reported higher levels of interpersonal distress than the other two groups. Presumably, secure subjects had little distress because of good relationships with others, and detached subjects experienced little interpersonal distress because of a successful strategy for avoiding it: striving for personal achievement while ignoring relationships that might cause anxiety.

There were parallel results for self-esteem, which was higher in the secure and detached groups than in the other two groups. (Adult attachment relates to self-esteem even when the threefold classification is used, with securely attached people reporting higher self-esteem than insecurely attached people [Bylsma, Luhtanen, & Rothbard, 1992].) Presumably, secure subjects, having been accepted and cared for by others who are dependable, feel that they are worthwhile. Detached subjects avoid relationships as a source of self-esteem and feel competent because of individual achievements. The ambivalent and fearful groups, having been rejected by others they cannot trust, blame themselves, reasoning that they are not worthy of receiving attention or acceptance. This interpretation—that the level of self-esteem derives from the history of adult relationships—is essentially that of Bowlby (1973).

An opposite direction of effects is possible, however. People who are already high in self-esteem confidently expect others to accept them, and believe that they can trust others for help when they need it. If their expectations are met, they will be called secure. If their expectations are repeatedly not met and they are neglected or rejected, they will turn away from social sources of self-esteem to personal sources; they will be called *detached*.

Those low in self-esteem, other things being equal, expect little attention or affection from others. Lacking self-worth, they believe that others will also find them unworthy. If they occasionally obtain the social rewards they seek, this schedule of partial reinforcement sustains their attempts to find the approval and acceptance they need to bolster their self-esteem; they will be called ambivalent. If their lack of self-esteem is validated by consistent inattention or rejection by others, they will give up trying to establish relationships and remain lonely; they will be called *fearful*.

These two interpretations are not mutually exclusive. Indeed, there may be a vicious cycle for ambivalent and fearful people, in which low self-esteem leads to interpersonal problems, which cause low self-esteem. Also, the parent-child relationship during the first year of life may be decisive in determining the level of self-esteem that may endure into adulthood (see Chapter 8).

Duggan and Brennan (1994) also demonstrated the importance of distinguishing between fearful and detached attachment types. They had college students read four paragraphs, each describing one of the attachment types, and choose the type that best portrayed them. Next, sociability and shyness questionnaires (Cheek & Buss, 1981) were administered. Secure subjects received the highest sociability scores, followed by lower scores for ambivalent and fearful subjects, and the detached subjects received the lowest scores. The shyness questionnaire yielded different findings: the ambivalent and fearful subjects had the highest scores, followed by detached subjects, and the secure subjects had the lowest scores.

Thus secure subjects were high in sociability and low in shyness. Ambivalent and fearful subjects were average in sociability and high in shyness. Detached subjects, being different from fearful subjects, were low in sociability and below average in shyness.

These findings may be interpreted from a temperament perspective. The findings of Duggan and Brennan (1994) connect with the two dimensions that emerged from research on attachment (Collins & Read, 1990). The first dimension, seeking and maintaining contact, is analogous to sociability, though with a narrower focus on close relationships. The second dimension, fear of abandonment or not being loved, is analogous to the fear component of emotionality, though with a narrower focus on fears involving close relationships. This analogy rests on the assumption that when emotional people are involved in social interaction, they tend to be shy.

The temperaments of emotionality and sociability may also explain why the original three attachment types differ in their attitudes toward work (Hazan & Shaver, 1990). Securely attached persons, being sociable and not very emotional, have few work worries and do not let work interfere with the social relationships they need. Ambivalent persons, being sociable but also emotional, are afraid that they will be rejected at work for poor performance. Avoidant persons, who include both fearful and detached persons in the Hazan-Shaver formulation, are not very emotional or sociable. They are only too glad to use work to preclude social interaction.

Temperaments may also be involved in reactions to danger (Mikulincer et al., 1993). Secure people reacted to missile attacks by seeking out other people (sociability). Ambivalent people, being high in emotionality, became especially upset. And avoidant people, also high in emotionality, coped with their anxiety by suppressing thoughts about danger.

This temperament model may be appropriate to the research on work situations and confrontation of physical threat. But it is obviously an incomplete explanation of relationships and must be supplemented by the more traditional models of attachment theorists. These models focus on the impact of behavior of mothers on their infants, and, later, on the behavior of adults in close relationships. Thus even a person low in emotionality, if faced with repeated inconsistent attention and affection in intimate relationships, might develop an ambivalent style. The role of temperament is that of a predisposing tendency: Emotional people are more sus-' ceptible to the effects of being ignored or unloved, which can tilt them toward the ambivalent and fearful types. And unsociable people, needing others less, are unwilling to put up with the negatives of relationships. They put up a stone wall between themselves and others (detached type).

Matches and Mismatches

Two of the matches in attachment types should lead to pleasant and enduring relationships. Two secure people will obviously be satisfied with each other. Two detached people should develop a solid relationship that avoids intimacy and emphasizes the independent careers of each. If both partners are workaholics, they will have little time for the closeness or the display of warmth and affection that neither wants.

The other two matches are more problematical. Two ambivalent people, both wanting special care and attention and being low in self-esteem, cannot meet each other's needs. The fearful-fearful match is even worse. Each expects rejection from the other and is chronically anxious about being abandoned. At the first sign of difficulty, both are ready to believe the worst, setting off a vicious cycle of feeling rejected, resulting in avoidance, which leads the partner to feel rejected. And jealousy is likely even when it is based on nothing more than a friendly interaction with another person.

If one partner is secure, one of the mismatches might work. A secure person is able to offer enough comfort, affection, and dependability to resolve some of the fears of the ambivalent person. If the relationship endures, the ambivalent person may eventually become confident enough in it to relax and enjoy it.

The secure-fearful mismatch is more of a gamble because avoidant persons tend to be low in self-esteem and sociability and high in fear. Such neurotic tendencies might be too much for even a secure partner to overcome.

If neither partner is secure, any mismatch will probably not work at all. Detached persons, having given up on close relationships, might get along with other detached persons but not with those who are fearful or ambivalent. And ambivalent persons have too many of their own problems to handle the neurotic behavior of the fearful type.

Dimensions of Attachment

In the original work on infant attachment and in the more recent work on adult attachment, subjects have been categorized as one of three or four attachment types. The alternative to types is dimensions of attachment. Recall the two dimensions of trust and self-esteem, which underlie the fourfold classification of adult attachment types (Bartholomew & Horowitz, 1991).

At about the same time, in research mentioned earlier, Collins and Read (1990) broke down each question of Hazan and Shaver (1987) into individual statements. Then they added statements on the dependability of others and reactions to separation to form a twenty-item questionnaire. When administered to college students, it yielded three factors: Depend, or being able to depend on others being there when needed; Anxiety, or fear of abandonment or of not being loved by one's partner; and Close, or the desire to be close to others.

A discriminant analysis provided two dimensions. The first consists of the Depend and Close factors and is highly similar to the dimension of seeking and maintaining contact, which was found in infant attachment (Ainsworth et al., 1978). The second dimension, Anxiety, is conceptually equivalent to the infant attachment dimension of separation anxiety.

Next, Collins and Read explored whether dating couples were matched on these dimensions, a reasonable expectation. People who sought and maintained contact tended to date others who matched them, with one exception: They tended not to date those who were anxious. And there was no match for anxiety—that is, anxious subjects might date any kind of partner.

These various findings led to this conclusion: "These dimensions can be seen as guiding principles that determine how the attachment system manifests itself in adult relationships. They concern beliefs and expectations that are fundamental to feelings of security in adulthood, such as whether a partner will be responsive and available when needed, whether one is comfortable with close contact and intimacy, and confidence about whether a partner will continue to be loving. And, like childhood attachment, beliefs and expectations about these security issues should have important implications for behavior in a wide range of relationships and situations" (Collins & Read, 1990, p. 650).

Dimensional analyses of attachment raise the issue of whether we should use attachment types or dimensions. Assigning people to particular attachment types has the advantage of offering concrete descriptions of people, who either show characteristics of a particular type or do not. Research with attachment types has also offered valuable information.

But either-or categories have their problems. The use of types assumes that people are well located within any one category and do not overlap other types of attachment. Such people may be rare, for even people who are basically secure may be partly ambivalent, avoidant, or even detached.

A second problem is subtypes. Ainsworth et al. (1978), for example, distinguish several subtypes for each of their attachment types. If there are sufficient differences between subtypes within a category, this variability renders the types less useful. Classify or use dimensions? This question will be discussed in Chapter 13.

Chapter 6

Prosocial Behavior

History

Philosophers have reflected about the prosocial behaviors of *altruism* and *empathy* for many centuries, and the ideas of two commentators are especially apt here. Adam Smith (1759/1976) noted, "How selfish soever man may be supposed, there are evidently some principles in his nature, which interest him in the fortune of others, and render their happiness necessary to him, though he derives nothing except the pleasure of seeing it. Of this kind is pity or compassion, the emotion we feel for the misery of others" (p. 47). Almost a century later, Compte (1851), in referring to the unselfish desire to help others, coined the term *altruism* (from the Latin *alter*, meaning "other").

More than fifty years after Compte, Titchener (1909) translated a German word into English as *sympathy*, which referred to the act of imagining the emotions of another person. About the same time McDougall (1908) distinguished between two emotions felt when viewing another person's distress. One is sympathetic pain, which leads to self-centered motivation. The other is tender emotion, which leads to altruistic motivation. This distinction has been revived in the modern era, generating theoretical dispute and empirical attempts to resolve the debate.

The modern study of altruism and empathy dates to the 1960s. Hamilton (1964) observed the self-sacrificing behavior of social insects. Empathy, in the form of distress about others' misfortune, was examined in young elementary-school children (Feshbach & Roe, 1968). In a series of studies summarized in a later book (Stotland, Mathews, Sherman, Hanson, and Richardson, 1978) empathy was measured by physiological reactions to another person's pleasure or pain.

Krebs (1975) suggested and then demonstrated that empathic reactions were linked to altruism. Cialdini, Darby, and Vincent (1973) denied this linkage and provided evidence that seemingly altruistic behavior is in reality hedonistic. Empathy was also related to moral development (Eisenberg-Berg & Mussen, 1978). Social norms, especially involving responsibility, were suggested as leading to altruism (Schwartz, 1975). The major review of altruism and other prosocial behavior was Staub's (1978, 1979) two-volume compendium.

This historical background has left us with these empirical questions:

What is the nature of empathy?
Is empathy a necessary condition for altruism or are there other antecedents?
Does truly altruistic behavior occur, or is all behavior fundamentally egoistic?
Is altruism a species-wide tendency?
Is there a trait of altruism?

Components

Prosocial behavior originates in another person's need, and there are three related reactions to this need. They are *instrumental acts* of helping, *affective reactions* to the other's problem, and *cognitive reactions* to the distressing situation.

Instrumental Reactions

Helping behavior starts with a person who has a problem that can be solved by the helpful action of another person, this action typically having a *potential cost.* Thus if the problem is hunger, it can be solved by the donation of food. If the donor has a sufficient supply of food or a surplus, there is no cost, but if the donor's food is severely limited, sharing it causes the donor to go hungry. In Somalia, for example, the famine was so profound that some parents starved to death while keeping their children alive with their meager rations. Similarly, some parents beggar themselves in order to provide an expensive education for their children. And if a good friend needs our time and effort, we may give them freely, thereby allowing our own tasks to go unfinished. In these examples, the potential cost is deprivation or reduction of a reward.

In other instances, the potential cost involves immediate danger to the donor. Someone who donates an organ loses a valuable part of anatomy. Attempting to rescue or offer assistance to other people in dangerous situations is risky. When an airplane crashed into a river in winter, a stranger dove into the water twice to rescue passengers, but he drowned the third time he went in. During World War II anyone who shielded Jews from the Nazis risked being thrown into a concentration camp or being executed, but some altruistic Christians saved Jews anyhow (P. London, 1970).

In another kind of risk an altruist may take the place of someone who is under severe threat. Parents have been known to confess to crimes committed by their children to save them from going to jail. Husbands have protected their wives from attack, knowing that they will themselves be injured.

In brief, there are three kinds of potential costs for helping behavior: (1) self-denial to satisfy another's needs, (2) risk of harm or even death in order to rescue or offer solace to another, and (3) acceptance of another's punishment to save that

person from suffering (see Table 6.1). When there is a high probability of deprivation or aversiveness suffered by the donor, it is appropriate to call the helpful
behavior altruistic. The focus here is specifically on altruism, not on the broader
topic of helping behavior.

Affective Reactions

When confronted with another person's suffering, we often react emotionally. There
are several such emotional reactions, which experimentation has specified. In one
study (Fultz, Schaller, & Cialdini, 1988) women listened to a tape recording of a
woman in need and checked adjectives that conveyed their feelings. A factor analysis revealed three separate though slightly overlapping sets of adjectives. One set,
labeled *empathy*, included adjectives such as *sympathetic* and *softhearted*; the second,
called *sadness*, included the adjectives *low-spirited* and *heavyhearted*, for example; and
the third, *distress*, was characterized by adjectives such as *disturbed* and *troubled*.

These various emotional reactions may lead to helping behavior. You might
offer help to relieve your own distress or because helping another person would
lift your spirits and you would no longer feel sad. Or you might feel so sympathetic that you would have to help. If you help to assuage your own emotional
reaction, should that help be called altruistic? As we shall see, psychologists disagree on the answer to this question.

Cognitive Reactions

When faced with a man who is in need, you might put yourself in his shoes and
wonder what it would feel like—that is, you might adopt the perspective of the
other person. In one experimental approach to altruism, subjects were asked to
take the perspective of another, imagining what it would be like to be a person who
is receiving electric shock (Batson, Duncan, Ackerman, Buckley, & Birch, 1981).
Doing so led to altruistic behavior.

There is another cognitive reaction: feeling responsible for the other person.
Virtually everyone is taught to take care of those in need. This moral precept

TABLE 6.1   Helping Behavior

Problem	Helpful action	Potential cost
Hunger	Donate food	Deprive self
Poverty	Donate money	Impoverish self
Cooperation needed	Offer effort, time	Own tasks suffer
Contagious disease	Provide nursing care	Risk illness
Body organ needed	Donate organ	Suffer anatomical loss
Danger	Rescue	Suffer injury or death
Punishment	Trade places	Self suffers

applies especially to children in need and perhaps to women. The injunction "Women and children first" captured the precept earlier in the century. When the *Titanic* was sinking in icy Atlantic waters in 1912, many men gave up their places on lifeboats to women and children. The men's moral code had been so strongly inculcated that they were willing to sacrifice their lives in its service.

Measures

There are numerous measures of the instrumental and affective components of prosocial behavior, in fact too many to cover here. A sampling follows.

Altruism

Dependent Variables

Recall the three kinds of altruistic behavior: donating a reward, placing oneself at risk, trading places to assume another's punishment (see Table 6.1). It would be unethical to tempt subjects to place themselves at risk, but it has been possible to assess the other two kinds of altruism.

For instance, in an assessment of the first kind of helping behavior children were requested to donate crayons or money to a needy child (Hetherington & Brackbill, 1963), and in subsequent research were asked to give up a prize to another child (Knudson & Kagan, 1982). Adults have been offered the opportunity to tutor an injured student (Toi & Batson, 1982) or spend time with a lonely student (Fultz, Batson, Fortenbach, McCarthy, & Varney, 1986).

In a test of the altruistic behavior in which a person trades places with another, a woman subject watched on a television monitor a woman receiving electric shock (Batson et al., 1981). As the shocks continued, the televised woman reacted more intensely. During a pause, the subject was asked if she would trade places and receive the shock. In the *easy-escape condition*, the subject is allowed to leave immediately if she decides not to trade places. In the *difficult-escape condition*, the subject must continue watching until the end. After a subject volunteers to trade places, the experiment ends, and she does not receive shock.

It is important to distinguish between easy and difficult escape when deciding whether the volunteer is acting altruistically or egoistically. If escape is easy, subjects can leave without having to deal with the situation. If they still decide to volunteer, their motive is altruistic. If escape is difficult, subjects might volunteer because they are stuck and feel pressured to volunteer; thus their motivation is egoistic.

Questionnaires

The Personality Research Form (Jackson, 1974) has a nurturance scale (in effect a measure of altruism) that taps these behaviors: offering assistance and sympathy, caring for children and the disabled, cooperating, and doing favors. Those who score high are described as helpful, caring, supporting, consoling, protective, and charitable.

The altruism questionnaire of Rushton, Chrisjohn, & Fekken (1981) contains highly specific items, for example, "I have given money to a charity" and "I have donated blood." Respondents are asked how often these behaviors have occurred.

Empathy

Dependent Variables

In the first experiment carried out by Batson et al. (1981), described above, some subjects were told that they were similar to the woman receiving the shocks, a procedure that might induce empathy. In a second experiment, in an attempt to induce empathy, subjects were administered a drug that ostensibly had a side effect of uneasiness and discomfort of the kind one might have when reading a distressing novel. These subjects reported being more empathic, and they were especially likely to trade places even in the easy-escape condition (altruism).

The empathic reaction itself has been assessed in various ways. Women watched a silent videotape of a child crying, and their emotional distress was evaluated by changes in heart rate and skin conductance (Weisenfeld, Whitman, & Malatesta, 1984). Women higher in empathy, preselected by a questionnaire (Mehrabian & Epstein, 1972), displayed greater physiological reactivity to the child's crying.

When children viewed a videotape of a child in distress, the latency and intensity of their facial reactions and the intensity of their gestures were observed (Lennon, Eisenberg, & Carroll, 1986). In earlier research, children read a story (with pictures) about children in an emotional event and were asked to describe how they felt (Feshbach & Roe, 1968). And, in a previously mentioned experiment, adults listened to a tape of a woman in need and checked adjectives denoting empathy, sadness, or distress (Fultz et al., 1988).

Questionnaires

There are a number of empathy questionnaires (Chlopan, McClain, Carbonnell, & Hagen, 1985), but only two are frequently used. An early questionnaire was divided into several subscales, some of which are especially relevant to empathy: appreciating others' feelings, being emotionally responsive, and being sympathetic (Mehrabian & Epstein, 1972). A later empathy questionnaire (Davis, 1983), on being factor analyzed, yielded four factors:

> Fantasy: for example, "After seeing a play or movie, I have felt as though I were one of the characters."
>
> Perspective taking: for example, "I sometimes try to understand my friends better by imagining how things look from their perspective."

Empathic concern: for example, "I feel bad when I see a lonely stranger in a group."

Personal distress: for example, "In emergency situations, I feel apprehensive and ill at ease."

Scores on these scales were compared with the emotional reactions of subjects who were shown a video of a disabled child (Eisenberg, Fabes et al., 1991). Perspective taking correlated in the thirties and forties with reports of sympathy, sadness, and distress. Personal distress correlated positively with the report of distress and negatively with the report of sympathy. The other two scales were unrelated to subjects' reactions to the film.

Prosocial Cognitions

Prosocial cognitions are regarded as mediators or motivators of altruistic behavior and therefore are not used as dependent variables. Accordingly, one kind of cognitive mechanism, taking the perspective of another, has been used as an independent variable. Toi and Batson (1982) had a group of college women listen to a tape of a woman student who had broken both her legs in an accident. As they listened, they were to take her perspective and imagine how she felt. This manipulation led to more helping responses—going over lecture notes from the past month—than a control condition.

In addition, several items dealing with altruistic cognitions were included in a questionnaire on social responsibility for eight- to eighteen-year-olds (Harris, 1957). Two such items were "Every person should give some of his time for the good of his town or city" and "People have a real duty to take care of their parents when they are old, even if it costs a lot."

Motivation

There are many different motives for helping others, and there are two positions for interpreting the facts. One position assumes that all helping behavior is selfish, motivated by sheer hedonism. Cialdini and his colleagues (Cialdini, Darby, & Vincent, 1973; Cialdini & Kenrick, 1976) have forcefully advanced this view and generated research bearing on it. The opposing position assumes that we often help others for their own sake, with no egoistic motivation. Batson and his colleagues (Batson, 1987, 1991; Batson & Shaw, 1991) have proposed, also with an accompanying body of research, that empathically motivated helping is altruistic.

We know that people often have selfish motives for helping others, and other motives that, at least on the surface, are altruistic. As an aid to understanding I shall align the various motives on a dimension, from the most selfish to the most altruistic. Such a dimension enables us to discover where different theorists draw the line between selfishness and altruism. Cialdini does not draw a line, believing that all seemingly altruistic actions are at bottom selfish. Batson draws the line when empathy comes into play.

Rewarded Helping

Material Incentives

In everyday life people are often rewarded immediately for helping others. For example, a reward, such as money, for something that has been lost, is often promised to the finder. Many people who return wallets expect some kind of reward because typically one is offered.

Children can be induced to donate goods if they are suitably reinforced (Fischer, 1963). Preschool children were given marbles and told that they could keep them. They were shown a picture of a child and told that the child had no marbles and would like some. Whenever subjects donated a marble, they were either given a stick of bubble gum or verbally praised ("That's nice"). Bubble gum was highly effective in generating donation of marbles, praise only marginally effective.

Of course, the reward may sometimes be distant. Zuckerman (1975) provided an indirect test by asking college students just before an exam to volunteer for a time-consuming experiment or to read to blind students. Those who believed in a just world volunteered more than did those who did not believe in a just world. Presumably, in a just world their helpful behavior would be rewarded by a good grade on the subsequent exam.

There are more direct examples of the promise of distant rewards in everyday life. In the rural tradition of barn raising, neighbors offer considerable time and effort to help one family build their barn. Another tradition is a "baby shower," during which the new mother is provided with clothes for her baby and related goods. In both instances, there is a strong implicit promise that those who help will later take their turn at receiving benefits.

Praise and Censure

The Fischer (1963) experiment showed that praise was not especially effective in getting preschool children to donate marbles. However, older children are more susceptible to verbal rewards and not as selfish about material goods. And adults may expect lavish praise for altruistic behavior.

Another motive for altruism is to avoid censure—for instance, from the person needing help. This motive was evaluated by Fultz et al. (1986), who had college women listen to the plaint of a fellow student who had no one to talk to. She appealed for someone to spend time talking with her. In the experimental condition she would find out if the subject volunteered. The implication was that she would think ill of a subject if she did not volunteer. In the control condition, the woman in need would not know. But her knowing—the experimental condition—did not result in any more volunteering to help than in the control condition.

Perhaps the reason for this failure was that the subjects did not have to face the woman in need, which meant that they did not have to deal with censure. In an experiment that offers indirect evidence, college men were told that they and an unseen partner would engage in a task that paid off in money and that they would allocate the money (Shapiro, 1975). When they expected not to see the partner later, they selfishly gave themselves more money and the partner less. When they expected to see the partner later (potential censure), they gave more money to him. Clearly, we need an experiment on volunteering to do something aversive in which subjects expect to see the person making the plea. That would be a better test of whether the prospect of negative social evaluation increases helping behavior.

Praise and censure do not always come from others but may be self-directed. Thus when you engage in behavior that helps others, say, volunteer to give blood, you may tell yourself what a good and upright citizen you are. Is this altruistic behavior? The test is whether you are doing it only (or principally) for self-praise. If so, it is selfish; if not, it is altruistic. And no one else will know.

Affect

Empathy and Distress

Laboratory evidence agrees with casual observation in everyday life that empathy often leads to altruistic behavior (see Eisenberg & Miller, 1987, for a review). But when we see another person severely hurt or in excruciating pain, our reaction may be not only empathy but also personal distress. We are both sympathetic and upset. Suppose that we help the other person at some cost to ourselves, but by doing so we reduce our own distress. Obviously, reducing personal distress is rewarding. Does that mean that the altruistic behavior is at bottom selfish? For some psychologists, the answer is no. Hoffman (1981) offers three reasons for regarding empathic distress as an altruistic motive: "First it is aroused by another's misfortune, not just one's own; second, a major goal of the ensuing action is to help the other, not just the self; and third, the potential for gratification in the actor is contingent on the actor's doing something to reduce the other's distress" (p. 134).

Batson (1987, 1991) agrees that altruism is not ultimately selfish, but he regards distress as motivating not altruistic behavior but egoistic behavior. He and his colleagues tested the hypothesis in a series of studies (see Batson, Fultz, & Schoenrade, 1987; Batson et al., 1988). In this research, some subjects reported being personally distressed, checking such adjectives as *upset*, *disturbed*, and *troubled*. Others reported feeling empathic, checking such adjectives as *sympathetic*, *moved*, and *compassionate*. The results converged on two conclusions: "Personal distress seems to evoke egoistic motivation to reduce one's own aversive arousal. . . . Empathy does not. The motivation evoked by empathy may instead be altruistic, for the ultimate goal seems to be reduction of the other's need, not reduction of one's own aversive arousal" (Batson et al., 1987, p. 19).

Empathy and Sadness

Recall that one reaction to observing a person in need is sadness. Early on, Cialdini suggested that such sadness could be remedied by an act of helping, which enhances mood (Cialdini et al., 1973). He and his colleagues elevated their subjects' mood by praise or an unexpected gift of money, which diminished helping behavior. In a later study, the inducement of sadness in high-school students led to increased helping (Cialdini & Kenrick, 1976). Still later, Cialdini, Schaller, Houlihan, Arps, and Fulz (1987) produced evidence that led them to conclude that it is only sadness that leads to helping behavior. We help others to get over being sad about their plight. The title of their paper was "Empathy-based helping: Is it selflessly or selfishly motivated?" Their answer was that it is selfishly motivated.

If this is so, can there be truly altruistic motivation? Batson, Batson, Griffitt et al. (1989) answered yes. After observing a person in need, subjects reported their own emotional reaction, yielding two groups: those experiencing personal distress or sadness and those experiencing empathy. Empathic subjects helped more than distressed subjects. Batson, Batson, Griffitt et al. observed, "Apparently, the empathy-helping relation is not simply a product of an egoistic desire for negative-state relief. There is more to it than that" (p. 932). What needs to be added is that empathy leads to a wish to help victims for their own sake.

Experiments by other researchers strengthened this conclusion. Reacting to another's need with facial distress was negatively related to intentions to help (Eisenberg et al., 1989). Facial concern, presumably empathy, was positively related to intentions to help. Finally, Dovidio, Allen, and Schroeder (1990) showed that empathy led to helping behavior over and above the helping behavior that originated in sadness.

These issues reflect two personal-social dichotomies discussed in Chapter 1 (see Table 1.4). When others are in need, people may react with distress or sadness, which are egocentric, or with empathy, which is sociocentric. And helping behavior may be self-directed—to relieve a negative state or, as we saw earlier, to achieve a reward—or it may be altruistic, that is, other-directed.

Morality

Responsibility and Norms

Kohlberg (1969) classified morality into six sequential stages. The fourth stage, called duty and responsibility, is where most adults are located. Duty and responsibility are central to a social-sociological approach to altruism (Schwartz, 1975). First, the person becomes aware of the person in need and of actions that would alleviate that need. This awareness arouses a sense of responsibility because the person reacting is available or has a social role that involves giving aid—being the parent of an infant or belonging to one of the helping professions, for example. This sense of responsibility activates obligations or the expectations of others, as well as such personal feelings as pride or guilt. Then, if the costs are not too great, altruistic action is taken. If the person has not developed the kind of morality called responsibility, however, the sequence will be short-circuited, and no altruistic behavior will occur.

Religion

Are religious persons more altruistic? To find the answer to this question we must distinguish the various ways in which people are religious. We start with a distinction drawn by Allport and Ross (1967). At one pole are those for whom religion is a means to an end; these people have an *extrinsic orientation*: "Persons with this orientation may find religion useful in a variety of ways—to provide security and solace, sociability and distraction, status and self-justification" (p. 434). At the other pole are those for whom religion is an end in itself; these people have an *intrinsic orientation*: "Persons with this orientation find their master motive in religion. Other needs, strong as they may be, are regarded as of less ultimate significance, and they are . . . brought into harmony with the religious beliefs and prescriptions" (p. 434).

A meta-analysis of six studies revealed that, as expected, those with an intrinsic orientation tended to be altruistic (Trimble, 1993). What was not expected was a *negative* relationship between an extrinsic orientation and altruism.

Batson (1976) added a third kind of religiosity, called the *quest*. Those with this orientation view religion as the examining and questioning of basic values and beliefs.

How do these three kinds of religiosity relate to altruism? To answer this question, Batson and Gray (1981) confronted college women with a woman who was desperately lonely. In one experimental condition she wanted help in the form of companionship; in the other condition, she wanted no help. Those with an extrinsic, means orientation did not offer help when it was asked for. Those with an intrinsic, end orientation offered a little help not only when it was wanted but when it was not wanted. Presumably, they were driven by an inner (selfish?) need to help, not by altruism, for they insisted on helping whether the other person needed it or not. Only those with a quest orientation abided by her wishes, offering help when it was asked for and not offering help when she did not want it, which suggests that they were altruistically motivated.

Batson, Oleson et al. (1989) followed with two similar experiments. The first again revealed that those with an extrinsic, means orientation and those with an intrinsic, end orientation were not altruistic, but neither were those with a quest orientation. The second experiment confirmed this pattern, except this time the quest orientation subjects behaved altruistically.

Social Bonds

Attachment

As we saw in the last chapter, parents quickly establish an intense emotional bond with their infants. Parents put up with considerable discomfort to nurture their young. They rise in the middle of the night to feed or comfort their infants; they stay up all night, if necessary, with a sick child; they change diapers; and they tolerate the aversive sound of an infant crying.

In their role as caretakers, parents feed, clothe, and nurture their young, often at cost to themselves. Many women postpone having a career or just surrender the goal. Some fathers have lost their jobs to stay with a seriously ill child. When my younger son was a college student, he said "No children for me," because he saw how many sacrifices his parents had made in raising children. (He now has two children.)

Parent-child attachment is altruistically a one-way street, from parent to child. But romantic love is altruistically a two-way street. The attachment bond is so strong that each lover is willing to make sacrifices for the other. This bond continues in a committed relationship long after the infatuation phase has waned, for spouses may be as altruistic as romantic lovers. In both kinds of relationship, though, gift giving and sacrifice are usually not purely altruistic, for the recipient is likely to reciprocate and to be especially loving.

Social Identity

Nationality is a potent source of social identity, most people being patriotic. In an experiment to be discussed in Chapter 9, college men were told that Russian men tolerated more pain from electric shock than did American men (Buss & Portnoy, 1967). The men immediately tolerated higher levels of pain to demonstrate that American men can take it at least as well as Russians. They were willing to endure pain for the sake of patriotism.

Real-life examples are more poignant. During wartime, American men have volunteered for highly risky missions. The ultimate sacrifice is of course a suicide mission. Toward the end of World War II, some Japanese aviators volunteered to crash their planes into American aircraft carriers, causing enormous damage at the cost of the aviators' lives.

Certain charismatic religious figures have led their followers to commit suicide. Jim Jones, leader of a fringe religious group that moved from the United States to Guyana, ordered his followers to commit suicide when federal authorities mounted an investigation into the activities of the group. After those who would not obey were killed, a significant minority of Jones's followers committed suicide in the name of their religious identity. More recently, some followers of David Koresh, leader of the Branch Davidian cult in Waco, Texas, willingly committed suicide on his orders.

Which Motives Are Altruistic?

The various motives for helping others are compared in Table 6.2. The five broad classes of motives may be regarded as a continuum that starts with the more egocentric reasons for helping (at the top of the table) and ends with the more altruistic reasons (at the bottom). Helping others because you will be materially rewarded immediately or in the future is obviously egoistic. Helping others to receive praise or avoid criticism is perhaps a shade less self-centered. Offering aid in order to praise yourself seems to be less hedonistic but is still self-centered.

Affect represents a gray area between egoism and altruism. Suppose you become distressed or saddened and alleviate another person's pain in order to relieve your own distress or misery. This behavior appears to be another step away

TABLE 6.2   Motives for Helping Others

Motive	Example or elaboration
Material incentive	
Immediate reward	You find and return a wallet; you expect a monetary reward
Distant reward	You help now; you will be helped later
Praise or censure	
Praise from others	You are praised for your courage or charity
Censure from others	You are censured for your cowardice or miserliness
Praise of yourself	You praise yourself for donating blood
Affect	
Distress	Comforting another makes you feel better
Sadness	Helping another lightens your mood
Empathy	Helping another is its own reward
Morality	
Responsibility and norms	You help others because you are supposed to
Religion	Your beliefs require "good works"
Social bonds	
Attachment	Relieving your loved one's suffering is its own reward
Social identity	You risk your life for your country

from complete hedonism. If your empathy motivates you to help and the other person's benefit is its own reward, your behavior is unequivocally altruistic.

Though empathy has been the focus of most of the experimental research, there are other reasons for altruistic behavior. If you help because of a strong sense of social responsibility, your behavior is other-centered. Religiosity is another reason for helping. But not just any kind of religious feeling will do. The available research suggests that only the questing attitude leads to altruism, though the results are not entirely consistent (Batson & Gray, 1981; Batson, Oleson et al., 1989).

Researchers have focused almost exclusively on the first three classes of motives—material reward, verbal reward or punishment, and affect—perhaps because this part of the continuum has been controversial. One view is that all helping behavior is motivated by egoistic concerns, and it matters not whether there is any accompanying affect (Cialdini & Kendrick, 1976). Another assumes that the presence of some kind of feeling caused by the other person's plight, whether it is distress, sadness, or empathy, is a sufficient basis for calling the helping behavior altruistic (Hoffman, 1981). A third view regards empathy as the sole affect that motivates altruistic behavior (Batson, 1991).

The last class of motives shown in Table 6.2 will be familiar. We are likely to behave altruistically toward those we love. In addition, when a particular social identity is strong—the feeling we have as U.S. citizens, for example—we are likely to make sacrifices in its cause. The two subclasses of social bonds—attachment and social identity—have not been the subject of debate among researchers, probably because they cannot easily be investigated in the laboratory. In everyday living there are instances of altruism, especially those involving risk of life and limb, that cannot be manipulated by experimenters for obvious ethical and practical reasons.

Personality Traits

Helping Behavior

Do relevant personality traits affect helping behavior? Several studies offer evidence that they do. Clary and Miller (1986) studied people who volunteered to answer telephones in a crisis-counseling agency for six months. Those who completed the six-month stint scored higher on an empathy questionnaire than those who left early.

Other investigators placed subjects from the previously mentioned easy- and difficult-escape condition and asked them whether they would replace a woman who was receiving electric shock (Batson, Bolen, Cross, and Neuringer-Benefiel, 1986). The traits of self-esteem, responsibility, and empathic concern correlated with volunteering to replace the woman but only in the difficult-escape condition (egoism), not in the easy-escape condition (altruism). However, these negative findings on traits and altruism appear to be specific to this especially stringent test of altruism: receiving electric shock.

In a later experiment, subjects observed a woman who read descriptions of assaults (Carlo, Eisenberg, Troyer, Switzer, & Speer, 1991). In the *high-evocative condition*, the reader was visibly shaken and choked back tears. In the *low-evocative condition*, the reader displayed only mild distress. There was also an easy-escape condition (leave early) and a difficult-escape condition (observe the reading of all the assault descriptions). A factor analysis of the personality measures yielded two factors. The prosocial factor consisted of measures of empathy, perspective taking, and responsibility. The other factor, called arousability, consisted of two scales of distress.

The measure of helping was whether subjects would volunteer to replace the reader and read the rest of the distressing descriptions of assaults. Volunteering in the high-evocative, easy-escape condition was the measure of altruistic motivation. It correlated .48 with the prosocial factor (and even higher for women subjects), but there was only a chance correlation with the arousability factor. Thus with a less stringent test of altruism—reading upsetting material, as opposed to receiving electric shock—the trait composite called prosocial behavior did lead to altruistic behavior.

Romer, Gruder, and Lizzadro (1986) found that affirmative evidence emerged from a different way of conceiving the disposition to be altruistic. They used a questionnaire that asked respondents what they would do when someone needed help in realistic situations. Each question had four possible responses, but only two are relevant here. The *receptive-giving response* involved a desire to help if there would be compensation. The altruistic alternative involved desiring to help without being compensated. Subsequently, the request for help was mild, involving only the expenditure of time: An experimenter telephoned each subject, explained her need for subjects, and asked each how many hours he or she would volunteer. There were two groups. One would be compensated with course credit; the other would not.

When there was compensation, a larger number of receptive givers than altruists volunteered to help, and they offered more hours of help. But when there was no compensation, more altruists volunteered than receptive givers, and the altruists volunteered more hours of help. These findings are important because they specify one of the conditions under which those high in the trait of altruism will help: not being compensated.

These experiments show that the situation determines whether there will be a relationship between personality and helping others. When the cost of helping is especially high, as in taking another person's place to receive electric shock, there is no relationship. But when the cost is not high, as in fulfilling an obligation to answer telephones, reading upsetting material, or participating in an experiment, there is a relationship. When there is anticipated compensation for helping, there is no relationship, but in the absence of compensation, there is a relationship. Bear in mind, though, that this research involved helping strangers. We do not know whether personality would be more or less important in determining empathy or altruism toward those we like or love.

Empathy and Altruism

In a sample of more than a thousand twins, Rushton, Fulker, Neale, Nias, and Eysenck (1986) assessed empathy (Mehrabian & Epstein, 1972) and altruism (Rushton, Chrisjohn, & Fekken, 1981). The correlation was .15. If nontwins had been used or if other measures of empathy had been used, the correlation might have been higher. But it is a reasonable guess that empathy and altruism are not closely related. It follows that if we consider only the extremes (the top and bottom thirds) of the distributions of the traits of empathy and altruism, there are four kinds of people.

Some are high in both empathy and altruism. If another person is in need, their hearts go out to that person, and they will help. Such people are beloved. Others are high in empathy but low in altruism. When confronted with a person in need, they feel for the other person and wish they could help, but they are just not in a position to do so. We like them for their sympathy but cannot depend on them. Still other people are low in empathy but high in altruism. In dealing with a person in need, they are unsympathetic and may demand that the other person stop complaining. But whether or not they hurt the needy person's feelings, they do offer help.

The existence of the second and third kinds of persons poses an interesting dilemma. Suppose you could choose only one of them if you were in need. Would it be a sympathetic person who is friendly, tender, and makes you feel better to know someone cares, but who does not help? Or would it be someone who might be brusque and hurt your feelings, but who would help?

The fourth kind of person is neither empathic nor altruistic. Such people are too egocentric to take the perspective of others, sympathize with others, or engage in any instrumental behavior that is not selfish. Clearly, they have not learned the lessons of socialization. Perhaps they are immature and will never grow up. Or perhaps they see others only as persons they can use to obtain material rewards. At the extreme of this dimension are those who were once called psychopaths but now the label is antisocial personality disorder.

Origins

Heredity

The traits of empathy and altruism are not represented on omnibus personality inventories, nor are they part of the Big 5 superfactors of personality traits (see Chapter 13). This omission, and perhaps the belief that these traits derive solely from the environment and personal experience, may explain the paucity of behavior genetics research on these topics. I have located only two twin studies.

Rushton et al. (1986) used an empathy questionnaire (Mehrabian & Epstein, 1972) and an altruism questionnaire (Rushton et al., 1981). These were the correlations: empathy, identical twins .54 and fraternal twins .20; altruism, identical twins .53 and fraternal twins .25.

The other study used a set of adjectives denoting empathy and altruism: *emotional, generous, helpful, kind, sensitive, softhearted, sympathetic,* and *warm* (Matthews, Batson, Horn, & Rosenman, 1981). For a composite of these adjectives, the correlation for identical twins was .34 and for fraternal twins, .13. Then the following adjectives, denoting the opposite pole of empathy-altruism, were added: *cold, hardhearted, self-centered, selfish,* and *unemotional.* For a composite of the total list of both kinds of adjectives, the correlation for identical twins was .41 and for fraternal twins, .05.

Thus there is evidence of the heritability of empathy and altruism, though it would be preferable to be able to rely on more studies. Bear in mind, though, that the presence of a heritable component does not deny the influence of environment. As we shall see, there are data on socialization that suggest an environmental input. However, there appears to be little socialization of prosocial behavior during the first two years of life, although there are individual differences in empathy by the age of two years (Radke-Yarrow, Zahn-Waxler, & Chapman, 1983). Such early individual differences may be taken as indirect evidence of the inheritance of empathy.

Species-Wide Innateness

The theory of evolution assumes that each individual attempts to survive and reproduce. Those that are better adapted leave behind more offspring, who in turn leave behind more offspring. Each individual competes for resources and mates and therefore has a built-in selfishness, which obviously is adaptive. It follows that altruism must be maladaptive. But altruism does occur, for example, when parents defend their offspring even at the risk of their own lives. Thus evolutionary theory was confronted with the paradox of seemingly maladaptive behavior: altruism.

Inclusive Fitness

This paradox led to the modern evolutionary thesis that Wilson (1975) called *sociobiology*. The basic assumption is *inclusive fitness:* that individuals act to sustain not only themselves but also their blood relatives. It is the genes that are selfish, not the individual. The closer the genetic relationship, the more altruistic behavior will occur. A sister is more likely to sacrifice for a brother than for a cousin; a parent is more likely to sacrifice for a child than for a niece or nephew.

Precise predictions can be made on the basis of the degree of genetic overlap. Suppose a man has three children, each of whom represents 50% of his genes. If he can save all three of them (total = 150% of his genes), he will do so by sacrificing his own life (100% of his genes), because more of his genes will survive.

Individuals must recognize who their blood relatives are. Mothers know who their children are, but fathers cannot be as certain about blood relatives, nor can siblings. Another mechanism is needed: "What therefore must have been acquired through natural selection is a predisposition or motive that, although biologically based, is nevertheless amenable to control by perceptual and cognitive processes" (Hoffman, 1981, p. 128). The mechanism is empathy. Presumably, individuals are more empathic toward closer relatives than toward those with less genetic overlap. Of course, empathy does not always lead to altruism, but it may be argued that adaptive mechanisms are far from perfect.

Reciprocal Altruism

Recall that one selfish motive for helping another person is the anticipation of distant reward. Such anticipation means that it is adaptive to help another individual, even at temporary cost to oneself—a hypothesis called *reciprocal altruism* (Trivers, 1971). If each seemingly altruistic act were repaid later so that the altruist eventually benefited, both donor and recipient would benefit. Thus there would be an adaptive payoff for reciprocal altruism, resulting in those who participated leaving behind more offspring. If this tendency were to continue generation after generation, it would eventually become part of the biological heritage of the species.

There are several conditions that would foster an altruistic tendency being built into the genes (Trivers, 1971). There must be repeated social interaction, so that earlier altruism is reciprocated later. Such enduring interaction will occur only if the group is relatively small and stable over time. When these conditions are met, cooperation pays off, for *inter*dependence is more adaptive than independence.

Reciprocal altruism assumes no necessary blood relationship between the donor and the recipient. Donors are altruistic toward others not because they share genes but because cooperation is adaptive. This perspective is of course different from that of inclusive fitness, which assumes that we are altruistic only toward those with whom we share genes. Wilson (1978) attempted to reconcile these different views: "The altruistic impulse can be irrational and unilaterally directed at others; the bestower expresses no desire for equal return. . . . I have called this form of behavior 'hard-core' altruism. Where such behavior exists, it is likely to have evolved through kin selection or natural selection, operating on the entire, competing family or tribal units. We would expect hard-core altruism to serve the altruist's closest relatives and to decline steeply in frequency and intensity as the relationship becomes more distant. 'Soft-core' altruism, in contrast, is ultimately selfish. The 'altruist' expects reciprocation from society for himself or his closest relatives. . . . The capacity for soft-core altruism can be expected to have evolved primarily by selection of individuals and to be deeply influenced by the vagaries of cultural evolution" (pp. 155–156).

These biological approaches to altruism are complemented by the psychological and social approaches discussed earlier. The various explanations of the origins of altruism are listed in Table 6.3.

Development

Empathy

Hoffman (1981) has offered a developmental account of empathy. It starts with distress at the sound of another infant crying (Simner, 1971). This innate emotional reaction is regarded as a precursor of empathy. The more mature reaction may occur through classical conditioning: "Cues of pain or pleasure from another per-

TABLE 6.3   Theories of the Origin of Altruism

Explanation	Author
Empathy	Batson
Inherited trait	Rushton
Socialization	
Learning (reinforcement)	Cialdini
Moral rules	Kohlberg
Evolutionary heritage	
Inclusive fitness	Wilson
Reciprocal altruism	Trivers

son or from his situation evoke associations with the observer's own past pain or pleasure, resulting in an empathic affective reaction" (Hoffman, 1981, p. 130).

This suggestion connects with everyday events in life. After having a wisdom tooth removed, you are more likely to empathize with a friend who is having the same operation. The same kind of shared feeling is likely to occur among men who have been wounded in battle or women who have experienced the pain of childbirth. After having had a particular emotional experience, the same or similar emotion in another person is likely to induce empathy.

The family would seem to play a role in the development of empathy. Subjects watched a sympathy film and then reported on family cohesiveness and expressivity (Eisenberg, Fabes et al., 1991). Both cohesiveness and expressivity correlated modestly with sympathetic and sad reactions to the film.

Parental practices would also seem to be important in the development of empathy, but there have been few studies confirming this. College students were asked how their parents behaved toward them during the students' middle childhood (Barnett, Howard, King, & Dino, 1980). The students were divided into high- and low-empathy groups on the basis of an empathy questionnaire. High empathizers reported that their parents had been more affectionate and spent more time with them.

Such retrospective reports provide some evidence, but obviously a longitudinal study would be better. Such a study was supplied by Koestner, Franz, and Weinberger (1990), who compared the empathic concern of thirty-one-year-olds with the reports of parental practices made twenty-six years earlier. The level of empathy in the thirty-one-year-olds was assessed with self-reported adjectives. Only two relationships were significant for both sexes: empathy at thirty years correlated .38 with parents' involvement with child care, and .23 with the mother's tolerance for dependency. For women only, empathy correlated .44 with maternal strictness and .46 with maternal inhibition of aggression. These findings confirmed one fact from the Barnett et al. (1980) retrospective study: Time spent with the child does correlate with empathy. But it refuted another fact: Parental affection is *not* related to empathy.

Moral Rules

Recall that Kohlberg (1969) offered a developmental sequence of moral rules that bear on altruism. In the first stage, young children are selfish and completely egocentric. As they mature, they enter the second stage, *reciprocity*. This kind of morality involves the familiar distant-reward basis for helping behavior: You help me now in the expectation that I will help you later. Children then move up to the third stage, *good-boy orientation*. Here they help to obtain praise or to avoid punishment, and in the absence of these consequences, there will be little or no helping behavior. Gradually, they adopt a more adult morality, and the fourth stage, *duty and responsibility*, is reached. If you are in a position to help and are competent to do so, society demands that you help. To do otherwise is an affront to constituted authority and signals a severe disruption of society. The fifth stage, *rights of others*, is based on the underlying assumption of fairness. In a just world, we must share what we have and care for those less fortunate. We cannot eat while others starve, and we must donate blood if there is a shortage.

In a series of longitudinal studies, Eisenberg and her colleagues followed children from preschool to the middle of high school (Eisenberg, Lennon, & Roth, 1983; Eisenberg, Shell, Pasternack, Lennon, Beller, & Mathy, 1987; Eisenberg, Miller et al., 1991). They interviewed them, asking about four moral issues (for example, whether they would donate blood when it was needed). The developmental sequence more or less followed that laid down by Kohlberg. Egocentric reasoning predominated in preschool children, waned thereafter, but was still present in some high-school males. The good-boy orientation started and continued during elementary school but decreased in high school. Direct reciprocity followed the same developmental trajectory. High school saw the beginning of empathy and reasoning that used social norms and moral rules.

Among adults, there are marked individual differences in the dominant stage of morality, as an intriguing study by Erkut, Jaquette, and Staub (1981) revealed. These researchers presented moral dilemmas in which the good-boy orientation (stage 3) and duty and responsibility (stage 4) were opposed by the rights of others (stage 5). In the midst of the experiment, another "subject" (really an experimental accomplice) evinced considerable distress by moaning and groaning. The real subjects wanted to help the confederate (rights of others), but they also wanted to complete the experiment to avoid punishment or because it was their duty. Subjects known to be in stage 5 helped more, at the expense of interrupting the experiment, than did those in stages 3 and 4.

Altruism

At what age do children begin to display altruism? Observations of two-year-olds revealed that they became upset at another's distress but did nothing about it (Bridges, 1931). Children in the three- to four-year-old range also became upset but tried to help. Of course, the fact that some children at this age occasionally behave altruistically does not mean that most children do. Furthermore, we may question whether their helping is egoistic or truly altruistic.

Pairs of children of different ages were asked to divide nuts between themselves (Ugurel-Semin, 1952). Most children in the four- to six-year-old range were selfish, but this tendency dropped sharply thereafter and disappeared by ten years of age. There was little equality or generosity at the early ages, but by the age of eight generosity reached a peak that was maintained subsequently, and equality reached that level in twelve-year-olds.

Recall that the relief of sadness can motivate altruistic behavior in adults, but there is evidence that this effect does not occur in children (see Cialdini & Kenrick, 1976, for a review). These researchers, noting the possibility of a developmental sequence here, tested the hypothesis with children in three age ranges: six to nine years, eleven to fourteen years, and fifteen to eighteen years. They participated in a bogus task and were rewarded with coupons that could be exchanged later in the week for a prize. They were told that some children would not receive any coupons but that the subjects might share some of their coupons with those less fortunate. Meanwhile, half the subjects were asked to imagine and reminisce about sad experiences; the other half, about neutral experiences. The youngest children contributed virtually no coupons in either condition. Children in the middle range contributed slightly more coupons when sad than when in a neutral mood. And in the oldest group, sadness resulted in considerable altruism, and the neutral mood, almost none.

These data provided a springboard for a developmental model of altruism as hedonism (Cialdini, Baumann, & Kenrick, 1981; Kenrick, Baumann, & Cialdini, 1979). The first stage occurs in young children who have not yet been socialized and therefore do not possess any norm for the sharing of material goods. Any time they give away something, they deprive themselves, so they do not share with the needy. In the second stage, children have been socialized and know that they are expected to share. But they have not yet learned that altruistic behavior is intrinsically rewarding. In the third stage, late adolescence, "helping has been so frequently paired with direct reinforcement that it has become a reinforcing event in itself. Under these circumstances, altruism . . . will appear under the same conditions that produce other forms of gratification" (Cialdini et al., 1981, p. 221).

One limitation of this model is that it applies principally to the sharing of resources. Its application to helping behavior that costs time or risks danger is doubtful. And it completely omits empathy, which is one of the motives for altruism.

Person-Environment Interaction

Passive Model
Though it was not highlighted, the passive model was implicit in the foregoing section on development. Thus as mentioned earlier, empathy may be *classically conditioned* (Hoffman, 1981).

Reciprocal altruism is acquired through instrumental conditioning. When the reward is immediate—you help me and I turn around and help you—learning occurs quickly. When the reward occurs weeks or months later, learning is slowed by the need for verbal mediators to bridge the gap in time. Even when a distant reward is unlikely, altruistic behavior can be instrumentally conditioned by using verbal rewards, leading to the good-boy orientation. As was just mentioned, Cialdini and his colleagues believe that instrumental conditioning may eventually lead to intrinsic, unselfish altruism.

Observational learning bypasses the slower trial-and-error learning. Children who watch their parents reacting empathically to another's distress may quickly acquire empathic behavior. After watching others behave altruistically, observers may be more likely to behave that way themselves. Clary and Miller (1986) asked adults to answer telephones in a crisis center. Those who reported that their parents modeled altruism volunteered more hours than those whose parents did not model altruism.

Norms for helping, the need to take responsibility, and moral rules are acquired through cognitive learning. As children become capable of more advanced cognitions, they are able to learn a more mature morality, which is likely to lead to altruistic behavior. Cognitive learning is also involved in making the cost-benefit analysis that typically precedes the decision to behave altruistically or selfishly.

Active Model

Setting the tone and modifying the environment are most likely to occur in close social interaction. Therefore they will be discussed in the next section, Matching.

Children may have few options in selecting environments for prosocial behavior, but there are many possibilities for adults. They may choose to become parents, and consequently play the caretaker role, with its many requirements for altruistic behavior toward children. Or adults may decide not to have children because the inevitable sacrifices cramp a preferred life-style; the dominant cultural norm suggests that this decision is self-centered.

Some people volunteer to answer telephones in a crisis center. Church groups offer breakfast for the homeless; some members rise early enough to prepare breakfast at 5:30 A.M., whereas others will not volunteer for this duty. Some people periodically donate blood without recompense; some never do. Church groups also have outreach programs, in which, for example, volunteers travel to such poor regions as Appalachia to build such things as bathrooms.

Some people select temporary environments such as those described, while others make more enduring choices. Some choose to pursue a career in one of the helping professions, as physician, nurse, social worker, or teacher, for instance. And within these professions, people choose environments that vary in degree of altruism. Thus a physician or nurse might volunteer to work with AIDS patients, which is riskier than working with other patients. There are also occupations that involve helping others at considerable cost of time, material rewards, and personal comfort. A prime example is missionary work in technologically undeveloped countries.

At the opposite end of the dimension of prosocial behavior are people who systematically deprive others, such as scam artists and confidence men. These people have chosen a work environment in which everyone is completely selfish and out for their own benefit in a dog-eat-dog world. Some are cynically egocentric when they enter this environment, but all inevitably become coldhearted once they have spent time in it. Some are antisocial; others are merely asocial.

Matching

I shall deal only with matches and mismatches between adults who are married or in a similar relationship. If both are prosocial in their orientation, the relationship should be harmonious. Each will do things for the other, and each will sympathize with the other's difficulties and delight in the other's successes.

The opposite match, neither person being prosocial, sets up the possibility of a vicious cycle of increasing selfishness. When the husband, for example, does not lend a hand, refuses to cooperate, and never sacrifices his comfort or well-being for his wife, she would reasonably be motivated to act solely in her own interest. But since she is already selfish, his behavior will reinforce and intensify her self-serving orientation. Seeing her selfishness may make him even more egocentric, thereby keeping the cycle going. The partners in such a marriage (for as long as it lasts) resemble two strangers who happen to reside in the same home and who continually play zero-sum games: if one wins, the other must lose.

A mismatch also poses problems. Let us assume, going with the stereotype, that the wife is prosocial and the husband is not. She will justifiably complain that he never sympathizes with her when she needs a shoulder to cry on. She will notice that she makes sacrifices for him, but he never goes out of his way for her. She can settle for this state of affairs, rationalizing that in other ways he is a good husband. Or she can leave him.

Another option is to try to change him. If he refuses to change or cannot, the first two options are still available. But he might change, for mismatches are prime motivators of shifts in personality. Perhaps he was unaware of how self-centered he is, and, becoming aware, decides to change. Perhaps he has always been doted on by his parents, always the recipient of altruism but never the donor. Some people are late maturers, and he might move toward a more prosocial orientation.

Sex Differences

In examining sex differences, it is crucial to separate the three components of prosocial behavior. No sex difference has been reported for the cognitive component, either in moral rules or in responsibility.

The research literature on altruism, the instrumental component, is mixed. Men are more likely to help a stranger in distress, especially if the victim is a woman and especially when there are onlookers (Eagly & Crowley, 1986). The same study suggested that male altruism is stereotypically heroic, consisting of rescuing others from risky situations, especially women and children.

But in the various laboratory experiments reviewed earlier, on sharing behavior in children and adults volunteering for onerous tasks, there are no consistent sex differences. And across seven different cultures, it is almost exclusively women who occupy the nurturing roles in which altruism is likely to occur (Whiting & Edwards, 1973). In our society, "women are expected to care for the personal and emotional needs of others, to deliver routine forms of personal service, and, more generally, to facilitate the progress of others toward their goals. The demand for women to serve others is especially strong within the family and applies to some extent in other close relationships, such as friendship" (Eagly & Crowley, 1986, p. 284). Thus the laboratory evidence on helping strangers suggests either that men are more likely to offer assistance or that there is no sex difference. Observations of everyday social roles suggest that women tend to be more altruistic but only in relationships.

As for the affective component, empathy, research findings converge with everyday observations. Eisenberg and Lennon (1983) summarized a large body of literature and concluded that women and girls are clearly more empathic than men and boys. When the issue has been examined more recently, the same sex difference in empathy is found (see Eisenberg, Miller et al., 1991; and Koestner et al., 1990, for example).

I selected one study to illustrate this sex difference because adolescents were observed in mixed-sex groups in an everyday situation, during an extended bicycle trip (Zeldin, Small, & Savin-Williams, 1982). Girls were more likely to help when someone needed comforting, boys when someone needed physical assistance: "The observed sex differences in verbal support and physical assistance may thus reflect the adolescent's response to the cultural expectation that girls express comfort or empathy and that boys react in a nonemotional, instrumental manner" (p. 1497).

Origins

The foregoing discussion of women's roles is part of the socialization approach to sex differences in altruism and empathy. Girls are trained to be altruistically nurturant toward infants and young children, and they imitate their mothers in reacting empathically to the plight of those they love.

But there is another approach: sociobiology. It starts with the fact that women have a much larger biological investment in their offspring than men do: "A woman can expect to produce only about four hundred eggs in her lifetime. Of these a maximum of about twenty can be converted into healthy infants. The costs of bringing an infant to term and caring for it afterward are relatively enormous. In contrast, a man releases 100 million sperm with each ejaculation. Once he has achieved fertilization, his pure physical commitment has ended" (Wilson, 1978, p. 124). In addition, a man may sire as many as a hundred or so children, which would spread his altruism somewhat thin.

Having a greater investment in their children, mothers are strongly motivated to ensure their well-being, even at a biological cost to themselves. Furthermore, having borne their children, nursed them, and nurtured them, mothers tend to become more attached to their children than do fathers (see Chapter 5). Close attachment is a strong motive for altruism.

The last reason for the sex differences, admittedly minor, is the issue of whose child it is. Mothers always know, of course, but some fathers are unsure. If they suspect that the baby is not theirs, they are not motivated to behave altruistically. For mothers, such motivation is always present.

The sociobiological approach has greater generality: It applies to both humans and animals. But it is limited to altruism and ignores the fact that women are more empathic than men. The socialization approach is broader in that it applies to sex differences in both altruism and empathy.

There is one last point of comparison that goes beyond sex differences: individual differences. Sociobiological theory deals with species-wide tendencies and is silent about the personality trait of altruism. Socialization theory easily explains such individual differences in altruism by invoking the training of children for adult social roles and observational learning of adult role models. Neither theory attempts to deal with the fact that the personality trait of altruism is to some extent inherited.

Answers

At the beginning of the chapter, I posed five questions, which now can be answered:

1. What is the nature of empathy? Empathy is essentially sympathy for another person. When another person is suffering or in need, an observer may become upset or sad. But empathy is a different emotional reaction, denoted by the terms *touched* and *concerned*.

2. Is empathy a necessary condition for altruism? Empathy often precedes altruism, but altruism may occur in the absence of empathy. Thus a person who has a strong sense of responsibility might not be empathic but would engage in altruistic behavior. Recall that empathy is an affective reaction, whereas altruism is an instrumental response. The affective reaction does not always lead to the instrumental act. Furthermore, there are causes of the instrumental act of altruism other than empathy. So the answer to the question is no, empathy is not a necessary condition for altruism.

3. Does truly altruistic behavior occur? The answer appears to be yes. People do act in the service of others in the absence of egoistic motivation. One can always come up with a possible egoistic motive for helping others, but there are enough instances in everyday life and data from the laboratory that indicate altruism far outweighs any potential selfishness. True altruism does occur, though it may not be frequent.

4. Is altruism a species-wide tendency? There is clear evidence of altruism in animals, including those in the line that led to our species (Buss, 1988, chap. 7). By extrapolation, the same innate tendency might occur among humans, and some of the human evidence can be interpreted in this light. But there is also strong evidence for socialization of altruism. So the answer to the question is perhaps.

5. Is there a trait of altruism? There is an altruism questionnaire and several adjective checklists that contain altruism items. But the relation of these self-report measures to altruistic behavior is unclear. There is at present no unequivocal evidence of a trait of altruism. There are, however, several personality tendencies that dispose people to behave altruistically.

Chapter *7*

Dominance

History

Research on dominance, in both primates and humans, began about sixty years ago. Maslow's (1936, 1937) research on zoo primates led him to distinguish two kinds of dominance. *Face-to-face dominance,* seen in both humans and other primates, is the result of an interpersonal challenge in which one individual predominates. *Cultural dominance,* seen only in our species, is established through a title, wealth, or being the boss over workers.

In this early era, Yerkes (1943) systematically observed chimpanzees and offered this description: "Dita and Fifi, both aggressive adult females, long acquainted but usually living apart, struggle for dominance whenever they are caged together. . . . Dita has the advantage of greater size and strength, but Fifi by fearless and persistent attacks can sometimes achieve mastery. So evenly matched are they that neither may confidently assume superior social status, for it is usually challenged by the other" (p. 47).

Jane Goodall, who started watching chimpanzees in the wild during the 1950s, collected her observations in a more recent book. Her account has implications for humans: "Factors other than age which determine the position of a male in the dominance hierarchy include physical fitness, aggressiveness, skill at fighting, ability to form coalitions, intelligence, and a number of personality factors such as boldness and determination. . . . At Gombe some males strike with much energy to better their social status over a period of years; others work hard for a short while, but give up if they encounter a serious setback; a few seem remarkably unconcerned about their social rank" (1986, p. 415).

In humans, dominant behavior in preschool children was systematically observed more than sixty years ago (Parten, 1933). A factor analysis of children's behavior yielded a factor called ascendance-submission, which of course is dominance (Williams, 1935). Bossiness and leadership were found to correlate only .20

in young children (Ackerson, 1943). And in adolescents, Tryon (1939) found a factor called ascendance, which is similar to dominance.

Dominance is a major means of controlling others, which has been labeled *power*. Individual differences in power were first studied by Veroff (1957), using the Thematic Apperception Test (TAT). Stories were scored for power if they had these themes, which were selected because they are closest to dominance: "feeling good about winning an argument or feeling bad because he was unable to have his way, . . . wanting to win a point, or showing dominance, wanting to gain control (such as by a political or executive position) . . . being humiliated in a status position, being ashamed of an incapacity to assert one's self or become dominant, resenting the influence of another and wanting to overcome this . . . dispute a position, argue something, demand or force something, try to put a point across" (p. 3).

There were later books on power by Winter (1973) and McClelland (1975), but research on power by psychologists has been sparse. One reason may be that the TAT is an unwieldy instrument for discovering individual differences. Another possibility is that power is too broad a concept, encompassing not only interpersonal dominance but also economic power, political clout, and social status.

Components

In the research literature, dominance is defined by the way it is measured. When observed in children and adolescents, dominance is scored when subjects are either aggressive or bossy (Savin-Williams, 1976). In questionnaires administered to adolescents and adults, items primarily on leadership and bossiness are used to assess dominance. When college students were asked to nominate dominant acts, they suggested actions denoting both bossiness and leadership (D. M. Buss & Craik, 1980).

These different operational definitions of dominance lead to several conceptual options. One is to include all three kinds of behavior—bossiness, leadership, and aggression—under the heading of dominance. The second is to include only bossiness and leadership because they have appeared together in both questionnaires and consensual acts supplied by subjects. The most exclusive option is to define dominance solely in terms of bossiness, the common element in the way dominance has been measured. This third option is my choice. Leadership and aggression, along with a third kind of interpersonal behavior, are regarded as paths to dominance (bossiness). The conceptual and empirical bases of this decision will be offered shortly.

Dominating Behavior

Bossiness represents the high end of a dimension of direct and emphatic control over the behavior of others: telling them what to do, when to do it, and how to do it. The clearest examples of this extreme of control by one adult of another may be found in the military or in prisons. Enlisted personnel and prisoners are told what to wear, where to reside, when and what to eat, when to rise and retire, when they can take time off, and so on. Parents, in their roles of caretaker and disciplinarian, exercise a similar degree of control over young children, though it is more benevolent and flexible.

As examples of dominant behavior, consider these acts nominated by college students (D. M. Buss, 1981):

1. I yelled in order to get my way.
2. I demanded that he run an errand.
3. I told her to get off the phone so that I could use it.
4. I forbade her to leave the room.
5. I told him which item to purchase.
6. I chose to sit at the head of the table.
7. I decided which programs we would watch on TV.
8. I monopolized the conversation.
9. I interrupted a conversaton.

Items 1 through 5 have to do with ordering people around, 6 and 7 are about seizing first choice of something, and 8 and 9 are about dominating conversations. These actions define dominance.

Taking charge of conversations touches on another aspect of interpersonal behavior, politeness. Is it not impolite to interrupt others or to give them little opportunity to talk? Dominant people may know the rules, but the press of their personality is so strong that they break the rules.

Extraverts tend to talk more than others, which means that they also dominate conversations. Does this mean that extraverts are dominant persons? Not necessarily. They may talk a lot, denying others the floor, but manifest none of the other signs of dominance: telling others what to do and insisting on being first in line for rewards. However, many extraverts are dominant, and introverts tend not to be dominant. These relationships are strong enough for dominance to be included as part of the *surgency* (extraversion) superfactor of the Big 5.

Submission

In the face of dominant behavior the other person may yield, bending to the other's wishes. Why would one man capitulate to another man? The submissive one may lack the persistence to struggle in a contest of wills. He may lack confidence, his low self-esteem leading to a defeatist attitude. He may be insecure and not want to jeopardize a friendship. Or he may simply not care enough to put up a struggle.

In addition to these personal reasons for submission, there may be *inter*personal reasons. Children find it difficult to resist the domination of their parents, a worker must listen to the boss, and a subordinate in any military or quasi-military organization has to follow orders. Thus people may be in a position that leaves no alternative but to obey. Whistle-blowers, who refuse to go along with the cover-up of illegalities, are routinely fired by their companies. And children who defy their parents suffer withdrawal of privileges or even physical punishment. Disobedience then becomes futile.

Overt capitulation is not the whole story, though, for covert retribution is available. Thus the person who capitulates may complain to others about the perceived ill treatment, damaging the reputation of the dominant person. Another option is to withhold affection, which is typical of children, who also may sulk and pout.

Resistance

In the face of dominance, the other person may opt for defiance. People who are confident, secure, and what might be called strong-willed tend not to go along with the bossy behavior of others. Indeed, they may typically be the ones who predominate. When two dominant people meet, they tend to struggle for the upper hand, and this contest can lead to several kinds of interpersonal conflict, which will be considered shortly.

People who resist being dominated are not necessarily dominant themselves; they may merely be *autonomous*. When confronted with an overbearing person, they do not struggle to achieve dominance. Rather, they resist being bossed and insist on going their own way. Such resistance may contain elements of a spiteful obstinacy, as exemplified by items on the *negativism* scale of an early hostility inventory (Buss & Durkee, 1957):

> Unless someone asks me in a nice way, I won't do what they want.
> When someone makes a rule I don't like, I am tempted to break it.
> When people are bossy, I do the opposite of what they ask.
> When people order me around, I take my time just to show them.

In brief, there appears to be a continuum of reactions to others' attempts to dominate. In order of least to most resistance, the reactions are the following:

1. Complete submission
2. Submission, accompanied by covert retribution toward the dominant one
3. Autonomous refusal to be bossed, which may shade into negativism
4. Defiance, accompanied by an attempt to dominate the other person

Paths to Dominance

Since resistance is one reaction to attempted dominance (bossiness), this resistance must be overcome if the dominant person is to prevail. Just continuing to give orders, seizing perquisites, and monopolizing the conversation, by themselves, would not work, because the other person could just refuse to go along: "No, I won't take orders. No, you can't have the best seat. No, I will not allow you to interrupt me." Dominance needs to be backed up by other behavior. Thus a dominant woman, for example, may have established that she is a leader or that she is in some way superior, and she can use these facts to sustain her claim to dominance. If these methods fail, she can fall back on coercion.

In other words, when dominant behavior is challenged, dominance cannot be sustained merely by more dominant behavior. This conception raises the issue of how dominance is achieved. The three ways of sustaining dominance mentioned above—leadership, superiority, and coercion (aggression)—must be considered as interpersonal paths to dominance. Once these means are successful, it becomes possible to issue orders and get one's own way. Without them, it is difficult to assume dominance or maintain it.

This is a behavioral formulation of how dominance is achieved, but there are other ways of dominating others. Others can be hired, and thus money is used as a basis of control. Another way to dominate others is to be appointed to a position that carries with it unequivocal control over others—a judgeship or high-ranking military office, for example. These two kinds of control fall in the province of a more general sociological-economic concept of power (Wrong, 1979) rather than within the confines of the more specific psychological concept of dominance. Control by money and ascribed status do not apply to peer relationships, and their linkage to the trait of dominance is unclear. In contrast, leadership, superiority, and coercion are paths not only in transitory dominance but also in the trait of dominance.

It would seem then that the trait of dominance is best established by examining behavior with peers. A boss may give orders to her workers but may not be dominant at home or with friends. A girl may have the upper hand over her younger, weaker sister but not over girls her own age. The true test of dominance as a personality trait requires a level playing field.

Leadership

Organized groups vary a great deal in their composition, goals, and formality. Here we will focus on less formal assemblies of people, such as friends, kin, and clubs, that exhibit a wide latitude of interpersonal behavior. In such groups, personality plays an important role. In this instance we will consider a specific aspect of personality, the qualities involved in leadership.

I conceive of three such qualities. The first is taking the *initiative*. When the way to proceed is not clear, someone will step forward with a suggestion. Leaders have action-oriented ideas about what to do next and step right up to say what they think the group should do. Furthermore, they do not command others but say in effect, "Follow me." They say, "Let's go to this movie" or "I know a trip that all of us will enjoy." They obviously have knowledge, motivation to act, and willingness to rise to the occasion.

Decisiveness is evident in a leader. Decisiveness on one person's part is likely to make others want to follow. Thus when there are several possibilities and others cannot make up their minds, one person may step forward and say in effect or literally, "Do it this way."

Having made a choice, the decision maker must subsequently take *responsibility* for the group's action. Those less willing to take risks typically are glad to have someone else assume them, on the assumption that the one who made the suggestion and was decisive should be accountable. Leaders are expected occasionally to make mistakes, but followers also expect them to own up to their mistakes.

The three components of leadership are separable. One person may manifest initiative but be too tentative in making suggestions. Another might be decisive but back away from responsibility. But if such people become leaders, their tenure is brief. All three components must be present for leadership to be effective. In successful leaders these three behaviors are correlated.

Occasionally, a leader's initiative, decisiveness, and sense of responsibility may be in full view for the public. When President Ronald Reagan was shot and Vice President George Bush was not available, Secretary of State Alexander Haig stepped in immediately, told others that he was in charge of the government, and started giving orders. As the third in command, he took over in the absence of the president and vice president. Though Haig was chided for his ambition—he was not, after all, an elected official and did not actually stand next after the vice president in the line of succession—the incident is an excellent example of the qualities involved in leadership. Not coincidentally, Haig had previously been a high-ranking military officer.

In brief, leadership comprises three associated behaviors: initiative, decisiveness, and responsibility. People who are high in the temperament of activity are especially likely to initiate. Leaders are optimally in at least the mid-range of the temperament of impulsivity, for those at the low end of the dimension are too obsessive to be decisive. Leaders also usually have a strong sense of responsibility, which as we saw earlier, is an aspect of prosocial behavior.

Reaction of Others.   The reaction of others to leadership determines the leader's degree of control. If others allow someone to assume leadership, and follow that lead, they are being controlled. But in this conception of leadership, there are no commands to be obeyed; thus one reaction is simply not to follow. The only penalties for not following are being isolated from those who do follow and being denied any benefits of group action.

Another reaction is to counter with a different initiative in an attempt to assume leadership, which constitutes a rebellion against the leader. Then it becomes a matter of group choice as to who will lead, a choice made on the basis of the comparative qualities of the aspiring leaders.

The choice depends not only on the personality traits mentioned earlier but also on that elusive personal quality called *charisma*. In this conception, leadership is decided not by competition or aggression, which require explicit submission, but by whether the group will follow. They accede to leadership not because they must but because they may benefit. The voluntary nature of the group's homage and submission ensures that leadership, as defined here, involves only weak control over others. The only occasion when leadership involves strong control over a group is when there is danger. Then the group must act quickly and cohesively or suffer grievous consequences, so the leader assumes more complete control.

Superiority

The second path to dominance is through a demonstration of *superiority* in competition. The challenge may involve aggression but only under the specific rules that govern athletics as in boxing, wrestling, and karate, for example. Typically, however, the competition involves no bodily harm but a demonstration of talent, skill, and determination. (Interpersonal aggression is part of the third path to domination, and thus must be distinguished from competitiveness.)

The competition may be explicit, with two individuals struggling to determine who wins and who loses. Explicit competition typically has rules. For example, in debating, each person is allotted equal time, and in beauty contests there are dress codes. Being human, we acquiesce easily to contests with rules, and being human, we may attempt to bend the rules.

The competition may be implicit and therefore without an overt set of regulations. Students compete for grades; assistant professors compete for tenure. In industry, schools, athletics, and the arts, individuals strive for prizes dangled before them: eating in the executive dining room, a scholarship, an Oscar. The actual contest for these rewards often remains beneath the surface, unacknowledged, as though it is in bad taste to mention competition.

Reaction to Losing.   The reaction of the loser depends on the degree of loss. In a debate, beauty contest, or competition for grades, the outcome may be so one-sided that the loser is humiliated. Then there is no viable alternative but to admit inferiority, for it is hard to challenge a clear loss.

Of course, if the outcome is close, the loser may deny being inferior, explaining that the difference is too trivial to be of any importance. Here the loser refuses to accept the verdict of inferiority and continues struggling to achieve superiority. The outcome can be appealed, or a demand can be made for a rematch. A person can temporarily retreat in order to practice and develop sufficient talent to win the next time. Anyone who wishes to renew the contest must be considered competitive—that is, have an enduring disposition to demonstrate superiority by challenging others and refusing to accept losing.

Superiority in competition leads to a weaker dominance over others than does leadership. The defeated competitors may admire the winner and display some deference, but they will not necessarily surrender to another's domination. There are exceptions, of course. If there is an election for sheriff, the winner attains a control over others that is backed up by the law. But most elections, such as for president of a club, do not yield such power to the winner, who, though acknowledged to be dominant in the sense of being superior, exerts only modest control over others.

Coercion

Dominance may also be achieved through coercion, that is, the use of aggression, either actual or threatened, physical or verbal. Both angry and instrumental aggression can produce dominance. But dominance is an extrinsic consequence of aggression, and therefore instrumental aggression is more likely to be a precursor of dominance. Hurting or harming the victim is intrinsic to angry aggression, which means that dominance over the victim must be regarded as a by-product, albeit a powerfully rewarding by-product. Thus angry aggression often occurs without leading to dominance. In one particular context, however, both kinds of aggression occur: when a dominant individual is attacked. The typical reaction is counteraggression, which includes both anger at being attacked and instrumental aggression to maintain or restore dominance.

Such resistance to being coerced continues until the initial attacker wins or gives up the attempt to dominate. Who resists coercion? Those who are dominant themselves and therefore find it impossible to give in to the other, and those who are not necessarily dominant but who are so autonomous that they will not knuckle under to anyone. Repeated attempts to intimidate an independent person who cannot successfully counteraggress may lead to negativism: a stubborn refusal to go along, rather than an outright attempt to overthrow the dominant person. If the resistance is sufficiently passive and does not openly challenge the dominant person, it may be grudgingly allowed to continue.

The other major reaction to coercion is simple submission. Youngsters must tolerate being controlled by their larger, stronger elders. But such submission may be tentative in that the youngsters are observing the dominant behavior of others while awaiting sufficient maturity to rebel: A girl may be counting the years until she has grown strong enough to challenge her older sister. Of course, the submissive response may continue for so long that it becomes habitual, and the individual remains submissive throughout adulthood.

Coercion results in extremely strong control over the behavior of others. The ultimate threat was popularized by the movie *The Godfather*: "Make him an offer he can't refuse," meaning "Kill him if he will not go along." Most coercion is not so extreme. In youth gangs, members follow the dictates of the gang leader or risk being beaten, not killed. Older siblings may occasionally beat up younger ones, threaten to do so, or threaten to embarrass them, but will do no serious harm.

Three Paths

Dominance may be achieved by acquiring leadership, by establishing superiority in competition, or by fighting successfully or threatening to fight (see Table 7.1). Other species are limited to fighting or threatening as a means of attaining dominance, but humans can also try the nonviolent paths of leadership and superiority.

TABLE 7.1   Paths to Dominance

	Leadership	Superiority	Coercion
Behavior	Initiate, decide	Compete, win	Hurt, threaten
Control of other	Moderate	Weak	Strong
Reaction of other			
Resists	Refuses to follow	Challenges results	Counterattacks
Submits	Follows	Admits inferiority	Yields

Leadership is assumed to have a moderate linkage to dominance, for others may refuse to be led by the person who seeks to do so. Superiority is assumed to have a weaker link to dominance, for losers may deny that losing is a basis for submission. Aggression is by far the most powerful path, for it virtually guarantees control of others. Such control is not absolute, however, for others may respond with counteraggression or the more passive negativism. Thus the reaction of the other is a major determinant of whether any given path succeeds in establishing dominance.

Differentiation.   People are expected to differ in which path to dominance is available to them. Some people are good leaders and therefore need not compete or aggress to attain dominance. Others are so skilled at the competitive tasks that are valued by the group (especially adolescent males) that they need only to demonstrate superiority in competition in order to dominate. And if neither of these avenues is open, a person can resort to aggression. It is likely, then, that among those at the high end of the trait dimension of dominance, some will be aggressive, others will be competitive, and still others will display leadership.

Those at the low end of the dimension are assumed to have relatively undifferentiated submissive behavior. They tend not to aggress or compete, and they follow the lead of others. It follows that for submissive people, the correlations among aggressiveness, competitiveness, and leadership are considerably higher than for dominant people.

Regardless of which path to dominance is used, there is always at least one target. Adults are more likely to dominate children than other adults, and some adults dominate only children, never adults. Similarly, women who dominate other women may be reluctant to dominate men. And there are men who dominate other men but are submissive to their wives. In brief, dominance behavior may differentiate in relation to targets.

Measures

Dominance has not previously been analyzed into three paths, hence most measures assess overall dominance, though some measure leadership. The most popular way to measure dominance is to count the frequency of dominant acts. It is more difficult to assess the intensity of dominant behavior because it is so hard to quantify. Another measure is the choice a subject makes when there is an option to gain an advantage over another individual. The last response measure is the degree of resistance to being dominated, which often takes the form of negativism.

Observation

Dominance may be observed in adults, mainly in situations involving ascribed social roles, such as boss and worker. But, as mentioned earlier, the true test of dominance is assertion with peers, and there are few contexts in which researchers can watch while one peer dominates another. In a summer camp, however, psychologists can watch adolescents work out their social relationships. Acting as a counselor, Savin-Williams (1976) observed a cabin of thirteen-year-old boys during their five weeks at a summer camp. The indicators of dominance were the following:

1. Verbal command or order
2. Verbal ridicule
3. Pushing, shoving, or hitting, earnestly or in fun
4. Verbal battles
5. Verbal or physical threat
6. Taking away an object
7. Ignoring or refusing to comply
8. Recognized status (for example, others wait for a subject)

By the third day of camp there was a dominance hierarchy among boys who entered the camp as strangers. The most dominant boy domineered about three quarters of the time, the second-ranked boy domineered about half the time, and so on. And, as Savin-Williams (1976) observed, "Perhaps most surprising in these initial human studies is the rapidity with which stable, ordered dominance hierarchy is formed. . . . Disagreements and shifts may have occurred during the first few weeks, but by the end of camp everyone knew his place" (p. 977).

The early disagreements occurred while the boys sorted out who was higher in status and who was lower. Once the hierarchy was established, the number of conflicts decreased. Thus the most dominant boy made sure that his bed was closest to that of the counselor (associating with a high-status individual), and the rest of the hierarchy determined the remaining bed distances from the counselor's. After that, there was no disagreement about who was sleeping where.

These events appear to confirm what observers of animal behavior have concluded: Among social animals a dominance hierarchy serves to organize the group, diminishing conflicts among individuals. Presumably, this conclusion may be extrapolated to our highly social species.

Experimentation

Laboratory research offers the advantage of close control and ease of measurement at the expense of naturalness. Experimenters need to be creative in arranging for a conflict in which only one subject predominates.

One method is to have a scarcity of resources. Eisenberg and Giallanza (1984) made available to trios of same-sex preschool children a fascinating toy, an animal that jumped when a rubber ball was squeezed. Videotapes of the interaction were examined for these indicators of dominance: seizing the toy, pulling it back if someone else took it, ordering another to hand over the toy, and complaining about another monopolizing the toy. Dominant children, as rated by the preschool teacher, tended to grab the toy more than did submissive children.

Omark and Edelman (1976) paired nursery-school children and asked each twosome to draw a picture jointly. Each member of the pair was given a different colored crayon. The experimenters could then see which child's color established the main outlines of the picture, an unobtrusive measure of dominance.

Megargee (1969) also used pairs of subjects to study leadership in adults. The subjects were told to decide which one would be the leader and which the follower. Dominant subjects, as assessed by a previous questionnaire (Gough, 1956), tended to assume leadership.

This paradigm can be extended by having the subjects actually carry out a task (Nyquist & Spence, 1986). In a subsequent study the experimenters recorded the discussion about who would assume leadership, and verbal interaction during the task. Again, dominant subjects tended to take over the leader's role.

Another variant of this procedure is to assign one member of the pair the role as leader and obtain self-ratings of dominance behavior during the task (Snodgrass & Rosenthal, 1984). The leader taught the follower several letters of the alphabet in sign language, after which the leader tested and graded the follower's performance. Observers judged women's dominance behavior as leaders to be no different from men's.

Self-Reports

The trait of dominance is represented in the major omnibus personality inventories such as the California Psychological Inventory (Gough, 1956) and the Personality Research Form (Jackson, 1974). As noted earlier, the dominance items on these scales emphasize leadership and bossiness, virtually neglect competitiveness, and omit aggressiveness.

There are also questionnaires that assess individual components of dominance. The Aggression Questionnaire (Buss & Perry, 1992) contains scales of physical and verbal aggression (see Chapter 1). In Lorr and More's (1980) assertiveness questionnaire, one factor is called directiveness. The positively worded items that load on this factor are

1. I work best when I'm the person in charge.
2. I seek positions where I can influence others.
3. I am usually the one who initiates activities in my group.
4. In an emergency I get people organized and take charge.

Notice that the behaviors involve initiating activities and being decisive, which are crucial to assuming leadership.

The third avenue to dominance, competitiveness, has been assessed by Spence and Helmreich (1983), who used these items:

1. I enjoy working in situations involving competition with others.
2. It is important for me to perform better than others on a task.
3. I feel that winning is important in both work and games.

4. It annoys me when people perform better than I.
5. I try harder when I'm in competition with other people.

Dominance may be assessed by items selected from an assertiveness questionnaire of Ray (1981):

1. I'm the sort of person who likes to get my own way.
2. I tend to boss people around.
3. I dislike telling others what to do.
4. I tend to dominate the conversation.
5. I'm pretty good at getting my own way in most things.

Correlation

If there are three paths to dominance—leadership, superiority, and coercion—each of the three corresponding personality traits—leadership, competition, aggression—should correlate with the trait of dominance (bossiness). Moreover, the correlations between each trait and dominance should be higher than the correlations among the three traits.

The self-reports of 499 college students were obtained for the four relevant traits (Gallaher & Buss, 1987). Typical leadership items were "I seek positions where I can direct others" and "I am the one who usually initiates activities in my group." Typical competitiveness items were "I need to be the best in my group" and "I get a kick out of matching my abilities against other people's." Typical aggression items were "If I need to, I will threaten people to get them to comply" and "I have been known to get into arguments." Typical dominance items were "I tend to boss people around" and "I tend to dominate the conversation."

The correlation matrix is presented in Table 7.2. All the traits are significantly intercorrelated, but the correlations between dominance and the other three traits are significantly higher than the correlations among the other three traits. However, any single correlation might have been affected by other correlations among the traits. The correlation between dominance and aggression, for example, might have been affected by the correlation of each of these traits with competition and

TABLE 7.2   Correlations among the Three Paths and Dominance

	Leadership	Competition	Aggression	Dominance
Leadership		.38	.30	.62
Competition	.23		.38	.50
Aggression	.15	.27		.53
Dominance	.50	.52	.46	

Note: Correlations for men (*N* = 233) are upper right. Correlations for women (*N* = 266) are lower left. All correlations are significantly different from zero.

TABLE 7.3   **Partial Correlations among the Four Dominance-Related Traits**

	Leadership	Aggression	Competition
Aggression	−.11		
Competition	.06	.17	
Dominance	.50	.40	.29

leadership. Therefore, partial correlations were computed, in each instance with the correlations with the two remaining traits controlled statistically.

The resulting correlational matrices were similar for men and women, so their data were combined to form a single matrix, which is presented in Table 7.3. The partial correlations between dominance and the other three traits remained relatively high, but the correlations among the other three dropped so low as to suggest that they are hardly related or unrelated.

Thus leadership, competitiveness, and aggressiveness do seem to be related, as the correlations in Table 7.2 demonstrate, but only through their link with dominance, as the partial correlations in Table 7.3 show. These facts are consistent with the path hypothesis.

In discussing the paths to dominance, I suggested that aggression would be strongly linked to dominance, leadership moderately linked to dominance, and competition only weakly linked. The partial correlations shown at the bottom of Table 7.3 are consistent with these suggestions.

Negativism is one reaction to domination by another. We expect negativistic people to be, if not dominant, then certainly not submissive. If so, there should be a positive correlation between negativism and dominance. But what about the relationship between negativism and the three paths to dominance? The correlations are shown in Table 7.4 (Gallaher & Buss, 1987).

Negativism does not correlate with leadership but has a moderate correlation with the other two paths and also with dominance. Notice that the strongest correlation is with aggression. This relationship makes sense. Aggression is the most aversive path to dominance and, as such, arouses the strongest reaction in the other person, one that is in a sense a kind of passive counteraggression.

TABLE 7.4   **Correlations between Negativism and the Four Dominance-Related Traits**

	Men	Women
Leadership	−.02	−.08
Competition	.18	.36
Aggression	.29	.46
Dominance	.19	.35

Origins

Heredity

There are only a few twin studies of dominance, but their findings consistently implicate inheritance (see Table 7.5). Three of the investigations warrant special attention. The first (Loehlin & Nichols, 1976), using high-school students taking a college entrance examination, was perhaps the largest personality study of twins, involving 490 pairs of identical twins and 390 pairs of fraternal twins. The dominance scale of the California Psychological Inventory yielded a clear difference in the correlations for identical versus fraternal twins.

In two rare longitudinal studies, twins were tested twice over an average interval of ten or eleven years. In the first study (Dworkin, Burke, Maher, & Gottesman, 1976) there was a large drop in the correlation for fraternal twins over eleven years. But in the second study (McGue, Bacon, & Lykken, 1993) there was a large increase in the correlation for fraternal twins over ten years. These differences reflect the variability of correlations for fraternal twins not only over time but, as can be seen in the table, from one study to the next. In addition, different studies employ different personality measures. In this context, we need to remember that fraternal twins share 50% of their genes on the average; thus samples of fraternal twins may vary considerably in their resemblance. Identical twins, of course, always share all their genes, so we expect their correlations to vary less over time and across studies.

TABLE 7.5   Correlations in Twin Studies of Dominance

	Identical twins	Fraternal twins
Loehlin & Nichols (1976)		
High-school seniors	.53	.25
Dworkin et al. (1976)		
16 years old	.62	.45
27 years old	.70	.09
McGue, Bacon, & Lykken (1993)		
20 years old	.70	–.16
30 years old	.57	.33
Tellegen et al. (1988)		
Adults		
Reared apart	.56	.27
Reared together	.65	.08

The Tellegen et al. (1988) research is unusual in including twins who were reared apart as well as twins reared together. Paradoxically, the difference in correlations for dominance was greater for twins reared apart than for those reared together. An explanation of this discrepancy foreshadows the discussion of matching below. If both twins are dominant, after living together for years one might accede to the other at least a little in order to avoid conflict. The other twin would then become slightly more dominant. As a result, twins reared together would be less alike than twins reared apart, who do not have to deal with such a conflict and therefore are freer to develop the dominance established by their heredity. But caution is advised here, for these differences in correlations may be evidence of nothing more than the random variability just discussed.

Notice that the correlations vary from one study to the next, even when the same questionnaire is used. Whatever the explanation for variability in correlations across studies, in every instance the correlation for identical twins was clearly and significantly higher than that for fraternal twins—unequivocal evidence for the heritability of dominance.

Person-Environment Interaction: Passive Model

Ascribed Status

Some people are given little choice but to be submissive, because of their relatively low status. Children are physically smaller and weaker than adults and so are easily controlled by them. Parents, teachers, and other authority figures are put in charge of children, who are expected to obey or suffer punishment.

For the most part, women tend to be smaller and weaker than men, who are therefore more likely to intimidate them. The traditional woman's role is that of a subordinate, which means that in the workplace, for example, the boss is usually a man. Traditional men are socialized to regard this state of affairs as natural and right. They may consider women to be inferior and may not be willing to work for women. Members of various minority groups, victims of prejudice, are also often stuck in lower status positions in which they must defer to authority.

One's status as a child, a female, or a minority member is of course determined biologically, but the pressure from others to submit is an environmental, not biological, consequence of such status. Most people of low status do submit, though women and minorities have been challenging their lower status. Children just have to wait until they mature.

This is not to deny individual differences in dominance, especially in light of the hereditary basis for the trait. Anyone who is forced into a submissive role by environmental pressure has options other than knuckling under: rebellion and indirect means of resisting domination.

Rewards

We know that dominant male primates gain better access to females, and the same may be true in our species as a privilege of men who attain high social status. The issue is complicated, however, by the availability of nonbehavioral means of attaining high status: through appointment, wealth, or social class.

Dominant humans do not necessarily have better access to food, but they may get the better-tasting foods, and they have available a variety of perquisites, which are the rewards of those who win in competition or lead others. Savin-Williams (1980a) observed these advantages of dominant adolescents: "sleeping sites, preferred sitting and marching positions, and desirable food—the scarce resources at summer camp" (p. 229).

Those who are dominant also receive an inordinate share of attention from others (Exline, 1971). A strong relationship has been reported between dominance and attention in children six to seven years old (Abramovitch & Grusec, 1978). When teachers ranked two groups of children for dominance and attention received, the correlations were .73 and .94. The problem with these findings is that the teachers may have used the amount of attention received as an index of dominance. However, if this confound were eliminated, there probably would still be a relationship between dominance and attention from others.

The issue of deference is complex because of the various social rules that govern social status. But deference may be observed among nursery-school children, whose interactions are not yet governed by the formal status considerations that will later come into play. Submissive preschool children adopt deferent postures and give way to their dominant peers.

Dominant humans know that they can control the behavior of others. The knowledge that one has impact has been called *effectance* (White, 1959). Effectance is not only intrinsically rewarding but contributes to self-esteem. Dominance then is expected to correlate with self-esteem, but what about the three paths to dominance? The correlations are shown in Table 7.6 (Gallaher & Buss, 1987).

The self-esteem correlations are similar for men and women: a fairly strong relationship with leadership, a moderate relationship with dominance, and a nonsignificant relationship with competition and aggression. Leadership and dominance, as we saw earlier, are highly correlated, which means that partial correlations are needed here. In the absence of sex differences, the men's and women's data were combined to yield a larger N. With leadership partialled out, the correlation between self-esteem and dominance dropped to .02. With

TABLE 7.6   Correlations between Self-Esteem and the Four Dominance-Related Traits

	Men	Women
Dominance	.30	.25
Leadership	.48	.42
Competition	.17	.02
Aggression	.01	−.09

dominance partialled out, the correlation between self-esteem and leadership dropped only slightly, to .38.

Thus ordering people around (dominance) is not related to self-esteem, nor is competition or aggression. Only leadership is related to self-esteem, and the direction of causality might go either way. Confidence would seem to be required to attempt to lead others, and leading others would enhance self-esteem.

Other data suggest a stronger dominance–self-esteem relationship, however. Hamilton (1971) reported a correlation of .67 between self-esteem and dominance scales of the California Psychological Inventory. This dominance scale contains many leadership items—for example, "When I work on a committee, I like to take charge of things" and "I think I am usually a leader in my group." There are also extraversion items—for example, "In a group, I take responsibility for getting people introduced" and "I must admit I am a pretty fair talker—and extraversion correlates with self-esteem (see Chapter 8). There are also self-esteem items—for example, "I am certainly lacking in self-confidence" (reversed)—which overlap those in the self-esteem scale. It follows that the .67 correlation is inflated by these extraneous items. If the contribution of these items were partialled out, the correlation between self-esteem and leadership would probably be close to the .38 we obtained.

Learning

Clearly, there are rewards for attaining dominance status through one or another path. One learning mechanism is instrumental conditioning. Assuming leadership, winning in competition, and aggressing are reinforced by the positive consequences outlined above. And bossiness has its own rewards. These various actions may have costs: others' refusal to follow, loss in competition, or defeat in aggressive encounters. However, the rewards are sufficiently potent for many people to make an attempt to assume dominant status.

Dominance may also be acquired through *observational learning*. Children watch older children and adults attain dominance by fighting, competing, or leading. Even if dominant behavior is acquired through imitation, however, it can be maintained only by its reinforcing consequences—that is, by instrumental conditioning.

Development

Dominance hierarchies are known to develop among preschool children. Playroom dyads of four- to six-year-old children were observed three different times, revealing a stable pattern of dominance and submission for the majority of children (Gellert, 1961).

However, dominance-related behavior may appear at an even earlier age. Aggression starts as soon as an infant has the motor control to achieve it, late in the first year or early in the second year. Dominance appears in the form of negativism during the second year of life and flourishes during the third year of life (after the second birthday), a phase appropriately called the terrible twos. Competition awaits the child's understanding of the rules of games, sometime in the fourth year of life or shortly thereafter. Leadership begins during the elementary school years. There is usually a gap in time, however, between the first appearance of these actions and their frequent use.

This developmental sequence may be the reason that research on dominance in preschool children has focused mainly on aggression. For example, the dominance hierarchy of preschool children predicted 96% of the observed physical aggression, 80% of the threat gestures, and 76% of the struggles for a seat or an object (Strayer & Strayer, 1976). Competition and leadership were not yet salient issues for these three- to five-year-old children.

Once children are in school, though, competition becomes important. Children were administered items about wanting to perform better in school than others (Ahlgren & Johnson, 1979). There was a downward trend from the first through the twelfth grade, reflecting decreasing interest in school or perhaps waning parental concern or influence.

By adolescence, the attributes associated with dominance have assumed considerable importance. Peers nominated each other for dominance, and their size, leadership, and athletic ability were independently assessed (Savin-Williams, 1976, 1979). The ranges of correlations were physical size, –.31 to .77; leadership, .83 to 1.00; and athletic ability, .71 to .94.

The correlation of .77 between dominance and physical size makes sense, for we expect larger adolescents to be the more dominant ones. However, the –.31 correlation tells us that sometimes smaller individuals have enough of the other attributes necessary for dominance.

The extremely high correlations between dominance and leadership contrast with the more modest correlation found in the self-reports of college students, described earlier. The crucial difference may lie in the age of the subjects. In young adolescents, leadership may be a more potent path to dominance than in older adolescents and adults, especially when the setting is a small group, as in the Savin-Williams (1976, 1979) research.

The same appears to be true for athletic ability, which is important for both sexes in high school (Weisfeld, Omark, & Cronin, 1980). When athletic ability was correlated with dominance and leadership, both sets of relationships were strong in the ninth and tenth grades (see Table 7. 7). However, in the last two years

TABLE 7.7   Athletic Ability, Dominance, and Leadership

| | Correlations between Athletic Ability and: | |
High School Grade	Dominance	Leadership
9	.82	.74
10	.73	.70
11	.20	.56
12	.49	.27

of high school, athletic ability was not as closely associated with dominance and leadership.

In this study, intelligence was unrelated to dominance all through high school. Similarly, intelligence was unrelated to leadership through the junior year of high school, but in the senior year the two correlated .69. Thus, as athletic ability wanes in importance, it is replaced by intelligence as a cause of leadership. Though the data are correlational, there is a logical basis for the direction of causality. Being bright might help a person to become a leader, but it makes little sense to think that being a leader might increase intelligence.

Person-Environment Interaction: Active Model

Choosing Environments

All three paths to dominance are relevant here. A person high in aggression, especially physical aggression, may seek social contexts in which fighting is likely to occur (see Chapter 2). Some political figures, who are known for their verbal aggresssiveness, seem to welcome political conflict as a means of demonstrating their ability to dominate.

Competitive people are attracted to social contexts that involve head-to-head contests without violence. Many free-time pursuits feature such competition: poker, bridge, rummy, and other card games; checkers, chess, dominoes, and other table games; and tennis, squash, golf, and other sports. Competitive people are also drawn to vocations that offer the excitement of competition, such as professional gambler, athlete, or trial lawyer.

Those high in the trait of leadership tend to find groups that need to be organized and led. They may start a new business or take over one that is faltering in order to lead it toward profit and expansion. Another option is to become a religious leader, either the head of a traditional congregation or, even better, the charismatic leader of an evangelical group. If those high in the trait of leadership lack the ability needed to lead peers, they may choose to associate with children or those of lower social status, thus ensuring the opportunity to initiate activities and make decisions.

Such people are complemented by those low in leadership, who want to be led. Erich Fromm was so struck by the human tendency to follow strong leaders, even at the cost of independence, that he titled one of his books *Escape from Freedom* (1941).

Setting the Tone

A person's place on the dominance-submission dimension can be signaled by non-verbal cues (Argyle, 1969). Erect posture with head held high, looking down at another person, a serious expression, and a loud, confident voice all convey dominance. Submission is signaled by a slumping posture, looking up at another person from under lowered brows, a nervous, apologetic smile or laugh, a softer voice, and sputtering speech. Thus, by their nonverbal behavior, dominant and submissive persons may establish an ambience at the beginning of an interaction. In setting the tone for social interaction, they partially determine their own social environment.

Matching

As caretakers and disciplinarians, parents are expected to control the behavior of their children, but parents vary in how strictly they exercise such control. Recall that in Chapter 2 parents were described as authoritarian, authoritative, or permissive (Baumrind, 1971). Parents at the authoritarian end of the spectrum tend to be extremely dominant, and those at the permissive end, nondominant.

If the parent is permissive and the child is submissive, the relationship should be harmonious. If the parent is permissive and the child is dominant, the relationship will be relatively peaceful, for the child is not pressured by strong parental control. There is a risk, however, that the child may not learn to obey the commands of adults when they are appropriate, leading to problems with schoolteachers and other authority figures.

If the parent is authoritarian and the child is not dominant, this mismatch should cause no problems, for the child submits to parental control. A match between an authoritarian (dominant) parent and a dominant child inevitably causes conflict. The child may become so resistant to adult authority, perhaps so negativistic, that teachers label the child as difficult (Bates, 1980).

What about matches and mismatches involving the paths to dominance? Matches and mismatches in aggression were discussed in Chapter 2, the worst combination being an aggressive parent and an aggressive child.

Matches and mismatches in leadership cause no problem. The parent's role requires not blind obedience from the child but a reasoned following of the parental lead. The child is asked to behave in certain ways, and a logical basis for the actions is offered. This kind of parental control is roughly equivalent to Baumrind's (1971) authoritativeness.

If the parent is not competitive, there should be no problems in the relationship, whether the child is competitive or not. If the parent is competitive and the child is not, again there is no reason for conflict. But conflict will occur if both are competitive. The danger is that when the parent competes with the child, he or she adopts a peer role. This peer role conflicts with the other parental roles of caretaker and disciplinarian, causing the child to be confused. Moreover, in virtually any competition, the parent inevitably wins, causing the child to be frustrated.

Parents are expected to play a dominant role with their children, but in marriage the playing field is level. If both spouses are competitive, they may be able to evade problems if they restrict the competition to games. Games have clear rules, and most adults take a mature approach to losing. Problems may arise, however, if the competition becomes too keen and develops into a means of asserting dominance over the other person. Thus a husband, for example, might become boastful after winning a game with his wife, teasing her for her incompetence. Such behavior is likely to elicit a similar reaction from her when she wins, escalating the conflict.

When both spouses are competitive, they are likely to take competition seriously. For example, if they are bridge partners, and the husband plays a hand poorly, the wife may be so annoyed at losing that she will be sharply critical of him. I know of a couple whose solution to this problem is to play with other partners, never with each other.

The most common problem when both spouses are competitive derives from traditional socialization. Boys are taught that they are superior to girls, especially in games, and this prejudice carries over into adulthood for many men. Some men would have trouble being married to a woman who earned more than they did, and would feel inferior if their wife had a position of clearly higher status, say, mayor or governor.

Traditional adult men also become upset when defeated by a woman at table games and especially in athletic games. Women's reactions depend on whether they have been traditionally socialized. I have asked college women what they would do if a date became upset because he was losing to her at bowling or table tennis. Traditional women reply that they would then purposely lose to make the man feel better. Nontraditional women disdain such acquiescence and suggest that the man grow up.

A central issue in marriage concerns a match in dominance itself. Two nondominant people pose no problem. If one is dominant and the other is submissive, this is a mismatch that works well: "The purpose of interpersonal behavior, in terms of its security-maintenance functions, is to induce from the other person behavior that is complementary to the behavior proffered" (Carson, 1969, p. 112). Thus the dominant person elicits the compliant behavior that the submissive person is only too willing to provide.

Problems arise, though, when both spouses are dominant. Each tends to be bossy, but neither tolerates being bossed (recall the two dominant chimpanzees mentioned at the beginning of this chapter). The solution is to divide the interpersonal arena into segments, the husband being in charge of some segments, and the wife in charge of others. Unless this solution is adopted, the marriage will have to endure a continual battle of wills.

If both spouses are nondominant, there should be no trouble in the relationship, for neither will contest for dominant status. A problem will arise, though, if both are so extreme in their submissiveness as to fit the diagnosis of dependent personality disorder (American Psychiatric Association, 1987). Such people, who are virtually as clinging and helpless as infants, cannot manage by themselves. They need another person to take care of them and tell them what to do, so they welcome being subservient. If both spouses are that dependent, would they survive in an adult world?

Sex Differences

A sex difference in competitiveness starts as early as seven years of age, as demonstrated in a cross-sectional study of children from grades two through twelve (Ahlgren & Johnson, 1979). Boys were slightly more competitive in every grade, starting with the second. In the eighth grade, the start of adolescence, girls' competitiveness dropped sharply, and from then on the sex difference was greater.

Other sex differences have been observed in early adolescents in summer camps (Savin-Williams, 1980b). Dominant boys attacked physically and verbally, made threats, and seized perquisites, whereas dominant girls tended to give directives to other children and act in subtly aggressive ways.

There are consistent data from college students. Dominant men "managed to persuade others to perform their menial tasks, boasted about their accomplishments, surreptitiously controlled meeting outcomes, and sometimes used their fists to get their way. Dominant women reported expressing their dominance primarily in group-oriented actions: settling disputes among members, introducing people, involvement with community activities, and organizing projects" (D. M. Buss, 1981, p. 152).

Supplementary data come from questionnaire research on relevant personality traits. Men are considerably more physically aggressive than women and slightly more verbally aggressive (Buss & Perry, 1992). In the Gallaher and Buss (1987) study, men were found to be higher than women in aggression and competition, but there was no sex difference for leadership or dominance. One further sex difference emerged in that study, in which negativism was correlated with dominance and the three paths to it (see Table 7.4). Negativism correlated higher with competition, aggression, and dominance for women than for men. The explanation may lie in the well-documented fact of women's lower status in society. The major options available to persons of lower status who nevertheless have dominance tendencies are passive and indirect means of challenging those of higher status. Therefore, negativism should be more closely linked to dominance and its paths for women than for men. But what about leadership? As Table 7.4 shows, negativism and leadership are unrelated for both sexes.

It is well known that in the animal kingdom females prefer dominant males. Do human females prefer dominant males? In each of several experiments, college women were given vignettes of men who were described as dominant or nondominant (Sadalla, Kenrick, & Vershure, 1987). The dominance vignette contained such words as *powerful, commanding, strong,* and *competitive*. The nondominance description contained such terms as *yielding, obedient, not competitive,* and *not authoritative*. Women found the dominant man to be sexually more attractive than the nondominant man. Evidently, dominance plays the same role in our species as it does in other animal species. When men were presented with vignettes of a dominant and a nondominant woman, however, it was found that dominance played no role in sexual attractiveness.

Men versus Women

Given the sex differences in dominance and some of its paths, when there is a contest between a male and a female, the male is expected to prevail. A review of sex differences in children concluded, however, that there was little evidence that boys dominate girls, especially since the sexes are usually segregated during play (Maccoby & Jacklin, 1974).

But there is behavioral evidence from several experiments that men predominate when there is question of leadership. Recall the Megargee (1969) paradigm in which two adults were to decide who would be the leader and the follower in a task. In mixed-sex pairs, when the man was high in the trait of dominance and the woman was low, the man was chosen roughly nine times out of ten. When the woman was dominant and the man not, the woman was chosen only one time in four. Since then there have been three experiments, each with a slightly different procedure, but with highly similar results (Carbonell, 1984; Fleischer & Chertkoff, 1986; Nyquist & Spence, 1986). Dominant women apparently become less assertive when confronted by a man. There is another possibility, though: Perhaps women wish not to be seen as dominant over a man.

These two explanations were evaluated by Snodgrass and Rosenthal (1984). This time the experimenter decided which of two persons would lead, and the leader's behavior during the task was watched. Observers saw no difference in dominant women, whether they led a man or a woman. But the women leaders rated themselves as less dominant when they led men than when they led women. Surely we can take the neutral observer's evaluations as veridical—in other words, the women leaders merely perceived themselves as less dominant over male followers than over female followers. The authors suggested that dominant women experience conflict when they are called on to lead men. Their personality disposes them to be dominant, but such behavior is inconsistent with traditional sex stereotypes. Evidently, their behavior follows from their personality, but their self-perceptions reflect society's traditional view that women are in a position of lower status than men.

Perhaps one basis for the sex difference is the nonverbal behavior that accompanies dominant instrumental acts. Men and women were watched in public places, but the observers saw no sex differences in dominance-related nonverbal behavior (Halberstadt & Saitta, 1987). The authors of the study suggested that sex stereotypes may be at work: "It may be that when we look at an event or image involving the two genders, we tend to see what the male is doing and identify him as the leader. When, however, we see the female enacting the same behavior, we interpret her behavior so that those same actions no longer imply leadership or control" (p. 270).

But there is another issue: the goals of groups. Eagly and Karau (1991), after an extensive review of the literature on leaderless groups, concluded that when the group has a task, men are likely to be chosen as leaders. But when the focus is on interpersonal aspects, such as group harmony, women are likely to become leaders. According to Eagly and Karau, groups tend to choose men to lead when getting the job done is paramount but tend to choose women to lead when interpersonal skills are sorely needed.

Hormones and Socialization

It has been established that testosterone is a crucial determinant of dominance in animals (see the review by Ellis, 1986). Virtually the only animal path to dominance is aggression, so the testosterone-dominance connection may derive solely from the hormone's role in aggression.

What about human dominance? There is some evidence for a role of testosterone in men's aggression (see Chapter 2), and it has been speculated that male hormones potentiate competitiveness (Hutt, 1972). There is no evidence that male hormones influence leadership. Thus testosterone may play a role in the human sex difference in dominance, again largely through its effects on physical aggression.

The alternative hypothesis about sex difference in dominance is socialization, and findings have already been presented that are consistent with this explanation. In our society, men are taught to believe that they have higher status than women, and the young are inculcated with beliefs consistent with this imbalance. Through the media and the actions of parents, teachers, and other authority figures, boys and girls learn that males are in some way superior and deserve higher status. Children can also observe what often happens when adults behave assertively: A man is called a real man, and a woman, a bitch.

In brief, there is research implicating both hormones and socialization in the origin of these sex differences in dominance. Men are usually stronger than women and therefore can more easily dominate them through physical aggression. Witness the many instances of wife abuse and rape. Male strength is known to originate in male hormones.

At the same time, women are assigned lower status than men, and children are socialized to adhere to this status difference. As we have seen, women tend to defer to men in a contest for leadership because men have higher status. But our society is slowly changing, and more women are demanding and achieving equal status with men. If socialization is the primary contributor to sex differences in dominance, then these differences should narrow in the next generation or two. The hormonal explanation seems reasonable only for the aggressive path to dominance. The socialization explanation, on the other hand, can account for sex differences in the other paths to dominance—leadership and competition—and, it appears, in dominance itself.

Part II Commentary

Social Motivation

This discussion of social behavior in Part II, together with the treatment of the temperament of sociability in Part I, suggests answers to the question, Why do we want to be with others? One reason is the stimulation rewards of sharing activities, attention from others, and responsivity. The relevant trait here is sociability, for sociable people seem to be especially motivated to obtain these stimulation rewards, especially responsivity.

The affective social rewards of praise, soothing, and love also motivate us to seek out others. These rewards occur mainly in friendships and close relationships, and these social ties are intensified by the delivery of affective rewards. Attachment is particularly relevant here, for people with insecure attachment seem desperately to need praise, soothing, and love. However, securely attached people also seek these social rewards, though their need for them is less intense.

We also move toward others so that we can control them, a motive especially strong in those high in the trait of dominance. The mirror-image incentive is the need to be controlled by others, especially to be led or told what to do. Submissive people welcome the leadership of others and are reassured by knowing that they can rely on another person for direction.

The complementary question to that above is, Why do we move away from others? One reason is to escape the excesses of the stimulation rewards. When others share an activity, there may be crowding. Receiving attention from others risks the aversiveness of feeling conspicuous. And the responsivity of others may become intrusive. These excesses may drive us away from others, and the people most likely to seek privacy tend to be low in the temperament of sociability.

We may also avoid relationships because of a fear of criticism or of being abandoned or rejected. Insecurely attached people, especially those called avoidant, having been spurned in a close relationship with a parent or in adulthood with a lover, tend to react by staying remote from others so as not to be burned again.

However, as mentioned in Chapter 5, the temperaments of emotionality and (low) sociability also play a role here.

Another reason for staying away from others is to avoid being dominated. Most of us do not like to be under the thumb of another person, but for some people this need for autonomy is intense. They may not wish to control others, but neither can they suffer being dominated. If they are stuck with the presence of controlling others, they may rebel. But if possible, they will just get off by themselves.

A related reason is to escape competition. Some people expect to do poorly in a contest, either because they lack competence or are low in self-esteem. Others might perform well in competition but do not like situations in which there is always a winner and a loser. In our society, most children learn to compete, but the lesson does not take for a minority who prefer to remain on the sidelines.

Winners and losers occur in the context of zero-sum games: one person's gain is another's loss. Dominance is of course such a game, in which one person's dominance is achieved only by the other's submission. The opposite of such self-rewarded behavior (dominance) is the selflessness of altruism, which is also a zero-sum game: the altruist's loss is the helped person's gain. The way out of this game is reciprocal altruism, in which an immediate loss is compensated by a later gain.

Combinations of Personality Dispositions

Let us start with the combinations of high sociability with the other social dispositions. People who are sociable and securely attached tend to be not only friendly and warm (sociable) but also affectionate, trusting, and self-disclosing (securely attached). Those who are sociable but insecurely attached, especially avoidants, tend to be friendly and polite, but they are too wary of rejection to risk being affectionate or trustful, and they are reluctant to share feelings.

People who are sociable and empathic sympathize intensely not only with their friends and relatives but also with strangers in distress, whom they are likely to help. Those who are sociable but not empathic lack sympathy for others, by definition, but nevertheless may be instrumentally helpful. And those who are sociable but not at all altruistic seek the stimulation social rewards from others to satisfy only their own selfish needs.

People who are sociable and dominant tend to seek high social status through competition or leadership, for these means involve sharing, attention, and responsivity from others. They are less likely to seek dominance through aggression, because it would deny them these stimulation rewards. Those who are sociable and submissive are the ones likely to volunteer as followers of a strong leader.

We now move on to combinations involving low sociability. Unsociable people who are securely attached have few friends but close relationships with one or two of them, with family members, or with a spouse. Those who are insecurely attached have few friends and miss having close relationships. They are expected to be lonely.

Unsociable people who are altruistic tend to help others because of a moral code or a sense of responsibility, not because of empathy, which they lack. Being unsociable, they prefer to offer help at a distance, for example, by giving money, rather than help involving close personal contact. Those with no altruistic tendencies are content to satisfy their own needs in isolation from others.

Unsociable people who are also dominant are expected to achieve dominance interpersonally through aggression or through competition that is not face-to-face, for example, by taking tests or displaying better vocational credentials. They are also expected to resist being dominated by nonsocial means. They seek autonomy by going their own way, leaving the group quickly at the first sign of demands for their conformity. A likely alternative avenue to interpersonal dominance is through money or ascribed status.

Unsociable, submissive people have a weak need to be with others and therefore would just as soon leave the group as comply to the demands of dominant others. However, when escape is difficult, they are expected to be among the most conforming.

The last set of combinations involves attachment. Those who are securely attached, having a solid base of acceptance from significant others, are expected to be empathic and altruistic. Those who are ambivalently attached may become distressed at another's plight but, having pressing personal needs, are unlikely to be altruistic. Avoidants might help others because of morality or a sense of responsibility, but they will surely lack empathy.

People who are securely attached and dominant are expected to lead or direct significant others. If they are challenged for dominance, say, by a spouse, they are assured enough to surrender some of their higher status in the interest of a tranquil relationship. Those who are submissive are satisfied to follow the lead of a more dominant partner or at least a partner who is not as submissive.

Insecure people lack the confidence to assert dominance, so the insecure-dominant combination is rare enough to be ignored. The same reasoning suggests that the insecure-submissive combination is common. Desperately needing affection but unsure of receiving it, such people tend to cling to the other person in a close relationship. If the affection is not forthcoming, they are expected to become negativistic and hostile.

Sex Differences in Social Behavior

Aside from the sex difference in sociability, mentioned in the Part I Commentary, there are several sex differences in social behavior (see Table II.1). The only predicted sex difference in attachment is that men are more likely to fall into Bartholomew's (1990) avoidant (detached) category than are women. The underlying assumption is that men tend to strive for status even if it means putting a relationship in second place, whereas women are more likely to surrender status, achieved, for instance, through vocational success, in favor of maintaining a close relationship.

Concerning prosocial behavior, there is evidence that men are more likely to offer physical assistance to someone in need of it. Women, however, are more likely to offer sympathy and comfort, and they display more empathy.

There is also evidence of sex differences in dominance. Men are more competitive and physically aggressive than women. There is also evidence that men are

TABLE II.1   Sex Differences in Social Behavior

	Men	Women
Detachment	More	Less
Physical assistance	More	Less
Empathy	Less	More
Sympathy	Less	More
Competitiveness	More	Less
Physical aggressiveness	More	Less
Dominance with opposite sex	More	Less

more dominant with the opposite sex than are women, and there are good reasons for this state of affairs. Being physically more aggressive, men commit more spouse abuse. They are socialized to seek high status, a tendency that spills over into dominating the personal relationship of marriage. And women are socialized to achieve control by charm, persuasion, and other nonconfrontational means. As a result, they are more likely to be dominated by men, who are more willing to argue, curse, and threaten harm to get their way. Furthermore, most men believe that it is unmanly to be dominated by a woman, whereas women tend to accept submission to men as having no bearing on their femininity.

Dichotomies of Behavior

Dichotomies of behavior were discussed in Chapter 1 (see Table 1.4). Several of these dichotomies are relevant to topics covered in Part II.

The active-passive dichotomy applies to the close relationships discussed in Chapter 5, Attachment. People who are securely attached reach out to others, actively seeking to establish an enduring connection with one special person and perhaps a few close friends. Insecurely attached people, especially those who are ambivalent or fearful, tend to wait passively for the other person to make the first overture because of a fear of rejection.

Several dichotomies apply to prosocial behavior. The direct-vicarious distinction is relevant to empathy, in which we vicariously feel something of what the suffering person is experiencing. Next, we may be pushed to help by our own emotional distress or pulled to help the other person by the need to alleviate his or her suffering. The bottom line is whether we are sociocentric in altruistically helping the other at cost to ourselves or are egocentric in refusing to help because of selfish concerns.

Dominant people actively seek to prevail over those around them, whereas submissive people passively accept being led or bossed by others. And the master-pawn dichotomy is also relevant here. Dominant people have the perspective of a master who is in control of personal destiny. Submissive people feel like pawns that are being manipulated on the chessboard of life.

$Chapter$ *8*

Self-Esteem

History

There has been a flood of literature on the *self* over the past 100 years (see Wells & Marwell, 1976; Wylie, 1974). Work on the concept of *self-esteem* has been sparse, however, and for our present purposes only two psychologists need to be mentioned.

William James (1890) regarded self-esteem as the ratio of pretensions to successes, a commonsense notion that still carries weight today. People with grandiose ambition tend to fail even when accruing considerable success. Their self-esteem is low because their pretensions are too lofty for them to match. People with modest pretensions, however, need little success for their self-esteem to be high.

Carl Rogers (1951) modified James's ideas, preferring a concept of *self-ideal discrepancy*. He emphasized who people are (the real self), not what they can accomplish. A congruence between real self and ideal self means self-acceptance, which can occur in two ways: (1) the ideal self is lofty, but the real self matches it, or (2) the ideal self is set so low that the real self easily matches it. When the two are congruent, there is self-acceptance, which Rogers viewed as equivalent to good mental health. He regarded most problems of adjustment as being caused by a lack of self-acceptance.

The concept of ideals requires comment. Ideals are what we strive for, but they are distant and virtually unattainable. The ideal of complete and unwavering honesty can be met only by a saintly few, for example. A *standard* is more realistic, and there is a consensus on a standard that is more tolerant than the ideal: We are allowed little white lies (for instance). When we fail to meet a reasonable standard of honesty, we are criticized and may feel guilty, but no one would be censured for failing to achieve the ideal.

Of course, if a personal standard were so high that it was extremely difficult to attain, it would approach an ideal. But standards also differ from ideals in being more specific, especially when they relate to ability and performance. Because of their greater realism and specificity, standards rather than ideals are preferred here in analyzing self-esteem.

The history of ideas about self-esteem has left us with two meanings of this concept: *self-love* and *confidence*. The two are linked but separable. You can like yourself but lack confidence, especially about performing a particular task, say, dancing. Or you can feel confident but not intrinsically worthwhile.

Components

Various components of self-esteem have been identified by psychologists. Cooper-smith (1967) mentioned four: "On the basis of extended interviews and the results of previous studies, we propose that there are four different types of experiences that may be employed to define success. . . . These four sources of self-esteem, and the four criteria employed for defining success, are the ability to influence and control others—which we shall term *Power*; the acceptance, attention, and affection of others—*Significance*; adherence to moral and ethical standards—*Virtue*; and successful performance in meeting demands of achievement—*Competence*" (p. 38).

Since Coopersmith (1967), several different lists of the components of self-esteem have been suggested in research on possible factors of self-esteem or the importance of any single source for global self-esteem (Fleming & Courtney, 1984; Fleming & Watts, 1980; Hoge & McCarthy, 1984; and Wells & Marwell, 1976). As might be expected, the longer the list, the more specific the items on it. Some of the items on Marsh's (1986) list, for instance, are extremely narrow: physical appearance, opposite sex, same sex, parents, emotional, spiritual, honesty, verbal, math, academic, and problem solving.

Notice that the words *components* and *sources* are used interchangeably. Presumably, the components of self-esteem are the sources of *global* self-esteem, an assumption shared by everyone who studies this topic. This usage does not mean that global self-esteem is nothing more than the sum of its sources, an issue to be discussed later.

The components of self-esteem have been divided into two sets. The first set—appearance, ability, and power—relates to the confidence aspect of self-esteem. The second set—social rewards, vicarious sources, and morality—relates to the self-love aspect of self-esteem.

Appearance

A large body of research has been summarized under the epigram "What is beautiful is good" (Berscheid & Walster, 1978). Though parents love their children regardless of their physical features, they are proud of good-looking children. Beauty is considerably more important in adults, especially as men view women and vice versa, but it also affects judgments of children's personality (Langlois & Downs, 1979) and even which infants are preferred (Langlois, Roggman, Casey, Rieser-Danner, & Jenkins, 1987). Attractiveness makes a strong first impression that may endure in subsequent personal relationships.

If attractive people are sought and liked by others, it follows that beauty is an important source of self-esteem and therefore should correlate with global self-esteem. The correlations have ranged from a high of .52 (Rosen & Ross, 1968) to a low of −.08 (Major, Carrington, & Carnevale, 1984). This wide range of correlations is puzzling, but perhaps no explanation is needed, for the research appears to have a basic flaw. The same subjects who evaluated self-esteem also evaluated their attractiveness.

This confound can be removed by having others rate subjects for attractiveness. When this procedure was followed, the correlations between attractiveness and self-esteem were .24 for men and −.04 for women (Mathes & Kahn, 1975). These low correlations pose a conceptual question: If attractiveness is a source of self-esteem, why is the relationship so weak?

One possibility is that only the extremes of attractiveness can elevate or depress self-esteem. When the upper 10% of beautiful women and handsome men gaze in the mirror or receive compliments from others, their attractiveness becomes salient, and they feel good about themselves. The lower 10%, after looking in the mirror or receiving taunts and ridicule from others, have their unattractiveness made salient, and they feel bad about themselves. The appearance of the remaining 80% of the population is not striking or deviant enough for it to become salient and therefore contribute significantly to self-esteem. This hypothesis has two parts. First, attractiveness and self-esteem are correlated for only the extremes of the distribution of attractiveness, where beauty or plainness are too extraordinary to dismiss. Second, the correlation is absent for most of us, yielding a low overall correlation. To test this hypothesis it is necessary not merely to evaluate beauty but to place people at the upper and lower extremes of attractiveness.

What about people who are plain but not so unattractive as to fall in the bottom 10%. Even if a person were in the lowest 25% of attractiveness, this fact might not depress self-esteem. After all, there are other components of self-esteem, and one has only to concentrate on positive sources to the neglect of negative ones. Most people do accentuate the positive.

Consider for a moment the minority of lovely people whose self-esteem rests mainly on being attractive—models and actors, for example. Their beauty deteriorates as they age, depriving them of the principal source of self-esteem. They may fear aging as much as dying, and in later years they may suffer a large enough drop in self-esteem as to become seriously depressed. Aging tends to even out youthful differences in beauty, which means that when older, those who were plain in youth typically need no longer suffer in comparison to their (previously) more attractive peers.

Ability and Performance

Ability

Ability is represented on a dimension marked at the high end by the broadest capabilities and at the low end by the narrowest, say, the ability to pass a Spanish exam. The considerable research on *self-efficacy* sheds light on the narrow end of the spectrum: "Perceived self-efficacy is a judgment of one's capability to accomplish a certain level of performance, whereas an outcome expectation is a judgment of the likely consequence such behavior will produce. For example, the belief that one can high jump six feet is an efficacy judgment; the anticipated social recognition, applause, trophies, and self-satisfactions for such a performance constitute the outcome expectations" (Bandura, 1986, p. 391).

Bandura (1986) and others have shown that confidence about completing a particular task often leads to success, and lack of confidence to failure. Such self-efficacy refers directly to perceptions about performance of highly specific tasks. But, typically, only the more general abilities contribute to global self-esteem.

Perhaps the broadest ability we possess is intelligence. In school, bright children are at first rewarded with gold stars and later with high grades. There is even an organization, Mensa, for those with high IQs. Given this strong social support, it follows that intelligence is an important source of self-esteem.

The correlation between self-esteem and intelligence has been found to vary from nearly zero to .50, but typically it is in the thirties (Wylie, 1974). Again we can ask why the correlation is not higher. One answer is that the measures of intelligence ordinarily used are achievement tests or grades in school, and the subjects usually are young. Perhaps if intelligence were measured directly by individually administered IQ tests, the correlation might be higher; or it might be higher in adults than in children or adolescents.

As we saw in the last chapter, intelligence is unrelated to leadership in highschool students until the senior year (Weisfeld, Omark, & Cronin, 1980). It is a fair assumption that leaders are high in self-esteem. If so, these data mean that intelligence is only a weak source of self-esteem early in adolescence but becomes a significant source by the senior year of high school, at least for males. By extrapolation, intelligence would become a more potent source of self-esteem as the years pass and cognitive ability assumes greater importance in adult life.

The list of other abilities that can be a source of self-esteem is fairly short. Professions such as physician, therapist, and architect require talents beyond intelligence, and vocations such as truck driver and mechanic require manual skills. Talent is a requisite for painting; sculpting; playing or composing music; writing plays, novels, or poetry; acting; and directing. In addition, social skills, which smooth social interaction and make it more pleasant, should not be ignored. Aside from the value placed by others on these various pursuits, possessing the talent required to succeed in them can be a source of self-esteem.

Lack of ability in any particular domain usually poses no problem for self-esteem. People with no musical talent, for example, can turn to athletics or acting in plays. Intelligence is another matter, though. It is a crucial determinant of success in school, and children who perform poorly in school cannot easily escape the negative impact of failure on their self-esteem. In adolescence, they observe brighter peers going on to advanced education, and as adults, they see their more intelligent contemporaries moving into better and more prestigious jobs. No matter what other attributes people possess, no one wants the stigma of being labeled as unintelligent.

Standards and Goals

Talent, skill, and performance can be sources of self-esteem only when measured against a standard of comparison. Criteria for judging performance vary. We have low criteria for young children, praising them for being barely able to read or for producing drawings that only a parent could love. With each passing year, performance norms escalate. Similarly, in athletics we do not judge women by the same criteria as men—the best woman tennis player in the world would probably be beaten by fifty to a hundred of the best male tennis players—and professional athletes are expected to perform better than amateurs. Usually, when competition is organized, each person competes only with those on the same rung of the competitive ladder. If a person loses to a higher-ranked opponent, self-esteem is not damaged.

Criteria for accomplishment also change over time. Thus fifty years ago in this country, it was a significant accomplishment to graduate from high school, because only a minority of the population did so. Now it is merely a moderate sign of success to graduate from college, and only an advanced, postgraduate degree is regarded as a significant achievement. Of course, one's own reference group may be important; one might have the honor of being the first member of the extended family to graduate from college, for example.

Standards are routinely acquired during the course of development. In the innocence of youth, young people may think they will succeed in anything they attempt. They have little idea of the talent and hard work required for what appear to be simple accomplishments.

Some children are trained to have excessively high standards, which they are unlikely to meet. As adults, they are faced with repeated negative discrepancies between ability and internalized norms. The result may be an enduring lack of self-esteem because of inability to measure up. For others there is the handy excuse that the standards are just ideals to be sought but rarely attained: "Man's reach must exceed his grasp, else what's a Heaven for?" There are scientists and writers who set the bar so high that they are never completely satisfied with their work and refuse to publish it. By avoiding publication, they escape a realistic evaluation that might threaten their self-esteem.

At the opposite pole are amateur writers and painters whose standards are so low that they believe their work to be of high quality when it reveals little talent or skill. They can maintain their self-esteem as long as they are protected from a clearly negative evaluation, or they can dismiss such an evaluation as subjective and therefore incorrect. In all these examples, the trait of self-esteem is crucial. People with high self-esteem find a way to sustain it, whereas those with low self-esteem are too ready to believe the worst about themselves.

Sometimes a choice is available between alternative goals that are either more or less ambitious. In universities such as Oxford and Cambridge, students can decide in advance whether to be examined for a "first" (honors) or merely a "pass," which will allow them to graduate. When people are allowed such control over their attempts to achieve, choosing an easier goal hardly damages self-esteem. After all, one can admit to limited talent without destroying self-esteem, for there are other sources. But if the choice were made by someone else and a person was told to try for the lower standard, there would be a strong implication, backed up by an impartial evaluation, that ability is lacking. That might lower self-esteem.

Dichotomies

The impact of performance or achievement on self-esteem depends on the cause assigned to the outcome and on the person's goals. In attributing causality, there are several possibilities (Weiner & Kukla, 1970). An achievement may be attributed to innate talent or to a combination of motivation and hard work. Some people derive self-esteem from being blessed with talent, and they need not work at what they do well. Some highly talented people deride those who have less talent but compensate by working harder.

Ability and performance are of course related, but the correlation is far from perfect. Some people of high intelligence, for example, do not approach their expected potential. This discrepancy between ability and performance may cause no drop in self-esteem, for several excuses are available: bad luck, lack of opportunities, excessively high standards, and reference to other talented people who were late bloomers. Attributions about oneself need not be veridical, for they are subjective and typically motivated by a need to maintain self-esteem.

The distinction between ability and performance is also prominent in work by Dweck (Dweck & Leggett, 1988; Elliott & Dweck, 1988), who hypothesized two kinds of individuals. The first kind use performance to make judgments about their ability, which is assumed to be a fixed entity. Called *entity theorists*, they seek evidence that they are able. Evidence that they lack ability devastates their self-esteem, and so they try to avoid it. The second kind, called *incremental theorists*, use performance to make judgments about mastery: whether they have shown any improvement. They view ability as something that can be increased through effort over time, so they look for challenges in the enduring quest for a distant goal. "For the entity theorist self-esteem will be fed by performance goals. Outcomes indicating the adequacy of one's attributes will raise and maintain self-esteem. However, for the incremental theorist, self-esteem will be acquired and experienced via learning goals. Pursuit of, progress on, and mastery of challenging and valued tasks will raise and maintain self-esteem" (Dweck & Leggett, 1988, p. 266).

In a relevant study, children were identified as entity theorists or incremental theorists and asked when they felt smart in school (Elliott & Dweck, 1988). Entity theorists reported that they felt smart when the work was easy and when they performed better than others, or made no mistakes. Incremental theorists felt smart when they worked on difficult problems and when they figured things out for themselves, without any help. Thus the self-esteem that accrues from engaging in tasks depends on whether the evidence sought is of fixed ability or of personal mastery or improvement.

Another dichotomy, skill versus luck, applies mainly to competition. Chance may determine who wins, offering an explanation that can maintain self-esteem. Thus if I win, it was because of skill; if I lose, it was due to bad luck. A closely related dichotomy is temporary versus enduring: If I lose, I had a bad day; if I win, it was because of enduring skill.

A sex difference has been found in these attributions (Dweck, Davidson, Nelson, & Enna, 1978). When boys failed, they said it was because of bad luck. When girls failed, they said it was because of a lack of ability. As we shall see later, the boys' attributions are typical of those who have high self-esteem, and the girls' attributions are typical of those with low self-esteem. However, we must bear in mind a sex difference in the sources of self-esteem: males' self-esteem derives more from success at tasks, and females' more from social rewards.

The issue of recognition raises a personal-social dichotomy. There are talented people whose performance or skill is appreciated only by themselves and precious few others. There have been occasions when one person has stolen another's invention and received credit for it. The rare brilliant speech delivered by a president is not written by him but by an unknown speech writer. Those in the public eye sometimes put their names to "autobiographies" that are the work of ghost-writers. In Hollywood, stuntmen and -women replace actors in dangerous scenes, and in several recent movies, actors have been replaced by dancers in scenes requiring dancing skill. Perhaps the least recognition goes to singers whose glorious voices appear to emerge on the screen from actors who merely mouth the words.

Self-esteem can be pumped up if one has the appropriate talent and knows it (personal) even if the credit goes to someone else (social). But what is the impact on the person who receives the applause? Recognition may have no effect on self-esteem, in this case, because the person who receives it knows that he or she was not responsible. Alternatively the person may experience a boost in self-esteem deriving from the social recognition of the performance, no matter who was ultimately responsible, for public acclaim is hard to resist. Self-serving attributions can contribute so powerfully to self-esteem that the tendency to make them may overcome any issue of fairness or truth.

The personal-social dichotomy is especially relevant to the contrast between team performance and the ability of each team member. For example, if a women's basketball team succeeds, the esteem of each player is enhanced, a boost that may endure because of trophies and memories of past achievements. But what is the reaction of a member of the team who plays below the level of the others and contributes little to the team's success? Her self-esteem will escalate only if she depends mainly on social sources of self-esteem. In the opposite case, a superb basketball player may be on a team of poor players. She feels good about herself because those with talent tend to depend mainly on personal sources of self-esteem, but she derives no self-esteem from the team's performance.

The various dichotomies that relate to ability and performance are shown in Table 8.1. Standards may be personal, applying only to oneself, or social, established by a consensus and applying to everyone. Performance may be determined mainly by innate talent or by training and discipline; both contribute to self-esteem. If the goal is to demonstrate fixed ability, good performance increases self-esteem, and one defends against evidence of poor, unchangeable ability. But

TABLE 8.1   Dichotomies of Ability and Achievement

Basis of comparison	Dichotomy
Standards	Personal versus social
Performance	Innate talent versus discipline, hard work
Evidence sought	Fixed ability versus mastery of challenge
Attribution	Me (skill) versus not-me (luck) Credit/blame to me versus to others
Recognition	Personal (not recognized, though I achieve) versus social (recognized, though I do not achieve)
Who achieves	Personal (I achieve) versus social (my team achieves)

if the goal is mastery of a difficult challenge, self-esteem is enhanced by attempting difficult tasks or by showing improvement over previous performance.

Self-esteem can be elevated by attributing successful performance to oneself, or it can be defended by attributing poor performance to luck. One can demonstrate considerable talent that receives no public recognition, thus tapping a personal source of self-esteem; or one can receive credit for another's talent, the public acclaim being a social source of self-esteem. Self-esteem can also be enhanced by personal success in the midst of group failure (personal source) or by group success to which one contributed little or nothing (social source).

Whether ability and performance contribute to self-esteem depends on prior learning. As we try various activities, we discover those that fit our talents, and we tend to stick to them, improving performance as we practice. Improved performance can lead to success and rewards for succeeding. As a result, we tend to like what we are good at and are good at what we do, a situation that holds mainly for persons whose self-esteem is positive. But those who are low in self-esteem may seek activities for which they lack talent, and simultaneously devalue activities for which they might have talent.

Power

Dominance

Every day we control others and are controlled by them. When control is achieved in the course of social interaction, it involves domination that is earned by the individual. Three major paths to dominance, discussed in Chapter 7, are coercion, competition, and leadership. Each path enhances self-esteem. Successful aggressors exert physical or verbal power over others. Successful competitors display superior skill and motivation, and leaders show that they are the ones to be followed.

Does one path to dominance lead to more self-esteem than the others? When superiority is demonstrated through aggression or competition, the arenas are narrow: physical force, verbal abuse, or a specific contest. Furthermore, the admission by others of the aggressor's or competitor's superiority may be grudging. This is not the case with leadership, in which others in the group voluntarily follow *because they believe that the leader is superior*. Leadership adds social approval to one's personal self-evaluation, and so offers a greater boost to self-esteem than the other two paths.

Those who are the victims of aggression or who lose in competition are likely to have lower self-esteem. They lack the strength or ferocity to resist aggression or the talent and motivation to win in competition. Their defeat in these two arenas of social behavior is so explicit that defeat surely causes a drop in self-esteem. The outcome for followers of leaders is different. Followers have not been defeated; thus their self-esteem is untouched. To the extent that followers also tend to shy away from competition and to lose in aggressive encounters, however, their self-esteem may be relatively low.

Status and Money

Power can derive from ascribed status. Parents can control their children because of their legal and moral status, and they are held responsible for their children. Judges can sentence people to jail or set a fine for offenders, and bureaucrats make decisions that affect members of the community. Their impact on the lives of others must be a source of self-esteem. Notice that their status is ascribed, occurring by appointment. If status is earned—that is, achieved through one's own efforts in, say, a political election—self-esteem has a double source: it derives first from winning a competition, and second from status, which enables one to assert power.

The other source of power, money, requires little comment. Those with money can hire and fire others and give orders. Is economic control as much a source of self-esteem as ascribed status? Probably not. Ascribed status has the advantage of being socially accepted, because society needs people in control, and we are taught to esteem those who possess such societal power. Rich people may be envied but not necessarily valued. Those who are controlled by others' money or who submit to control by those with ascribed status need suffer no loss of self-esteem, though some do.

Varieties of Power

The different kinds of power that enhance self-esteem are listed in Table 8.2. Power may be earned by any of three interpersonal paths to dominance—aggression, competition, or leadership—which allow the successful person to assert control

TABLE 8.2   Kinds of Power as Sources of Self-Esteem

Kind	Example
Domination (earned)	Interpersonally order others around
Ascribed status (appointed)	In a social role order others around
Money	Hire and fire others
Environmental effectance	Build houses, dams

over others. Power can derive from an appointed position of status, which leads to control over others. Power can also accrue from having the money that allows the hiring of workers or servants.

People can also have an impact on the environment; this kind of power is called *environmental effectance* in the table. Architects who are instrumental in erecting skyscrapers profoundly alter a city, and dam builders change the course of rivers, leaving a lasting imprint on the geography of a region. Having such an impact must enhance self-esteem. Thus power, as a contributor to self-esteem, can be social or nonsocial.

Social Rewards

Relationship Rewards

Recall the affective social rewards, which occur mainly when there is a relationship—among friends, family members, spouses, or coworkers—and which tend to intensify any social relationship (see Chapter 4). The most powerful of these rewards is affection. Children are loved by parents and doting grandparents, adolescents and adults may be loved by an infatuated romantic partner, and there is the more realistic affection between siblings and spouses. The effect of affection on self-esteem appears to be straightforward. In effect, the recipient says, "If others like me, I must be worthwhile; if others love me, I must be a special person to deserve it."

Self-esteem obviously can also be enhanced by praise. Why are people admired? Several attributes that elicit praise have already been discussed: appearance, talent, superiority in competition, and leadership. These qualities can be observed by oneself, but such self-evaluations are known to be self-serving. Praise from others is more objective and realistic. (Of course, the praise may be delivered as part of the tactic of ingratiation and be no more veridical than a self-evaluation.) However, others may have such low standards that their evaluation has little meaning—parents complimenting their young children on their drawing, for example. But recipients of praise rarely question the motives of others. Again, the contribution to self-esteem is straightforward: If others admire me, I must be praiseworthy.

There is an added complexity, however: the identity of the person offering the praise. Thus in some families older children and adolescents learn that their parents tend to overpraise them, and as a result they do not trust parental praise. Some peers have such low standards that they may praise even shoddy work. Such praise adds little to the recipient's self-esteem.

Another complexity derives from individual differences in self-esteem. People high in self-esteem tend to accept praise, for it is consistent with their self-evaluation. For the same reason, consistency, those low in self-esteem may find it difficult to accept praise, and thereby prevent it from adding to self-esteem.

The third social reward that influences self-esteem is respect. Just as praise is linked to ability or performance, respect is linked to status. When the status is earned, for instance, by election or by winning an acclaimed or revered prize, more respect accrues to the individual than when the status is ascribed. A recent example of "I don't get no respect" was the selection of Dan Quayle to be George Bush's vice presidential candidate. Public opinion polls suggested that Quayle was seen as a lightweight by most people, and he was the object of demeaning humor while vice president. At the other extreme, a person can have only minimal formal status but receive enormous respect from others—Martin Luther King, Jr., was such a person.

The three social rewards have been discussed in descending order of their impact on self-esteem. One does not have to accomplish anything special to be liked, which means that affection is directed to the most intrinsic aspects of the person: I am liked (loved) because I am me. The resultant boost in self-esteem is therefore likely to be greater and more enduring. One does not need positive attributes to be praised, but the belief that one has these qualities obviously contributes to self-esteem, though not as much as affection. Respect is typically offered on the basis of social position, a more peripheral part of the self, which is an indication that respect is a less potent enhancer of self-esteem.

Each of the social rewards has an opposite that devalues the recipient: the opposite of affection is dislike; praise, criticism; and respect, insolence. The opposites of the social rewards also vary in their impact on self-esteem. Being disliked can be devastating to self-esteem, criticism can cause self-esteem to drop, and insolence may have only the slightest negative impact.

Vicarious Sources

Basking in Reflected Glory

Why do people boast about meeting or shaking hands with well-known athletes? Why are the walls of some offices filled with photographs of the proprietor together with movie actors or senators? The obvious answer has been stated in explicit terms: "It is a common and understandable tendency for people who have been successful in some positive way to make others aware of their connection with that accomplishment. However, there appears to be a less rational but perhaps more interesting tendency for people to publicize a connection with *another person* who has been successful. This latter inclination might be called the tendency to bask in reflected glory (BIRG). That is, people appear to feel that they can share in the glory of a successful other with whom they are in some way associated" (Cialdini et al., 1976, p. 376).

Cialdini and his colleagues related the behavior of college students to the success of the Arizona State University football team. After a win, more students wore buttons, jackets, sweaters, or shirts with the name or insignia of the university than after a loss. When describing a victory, they used the pronoun *we* more often than when describing a loss. This research provides an empirical basis for a phenomenon informally observed in everyday situations. When a team wins the Superbowl, for example, its fans swell with pride, and gold medals won by U.S. athletes at the Olympics are occasions for national pride. Individual accomplishment is also hailed. Arkansans are proud that one of their own is president, as were Texans when Lyndon Johnson was president.

One advantage of this source of self-esteem is that it is mainly positive. Notice that after the success of their university football team, college students basked in reflected glory, but after a defeat, they dissociated themselves from the university: We won; they lost.

When the affiliation is personal, such as being a family member, the involvement is more intense, and failure is not easily ignored. It is commonplace for children to share in the fame of parents or siblings: Think of the spouses and children of presidential candidates. When the famous family member fails, the close association causes a drop in the self-esteem of the rest of the family. Parents have a larger stake in their children than the reverse; after all, the parents have contributed genes and reared their children. It follows that parents typically derive more vicarious self-esteem from their children than children do from parents. Similarly, there may be more vicarious self-esteem for teachers and coaches than for their students or athletes.

Reflection and Comparison

Within families, competition may be intense among siblings, and less often between parent and child. Tesser (1980, 1991) has generated several intriguing ideas about such family dynamics. If I do not compete with my brother and he is successful, I can bask in reflected glory, which enhances my self-esteem. If I compete with my more successful brother, the comparison between his relative success and my relative failure diminishes my self-esteem. One way to compete and not suffer a loss in self-esteem is to put psychological distance between him and me. Of course, if I am the more successful sibling, I will feel close to my rival, for closeness enhances the value of my superior performance.

Tesser (1980) tested his theory, called Self-Esteem Maintenance, in several ways. College men and women were asked how much they resembled their siblings in ability and ways of thinking. When men performed better than siblings, the men reported being closer in ability and feeling, thus intensifying rivalry and elevating their self-esteem. When they performed worse, they reported feeling closer to a more distant sibling than to the successful one, thereby minimizing rivalry and maintaining their self-esteem. There were no comparable findings for women, which suggests that this formulation holds only for men.

Next, biographies of eminent scientists were examined to discover whether a less successful father and a more successful son were close or did not get along. When their occupations were dissimilar, they tended to be close, but when their occupations were similar, there was friction.

Tesser (1980) referred to similarity of occupations or of tasks requiring ability as *relevance:* "When relevance is high, comparison processes are relatively important. A good performance by the other is threatening to self-esteem, and the closeness of that other increases the threat. When relevance is low, the reflection process is relatively unimportant, and the other's good performance will bolster the person's self-esteem, especially when the other is close" (p. 78). Subsequent research has found other data consistent with this formulation (Tesser & Campbell, 1983), including evidence that the most pleasant affect is observed when a subject is outperformed by someone close on a task that is low in relevance, a situation favoring vicarious self-esteem (Tesser, Millar, & Moore, 1988).

The theory has been extended to dating couples (Pilkington, Tesser, & Stephens, 1991). Subjects filled out questionnaires listing a variety of activities, rating each for importance—in Tesser's terms, relevance. They also evaluated whether they or their partner performed each activity better. Self-esteem was maintained by claiming superiority for relevant activities, but, as it was observed, "When relevance was high for one partner and low for the other, the superior performance was most often attributed to the first partner. This allows the 'high relevance' person to benefit from the comparison of performance and the 'low relevance' person to bask in the reflected glory of his or her partner" (Pilkington et al., 1991, p. 500). By using this kind of strategy, couples can boost or maintain each other's self-esteem and avoid conflict. This strategy might also be useful for parents in dealing with their children's various pursuits.

Possessions

Another source of vicarious self-esteem is possessions. Some people are proud of their cars; others, their homes or their clothes; and some men, regarding their wives as possessions, are proud of how their wives look. Others collect valuable paintings, stamps, or rare books, all of which are a source of pride. The underlying psychological rationale appears to be the following: The excellence of my collection reflects on me, establishing that I am a worthwhile person. We not only bask in the reflected glory of the accomplishments of those close to us but use possessions as a mirror of our own value.

Morality

One component of morality is fair and honest treatment of others, but fairness and honesty would seem to contribute only weakly to self-esteem. A possibly more potent asset is altruism: helping others at some cost to oneself. But the component of morality most frequently used to boost self-esteem may be religiosity. A person who is deeply involved in religion, worships faithfully, and scrupulously follows religious tenets can claim to be a good person, one who is worthy in the eyes of God. For those who can substantiate such a claim, at least to themselves, religiosity is a powerful source of self-esteem.

The private-public dichotomy may be relevant here. One can be religious in private, whether alone in a church or at home, and one can engage in altruistic acts anonymously. Even if no one else knows, the person who is having the experience knows, and this knowledge can contribute to self-esteem. Alternatively, one can practice religion publicly or ensure that everyone knows about one's altruistic acts. Public knowledge of such morality offers an additional, social source of self-esteem. Private morality is a personal source of self-esteem, whereas public morality is a social source.

It should be added that religiosity itself, separated from moral acts, can enhance self-esteem. Regardless of someone's social behavior, if they are religious, they can take solace in the belief that God loves them. Even if they sin, appropriate religious rites can lead to forgiveness and blessing by God or his vicars: "If God loves me, I must be worthwhile." By the same token, when those who are religious do not pray or attend church, they are shutting out God, and this knowledge can diminish self-esteem: "I am not worthy of His grace."

Six Components

The six components of self-esteem, then, are appearance, ability, power, social rewards, vicariousness, and morality. They first occur at different times during childhood. Very young infants accomplish little, but they can receive social rewards. Affection comes first, followed by praise. Attractiveness is the next component, emerging probably by the second year of life, and then vicariousness, as young children borrow esteem from parents and older siblings. As children develop skills during the preschool period, they can derive self-esteem from demonstrated ability. The assertion of interpersonal power to a significant degree starts later in the preschool period, but morality awaits later developments in cognition.

At the other end of life, age takes its toll on attractiveness, ability, and power, and these are no longer available as sources of self-esteem for older persons. But their self-esteem can still be maintained by affection, respect, morality, and especially by vicariousness, the latter through their children or former students and any social clubs or institutions to which older persons belong.

No research has included every one of the six components of self-esteem named, but there are data on several of them (Buss & Perry, 1991). College men and women were asked to rate seven attributes for their importance as sources of self-esteem (see Table 8.3). For men, intelligence is the most important source, followed at a distance by character/morality. For women, intelligence and character/moral-

TABLE 8.3   Sex Differences in Sources of Self-Esteem

Source	Men	Women
Intelligence	8.6	8.2
Character/morality	8.0	8.3
Being liked	7.8	7.9
Physical attractiveness	7.3	7.0
Ability to influence others	6.6	6.4
Artistic ability	5.1	5.9
Athletic ability	5.2	4.8

Note: The data are based on a total *N* of 499 subjects, who rated the sources from 1 to 9, with 9 being the highest in importance.

ity are the two most importance sources. After these first two sources, both sexes agreed that being liked is more important than physical attractiveness, which is more important than the ability to influence others. There is an expected sex difference for the least important sources: Women value artistic ability more than men, and men value athletic ability more than women.

These norms apply to college students. No one would be surprised if different sources were more important for children or for older adults. We know that during the early school years, athletic ability is more important as a source of self-esteem than it is later. And as older adults accrue power, the ability to influence others might assume greater importance.

Bear in mind that these various facts and conjectures are *normative*. Individuals are expected to differ considerably in their ranking of these components. Thus bright students tend to overvalue intelligence, and good-looking students tend to overvalue appearance. Those who are deeply religious surely place character/morality at the top of the list. And for those who cannot depend on themselves, vicarious sources may be the most important. Thus in applying our knowledge about sources of self-esteem to individuals, we should search for patterns that vary from one person to the next.

Personal-Social Distinction

Of the various dichotomies that apply to the six components of self-esteem, the personal versus social distinction stands out as the most general. Appearance, ability, and morality are attributes of individuals and therefore are personal sources. Power can be earned (personal) or ascribed as a societal role (social). Social rewards and the vicarious claim of esteem through association are social, by definition, with the exception of possessions, a personal source. These differences are summarized in Table 8.4.

Psychologists have speculated that men and women differ in their respective emphases on the personal or social aspects of themselves. For example, Bakan (1966) suggested that men are more individualistic and women more socially centered. This dichotomy was recently applied to self-esteem, the idea being that

TABLE 8.4   Personal and Social Components of Self-Esteem

Personal components	Social components
Appearance	Social rewards
Ability	Vicariousness
Power (earned)	Power (ascribed)
Morality	
Possessions	

Note: There are more than six components here because power has been subdivided and possessions have been separated from other (social) vicariousness.

men's self-esteem would depend on "being independent, autonomous, separate, and better than others. For women, feeling good about one's self . . . should derive, at least in part, from being sensitive to, attuned to, connected to, and generally interdependent with others" (Josephs, Markus, & Tafarodi, 1992, p. 392). It follows that men with high self-esteem would differentiate themselves from others in ability more than men low in self-esteem, and women high in self-esteem would feel more connected with others than women low in self-esteem. These hypotheses were tested in two experiments.

In the first experiment, subjects wrote down their best skill among four (social, athletic, academic, and creative) and the percentage of local students who were good at that skill. The lower the percentage, the more subjects would regard themselves as possessing superior abilities. Among men, those high in self-esteem believed that they were superior in every ability, as compared with those low in self-esteem. For women, there was no similar difference between those high and those low in self-esteem. The second experiment involved memory for words. For women, those high in self-esteem remembered words involving friends or groups better than did those low in self-esteem. For men, those high and low in self-esteem did not differ.

These two sets of findings confirm the authors' hypothesized sex differences. In our society at least, men seem to derive more of their self-esteem from personal sources, whereas women derive more of their self-esteem from social sources.

The Trait of Self-Esteem

Global Self-Esteem

Any measure of self-esteem that includes all six sources would provide detailed information about individuals. A global measure of self-esteem ignores its various components and offers only a single score. Can a global measure be of value?

For some researchers, the answer appears to be not much. They prefer to investigate self-confidence applied as narrowly as possible, say, on a particular task. The best-known example of this preference for specificity is the concept of self-efficacy, as already noted above. Self-efficacy refers directly to perceptions about a specific anticipated performance. As such, it is even narrower than self-perceptions of ability or power.

Self-efficacy is an excellent predictor of performance (see Bandura, 1986, for a review); thus some psychologists question whether global self-esteem is worth measuring. They might ask the same question about intellectual ability. Intelligence tests assess several components of intelligence, offering information about several different cognitive abilities. For example, one person might be more competent in verbal skills than in imagery, whereas the next person might show the reverse pattern. The global IQ score ignores these details but still provides important information. It is an excellent predictor of academic performance, for instance, and it is fairly reliable in assessing competence for jobs requiring cognitive skills.

Just as global intelligence provides important information beyond that offered by its components, so does global self-esteem.

Furthermore, as will be seen shortly, global self-esteem is a crucial determiner of how people react to positive and negative feedback, and global self-esteem has been found to be a crucial aspect of an individual's personality. Self-esteem has a strong impact on certain other personality traits and is strongly affected by them. Indeed, self-esteem is one of the most pervasive personality traits.

A Questionnaire

The following measure was used to obtain most of the correlations to be reported (Cheek & Buss, 1981):

1. I have a low opinion of myself.
2. I often wish I were someone else.
3. Things are all mixed up in my life.
4. I'm fairly sure of myself.
5. There are a lot of things about myself that need to be changed.
6. I am a failure.
7. I am basically worthwhile.

Notice that most of the items are in the direction of *low* self-esteem. We assumed that this tactic might counteract a tendency to be modest about oneself when asked by others. Evidently, though, it does not matter how the items are written, for this questionnaire correlates .88 with that of Rosenberg (1965), the most popular self-esteem questionnaire currently in use. Indeed, the correlations among virtually all questionnaires on self-esteem are so high—in the eighties—that any one can substitute for the others.

A cautionary note, however: When the items of various self-esteem questionnaires were examined, and a conceptual midpoint was determined, it was found that the means and medians were clearly higher than this midpoint (Baumeister, Tice, & Hutton, 1989). These authors justifiably concluded that low scores on such questionnaires might include people with intermediate self-esteem as well as those with low self-esteem. As a result, it would be inappropriate to use a median split to select subjects high and low in self-esteem. The problem could be solved by selecting those in the top and bottom thirds of the distribution. In any event, the skewness of distributions toward the high end of self-esteem does not affect correlational research.

Relation to Other Personality Traits

Global self-esteem was correlated with several other personality traits: sociability and shyness (Cheek & Buss, 1981), loneliness (Russell, Peplau, & Cutrona, 1980), fearfulness (Buss & Plomin, 1975), and optimism (Scheier & Carver, 1985). The correlations are shown in Table 8.5. In these correlations and in the means for self-esteem, the sex differences were trivial.

TABLE 8.5   Correlations of Self-Esteem with Other
Personality Traits

Sociability	.28
Shyness	−.51
Social loneliness	−.59
Fear	−.43
Optimism	.64

Note: $N = 499$ for optimism; for all others, $N = 912$.

Self-esteem is only modestly related to sociability, but its correlation with shyness is strong and of course negative. People who lack confidence tend to be reticent and inhibited in social situations. Feeling that they are not especially worthwhile, they tend to expect rejection from others and so are tense and avoidant when with others. Of course, shyness can contribute to low self-esteem. Shy people are aware of their poor social behavior when with others and are less likely to receive attention, praise, or respect from others. Such awareness of one's social failings and the relative absence of social rewards can devalue one's sense of self-worth.

The negative correlation between self-esteem and loneliness may be explained by the impact of loneliness on self-esteem. Lonely people miss the companionship of sharing activities with others, or close relationships, or both (Weiss, 1973). If one asks why these important elements in life are missing, an obvious answer is that one lacks the personal attributes that attract others—that is, one is not worthwhile.

Of course, the direction of causality might be reversed. Those with high self-esteem expect others to accept them. As a result of their confidence, their social interactions are often successful, and they are not lonely. Those with low self-esteem do not expect acceptance and therefore are less willing to be socially assertive or to risk the rejection. As a result, they tend to be lonely.

The negative correlation between self-esteem and fear seems also to require a bidirectional explanation. Those with low self-esteem are unsure whether they can cope with a variety of situations, including those that might induce fear. Lacking confidence, they do not even try and tend to avoid potentially frightening environments. Thus low self-esteem can lead to fearfulness. People who are self-confident assume that they can deal with threat and so are less likely to be fearful.

Experimental findings appear to confirm this idea (Greenberg et al., 1992). Subjects were given a positive or neutral evaluation of their personality, the positive evaluation boosting their self-esteem. Then they were shown a video of autopsies and electrocutions, which obviously are threatening. The subjects whose self-esteem had been raised reported less anxiety than the other subjects. In a second experiment, subjects were threatened with having to experience painful electric shock. Those whose self-esteem had been raised were less aroused physiologically (electrodermal reaction) than the other subjects. These experimental findings may be extrapolated to the trait of self-esteem, which presumably helps in dealing with threat.

From the opposite perspective, people who are fearful usually realize that they cannot cope with an environment they see as threatening and uncontrollable. Compared to others who do not find so many situations scary or who can deal with potentially frightening situations, fearful people feel helpless and inept—feelings that lower self-esteem. Those who are low in fear are less frightened by potential threat, and knowing they do not scare easily tends to increase their confidence in themselves.

There may be a reason for favoring the impact of fear on self-esteem rather than the opposite causation. Fear is one of a group of temperaments, defined as inherited traits that first appear in infancy (see Chapter 3). Self-esteem first appears later, several years after infancy. Given the developmental precedence of fear, it seems logical to conclude that it might lead to (low) self-esteem rather than the reverse. However, only a longitudinal study would provide a definitive answer about the direction of causality.

People high in self-esteem might have tendencies toward grandiosity and narcissism, and this relationship has been confirmed (Raskin, Novacek, & Hogan, 1991). These findings make sense, but the researchers also reported a negative correlation between self-esteem and aggressiveness when grandiosity and narcissism were partialled out. Their measure of aggressiveness included not only hostility (resentment and suspicion) but also anger and verbal and physical aggression.

The findings of a large-scale study (*N*=1,253) were more specific (Buss & Perry, 1991). Self-esteem correlated –.49 with hostility but was weakly (negatively) related to anger and unrelated to physical or verbal aggression. Evidently, people who are low in self-esteem tend to be highly resentful and suspicious, a little angrier than average, and neither high nor low in aggression. There is experimental evidence of a link between self-esteem and anger (Kingsbury, 1978). Insult led to more angry aggression by low self-esteem subjects than a control condition (no insult). For high self-esteem subjects, insult did not affect angry aggression.

The last correlation in Table 8.5, deriving from a study by Buss and Perry (1992), is between self-esteem and an optimism scale developed by Scheier and Carver (1985). I regard optimism, which in this scale refers only to events that might happen to oneself, as the cognitions that derive from self-esteem. If one feels confident, there is reason for optimism; if one lacks confidence, there is reason for pessimism. It might be argued that those who lack confidence might still be optimistic because they somehow feel lucky. But when people feel that luck favors them, they might ask why. The usual answer is that luck comes to those who deserve it, and those who deserve luck must in some way be worthwhile. The issue here is not the source of self-esteem—whether it is based on past demonstrations of ability, being liked by others, or merely a feeling that one is worthwhile—but the level of global self-esteem. If it is high, cognitions about the future should be positive, that is, optimistic. If the level of self-esteem is low, pessimism would seem to follow directly. The correlation of .64, in light of the reliabilities of the two questionnaires, is high enough to suggest that optimism is evidently nothing more than the cognitive aspect of self-esteem—in other words, high self-esteem causes optimism.

For most of the relationships shown in Table 8.5, however, causality might go either way, which suggests the possibility of vicious cycles. The cycle might start with either trait of the pair, but for simplicity, let us assume that the starting point is not self-esteem. Thus a very shy person would be so reticent and inhibited as to behave poorly in social interactions and thereby be neglected or rejected. Either outcome would diminish self-esteem, making the person even less confident of future social interaction, the result being greater shyness—a vicious cycle.

People who are low in self-esteem have so negative a perception of themselves that they misinterpret the reactions of others. Brockner and Lloyd (1986) paired unacquainted men and women and asked them to get acquainted. Before and after becoming acquainted, they completed a likability questionnaire on themselves and their partners. Compared to those high in self-esteem, subjects low in self-esteem liked themselves less and believed that their partners liked them less. But low self-esteem subjects were rated no less likable by their partners than were high self-esteem subjects. Brockner and Lloyd concluded, "If, as in the present study, . . . low self-esteem persons underestimate their likability, then it may be that some of the low self-esteem persons' interpersonal problems reside in their perceptions of their social behavior, rather than the actual behavior itself" (p. 507).

How Failure Affects Performance

What is the effect of failure on subsequent performance? Previously confident people might lose heart and perform worse thereafter. Or people lacking confidence would have their prior beliefs verified and just give up afterward.

Level of self-esteem is a strong determinant of the reaction to failure. Compared to high self-esteem subjects, those low in self-esteem (1) are less willing to say they would be successful on a future task (McFarlin & Blascovitch, 1981); (2) attempt to lower the expectations of others when there will be continuing evaluation (Maracek & Mettee, 1972); and (3) downgrade themselves on dimensions that are irrelevant to the task just completed (Baumeister, 1982).

These cognitive reactions to failure will be discussed shortly, but for now the question is whether they have any impact on subsequent performance. They do. Brockner, Derr, and Laing (1987) reviewed laboratory research showing that negative feedback deteriorates the subsequent performance of persons who are low in self-esteem. In their own research they tracked the impact of one exam's outcome on performance on the next exam. Positive feedback (doing well on the first exam) had no impact for either high or low self-esteem students. Negative feedback left the high self-esteem students unaffected but caused a significant drop in the second exam's score for low self-esteem students. Persons low in self-esteem, devastated by negative feedback, lose confidence and perform worse afterward.

If a poor reaction to negative feedback causes deterioration of performance as the month and years pass, those with low self-esteem are likely to develop enduring problems of adjustment. Could problems of adjustment cause a drop in self-esteem? There is evidence from a cross-lagged study that low self-esteem causes adjustment problems, and not the reverse (Kahle, Kulka, & Klingel, 1980).

Why does the performance of low self-esteem subjects worsen after failure? Perhaps they overgeneralize and conclude that they will perform poorly everywhere, a suggestion of Kernis, Brockner, and Frankel (1989). They used a questionnaire, developed by Carver and Ganellin (1983), that measures the tendency to overgeneralize after failure. Sample items are "How I feel about myself overall is easily influenced by a single mistake" and "If something goes wrong—no matter what it is—I see myself negatively." This tendency to overgeneralize correlated −.61 with self-esteem: The lower the self-esteem, the greater the tendency to overgeneralize after failure. Thus failure feedback confirms what low self-esteem persons have believed all along: that they are just no good.

Performance can be affected even by hypothesized failure (Campbell & Fairey, 1985). Experimental subjects were shown an anagrams task and asked to imagine that they had done poorly and to explain this failure. Then they were asked how well they expected to do on the task, and, finally, they worked on the anagrams task. Control subjects merely performed the task without imagining failure or explaining it. The hypothesized failure condition caused low self-esteem subjects to perform worse and high self-esteem subjects to perform better. Evidently, even imagining failure is devastating to the confidence of people low in self-esteem, causing them to do poorly on a task. In contrast, imagined failure seems to spur high self-esteem people to redouble their efforts and perfom better.

Clearly, those high in self-esteem react differently to failure than those low in self-esteem. Brown and Mankowski (1993) suggested that "many of the outcome effects observed in previous research might be mediated by responses to the mood states they occasion. For example, rather than responding differentially to failure per se, the two self-esteem groups might be responding to the sadness that failure engenders" (p. 428). In one experiment, positive or negative moods were induced by having subjects read positive statements ("I feel cheerful") or negative statements ("My life is tiresome"), followed by self-evaluations. The positive mood affected high and low self-esteem subjects about the same, but the negative mood caused lower self-evaluations in the low self-esteem subjects than in the Highs.

In a second study, subjects filled out measures of mood and self-evaluation over a six-week period. Positive mood correlated (positively) with self-evaluations comparably for the two self-esteem groups. But negative moods correlated higher (negatively) for low self-esteem subjects than for Highs.

These two studies by Brown and Mankowski (1993) appear to confirm their hypothesis. Their explanation is that people with high self-esteem cope better with negative moods than Lows. This idea is consistent with the fact that depressed people are low in self-esteem, an issue we shall explore in Chapter 14.

Cognitive Mechanisms

Self-Enhancement versus Consistency

Common sense suggests that each of us wants to maintain self-esteem and even increase it, a tendency called *self-enhancement*. It follows that we should prefer positive feedback, which maintains or elevates self-esteem, to negative feedback, which diminishes it. But there is another approach to such feedback, popular in social psychology, which assumes that we strive for consistency. To be consistent, those high in self-esteem should prefer positive feedback, but those low in self-esteem should prefer negative feedback.

Though the consistency position opposes common sense, at least for the prediction about people low in self-esteem, there is considerable evidence for it. One study will illustrate the issue. Subjects were either flattered or evaluated neutrally and then asked to rate the evaluator (Colman & Oliver, 1978). High self-esteem subjects, as might be expected, rated the flattering evaluator more favorably than the neutral evaluator, which reflects both enhancement and consistency (high self-esteem people in a sense engage in self-flattery). But low self-esteem subjects rated the neutral evaluator more favorably than the flatterer, presumably because the neutral evaluation was more consistent with their self-evaluations.

Although psychologists who emphasize one or the other of these perspectives differ sharply in their predictions about people who are low in self-esteem, the two approaches can be reconciled. After reviewing the literature on this topic, Shrauger (1975) concluded that when cognitions were assessed, the data tended to support the consistency position, but when affect was assessed, the data tended to support the enhancement position.

Later data confirmed this hypothesis (Swann, Griffin, Predmore, & Gaines, 1987). Subjects low in self-esteem reported that unfavorable feedback was more self-descriptive than positive feedback. At the same time, they were depressed and distressed (negative affect) after receiving unfavorable feedback. Swann et al. concluded, "Our data therefore provide strong support for Shrauger's (1975) hypothesis that cognitive reactions to social feedback conform to self-consistency theory and affective reactions conform to self-enhancement theory" (p. 886). As these authors pointed out, negative feedback elicits intense conflict in persons with low self-esteem, which they called *cognitive-affective crossfire*.

Thus self-esteem has both affective and cognitive components. When people with insufficient self-esteem succeed, they feel good just as anyone would but cannot believe that they really are competent. When people with adequate self-esteem succeed, they feel good and construe the success as further evidence of their competence.

But what happens when people fail? High self-esteem subjects, after failing in an achievement task, exaggerated their positive social characteristics, being altruistic, for example (Brown & Smart, 1991). In contrast, low self-esteem subjects depreciated their social characteristics after failure. Thus people high in self-esteem do not challenge the fact of failure. Instead they maintain self-esteem by exaggerating their accomplishments elsewhere, saying in effect, "I may not be good here but I'm great elsewhere." People low in self-esteem do not use this compensatory mechanism, and failure depresses their self-esteem even farther. They say in effect, "Failure is just more evidence that I'm no good."

What happens if after failure, subjects are given another opportunity to demonstrate ability. College men and women were given tests that ostensibly measured two kinds of ability (Josephs, Markus, & Tafarodi, 1992, experiment 3). One kind supposedly involved independent thinking: unique and able to achieve individually. The other kind presumably assessed interdependent thinking: capable of nurturance and group achievement. After being told that they scored low in these abilities, subjects were asked to guess how much they would improve if they took the test again. In line with other research, high self-esteem subjects predicted considerably more improvement than did low self-esteem subjects. But Josephs, Markus, and Tafarodi also discovered a sex difference: "Evidence of poor independent thinking ability prompted the highest predictions by high self-esteem men, whereas evidence of poor interdependence thinking ability was answered with the highest predictions by high self-esteem women" (p. 399). The authors suggest that this sex difference originates in the socialization of traditional sex roles. The traditional male role emphasizes independence and achievement; the typical female role emphasizes affiliation and relationships. Among those with high self-esteem, men respond more to failure in individual achievement, and women respond more to failure in the interpersonal sphere. Those low in self-esteem, as might be expected, predict little improvement, for low self-esteem persons of both sexes are more ready to accept failure as consistent with their self-views.

In brief, all people appear to maintain their enduring level of self-esteem. Those with high self-esteem develop mechanisms to sustain it in the face of threats to their self-worth. They believe that what they are good at is important to them and what they are poor at is not. Those with low self-esteem seem unable to deny the importance of whatever they are poor at and deny the importance of what they are good at, thereby sustaining their low level of self-esteem.

Swann (1984) has suggested that all of us seek information that confirms who we think we are. This theory of *self-verification* leads to the interesting prediction that those who are low in self-esteem will prefer people who confirm that they really are low in self-esteem. Subjects who were either socially confident or not confident were allowed to choose one of two partners with whom they would spend several hours (Swann, Stein-Seroussi, & Giesler, 1992). They were told that one partner thought that they were high in social confidence (favorable) and the other partner thought they were low (unfavorable). Those who were socially confident chose the favorable partner 72% of the time, and those who lacked social confidence chose the unfavorable partner 78% of the time, strong evidence for self-verification. The subjects verbalized two main reasons for making the choice. One was a preference for someone who confirmed their views of themselves. The other was the expectation that a partner who agreed with their self-views, even when these were negative, would lead to more harmony in the interaction. The motives for self-confirmation and harmony sometimes outweigh the desire to obtain positive feedback.

Other research is not as supportive of self-verification. Sedikides (1993) had subjects select questions they would ask themselves about personality traits. The traits were either positive or negative and either central or peripheral to the subjects' personality. The questions varied in diagnosticity, that is, how much they distinguished between people high in the trait and those who were low. In several experiments, subjects selected questions high in diagnosticity more when the traits were positive than when they were negative. This is evidence for self-enhancement.

The self-verification view assumes that subjects prefer information about central traits rather than peripheral traits even when the traits are negative. It follows that they would select questions about central traits even when the traits were negative. This prediction was supported in only one experiment; in the other five experiments it was not supported, leading to this conclusion: "The general trend of the comparative tests was to support the notion that the self-enhancement motive is more influential than the self-verification motive in steering the self-evaluation process" (Sedikides, 1993, pp. 334–335).

Enhancement versus Self-Protection

It has been suggested that high self-esteem people have a different strategy for dealing with threats to self-esteem than those low in self-esteem (Baumeister et al., 1989). Those high in self-esteem attempt to boost their self-esteem in their own eyes or the eyes of others. Those low in self-esteem lack the confidence to attempt enhancement and therefore settle for protecting the little self-esteem they possess.

If people with low self-esteem are so motivated, they should be less likely to take risks, because a negative outcome would be too threatening. Subjects were told that they would gamble for real money, and they chose risky or safe options (Josephs, Larrick, Steele, & Nisbett, 1992). Low self-esteem subjects selected safer bets than high self-esteem subjects. The authors argued that high self-esteem subjects take risks because they have self-protective mechanisms when their self-esteem is threatened, in this case, by losing. Low self-esteem subjects lack such protection, so they play it safe.

In a related experiment, subjects practiced a video game and then bet on how well they would do when they played it again (Baumeister, Heatherton, & Tice, 1993). Those high in self-esteem set higher goals and met them, winning more money than those low in self-esteem. There was also an ego threat condition in which the experimenter suggested that subjects might choke under pressure and therefore should make safer bets. Under ego threat, high self-esteem subjects bet too much and wound up losing more than low self-esteem subjects, who hedged their bets. Thus under ego threat, those high in self esteem "cease to base their goal-setting on rational, appropriate self-prediction and instead become concerned with making a good, self-enhancing impression. . . . Meanwhile, people with low self-esteem responded to ego threat with cautious, conservative, self-protective responses. They set low, safe goals" (pp. 152–153).

Merely having one's performance evaluated may be threatening, eliciting the strategy called self-handicapping: placing barriers to performing well, which can then be used as an excuse for poor performance (Jones & Berglas, 1978). Tice (1991) allowed subjects to decide how much time they would practice for a forthcoming performance. If they practiced less, they could attribute failure to the lack of practice, a self-handicapping strategy. In the self-enhancement condition, subjects were told that the task would identify only those extremely high in ability. Then subjects answered questions about the meaning of how well they would perform. High self-esteem subjects endorsed this attribution much more than low self-esteem subjects: "If I do not practice much and do very well on the evaluation, that suggests that I have extremely high ability."

In the self-protective condition, subjects were told that the task would identify only those extremely deficient in ability. Low self-esteem subjects endorsed this attribution more than high self-esteem subjects: "If I do not practice much and do very poorly, that does not say much about my ability because I might have done better if I had practiced longer." In brief, people with low self-esteem used self-handicapping to protect against a drop in self-esteem. High self-esteem people used self-handicapping to enhance their self-esteem.

Another way of dealing with threats to self-esteem is *self-presentation*: managing the impressions others have of one's behavior. Baumeister (1982) suggested that people high in self-esteem present themselves differently than those low in self-esteem. This idea was tested by having subjects account for their performance under conditions of high or low motivation to succeed (Schlenker, Weigold, & Hallam, 1990).

> As hypothesized, high self-esteem subjects were most egotistical when social evaluation was greatest, that is, when high motivation to impress an audience was combined with the opportunity to account publicly for their performance. In contrast, low self-esteem subjects became less egotistical as evaluation pressures increased (i.e., when they were motivated to make a good impression and had to account publicly). . . . People with high self-esteem become more boastful as the social stakes increase, whereas those with low self-esteem become more timid. (pp. 860–861)

Downward Comparison

Suppose you received a grade of C in a course and felt bad about it. If you discovered that a friend had failed the course, you would probably feel better about yourself. Downward comparison can improve subjective well-being (Wills, 1981).

College students were asked to write about problems in adjusting to college, after which they read about a member of their group who either had problems (downward comparison) or did not (Gibbons & Gerrard, 1989). Downward comparison improved the mood of subjects low in self-esteem but not of those high in self-esteem.

In a follow-up experiment, Gibbons and McCoy (1991) told subjects that they had done poorly on a task and then had them hear about a student who was having academic and social difficulties. Again, the mood of low self-esteem subjects, but not high self-esteem subjects, improved after making the downward comparison. Evidently, the low self-esteem subjects were satisfied to discover that others were worse off. Those high in self-esteem derived no apparent benefit from the downward comparison, but it did offer them an opportunity. They responded by derogating the student with academic difficulties, displaying a sex difference: Men typically derogated on the competence (academic) dimension, women on the social dimension.

High versus Low Self-Esteem

The various differences between people low in self-esteem and those high in self-esteem are summarized in Table 8.6. Those low in self-esteem, being pessimistic, tend to protect whatever level of self-esteem they have and therefore set low standards for their own performance. When confronted with a specific lack of ability, they cannot deny its importance. When confronted with failure, they perform worse and assume that they tend to fail in everything. But they find consolation in the fact that others are inferior (downward comparison).

Those with high self-esteem, being optimistic, seek to enhance their already high self-esteem and therefore set high standards for themselves. They dismiss evidence of inability as being important. They react to failure by trying harder and by telling themselves and others of their other abilities and successes. And already feeling superior, they do not benefit from knowing that others are inferior.

Person-Environment Interaction

Choosing Environments

People with good self-esteem are likely to seek challenges, because they are secure in their own abilities. Confident of success, they are willing to reach for the brass ring, whether the arena is personal achievement or social rewards. For example, they are likely to seek a job that is risky but has great potential for personal

TABLE 8.6   High versus Low Self-Esteem

	Low self-esteem	High self-esteem
Outlook	Pessimistic	Optimistic
Self-cognitions	Protective	Enhancing
Goals	Set low	Set high
Specific low ability	Deemed important	Deemed unimportant
Reaction to failure	Poorer performance Overgeneralize	Try harder Compensate: other success
Downward comparison	Benefit	No benefit

advancement or money. At times their optimism may be excessive, and their abilities not up to the task, especially when their ego is threatened, as we saw earlier. When their ego is not threatened, their self-assurance is usually a positive attribute, for, as Bandura (1986) and others have documented, a feeling of self-efficacy can contribute to success.

People with poor self-esteem avoid challenges, because they are insecure about their abilities. They seek sure bets, tasks that are so easy as to guarantee success. If those with high self-esteem take the offensive in the expectation of success, people with low self-esteem adopt a defensive strategy of not failing. They will not take chances and desperately seek to avoid mistakes that, in their pessimism, they feel are likely to occur. In choosing environments, they play it safe, for example, preferring a secure job to a riskier one with greater potential.

Setting the Tone
Let us start with a small, task-oriented group. People who are high in self-esteem exude optimism with regard to both their own abilities and the chances of group success. Their confidence is often contagious, and others appreciate their buoyant self-assurance. They set a positive tone for the group.

Those low in self-esteem tend to be more pessimistic, and if this attitude prevails, it sets a negative tone that is not appreciated by other members of the group. People in task-oriented groups tend not to like gloomy predictions or those who question their own abilities; thus those low in self-esteem are likely to be pushed aside and ignored.

The situation may be reversed in interpersonal contexts, when there is no specific task but only social interaction. Here those with high self-esteem, who convey their intrinsic self-worth, may be seen as conceited. Thus some people who are high in self-esteem set a tone of superiority and so ask for rejection by others.

Those with low self-esteem fare better in interpersonal situations. Most of us are socialized to be at least superficially modest. We prefer those whose opinions of themselves are lower than our opinions of them, perhaps because it also contributes to our own feeling of superiority. Thus when those with low self-esteem set a tone of humility, they may gain acceptance by people who prefer this attitude in others and are only too willing to offer reassurance. In brief, we may prefer those high in self-esteem as members of a task-oriented group because they set a tone of optimism, but we like those low in self-esteem interpersonally because their tone of modesty is more socially acceptable and makes us feel good about ourselves.

Matching
When a husband and wife are both high in self-esteem, it should be good for the relationship. Each one's confidence sets a tone of optimism that is reinforced by the other's optimism. If the wife, for example, felt slighted by the husband, her strong feeling of self-worth should allow her to cope with this negative situation. And if the husband suffered reverses on the job, her optimism should help him to rebound.

When both members of the pair are low in self-esteem, we expect problems. Each will react to the other's slights or rejection with a devastating loss of self-worth. And the pessimism of the husband, for example, will resonate to the wife's dark assessments, creating a regime of gloom and doom.

A mismatch is not as bad. If the wife is high in self-esteem, she will be able to offer her husband the praise and affection he so desperately needs. And the husband will feel better about himself, knowing that he is married to such a self-assured person. His contribution is a consistent doubting of outcomes, which provides a needed counterweight to his wife's excessive optimism.

Development

It is not clear whether preschool children have the requisite cognitive ability and experience for an enduring, global sense of self-esteem, but it is present in elementary-school children (Harter, 1982). Harter constructed a questionnaire that has four correlated factors: *cognitive competence* (intelligence and doing well in school), *social competence* (having many friends, being liked, and being popular), *physical competence* (ability in sports and games), *general worth* (being sure of oneself, being happy as one is, and being a good person). Physical competence was the only factor to show a sex difference; boys were higher in this factor.

In cross-sectional research, Harter (1982) found that self-esteem held steady from grades three through six, dropped slightly at grade seven, and then held steady through grade nine. The gradual increase in self-esteem was confirmed in a longitudinal study by Simmons (1987). She also verified the drop at grade seven, but only for girls who were starting junior high school. Simmons argued that girls start puberty at about when grade seven begins, and that event, together with the shift from elementary school to junior high, caused the drop in self-esteem. To buttress her case, she counted the major changes that might occur for girls at the start of adolescence: entering junior high school, puberty, early onset of dating, geographical mobility, and death or divorce of parents. As the number of changes increased from one to three, self-esteem dropped sharply. Such changes had virtually no effect on the self-esteem of boys, however, perhaps because they enter adolescence later.

The developmental story continues with a longitudinal study by Block and Robins (1993), who followed adolescents from an average age of fifteen years to twenty-three years of age. There was moderate consistency over the eight-year period, some individuals being stable and others changing considerably. An examination of the personality of those who changed led to this conclusion: "Self-esteem change among females seems to be related to prior interpersonal qualities such as warmth and nurturance, whereas self-esteem change among males seems to be more strongly linked to prior self-focused characteristics such as ability to control personal anxiety level" (Block & Robins, 1993, pp. 920–921). The other sex difference involved the average direction of change over the eight-year period: Males increased slightly in self-esteem, but females dropped.

Developmental Theory

Discrepancies

The simplest assumption about a person's global self-esteem is that it consists of the sum of the components or sources of self-esteem, but is this assumption correct? Pelham and Swann (1989) had college students rate themselves for such components of self-esteem as intelligence, appearance, leadership, and emotional stability. A composite of these sources correlated only .50 with global self-esteem. Clearly, overall self-esteem is considerably more than the sum of its components.

Another perspective on this issue is to compare self-evaluation with a less subjective evaluation, that of friends and family who know the person. When these two evaluations match, there is nothing to explain. But what if a person's self-esteem is considerably higher than the evaluation made by others? An example might be a man who can make no special claims about his appearance, ability, or morality, is not especially liked or respected by others, cannot dominate them, and has little basis for vicarious self-esteem. Still, his self-esteem is enormous. Such conceit might be explained with the observation that people are egocentric and view themselves through rose-colored glasses. But how would we account for people whose self-esteem roughly matches the evaluations of them made by others? One possible answer is that they are not egocentric and do not wear rose-colored glasses. But this explanation begs the question, for we have not explained why only some people are egocentric.

Furthermore, the explanation would not account for persons whose self-esteem is clearly lower than the evaluation made of them by knowledgeable others. An example might be a man who is attractive, intelligent, receives affection from friends and family, and has some measure of status in a career. Yet, his global self-esteem does not come close to the sum of these sources. Perhaps he is clinically depressed, and his negative mood might explain his excessively low self-esteem. But most people with such humility are not pathologically depressed, and we are left with no explanation for their low self-evaluation.

For most people there is not much of a gap between self-esteem and evaluation by others. For an important minority, though, there is a discrepancy between these two evaluations. In this minority, some are conceited, and it is difficult to understand why their self-esteem is so high. Others show surprising humility, and it is puzzling why they cannot take account of their rich personal and social sources of self-esteem. Again, there must be more to global self-esteem than its individual components.

A Thought Experiment

Most of the misfortunes of life are spread out over time, but many calamities can pile up suddenly. Think of a single, middle-aged airline pilot of average appearance. He realizes that his ability to fly might be slipping but somehow convinces himself that he can still do the job. He is wrong, however, and is rightfully blamed for a crash that spares him but kills or maims a number of passengers. When the full truth is revealed, he loses his job, his friends and family shun him, and he realizes that he is guilty of causing the loss of life. None of the usual sources of self-esteem are now available to him. His ability to fly is diminished, he no longer can exercise command in the cockpit, others criticize him and are hostile, he can no longer depend on vicarious esteem from being a pilot, and he is ashamed of his own incompetence.

His self-esteem drops sharply, but does it go down to zero? Is there any self-esteem remaining after the usual sources of self-esteem are removed? When people are asked to place themselves in the shoes of this pilot, the typical answer is that some self-esteem remains. For the moment let us take this answer at face value and assume that there is a residual of self-esteem that does not depend on the six sources.

Core and Periphery

What would make a person feel intrinsically worthwhile? One answer that comes to mind is the love of others. But the affection offered by others is too inconsistent to be depended on. In close relationships there is inevitable friction, annoyance, and dislike, and today's loving friend can turn into tomorrow's angry acquaintance. Furthermore, being liked by others depends in part on attractiveness, ability, friendliness, and other desirable qualities. Being liked for such attributes means that when these attributes are no longer present, one will no longer receive affection. What is needed is affection that endures even when one does not display the positive qualities esteemed by others.

An individual can acquire intrinsic self-worth only if love is delivered consistently and without conditions. Such unconditional love rarely occurs in life, but it is typically offered in early infancy (see Chapter 5). Infants are tiny and helpless; they stimulate nurturance by parents. But newborn infants tend to be bald and wrinkled, and they display little of the physical attractiveness they may later have. They sleep most of the time and wear out parents with their need for constant care and their nighttime waking. Why, then, are infants so intensely loved by their parents? Because the infant is theirs. Needing no beauty or accomplishment, the infant merely has to be there to receive generous love and care.

During the first year of life, the infant learns that the most important and powerful figures, the parents, offer the best care and the greatest love without any conditions. The learning process is imitation, the parents being the model and the infant being the copier. Such imitation is different from most observational learning in that what is learned is directed toward the learner. There is the implicit, unverbalized attitude "If they love me, I must be great." From another perspective, that of symbolic interactionism (Mead, 1934), there are reflected appraisals coming from the parents, and these are internalized by the infant.

The infant need not do anything, just be there to be loved. Under this benevolent regime the infant acquires a core of self-esteem that does not depend on any specific sources: to paraphrase a philosopher, "I am, therefore I am worthwhile."

Infants who are loved unconditionally and consistently during the first year of life are expected to develop a robust core of self-esteem. In rare instances, unconditional parental love continues well beyond the first year of life, producing an insufferably conceited child who expects to be liked regardless of selfishness and nastiness. However, if the period of unconditional love is too short and parental love becomes conditional too early, the core will be smaller and weaker. Such children are expected to lack confidence in themselves.

These ideas are related to mother-infant attachment (Ainsworth, Blehar, Waters, & Wall, 1978). Securely attached infants are likely to approach strangers and other infants confidently, using the mother as a reliable base. Insecure infants lack this confidence and tend to be more fearful. Confidence, it will be recalled, is one of the major aspects of self-esteem, the other being self-love.

Sooner or later, unconditional love ends (though Carl Rogers [1951] assumes it continues). Parents and other caretakers do not show affection when the child acts badly. Hugs and kisses become less spontaneous and more in response to the child's good behavior. And parents may become angry and rejecting. Young children typically learn the contingencies of social reinforcement, for mere existence is no longer sufficient to generate praise and affection. Parental love is now mainly conditional, and any subsequent additions to the child's self-esteem depend on the sources discussed earlier.

Any and all of these sources can potentially be lost, which means that they contribute only to *peripheral self-esteem*. As these various sources accrue over the years, they become part of an enduring periphery around the core of self-esteem. An adult forty years old, for instance, may be able to look back on a history that includes some measure of attractiveness, ability, status, affection, praise, and respect from others, morality, and the value that comes from being part of successful groups. This accumulation over decades of life may be regarded as the stable portion of peripheral self-esteem. Older adults with good peripheral self-esteem can reflect on many decades of performance, power, social rewards, or morality. Time lends stability to such self-esteem.

There is also a transient portion of self-esteem that varies from day to day, from week to week. The familiar ups and downs of daily life, the temporary victories and defeats, acceptance and rejection, and success and failure all contribute to an unstable periphery. This part of self-esteem bobs up and down like a cork in water. In contrast, the stable part of peripheral self-esteem is less affected by daily events.

In summary, peripheral self-esteem derives from the various external sources of self-esteem. It consists mainly of an enduring, stable part that is built up over many years, and to a lesser extent, of an extremely unstable part that fluctuates daily or weekly. Core self-esteem derives from the unconditional love delivered by parents to their infants. The core accounts for the residual, implicit faith in one's worth that can be relied on when all external sources of self-esteem are removed. It is assumed to be resistant to forces that might diminish it or enhance it.

Romantic Love

Romantic love offers a possible exception to the immutability of core self-esteem. Recall that except for the sexual element such love is similar to the mother-infant bond of attachment (see Chapter 5). In both relationships there is mutual gazing, touching, intimacy, and unbounded love. The most relevant similarity for self-esteem is that each partner basks in the glow of the other's adulation. Like the love of parents for their infants, the love of romantic partners is unconditional.

Like unconditional parental love, the infatuation phase of adult love does not last. Eventually, each lover's eyes open. Minor slights and rejections show up, one partner may become jealous and temporarily hostile, and affection becomes contingent on how the other person behaves. The honeymoon ends, and more realistic and enduring adult love becomes a possibility.

Meanwhile, there has been a period of unconditional love between two adults during which their self-esteem goes through the ceiling. Does it add to the core of self-esteem? Insofar as the unconditional love of romantic partners resembles that of the parent-infant pair and other things are equal, the tentative answer must be yes.

But other things may not be equal. First, the infant is helpless and completely dependent on the parents, which makes the child a more powerful influence than an adult lover might be. Second, the infant has no basis for comparison with other relationships, and the primacy of the parent-infant bond (the first relationship) makes it enormously powerful. Adults have experienced other attachments and maintain the bonds of friendship and family relationships throughout the course of romantic love. Third, the infant knows virtually nothing about the world and is therefore more likely to imitate than are more experienced adults.

For these reasons, the answer becomes no; romantic love does not necessarily enhance core self-esteem. This position has the added advantage of parsimony: The simplest assumption is that core self-esteem is established in infancy and endures as a permanent, unchanging part of the self. Simplicity, however, is not the most important characteristic of a theoretical position, and we must be ready to accept the possibility of complexity. Thus romantic love might add to the core of self-esteem, and for completeness we might consider other complexities. The duration of romantic love might determine whether it adds to core self-esteem. Romantic love might add to core self-esteem for those high in total self-esteem but not for Lows. Or there might be more than one kind of romantic love, only some kinds contributing to core self-esteem.

Individual Differences

The theory requires an additional assumption to explain discrepancies in self-esteem: The size of the core in part determines the size of the periphery. The man with a large core engages in self-serving judgments about himself that are far in excess of the normal tendency to favor oneself. He places a higher value on the six sources of self-esteem as they apply to himself than would neutral observers. His periphery thereby becomes larger in his own eyes than it is when judged by others. As a result, his self-esteem is higher than the esteem he receives from others; he is conceited.

The man with a small core does not value himself intrinsically and therefore downgrades his appearance, ability, and other sources of self-esteem. His judgment of the size of the periphery is considerably less than that of neutral observers; he displays humility. These conjectures are based on research, reviewed earlier, showing how those high and low in self-esteem maintain their respective levels of self-esteem.

Most people are neither conceited nor humble, but they do engage in some self-enhancement. In terms of this theory, most people have an adequate core, not an excessive one, because most people receive unconditional love during infancy for a sufficient, though not excessive, length of time. If most people are not especially conceited or humble—that is, there is no particular discrepancy between core and periphery—does the theory apply at all to most people?

The answer is yes, but only the core is relevant. Recall the thought experiment, in which all sources of self-esteem were removed. Such a catastrophe must be extremely rare, but less extreme misfortunes do occur. People can lose their beauty because of an accident or illness, fail in school or on the job, be rejected by others or lose their respect, or behave so as to induce shame or guilt. What is the reaction to these threats to self-esteem? Those with a small core suffer a huge drop in self-esteem, because they cannot fall back on a feeling of intrinsic self-worth. Those with a large core rebound from disaster with minimal loss of self-esteem, for they can rely on a residual feeling of self-worth that requires no external sources.

Depressed people are known to have low self-esteem. Among college students, the correlation between self-esteem and scores on a well-known depression questionnaire was −.39 (Tennen & Herzberger, 1987). Self-esteem was also related to attributions for success and failure: "The tendency to make internal attributions for failure and external, unstable, and specific attributions for success is characteristic of individuals with low self-esteem independent of depression status" (p. 77). Low self-esteem shares a cognitive tendency with depression: Depressed college students, just like those low in self-esteem, overgeneralize after failure (Kernis, Brockner, & Frankel, 1989).

Low self-esteem is prevalent not only among depressives but among most clients who seek psychotherapy. Successful therapy is known to elevate self-esteem, and the major reason for this change is clear: a feeling of competence that derives from having mastered an issue and having removed a problem area from one's life. In terms of core-periphery theory, there is an addition to peripheral self-esteem.

But therapists know how difficult it is to alter the self-esteem of their clients. One reason is the attributional tendency mentioned above: " I am not responsible for success, but failure is my fault." Why is this tendency so strong, and why is low self-esteem so resistant to change? An answer to both questions may be the stability of core self-esteem. People with a weak core have difficulty taking credit for success because believing themselves to be competent or talented conflicts with their fundamental sense that they are not intrinsically worthwhile.

Can psychotherapy also enhance core self-esteem? The answer may be yes for relationship psychotherapies. The therapist is important, powerful, and interested in the client's welfare, features shared with the parents of infants. The client may defer so frequently and thoroughly to the therapist's judgment and evaluations as to be in the position of a young child with a parent. And the therapist, though not affectionate, offers virtually unconditional acceptance of the client and views the client as intrinsically worthwhile. These parallels between client-therapist and infant-parent, though far from complete, may be close enough to reinstate the conditions that enhance core self-esteem. Such an addition to the core is most likely to occur when the therapist comes closest to the parental role and when the therapy is of longer duration.

Like these particular comments about psychotherapy, the more general theory of core and periphery is speculative, but its assumptions are grounded in known facts about imitation, parent-infant attachment, and self-serving human tendencies. It relates parent-infant attachment to adult romantic love , and it accounts for the top-of-the-world feeling of infatuated adults. Finally, it offers a reasonable explanation for conceit, humility, and differential reactions to threats to self-esteem. Though the theory is difficult to test, requiring a longitudinal study starting at birth, it does offer an account of the otherwise puzzling phenomena of conceit and excessive humility.

Why Self-Esteem?

There are several possible responses to the question of why there is self-esteem. First, we are egocentric. We start life that way and, despite socialization, remain self-centered. Such egocentricity makes oneself more important than anything else. If oneself is important, it must be valuable, hence self-esteem.

Why are we so egocentric? There is an adaptive payoff in an ultimate sense, within the broader context of adaptiveness in evolution. Animals who selfishly look after themselves first are likely to be successful surviving and propagating their genes. Less selfish animals would be less successful. Even when we take into account inclusive fitness—altruism because others share genes (see Chapter 6)—each animal has 100% of its genes, whereas others have a lesser percentage, by definition.

Like all animals, we are reward seekers and punishment avoiders. When we receive rewards from the environment or from others, we experience pleasure. So we should be motivated to reward ourselves, and one way of doing so is by proclaiming self-esteem.

When we evaluate ourselves poorly, that is self-punishment. Why do people have low self-esteem, then? One answer is that others have treated them badly, especially parents early in life, as was suggested in core-periphery theory. Or perhaps there is an inherited tendency toward low (as well as high) self-esteem. If the question is, "How would such a maladaptive tendency remain in our gene pool?" the answer is that we also have inherited tendencies toward depression, which is maladaptive (note that low self-esteem accompanies depression).

Good self-esteem is also adaptive in a narrower sense in everyday life. Those high in self-esteem expect to succeed. Expecting success, they are more likely to persist in the face of failure than people with low self-esteem, who are more likely to give up. Recall the research on self-efficacy (Bandura, 1986).

Finally, a terror-management theory has been proposed, which assumes that self-esteem is needed primarily as a means of dealing with threat: "People need self-esteem because it is the central psychological mechanism for protecting individuals from the anxiety that awareness of their vulnerability and mortality would otherwise create" (Greenberg et al., 1992, p. 913). There are data consistent with this assumption, both the experimental findings of these authors reviewed earlier and the strong negative relationship between self-esteem and fear. However, the theory focuses exclusively on the defensive value of self-esteem in coping with threat and cannot account for its positive attributes: Those high in self-esteem tend to be more successful even in challenges that involve no threat.

Chapter 9

Identity

History

Most of the history of the self can be found in the writings of sociologists, who equated self with what is here called identity. At the turn of the century Cooley (1902) developed the idea of the looking-glass self: identity based on the appraisals of others. He assumed that we use the reactions of others as we might use a mirror, to determine who we are.

This notion was elaborated by Mead (1934), who suggested that identity arises from being able to take the perspective of others. The individual develops an identity "in so far as he can take the attitude of another and act toward himself as others act" (p. 171). As will be seen in the next chapter, Mead assumed that public self-awareness was the source of identity.

The work of David Riesman (1950) also provides a history of identity, although it is not so named. In the Middle Ages, virtually every aspect of life was controlled by a rigid set of rules. Identity was more or less fixed at birth by one's gender and social status, lending stability and a strong sense of continuity, for little changed over generations. People were so immersed in society that they just belonged, and no one was aware of the issue of identity any more than a fish is aware of water. Nevertheless, people had an identity that was determined by tradition. In Riesman's words, "The tradition-directed character hardly thinks of himself as an individual. Still less does it occur to him that he might shape his own destiny in terms of personal, lifelong goals" (p. 17).

The Renaissance and the Industrial Revolution tore apart the fabric of medieval society, and the changes they brought about increased mobility and opportunity for individuals. Now there were fewer rules and more choices. Parents and other authority figures trained their children to move toward goals, which become internalized. Riesman, using the metaphor of an internal gyroscope, suggested that these people set their sights on achieving and making individual choices, but the internal stabilizer is established by adolescence, and adults' choices are limited by it. Called inner-directed, these individuals' identity is defined by their individual commitments and achievements.

As industrial societies became centralized and increasing numbers of people moved to the more densely populated urban areas during the present century, they came into close contact with each other. Now people needed to be more sensitive to others, more attuned to cues from others. Family and local community waned as significant influences and sources of stability. Peer groups and other affiliations began to assume greater importance. People became other-directed. As Riesman (1950) points out, "What is common to all other-directeds is that their contemporaries are the source of direction for the individual—either those known to him or those with whom he is indirectly acquainted, through friends or through the mass media" (p. 22). Social roles, relationships, and affiliations now defined identity. Thus Riesman describes three sources of identity: traditional, having been born into a category; inner-directed, with individual achievements and a unique history; and other-directed, with social roles and affiliations.

Baumeister (1987) offered a similar history of a concept close to identity: self-definition. Again, in the medieval era, identity was defined by gender, kin, and social status. Gradually, these waned as determinants of identity, and during the middle and late nineteenth century the political and economic upheaval made absolute guidelines obsolete. Now adolescents had to arrive at an identity on their own, through commitments made with the knowledge that change was inevitable and there was little stability in the world. This development has since become known as the adolescent identity crisis.

The crisis was popularized in the twentieth century by Erik Erikson (1950), who revised Freud's psychosexual stages and added an adolescent stage of *identity versus role diffusion*. In his developmental theory of identity, the child identifies with adults and older peers, imitating them and wanting to be like them. Some of these models are rejected and some retained as the child matures, as the child and then the adolescent tries on this or that identity as one would clothes. "The final identity, then, as fixed at the end of adolescence, is superordinated to any single identification with individuals of the past: it includes all significant identifications, but it also alters them in order to make a unique and reasonably coherent whole of them" (Erikson, 1968, p. 161).

Clearly, Erikson emphasized personal relationships and the unique history of each person at the expense of the more sociological variables of gender, status, and ethnicity. In line with this emphasis, Erikson defined identity as a sense of individuality and a sense of sameness or continuity over the course of one's life. He was following the earlier lead of William James (1890), who suggested that by the word *I* we mean something that is always the same, though this feeling of continuity is lowest during adolescence.

Self-Esteem versus Identity

This historical account suggests that there are both personal and social components of identity. In this respect, identity is like self-esteem. There are other similarities; for example, ascribed status adds to self-esteem and is a source of identity. But identity and self-esteem also differ, and one way to clarify the concept of identity is to contrast the two.

The basic question relevant to self-esteem is "Am I worthwhile?" If the answer is positive, it adds to pride in oneself. If the answer is negative, the result is self-effacement. The basic question relevant to identity is "Who am I?" If the answer is positive, it lends meaning to life. If the answer is negative, reflecting a weak sense of identity, the result may be existential anxiety or a feeling of rootlessness.

We play a variety of social roles in our family, at work, and among friends. When roles are enacted satisfactorily, self-esteem is enhanced. A social role contributes to identity only if there is a personal investment in it. More generally, a basic question concerning self-esteem is "How well am I doing?" A basic question regarding identity is "How committed am I?"

Self-esteem is enhanced by romantic love, which offers unconditional love from a valued partner. Identity is enhanced by marriage, which adds a strongly committed social role and establishes a place for a person in the eyes of the community.

Being a member of a group can add to self-esteem through vicarious sharing in the group's triumphs. Being a member of a group can add to identity through a feeling of belonging to an entity larger than oneself, a group typically accorded recognition by the community. If the group is attacked, vicarious self-esteem is weakened, and total self-esteem is thereby diminished. If the group is attacked, one comes to its defense with a stronger sense of belonging, thereby enhancing identity.

Finally, there is the intriguing problem of amnesia. Can it affect self-esteem? Probably not, for self-esteem does not depend on any particular memory, only an intrinsic feeling of worthwhileness. But amnesia all but destroys identity, virtually by definition. In the absence of a history, there is no good answer to the question "Who am I?"

The various differences between self-esteem and identity are summarized in Table 9.1. Clearly, there are sufficient bases for distinguishing between the two, and in so doing we can discern the boundaries of the concept of identity. Yet there is a

TABLE 9.1   Self-Esteem versus Identity

Self-Esteem	Identity
How worthwhile am I?	Who am I?
Positive: adds pride in self	Positive: lends meaning to life
Negative: self-effacement	Negative: unease, rootlessness
How well a social role is played	Investment in a social role
Performance	Commitment
Romantic love adds to it	Marriage adds to it
Group: vicarious self-esteem	Group: a feeling of belonging
Group attacked: lower self-esteem	Group attacked: stronger identity
Amnesia has little effect	Amnesia obliterates it

crucial similarity between self-esteem and identity: the dichotomy between personal and social components.

The distinction between personal and social identity was the crux of Angyal's (1951) model of personality. Personal identity involves the seeking of autonomy and self-determination. Individuals wish to pursue their own goals relatively free of constraints. The extreme of this tendency, as we shall see later, is the seeking of uniqueness. In social identity the individual "strives to surrender himself willingly, to seek a home for himself and *to become an organic part of something that he conceives as greater than himself*" (p. 132). The social unit that provides a "home" may be family, clan, country, or religion.

Personal Identity

Personal identity may be roughly equated with individuality: how each of us is different from everyone else. In this age of computers, telephone answering machines, and mailings sent to "occupant," many people feel that they are regarded as nothing but ciphers. In crowded cities, many citizens feel that their individuality is buried beneath the weight of hordes of people. Yet in spite of these tendencies toward deindividuation, many people are motivated to regard themselves as special and take pleasure in the feeling of uniqueness.

The Public (Observable) Self

The term *personal* implies features that are intrinsic to the person and therefore, in a sense, private. If so, how can personal identity include public, observable aspects of the self? The answer is that observable characteristics can be used to differentiate oneself from everyone else, that is, to establish personal identity.

Appearance

Despite superficial resemblance , most people are easily recognized. Beautiful women and handsome men, many of whom become models or movie actors, are easily discriminated from most of the population. The movie star Cary Grant was so recognizable that he found it difficult to dine in a restaurant because other patrons stared or asked for autographs. And most people have no difficulty in identifying such celebrities as Michael Jordan and Michael Jackson. These are extreme examples that illustrate the more general point that each of us has a face and body that are distinguishable from those of other people and that therefore contribute to our uniqueness.

The need to be different may also be seen in individuals' use of cosmetics, hairstyles, and clothing, not only to enhance attractiveness but also to help establish individuality. At a party, a woman may become distressed to discover another woman wearing exactly the same dress. Some wealthy individuals are willing to pay exorbitant sums just to wear designer clothes that are one of a kind. Individuality in hairstyles and clothing are perhaps becoming as important to men as they historically have been to women. Consider the increasing range of hairstyles and clothing for men seen in recent years.

The need for individuality in appearance is closely tied to freedom of choice, a particularly salient issue among adolescents. Many schools still have dress codes, some of which specify length of hair for boys, length of skirts for girls, and such details as whether shirttails must be tucked into blue jeans. Parents may also restrict the hairstyles and clothing of their children. Adolescents tend to rebel against such regulations because they want the freedom of choice that allows them to establish their individuality.

Style

Each of us also possesses particular ways of doing things, a class of behaviors called *style* (see Buss, 1986b, chap. 8). Think about the variety of routine actions performed every day: walking, running, climbing stairs, standing, sitting, leaning, eating, brushing one's teeth, putting on or removing clothes, talking, smiling, frowning, grimacing, and so on through a list of instrumental and expressive behaviors. Each act is performed in a manner that is characteristic of the person. Some acts leave behind a record of individual style that is recognizably a product of that person. Obvious examples are handwriting and recorded speech, both of which have been analyzed in depth and are sufficiently distinctive to identify persons in a court of law.

Clearly, each of us has a unique set of behavioral styles that can be observed by others. But this stylistic pattern is at the same time a component of personal identity. Like other aspects of identity, behavioral style tends to remain out of awareness unless an event makes it salient. Such an event might be a video recording of one's actions or confrontation with the different style of an intimate other, which might happen, for example, when a couple move in together. Perhaps nothing elicits greater awareness of personal identity than contrast with another person.

Personality

Such contrast can also occur for personality traits. Consider two men: one an extreme extravert and the other shy. Both are so familiar with the way they are that it has long since been the focus of self-attention. But as they become acquainted, the enormous personality difference emphasizes the individuality of each. The shy person wonders how anyone can forge ahead and talk easily with strangers without being concerned about being intrusive. The extravert is puzzled about why anyone would be so self-conscious and constricted in social behavior. Each is made more aware of his personality, recognizing that it is an important part of his identity. But identity does not depend on awareness. Personality, like other components, may play a major role in identity without a person's being aware of its role.

Deviating from the norm in a positive direction is especially important for intelligence and, more specifically, for creativity. The artist, writer, musician, architect, cabinetmaker, or scientist who produces innovative and valuable work can stake a claim not only to enhanced self-esteem but also to personal identity. The sense of individuality that derives from creativity does not require the public acclaim of, say, a Nobel prize, only an awareness that one has been creative. Even an attempt to be original, whether or not it is successful, may produce at least a temporary feeling of individuality.

Most people, however, are neither creative nor at the extremes of personality trait dimensions. Their individuality resides in the particular pattern of personality traits and personal preferences that marks each person. There is a precise parallel with fingerprints, no two of which are alike. Fingerprints are identified on the basis of a small number of dimensions, along which people vary. When these dimensions are combined, the total number of patterns runs into many billions, enough to identify every person on earth. Similarly, each of us has a unique combination of personality traits and preferences, which provide a basis for personal identity.

Part of personality is a cluster of traits that are best called *character*. Its core is a sense of morality, but it is broader than just morality and may be summed up by Shakespeare's injunction "To thine own self be true." Thus a man of character could not cheat on his wife; a true scientist could not fake her data. The point is that most adults come to stand for something, and to act differently would be a betrayal of who they really are—that is, their personal identity.

Twins

In brief, appearance, behavioral style, and personality traits can contribute to personal identity because the pattern is unique. But there is an exception: identical twins, who are precisely the same in body, face, and style, and highly similar in personality. Some twins are sufficiently concerned with personal identity to alter their appearance by means of different hairstyles and clothing. Behavioral style and personality traits are difficult to change, but some twins, whether aware or not, do manage to diverge in personality traits. In a total sample of identical twins, the correlation for the trait of sociability was .51, but in a small group who were reared apart the correlation was .91 (Canter, 1973). Sociability is an inherited trait, but when identical twins are reared together, the correlation drops sharply. A reasonable conclusion is that at least one twin wishes to establish a distinct identity, which is achieved by differing in an important personality trait, as if to say, "Despite our obvious similarities, each of us is a distinct individual."

However, other identical twins cherish their sameness, deliberately dressing alike and enjoying the fact that others mistake one for the other. They often decide on the same college and the same career, and they may even marry similar people. Clearly, they share a personal identity and are delighted to do so. Being unique is obviously not important to them.

The Private Self

The Body

The most primitive identity issue is the dichotomy between me and not-me. Early in life infants come to know where their bodies end and the environment begins. As the months and years pass, they become familiar with the feel of their own bodies and gradually develop a sense of the importance of various body parts. No one thinks about which body parts are more central and which are more peripheral until there is serious injury or loss. For men, castration or the loss of the penis is a severe threat not only to the integrity of the body but to their masculine identity. In some states, convicted rapists are given the choice of castration or life imprisonment: male identity versus freedom. The removal of a breast may make a woman feel insecure about her attractiveness and femininity. For a woman without children, a hysterectomy may be equally traumatic in its denial of the possibility of motherhood.

Some parts of the body are psychologically and anatomically so peripheral that their loss poses no special threat to identity. When people are asked to choose a part of the body in the event that one part had to be amputated, most would start at the little toe of each foot, work their way through the other toes, move to the little finger of each hand, then to the earlobes, and so on.

This question is rarely asked, however, and most people do not suffer amputation of a body part. Ordinarily, then, we are not especially aware of the role of the body in our identity. But awareness is not the issue, only the importance of the body for identity. For most people, it is not only the earliest aspect of identity but one of the most basic.

Feelings and Daydreams

Infants express every irritation, every pain, and, generally, every experienced feeling. As the years pass, children gradually suppress some emotions and learn the value of secretiveness. They become aware of a private self, aspects of which are unknown to others. They experience body sensations and private feelings that remained unshared. Most people at one time or another develop a crush or generate an intense hatred for another person, experience awe at the grandeur of nature, or feel a communion with God. There are people who talk to God, have fantasies in which God or other heavenly beings appear before them, or experience a related epiphany. Such cognitions are assumed to contribute to personal identity.

These various feelings are difficult to express, hence the need for poets. Typically such experiences are suppressed, perhaps for fear of ridicule. But we are intensely aware of these various aspects of a rich inner life and know that they belong to ourselves and no one else. These experiences and the recognition of their covertness contribute to personal identity and the associated feeling of uniqueness.

Linked with feelings but nonetheless separable are daydreams: a journey to remote areas of the earth or a voyage to distant stars. More often a daydream is a romantic fantasy that involves a partner, sometimes with sex and sometimes not. And who has not had a fantasy of vaulting ambition: being president, an internationally known actor, painter, musician, or inventor, or a winner at the Olympics? Most dreams of glory are so grandiose that they risk ridicule if made public. By keeping them private, we not only avoid embarrassment but also maintain the myth that our fantasied goals are unique or at least rare, thereby enhancing personal identity.

Gender Identity

Gender identity involves both the public self and the private self. Other people can observe whether any individual is male or female (public), but, as mentioned above, each person has an inner sense of being male or female (private).

Gender identity starts with anatomy, which in turn begins with the action of sex hormones during prenatal development. Boys and girls differ not only in anatomy but in hormones that affect how the brain develops. Thus there is a biological basis for the feeling that one is male or female and the behaviors that accompany this feeling. There is also a psychological basis for personal gender identity. From birth onward, boys and girls are labeled appropriately, treated differently, and develop slightly different personality traits. By adolescence they are expected to become attracted to the opposite sex.

For most people, the inner feeling of being male or female (private) matches their sex-appropriate appearance, the gender labels, and the roles they typically adopt as adults (public). But for a minority there is a conflict between private and public gender identity: between the inner feeling and the body's sex characteristics. The problem may arise because of biological anomalies (Ehrhardt, 1985). During prenatal development, some females are exposed to a level of androgens that would be appropriate only for males. Such girls typically are tomboys who like active sports and prefer boys as playmates. Some children are genetically males (XY chromosomes) but are insensitive to androgens. They tend to be raised as girls, and in their play and preference for playmates they usually behave like girls. There are also people with the bodies of men who nevertheless feel like women. Some of them opt for a sex-change operation, which eliminates the conflict.

A conflict about gender identity may also arise because of the way children are socialized. Some parents, for example, do not emphasize sex differences in their children. Some mothers dress their young boys in girls' clothes and vice versa. The only boy in a large family of girls may develop some typically feminine tendencies, especially if the father is absent, or the only girl in a large family of boys may develop some masculine tendencies.

Gender identity has been assessed by questionnaires for each sex, the items deriving from a factor analysis of a large number of items relating to masculinity and femininity (Finn, 1988). The scale for men, which assesses their feminine gender identification, is presented in Table 9.2. Most of the items are the same as those on the women's scale, except for sex-appropriate substitutions. Thus the first men's item, "I often wonder what it would be like to be a woman," becomes "I often wonder what it would like to be a man" for women. The women's scale assesses masculine gender identification. For ease of exposition, the men's and women's scales will be called *gender misidentification*.

Only a minority of college men score high on the scale for men, and only a minority of women score high on the scale for women. But for this minority the way they feel about their sex identity conflicts with the way they are seen by others: Males are not sufficiently masculine, and females are not sufficiently feminine.

TABLE 9.2   Gender Identity Scale for Men

I often wonder what it would be like to be a woman.
I have thought about the possibility of a sex-change operation.
Several times I have dreamed I was a woman.
I have had sexual fantasies in which I was a woman.
I feel like part of me is male and part of me is female.
At times people in stores and restaurants have mistaken me for a woman.
I pride myself on being feminine.
I don't feel very feminine. (reversed)
I feel more comfortable around women than men.
In general, I understand women better than men.
I'm very different from most other men.
People think I should act more masculine than I like to.
I feel like I am more "fatherly" than "motherly." (reversed)
I would make a better husband than a wife. (reversed)
As a child, I sometimes wanted to be a girl.
My parents were hoping that I would be a girl.
I preferred to play with girls when I was a child.
As a child I rebelled against girlish things. (reversed)
As a child I was a "sissy."
It would be fun to go to a costume party dressed as a woman.
Putting on women's clothes would be a turn on.
I have been tempted to get my ears pierced.
I think men who wear an earring are sexy.
I'm glad they're finally making cosmetic products for men.
The idea of wearing make-up doesn't appeal to me. (reversed)
I would like to have longer eyelashes.

As might be expected, high scores on these scales are associated with low scores on traditional scales of masculinity and femininity. For men, the correlation between the gender misidentification and masculinity is –.41; for women, the correlation between gender misidentification and femininity is –.27 (Finn, 1988). Having a gender-inappropriate identity is also associated with homosexuality (Finn, 1988). The correlation between gender misidentity and homosexual tendencies is .58 for men and .34 for women. Men with a feminine orientation often tend to be homosexual, whereas for women with a masculine orientation the relationship between gender misidentity and homosexuality is much weaker.

We can only speculate about this sex difference. Socialization may be relevant, masculinity being more stringently socialized than femininity. If boys dress up in girls' clothes, they likely will be reprimanded or teased more severely than girls who dress up in boys' clothes. Blue jeans are available to girls, but dresses are forbidden to boys. It is merely mild teasing to call a girl a tomboy but strong ridicule to call a boy a sissy.

Gender roles are a powerful source of identity for a number of men and women. Some men view it as the height of masculinity to serve as the protector, the provider, and the decision maker; in this traditional role, sexual and physical prowess may be means of demonstrating *machismo*. Some women identify strongly with the traditional female role, in which the woman is the caretaker and obedient and supportive of the man; qualities such as physical beauty and fertility may be significant in demonstrating femininity.

Gender identity may be more crucial for men than for women because, generally, the masculine role is more sharply defined and more valued by society than the feminine role and masculine traits are more highly rewarded. Therefore, any boy who resists masculine socialization and tends to adopt a feminine gender identity must be more strongly driven to do so than a girl who resists feminine socialization and adopts a masculine orientation. Research has found that boys who are seen as sissies are more likely to become homosexuals than are girls who are seen as tomboys (Green, 1985).

To what lengths will men go to establish their masculinity? In the 1960s, college men were tested for tolerance of painful electric shock and then told that women could take more painful shock than men (Buss & Portnoy, 1967). After hearing that, the men were willing to tolerate considerably more painful shock than previously.

In recent years, however, the qualities that constitute appropriate gender identities for men and women seemingly have become less specific and maybe even more universal. That is, more men and women are adapting or even abandoning traditional roles and opting for more egalitarian roles in which women are entitled to be successful and decisive and men are entitled to be nurturing and emotional. As a result, more women are enjoying careers and more men are enjoying parenting.

Perhaps one of the major forces in creating these changes has been the women's liberation movement, which originated in the early 1970s. Supporters of this movement, called *feminists*, assert that women are just as capable as men, that women deserve equal rights in all walks of life, and that female gender identity should be valued as much as male gender identity. These ideals can be traced back to the suffragists of the nineteenth and early twentieth centuries, who earned the right to vote for American women. It will be interesting to see where feminism leads Americans—men and women—in the next fifty or one hundred years.

Public and Private Components

The public and private components of personal identity are listed in Table 9.3. Appearance, style, and personality traits, being public, may be seen differently by others than by self-examining persons. When there is a difference in perspective, individuals may defend their view of themselves: "The basic argument here is that people are highly motivated to verify their self-conceptions, and this motivation shapes the nature of the identity negotiation process. Some strategies of self-verification are interpersonal, involving people's efforts to bring others to see them as they see themselves. Other strategies are intrapsychic, involving processes through which people see more self-confirmatory evidence than actually exists" (Swann, 1987, p. 1047). Such self-verification deals only with the public aspects of

TABLE 9.3   Components of Personal Identity

Public components	Private components
Appearance	Body
Behavioral style	Feelings, daydreams
Personality traits	Gender identity

personal identity, for no one needs to confirm awareness of one's body, feelings and daydreams, and one's experience of gender identity, which cannot be observed by anyone else.

Like virtually every component of personality tendencies, there are individual differences in the importance of the six components of identity. Appearance surely ranks higher for an attractive person than for a plain person, and daydreams are more important for most adolescents than for people who are aged. For some people the external, observable features of themselves are more important: appearance, style, and personality traits. Other people are more attuned to the internal, covert parts of themselves; thus the private aspects of personal identity (body, feelings, daydreams, and gender identity) contribute more to identity.

But the fact that people differ does not deny general tendencies. Which components are likely to be the source of a feeling of individuality for most people? In U.S. society, a reasonable guess is the private components. Being unobservable, our inner experiences can be regarded as unique and therefore constitute more important sources of personal identity than the public features of ourselves. Among the private sources, body would seem to rank first, followed by gender identity, feelings, and daydreams.

Social Identity

Social identity derives from a variety of sources, which may be divided into two classes. The first consists of universal social entities: kinship, ethnicity, religion, and nationality. The second class consists of organized groups in the mainstream—clubs and vocations—and outcast groups that have a negative identity.

Kinship

Marriage

In all societies, marriage is marked by ceremony. Until recently in U.S. society marriage was regarded as the natural consequence of reaching adult status. Older single women were considered old maids, incapable of attracting men. Older single men were considered playboys, incapable of love and commitment. Divorce was difficult, and children born out of wedlock were demeaned. Now, many men and women choose not to marry and are not censured for it, even when they become single parents. Divorce is easy. As a result, being a husband or wife is not as important a source of identity as it once was.

Until recently, the change from single to married status was perhaps greater for a woman because she usually took her husband's name. Now, some women retain their family names, some because they already have professional identities, and others because they believe it marks their individuality: I am a person in my own right, not just someone's wife. Does a woman who retains her family name have less of a social identity as a wife? Not necessarily, but it is an interesting question for researchers.

However, for most adults, being a husband or wife is still a major way of defining themselves. This fact is underscored when a marriage is dissolved. Married people have a secure place in the community, which recognizes them as basic to the core family. After divorce, the man and woman revert to the now-unfamiliar identity of a single person. Some people, especially those raised in traditional families, feel a loss of social identity. And whenever there is such a loss or the threat of such a loss, the issue of identity becomes salient: What was previously taken for granted now breaks into awareness.

In divorce, women again are faced with the issue of their surname. The woman's retention of her married name might imply a partial retention of the married identity. A return to her family name might represent a complete rejection of the marriage and any identity attached to it.

Of course, there is now a new social identity: divorced person. Men and women are clearly labeled this way, and friends attempt to fix them up with dates or potential spouses. There are various support groups and clubs for divorced people and more specialized groups for single parents. As with any new identity, it takes time to adjust to being labeled a divorced person.

The death of a spouse also brings marriage to an end. In addition to the loss of a loved one, there is the loss of identity as a married person. The community and the law recognize survivors as widows or widowers. There is no sense of personal responsibility for the loss, as there is in divorce. But widowhood usually occurs after many decades of marriage, so the loss of social identity may be felt even more keenly. After so many years of being a married person, it feels strange to be a widow or widower.

Parents

Like the role of married person, the role of parent is recognized by the community and its laws and is strongly supported by both. In all societies, boys and girls are socialized to become parents, a role that is willingly adopted by most adults. It is a potent source of identity; for many parents it is so powerful that they work harder just to make a better life for their children. The father of two teenage children told me that he honored their desire to attend an exclusive, expensive private college. Asked how he and his wife could afford that, he replied that they would be out of debt in about fifteen years. An example of an even greater sacrifice is the donation of an organ to one's child.

Which is generally a stronger identity, that of mother or father? When parental identity is defined as nurturing and caretaking, it seems that being a mother is the stronger role. Mothers have a much greater biological investment in their children and usually do most of the child rearing. There are exceptions, of course, including fathers who receive custody of their children after a divorce and assume the primary caretaking role, but these situations are not the norm. The belief that maternal identity is stronger than paternal identity is a popular one.

The single parent, who must be both mother and father to the children, bears a much larger share of responsibility for them than a married parent. It follows that parenthood is a stronger source of identity for a single parent than for a married parent.

One manifestation of parental identity is altruism. Recall that most parents work for a better life for their children, often sacrificing their own well-being (see Chapter 6). Though such altruistic behavior is also driven by the fact of shared genes, parental identity is a strong contributor.

Children

For children of an intact family, family is a strong source of identity, for they have yet to develop other sources that will accrue later. For this reason, divorce may be as much of a problem for children's identity as for their parents'. Certainly, there is some confusion and a diffusion of roles and relationships. If the mother remarries, they now have both a stepfather and a biological father. If the mother assumes the name of her new husband, do they change their name or retain the name of their biological father? If the children are young and the stepfather assumes the paternal role with them, do they now identify with this new family, retain their previous familial identity, or, more likely, have a split familial identity? Whatever the outcome, familial identity is chaotic while they adjust to the new reality.

Familial identity is more problematical for adopted children who know that they are adopted. If they are adolescents when they discover that they are adopted, there may be an identity crisis. In an English study called "Now I know who I really am," such adopted children split on their reaction (Haimes, 1987). One group was profoundly affected and changed their name back to that of the biological parent. Then they reconstituted the sequence of their life this way: original (birth) identity, altered by adoption to a false identity; discovery of birth identity, reappraisal of situation; return to original, true identity. The other group was minimally affected. They merely added their original identity to their adoptive family identity and reported that the discovery of their adopted status made little difference in who they were.

Extended Family

In these days of great mobility, many people lose contact with grandparents, aunts, uncles, and cousins. Those who do maintain a continuing, close relationship because of geographical proximity or regular family reunions tend to develop a strong sense of their place in the context of a broader familial unit. This familial identity is especially strong in families who trace their roots back over a number of generations—whether that leads to England or Africa. Historic organizations such as Daughters of the American Revolution and other more contemporary groups with ethnic and religious affiliations unite families who can trace their heritage to past events or groups and thus further strengthen familial identity. I once received a letter from a woman who was tracing those with the Buss name back nine hundred years to migrants from Holland to England.

In some families, traditions are handed down from one generation to the next. Some families can trace the tradition of military service through several generations. In each generation, for instance, at least one son has entered the Naval Academy. Similar traditions may be found in other fields—medicine, teaching, or government service, perhaps. As women's roles continue to evolve, there are related expectations of daughters, including vocational and even military traditions. The more the family values traditions, the stronger the contribution of family roots to each person's identity.

An adult member of an extended family has a network of relationships. A woman, for example, can be a wife, mother, sister, daughter, cousin, aunt, niece, and granddaughter. These varied relationships have posed a problem for some women. As one woman observed, "I was a daughter, then a wife, and then a mother. My identity was defined by my relationships with others. When do I get to be an individual in my own right?" The sources of her identity were mainly social, and she was appealing for personal sources of identity.

Ethnicity

We start out life as members of an ethnic group, a nation, and a religion. We can alter our original nationality and religion, but ethnicity is almost always permanent. One's physical characteristics, especially facial features and skin color, often lead to immediate labeling by others and are a major contributor to ethnic identity. But there is also a more private aspect. At issue here is not how others regard a person but the feeling that one belongs, as reflected in such verbalizations as "My fate and future are bound up with my own group," "I feel attached to my group," and "I feel strong bonds toward my group" (Phinney, 1990, p. 504). As might be expected, there are marked individual differences in this commitment to an ethnic identity.

Most whites are unaware of their ethnic identity, because they swim in a sea of white people. Housing in U.S. society is still largely segregated, each ethnic group having its own enclave. At school, however, there is some mixing of the races, and this is expected to cause those in the minority to become more aware of their ethnic identity. When schoolchildren were asked to tell about themselves, white children hardly mentioned ethnicity at all, whereas minority children mentioned ethnicity with some frequency (McQuire, McGuire, Child, & Fujioka, 1978).

The salience of being identified as Black in the United States may be one reason many Blacks prefer to attend Black colleges. There, they seldom or never see a white face and can therefore develop a collective identity in a way similar to that of whites who attend predominantly white colleges.

The feeling of belonging is strengthened when the minority group is subjected to bigotry on the part of the group that predominates. Though the United States has the reputation of being a melting pot, nonwhites have never been truly integrated. Here, the ethnic identity of Caucasians is weak, except for members of hate groups (see below). There are much stronger group identities among Blacks, Asians, and Native Americans. Why?

There appear to be two reasons. First, because they may have different physical characteristics, members of these groups may be readily identifiable and therefore quickly labeled. When they mix with the white majority, their ethnicity may be brought home strongly. Second, as mentioned earlier, attacks on a group may lead to a "circling of wagons" to defend the group against the attacks. This we-versus-them attitude usually strengthens group identity.

Religion

Virtually everyone is born into a family that has a specific religion. The United States is predominantly Christian, and within this religion there are enormous variations in the strength of this identity. There are people who not only attend church regularly but also read the Bible daily, contribute money by tithing, and would not consider marrying outside the faith. At the other extreme are those who have drifted away from the church, which has no special hold on them, and they often intermarry.

Religious identity is expected to be stronger when the particular religion commands obedience in everyday details. Thus until a few decades ago Catholics were forbidden to eat meat on Friday, and to this day they are not supposed to use any kind of artificial birth control. The everyday routine of Orthodox Jews is specified in even greater detail: the time of prayer, the allowable food and how it is prepared, and the precise dishes and cutlery to be used. Orthodox Jews are estimated to have the strongest religious identity of any religious group. It is further strengthened by a prevailing anti-Semitism, another example of intensified identity when a group is attacked.

Religious identity is magnified when members of two religions occupy the same country and contend for dominance, as may be seen in Ireland. When both religious and cultural backgrounds clash, group identity is even more intensified: Witness the struggles within Israel between the ruling Jews and the subordinate Palestinians, most of whom are Muslims. Or consider the conflict between the Christian Serbs and the Muslim Croats in what was once Yugoslavia.

Place

Place includes more than identity with one's country, but nationalism is surely the more pervasive of the sources of identity involving place or citizenship. Most U.S. citizens, indeed, citizens of most countries, have strong feelings of patriotism, for our children are brought up to be patriotic. We are taught to salute the flag. Some people burned the American flag as a protest against international policies, especially during the Vietnam War. This flag burning elicited a storm of patriotism and demands for punishment of the protesters. Any war, justified or not, brings out the latent patriotism of citizens: Think of the men and women who volunteered for duty when Pearl Harbor was attacked in 1941 and the sense of national unity aroused by the Gulf War in 1991.

Aside from war, competition elicits patriotism. One example is our enthusiasm for our Olympic team and our national pride when medals are won. Another example is the Japan bashing and "Buy American" trend that have developed because of economic competition with Japan.

Patriotism demands that we sacrifice in the name of our country, not only in war but in any competition. In another part of a study mentioned earlier (Buss & Portnoy, 1967), college men were tested for tolerance of painful electric shocks and then told that Russian men had been found to tolerate more pain than men from the United States. Subsequently, these subjects tolerated more intense pain than before. However, such shows of patriotism are not as important for competition with every country. After all, when the study was conducted, during the 1960s, the Russians were the United States' main enemy in the Cold War. In the same study, when men were told that our friends the Canadians tolerated more shock, the subjects increased their pain tolerance only a little.

In the United States, we have a particular source of identity that most foreigners cannot comprehend: as citizens of a particular state. Thus a person has to be born in Indiana to qualify as a Hoosier. Texas is more lenient and will allow latecomers to be known as Texans if they have resided there long enough and love the state. And in that large state, an important part of identity is being a Texan.

Foreigners can more easily understand the strong bond that exists between some cities and their citizens. New Yorkers and Bostonians are known for it, and San Franciscans may also fall into this group. Parisians certainly do. Citizens of each of these places openly criticize the city but defend it against criticism by anyone else and feel that it is the best city in the world. If they had to move to another city, they feel they would lose a piece of their identity.

In the United States, this feeling of allegiance is strengthened by the presence of professional baseball, football, and basketball teams. The identity does not necessarily depend on the team's winning: Chicago has a love affair with the Cubs even though they have not been champions in living memory.

Organized Social Groups

Fraternities and sororities are a prime source of social identity. College students live together almost like siblings, and there is an analogue of the extended family: the national fraternity. Once a student becomes a member, he or she is there for life. Fraternity brothers and sorority sisters, even when they are strangers, are expected to help each other.

The feeling of belonging is enhanced by the selection process ("You have been chosen") and the punishment of initiation. The more severe the initiation rites, the more the group is liked (Aronson & Mills, 1959). There are secret ceremonies and secret handshakes. Rivalry is prominent, and the competition intensifies commitment and the group feeling. Members are expected occasionally to submerge personal needs to the needs of the group. For some members, especially officers, the fraternity or sorority is a major component of their social identity.

Despite some obvious differences, there are similarities between fraternities or sororities and gangs. Just as fraternities and sororities offer places for students who might get lost in the crowd, so gangs offer a place for adolescents who wander unprotected in poor neighborhoods. Like fraternities and sororities, gangs have initiation rites, a hierarchy of older and newer members, status among access to members of the opposite sex, pressure for individuals to subordinate personal goals to group goals, and competition with peer groups. Gangs also engender a strong sense of belonging to a group, often identifying themselves by the jackets worn by members and the territory they stake out. Also like fraternities and sororities, gang membership may extend into adulthood, at least in terms of one's affiliations and loyalties, but gangs may have little enduring value as a component of identity among older adults.

Let us return to educational organizations. For some people, the college experience is one of life's highlights, and the particular college contributes to their social identity. For some students, the university may be regarded as an extension of themselves, and this is especially true of die-hard fans of athletic teams. At Indiana University, basketball is the major sport, a fact that was used to study how students identified with the university (Hirt, Zillman, Erickson, & Kennedy, 1992). Students watched a live basketball game on television, during which their team either won or lost. The team's success or failure significantly affected only the truly dedicated fans: "[Their identity] is so integral to their sense of self that they respond to team outcomes as if they directly affected the self. Success on the part of their team led these fans to assess *their own* abilities more positively, whereas team failure resulted in lower estimates of *their own* abilities" (p. 736). Notice that these findings are related to the fact that self-esteem may be maintained or boosted by basking in reflected glory (Cialdini et al., 1976).

After graduating, some people become boosters and root for their college's athletic teams, contribute money, return for reunions, and display their status as alumni, putting a "Texas Exes" sticker on their car, for example. This identity is even stronger when both spouses are from the same college, which occurs frequently. They may become active in college affairs, perhaps even serve on the board of trustees; they may want their children to attend the same college. Their college affiliation continues to play a major role in defining who they are long after graduation.

Vocation

Why is vocation a source of identity? To answer this question, we might start with medieval guilds, where a young man would apprentice to a master, perhaps a stonemason. After years of apprenticeship, increasing skill, and maturity, the man would eventually be admitted to the guild. It was a life appointment; only members of the guild were allowed to engage in stonemasonry. Being a stonemason became a crucial part of the guild member's social identity.

One analogue of guilds in our time are the professional societies that oversee licensing. No one can practice law, for instance, without having completed the special education required and passing a licensing exam. Generally, people who enter a profession must pass through a selection process and a period of study. Like immigrants who want citizenship, they have to work to become a professional. Licensed plumbers, for example, must first apprentice in somewhat the same way their forebears did in the Middle Ages.

Once people attain the required skills, most of them work in that job or profession for decades, probably most of their adult life. What is the relevance for identity? Ask teachers this question, and most of them will offer this kind of reply: "I have a strong commitment to helping students to learn, and I make my living doing that. Having done it for years adds to my sense of sameness. Commitment and continuity contribute strongly to my social identity: Ask me who I am and an important part of the answer is teacher."

Negative Identity

Most social identities are part of mainstream society and are regarded as positive or at least neutral. But some groups are outside the mainstream, and their members are branded as outcasts. They may be said to have a negative identity, and it typically is a stronger identity than the collective identity of those in the mainstream, because they are continually being attacked.

Perhaps the largest group in the United States with a negative identity are homosexuals. Earlier, gender identity was called a personal identity, but homosexuals also have a social identity thrust on them because they are often branded as deviants. Some homosexuals react by keeping quiet about their sexual preference, because of the bigotry of others. Others react by flaunting their homosexuality in provocative dress and behavior. In the last decade or two, many have become militant in fighting against prejudice, which of course strengthens their social identity. In San Francisco, for instance, the gay community is a significant political force.

Homosexuals are one of a number of social groups targeted by *hate groups:* skinheads, neo-Nazis, members of the Ku Klux Klan, and so on. These individuals are easily recognized by their haircuts, uniforms, or sheets, respectively. The Nazis and KKK members tend to have initiation rites and secret ceremonies, which help solidify the group. Their negative social identity is further enhanced by the opposition they encounter, which engenders a we-versus-them attitude.

The best-organized of the social groups with negative identities is the Mafia. Its members are initiated and sworn never to testify against other members on pain of death. Most Mafia members marry within the clan and have a strong sense of family; in a way the Mafia is like an extended family. These various characteristics make this social identity the strongest of any social identity, whether positive or negative.

Mafia members are mainly Italians, and especially Sicilians; on account of this identification the great majority of Italian Americans have been subjected to the prejudicial view that most Italians are criminals. In fact, though, organized crime is not exclusive to Italian Americans or the Mafia.

Convicted felons have a much looser social identity. Cast out of mainstream society by the law, they develop their own subculture and language idioms. Criminality is often a way of life for them, an intrinsic part of their social identity, which is part of the difficulty of "going straight."

Sources of Social Identity

The sources of social identity are listed in Table 9.4. We are born into kinship and race ethnicity and cannot escape from them. We are born into a nationality and a religion, but we can relinquish both or change them. However, most people retain their original nationality and religion. Thus the first four sources may be regarded as our roots.

The last three sources are voluntary except for the negative identity of homosexuality. The rest of these sources may be transitory, ending with adulthood. Organized social groups, vocation, and negative identity do not involve our roots

---

TABLE 9.4   Sources of Social Identity

Kinship

> Core family: spouse, parent, child
> Extended family: roots

Race/Ethnicity

Place

> National
> State

Religion

Organized social groups

> Fraternity
> Gang
> Alumni

Vocation

Negative Identity

> Sexual orientation
> Hate groups
> Criminals

---

and therefore are expected to be less important aspects of social identity for most people, though of course there are individual differences.

These various sources also differ along several dimensions. We are born into kinship groups, religion, and nationality but voluntarily join clubs, vocational groups, and outcast groups. Some involve face-to-face contact. Kinship certainly does, as do fraternities and sororities, gangs, hate groups, and criminal partnerships. Ethnicity, religion, and place are more distant, enormous affiliation groups. The closeness of contact, however, does not determine how powerful the source is as a contributor to social identity. Thus for some people the most important source is religion, and for others it is national identity. The strength of affiliation with any group is intensified when the group is attacked; this holds especially for racial, ethnic, religious, and national minorities and the various groups with a negative identity. And awareness of any source of identity varies from person to person. Identity also depends on events that can render it salient, such as attack from outside. In brief, there are four dimensions of social identity: (1) origin, innate versus voluntary; (2) interaction, close versus distant; (3) commitment, intense versus casual; and (4) awareness, keen versus vague.

There is no research on all the sources of social identity, but two studies come close to covering all (Buss & Portnoy, 1967; Buss, 1992). The former was conducted at the University of Pittsburgh, the latter, at the University of Texas, each with more than three hundred subjects. Reference groups appropriate to college students were selected, and subjects were instructed to rank them for how strongly committed they were, how important it was to belong to the group, or how strongly they felt as members of the group. The groups were listed in alphabetical order: age, American, club, college, gender, religion, state, and vocation. For age, subjects were to contrast their peer group with those younger and older. For club, they were to consider current, past, or future fraternities, sororities, or other meaningful clubs. For vocation, they were to consider the one they were aiming for.

The rankings, presented in Table 9.5, are in order of the ranking for men in the 1967 study. Notice that a rank of 1 is the highest and a rank of 8 is the lowest. In 1967, the strongest identification was for nationality, followed by gender and religion, and then vocation and age, with college, club, and state being the lowest ranked. The only sex difference was for vocation, women ranking it higher than men.

The pattern was different in 1992, so let us compare the two sets of ranks that are separated by twenty-five years: the rows of the table. The significance of being American dropped sharply, and so did that of religion. The peer group (age) became more important, and so did gender. Could these differences be due to the different regions of the country in which the studies were carried out, North versus Southwest? It is hard to believe that patriotism and religion are weaker in Texas than in Pittsburgh, and there is no obvious reason why the peer group would be stronger in the Southwest than in the North. Therefore, these shifts in sources of identity are probably due to changes over more than a generation, not to regional differences.

There were other shifts that might be attributed to region. Thus for women only, vocation became less important, perhaps not because of a generational dif-

TABLE 9.5   Rankings* of Social Identity

Reference group		Pittsburgh (1967)	Texas (1992)
American	Men	2.3	3.5
	Women	2.5	4.0
Gender	Men	3.3	3.3
	Women	3.2	2.0
Religion	Men	3.3	4.8
	Women	3.0	4.6
Vocation	Men	4.3	4.6
	Women	3.0	4.9
Age	Men	5.0	4.2
	Women	5.2	3.7
College	Men	5.3	4.2
	Women	5.0	4.5
Club	Men	5.7	5.8
	Women	6.4	6.2
State	Men	6.5	5.5
	Women	6.2	5.8

*Note: 1 = highest rank, 8 = lowest rank.

ference but because women might be more conservative in Texas. Among the lower-ranking reference groups, college and state were ranked higher by Texas students than by Pittsburgh students. Again, region probably played a role. Texas residents are known more for state pride than are Pennsylvania residents, and, as one of the prime universities in the state, the University of Texas may be more valued among its students than the University of Pittsburgh. Notice, however, that none of these reference groups were ranked especially high for social identity.

Now examine the righthand column, particularly the sex differences in the current rankings of identity. A rank difference of .5 appears to be meaningful. On this basis, women ranked gender much higher than men. For men, the highest ranks were for American and gender, with little difference between them. For women, gender received the top ranking, with American far behind. The only other sex difference was a minimal one, women ranking age a little higher than men.

A few words of caution are needed. First, these are college students and a very limited sample at that. Noncollege people of the same age might have a different kind of social identity, and even college students are expected to shift as they mature. Second, these are average rankings, with a fair amount of variability. Third, if we sampled a church group, religion would likely assume a higher ranking; if we sampled a military group, American would probably rank higher; and if we sampled fraternity officers, club would likely rank higher. Still, these data represent virtually the only available findings that compare the strength of various social identities, and, as such, they are useful in drawing tentative conclusions.

The past several decades have seen women stream into the work force, and everyone today seems much more aware of what are called women's issues. Similarly, in 1967 the Vietnam War made most people aware of their patriotism, even those who were opposed to the war, and this may explain why nationality was predominant at that time. Events since then have made many people in the United States wary of the excesses of patriotism. Young people are no longer as proud of their country, nor do they identify with it as strongly, though nationality still ranks relatively high, especially for men. And religion has dropped as a source of identity, even in Texas, which is part of the Bible Belt. It will be interesting to see how these patterns change over the next generation.

Personal and Social Identity

So far, each component has been described as a source of either personal or social identity. This either-or dichotomy holds for most of the sources, but a few are the source of *both* personal and social identity. Homosexuality is one example. Religion is another. Religion is a source of social identity, one that most of us are born into and retain throughout life. But religion may be more than just belonging to a particular sect or attending a particular house of worship. Some people maintain a personal relationship with God. They talk to God and believe that he reveals himself to them in direct or indirect ways. It is a private matter for them, linked to organized religion but separable from it. For such people, religion is a source of both social and personal identity.

Continuity and Discontinuity

Continuity of identity, the feeling of sameness over time and across situations, can be either personal or social. As evidence of personal continuity, feelings, daydreams, and ambitions can be recalled with amusement, sadness, pride, or regret. These memories alone or together with the autobiography that each of us constructs, whether veridical or fictional, elicit a feeling of continuity that defies changes in appearance, values, and even personality. Recall the adopted children who discovered their biological parents (Haimes, 1987). Some of them saw the event as part of a continuous identity, with new knowledge merely supplementing the same identity. Others saw their identity as discontinuous, and they marked this by changing their names.

But there are also social sources of continuity: the same set of relatives, perhaps of friends, the same race, nationality, and religion. The commitments each of us makes to social roles, social organizations, and vocation tend to change little in adulthood. Most adults settle into a life that is organized around the various social groups they were born into and those they chose. One's place in these stable entities offers a sense of being the same now as decades ago.

The other side of the coin is *discontinuity:* the sense of a break with one's past identity. Discontinuity sensitizes people to the issue of identity, which otherwise remains largely out of awareness for most people (R. H. Turner, 1975). Discontinuity tends to occur when there are threats to one's personal identity that trigger defenses of it, changes in appearance or the inside of the body, or a desired change in identity, the extreme of which would be a sex change. And there are other causes. The death of a spouse or divorce challenges the identity of the remaining spouse and any children. A move to a different part of the country or emigration to another country disturbs national identity. A person's belief in the family religion or faith in God may be shaken and religion abandoned. Body integrity may be threatened by amputation of a limb or by a mastectomy.

Aside from such adventitious events, there are two times during life when identity is likely to be unstable. One is during the teenage years, when adolescents are leaving childhood and are in the process of establishing an adult identity. The other time is the forties, when the makeup of the family is changing, there may be career problems, and the aging process starts to take its toll.

There may also be a sense of discontinuity across the various social roles that adults assume on an everyday basis. Some people see themselves as behaving very differently as they move from one role to another (discontinuity), but others see consistency and integration of behavior across roles (continuity). Those with self-reported discontinuity across roles tend to be low in self-esteem, anxious, depressed, and neurotic (Donahue, Robins, Roberts, & John, 1993). These tendencies were no transient phenomenon of early adulthood, for the relationships between discontinuity and maladjustment tended to be stable over several decades.

Conflict

Recall that one source of personal identity is the aspect of personality called character. A person's moral stance can collide with his or her social identity. Consider a patriotic man who is also a pacifist. He loves his country but is against war on principle. Does he go along with his patriotism and join the armed forces, or does he refuse to fight and risk prison or at least social censure? That was the dilemma faced by some men in both world wars and in the Vietnam War. Some joined the armed forces, some resisted, and some left the country.

A conflict over pacifism occurs only periodically, but another conflict is always with us. Consider religious Catholics who on principle believe that only a woman should decide whether to terminate her own pregnancy. As good Catholics, they should respect the antiabortion stance of their church, but as persons who believe in the sanctity of a woman's body, they are pro-choice. Most of them resolve the conflict in one direction or the other but remain conflicted and ambivalent.

Multiple Personality

Multiple personality represents a bizarre, abnormal kind of discontinuity of identity. Historically, multiple personality was popularized in psychology by Morton Prince (1906), who reported on a case at the turn of the century. But perhaps the best-known case was described by Thigpen and Cleckley (1954) and was later made into a movie, *The Three Faces of Eve*. Eve originally had two separate identities, each with its own personality features. These merged into one, but years later she reported more than twenty. She was puzzled by this array of different personalities and asked, "Did the others come because I could not live with my reality? But other people face these same realities. Why was I different?" (Sizemore & Pittillo, 1977, p. 38).

No one has yet answered Eve's question satisfactorily, and multiple personalities continue to seek psychological help. They may be placed on a continuum of dissociation. Let us start with normal people who, when they assume different roles, behave differently and think of themselves differently. Consider a woman who is a mother, wife, daughter, aunt, niece, boss, employee, athlete, and choir singer. She not only behaves differently in these different roles and contexts but assumes different *sub*identities and thinks of herself differently. At the same time, she knows that she is the same person despite these subidentities.

Next, consider man who has an epiphany, and this religious experience results in his being "born again." He feels different from before, and religion has suddenly become a major component in his identity, but he knows that he is still the same person as before. If he denied his previous identity, that would come close to a multiple personality, but it would still be a step away.

Finally, consider a quiet, unassertive man who drinks too much, becomes boisterous and aggressive, and the next day remembers so little of what happened that he has to be told of his strange behavior. Clearly, he was behaving out of character, and he thinks, "But that's not really me." Add denial that it was himself, and the discontinuity becomes multiple personality.

Tilt

If our identity derives from both personal and social sources, in some people the personal sources will predominate, and in others the social sources. When the personal sources largely determine identity, the person tends to feel special and different from others: "I am not just another cipher on this planet of billions of people. I am uniquely me." But there is an unfortunate consequence of this tilt toward a personal identity. If you are indeed unique, everything you are is completely wiped out when you die. Thus the stronger the emphasis on personal identity, the greater the existential anxiety.

Existential anxiety does not concern people whose identity is predominantly social. Their family, country, religion, and the other sources of social identity existed before they were born and will remain after they die. Therefore, the part of these people that belongs to these various social entities does not die. There is a place for everyone in the sense of belonging to a group that continues from one generation to the next.

A related advantage of a predominantly social identity is a feeling of belonging to something larger than oneself. If you sometimes feel small and lonely, here is a place for you in the larger scheme of things; you belong. But you will have difficulty in proclaiming your individuality.

In another book, I suggested a link between personal identity and private self-consciousness, and between social identity and public self-consciousness (Buss, 1980). These hypotheses were tested by Cheek and Briggs (1982), who correlated the two kinds of identity with the two kinds of self-consciousness. On the self-consciousness questionnaires, which are included in the next chapter, subjects were asked about their self-awareness. On the identity questionnaires, they were asked about the importance of each item for their identity. Typical social identity items were "Memberships I have in various groups" and "My popularity and attractiveness to others." Typical personal identity items were "My intellectual ability" and "My emotions and feelings." Private self-consciousness correlated .37 with personal identity, and public self-consciousness correlated .30 with social identity; the other two correlations were nearly zero. Evidently, a tilt toward the personal or the social aspects of oneself encompasses both self-consciousness and identity.

Two subsequent studies confirmed these findings with only minor differences in the correlations. Private self-consciousness correlated .40 with personal identity, and public self-consciousness correlated .46 with social identity (Schlenker & Wiegold, 1990). In later research, private self-consciousness correlated .29 with personal identity, and public self-consciousness correlated .41 with social identity (Britt, 1993).

People who are high in social identity report being more sociable than Lows (McKillop, Berzonsky, & Schlenker, 1992). These subjects were asked to present themselves in either a positive or a negative light during a face-to-face interview (public) or on an anonymous questionnaire (private); afterward they made self-ratings. Those high in social identity shifted their self-ratings in the direction of their self-presentation, positive or negative, but only in the public condition. In the private condition, they saw their negative self-presentations as dishonest. Those low in social identity showed an opposite pattern, dismissing their negative self-presentations in the public condition as dishonest. Self-presenting in the public condition did not affect their later self-ratings. The authors of the study concluded, "People high in Social Identity are affected by their face-to-face self-presentations, whereas people low in Social Identity are more likely to be affected by their private, positive thoughts about self" (p. 806).

There may well be a sex difference in whether personal or social components prevail in determining identity (Josselson, 1988). Men tend to seek independence and strive to achieve, both of which are related to a sense of distinctiveness and, more broadly, personal identity. Women tend to seek affiliations and find satisfaction in a network of personal relationships, which are related to social identity: "Intimacy, or interpersonal development, among women *is* identity" (p. 99).

Individualism and Collectivism

Societies may be aligned along a dimension of individualism-collectivism, which is relevant to the personal-social distinction (Triandis, 1989). In an individualist culture such as that in the United States, personal goals are placed ahead of the goals of the group. There is an emphasis on autonomy, self-reliance, and achievement, together with a desire to be distinct and different from all others, often at the cost of loneliness. In a collectivist culture, such as that of Japan, group goals are placed ahead of individual goals. There is an emphasis on conformity, harmony, reliability, and being nice to other members of the group.

Sampson (1988) refers to the individualist-collectivist dimension in terms of whether the self is exclusionary or inclusionary: "Although all cultures draw a line between a region defined as belonging intrinsically to the self and a region defined as extrinsic or outside the self and hence belonging to 'the nonself other,' where that line is drawn varies extensively" (p. 15). Our culture tends to be extremely individualistic in drawing a sharp boundary between self and other. At the other extreme are cultures so collectivistic that persons define themselves solely by their attachments to family and society, and the concept of individuality is foreign to them.

In addition to these differences from one society to another, there are analogous differences within a society. R. H. Turner (1976) divided people into *institutionals* and *impulsives:* "People accept as evidence of their real selves either feelings and actions with an *institutional* focus or ones they identify as strictly impulse" (p. 990). Institutionals fit well into a collectivist culture; impulsives thrive in an individualist culture.

Triandis (1989) suggested that identity is defined differently in these two kinds of culture: "Individualistic cultures tend to emphasize elements of identity that reflect possessions—what do I own, what experiences have I had, what are my accomplishments (for scientists, what is my list of publications). In collectivist cultures, identity is defined more in terms of relationships—I am the mother of X, I am a member of family Y, and I am a resident of Z" (p. 515). The message is clear: For those living in an individualist culture, the major sources of identity are personal, but for those living in a collectivist culture, the major sources of identity are social.

Individualist cultures raise their children to seek independence and, eventually, self-actualization. Considerable attention is directed toward the private, personal aspects of the self. Collectivist cultures raise their children to be respectful and to fit in with the group and conform to it. An emphasis on personal goals is regarded as selfish and immature. Such child rearing sets the stage for the differing emphases on identity: on the personal aspects in individualist cultures and on the social aspects in collectivist cultures.

Sociologists and anthropologists find that U.S. culture is too individualistic and attribute many of our current problems to self-centeredness (Sampson, 1988, for example). A social psychologist concurred, suggesting that an optimal identity would be a collective, "at some intermediate range of inclusiveness, one that provides both shared identity with an in-group and differentiation from distinct out-groups" (Brewer, 1991, p. 478). Whatever one's opinion on this issue, two kinds of identity needs must be satisfied even in our individualist culture: the need to be distinctive (personal) and the need to belong to something larger than oneself (social). Herein lies the special relevance to personality: individual differences in the balance between these needs.

Development

The first step in establishing identity is differentiating between me and not-me. During the first year of life, infants learn the boundary between self and nonself, between their bodies and the external world. The fact of a separate body establishes that they are different from other things and other people.

During childhood an analogous differentiation between self and nonself occurs, this time based on psychological features: behavioral style, personality traits, gender identity, and a private, inner world. These features are recognizable as the components of personal identity, which also contribute to a sense of continuity.

Childhood through Adolescence

In a developmental study, subjects were asked to describe themselves (Peevers, 1987). All the six year olds mentioned continuity, especially lack of change over time. The percentage mentioning continuity dropped to 70% in nine year olds, bottomed at 50% in thirteen year olds, and rose only slightly among seventeen and twenty-one year olds. Few subjects at any age mentioned distinctiveness, perhaps because distinctiveness is not salient in free reports.

An alternative is to ask subjects directly about continuity and distinctiveness. Adopting this tactic, Hart, Maloney, and Damon (1987) interviewed subjects ranging from first graders to sophomores in high school. They discovered four developmental stages of continuity:

1. Physical characteristics: eye color
2. Psychological features: intelligence
3. Social recognition: recognized by friends as the same person
4. Relative sameness: though slightly different, essentially the same

The researchers also discovered four developmental stages of distinctiveness:

1. Physical features: taller than anyone in the class
2. Psychological features: smarter than anyone
3. Unique combination: smart, friendly, short
4. Unique inner world: private thoughts and feelings

These four developmental stages of continuity and distinctiveness have been ordered this way: (1) is early childhood, (2) is the rest of childhood, (3) is early adolescence, and (4) is late adolescence. Notice that for both continuity and distinctiveness the first progression is from physical to psychological characteristics. After that, continuity depends on the social environment and finally on being somewhat the same as earlier. The feeling of distinctiveness progresses to a dependence on a unique combination of features and then moves on to a focus on the private self.

Notice also that virtually all these characteristics fall under the heading of personal identity, but the sources of social identity are hardly mentioned. One reason is that the subjects were interviewed about continuity and distinctiveness at the same time. When asked how we are different from others, most people will answer with personal characteristics. Another reason may be that youngsters are more preoccupied with personal identity. Attention to the social components of identity may have to await their moving from the relatively cloistered world of family and school to the larger stage of the adult world.

Recall that Erik Erikson (1950) initiated modern thinking about identity by specifying an adolescent stage called identity versus role diffusion. The adolescent must deal with two basic problems of identity. First, puberty initiates rapid changes in size and secondary sex characteristics. In just a few years, the individual's appearance changes from that of a child to that of an adult. The prior continuity of body is shattered, making the question "Am I the same person I was before?" especially salient.

Second, there are many different role models, and the adolescent has difficulty in choosing appropriate ones. There is also the discomfort that attends trying out any new role, whether on stage or in everyday situations. Remember, too, that an adolescent has one foot in childhood and the other in adulthood. Yearning for the past that is now perceived nostalgically as an easier time, the adolescent is expected to move forward into adult roles.

Thus identity can become confused by complexity, rapid change, and multiple expectations. In the past the solution lay in moving to a stable identity through marriage, career, and place in the community. For many young people today this solution is more difficult to attain, and the confusion over identity that Erikson labels role diffusion has become an enduring problem.

Building on this framework, Marcia (1966, 1987) laid out a sequence of four identity statuses during late adolescence. In his research, subjects are interviewed about occupational choice, religious and political beliefs, sex roles, and sexuality. The focus is on how much the subjects are exploring identity options and to what extent they have made a commitment. The outcome is assignment to one of the four identity statuses:

1. Identity diffusion. In this most immature status, adolescents are not committed to any social roles, vocations, or, generally, to any direction in their lives. They often feel rejected by their family and have few or no close personal relationships.

2. Foreclosure. There has been no adolescent exploration of options because the adolescent is strongly committed to values acquired during childhood and not subsequently examined. These individuals tend to retain the childhood absolutes of right and wrong, good and bad, and they have trouble being flexible in their close relationships.

3. Moratorium. These adolescents have temporarily given up the struggle to achieve a mature identity because they are still exploring and are not ready to commit themselves to a particular direction. They are the most conflicted group, inconsistently being anxious, acquiescent, and rebellious by turns.

4. Identity achievement. Having explored and resolved the issue of selecting from many options, these individuals have committed themselves to an adult

identity. By definition, they represent the most mature and flexible identity status.

Unfortunately, Marcia (1966, 1987) did not distinguish between the various sources of identity. Consider a young woman who aims for personal achievement and intends to become a physician. Let us say that she fails in her premedical studies and cannot become a physician. Now she reverts to the diffusion stage, as she reconsiders her vocational identity. A second woman wants to be a homemaker and mother. She is likely to marry and have children, and she can remain in the identity achievement stage. Thus an original vocational identity, depending as it does on ability, may not be realized; but the identity that derives from social roles, which does not depend in any important sense on ability, is more likely to be realized. Furthermore, in people in traditional sex roles, vocational identity may be more an issue for men, and social identity may be more crucial for women. Here, as elsewhere, it is important to analyze identity according to its components or sources, for a generalized concept of identity may be misleading.

A different approach has been taken by Berzonsky (1992), who proposed three cognitive styles as the bases of Marcia's (1966, 1987) four identity statuses. These styles presumably transcend identity and typify the person's general cognitive tendencies. Adolescents in the diffuse identity status tend to avoid dealing with problems, procrastinating until the problems become too pressing. Those who have foreclosed identity use a normative orientation, depending on societal norms and the teachings of parents and other socializing agents. Those in the last two identity statuses, moratorium and identity achievement, seek information about themselves in solving personal problems. An attempt to validate these ideas, using a factor analysis of coping strategies, met with mixed results too complex to be discussed here (see Berzonsky, 1992).

Maturity

Marcia (1987) acknowledged that the issue of identity continues throughout adulthood: "Unsuccessful identity resolutions at late adolescence do not necessarily mean that an identity will never be constructed. Even if one has not moved out of Foreclosure during late adolescence, there are plenty of disequilibrating events in a life cycle to elicit identity crises" (p. 165).

Let us assume that individuals achieve an adult identity in their twenties. In Marcia's (1987) terms it is identity achievement; in my terms it is a stable combination of personal and social sources of identity. Most adults settle into an occupation, marry and raise a family, continue in stable affiliations (race, religion, nationality), and join one or another social organization.

Now move the calendar forward twenty to twenty-five years and consider the social sources of identity. Many married partners have grown apart, and a fair percentage have divorced. The children have left the home or are about to do so, attenuating the parental role. Parents and members of the extended family's older generation are starting to become decrepit or have already died. The limits of vocational status have been reached or are about to be, and there are few signs of progress along this line. Significant sources of social identity remain but fewer than previously, and one's commitment to them tends to wane.

Next, consider the personal sources of identity. The face is becoming lined, hair is turning gray, and the body is sagging with the weight of age. Earlier daydreams have not been realized. The feeling of continuity has been weakened by these changes, which are not for the better. And by the late forties, one senses that there are fewer years ahead than there are behind. The clock is ticking, and if the personal sources predominate, existential anxiety becomes more salient.

These developments may cause a problem that has been variously labeled mid-life crisis, burnout, or the empty nest syndrome. The response varies: wanting to start another family, getting divorced, marrying again, changing careers, becoming more religious, being "born again" or changing religions, taking up a national or political cause, or entering psychotherapy. In the last generation or so, some women at this stage of life have embraced feminism, for a number of reasons. Similarly, some men in mid-life have chosen to share interests and concerns through newly started men's groups.

I should not overstate the case, however. Many people, perhaps the majority, do not experience this identity crisis. Perhaps they have foreclosed on an identity and are rigidly sticking to it. Perhaps they have a mature identity that allows them to deal flexibly with the changes wrought by advancing age. Or, in my terms, they have sufficient personal and social sources of identity to handle this kind of problem. Then again, perhaps they are part of a collectivist culture or subculture, where there is a place for everyone from birth to death. Safely located in a web of societal structures and familial roles, such people do not have an identity crisis in middle age. But in our individualist culture there may be such a crisis—Erikson (1950) dichotomized it as generativity versus stagnation—which may be one reason why some social commentators have criticized our way of life.

Chapter 10

Self-Consciousness

History

The topic of self-consciousness has occupied philosophers and psychologists for a long time, but the scientific study of it is more recent. Modern research begins with a book by Duval and Wicklund (1972) on self-focused attention. Such self-awareness, they assumed, causes an immediate self-appraisal, which typically reveals a discrepancy between one's current behavior or feelings and one's standards or goals. This discrepancy is sufficiently aversive to motivate attempts to escape it by leaving the situation or directing attention away from the self. If escape is not possible, the person tries to reduce the discrepancy by making behavioral adjustments.

The underlying assumption is that we all strive for consistency, which means that any internal discrepancies must either be resolved or avoided by not thinking about them. Accompanying the theory was research demonstrating the impact of manipulations that make people self-aware, especially mirrors and cameras.

The next step was the construction of a questionnaire to assess individual differences in self-consciousness as a trait. The questionnaire revealed that there are two kinds of self-consciousness: private and public (Fenigstein, Scheier, & Buss, 1975). Since then, researchers have produced a body of work on transient self-awareness and the traits of private and public self-consciousness. The earlier work was reviewed in two books (Buss, 1980; Carver & Scheier, 1981a).

Meanwhile, Gallup (1970) showed that chimpanzees would recognize themselves in a mirror, which he attributed to their having self-awareness. "To the extent that self-recognition implies a rudimentary concept of self, these data show that contrary to popular opinion and preconceived ideas, man may not have a monopoly on the self-concept. Man may not be evolution's only experiment in self-awareness" (Gallup, 1977, p. 333).

Primitive versus Advanced Self-Awareness

Gallup (1977) concluded that humans have self-awareness in common with other animals, especially the great apes. This statement appears to contradict other facts about animals. Do they introspect as we do? Do they have self-esteem and a sense of identity as we do? There is no evidence that they engage in these self-related cognitions, but the great apes are capable of mirror-image recognition. My answer to the paradox is to suggest two kinds of self-awareness: primitive and advanced.

Primitive Self-Awareness

Body Boundary

I am aware of the boundary of my body: where my feet end and the floor begins. This distinction between me and not-me, which is acquired early in life, involves a particular kind of awareness. It is a *sensory* separation between the body and the enveloping environment. Presumably, all animals possess this sense of body boundary.

Double Stimulation

If someone were to put a hand on my arm, I would duly record being touched. If I put my right hand on my left arm, the left arm registers being touched, and the right hand registers that it is touching the arm. In this self-induced stimulation, part of me is active, and part passive. Clearly, such double stimulation is different from the single stimulation of being touched by another person or of touching another person. Presumably, any animal with limbs can experience double stimulation and distinguish it from single stimulation.

Mirror-Image Recognition

When I look in a mirror, I know that the image is mine. How do we know that the great apes are capable of such self-recognition? Gallup (1970) placed young, wild-born chimpanzees in a small room that had only a mirror in it. For the first few days, they responded to the mirror image with social behavior, which implies that they perceived the image as another animal. Thereafter, they groomed parts of the body they could not otherwise see, picked food from their teeth, blew blubbles, and made faces—behavior that strongly suggests recognition of self.

In a more objective test, older chimpanzees were anesthetized, and red dots were placed above one eyebrow ridge and at the top of the opposite ear of each unconscious animal. After the chimpanzees regained consciousness, the mirror was again introduced. They repeatedly attemped to touch the red dots on their own heads and spent an inordinate amount of time looking at themselves in the mirror.

Gallup's (1977) summary of his own and others' experiments on mirror-image recognition in other animals revealed that it had been demonstrated in chimpanzees and orangutans, but not in baboons or any species of monkeys. The home-reared gorilla Koko has been reported to show mirror-image recognition, though the observations were made informally and without laboratory control. Thus self-recognition appears to be limited to the higher primates: humans, chimpanzees, orangutans, and probably gorillas.

Research on humans has shown that there are several varieties of recognition of mirror images, and that they follow a developmental sequence in early childhood (Amsterdam, 1972; Bertenthal & Fischer, 1978; Lewis, Sullivan, Stanger, & Weiss, 1989; Schulman & Kaplowitz, 1977). At about six months, infants can touch a part of themselves while looking at their mirror image. At about eight months, when an infant is placed in front of a mirror while dressed in a vest with a hat projecting over the head, the infant immediately looks up or tries to grab the hat. At roughly ten months, when a toy that can be seen only in a mirror is lowered from the ceiling, an infant turns directly toward the toy rather than looking at the mirror image. At approximately eighteen months, when a dot of rouge is applied to the face and the infant looks in the mirror, he or she touches the face and says that there is something different about it. Finally, a two-year-old child, when asked, "Who's that?" and directed to the child's mirror image, says, "Me," or states his or her name.

Advanced Self-Awareness

The facts of body boundary, double stimulation, and self-recognition lead to the conclusion that our species shares self-awareness with the great apes. If only body boundary and double stimulation are considered, other mammals may also possess this kind of self-awareness. But it is *primitive self-awareness*, at least in relation to the *advanced self-awareness* that is seen only in humans, and among them only in older children and adults who possess the necessary cognitive capabilities. "From a developmental standpoint, to be self-aware (in the sense of being able to recognize yourself in the mirror) is not necessarily the same as being able to attribute intentions and beliefs to others or yourself in the same way as adults or even older children do" (Povinelli, 1993, p. 503). The advanced self-awareness of older children and adults may be seen in three kinds of behavior, each a cognitive analogue of the more sensory behavior we share with animals.

Covertness

The first kind of behavior is covertness: awareness of a private self, consisting among other things of daydreams, feelings, memories, and grandiose ambitions that no one else can know directly. Early in childhood, we learn to keep most of these cognitions to ourselves. We also gradually learn that covert feelings of affection or love may cause embarrassment if expressed openly and that the emotions of fear and anger may cause ridicule or anger on the part of others if they become aware of them.

When we are suppressing cognitions, feelings, or just opinions (the hostess's dinner was awful, but the opinion cannot be expressed), we become especially aware of the dichotomy between the private self and the public self, between an inner, covert psychological world and an outer, overt world of the everyday. This sense of covertness or being aware that one's psychological insides do not match overt behavior is analogous to the distinction between me (inside) and not-me (outside).

Self-Esteem

Another kind of behavior occurs when we evaluate ourselves. This of course is self-esteem. When one person praises another or thinks that person worthwhile, the evaluator and the recipient are two different people. But in *self*-esteem the evaluator and object of evaluation are the same person. In this respect self-esteem is analogous to double stimulation (one's hand touches one's arm).

Identity

The last kind of behavior that justifies a concept of an advanced self involves identity (see Chapter 9). We humans tend to know who we are, or we try to discover who we are. The search may involve discovering affiliations, the nature of character, or the continuity of life. It may extend into seeking the meaning of life or descend into existential anxiety. The issue of identity is parallel to self-recognition, but there is a crucial difference. In self-recognition, there is a *perceptual* match between one's own body and the image in the mirror, a sensory self-awareness. In identity, there is a higher-order, cognitive characterization of oneself or a search for such a characterization that goes beyond perception and into *conception*. That is to say, identity requires the kind of advanced cognitions that are not necessary for mirror-image recognition.

Analogies

The three kinds of advanced self-awareness are each analogous to a kind of primitive self-awareness (see Table 10.1). Among humans, primitive self-awareness develops in infancy, starting with the distinction between me and not-me. After a body boundary has been established (covertness), the infant becomes aware of the difference between single stimulation and double stimulation (self-esteem). The last kind of sensory self-awareness to appear is self-recognition (identity), which occurs during the second year of life.

TABLE 10.1   Primitive versus Advanced Self-Awareness

	Primitive self-awareness	Advanced self-awareness
Type	Sensory	Cognitive
Basis	Body boundary Double stimulation Mirror-image recognition	Covertness Self-esteem Identity
Occurrence	Animals, human infants	Children, adults

Advanced self-awareness is so named because it requires the higher capabilities that are seen in human children during the period of *representative intelligence* (Piaget, 1962). A sense of covertness would seem to develop first, as the child learns the art of prevarication and therefore becomes keenly aware of the discrepancy between the private and the public self: between covert truth and overt lies. A sense of self-esteem probably emerges next, followed somewhat later by an interest in identity.

Animals can of course distinguish between me and not-me, but they lack the human cognitions that would make them aware of an internal psychological life and therefore of covertness. Similarly, animals are aware of double stimulation, but, as far as we know, they do not evaluate themselves. It might be argued that though we have no evidence that animals have self-esteem, they may be capable of this self-reaction. Admittedly, animals might be capable of more than we know, but we must be wary of the seductive trap of attributing human qualities to animals. Until there is evidence that animals have self-esteem, we can only assume that they do not. Finally, the great apes are capable of mirror-image recognition, but there is no evidence that they are aware of a personal or social identity.

On the basis of present knowledge, then, it is concluded that animals possess a more primitive, sensory self-awareness, and only humans possess a more advanced, cognitive self-awareness. In this chapter, I discuss only the advanced, cognitive kind of self-awareness, the kind present in older children and adults.

Before proceeding, I need to pin down vocabulary. There are brief periods when we turn attention toward ourselves: when writing a diary or gazing in a mirror, for example. This temporary focus on the self will be called *self-awareness*. Some people have a strong tendency to focus on themselves, and others only a weak tendency. The enduring disposition will be called *self-consciousness*. These terms should help communication. Self-awareness refers to the transient state, and self-consciousness refers to the trait.

Two Traits

Are there two kinds of self-consciousness, one private and one public? A moment's thought suggests that there are. We can focus on the covert aspects of ourselves that cannot be observed by anyone else: sore muscles, feelings of anger or love that remain unexpressed, romantic daydreams too embarrassing to disclose, and feelings of religious awe. Or we can focus on aspects of ourselves that are open to observation by others: face, body, or clothes; expressive behaviors of gesturing, smiling, frowning, or blushing; and the social behaviors of speaking, offering respect, and more generally, paying attention to the social rules called manners. This armchair analysis of self-consciousness may seem compelling, but it needs to be confirmed empirically.

A questionnaire was constructed and administered to several samples of college students, totaling more than two thousand subjects (Fenigstein, Scheier, & Buss, 1975). Factor analyses of successive samples yielded two distinct factors, called private and public self-consciousness on the basis of the content of the items (see Table 10.2). A third factor, social anxiety, is not relevant here.

The items in each scale illustrate that the focus of attention can be directed to either covert or overt aspects of oneself. The items in the private self-consciousness scale reflect either the process of attending to oneself (figuring oneself out, scrutinizing oneself) or the object of the attention to oneself (fantasies, feelings, motives, and moods). The items in the public self-consciousness scale refer to awareness of style, appearance, self-presentation, and a concern about what others might think.

At first glance the wording of several of the public self-consciousness items might pose a problem. Note in particular the words *concerned* and *worry*. Items with such words might tap social anxiety rather than public self-consciousness. However, none of these items loaded on the social anxiety factor, which deals mainly with shyness, embarrassment, and public-speaking anxiety.

Public self-consciousness correlates in the low thirties with private self-consciousness. An after-the-fact explanation of this moderate correlation assumes that there are three kinds of people. Some turn inward and examine themselves, both the inner and outer aspects; this would yield a high positive correlation. Some simply do not examine either aspect of themselves, which again would yield a high positive correlation. And some people attend to one aspect but not the other, which

TABLE 10.2   The Self-Consciousness Questionnaire

Private self-consciousness

1. I'm always trying to figure myself out.
2. Generally, I'm not very aware of myself. (reversed)
3. I reflect about myself a lot.
4. I'm often the subject of my own fantasies.
5. I never scrutinize myself. (reversed)
6. I'm generally attentive to my inner feelings.
7. I'm constantly examining my motives.
8. I sometimes have the feeling that I'm off somewhere watching myself.
9. I'm alert to changes in my mood.
10. I'm aware of the way my mind works when I work through a problem.

Public self-consciousness

1. I'm concerned about my style of doing things.
2. I'm concerned about the way I present myself.
3. I'm self-conscious about the way I look.
4. I usually worry about making a good impression.
5. One of the last things I do before leaving my house is look in the mirror.
6. I'm usually aware of my appearance.

Source: From "Public and Private Self-consciousness: Assessment and Theory" by A. Fenigstein, M. F. Scheier, and A. H. Buss, 1975, *Journal of Consulting and Clinical Psychology*, 43, p. 524. Copyright 1975 by the American Psychological Association. Adapted by permission of the publisher.

would yield a high negative correlation. When all three kinds of people are combined, the result is a moderate positive correlation between the two kinds of self-consciousness.

Despite the correlation between the two kinds of self-consciousness, they have different relationships with other traits. People who are very high in public self-consciousness may be so distressed about the observable aspects of themselves that they shade over into shyness. Or they may think so little of their observable aspects that their self-esteem is diminished. Public self-consciousness correlates .34 with shyness and −.21 with self-esteem (Perry & Buss, 1990). Private self-consciousness, in contrast, has no conceptual link to either shyness or self-esteem, and it is uncorrelated with them.

Much of the research to be discussed has used both the private and public self-consciousness scales. In virtually every instance, when one of these traits has had a significant impact, the other has not. Therefore when one self-consciousness trait is discussed, the other will not be mentioned except for the rare instances when it too has an impact. Also, the research on both traits typically splits subjects into Highs and Lows on the basis of their scores on the questionnaire.

Private Self-Consciousness

Self-Knowledge

Veridicality

Those who score high on the trait of private self-consciousness report that they regularly try to figure themselves out, reflect about themselves, scrutinize themselves, examine their motives, and, generally, focus on the personal aspects of themselves. As a result, they are likely to know themselves better than those who are low in private self-consciousness. Other things being equal, it follows that those high in private self-consciousness should produce more veridical self-reports.

College men and women filled out questionnaires on the trait of aggressiveness, and later their instrumental aggression was assessed in the laboratory with the aggression machine (Scheier, Buss, & Buss, 1978). For subjects high in private self-consciousness, the correlation between the self-report of aggressiveness and aggression machine performance was .66; for those low in private self-consciousness, the correlation was .09. Presumably, those high in private self-consciousness knew themselves well enough for their self-report of aggressiveness to be veridical, and therefore it correlated strongly with behavioral aggression.

In another questionnaire study, subjects reported on their own altruism and were given the opportunity to offer help (Smith & Shaffer, 1986). For those high in private self-consciousness, the correlation between self-reported altruism and helping behavior was .56; for the Lows, it was .12.

In a variation on this theme, subjects wrote stories about how dominant they would be and then were placed in a group situation and told to be as dominant and assertive as possible (R. G. Turner, 1978a). For those high in private self-consciousness, story dominance correlated .67 with behavioral dominance; for the Lows it was .33.

An alternative way of checking on self-knowledge is to determine whether others see you as you see yourself. Subjects were asked to imagine that a friend had angered them and they were to act out what they would typically do as a consequence (Klesges & McGinley, 1982). Their aggressive behavior with a Bobo doll as the victim was rated. At the same time a friend was asked how the subject would react. There was much closer agreement between subjects' behavior and friends' predictions for subjects high in private self-consciousness than for Lows.

In an analogous behavioral study, subjects were asked to write down three words that described themselves without using words referring to appearance (Bernstein & Davis, 1982). Then they were videotaped in a discussion group, and the tape was shown to judges. These judges were to match what they saw on the tape with the three-word descriptions. The matches were considerably closer for subjects high in private self-consciousness than for Lows.

These findings were confirmed by another matching experiment (Franzoi, 1983). Subjects completed an adjective checklist about themselves, and friends evaluated them, using the same adjective checklist. There was greater agreement between the self-reported adjectives and the friends' adjectives for subjects high in private self-consciousness than for Lows.

Self-Cognitions

If you have been reflecting about yourself, the resulting personal knowledge should be more accessible than if you have been ignoring yourself. Subjects were asked whether trait terms applied to them (R. G. Turner, 1978c). Those high in private self-consciousness took less time than did the Lows.

Similarly, subjects high in private self-consciousness made self-descriptive judgments and self-reference decisions faster than Lows (Mueller, 1982). When asked to list trait adjectives that applied to themselves, those high in private self-consciousness listed more terms than the Lows (R. G. Turner, 1978b). In a memory task, subjects high in private self-consciousness remembered more self-relevant words than did the Lows (Hull, Levinson, Young, & Sher, 1983).

Better access to the private aspects of oneself should also lead to better memory for self-related material. Subjects were given words that described either traits or nontraits (R. G. Turner, 1980). A surprise memory test later revealed that those high in private self-consciousness remembered more trait words than did Lows. Presumably, the Highs are more attuned to issues involving self-reference, in this instance, trait words.

Internal Focus

If you regularly turn your attention to the private aspects of yourself, this internal focus should be decisive behaviorally. Consider three relevant studies. Subjects drank a peppermint-flavored drink, rated it, and then drank a second drink (Scheier, Carver, & Gibbons, 1979). Half the subjects were told that the second drink was stronger in flavor, and the other half, weaker. Those low in private self-consciousness were swayed considerably by these suggestions, rating the second drink stronger or weaker, respectively. But those high in private self-consciousness, focusing internally on the actual taste, changed their ratings hardly at all.

When subjects are pressured to change their opinions, they often resist and hold their ground in an attempt to demonstrate that they still have freedom of choice. This phenomenon, called reactance, is expected to be stronger in those who focus on the private aspects of themselves. Thus subjects high in private self-consciousness display more reactance when pressured to change their attitude than do Lows (Carver & Scheier, 1981b).

Field-dependent people tend to rely on external cues in making perceptual decisions such as how upright they are, but field-independent people tend to use internal cues (Witkin, Dyk, Faterson, Goodenough, & Karp, 1962). Davies (1984) saw the parallel with self-consciousness and administered the rod-and-frame test and the embedded-figures test, two measures of field-dependence–independence. Private self-consciousness correlated with these tests –.32 and .45, respectively. Davies concluded, "Field-independent persons and high scorers on private self-consciousness tend to have a more articulated concept of the self; a greater sense of separate identity; a greater awareness of and reliance on personal standards, feelings, motives, and other internal referents" (p. 546).

Intensified Emotions and Moods

Imagine that you are soon to take an important exam, and you are worried about the outcome. The more you think about the exam, about how difficult it might be, about the odds that you might fail, and the consequences of failing, the more anxious you become. Now imagine that you have just fallen in love with someone. The more you think about that person, the stronger is your feeling of love. The point of these examples is that a focus on emotions tends to intensify them. If you are having an emotional experience, turning your attention inward should result in the emotion being experienced as more intense. It follows that those high in private self-consciousness, who by definition chronically focus on their psychological insides, should experience both positive and negative emotions more intensely.

Anger is a powerful emotion, which presumably would be intensified by focusing on the experience of it. College men were angered by a confederate, and then the aggression machine was used to determine the intensity of their aggression (Scheier, 1976). Those high in private self-consciousness aggressed intensely more than the Lows. The explanation does not lie in an association between self-consciousness and the trait of physical aggression, for they are uncorrelated. Rather, those high in private self-consciousness focused on the experience of anger, thereby amplifying it and expressing the heightened anger in greater aggression.

College men were shown slides of nude women and slides of atrocities (for example, a pile of dead bodies), and they rated the slides on a scale from extremely unpleasant to extremely pleasant (Scheier & Carver, 1977). Compared to those low in private self-consciousness, the Highs rated the nude slides as more pleasant and the atrocity slides as more unpleasant. In a follow-up study by the same researchers, positive and negative moods were induced by having subjects read lighthearted statements or depressing statements. (Previous research had demonstrated that this mood induction works.) After reading the negative statements, those high in private self-consciousness reported being more depressed than the Lows. After reading the positive statements, the Highs reported being more elated than the Lows.

These various reports on moods and emotions have been supplemented by behavioral observations. Subjects listened to audiotapes of humorous errors, called bloopers, and their laughter was tape-recorded (Porterfield et al., 1988). The correlation between private self-consciousness and laughter was .34. The authors concluded, "The laughter findings support the affect intensification hypothesis. The amusement induced by bloopers was intensified by dispositional self-consciousness, resulting in more laughter in high private self-conscious than in low private self-conscious subjects" (pp. 416–417).

Subjects were asked to volunteer for an experiment in which they would be given electric shock, the rationale being that such research would have medical implications such as using electric shock to cauterize blood vessels (Scheier, Carver, & Gibbons, 1981). When told that the electric shock would be weak, 100% of those high in private self-consciousness volunteered, compared to 75% of the Lows. When told that the electric shock would be very strong, the percentage of Lows remained about the same, but now only 50% of the Highs volunteered, presumably because of their more intensely experienced fear.

One way of minimizing intense negative emotions is to avoid thinking about them. Drinking alcohol may accomplish this end by minimizing self-awareness (Hull, 1981). If so, when people experience negative emotions, those high in private self-consciousness, who by definition are more aware of their private selves, should drink more. In a laboratory study, subjects either succeeded or failed in a task and then drank wine, presumably as part of a taste test (Hull & Young, 1983). The subjects could drink as much wine as needed, the taste test of course being bogus, the real purpose being to discover how much alcohol was consumed. Those high in private self-consciousness drank more wine after failure than after success, but the Lows showed no such difference. Evidently, only the Highs felt the need to minimize self-awareness after failure by consuming more alcohol.

Subsequently, alcoholics who had abstained from drinking for at least three weeks completed a life events survey that included positive and negative events of the previous year (Hull, Young, & Jouriles, 1986). Three months later, the subjects' drinking behavior was evaluated. Among those high in private self-consciousness, the relapse rate for those who had experienced mainly negative events the year before was 70%, and for those who had experienced mainly positive events, it was only 14%. For the Lows, the relapse rates were 40% and 38%, respectively. Thus private self-consciousness intensified the impact of both positive and negative events. Apparently, negative events so depressed the Highs that they tried to minimize the emotion by drinking, but when the events were positive, there was little need for drinking, because there was no negative emotion. We know from previous research that those low in private self-consciousness do not experience emotions as intensely as Highs do, and this fact is reflected in the drinking behavior of Lows: unaffected by positive or negative experiences.

Blue-collar workers often toil under conditions of noise, breakdown of machinery, and time pressure. Frone and McFarlin (1989) suggested that those high in private self-consciousness should react more intensely to the stresses of work. They found that workers high in private self-consciousness report more work stress and more somatic symptoms than do the Lows.

Summary

These various findings are sufficiently complex to require a summary. People who are high in private self-consciousness know themselves better and therefore

1. offer more veridical self-reports,
2. respond more quickly to self-descriptions and offer longer self-descriptions,
3. cannot be fooled by suggestions about internal events,
4. tend to resist pressure to change attitudes, and
5. rely on internal cues in making perceptual decisions.

People who are high in private self-consciousness experience emotions and moods more intensely; thus

1. when angered, they aggress more intensely;
2. they have more extreme reactions to pleasant and unpleasant stimuli;
3. they respond to mood inductions more strongly and laugh more at jokes;
4. they respond to threat with more anxiety; and
5. they respond more deeply to both positive and negative life events.

Public Self-Consciousness

People who are high in private self-consciousness know themselves well, but there is an analogous kind of self-knowledge in those who are high in public self-consciousness. They concentrate on the overt, social aspects of themselves and therefore should know what kind of impression they make on others. College women were videotaped while talking to a researcher (Tobey & Tunnell, 1981). They were asked how viewers of the videotape would regard them. Then judges watched the tapes and evaluated the women's personalities. Women high in public self-consciousness were better at predicting the impression they would make than were Lows.

Gallaher (1992) had observers watch subjects moving about and rated them for expressiveness (for example, lots of gestures) and expansiveness (for example, broader gestures). The subjects also rated themselves for these two stylistic features. For subjects high in public self-consciousness the correlations between observers' ratings and self-reports were .67 for expressiveness and .55 for expansiveness. For the subjects low in public self-consciousness, the correlations were, respectively, .07 and −.05. Evidently, those low in public self-consciousness had paid no attention to an important aspect of their overt behavior, style of movement.

Clearly, focusing on oneself leads to greater self-knowledge. If the focus is on the private aspects of self, there is better understanding of one's emotions, motives, attitudes, and personality. If the focus is on the public aspects, there should be better understanding of the perspective of others about oneself. Subjects were asked to draw an *E* on their forehead (Haas, 1984). They drew it either from their own perspective, which would look reversed to an observer, or from the observer's perspective. Those high in public self-consciousness were more likely to draw it from an observer's perspective than were Lows.

Appearance

People who have a keen sense of themselves as social objects are likely to be concerned with their appearance. College women were told in advance that their pictures would be taken in the laboratory (Miller & Cox, 1982). Judges examined the pictures and evaluated how much makeup had been applied. The amount of makeup correlated .32 with public self-consciousness. Public self-consciousness also correlated .40 with subjects' beliefs that makeup enhances appearance and social interactions and .28 with judged attractiveness of the subjects. Other researchers have also reported that women high in public self-consciousness are more attractive than Lows (Turner, Gilliland, & Klein, 1981). These investigators also found that when asked to express like or dislike of their physical features (for example, hair and eyes), women high in public self-consciousness reacted faster than Lows. Clearly, those high in public self-consciousness are especially attuned to their overt features.

Self as Target

College women participated in an experiment with two other ostensible subjects who were in reality experimental accomplices (Fenigstein, 1979). These accomplices, who seemingly were strangers, completely ignored the subject while having a conversation between themselves. All this happened in a "waiting room," and afterward the subject was given a choice of continuing in the experiment with these two "subjects" (accomplices) or obtaining two new partners. Those high in public self-consciousness chose other partners (avoided those who shunned them) to a much greater extent than the Lows. In replies to later questions, the Highs liked the accomplices less than did the Lows, but the Highs felt more responsible for the way the others behaved than did the Lows. Thus when the Highs were the targets of shunning, they directed some of the blame toward themselves, which is exactly what we would expect from people who have an acute sense of themselves as social objects.

Small groups of students were told that some of them had been chosen randomly to participate in an experiment, and each student was asked to estimate the probability that he or she had been so selected (Fenigstein, 1984). Those high in public self-consciousness exaggerated whether they had been chosen. The estimates of self as target correlated .34 with public self-consciousness.

Then Fenigstein (1984) had a new sample of subjects fill out a self-as-target questionnaire. A typical item was "You are giving a public lecture, and before you finish some people get up and leave." There were two responses to each item, one involving the self as target: for example, "The people left because the lecture was boring." Again those high in public self-consciousness answered more of the questions in the direction of self as target than did the Lows. Evidently, a focus on the public aspects of the self can make one somewhat self-centered.

Fenigstein carried this idea one step farther: "To see oneself as an object of attention, especially to others, may leave one susceptible to the idea that others are more interested in the self than is the case; the self-referent perception of the behavior of others is one of the hallmarks of paranoid thought" (Fenigstein & Vanable, 1992, p. 136). Fenigstein and Vanable constructed a paranoia scale (typical item: "Someone has it in for me"), and it correlated with public self-consciousness from .37 to .41 over four successive samples of subjects. These correlations were confirmed in research by Buss and Perry (1992) on aggression. The correlations between public self-consciousness and hostility were .32 for men and .49 for women. Among the items on the hostility scale were several that tapped suspicion: for example, "I am suspicious of overly friendly strangers."

Paranoia would seem to be the extreme end of a focus on oneself as a social object. Though public self-consciousness correlates with paranoia, a strong sense of oneself as a social object is best regarded as a requisite for paranoia but not as equivalent to it.

Private and Public Self-Consciousness

In the studies reviewed so far, when one kind of self-consciousness has had an impact, the other kind has not. Additional research has demonstrated the contrasting effects of private self-consciousness and public self-consciousness.

Relation to Other Traits

Private and public self-consciousness correlate from the low twenties (Fenigstein, Scheier, & Buss, 1975) to the low thirties (Perry & Buss, 1990). Despite this relationship, they correlate differently with other personality traits (see Table 10.3). Private self-consciousness is unrelated to self-esteem, sociability, shyness, and fear. It is only modestly related to hostility, perhaps (speculatively) because self-consciousness leads to the intensification of all affects, including the negative ones involved in hostility.

In contrast, *public* self-consciousness is correlated with all five of the other personality traits. It is modestly (negatively) related to self-esteem and more strongly related to the other four personality traits. The negative correlation with self-esteem may derive from the fact that attention to oneself as a social

TABLE 10.3   **Self-Consciousness and Other Personality Traits**

	Private self-consciousness	Public self-consciousness
Self-Esteem	.02	−.21
Shyness	.10	.34
Fear	.09	.41
Sociability	.09	.41
Hostility	.24	.41

object is usually associated with criticism, as when a person is unclean, untidy, or embarrassed (see below in the section Socialization). This assumption may also account for the correlation with shyness and perhaps with fear as well. Heightened awareness of the self as a social object may be a consequence of an interest in others, hence the correlation with sociability. The correlation with hostility—the .41 combines .32 for men and .49 for women—has already been discussed.

Laboratory Research

When subjects are pressured to comply with a group consensus, they can stick to their guns and depend on what their senses tell them or they can comply and distort their own perceptions—the well-known Asch conformity paradigm. In an auditory perception study, subjects' error scores (indicating compliance) were correlated with the two self-consciousness traits (Froming & Carver, 1981). The error scores correlated negatively with private self-consciousness: Those higher in private self-consciousness made few errors, because, knowing what they heard, they refused to comply with group pressure. The correlation between error scores and public self-consciousness was positive: Those higher in this trait conformed more to group pressure, and this resulted in more errors.

When asked to register like or dislike of their physical features, those high in public self-consciousness reacted faster than did Lows (Turner, Gilliland, & Klein, 1981). Perhaps each kind of self-consciousness causes sensitivity to different kinds of self-reference. Subjects were shown a list of words serially and asked to say yes or no for three questions: Is it a long word? Does it describe how you typically feel or think? Does it describe the way people typically see you? (Agatstein & Buchanan, 1984). Notice that the questions involve, respectively, no self-reference, private self-reference, and public self-reference. A few minutes later there was a surprise recall test. Subjects high in private self-consciousness and low in public self-consciousness recalled more private self-reference words than the other two kinds. For subjects high in public self-consciousness and low in private self-consciousness, recall was best for public self-reference words.

Nasby (1989) confirmed these findings in a recognition task. Subjects high in private self-consciousness had more intrusions, called false alarms, of private self-reference words than did Lows. Subjects high in public self-consciousness had more intrusions of public self-reference words. Presumably, such intrusions indicate a more articulated self-schema. On this assumption, Nasby concluded that his results demonstrated that "private self-consciousness (but not public self-consciousness) predicts the extent to which individuals have articulated the private component of the self-schema, whereas public self-consciousness (but not private self-consciousness) predicts the extent to which individuals have articulated the public components of the self-schema" (p. 121).

In everyday situations, personal standards of fairness may conflict with social pressure to be regarded as a nice person, a conflict examined by Greenberg (1983). Subjects were asked to divide $10 between a high-output worker who did 75% of the work and a low-output worker who did 25% of the work. Fairness suggests an equitable distribution of the money: $7.50 to the high-output worker and $2.50 to the low-output worker. But all subjects were told that they would meet with the low-output worker after the money was allocated. The social pressure of dealing with this person might lead to an equal distribution of money. Subjects high in private self-consciousness tended to offer more money to the high-output worker and reported less concern about making an impression on the low-output person. Those high in public self-consciousness tended to offer about the same amount to each worker and reported being less concerned about doing what seemed fair.

These findings were conceptually replicated by Kernis and Reis (1984). Evidently, people high in private self-consciousness focus more on personal standards of morality, whereas those high in public self-consciousness focus on themselves as social objects and therefore are concerned with the impression they make on others.

A related study used ratings of behavioral intentions to assess the strength of personal attitudes and social norms for each subject (Davis, Kasmer, & Holtgraves, 1982). In predicting behavioral intentions, private self-consciousness correlated positively with the strength of personal attitudes and negatively with social norms. The findings for public self-consciousness were more complex, this trait having an impact on behavioral intentions only when normative influences became stronger.

An experiment on cognitive dissonance is especially relevant (Scheier & Carver, 1980). Subjects were induced to write counterattitudinal essays, which set up a conflict between their original attitude and the one they were induced to write. A focus on the private aspects of the self would make subjects attend to their original (private) attitude, which in turn would make the attitude more resistant to change. A focus on the public aspects of the self would make subjects attend to their public behavior (writing an essay in the opposite direction), which in turn would make the attitude more susceptible to change. The results were as expected. Subjects high in private self-consciousness, focusing on their original attitude, resisted change. Subjects high in public self-consciousness, focusing on their public behavior, changed their attitude in the direction of the essay they wrote.

In each of these experiments, subjects high in private self-consciousness were oriented toward the covert, personal aspects of the self, and subjects high in public self-consciousness were oriented toward the overt, social aspects of the self. This divergence is especially interesting in light of the fact that the two kinds of self-consciousness correlate in the thirties. Clearly, when we know that a person focuses on the self, this knowledge is too vague, and it may be misleading: A focus on the internal aspects of the self leads to very different behavior than a focus on the external aspects of the self.

The distinction between personal and social surely is familiar by now. It appeared in the chapter on self-esteem, where the personal versus social sources of self-esteem was discussed. And it appeared in the chapter on identity, where we saw what a difference it makes whether one's identity is more personal or more social.

Transient States

Private Self-Awareness

Immediate Causes

Private self-awareness can be self-induced. One way is to daydream about oneself either when alone or in public, as students are wont to do when trapped in a dull lecture. Another way is to introspect and examine one's motives, moods, recent history, or ambitions.

A common inducer of private self-awareness is writing in a diary. Many diarists include private thoughts, feelings, and reflections about the past and the future. When writing, they are in a state of high private self-awareness. Of course, if the diary is nothing more than a recital of the day's events—jobs performed, people met, meals eaten, and the details of everyday living—there is only minimal attention to the private self.

Certain kinds of psychotherapy turn on private self-awareness, especially the uncovering varieties of psychotherapy. Clients may be asked to say whatever comes to mind, and then the therapist selectively attends to daydreams, night dreams, and the most personal aspects of what clients report about themselves. Alternatively, clients are asked directly to introspect about topics usually not revealed to others. During such sessions, the clients are in a state of high private self-awareness

Eastern philosophies have enjoyed considerable popularity in the United States. One aspect of these philosophies is the injunction to meditate. Certain kinds of meditation can induce private self-awareness, the person attending to whatever mood, feeling, or other self-topic that comes to mind.

The Special Case of a Small Mirror

A small mirror has been used to induce private self-awareness. It might seem paradoxical that a mirror would cause private self-awareness rather than public self-awareness. After all, it is the overt, public face that is seen in the mirror. The explanation may lie in habituation. How many times have we seen the image of our head and shoulders in a bathroom mirror? Even if we view this image as little as once a day, the frequency must run into many thousands. Eventually, this reflected visage has no impact of oneself as a social object. What is left is the other aspect of the self, the private self, and this aspect evidently does not habituate. If this explanation seems convoluted, another one will be needed, for the evidence for a small mirror's inducing private self-awareness is extremely strong. I shall review only those studies that demonstrate a parallel between the effects of the mirror (state) and the effects of private self-consciousness (trait).

Recall that those high in private self-consciousness, knowing themselves better, offer a self-report of aggressiveness that correlates strongly with observed laboratory aggression (Scheier, Buss, & Buss, 1978). In a related experiment, subjects who were opposed to electric shock or condoned its use were tested for intensity of aggression on the aggression machine (Carver, 1975). In the control condition (no mirror) these groups did not differ in aggression, but with a small mirror in front of them, the subjects who condoned electric shock aggressed more intensely than those who opposed it. Their attitudes were expressed in behavior only when they were made aware of the private aspects of themselves.

Similarly, self-reported sociability was compared with observed sociability in the laboratory (Pryor, Gibbons, Wicklund, Fazio, & Hood, 1977). When the self-report was made in front of a mirror, the correlation between self-reported and observed sociability was .55; in the absence of a mirror, it was .03.

Patients in a Veteran's Administration hospital were asked about their hospitalization history (Gibbons et al., 1985). Those who had a small mirror in front of them recalled their history with better accuracy than a control group.

Research described earlier revealed that those high in private self-consciousness resisted pressure to alter their attitudes (Carver & Scheier, 1978). There are parallel findings for private self-awareness. When subjects are pressured to conform, if a mirror is present, they stick to their guns and resist the pressure more than in the absence of a small mirror (Carver, 1977).

In an experiment discussed earlier, subjects were made cognitively dissonant by a counterattitidunal essay (Scheier & Carver, 1980). Those high in private self-consciousness resisted changing their original attitude, as did those exposed to a small mirror.

When told otherwise, those high in private self-consciousness can detect the true flavor of a drink better than those low in private self-consciousness (Scheier, Carver, & Gibbons, 1979). In an analogous experiment, women were told that an inert powder would cause increases in heart rate, tightness of the chest, and sweating (Gibbons, Carver, Scheier, & Hormuth, 1979). Subjects in front of a small mirror did not report these sensations, presumably because they focused on their true internal sensations. Control subjects report some of the suggested sensations.

So far, the parallels have involved self-knowledge, but there are also parallels in intensification. When angered, men high in private self-consciousness aggressed more intensely than Lows (Scheier, 1976). That research also had two experimental conditions: a small mirror or no mirror. In a precise parallel to private self-consciousness, subjects who sat in front of a mirror aggressed more intensely than the control subjects.

In a study discussed above, men high in private self-consciousness rated pictures of nude women as more attractive than did the Lows (Scheier & Carver, 1977). In the same study, a mirror and a control condition were used. The mirror led to higher ratings of attractiveness. These researchers also used both the trait and the state to study the impact of mood-inducing procedures. Both the trait (high private self-consciousness) and the state (private self-awareness induced by the mirror) led to more intense ratings of mood.

Psychiatric patients were asked how anxious, hostile, and depressed they were (Gibbons et al., 1985). Those in front of a mirror reported more intense negative affects than those in a control condition.

These various findings, which demonstrate a parallel between private self-awareness and private self-consciousness, are summarized in Table 10. 4. In some experiments, exactly the same procedure was used to study both the state and the trait. In other studies, the procedures were closely analogous.

Public Self-Awareness

Social Attention

One of the most potent inducers of public self-awareness is receiving close attention from others. It may occur in front of an audience or simply because others are staring. This kind of self-awareness is also heightened when people are being filmed or tape-recorded.

Public scrutiny often elicits a feeling of exposure, either that one's clothes are somehow transparent, revealing nakedness, or that one's skin is transparent, revealing thoughts and feelings. For most people, being closely examined elicits at least a faint feeling that there is something wrong with the public self. Why is

TABLE 10.4   Parallels between Private Self-Awareness and Private Self-Consciousness

State	Trait
Attitude toward electric shock correlates with its use	Self-report of aggression correlates with its use
Pressure to conform is resisted	Pressure to conform is resisted
Original attitude is changed little by cognitive dissonance	Original attitude is changed little by cognitive dissonance
Suggestions about bodily sensations are resisted	Suggestions about the flavor of a drink are resisted
Angry aggression is intensified	Angry aggression is intensified
Nude pictures are rated more attractive	Nude pictures are rated more attractive

public self-awareness typically uncomfortable, almost like the feeling motorists have when they see a police car in the rearview mirror? Presumably because of the way we are socialized, a topic to be discussed below.

Too little attention is also an immediate cause of public self-awareness. Recall that shunning made subjects uncomfortable enough to request other partners (Fenigstein, 1979). When people are ignored, they often seek an explanation in their own appearance or behavior, thereby focusing on the self as a social object.

Perceptual Feedback

Modern technology offers us images that tell us how we appear to others. A tape recording of your own voice sounds different from your actual voice because bone conduction is missing. What you hear on the tape, though, is what you sound like to others. You hear aspects of your voice that ordinarily escape awareness: pitch, loudness, accent, inflections. And you may be dismayed to discover that your voice is shrill, hoarse, or whiny.

Perhaps even worse is the surprise provided by videotapes. Now there are views of yourself from the side, displaying facial and body profiles, or views from the back that may embarrass you: "Is my nose that funny-looking? Am I that fat? Is my hair such a mess? (alternatively, am I that bald?)." Now add facial expressions and posture that are not pleasing, and it is clear that perceiving yourself as others perceive you is usually a blow to self-esteem. Even physically attractive men and women find fault with what they see, for they tend to focus on their minor imperfections.

Most of the problem stems from the novelty of these views of yourself as others see you. Singers and announcers hear recordings of their voices so often that they habituate to the sounds and are not made aware of themselves as social objects. Similarly, movie actors see themselves on the screen frequently enough to habituate to the sight of themselves from all angles, and eventually the movies do not induce public self-awareness. Presumably, the same kind of habituation occurs to the visage we see in our bathroom mirror every day, the basic assumption (mentioned earlier) of why a small mirror induces private self-awareness.

Development (Origins)

At birth, infants possess neither kind of self-awareness, but by school age they are able to focus on both aspects of the self. The development of self-awareness continues throughout childhood, reaching a peak at adolescence. This discussion traces the sequence of milestones for most children. But some children are precocious, and some are laggards in development. As with walking unaided—the norm for first appearance is about one year with individual variations of six months on either side—so with self-awareness: We can offer norms accompanied by considerable individual variation.

Private Self-Awareness

Covertness

Private self-awareness starts with a developmental trend toward covertness. Infants are completely uninhibited in expressing emotion, and when distressed, they cry, scream, and thrash about. As children mature, they gradually inhibit expression of their emotions. They may still become frightened or angry, but as the years pass, these emotions are first partially suppressed and, later, sometimes kept completely covert. In older children and especially in adults, a placid exterior may conceal intense, private feelings and emotions.

Young children freely express their high opinion of themselves and their grandiose ambitions. Such conceit is gradually proscribed by parents and other socializing agents, for no one likes a braggart. Though the high self-evaluation and the soaring ambition are not typically expressed, they still exist as part of the private self, the part accessible to private self-focus.

The play of young infants is entirely overt: handling objects and playing such games as peek-a-boo. Gradually, children start using fantasy, and a stick becomes an imaginary horse. Later, all the overt elements may be dropped in place of play that occurs entirely in the imagination. Even more relevant to the private self, wish-fulfilling fantasies occur with the self as hero, and most of us rarely make them known.

When infants first learn speech, they sometime practice it alone, talking to themselves. As the years pass, the motor elements slowly disappear, and the lips no longer move, as self-talking becomes entirely covert. When talking to ourselves, we often focus on the internal aspects of the self that are not open to observation.

Thus there are four components of the developmental trend toward covertness: emotional inhibition, inhibition of overt conceit, self-directed fantasy, and talking to oneself. Once children learn to conceal some of their overt behavior, once they are capable of fantasy that is detached from reality, they are likely to turn attention inward toward the covert self. And their private self-awareness is especially acute when there is a clear discrepancy between inner feelings and behavioral expressions—one's private self-esteem versus the more modest self-esteem proclaimed in public.

Private Self-Consciousness

The developmental trend toward covertness occurs in all normal children, but the immediate task is to discover why some people eventually focus on their psychological insides more than other people do. In other words, what are the origins of private self-consciousness? The answer is made difficult by the absence of research on this question. And the problem is compounded by the realization that except for religion and psychotherapy, it is difficult to influence covert cognitive processes. Still, it may be worthwhile to examine several possibilities.

One that comes to mind is *fantasy*, a component of covertness. Children vary considerably in fantasy. Some have vivid imagery, which delights them and reinforces the tendency to daydream. They are likely to develop fantasies about themselves, as children who are read to and who are encouraged by books and other media to engage in fantasy. At the opposite pole, children with an impoverished imagination, which is not enhanced by being read to or other media, are less likely to develop private self-consciousness.

A second possibility is Jung's (1933) personality trait of introversion. Introverts, by definition, turn their attention inward onto plans, thoughts, and imagery. Not all these cognitions are self-directed, for they may involve composing music, constructing a theory, or planning a building, which means that not all introverts are necessarily high in private self-consciousness. Nevertheless, any time attention is directed inward, a focus on the self becomes more likely. Other things being equal, then, we expect introverted children to become high in private self-consciousness.

Other persons are an important part of the environment. When others are not available, a large piece of the environment is missing, which may turn children inward on themselves. Isolated children are likely to develop fantasies, sometimes imaginary playmates, and, in general, turn inward. Other things being equal, they are likely to become high in private self-consciousness.

Development does not end with childhood, so we should consider influences available to adolescents and adults. Recall that keeping a diary may turn on transient private self-awareness. Chronic diary-writing is likely to cause a habit of turning inward toward the self to develop, which of course is private self-consciousness.

Recall that meditation induces private self-awareness. People who regularly meditate and focus attention chronically on the covert aspects of themselves are likely to become high in private self-consciousness.

An analogous process occurs in the previously mentioned dynamic or uncovering psychotherapies, which ask clients repeatedly to review their lives. Clients are also asked to disclose their fantasies, feelings, thoughts, and emotions. Therapists often interpret these covert cognitions and feelings, focusing attention on the client's psychological insides. Clients are rewarded directly or subtly for examining their inner feelings. Consistent reward over time is likely to heighten the trait of private self-consciousness. It might be added that clients already high in private self-consciousness would appear to be the best bets for uncovering therapies, for they need little prodding to reveal their psychological insides.

Public Self-Awareness

Awareness of oneself as a social object requires assuming the perspective of another person toward yourself so that you can observe yourself as others do. This kind of social perspective-taking is emphasized by sociologists who use such concepts as *mirror-image self* and *generalized other* (Cooley, 1902; Mead, 1934). Notice that this is not a question of spatial perspective, that is, being able to envision what a scene looks like from another angle. Rather, it is knowing or guessing what others are thinking or concentrating on.

First Appearance

When can children first take the perspective of another person? A reasonable test is whether children know that others have different preferences than their own, not because of specific knowledge (knowing a mother's preference in foods, for example) but because of general knowledge about other people. Children were shown silk stockings, a necktie, a toy truck, a doll, and an adult book (Flavell, 1968, pp. 164–168). They were asked which would be a suitable gift for father, mother, brother, sister, and self. Three year olds tended to choose the same gifts for others as for themselves, suggesting that they could not take another's perspective. Some four year olds selected appropriate gifts for others, half the five year olds did, and all of the six year olds did. Evidently, by the age of about five years, children are cognitively mature enough to know that people different from themselves would want different gifts. They have acquired the ability to place themselves in another's shoes.

It follows that children who can take the perspective of another person can then view themselves from that perspective. Earlier in life children can view themselves only from their own egocentric perspective. As their cognitive ability matures, they can begin to see themselves as social objects, that is, from the viewpoint of another person. This is of course the definition of public self-awareness.

It would help to know when children first show signs of public self-awareness. There is evidence, but it relies on the assumption that embarrassment is an indicator of public self-awareness (Buss, Iscoe, & Buss, 1979). On this assumption, public self-awareness first appears around the fifth year of life (details of the study will be offered in the next chapter). This estimate of five years coincides neatly with the data on social perspective-taking, the study of gifts (Flavell, 1968).

Learning

How do children learn to take the perspective of another person? Another's perspective is likely to be acquired through an advanced form of imitation learning. Parents, for example, observe children and comment on their behavior, often asking plaintively, "What will people think of you?" After many repetitions, children may imitate their parents by asking the same question about themselves. Such imitation is strengthened by the knowledge that others are looking at them and either approve or disapprove of what they see.

Such contingencies raise the issue of instrumental conditioning. Once children can regard themselves as social objects, rewards and punishments not only affect behavior but signal whether the children are perceiving themselves as others see them. Rewarded behavior implies that children are perceiving themselves correctly, that is, in line with the views of others. Punished behavior may reveal a discrepancy between self-views and those of others. Notice that instrumental conditioning has now shaded over into cognitive learning. And certain kinds of punishment are effective only against someone who is capable of public self-awareness—ridicule, for example.

Socialization

When children are taught to attend to the observable aspects of themselves, what specifically are they asked to focus on? These components of the public self were mentioned briefly earlier in the chapter, but here they are described in more detail. The most obvious features involve appearance. Socialization training emphasizes minimal standards of grooming and teaches children and adolescents to be aware of others' scrutiny. Hair is expected to be combed and in a more or less acceptable style. The face should be clean and preferably unblemished. Hands should be clean; nails should be clean and trimmed.

There are also minimal standards for clothing. Clothes must conceal those parts of the body that ordinarily are not exposed to others. These body parts can be seen unless they are covered, and therefore are features of the public self, but certain features of this public self are exposed only to intimate others. Such modesty may be regarded as "public privacy" (exposed unless concealed) in contrast to what might be called "private privacy," which involves not disclosing to others what is metaphorically inside one's head (concealed unless disclosed).

Clothes are expected to be clean, neat (usually unwrinkled), and fastened properly, and not torn or excessively worn, except for occasional fads in fashion. They should be appropriate to the occasion, which varies considerably in formality.

The other component of the public self involves behavioral style. Individuals are expected to have a more or less erect posture and not slump. There is a minimal standard for coordination, and those who walk and sit awkwardly or clumsily handle utensils and tools are downgraded or even ridiculed. Coordination extends to speech, which is expected to flow evenly, without excessive hesitations or stammers. And in the venting of emotions—when a person laughs, for example—some modulation is preferred to wild and uninhibited expressiveness.

Behavioral style extends into social behavior in the rule-governed contexts called formal. Individuals are expected to be aware of status differences and to greet and leave people with appropriate phrases. The phrases "Thank you" and "I beg your pardon" should be part of one's vocabulary. Certain words or phrases are taboo.

Older children who have undergone the usual socialization are aware of the social regulations governing appearance and stylistic behavior. When these rules are abrogated, there are social penalties: ridicule, scorn, teasing, and rejection by others. When children become aware of a deficiency in appearance or a mistake in style, a frequent reaction is embarrassment, which represents an acute, negative awareness of the public aspects of oneself.

Adolescence

Puberty is marked by rapid body growth and development of secondary sex characteristics. Girls' hips spread, their breasts enlarge, and menses begin. Boys start growing facial hair, and their voice drops in pitch, though sometimes a boyish squeak breaks through the more adult baritone.

The body of an adolescent feels and looks different, not only to the adolescent but to everyone else. Parents and siblings comment on the rapid changes, often in a teasing fashion. Keenly aware that they feel different and look different, adolescents are certain that everyone is looking at them, examining them. When strolling down the street, they have something in common with movie or rock stars: a belief that they are the center of attention. For some, the attention is welcome, and they may even show off, perhaps with a female hip swing or a male swagger. For many, the attention is distressing in making them feel naked and exposed. Whether the reaction is positive or negative, public self-awareness reaches its peak during adolescence.

Adulthood

As the years pass, public self-awareness diminishes. People gradually become accustomed to their bodies and no longer assume that they are the center of attention. Social roles stabilize, there are fewer mixed expectations about social roles, as social identity becomes firmly established, and there are fewer role conflicts. Adults become more knowledgeable about social stimuli and appropriate social behavior. As these various experiences accrue, social behavior becomes more habitual. There may still be considerable awareness of one's self as a social object but certainly less than in adolescence.

Public Self-Consciousness

Parents vary considerably in how intensely they socialize their children. At one extreme, formal parents, sometimes labeled old-fashioned, lay down strict rules of appearance and deportment. Children's attention is firmly directed toward themselves as social objects. Such children are likely to become high in public self-consciousness.

At the other extreme are parents who are casual about appearance and demeanor. They are more likely to value independence in their children and only minimally direct attention to the externals of self. Such children are expected to become low in public self-consciousness.

Aside from explicit socialization, the social environment of children is relevant here. Consider children of ministers, politicians, and media stars. Family life is something like living in a fishbowl: There is a stream of visitors, and the public is intensely curious about everyone. Unless the children are protected by a wall of privacy, and that is rare, they learn early that others will closely examine them. Most of them will become high in public self-consciousness and retain it beyond adolescence.

The developmental determinants of private and public self-consciousness are listed in Table 10.5.

TABLE 10.5   Developmental Determinants of Private and Public Self-Consciousness

Private determinants	Public determinants
Covertness	Socialization
Fantasy	Formality
Introversion	Conspicuous family
Uncovering therapy	Changes in body

Person and Environment

Person Affects Environment

Private self-consciousness involves focusing on the unobservable aspects of the self. Being entirely covert, it plays no role in the interaction between person and environment. Public self-consciousness, in contrast, involves a focus on the observable aspects of the self, which means that it is an important determinant of social behavior. In what follows, it is assumed that people who are high in public self-consciousness tend to be social rules-followers. In other words, they are formal.

Choosing Environments

Those high in public self-consciousness, having been trained to focus on what others can observe, like social contexts in which they know exactly what is expected of them. They are concerned about the impression being made on others and therefore pay attention to their own dress and demeanor. The more formal the situation the more specific are the social rules and the greater is the expectation that the rules will be followed. I assume that those high in public self-consciousness prefer formal situations, for example, opting for a formal party over a casual one.

Those low in public self-consciousness, being relatively unaware of themselves as social objects, are assumed to be informal. They dress casually and tend not to be concerned with the rules of etiquette. When stuck in ceremonial settings such as weddings, funerals, or graduations, they are fidgety and uncomfortable. They prefer the give-and-take of social interaction in situations with few rules, where they can be themselves, maintaining their unawareness of themselves as social objects.

Modifying the Environment

When people high in public self-consciousness find themselves in a casual social environment, they may be uncomfortable at the lack of social structure. They might want to invoke more social rules, but it would be difficult because most people resist adding such rules. Therefore, they are limited in the ability to modify the environment.

It is much easier to relax rules and make a situation more informal, which is one reason that most people like to go on picnics or drop into bars. Therefore, those low in public self-consciousness are likely to attempt to modify the environment. A Low would probably be the first man to take off his coat and loosen his tie or perhaps sit on the floor. A Low is more likely to tell an off-color joke or suggest a wild party game. Lows not only chafe more when confronted with formal situations but are more likely to succeed in modifying them.

Matching

When husband and wife are both high or both low in public self-consciousness, the match bodes well for the relationship. They understand each other and have similar social preferences. Each High implicitly knows why the other person is so self-conscious. Each Low likes being able to be unself-consciously oneself without worrying about oneself as a social object.

But problems arise when there is a mismatch. The wife who is high in public self-consciousness becomes upset that her husband is so careless about the impression he is making. Why does he dress so inappropriately, and why are his table manners so poor? Being a Low, he wonders why she is so concerned about herself as a social object and why she is so fussy about manners. Does she not feel confident enough to be herself without constantly being concerned about the impression she is making? As in most mismatches, there will be little empathy.

Assuming the marriage is basically secure, we expect both extremes to modify their behavior at least a little. The wife may loosen up, for example, going to the supermarket in old clothes or without makeup. The husband may tone up his table manners, dress up a little more, and exercise caution about freely venting his opinions about politics or religion. Such modifications reduce the gap between husband and wife, making the relationship more tranquil. Of course, harmony ultimately depends on each accepting the other without demanding major changes.

Chapter *11*

Shyness

History

The history of research on shyness can be briefly related, for the topic was largely ignored until the last decade or two. Baldwin (1894) distinguished between two kinds of bashfulness in children. Other early papers on shyness, published in British journals, focused on it as maladjustment (Campbell, 1896; Hampton, 1927). As for shyness observed among normal people, Lewinsky (1941) wrote,

> We find shyness described as a character trait, as an attitude, or as a state of inhibition. The fact of inhibition as such is not a distinguishing mark, as the inhibition of impulses is commonly expected after the earliest phases of child-hood. However, inhibition in shyness is not volitional, but compulsory. . . . It is a state of hyper-inhibition, usually accompanied by physical symptoms like blushing, stammering, perspiring, trembling, going pale, accessory movements and increased urinary and faecal urges. The mental state is described by the individual as a feeling of inferiority, of not being wanted, of intruding; it is coupled with an inability to say the right thing at the right moment. (p. 105)

This description is as appropriate today as it was more than fifty years ago.

In the United States, Guilford and Guilford (1934, 1936) used factor analysis of self-reports to obtain a shyness scale. Some of the items appear to assess shyness: "Are you inclined to be shy in the presence of the opposite sex?" and "Do you feel ill at ease when with other people?" However, other items obviously tapped into sociability: "Do you like to mix socially with people?" and "Would you rather spend an evening reading at home than attend a large party?" As might be expected from the presence of both kinds of items on the shyness scale, Eysenck (1953) later demonstrated that shyness correlated with both introversion and neuroticism.

Shyness continued to appear as a factor on personality inventories—see Comrey (1965), for example—but there was no specific measure of shyness. Watson and Friend (1969) constructed a questionnaire assessing fear of negative evaluation, which had shyness items but also a variety of other items about concern about the impressions of others and lack of confidence, for instance. Thus the topic of shyness was not examined closely and systematically until the appearance of two books: Zimbardo's (1977) and my own (1980). These books spurred research on shyness that continues to this day.

Components

Overt Behavior

Lewinsky (1941) was on target when she characterized shyness as inhibited behavior. To be more precise, it is the *inhibition of normally expected social behavior.* There is less time spent talking, and conversations are not initiated. When a reply is called for, it is brief and halting. Others may regard this taciturn behavior as haughty, but it is nothing more than a shutting down of responsiveness.

The voice typically is soft, though sometimes it is strained and hoarse. Speech inflections are sparse, and there are few accompanying gestures. If there are gestures, they are likely to be nervous movements such as touching oneself or, at the extreme, tics. Facial expressions are absent, except possibly for an apologetic half-smile, a tightly clamped jaw, or other signs of tension. Gaze is averted, and sometimes the head is kept down. The handshake often is weak and tentative, and there may be nervous touching of the face or body.

Typically, there are signs of behavioral disorganization: stuttering, hesitation, and self-interruptions. Speech may halt in mid-sentence or trail off into silence. When two shy people meet, there may be long periods of silence as each waits for the other to start talking.

There is a tendency to escape from social situations, especially those with strangers or casual acquaintances. When people are shy, they keep their distance from others, typically remaining on the fringe of a conversational group. They are ready to leave long before anyone else.

Some people remain physically present but escape in their imagination. A woman related how she dealt with her extreme shyness at parties and other crowded social gatherings. She pretended that she was off by herself, enjoying a walk through the forest or reading a book of poetry. This stratagem enabled her to relax and smile as if she were enjoying the situation. She solved her immediate discomfort but of course never dealt with the enduring problem of her shyness.

Shyness is also evident in avoidance of social occasions: refusal to attend parties or dances and reluctance to go on dates. At the extreme, the tendency to avoid others, especially when social evaluation might occur, results in not applying for a job because the interview would be too painful.

Physiological Reactions

The body's reaction depends on which division of the autonomic nervous system is activated. If the person is anxious, the sympathetic division predominates, as manifested in the typical autonomic reaction of fear: increased heart rate, blood pressure, sweating, breathing. If the person is embarrassed, the parasympathetic division predominates, as manifested in facial blushing. More of this distinction later.

Cognitions

Shy behavior is typically accompanied by worry over one's own social performance: saying the wrong thing, not being able to think of something to say, or being physically clumsy. There is also concern about what others might think or feel, the assumption being that rejection is likely. Perhaps others will focus their attention excessively, causing one to feel conspicuous, or, worse still, one is ignored and feels shunned. If another person fails to respond warmly, then fault must be one's own. More generally, if anything in the social situation does go wrong, it will be attributed to oneself.

Patterning

The various components of shyness are summarized in Table 11.1. Typically, shyness is manifested in several components, but one component is likely to be predominant. Thus one person might display strongly inhibited overt behavior but have only a weak physiological reaction and few shy cognitions. For another per-

---

TABLE 11.1   Components of Shyness

Overt behavior

> Inhibition
>> Verbal
>> Expressive
> Disorganization of behavior
> Escape, avoidance tendencies

Physiological reaction

> Sympathetic reactivity (if anxious)
> Parasympathetic reactivity (if embarrassed)

Cognitions

> Worry over own mistakes or rejection by others
> Worry about excessive or insufficient attention
> Negative self-attributions

---

son it might be the physiological reaction that is most prominent. Such individual differences surely are worthy of study.

Suppose only one component is present. Should we label the behavior as shy? If a person displays inhibited social behavior but denies being concerned, and there is no evidence of physiological reactivity, is that shy behavior? If the overt social behavior is normal but the person reports being upset, is that shy behavior?

As a prelude to answering the question, consider fear of snakes. If a person shrinks back from snakes and avoids them, we conclude that fear has occurred even in the absence of the physiological and cognitive components. And if a person does approach snakes but reports feeling scared, we also infer the presence of fear.

Similarly, the answer to the questions about shyness must be yes. As with fear, anger, and other emotional reactions, we label the behavior as shy if any one component is present: overt behavior, physiological reaction, or self-reported cognitions.

Two Kinds of Shyness

The physiological reaction in shyness, as mentioned earlier, may be sympathetic-dominant or parasympathetic-dominant. This dichotomy mirrors a conceptual distinction between two kinds of shyness: *anxious shyness* and *self-conscious shyness*. These two labels describe the basic contrast between the two kinds of shyness, but the two kinds also differ in when they first occur during development, their immediate causes, and their relationship to personality traits.

But first a note on usage. In this chapter it will be simpler to use the term *self-conscious* to refer to (a) only public self-consciousness, and (b) both transient states and the enduring disposition.

Anxious Shyness

Development

First Occurrence

Recall the strange situation in which the mother leaves the room and a stranger attempts to interact with the infant (Ainsworth, Bell, & Stayton, 1971). During the second six months of the first year of life, many infants display fear and wariness toward the stranger. They may retreat or merely show a cry face. If the mother is present when a stranger is there, infants tend to cling to her or hide behind her. This *stranger anxiety*, fear of social novelty, marks the first appearance of anxious shyness.

It might be argued that the infant's fear response depends on who the stranger is, for adults vary considerably in physique and personality. In an unusual study, Smith and Sloboda (1986) used eight different strangers to demonstrate that infants' response to strangers was consistent. Those who were afraid of one stranger were afraid of all or most of them.

Childhood

As infants mature, they gradually achieve better motor control, become less emotional, and habituate to social novelty. Consequently, many infants who display stranger anxiety in the first year of life eventually grow out of it. Greenberg and Marvin (1982) reported that most preschool children no longer fear strangers, but a minority still do. They observed one group of preschoolers who withdrew from strangers, avoided gaze, and seemed to want only to escape though there was no outright fear. The second group were not only avoidant but cried and revealed other facial expressions of fear. Clearly, some children continue to be anxiously shy, some only with adults, others with peers. These developmental trends have emerged from several longitudinal studies.

The best-known research is that of Kagan and his colleagues at Harvard (Kagan, Reznick, Clarke, Snidman, & Garcia-Coll, 1984; Kagan, Reznick, & Snidman, 1987; Kagan, Reznick, Snidman, Gibbons, & Johnson, 1988), who use the terms *inhibited* and *shy* to characterize the avoidant behavior of children faced with social unfamiliarity. One cohort of children was observed initially at the age of twenty-one months with an unfamiliar examiner, unfamiliar toys, and when separated from the mother. From a larger group of children, two groups were selected, inhibited and uninhibited children. "The major signs of behavioral inhibition were long latencies to interact with unfamiliar adults, retreat from unfamiliar objects, cessation of play and vocalization, and long periods remaining proximal to the mother" (Kagan et al., 1988, p. 1580).

This cohort was observed again at four years of age, this time with an unfamiliar peer; again at five and a half years with an unfamiliar peer, an examiner, and a room full of unfamiliar objects (yielding a composite index of inhibition); and once more at seven and a half years in a play situation with seven to ten unfamiliar peers and a testing situation with an examiner. The index of inhibition at twenty-one months correlated .52 with inhibition at five and a half years. Next, the inhibition scores at twenty-one months were plotted against inhibition scores at seven and a half years, which yielded a slope of .50 (Kagan et al., 1988).

A second cohort, first observed at thirty-one months and again at the same ages as the first cohort, yielded corroborating findings. When children are identified as uninhibited in early childhood, many of them continue to manifest shy behavior through middle childhood.

In the research by Kagan and his colleagues, young children are exposed to both unfamiliar people and objects, which means that the children's inhibition is broader than shyness, which is specifically social. However, Kochanska (1991), using factor analysis, found that there are two independent patterns of inhibition. The first involves the young child's reaction to a new environment, the first ten minutes in the laboratory; this is nonsocial inhibition. The second involves the child's reaction to the first five minutes with an unfamiliar person; this is social inhibition or stranger anxiety.

These children, first seen as toddlers of one and a half to three and a half years, were followed up several years later (Kochanska & Radke-Yarrow, 1992). At the age of five years they were observed playing with an unfamiliar peer. Multiple regression analysis revealed that social inhibition in toddlers predicted their shy behavior at age five, but nonsocial inhibition did not. This finding, together with the appearance of two factors, means that we must separate wariness about unfamiliar objects and events from fear of social interaction, which of course is shyness.

In a Swedish study, children were tested for behavioral inhibition at sixteen months, and then the quality of their free play with peers in a child-care facility was evaluated two years later (Broberg, Lamb, & Hwang, 1990). The two correlated −.54: the greater the inhibition, the poorer was the quality of free play. Within a few weeks of the first test, these children were placed in a municipal day-care setting. This increased contact with strange adults for two years did not alter the children's inhibition at forty months, which led the authors to conclude, "Inhibition in the first years of life is best viewed as a stable dimension that is not systematically affected by ordinary life changes like those implicit in the initiation of out-of-home care" (p. 1161).

The other major longitudinal study, done in Munich, started with four year olds (Asendorpf, 1990, 1991, 1992). One measure was parental ratings, and the other was latency to first utterance. "Children's shyness at age 4 as measured by the aggregate of the parent scale and the latency measure . . . correlated .75 with the same measure at age 6 . . . and .62 with the same measure at age 8" (1992, p. 73). These correlations, higher than those of the investigations in the United States, may have been inflated by the use of parental ratings. Perhaps if only observations were used, the correlations would be in the fifties, comparable to those of Kagan and his colleagues.

Adolescence

The advent of adolescence marks crucial changes in social roles. Adolescents have one foot rooted in childhood and the other foot tentatively stepping toward adulthood. They are expected to relinquish childish behavior and social roles for more mature behavior and adult roles. As a further complication, there are mixed and conflicting role expectations from different sources: parents, peers, and media. Movies, television, books, and magazines tend to present idealized pictures of adolescent social role and behavior. Peers expect conformity to group norms, and parents want more responsibility and grown-up behavior.

Consider a fifteen-year-old boy on his first date. His head may be filled with the adult male images presented in movies and on television, but he lacks the skill and knowledge to play such roles. What do you say to the girl's parents? How late can you two stay out? How far can you go sexually? Will she like you? In the face of inexperience and at least implicit evaluation, certainly by the girl and perhaps by her parents, the boy is likely to be anxiously shy. Indeed, adolescence surely marks one peak of this kind of shyness (the other peak occurring in infancy as stranger anxiety).

Adulthood

With the passing of adolescence, social roles become stable. There are fewer mixed expectations, perhaps none. There are fewer conflicts about social roles, perhaps none. As the years pass, most adults become knowledgeable about social contexts and acquire the skills needed to deal with them. The lot of a minority, however, is chronic anxious shyness.

This minority was studied longitudinally, starting in late childhood and followed up thirty years later (Caspi, Elder, & Bem, 1988). In this cohort, childhood shyness posed no particular problems for women in adulthood, but it did for men. Men who were shy as children tended to take longer as adults to fulfill male adult social roles than nonshy peers. They were late in marrying, becoming fathers, and entering stable careers. "Thus, it appears that childhood shyness was evoked again in new settings that required these men to initiate action and social contacts. Their shy interactional style affected them most at precisely those transition points during which young adults are called on to make critical choices about work and family" (p. 829).

These subjects were first studied when they were eight to ten years of age; they may have had either kind of shyness or both. However, though the children were old enough to be self-conscious, this age range seems to be too young for the presence of the extreme public self-consciousness that constitutes shyness. Furthermore, it seems unlikely that self-consciousness would prevent the subjects from initiating action and social contacts as adults. It follows that what was being studied here probably was essentially anxious shyness.

Immediate Causes

At one time or another, most children and adults experience anxious shyness. There are two major classes of causes.

Novelty

The first, social novelty, starts with the now-familiar *stranger anxiety*. Infants and young children may become especially anxious when a stranger approaches closely and perhaps touches them. Clearly, what upsets them is physical intrusion, for as long as the stranger is far enough away, there is little fear. As children mature, such intrusion loses its ability to frighten them, and they tolerate strangers approaching them. However, in these days of escalating crime, many adults are wary of letting strangers get too close; women are especially careful.

Often we meet strangers on the job, at a party, dinner, or similar social occasion where there is no physical danger, so physical intrusion is not the issue. Rather, the cause of shyness is *unfamiliarity*. We are not sure what to say or what the stranger will say. We don't know what to expect or what the stranger expects of us. Some topics of conversation may be explosive, so we step carefully in the minefield of potentially taboo topics. Perhaps a humorous comment will backfire because it is unexpectedly offensive. Perhaps the stranger will quickly become bored. Can we latch on to a topic of conversation that is interesting but not offensive? The unknown may cause at least mild apprehension and inhibited social behavior.

Unfamiliar social settings may cause shyness. For many of us change is a way of life. In the military, men and women move from one post to another every several years. Employees are shifted from one city to another. Families move to different dwellings, and children change schools. Most of us can remember the trepidation of the first day at high school or college. Everyone seems to know everyone else, and no one is interested in getting to know you. There is a feeling of being out of place, for you are the stranger here. Little in your experience prepares you for this situation, and you are unsure how to behave. So you watch, listen, and say nothing. You remain on the fringe of any social group and inhibit your normal social behavior until you receive some cues about how to behave. And you may feel some social anxiety.

Even beyond adolescence, adults may move from one social role to another. A man or woman may be promoted to supervisor, now becoming in charge of those who were formerly fellow employees. Old patterns of peer social behavior must give way to the unfamiliar social behavior of a person with higher status. Divorce and widowhood have their own changed role expectations, and for those who remarry and have stepchildren, the role of a stepparent is new and offers its own perils. And the stepchildren must deal with a comparable novelty in how they relate to the new parent.

When there is novelty—a stranger, a social setting, or a social role—there is an initial conflict between the motives of security and exploration. In each instance, the way to deal with unfamiliarity is to explore the new environment and start coping with it. At first there is so little knowledge of the environment and appropriate behavior that the need for security predominates, leading to the inhibition of normally expected social behavior. As people, roles, and settings become familiar, the person becomes more secure. Instrumental social behavior now occurs as the person explores the social environment and responds more freely. The initial shyness wanes and then disappears.

Evaluation

Once past infancy, children are exposed to social evaluation. The appraisal occurs in situations that may be aligned along a continuum from explicit to implicit. The more explicit the evaluation, the greater the probability of shy behavior. Thus in a job interview, many people are stiff and inhibited; some freeze and have difficulty speaking normally. In a fraternity rush, the potential pledge knows that his every move is under scrutiny. When a young woman first meets her fiancé's parents, she realizes that she is being examined closely to see if she measures up.

The social evaluation that occurs on a date is less explicit. The major goals are having a good time and getting to know each other, but as the other person gets to know you, he or she is also evaluating you. Evaluation also may occur when same-sex people are introduced. They may never meet again, and there may be little motivation for getting to know each other. Still, there may be an undercurrent of implicit evaluation, though it is expected to be only a weak cause of shy behavior.

Among the major criteria of social appraisal are attractiveness, friendliness, social skills, and conformity to local social rules of comportment. When people are rejected or realize that they have failed a social test (or are likely to fail), they become worried and socially cautious. Such wariness and inhibition render it difficult for them to cope with evaluation-laden situations. They are unlikely to be friendly and therefore may be seen as cold and distant. And they are unlikely to add the social skills that would cope with social evaluation.

The fact of social evaluation has led some psychologists to offer *self-presentation* as a cause of shy behavior (Schlenker & Leary, 1982). They start with two related assumptions of self-presentation theory: (1) there is explicit or implicit evaluation in all social situations, and (2) people inevitably strive to sustain a favorable impression on others. But in some contexts, people may doubt that they can carry it off or that something will happen to ruin the impression they are trying to convey. Fearing negative evaluation, they become socially inhibited.

Arkin (1981) suggested that this shy behavior is regarded as protective self-presentation. He hypothesized two kinds of self-presentation. In the first kind, acquisitive, people take risks to attain social status and approval. In the second kind, protective, people take no risks and act cautiously so as to avoid social disapproval. Presumably, shy people engage in protective self-presentation as a way of minimizing the anticipated social disapproval.

Enduring Causes

The term *enduring* refers to causes that are maintained over months and years, or as we shall see, a cause that may be present at birth. All the enduring causes to be discussed here are assumed to be specific to anxious shyness. They do not apply to self-conscious shyness, because they involve inheritance, occur too early in life, or involve events known to affect only anxiety.

Heredity

The inheritance of shyness has been established by research on twins. In one of the earliest studies, mid-parent ratings of children's shyness correlated .58 for identical twins and .23 for fraternal twins. By the middle 1980s there were a dozen and a half twin studies, all with similar findings on shyness (Plomin & Daniels, 1986, table 1).

Most of this research depended on the ratings of parents or the self-reports of twins, but in several studies, observers evaluated twins' behavior directly. The inheritance of shyness shows up as early as one year. Matheny (1989) observed infants' fear during testing (shyness) and reported these correlations in one year olds: .76 for identical twins and .48 for fraternal twins. He also had comparable data on twins eighteen, twenty-four, and thirty months old, and at each age, the correlation for identical twins was clearly higher than that for fraternal twins. Across all ages the respective correlations were .75 and .21. In another study, fourteen-month-old twins were observed in the home and laboratory, the focus being on how they reacted to strangers (Emde et al., 1992). For identical twins the correlation for shyness was .70 and for fraternal twins, .45.

As with any inherited personality trait, the fact that anxious shyness is inherited does not imply that it is fixed for life. "Because these data describe population averages, it is certainly possible for a shy individual to change. The finding of genetic effects implies hereditary propensities, not predestination" (Plomin & Daniels, 1986, p. 76).

Temperament

Temperaments, it will be recalled, are inherited tendencies that appear early in life. Two temperaments would seem to be related to shyness: fear and sociability. Temperamentally fearful infants are likely to become insecurely attached, and, by definition, they are afraid of both social and nonsocial objects. Other things being equal, then, temperamental fear is a precursor of shyness. Two kinds of evidence are consistent with this hypothesis.

First, Bronson (1970) reported that crying and distress at visual novelty in infants four to nine months correlated with shyness .56 when the infants were two to three years old. Second, the research of Kagan and his colleagues (Kagan et al., 1984, 1987, 1988), mentioned earlier, demonstrated that social and nonsocial inhibition in infancy or toddlerhood tended to develop into shyness later in childhood.

The rationale for the relevance of temperamental sociability is different. Unsociable infants have a relatively weak need to be with others, by definition. Having only this weak motive, they are less tolerant of the negatives of social interaction. Strangers arouse less curiosity in them but a full measure of fear. Since others are less socially rewarding, again by definition, young unsociable children are likely to seek immediate escape from social novelty. As a result, they tend not to become familiar with strangers, and social novelty continues to be a stimulus for inhibited social behavior.

In brief, the two temperaments of fear and sociability may be seen as enduring causes of anxious shyness. One possibility is that the heritability of the trait of anxious shyness is entirely accounted for by these two inherited temperaments. The alternative is that shyness is inherited on its own, independently of the temperaments, but they contribute to the trait. The only reason for favoring the first alternative, shyness deriving from the two temperaments, is parsimony.

Attachment

Insecurely attached infants (see Chapter 4) lack the secure base from which they may explore social environments. Later in childhood they are likely to be anxious in the presence of those they do not know well, generally wary of others, and cautious in their social behavior—in other words, shy. Avoidant infants are especially at risk for anxious shyness for the same reason as unsociable infants: a readiness to cut and run at the first sign of social difficulty.

Learning

Social novelty, an immediate cause of anxious shyness, tends to wane as strangers become familiars. The process by which this occurs is habituation, the most primitive form of learning. The more children are exposed to new situations and strangers, the more likely they are to become accustomed to dealing with social novelty. Consider, for example, the children of men and women in the army, who are affectionately called army brats. As the military parent is shifted from one base to another, usually every three or four years, the children must abandon their old friends and join entirely new social groups, in which they know no one. As one of them once said, "You learn to cope with all the moving and meet new people or just sit in the corner and cry." Most army brats do learn to cope, because after several moves, new social environments and challenges are no longer a novelty. They have habituated.

But what if habituation is not allowed to occur? Some children are raised in rural isolation, their main social contacts being those that occur in school. Such insularity means that such children rarely see strangers. Unable to habituate, they maintain their fear of strangers and remain anxiously shy.

As with any chronic fear, the trait of anxious shyness can be acquired through *traumatic avoidance conditioning*. A young child may be treated roughly by strangers or sharply rejected by peers. It may require only a single bad experience for the child to acquire a lasting tendency to avoid social novelty: "Once bitten, twice shy."

Self-Conscious Shyness

Self-conscious shyness represents the extreme of awareness of oneself as a social object. It is a feeling of psychological nakedness, as though one were completely exposed to others. It is often accompanied by embarrassment, but one can experience keen public self-awareness without being embarrassed. However, embarrassment is always accompanied by acute public self-awareness. Thus embarrassment is a major component of self-conscious shyness, but the two are not precisely equivalent.

Development

When embarrassment does occur, it is a clear indicator of self-conscious shyness. Toward the end of the last chapter, a study on the development of embarrassment was mentioned (Buss, Iscoe, & Buss, 1979), with the promise that details would be offered here. The question concerned when embarrassment first occurs. It would be difficult ethically to induce embarrassment in children, so the study relied on secondhand reports. We sent a questionnaire to parents of elementary and preschool children, inquiring about blushing or other signs of embarrassment. We deliberately avoided defining embarrassment so that parents would not be constricted by our definition. Almost all the questionnaires were filled out by mothers.

Gender differences were trivial and subsequently ignored. The results for each age group are presented in Table 11.2. Embarrassment was reported in roughly a fifth of the three year olds, a tenth of the four year olds, half the five year olds, and most of the six year olds. The percentage then leveled off for older children, allowing for the normal, minor variation from one age sample to the next.

When does embarrassment first occur? It is present in a few precocious children who are three or four years old, but in half of the five year olds. A conservative interpretation is that the norm is during the fifth year of life, so that by the

TABLE 11.2   Development of Embarrassment

Age	Ratio (embarrassment/total)	Percentage
3	3/14	21
4	2/20	10
5	15/30	50
6	28/39	72
7	35/49	71
8	34/50	68
9	30/50	60
10	24/32	75
11	13/21	62
12	13/18	72

age of five years at least half the children have developed it. Some children manifest self-conscious shyness earlier, and some later. And some children have so little awareness of themselves as social objects that they never or rarely suffer from this kind of shyness.

This interpretation is based on more than these parental reports. Bear in mind the cognitive development that must precede public self-consciousness. Children must also be told and shown repeatedly that others are examining them until eventually children can develop awareness of themselves as social objects. Until then, there is no basis for embarrassment. Thus cognitive development and socialization training lay the foundations for the occurrence of embarrassment; so it makes sense that the process can take most children into the fifth year of life.

Edelmann (1987) assumes that embarrassment in the fifth year of life is primitive because children are not sufficiently mature to understand when they experience embarrassment, such understanding requiring the advent of self-presentation. Accordingly, he suggests that a more mature embarrassment develops at roughly eight years of age, and his entire developmental scheme has five factors:

1. An ability to understand that one is a social object with an outward appearance to others
2. An ability to see from someone else's viewpoint that impression-management styles influence the way an individual is perceived
3. Knowledge of what constitutes acceptable behavior within a given culture or subculture
4. An ability to understand that changes in appearance can be conveyed by various impression-management strategies
5. An ability to understand that one can make inferences about others on the basis of appearance (p. 119)

As was just mentioned, self-conscious shyness represents the extreme of public self-awareness: an acute focus on oneself as a social object. The end of the last chapter described public self-awareness in adolescence, when it peaks, and in adulthood, when it wanes. That description applies equally to self-conscious shyness.

Immediate Causes

Self-conscious shyness is of course intense public self-awareness. It follows that the immediate causes of this kind of shyness are the events that cause the intense awareness of oneself as a social object. Gross and Stone (1964) suggested three classes of causal events: misplaying identities, losing poise, and losing confidence. Several studies had subjects list the events that make them embarrassed. Several dozen causes of embarrassment were then grouped into three clusters: impropriety, incompetence, and conspicuousness (Sattler, 1965). Miller (1992) had high-school and college students describe their last embarrassment, and the large list that emerged was assembled into these categories: individual behavior, interactive behavior, audience provocation, and bystander behavior.

The events that subjects reported as causes of embarrassment have also been factor analyzed. One study yielded five factors: accidental foolishness, inability to respond, being the passive center of attention, watching someone else fail, and inappropriate sexual encounters (Modigliani, 1968). In his book, Edelmann (1987) reported four factors: embarrassment to others, vicarious embarrassment, others' behavior, and appearing foolish. At the risk of challenging empirical work, I find it difficult to understand some of these factors. Consider Edelmann's first factor, which consists of items on these topics:

1. calling for a first date,
2. overheard talking to yourself,
3. walking into a bathroom occupied by the opposite sex,
4. overpraising on a first date,
5. surprising a couple necking.

The first and fourth items deal with heterosexual relationships, but the first involves novelty, and the fourth overpraise. The second, third, and fifth items deal with a breach of the public/private distinction, but the second item involves only oneself, whereas the third and fifth items involve others. Thus the factor contains a mix of novelty, overpraise, and very different invasions of privacy, a mélange that makes little conceptual sense. This is not a criticism of the study, but it does suggest that the factors that emerge from subjects' reports of causes are likely to be blends of conceptually distinct causes of shyness.

The various classes of the immediate causes of self-conscious shyness mentioned above, despite problems with the factors and despite the different names given, clearly have much in common. They overlap an earlier grouping of mine (Buss, 1980, chap. 8), which I have revised and elaborated, as follows.

Conspicuousness

A prominent cause of self-conscious shyness is a feeling of being conspicuous. One reason for this feeling is excessive attention from others. As we saw in Chapter 4, social attention is rewarding in the middle range of the dimension but aversive at the high end. For some people, all it takes is being in a public place, such as a restaurant or dance floor. Somehow, every little gesture or comment, every aspect of clothes or behavior, will be noticed by others. Of course, there may be a good reason for feeling that you are the center of attention. Others at the table might be too noisy, or people at other tables may be staring. Perhaps attention is directed to you, as at a birthday party or because a host insists on introducing you to everybody in the room.

Too little attention is also aversive. If you are shunned by others, who for whatever reason will not talk to you—it may be adventitious or deliberate—this exclusion is likely to make you feel conspicuous and therefore self-consciously shy.

Another reason for feeling conspicuous is difference from others. You feel conspicuous when you are a minority of one in the midst of others who are strikingly different from you. You might be the only woman in a pilot training class or the only man assisting a Girl Scout troop. Being so obviously different calls so much attention to you that it surely inhibits social behavior. That is the time to keep quiet and not draw any attention to yourself.

Breaches of Privacy

Children are routinely taught the difference between public and private behavior. When the barrier between public and private is violated, that is, when private behavior occurs in public, the outcome is usually embarrassment. Three such breaches may be summarized as unseen, unheard, and untouched.

The most frequent and perhaps most intense embarrassment occurs over body modesty. If you are the one who is not fully clothed, you may be the only one who becomes embarrassed. But consider an event that most people have experienced: Someone inadvertently enters a room when you are not fully dressed. It is nobody's fault, but, having been strongly socialized in body modesty, both of you are intensely embarrassed.

Then there are body noises, best not fully described, that cause embarrassment when heard by others. And there are parts of the body that are not to be touched except when two people are intimate. If a stranger or friend accidentally touches these parts, say, a man brushes against a woman's breast or a woman against a man's genitals, both usually become embarrassed.

Being touched represents the endpoint of personal space, that circle of space around each of us (Hall, 1966). The intimate zone extends about two feet in front of the body. "This is the distance of lovemaking, and wrestling, comforting and protecting" (p. 110). When anyone but a lover or a family member gets too close, we tend to back up. On a crowded elevator or bus, everyone is asked to face forward so that no one is confronted with another's eyes only a foot away; it is too close for comfort. It might be expected that shy people stay farther away from others, but this expectation is only partially correct. Shy people maintain a greater personal distance only with those of the opposite sex (Carducci & Webber, 1979).

The *physical privacy* just described can be maintained only if others are not around or if they remain sufficiently far away. This domain is essentially that of the social self, which is relevant to public self-awareness. But there is a covert self as well, which is relevant to private self-awareness: thoughts, feelings, ambitions, love, and jealousy. This *psychological privacy* may be breached by yourself when you inadvertently blurt out a hidden feeling or make a Freudian slip, which is then interpreted by others. The usual reaction is acute embarrassment.

Actions of Others

The staring of others, causing conspicuousness, has already been mentioned, but there are more active behaviors by others that cause shyness. The most serious is teasing, which causes considerable discomfort to the victim to the considerable amusement of onlookers. People tease others with a nickname long ago abandoned as childish or about physical features such as baldness, excessive weight, or skinniness. They may ridicule another's name, clothes, or speech accent. Children, not having been taught consideration for others, may be especially vicious in their teasing, but such teasing does not stop at the end of childhood. A girl may be teased about being flat-chested or a boy about having a squeaky voice. A male adolescent may reveal a friend's crush on a girl or reveal to his friend that a girl has a similar crush. Such ridicule is designed to embarrass others, the hostility typically being justified as just another example of humor.

But even well-meaning social behavior can cause embarrassment, as in the case of overpraise. Overpraise is evidently a case of too much of a good thing, that is, compliments causing mild distress. One explanation is that overpraise inevitably involves being made conspicuous. Thus when a person receives a letter announcing their winning a prestigious award, there is no embarrassment. But when praised effusively by another, especially when others are present, there is embarrassment. For example, in her son's presence a mother brags about her son's accomplishments to neighbors. An example more familiar to psychologists is being lauded excessively in an introduction to a speech.

To check on conspicuousness as the explanation, L. Buss (1978) had a confederate individually tell college women subjects how attractive and sensitive they came across to her. Several months earlier the subjects had rated themselves for attractiveness and sensitivity, so the confederate could deliver overpraise, underpraise, or the same evaluation as the subjects'. Overpraise, as expected, elicited blushing in most subjects, but blushing was infrequent when there was criticism or when the evaluation agreed with the subjects' prior self-evaluation. The fact that there was some blushing even without overpraise confirms that conspicuousness can cause embarrassment, but overpraise elicits even more embarrassment.

The last action of others that can cause embarrassment is their own embarrassing behavior. When a child does something silly in public, the parents may be embarrassed. This is *empathic embarrassment*. As Miller (1991) demonstrated, even the foolish actions of a stranger can cause empathic embarrassment. And just as we react with distress at the distress of a Hollywood heroine on the screen while watching a movie, we may become embarrassed while watching her in an embarrassing situation.

Foolish Actions

Mishaps often lead to embarrassment, and even thinking about a specific example can cause wincing. Imagine that at a social gathering you trip and wind up sprawled on the floor, or you reach for food and spill wine on your hostess's gown. Suppose you are introducing a friend and suddenly forget her name, or you are greeted by someone who clearly knows you but you have no recollection of meeting him before. Worse still, you call him by the wrong name.

Then there are the inadvertent traps of ordinary conversation. You ask an acquaintance how his wife is, only to discover that they are divorced or, worse still, that she has died. Or you ask how his job is going, but he has just been fired. At such times, you may look for a place to hide.

Notice that in each instance the mistake is compounded by all the attention it draws to you. Such conspicuousness is especially marked when people are forced by public pressure to behave in ways that they believe are foolish or immature. Thus Apsler (1975) induced keen embarrassment in college men by requiring them to dance, laugh for thirty seconds, sing, and imitate a child's temper tantrum. This experiment is analogous to some parties at which guests are asked to indulge in silly or outrageous behavior that is likely to embarrass them. And adding insult to injury, they are likely to be teased about their behavior.

Embarrassment and Shame

Embarrassment and shame are similar in several ways. Both require the presence of others who realize that some kind of social mistake has been made. Both involve the most acute and psychologically distressing end of the dimension of oneself as a social object. In both there is a loss of self-esteem. And like embarrassment, shame causes the inhibition of social behavior that is the hallmark of shyness.

But the two emotions differ in many ways, and these differences help to illuminate the nature of embarrassment. The most important difference is that shame involves morality, that is, a moral lapse, but embarrassment involves more trivial social errors. Also embarrassment falls under the heading of self-conscious shyness, whereas shame has the added element of a strongly negative evaluation and therefore involves anxious shyness as well. The various differences between embarrassment and shame are outlined in Table 11.3, which also offers a review of the aspects of embarrassment.

Enduring Causes

Socialization and Ridicule

Some people who are high in public self-consciousness can use this self-focus in their attempts to manage the impression others have of them. However, most people who are high in public self-consciousness are likely to be easily embarrassed, which means that this trait is a major cause of self-conscious shyness. Excessive

TABLE 11.3   Embarrassment versus Shame

	Embarrassment	Shame
Reaction		
Blushing	Often	Rarely
Smiling, giggling	Yes	No
Feeling	Foolish	Depressed
Self-attribution	Mistake	Personal defect
Immediate causes		
Breach of manners	Yes	No
Conspicuousness	Yes	No
Teasing	Often	Infrequently
Overpraise	Yes	No
Letting others down	No	Yes
Immorality	No	Yes
Leakage/disclosure	Of affection	Of baseness
Vicarious	Yes	No
Consequences		
Importance to self	Minor	Major
Loss of self-esteem	Temporary	Enduring
Reaction of others	Laughter	Scorn
	Acceptance	Rejection

socialization can lead to high public self-consciousness, as described in the last chapter. Here the focus is on the methods used to socialize children that can lead to self-conscious shyness, especially ridicule.

Behavior that opposes the goals of socialization is punished verbally or physically. Laughter and teasing are especially potent punishments in that they cause children to feel uncomfortably foolish. Children are taught to conceal certain body parts in public and to reserve nakedness for the bathroom or bedroom. When children violate the nakedness taboo, they are laughed at.

Young children, being egocentric, believe they are better than anyone else and will tell the world about it. So they are taught modesty about their personal accomplishments, and any bragging is mocked, especially by peers. In our society, well-socialized people tout their own accomplishments at the risk of meeting with raucous laughter, scorn, and even caricature, all leading to embarrassment.

Children also learn about another area of privacy: images, feelings, and ambitions, which are the domain of the private self. When these covert feelings are verbalized, they are often met with laughter and teasing.

Children are taught not to have outbursts of emotion, especially when distress is accompanied by crying. When older children cry, they are accused of being babies. When boys cry, they may be labeled as sissies.

In brief, children learn about several kinds of privacy and two kinds of modesty. Presumably, such training can lead to the enduring trait of public self-consciousness. When ridicule and teasing are used excessively in socializing children, the outcome is likely to be a person high in self-conscious shyness.

One result of the socialization of children is the association between conspicuousness and embarrassment. Consider when parents, teachers, and peers single out a child for particular attention. Typically, it is because he or she has done something wrong: violated a taboo about privacy, demonstrated conceit, or had a childish outburst of emotion. The punishment is often teasing and ridicule, causing embarrassment. After many repetitions, a close link is forged between conspicuousness and embarrassment.

Personal Negatives

Public self-consciousness correlates −.21 with self-esteem (Perry & Buss, 1990), which suggests that among people who are concerned about themselves as social objects there is a (weak) tendency to have a negative self-image. Beyond this relationship, there is a rational basis for assuming that low self-esteem and self-conscious shyness are connected. Those with low self-esteem tend to be more susceptible to any kind of negative social reaction, which means that laughter and ridicule will be especially potent causes of embarrassment. People low in self-esteem are also more likely to believe that others will regard them as foolish and clumsy, even in the absence of teasing or other negative social reactions.

Another enduring cause of self-conscious shyness is an obvious physical defect—such as facial scarring or crossed eyes—or features so plain as to approach ugliness. Obese people are made keenly aware of bodily grossness, if not by others then by their own mirrors. In our society, which these days favors female slimness, overweight women are almost certain to be self-consciously shy. Given that men are not held to the same standard, they are less likely to feel shy about being overweight.

The defect may lie not in appearance but in behavior. Thus children who stutter are often teased unmercifully by playmates, and adult stutterers are acutely aware that their listeners are impatiently waiting for them to get the words out. Problems in maintaining bodily control may also cause self-conscious shyness. Some people sweat easily and profusely; others may have physical problems that make bladder control an issue; and others are subject to occasional convulsions and unconsciousness. Such biological problems are likely to cause self-conscious shyness.

Finally, some people never acquire the social skills that make it easy and often pleasurable to deal with others. A client told me that she had no idea how to ask another woman to come to her home for a cup of coffee and just talk. Similarly, some adolescents do not know how to ask for a date, or what to talk about when on a date. Most adults are expected to have acquired these skills: how to listen and seem attentive, maintain eye contact without staring, offer or receive a compliment, gain the floor, direct attention away from oneself, put someone at ease, introduce someone, deal with rebuff, or acknowledge making a mistake. There are also minimal rules of etiquette that everyone is more or less expected to know. Lack of these social skills and the various defects mentioned above may also contribute to low self-esteem, which can further intensify self-conscious shyness.

Two Kinds of Shyness

Contrasts

The two kinds of shyness differ in the kind of emotion involved, when they first appear, their immediate causes, and their enduring causes. These various features are shown in Table 11.4.

Emotion

The emotion in anxious shyness is fear, by definition, and the emotion in self-conscious shyness is embarrassment. The physiological reactions in these two emotions are widely believed to be mediated by the two divisions of the autonomic nervous system. Fear, an emergency emotion involving reaction to threat, is mediated by the sympathetic division. Embarrassment, which is not a reaction to threat, is mediated by the parasympathetic division.

There is evidence of this distinction (Buck, Parke, & Buck, 1970). College men were divided into two experimental groups. The fear group were told that they were about to receive intensely painful electric shock. The embarrassment group

TABLE 11.4   Anxious versus Self-Conscious Shyness

	Anxious shyness	Self-conscious shyness
Kind of emotion	Fear, distress	Embarrassment
ANS reaction (if any)	Sympathetic	Parasympathetic
First appearance	First year of life	Fifth year
Immediate causes	Strangers Novel setting Novel social role Evaluation Poor self-presentation	Conspicuousness Breach of privacy Teasing, ridicule Overpraise Foolish actions
Enduring causes	Heredity Chronic fear (Low) Sociability (Low) Self-esteem Insecure attachment Isolation Conditioning	Excessive socialization Public self-consciousness History of teasing, ridicule Low self-esteem Negative appearance Poor social skills

were told that they would shortly suck on the following objects: a baby bottle, a breast shield, a pacifier, and two nipples. Then physiological measures were recorded for two minutes, and the experiment ended without any shocks or objects being placed in the mouth. Skin conductance, a measure of physiological arousal was higher in fear than in embarrassment. Heart rate changed little in fear but dropped in embarrassment. These results are consistent with the hypothesis that fear is sympathetically mediated (high arousal) and embarrassment parasympathetically mediated (low arousal).

But there is another reason for believing that embarrassment is a parasympathetic emotion. When embarrassed, people tend to blush, a phenomenon caused by the engorgement of the capillary bed of the face, which is under the control of the parasympathetic division. We know little more about blushing than when Darwin wrote, "Blushing is the most peculiar and the most human of all expressions. Monkeys redden from passion, but it would require an overwhelming amount of evidence to make us believe that any animal could blush" (1873, p. 309). Animals and human infants do not blush, presumably because they lack the advanced cognitions and socialization training that would lead to a sense of oneself as a social object. Once this public self is attained, in our species by the fourth or fifth year of life, there is a basis for becoming embarrassed, and blushing appears.

Blushing and the silly smile that often accompanies it appear to be universal. The different situations that might cause embarrassment are sufficiently common that virtually no one has escaped that burning sensation in the face. It should be added that some people experience a facial temperature rise without the skin reddening (I observed this in pilot research on embarrassment). In one study, almost four-fifths of subjects reported that a rise in skin temperature characterized their embarrassment reaction, and about half of them mentioned blushing (Edelmann, 1987, p. 69).

Immediate Causes

The events that elicit the two kinds of shyness are different (see Table 11.4). The various immediate causes of anxious shyness may be grouped into two categories. The first is novelty: of persons, setting, and social role. The second is evaluation, which occurs because the situation is structured that way (a job interview) or because of failed self-presentation.

The immediate causes of self-conscious shyness are more complex, involving conspicuousness, breach of privacy, other's actions (teasing or overpraise), and one's own social mistakes. The reason for this longer list may be the strong emphasis in socialization on oneself as a social object. There are many different social contexts in which acute public self-awareness is salient, and the public/private distinction is drilled into children early in life. Add teasing and ridicule, and there are multiple situations with a potential for embarrassment.

Enduring Causes

Some anxiously shy people are born that way. The inheritance may be direct, or it may derive from a combination of the inherited traits of fear and low sociability (see Table 11.4). Others become anxiously shy because they are insecurely attached in infancy, though insecure attachment itself partly derives from fear and low sociability. Furthermore, problems of attachment can lead to low self-esteem, which renders anxiously shy people especially sensitive to evaluation and potential rejection. In addition, being isolated or suffering from avoidance conditioning are also precursors of this kind of shyness.

The enduring causes of self-conscious shyness center on the public self. An overemphasis on socialization can lead to the trait of public self-consciousness, establishing a strong potential for embarrassment, as will a history of teasing. A negative focus on the public self also may occur because of low self-esteem, defects in appearance, or poor social skills.

Overlap

In the interest of conceptual clarity, I have contrasted anxious shyness with self-conscious shyness. However, there is some overlap in their causes. Novelty is an immediate cause of anxious shyness (see Table 11.4), but in a strange setting or new social role, people sometimes feel conspicuous, which is a cause of self-conscious shyness. Social mistakes and teasing, which are immediate causes of self-conscious shyness, can also make people anxious about evaluation, which is a cause of anxious shyness.

Low self-esteem appears on both sides of Table 11.4. People low in self-esteem expect to fail, a cause of anxious shyness, but when such people make blunders, they may blame themselves and become embarrassed. In addition, poor social skills, which make people feel self-conscious, may also cause them to fear evaluation, a cause of anxious shyness.

Thus the contrasts in Table 11.4 must be interpreted in light of the various overlaps in the causes of the two kinds of shyness. But the similarities between the causes of anxious and self-conscious shyness should not be overinterpreted either, for they are minor compared to the major differences in causes. And perhaps even more important than causes are the crucial differences between the two kinds of shyness: their first appearance during development and their distinctive emotional reactions.

Can there be a blend of both kinds of emotions? Yes, it is possible to be anxiously shy and embarrassed at the same time. Does this mean that we cannot distinguish between the two kinds of shyness? Before answering this question, consider other emotions. We are sometimes simultaneously afraid and angry, ashamed and angry, or sexually aroused and afraid. The fact that two emotions can occur at the same time does not deny their distinctiveness. When people are shy, they may be anxious and self-conscious at the same time. It should be added that as in the case of other emotions, blends in anxious and self-conscious shyness are infrequent. Typically, at any given moment when one kind of shyness occurs, the other is usually absent.

Implications for Therapy

There are people whose shyness is so severe that it causes problems in everyday situations. They have trouble meeting people, are unsuccessful on dates, and perform poorly on jobs that require frequent contact with others. Some shy people will not apply for a job if it requires a hiring interview. The more severe the shyness, the more likely that anxiety predominates rather than self-consciousness. When shyness becomes extreme, it may be labeled social phobia, which, like other phobias, is characterized by anxiety. In milder shyness, though, acute public self-consciousness may be the salient aspect of the problem.

What is the appropriate psychotherapy for shyness? The answer depends on which kind of shyness predominates. If it is anxious shyness, the therapy would be similar to that used in other kinds of anxiety. It might be systematic desensitization, flooding, or a variety of cognitive behavior modification techniques.

If the major problem is acute public self-consciousness, it must be diminished. One way is to teach clients to direct attention elsewhere: for example, by directing the conversation to topics other than the self ("Are you wearing a new outfit?") or by having pictures or other objects that listeners might examine. Another way is to have clients learn that most of the time they are not the focus of attention: for example, by showing them videotapes of themselves in social interaction. A third option is to have clients learn to direct attention away from the self by concentrating on the current topic of conversation or on the physical and psychological characteristics of those around them. When attention is directed toward the social environment, there is a double benefit. Self-awareness is necessarily diminished, and people can more comfortably deal with the social context because their focus is where it belongs: on being socially responsive and on their social skills.

Evidence

There has been little research on the distinction between the two kinds of shyness, perhaps because the theory was published only recently (Buss, 1985, 1986). But there are two relevant studies.

College women who identified themselves as previously shy but not currently shy were asked when their shyness first occurred (Cheek, Carpentieri, Smith, Rierdan, & Koff, 1986). Roughly four-fifths said that their shyness started after the age of six, which suggests the late-starting self-conscious shyness. The other fifth said it started before the age of six, which suggests the early-starting anxious shyness. Presumably self-conscious shyness, which occurs because of socialization training and a history of teasing, can be more easily overcome than anxious shyness, which has an inherited component and is also caused by insecure attachment in infancy. On these assumptions, we should expect that more self-consciously shy people would become unshy than anxiously shy people, which is consistent with the above percentages: four-fifths and one-fifth for self-conscious and anxious shyness, respectively.

The other study divided college students into two groups of shy subjects (Bruch, Giordano, & Pearl, 1986). One, called fearful shy, was high in fear and low in public self-consciousness. The other, called self-conscious shy, was low in fear and high in public self-consciousness. Most of the fearful shy subjects reported that their shyness started before elementary school; most of the self-conscious shy subjects reported that their shyness started after they began elementary school. In addition, physiological arousal was reported more frequently by the fearful shy subjects.

The results of these two studies are consistent with the distinction between two kinds of shyness, but they depend on retrospective reports. Such research needs to be supplemented by longitudinal research. We already know that anxious shyness starts in the first year of life, when it is called stranger anxiety or inhibition, and self-conscious shyness starts a few years later. Thus the distinction is important in childhood, but is it important later in development, that is, does it make a difference whether adults are anxiously shy or self-consciously shy? To find out, we need research that tracks both kinds of shy children through to adulthood.

The Trait of Shyness

Questionnaires

There is no questionnaire that separates the trait of shyness into the anxious and self-conscious types. All extant questionnaires assess only overall shyness.

To my knowledge, the first questionnaire to deal with the trait of shyness uncontaminated with sociability or with other kinds of social anxiety was that of Cheek and Buss (1981). In fact, the questionnaire in Cheek and Buss's study was part of research designed to discover whether shyness is nothing more than low sociability. Shyness, of course, is discomfort and inhibition when with others; sociability is the need to be with other people. Accordingly, items were written to meet each of these two definitions. The resulting questionnaire, administered to 912 subjects, yielded separate factors for shyness and sociability (see Table 11.5).

The two scales correlated −.30 in this study, though a correlation of −.47 was reported in a study that used confirmatory factor analysis to substantiate the reliability of the presence of two factors (Bruch, Gorsky, Collins, & Berger, 1989). However, in light of a correlation of −.35 reported in a third study (Perry & Buss, 1990) and a correlation of −.35 based on mothers' reports about their second-grade children (Asendorpf & Meier, 1993) and a correlation of −.34 between shyness and extraversion (Jones, Briggs, and Smith, 1986), the best estimate is that shyness and sociability are correlated negatively in the middle thirties. Thus, though shy people, not surprisingly, tend to be lower in sociability, the relationship is moderate enough for us to conclude that the two traits are different.

There is other evidence supporting this distinction. In one study, shyness and sociability contributed independently to the inhibited behavior of interacting subjects (Cheek & Buss, 1981). In two other studies, shyness affected social behavior and experience, but sociability did not (Arkin & Grove, 1990; Bruch et al., 1989). The just-mentioned study by Asendorpf and Meier (1993) observed children during and after school. Compared to unshy children, shy children spoke less in unfamiliar and moderately familiar situations, but there was no difference in familiar situations; sociable and unsociable children did not differ here. However, as men-

TABLE 11.5   Shyness and Sociability Questionnaire ($N = 912$)

Item	Factor loading	
	Shyness	Sociability
Shyness		
1. I am socially somewhat awkward.	.54	−.15
2. I don't find it hard to talk to strangers.*	.50	−.07
3. I feel tense when I'm with people I don't know well.	.63	−.02
4. When conversing, I worry about saying something dumb.	.56	.09
5. I feel nervous when speaking to someone in authority.	.53	.17
6. I am often uncomfortable at parties and other social functions.	.55	−.13
7. I feel inhibited in social situations.	.59	−.13
8. I have trouble looking someone right in the eye.	.46	−.02
9. I am more shy with members of the opposite sex.	.49	.02
Sociability		
1. I like to be with people.	−.10	.76
2. I welcome the opportunity to mix socially with people.	−.32	.59
3. I prefer working with others rather than alone.	.00	.50
4. I find people more stimulating than anything else.	.02	.45
5. I'd be unhappy if I were prevented from making many social contacts.	.06	.44

Source: From "Shyness and Sociability" by J. M. Cheek and A. H. Buss, 1981, *Journal of Personality and Social Psychology*, *41*, p. 332. Copyright 1981 by the American Psychological Association. Adapted by permission of the publisher.
*Reversed item.

tioned in Chapter 4, sociable children spent more time with friends than unsociable children. As the authors suggested, "The results show that sociability affects the exposure, and shyness the reactivity, to situations, and that these traits are clearly distinct" (p. 1072).

There are several other questionnaires on shyness, and all of them appear to be interchangeable. Jones et al. (1986) reported that the correlations among five questionnaires, including the one in Table 11.5, range from .72 to .81: "Correlations among the scales approached the ceiling set by their respective alpha coefficients. Evidence of internal consistency met or exceeded conventional standards of measurement, and both convergent and discriminant validity were demonstrated" (p. 637).

Shyness and Other Personality Traits

Shyness in the Cheek and Buss (1981) questionnaire was correlated with other personality traits in that study and three others (Perry & Buss, 1990; Collan & Buss, 1991; Jones et al., 1986). The correlations are presented in Table 11.6. In describing these correlations with shyness, I shall mention only the other trait.

TABLE 11.6 Correlations between Shyness and Other Personality Traits

Trait	Correlation			
	Cheek-Buss	Perry-Buss	Collan-Buss	Jones et al.
Self-Esteem	−.51	−.53	−.54	−.52
Fear	.50	.47	.49	—
Public self-consciousness	.26	.34	.27	.22
Social loneliness	.58	.57	—	—
Emotional loneliness	.37	.40	—	—
Privacy	—	—	.51	—

The negative correlation with self-esteem is stable across all four studies, and the positive correlation with fear is stable in all three where it was computed. The correlation with public self-consciousness varies somewhat, and the best guess is that it is in the high twenties. Notice that the correlation with fear is higher than that with public self-consciousness, which makes sense when shyness is divided into the anxious and self-consciousness types. Anxiety would appear to be a considerably more intense experience than public self-awareness. It follows that those in whom anxious shyness predominates would have higher shyness scores than those in whom public self-consciousness predominates. The result would be a higher correlation with fear than with public self-consciousness.

Loneliness has been divided into two subtypes (Weiss, 1973). In social loneliness the person misses social contacts and the sharing of activities. In emotional loneliness the person misses intimate relationships, either romantic or familial (DiTommasso & Spinner, 1993). Shyness is much more closely linked to social loneliness (r = .58 and .57) than to emotional loneliness (r = .37 and .40).

People who are shy, either because of anxiety or because of self-consciousness, tend to draw a veil around themselves. The total score of a privacy questionnaire (Collan & Buss, 1991) correlated .51 with shyness. However, the privacy questionnaire consisted of three factors. The first was secretiveness, a typical item being "It is hard for me to talk about myself." The second was concealment (a combination of visual and auditory privacy), typical items being "I feel very uncomfortable when using a public restroom" and "I hate being in a room when the people next door can overhear you." The third was seclusiveness, typical items being "It is difficult to really concentrate on a problem when other people are around." Secretiveness had the highest correlation with shyness, .48; concealment was next, .38; and seclusiveness was only modestly related to shyness, .29.

These various correlations provide a description of shy people. They are low in self-esteem, anxious, and, to a lesser extent, highly aware of themselves as social objects. They tend to be unsociable (or introverted) and lonely, but they miss ordinary social contacts more than intimate relationships. And they are private persons, especially in not disclosing much about themselves, preferring not to be seen or heard by strangers or casual acquaintances, and, to a lesser extent, preferring to work alone.

Bear in mind that correlations do not tell us the direction of causality. People low in self-esteem may become shy, but shy people, lacking rewards in social contexts, may come to lose confidence in themselves. Fearful people may become shy, but shy people may develop generalized fears. Thus causality could go either way, and there may be a spiraling, positive feedback cycle: for example, self-esteem leads to shyness, which makes self-esteem drop, and so on.

There are rational grounds, however, for assuming that shyness leads to loneliness. Shy people, because they tend to avoid social contexts and remain relatively uninvolved when in social contexts, are likely to have few friends and to lack intimate relationships. Being shy, they become lonely. Unshy people are likely to have more social opportunities and therefore tend not to be chronically lonely. Thus, feeling lonely does not cause shyness; shyness leads to loneliness. And one reason that shy people are lonely is that they treasure privacy.

A last set of correlations, not in Table 11.6, bears on the distinction between shyness and sociability (Cheek & Buss, 1981). Self-esteem correlates negatively in the fifties with shyness but positively only .18 with sociability. Fear correlates in the fifties with self-esteem but is uncorrelated with sociability. These divergent correlations offer more evidence that shyness and sociability, though related, are distinct traits.

Extremes of the Dimension

Shyness represents one pole of a dimension of how people behave when with others. People at this end of the dimension tend not to initiate conversation and are often minimally responsive to others' social gestures. They prefer only a small amount of attention, just enough to ensure that they are not being ignored. Beyond that level, they start feeling conspicuous and shrink back. They tend not to offer others the intrinsically social rewards that make social interaction so rewarding, and so are considered boring.

At the other end of the dimension are those called extraverts. They talk to strangers and enthusiastically respond to others' social gestures. They offer others the intrinscially social rewards that most people seek, which is why they are considered so lively. At their best these self-starters get things going in a social group. At their worst, they may intrude on the privacy of those who would rather be left alone.

Though extraverts occupy the other end of the dimension, there are people even more extreme: *exhibitionists*. Exhibitionists thrive on attention and are delighted to feel conspicuous. Shy people abhor excessive attention. They feel exposed and naked when others stare, and they shrink back. Exhibitionists are delighted to be in the spotlight and may go to great lengths to remain there. No one likes being shunned, but shy people might tolerate it if the alternative is conspicuousness. In contrast, being ignored is the exhibitionist's worst nightmare.

It follows that the two ends of the dimension also differ in self-esteem. Shy people tend to think that they are in some ways lacking, especially in how they might appeal to others. Exhibitionists believe that they are so interesting that other people are delighted to look at them, and listen to them. Shy people tend to be modest; exhibitionists tend to be conceited.

Interpersonal Behavior and Cognitions

Laboratory experiments have examined the social behavior of subjects who vary in the trait of shyness. Pairs of college women, both of whom were either shy or unshy—sixtieth or fortieth percentile on a shyness questionnaire—were asked to get acquainted in a waiting room, where they were surreptitiously video-taped (Cheek & Buss, 1981, study 2). Compared to the pairs of unshy subjects, the shy subjects talked less of the time and engaged in more nervous touching of the face or body. Judges who were blind to the questionnaire scores watched the videotapes and rated the shy pairs as being more tense and inhibited, and less friendly.

Two similar experiments studied German male college students who varied in shyness and who interacted either with strangers or with friends (Asendorpf, 1987, 1989). Body posture was generally more closed with strangers, but this effect was especially strong for shy subjects. When viewing videotapes of the interaction, shy subjects mentioned more fear of being evaluated by the other person, but not more generalized fear.

These same-sex studies were complemented by one using persons of opposite sexes meeting for the first time (Garcia, Stinson, Ickes, Bissonette, & Briggs, 1991). The subjects' scores on a shyness questionnaire were correlated with their observed behavior. Shyness was associated with fewer and shorter verbalizations, less frequent initiation of conversation, fewer and shorter gazes directed at the other person, and fewer and shorter mutual gazes. Men's shyness correlated negatively with the mutual gazes initiated by women, leading the authors to suggest that "the shy men's unusual gazing behavior may have been responsible for such indirect effects as making the women feel self-conscious and uncomfortable, inhibiting the verbal and nonverbal behaviors of both dyad members" (p. 47).

Given that shy people tend to be low in self-esteem and high in both fear and public self-consciousness, it follows that their cognitions should be mainly negative and their social strategy, self-protective. Cheek and Melchior (1990), after reviewing research bearing on these issues, concluded that shy people

1. perceive that a social interaction will be explicitly evaluative
2. expect that their behavior will be inadequate and that they will be evaluated negatively
3. hold "irrational beliefs" about how good their social performance *should* be and how much social approval they *should* get from others
4. think about "Who does this situation want me to be?" rather than "How can I be me in this situation?"
5. adopt a strategy of trying to get along rather than trying to get ahead

6. become anxiously self-preoccupied and do not pay enough attention to others
7. judge themselves more negatively than others judge them
8. blame themselves for social failures and attribute successes to other factors
9. accept negative feedback and resist or reject positive feedback
10. remember negative self-relevant information and experiences (p. 68).*

If shy people tend to judge themselves as inadequate and expect to be negatively evaluated, it follows that they should disclose less about themselves than do unshy people. Shy and unshy women interacted with another subject, an experimental accomplice who disclosed a lot about herself or just a little (Meleshko & Alden, 1993). Unshy subjects responded to the accomplice's higher level of self-disclosure by telling more about themselves, that is, they reciprocated. But shy subjects did not reciprocate, instead keeping their self-disclosure to a moderate level and not revealing much about themselves. Subsequently, they reported fearing disapproval and said that they were protecting themselves during the interaction.

Person and Environment

Choosing Environments

Shy people do not so much choose certain environments as avoid them. The settings they stay away from are precisely those that elicit shy behavior. These include entering a new school or a new neighborhood and starting a new social role or a new job. As mentioned earlier, shy people may decide not to apply for a job if it involves an interview, because of the interviewer's higher status and the ensuing evaluation. Shy people often avoid meeting the opposite sex because of both novelty and evaluation. They also tend to skip situations in which they are likely to be conspicuous, such as giving a speech. They prefer and seek out social environments that are familiar and involve no conspicuousness or evaluation.

Setting the Tone

Shy people are typically passive, waiting for others to initiate conversation. Let me offer an example. At a party I introduced a young colleague to a distinguished psychologist who is extremely shy, and then I left. The young colleague related what happened. He was tongue-tied in the presence of so famous a psychologist and therefore said nothing. The famous psychologist rocked on his feet for a couple of minutes and then wandered away. He was dispositionally too shy to initiate conversation, and the young colleague was temporarily too shy to start talking, so

---

*From "Shyness, Self-esteem, and Self-consciousness" by J. M. Cheek and L. A. Melchior, 1990, in H. Leitenberg (ed.), *Handbook of Social and Evaluation Anxiety*, p. 68. Copyright 1990 by J. M. Cheek. Reprinted by permission.

there was silence. Shyness, either transient or trait, sets a tone of tension and inhibition that can be overcome only if there is an extravert present.

Matching

When both partners are not shy, they understand each other and encounter no particular problems in social situations. When both partners are shy, they understand each other, each sympathizing when the other either avoids certain social contexts or is inhibited during interaction. The problem is that they reinforce each other's shyness and never overcome it.

In a mismatch, the unshy partner, say, the wife, cannot understand her husband: Why won't he go to a job interview for a promising position? She wants to get out and see friends, but he wants to stay home. She loves parties; he hates them. They can compromise by socializing more than he wants and less than she wants. Of course, he may be uncomfortable or miserable when he has to meet people in these situations. Alternatively, the wife can accept the fact that her husband cannot change, and stay home with him or go out on her own, without him.

Part III Commentary

Combinations of Aspects of the Self

Self-esteem and identity overlap, as we saw in Chapter 9, but here the issue is combinations involving people who are high or low in each. We expect those who have good self-esteem to have a strong identity (High-High). It is a two-way street, confidence in yourself leading to a secure feeling of knowing who you are and knowing who you are leading to a feeling of confidence. Similarly, lack of confidence in yourself is expected to weaken your feeling of identity (Low-Low), and the opposite direction of causality also occurs.

However, a minority of people are high in one and low in the other. It is possible to feel good about yourself but be uneasy about who you are (High-Low). This scenario is likely if your self-esteem derives mainly from personal success that is achieved at the expense of relationships and other kinds of social support. Then you might feel confident about your abilities while lacking roots and being in a quandary about the meaning of your life. An example might be an executive who builds up her company into a giant only to discover that she has few friends and no contacts with her family.

The last possibility is low self-esteem but a secure identity (Low-High). You lack confidence in yourself and depend mainly on others as the source of your self-esteem. But you feel secure in the nest of your multigenerational family and can trace your roots back to ancestors who came over on the *Mayflower*. You may not think highly of yourself, but you know where you belong.

Self-esteem is unrelated to private self-consciousness but (modestly) negatively correlated with public self-consciousness, as we saw in Chapter 10. If you lack confidence in yourself, you may focus on yourself as a social object to ensure that you do not make a bad impression on others. In the opposite direction, a strong focus on yourself as a social object tends to make you aware of your deficiencies, lowering your self-esteem.

The correlation between self-esteem and shyness is high and negative. As discussed in Chapter 11, this relationship is also bidirectional: Lack of confidence generally breeds lack of confidence socially (shyness), and shy behavior often leads to being ignored or rejected, diminishing self-esteem.

Those who are low in self-esteem tend to play it safe in the interest of protecting what little self-esteem they have. But shy people, too, were shown to be "-driven by fears of disapproval and appeared to have adopted a strategy of protecting themselves during the interaction" (Meleshko & Alden, 1993, p. 1007). In their social behavior, shy people evidently have the same problems as do those low in self-esteem, and adopt the same solutions. Small wonder that the two traits are strongly correlated.

Of the remaining combinations, the link between (public) self-consciousness and shyness, discussed fully in Chapter 11, needs no further mention. That leaves the link between identity and self-consciousness, a connection that has an empirical basis. As we saw in Chapter 9, social identity correlates with public self-consciousness, and personal identity correlates with private self-consciousness. But there is also a conceptual connection between identity and private self-awareness. When there is an identity conflict—say, between two social roles or between two national identities (for example, a recent German immigrant who became a U.S. citizen just before World War II)—there is a heightened self-focus. And the familiar mid-life crisis of identity leads to greater attention to the private aspects of oneself.

Sex Differences

No sex differences have been reported on questionnaires of self-esteem, self-consciousness, or shyness, and there is no evidence of a sex difference in the strength of identity. But there are sex differences in specific aspects of these personality tendencies.

Recall that as sources of identity, men rated intelligence and athletic ability higher than did women, and character/morality and artistic ability lower than did women (see Chapter 9). It also seems likely that personal sources of identity are more important for men, but social sources, especially family and religion, are more important for women.

Concerning public self-consciousness, women have been socialized to focus more on how they look than have men. That seems to be changing, however, as more men become interested in clothes, hairstyles, and maintaining their weight. It follows that men may also become more aware of the appearance aspect of themselves as social objects, an aspect of which most women are acutely aware.

Dichotomies of Behavior

The dichotomy of behavior most relevant to the self is personal-social (see Table 1.4). There are personal and social sources of self-esteem and identity, and self-consciousness is generically either private (person) or public (social). More specifically, private self-consciousness is self-directed and egocentric, whereas public self-con-sciousness is at least implicitly other-directed and sociocentric.

The master-pawn dichotomy applies to self-esteem: Those high in self-esteem are confident they can control their destiny, whereas the Lows believe they are being controlled. The active-passive dichotomy also applies: Those who are high in self-esteem try actively to boost that level even higher, whereas the Lows passively protect the little they possess because of the threat that they might lose some.

Those who are high in private self-consciousness regularly turn their atten-tion to their psychological insides. Lows pay no attention to these aspects of the self. Those who are high in public self-consciousness focus on themselves as social objects. Lows are unaware of the observable self. The relevant dichotomy obvi-ously is conscious-unconscious.

People who are not shy freely disclose their feelings and opinions, and their behavior in social situations is relaxed and open. Shy people, being anxious or self-conscious, say little about themselves, keep a lid on their emotions, and restrict their social behavior. Thus the dichotomy of expressed-inhibited applies to the dimension of shyness.

C h a p t e r **12**

Disputed Issues

Are personality traits important? The negative answer, that they are of little importance, has been espoused by those who view manipulations and situations as the crucial determinants of behavior. Personality psychologists, defending their field, insist that traits are important, often crucial, determiners of behavior. One can measure importance quantitatively with estimates of power.

Power

In a study mentioned earlier in this book, the correlation between aggressiveness (trait) and aggression (behavior) was .34 (Scheier, Buss, & Buss, 1978). This moderate relationship between a trait and laboratory behavior is typical, such correlations usually not exceeding .40. Correlations in this range are regarded as weak relationships and have been used to support the argument that personality traits are unimportant in comparison to laboratory manipulations. The underlying assumption here is that laboratory manipulations are more powerful determinants of behavior than personality traits. Are there data on this point? Very few, because most researchers do not report the power of the effects they obtain. The statistics ordinarily reported in experiments—means, curves, and tests of significance—do not tell us how strongly the manipulations affected the dependent variables. In contrast, the correlation coefficients often used in personality research contain evidence of the power of the relationship.

To compare the impact of traits in personality research with the impact of manipulations in laboratory research, one can convert tests of significance into correlation coefficients. This is precisely what Funder and Ozer (1983) did in examining the results from three well-known experimental topics in social psychology: forced compliance, bystander intervention, and obedience. When converted, the tests of significance yielded correlations ranging from .36 to .42, leading these psychologists to write,

The effects of behavior on several of the most prominent situational factors in social psychology seem to average slightly less than .40. Moreover, because in most social psychological experiments only two or three levels of situational independent variables are studied, and because these levels are deliberately chosen to be quite different from each other, situational linear effects such as calculated here quite possibly *over*estimate the true state of affairs. (p. 110).

Undoubtedly, there are experiments that yield more powerful effects and therefore higher correlations than occurred in this social psychological research. Similarly, some of the personality research, mentioned earlier in this book, yielded correlations considerably higher than .40. In brief, personality traits appear to exert no less impact on behavior than do experimental manipulations.

Whether traits are important also comes up in everyday situations. Consider the example of professional baseball players, who vary in their ability to hit the ball. Batters who on the average get 3 hits every 10 times at bat (.300) are paid hundreds of thousands of dollars per year more than .200 hitters. One must wonder about this differential in pay when the difference between the players is 1 hit for every 10 times at bat, which if found in psychological research would be regarded as trivial. Furthermore, the best prediction is that a .300 hitter will *not* get a hit in any particular time at bat, a prediction that must be correct 7 times out of 10. If so, is hitting ability important? The answer lies in what happens over the course of a baseball season, when there are roughly 500 opportunities to get a hit: The difference between a .200 hitter and a .300 hitter is 50 hits, enough for the latter to win some ball games. Teams with several .300 hitters win pennants; teams with .200 hitters do not. Baseball managers and owners know what personality psychologists know: The impact of traits may be hard to see on a single occasion, but traits are crucial in the long run.

Two Disciplines

Underlying the challenge to traits and the response to the challenge are assumptions about behavior and implicit models about personality-relevant behavior. These assumptions and models derive from and influence how psychologists study people and which behaviors they study. The simplest division is between experimental psychologists and personality/differential psychologists (Cronbach, 1957).

Generally speaking, experimental psychologists study the impact of experimental manipulations on specific responses made in particular situations. In seeking to understand the psychological processes underlying the occurrence of the behavior, they search for all the determinants of behavior or at least all the important ones. In practice, only a single determinant (sometimes, two) is studied in any given experiment. One problem with this strategy, well known to experimental psychologists, may be the limited generality of any particular finding.

Personality traits usually are omitted because they are assumed to contribute nothing to the behavior being studied. This assumption is often correct, for the experimental procedure typically minimizes or eliminates the influence of personality traits. As a result, traits are rarely systematically varied or controlled. Allowing differences among subjects to vary randomly can contribute to the error term, but as long as independent variables have a significant impact on dependent variables, experimental psychologists feel safe in ignoring personality traits. In framing independent variables and seeking explanatory processes, they tend to focus on behavior that is influenced by short-lived laboratory manipulations and transient situational variables.

Generally speaking, personality psychologists search for the consistencies in behavior that allow them to infer traits. They investigate relationships among these traits, their origins, and the consequences of these personality dispositions for behavior. The goal is not to discover all the determinants of behavior but only those contributing to the enduring behavioral tendencies of individuals. Trait psychologists typically seek to discover the psychological dimensions along which people differ and how traits cluster within individuals. Though brief segments of behavior may be studied, the major focus is on enduring behavior: not one time at bat in baseball but the season's hitting average.

Personality psychologists typically ignore the impact of experimental manipulations. More attention is paid to the content of behavior than to the psychological processes underlying the behavior. Process is not completely ignored, but the focus typically is on the outcomes of process, not on process itself.

Concrete examples of the distinction being drawn may be found in research on aggression. In the study mentioned above, aggression and aggressiveness correlated .34 (Scheier et al., 1978). Subjects high in the trait of private self-consciousness, knowing themselves well, were assumed to furnish a veridical self-report, but those low in private self-consciousness might not. The correlation between intensity of laboratory aggression and the trait of aggressiveness was .66 for those high in private self-consciousness (well above the limit of .40) but only .09 for those low in private self-consciousness. This study deliberately had no experimental manipulation, and the crucial question was whether transient aggression against one person would correlate with the trait of aggressiveness for subjects varying in another trait (private self-consciousness).

In a social psychological experiment, the impact of frustration on aggression was investigated (Buss, 1966b). Frustration was manipulated by having the accomplice learn so slowly that the real subject's desire for money or a better course grade was blocked. Such frustration was found to have a weak but significant effect on aggression. This frustration study contained an experimental manipulation, and the crucial question was whether it affected the dependent variable, aggressive behavior. In contrast, the personality study of self-consciousness and aggressiveness had no experimental manipulation, and the question was whether the trait of aggressiveness would predict transient aggression. Clearly, the particular question asked led directly to the method of research and the importance attached to manipulations versus traits.

Traits versus Manipulations

Psychologists who ignore the fact that there are two distinct disciplines in psychological research have sought to oppose traits and manipulations to determine which are more powerful. Mischel (1968) claimed that when the manipulation is strong, it negates the effect of any trait; only when a manipulation is weak or absent would a trait have a significant impact on behavior. Mischel, Ebbesen, and Zeiss (1973) attempted to support this claim with an experiment on sensitizers and repressers (Byrne, 1961), the poles of a trait dimension that has people who admit psychological problems at one end (sensitizers) and those who do not at the other end (repressers). Subjects either succeeded or failed on a laboratory task and then were allowed to examine items about their own psychological assets or liabilities. The dependent variable was time spent on assets or liabilities.

Repressers and sensitizers reacted similarly in the failure condition and in a control condition, but they reacted differently to success. The authors concluded that traits are important only when there is no manipulation (control condition) or when the manipulation is weak (failure), but traits are unimportant when the manipulation is strong (success). Is failure a weak manipulation? The many investigators who have successfully used failure to frustrate and motivate subjects surely would say no. Mischel and his colleagues were so eager to emphasize a manipulation at the expense of a trait that they denied the impact of failure. Worse still, they virtually ignored differences between sensitizers and repressers. In all conditions, repressers paid roughly equal attention to their liabilities and assets. But in the control and failure conditions, sensitizers paid significantly more attention to liabilities than to assets. Clearly, the sensitizer end of the trait dimension determined the focus of attention.

Aside from this particular experiment, some traits may be important *only* when the manipulation is strong. Fearful people react with fear only when there is a threat, and shy people become inhibited only when meeting strangers or casual acquaintances. Television violence has been shown to have an impact on children who are already aggressive, making them somewhat more aggressive, but television has little impact on children low in aggressiveness (Eron, 1982). Other examples of how traits and manipulations interact will be offered below, but there is a more general issue here: how research can favor manipulations or traits. There are four points to consider.

Manipulations or Traits

Consider first the context of the study. Recall that in public and formal situations much of our social behavior is prescribed (Chapter 7). Thus dinner guests compliment the hostess even after a bad meal, and sworn enemies may be polite in public. Behavior is further circumscribed when the situation is novel or the others are unfamiliar and one is wary of making social mistakes. When our behavior is controlled mainly by context—formal, public, novel, and involving strangers—we must pay careful attention to social cues and suppress any tendencies toward individuality. It follows that people will be especially susceptible to social manipulations. Researchers who favor manipulations tend to study behavior in contexts that are formal, public, novel, and involving strangers—a characterization that fits many laboratory experiments.

In familiar situations with acquaintances, people are at ease, and their behavior usually reflects their habitual tendencies and personality dispositions. Similarly, informal situations, having fewer rules or expectations, allow people to act in line with their personality traits. When we are unseen or unheard by others, our individuality is most likely to be expressed. And in familiar situations we need not worry so much about making social mistakes and therefore can act in accord with habitual (personality) tendencies. Thus personality traits are more likely to have an impact in situations that are informal, private, and familiar: for example, in one's home or backyard.

Laboratory experiments tend to start with a detailed set of instructions for subjects, which offer them little choice and tend to restrict their behavior. The extreme case may be research in which the subject merely says yes or no. Such constriction is part of a laudable attempt at experimental control, but subjects can be so constrained by instructions that their personality traits are not allowed free play. Manipulations, however, are carefully chosen so as to have maximal impact.

Personality research tends to occur in relatively unstructured situations, sometimes even naturalistic ones. Subjects typically are allowed wide latitude in behavior and may even be permitted to select the context or a partner. Instructions are minimal or nonexistent; even when there are instructions, they often tell subjects only how to fill out questionnaires. Manipulations often are missing. Minimal instructions, greater choice, few restrictions on behavior, and the absence of manipulations all lead to personality traits strongly influencing behavior.

Human subjects will not remain in the laboratory for more than an hour or two, and long sessions produce fatigue. Laboratory experimentation on humans must therefore be brief. For short durations, subjects may behave as they think they are expected to behave, that is, in accord with demand characteristics, or they may conceal their habitual tendencies. Thus in a brief laboratory study, the role of personality traits is often minimized, and the role of manipulations is maximized (after all, one does experiments by manipulating independent variables).

It is difficult to maintain atypical behavior over time, however. A subject tires of acting in accord with the real or imagined expectations of the experimenter and cannot keep on suppressing habitual behavioral tendencies. For example, a mild, introverted, submissive man might play the role of a dominant boss for a while, but after an hour or so he would revert to his typical passive behavior. When students are videotaped, they may act self-consciously for a while, but eventually they ignore the camera and return to typical behavior. The behavior of a couple on a first date is known to involve the managing of impressions, but as the relationship continues, the couple revert to their typical behavior, which is determined to a great extent by their personality traits. Thus when the period of observation is extensive, especially over days and weeks, personality traits exert their expected influence on behavior.

Laboratory experimenters can select dependent variables so as to maximize precision of measurement. Narrowly defined responses are favored because they are easily recorded and quantified. But smaller units of behavior tend to be especially influenced by transitory, localized determinants. A major determinant is immediate experimental manipulations.

When responses are defined more broadly, behavior is less affected by momentary stimuli, including transient manipulations. The down side is a loss of precision of measurement. Personality psychologists are willing to tolerate some loss of precision because broadly defined responses are more likely to be affected by enduring variables, especially personality traits.

These various issues are summarized in Table 12.1. At one extreme, laboratory research can yield evidence of traits, and it has—for example, the research on aggressiveness and laboratory aggression (Scheier et al., 1978). Clearly, the way research is conducted can determine whether manipulations or personality traits are important. If one does experimental investigations and wishes to favor manipulations, research should be conducted in novel, formal, public settings, with detailed instructions to subjects who are allowed little or no choice, in a brief period of study of narrowly defined responses. If one wishes to favor personality traits, research can be conducted in a familiar, informal, relatively private setting, with few instructions and maximal choice by subjects, whose broadly defined responses are studied over an extensive period of time. Thus it appears futile to pit manipulations against traits and argue that one category is more important.

Traits and Manipulations Together

A reasonable alternative to opposing manipulations and traits is to investigate them jointly (Endler & Magnusson, 1976). When this strategy is used, there are many possible outcomes. To reduce a potentially bewildering complexity, only two levels of the trait and two conditions (experimental and control) will be considered.

In the most straightforward case, no interaction, the manipulation and the trait independently affect behavior, as in Scheier's (1976) experiment on aggression, for example (see Chapter 10). Recall that he angered subjects who were either high or low in private self-consciousness and allowed them to administer shock on the aggression machine. Subjects who were high in private self-consciousness aggressed more intensely than those who were low. The manipulation

TABLE 12.1   Manipulations

Issue	Favoring manipulations	Favoring traits
Context	Novel, formal, public	Familiar, informal, private
Instructions	Detailed, complete	General or none
Choice	Little or none	Considerable
Duration	Brief	Extensive
Response	Narrow	Broad

consisted of a small mirror, which was used to induce private self-awareness; there was no mirror in the control condition. Self-aware subjects aggressed more intensely than control subjects, and those high in private self-consciousness aggressed more intensely than Lows.

The other three cases involve interactions between manipulations and traits. Subjects who were either high or low in a trait called absorption (Tellegen & Atkinson, 1974) were given either biofeedback instructions or no instructions. There were no main effects. When given biofeedback, subjects low in absorption relaxed more than those who were high. Compared to the biofeedback condition, in the control condition the Lows were much less relaxed and the Highs were much more relaxed, so that now the Highs were more relaxed than the Lows. Thus the manipulation had opposite effects on those high in absorption than it did on the Lows.

In another kind of interaction, those high in the trait are more affected by the manipulation. An example is the link between public self-consciousness and a manipulation designed to induce transient social awareness. Fenigstein (1979) placed each subject in a waiting room with two other "subjects" who were really experimental accomplices (see Chapter 10). In the control condition these confederates responded to conversation by the subject, but in the experimental condition they shunned the subject. The dependent variables were postexperimental reports of discomfort and choosing whether to remain with these confederates in a second part of the experiment. Compared to those low in public self-consciousness, the Highs reported greater discomfort and tended to avoid choosing the confederates as subsequent partners—that is, the shunning manipulation had a much stronger impact on subjects who were high in public self-consciousness.

The manipulation may affect *only* subjects in one part of the trait dimension. Subjects who were either high or low in private self-consciousness, after being told about the medical usefulness of electric shock and the importance of the experiment, were asked to volunteer to receive electric shock (Scheier, Carver, & Gibbons, 1981). The manipulation was the presumed intensity of the forthcoming shock: intense in the experimental condition and very weak in the control condition. Compared to the control condition, the threat of intense shock markedly decreased volunteering among subjects high in private self-consciousness but had virtually no impact on the Lows.

Of course, a manipulation may affect only those low in a trait. A body of research has established that failure tends to depress persons low in the trait of self-esteem but has little impact on those high in self-esteem. For example, Brockner (1979) demonstrated that failure worsens the performance of subjects low in self-esteem but has little or no effect on subjects high in self-esteem.

These various cases, no interaction and several kinds of interaction, represent the major outcomes that occur when manipulations and traits are studied simultaneously. The empirical research cited for the various interactions shows clearly that traits determine behavior even when experimental manipulations significantly affect behavior. And there is a larger issue: Research that includes both traits and manipulations more closely maps everyday situations, in which individuals who differ (traits) are exposed to environmental influences (manipulations).

Units and Classes

Which behaviors are studied in the laboratory? Some responses are easier to observe or to record objectively and so are favored. Discrete responses can be identified precisely and measured quantitatively. Some researchers completely ignore differences among responses, assuming that studying one response is as good as studying any other response so long as the outcome is reproducible data. Though most experimental psychologists do not share this extreme position, they tend to ignore differences among responses on the implicit assumption that their findings for one response will generalize to all behavior, an assumption rarely tested.

If personality psychologists were to study only single responses, they would be faced with a numerical problem. There must be thousands of individual, narrow responses, and the number of combinations of responses is astronomical. To tame such large numbers we are forced to group responses into classes of responses. A class of responses and individual differences in the class are the two defining properties of a trait.

Consider the habit of smoking cigarettes. It may be regarded as one component of the broader response class of addiction, which includes other kinds of nicotine use (pipe, cigar, chewing tobacco), as well as alcohol consumption, the use of marijuana, cocaine, and the various psychoactive drugs that fall under the heading of addictive substances. Perhaps general addiction would not be the best way to group smoking and drug taking, but the solution would be to form other response classes involving individual differences in the taking of drugs. Similarly, some of the response classes that define the traits discussed in this book might need to be reformulated. But however response classes are formed, they would be necessary, and in this sense, traits occupy a central place in the study of personality.

Conceptual Response Classes

Responses may be assigned to a class conceptually. The responses that comprise verbal aggression share a common feature: the voice. Such topographical similarity is a logical basis for forming a response class. Thus the trait of tempo includes rapid talking, writing, typing, gesturing, and eating (Buss & Plomin, 1975). These various responses share the common surface characteristic of a high rate of responding, as the person hurries through a series of repetitive acts.

Otherwise disparate responses may have the same outcome. Aggression is defined as actions that have a high probability of hurting or harming the victim, for example, hitting, kicking, cursing, and insulting. There might be two related outcomes here: Kicking and hitting result in physical pain, whereas cursing and insulting result in psychological discomfort. Thus a generic outcome (hurt) can be differentiated into two related consequences, physical hurt versus psychological hurt. Such differentiation yields the narrower traits of physical aggressiveness and verbal aggressiveness.

Another conceptual basis for forming a response class is a commonality of process. Consider the response of examining one's motives, reflecting about one's past, examining one's present emotional state, and daydreaming about oneself. All involve the same cognitive process: focusing attention on the private aspects of oneself. Individual differences in this attentional focus define the trait of private self-consciousness (Fenigstein, Scheier, & Buss, 1975). Cognitive styles involve the processing of information, for example, field dependence (Witkin, Dyk, Faterson, Goodenough, & Karp, 1962).

A response class may also be formed on the basis of theory. Thus the authoritarian personality contains behaviors that superficially would not seem to go together: dominance and submissiveness (Adorno, Frenkel-Brunswik, Levinson, & Sanford, 1950). Authoritarians are assumed to be tyrannical with subordinates but fawning with superiors. The concept of ego control (Block & Block, 1979) includes this diverse set of behaviors: energy expenditure, delay of gratification, exploratory behavior, planfulness, and distractibility.

Empirical Response Classes

Conceptual response classes may be logically compelling, but do the various responses assumed to comprise the class actually cluster together empirically? The typical statistical method of assessing coherence is factor analysis.

Consider individual differences in self-consciousness (see Chapter 6). The first step was to identify behaviors that defined the domain of self-consciousness. The conceptual class included preoccupation with past, present, and future behavior; sensitivity to inner feelings; recognition of one's positive and negative attributes; introspective behavior; a tendency to picture or imagine oneself; awareness of one's physical appearance and presentation; and concern over the appraisal of others. Items assessing these various facets of self-consciousness were factor analyzed, yielding the traits of private self-consciousness (attention to nonobservable aspects of the self) and public self-consciousness (attention to the observable aspects of the self (see Chapter 10).

A novel way of obtaining empirical clusters of responses is the act frequency approach (D. M. Buss, 1981; D. M. Buss & Craik, 1983). For a potential trait such as dominance, each subject is asked to think of three dominant persons, and to write down five acts that reflect their dominance. Subjects are also asked to say of each dominant act how prototypical it is. These nominating procedures not only sample the domain of a variety of traits but also suggest which acts are more frequent and more prototypical. Identifying prototypical acts can be important, for if a behavior is central to the concept of the trait, a personality trait might predict the behavior of a single response.

The value of this approach also may be seen in a study of sex differences in dominance, mentioned in Chapter 7. "Men expressed their dominance in the entire range of dominant acts. They reported more often taking the lead in groups, initiating group activities, and talking considerably in public" (D. M. Buss, 1981, p. 151). Dominant women expressed their dominance by introducing others and mediating disputes.

Breadth

Behavior

Breadth may be regarded as a continuum. The bottom end is defined by a single response, such as hitting others. Add kicking, scratching, biting, shoving, and pinching, and there is a response class: use of the body to hurt others. Individual differences in this class define the narrowest aggressiveness trait: hurting others with hands, feet, teeth, or nails. Add the use of knives, clubs, guns, and other weapons, and the broader response class of physical aggression is formed. It can be further extended by indirectly aggressive acts such as letting air out of car tires or destroying another person's possessions. Finally, we might add the varieties of verbal aggression to form the most inclusive aggressiveness trait.

It follows logically that narrowly defined traits, having fewer responses in the class, tend to be homogeneous. As such, they tend to be better predictors of a particular behavior, just as tennis ability better predicts tennis performance than does general athletic ability. Baseball hitting ability can be differentiated into power hitting and singles hitting. When two batters have the same hitting average, the slugger hits many home runs but strikes out frequently, whereas the singles hitter hits few home runs but rarely strikes out. Dividing hitting ability into the narrower traits of slugging versus singles hitting can lead to a more precise prediction of what happens in a particular ball game when hitters are at bat.

However, the exclusiveness of narrow traits has a potential disadvantage. The few responses that comprise a narrow trait may occur so infrequently as to mask or eliminate differences in frequency from one person to the next. Rarely occurring responses are also difficult to study. For example, people blush so seldom that researchers cannot wait around until the response occurs. The solution is to add responses, thereby broadening the class to embarrassment, which includes not only blushing but also gaze aversion, giggling, covering the face, and a feeling of silly discomfort (see Chapter 11).

Broader personality traits not only allow a greater frequency of behavior but enable us to observe response alternatives that may have the same generic outcome. Consider a man who is high in the trait of weapons-defined aggressiveness but who has no weapon available. Presumably, he would then use his fists or hurt a victim verbally. These substitute responses, part of the broader trait of general aggressiveness, would be missed by the narrower trait of weapons-defined aggressiveness.

Thus the continuum of breadth offers trade-offs at either extreme. Narrow traits, being homogeneous and specific, are better predictors of particular behaviors, but the responses that define them may occur infrequently, and they may exclude important response options. Broad traits are heterogeneous and do not predict specific behaviors as well as narrow traits. They are, however, better predictors of a range of behavior, and their breadth allows researchers to include alternative responses and to study infrequent behavior.

It might be argued that in everyday situations, behavior consists mainly of narrowly defined responses: for example, whether a person is so fearful of flying that he or she will not travel on an airplane. But broadly defined behavior is just as important in everyday situations: the generic shyness of a man who does not seek dates, cannot function in a job interview, and shrinks back in most social groups. Important behavior in everyday situations may be narrow or broad.

If the goal is a comprehensive picture of personality, broader traits are preferred simply because there are fewer of them. Scientists prefer a few broad concepts that integrate a complex domain. One way of moving to the upper extreme of the breadth continuum is to factor analyze traits. This procedure can be continued until there are just a few factors or supertraits, which will be discussed in Chapter 13.

Even when traits covary sufficiently for them to cohere in a higher-order factor, there may be reasons for separating them. When extraversion was assessed in a questionnaire, it was found to consist of two main factors, sociability and impulsivity (Eysenck & Eysenck, 1963). Two boys who received identical middle scores on extraversion might be different in important ways. A high-sociable, low-impulsive boy would be easy to socialize on two counts. First, being sociable, he would be especially susceptible to the social rewards and punishments typically used by parents, teachers, and other socializing agents. Second, being low in impulsivity, he would already be partway toward one of the major goals of socialization, inhibitory control of impulses. A low-sociable, high-impulsive boy would have double jeopardy on the same two bases. Being low in sociability, he would be less affected by the social rewards and punishments typically used by socializing agents. And being high in impulsivity, he would have a longer road to travel toward the goal of impulse control. Thus the supertrait of extraversion can mask the very different outcomes of the combined traits of sociability and impulsivity.

Situations

If responses occur in only one context, that is not a sufficient basis for inferring a trait, because traits are expected to involve behavior in at least several situations. But situations elicit changes in behavior, so how can there be cross-situational consistency? Individuals do not necessarily maintain a fixed level of behavior from one situation to the next. Rather, they are expected to hold their place in relation to other individuals over a range of situations. Thus some contexts allow more aggression, which means that an aggressive child may attack more on the playground than inside the school building. But the trait of physical aggressiveness also determines behavior, which means that an aggressive child is likely to attack more in both places than a nonaggressive child.

Just as personality traits vary in breadth, so do situations. The trait of heterosexual social anxiety (Farrell, Mariotto, Conger, Curran, & Wallander, 1979) may be observed on a blind date, a date with someone already known, a computer date, or an arranged date. This list clearly is short, resulting in a narrow trait. Now add interviews, clubs, parties, and other social gatherings, the wider variety of contexts that do not involve dating but all other social interaction with either sex. The personality trait appropriate to this broader class of situations is shyness. Now add nonsocial contexts in which people may become fearful: hospitals, airplanes, snakes, learning to drive, and taking tests. The trait relevant to this broad class of social and nonsocial situations is fear.

Just as the number of responses determines the breadth of a personality trait, so does the number of situations. Smaller classes of situations tend to be more homogeneous and, other things being equal, should yield more cross-situational consistency than broader, heterogeneous situations. Baseball hitting offers examples. A .300 hitter might bat .350 against right-handed pitchers but only .250 against left-handers. He might hit better against some right-handers than others, better in day games than in night games, better in some ballparks than in others, better against some teams than others, and better with players on base than when the bases are empty. Baseball managers know these things about their players and take into account more than the overall batting average when deciding how to use their players.

Like responses, situations need to be clustered, and this is ordinarily accomplished intuitively. Indeed, situations are often sampled in personality trait questionnaires. Unlike personality traits, however, situations are ordinarily not subjected to factor analysis to discover empirical clusters, though there are exceptions (see Magnusson, 1971).

Aggregation

Without being labeled, aggregation was just mentioned in the discussion of baseball hitters. In personality, the issue has received the most attention from Epstein (1986):

> Aggregation is a powerful technique for extending the generality of an observation and for reducing the error of measurement. This is widely recognized when data are averaged over subjects. By averaging over subjects in a sample, it is possible to generalize the findings to other subjects from the same population and to cancel out unique reactions of different subjects, thereby reducing error of measurement. What is true of aggregation over subjects applies equally well to other forms of aggregation, including aggregation over stimuli, situations, occasions, modes of measurement, and judges. (p. 1203)

Time

In a study of dominance, nursery-school children were observed over four-minute intervals, each divided into ten-second units (Moskowitz & Schwarz, 1982). For each unit, observers counted whether a dominant act had occurred, and the child's dominance score was the sum of these ten-second units. Also, after the eight weeks of the study, the head teacher and other observers rated the children for dominance, and these ratings were averaged.

The correlation between the raters and the behavior counts of dominance depended on the number of weeks of observation: for one week, .38; for four weeks, .54; and for eight weeks, .59. The authors pointed out that dominant behavior is infrequent, which means that it may take many different observations to attain a good sample of a child's dominant behavior. As the period of observation increased and observations were further aggregated, the correlations between raters and behavior counts rose.

Situations

Magnusson and Hefler (1969) had small groups of soldiers perform six tasks: decision making, solving work puzzles, constructing a pump, planning a community, deciding a beauty contest, and constructing a toy ferris wheel. One group of psychologists observed three tasks, and a second group observed the other three tasks. Both groups rated the soldiers for the traits of leadership, cooperation, and confidence after observing each task. After the second task, they used information from both tasks; after the third task, they used information from all three tasks. Within each group of observers, the ratings correlated from .78 to .89, suggesting adequate interjudge reliability. The correlations between the two groups of observers were as follows: after observing one task, .01; after two tasks, .13; and after three tasks, .55.

What caused this increase in correlations? For any single task, each soldier's behavior would be influenced considerably by specific situational requirements. If a soldier behaved similarly in the other two situations, however, this consistency would allow an observer to infer a trait. Behavior specific to each situation would be canceled out, leaving behavior attributable to enduring dispositions. Thus when judges were allowed to include behavior from several situations, they could better evaluate each soldier's contribution to the tasks. This aggregation over situations elevated the correlation between the two groups of observers from chance to an adequate level.

College students wore timers telling them when (randomly) to record their present mood and behavior (Diener & Larson, 1984). They were also to record their present situation: work, recreation, dinner, and so on. The authors summarized their findings this way: "Aggregating data across occasions resulted in much higher stability and consistency estimates than those based on disaggregated estimates. . . . This indicates that there are consistent and stable long-term trends in mean level of responding for individuals, but in general single responses will show very low levels of consistency and stability" (p. 880).

Responses

The trait of activity consists of a number of specific acts that make up the response class. McGowan and Gormly (1976) observed several kinds of energetic behavior in college men when they were in class or on campus: walking speed, distance per step, speed while climbing stairs, rate of head movements, and rate of postural adjustments. Their fraternity peers also rated these subjects for activity. The correlations between these peer ratings and each specific behavior varied from .20 to .60. When the specific behaviors were aggregated to form an average, this average of behavioral observations correlated .70 with the peer ratings.

These findings extended an earlier study that remains unpublished (Gormly & Champagne, 1974). College men were given laboratory tasks that involved tempo and vigor, and they filled out a self-report on the trait of activity. When this self-report was correlated with each of the laboratory tasks, the average correlation was .22. But when the self-report was correlated with the average laboratory performance, the correlation rose to .78. Evidently, aggregation of responses is necessary to demonstrate how strongly personality sometimes affects behavior.

Implications

These empirical studies on aggregation demonstrate how important it is to group observations to yield a summary score. Aggregation over responses bears directly on the issue of response classes. Personality traits are defined as response classes for which there are consistent individual differences. If researchers collect data on merely a single member of a response class, they are neglecting other members of the class. That is to say, they have a poor sample of the behavioral domain they are attempting to study. For example, in McGowan and Gormly's study (1976) the rate of climbing stairs correlated .20 with peer ratings of activity. Clearly, climbing stairs is an inadequate sample of the class of energetic behaviors.

It appears to be just as important to aggregate over time and situations if the impact of personality traits is to be discovered. When behavior is sampled once in a single situation, momentary determinants of behavior may overwhelm any contribution of traits. A single at bat of a baseball hitter serves as an apt example. Whether he makes a hit on any one at bat is likely to be affected by fatigue (second game of a doubleheader), whether he is playing at home or away, whether it is a day or night game, whether the pitcher is right-handed or left-handed, whether there are runners on base or not, whether it is an early or late inning, and what the score is. When all these variables are summed, there is little room for hitting ability to make a significant contribution. But when the player's hits are aggregated over time, these transient variables cancel out, and his true ability is revealed by the season's batting average.

Like baseball managers, personality psychologists focus on enduring dispositions and therefore need to aggregate when studying personality traits. Thus personality questionnaires sample different responses made in different situations, and subjects are asked to report their enduring behavioral tendencies. Then single items are aggregated to yield a score for the particular trait, and in research the scores of all the subjects in a sample are aggregated to yield an average for the group.

Consistency

It is a plausible assumption that some people are more consistent in their behavior than others. Those who are consistent offer evidence of traits in their behavior, whereas in the case of those who are inconsistent the trait concept may not be useful. Knowing this, personality psychologists have attempted to identify who is consistent and who is not. The usual method has been to compare self-reports of subjects with how their peers rate them for personality traits. The aim is to discover characteristics of those subjects whose self-reports roughly match the evaluations of them by peers. These characteristics are called *moderator variables.*

Moderator Variables

One way to discover who is consistent is simply to ask subjects. Bem and Allen (1974), using subjects' ratings about the consistency of their own behavior, reported higher correlations between self-reports and the ratings by peers for two traits. Several attempts to repeat and extend these results failed (see Chaplin & Goldberg, 1985), as have attempts to use statistical variability within a questionnaire (Tellegen et al., 1988). Perhaps self-reported consistency, used alone, is worth little as a moderator variable.

Aside from self-reported consistency, two other moderator variables have proved to be important determiners of the correlations between self-reports and the observations of peers. One is the *observability* of the trait-relevant behaviors. If these behaviors tend to be covert, it will be difficult for an observer (peer) to judge them accurately. The other moderator variable is *relevance*. If a trait is unimportant for the person, he or she may not self-report it accurately, and others might have trouble observing it, but an important trait is more likely to be noticed by both subjects and observers.

All three moderators were evaluated in a large-scale study of 472 college students (Zuckerman et al., 1988). The subjects rated themselves and were rated by same-sex roommates on eleven sets of adjectives: *emotional-calm, reserved-outgoing, assertive-mild-mannered, conscientious-disregarding of duties, cautious-adventurous, suspicious-trusting, self-assured-worrying, group-oriented-self-sufficient, undisciplined-compulsive, driven-relaxed,* and *organized-disorderly.* The subjects also ranked the eleven sets of traits for relevance or importance. They rated the consistency of each pair of adjectives: "How much do you vary from one situation in terms of _____?" And they rated the observability of each pair of adjectives: "How publicly observable is your behavior on the _____ dimension?"

Higher consistency, observability, and relevance all served to elevate the correlations between the subjects' self-reports of the eleven traits and the ratings of their roommates. Unexpectedly, the combination of all three moderator variables yielded correlations much higher than would be expected merely by adding their contributions—that is, it had a synergistic effect. Consider the average correlations for all eleven traits. When the traits were ranked as inconsistent, and rated as relatively unobservable and not especially relevant, the average correlation between subjects' self-reports and peers' ratings was .27. But when the traits were ranked as consistent, and rated as observable and relevant, the average self-peer correlation rose to .53.

A follow-up study used similar slightly different trait pairs and had subjects both rank and rate the three moderator variables (Zuckerman, Bernieri, Koestner, & Rosenthal, 1989). The impact of the moderator variables was small when they were rated but much larger when they were ranked. This time, the effect of each moderator variable was small, and this was the authors' interpretation: "In an ideal case, then, an observable behavior would yield low self-peer agreement unless the behavior were also high in relevance and consistency; conversely, a relevant as well as consistent behavior may still result in low self-peer agreement unless it is also observable" (p. 290).

These two studies may explain the negative findings of some previous research, which used ratings and typically studied only a single moderator variable, usually self-reported consistency. Future research should include all three moderators and perhaps use rankings rather than ratings of the moderator variables. Researchers might be advised to go beyond self-reports of these moderator variables and try more behavioral assessments of consistency, observability, and relevance. One last point about moderator variables: They are not the only systematic determinants of consistent behavior (see Ozer, 1986). The place of subjects on any particular trait dimension might be important, as well as several personality traits that conceptually appear to be relevant to the issue of consistency.

Extremes

Any trait dimension may be divided into subjects at the high and low ends (*extremes*) and subjects in the middle (*moderates*). Paunonen (1989) discovered that whether subjects were extremes or moderates was related to the observability of traits: observability was greater for subjects both at the high and low ends of trait dimensions than for subjects in the middle. In explaining this curvilinear relationship, he wrote, "People who are more extreme on a bipolar trait, high or low, are more likely to behave in a trait-consistent manner across occasions and situations than those who are moderate on the trait; those extreme people are the ones, therefore, for whom the trait behaviors are more likely to be observed by others" (Paunonen, 1989, p. 825).

Research on achievement provides an example of the importance of where subjects are located on the trait dimensions. Those in the middle of the trait dimension of achievement tend to be less consistent in their behavior than those at either extreme. "Data from four studies and an extensive review of the literature reveal a pervasive inconsistency in the behavior of those who obtain moderate scores on various motive measures. Such individuals tend to behave at a higher or lower level on a number of measures than do those classified as either high or low in the same motive measure" (Sorrentino & Short, 1977, p. 478). Persons at the two extremes of the trait of achievement were more consistent on laboratory tasks, which raises an important issue. When behavior relevant to a trait is more observable, it can be more accurately observed by roommates and friends of the subjects and thus yield greater consistency. But when laboratory measures are used, observability of the trait-related behavior is not important, for experimenters can find ways to measure the behavior reliably in the laboratory. This is an important issue for some of the traits that are not particularly observable, such as self-esteem and cognitive styles. Observability of traits clearly is a dimension that is anchored at the high end by one of the most observable traits, activity, and anchored at the low end by one of the least observable traits, private self-consciousness.

Another trait, the temperament of sociability, offers an example of a conceptual analysis of extremes, which starts by dividing the trait dimension into three parts. At the low end are persons whose motivation to be with others is weak. They can take or leave discussion groups, parties, and other social functions. They are not hermits and prefer at least some social interaction, but they would just as soon keep their own company. Persons in the middle of the dimension have stronger social needs, tend to seek out others more often, and remain longer in the presence of others. They prefer being with others to being alone and are responsive to others' overtures. But they too like being in their own company, and a little social interaction may go a long way in satisfying their social needs. At the high end of the dimension are persons who seem driven to seek out the company of others. They are restless and bored when alone, may complain of loneliness, and crave the stimulation that can come only from other people. Their need for others is strong, perhaps insatiable, and they respond with great pleasure to overtures from others.

What are the implications for consistency? Those at the low extreme of sociability, by definition, tend not to seek out others and are minimally responsive to the approach of others. There is a "floor effect" operating here, for though these persons can be somewhat more sociable, they cannot be less sociable. It follows from this restriction of range that persons at the low extreme of sociability are more consistent in behavior relevant to this trait.

At the high end of the sociability dimension there is a ceiling effect. Persons at this end might be less sociable, but they cannot be more sociable, by definition. It follows from this restriction of range that those extremely high in sociability display greater consistency in behavior relevant to the trait of sociability.

Persons in the broad middle range of sociability can move in either direction, and this wider range of behavior may be one reason that they are less consistent. We should also consider the possibility that two kinds of persons are located in the middle of the dimension. One kind might display great variability in their sociable behavior: gregarious in some contexts and solitary in others. The average of these diverse behaviors places these people in the middle of the trait dimension. The other kind of person in the middle of the trait dimension displays low variability. Across most situations, they are somewhat companionable and agreeable to the approach of others. They are consistently more sociable than those at the low extreme and more sociable than those at the high end of the dimension.

In brief, dividing a trait dimension into segments reveals where we are likely to find consistency. First, persons at either extreme of the dimension will be more consistent in the behavior relevant to the trait than those in the middle range. Second, only some of those in the middle of the dimension are likely to be inconsistent in their trait-relevant behavior. Identifying them and their consistent counterparts requires further conceptual analysis.

Differentiation

Recall that personality traits may be divided into their component parts. Thus the trait of activity consists of both tempo and vigor, which are alternative means of expending energy. Two persons who are assessed as having the same level of activity might differ in which component predominates. One person rushes through various situations in a hurry and only sometimes is vigorous, whereas the other person occasionally moves quickly but generally moves slower, delivering responses of great amplitude. If one considers only the overall level of the trait, each person might be regarded as inconsistent with respect to the trait of activity.

Other traits provide further examples. The components of fear are avoidance, physiological arousal, apprehensiveness, and expressive behavior. For some sociable people, the crucial social incentive is sharing activities, whereas for others it is attention from other people. Impulsivity can differentiate into its components: control, discipline, and reflection. And dominance can be achieved through aggressiveness, competitiveness, or leadership. For each of these traits, two persons at the same level of the trait might display evidence of the trait through behavior involving more than one component. When this behavior is assessed in research, it would be regarded as inconsistent. This potential for inconsistency of behavior exists not only for the traits just mentioned but for all the traits discussed in this book.

Differentiation is unlikely to occur for people at the extremes of a trait dimension. Thus those at the bottom of the activity dimension appear to have little energy for either fast-moving behavior or vigorous behavior; they show neither tempo nor vigor in their behavior. Those who are extremely active tend to be high in both vigor and tempo, or they would not have been classified as extremely high in the traits. Most of the energy of those in the middle of the activity dimension, however, may go into quick actions or into vigorous actions, establishing a potential for inconsistency. What appears to be true for the trait of activity would seem to hold for the other personality traits: Differentiation into components is most likely to occur in the middle range of the dimension. The absence of differentiation promotes consistency, which means that persons at the extremes of a trait dimension are likely to be more consistent than those in the middle.

Traits

Inherited Traits

Let us consider whether inherited personality traits are likely to be more consistent than those that are not inherited. Is it likely that inherited tendencies would be specific to one or just a few situations? If people are high in the trait of activity, is it possible that they are energetic at work but not at home? No, we must assume that most inherited traits are broad dispositions, not limited to just one context. If this assumption is correct, behavior determined by an inherited trait is likely to occur in a number of situations, and therefore it will be especially consistent.

Inherited personality traits can of course be altered by the impact of different environments and the experiences of life. Recall the example of physique, which is inherited but can be modified. Other things being equal, however, inherited personality traits tend to be less affected by environmental contingencies than are traits that are wholly acquired. To the extent that environmental contingencies affect behavior, they produce inconsistency from one situation to the next. An inherited trait, being less subject to these contingencies, is likely to be more consistent.

Style

Stylistic traits refer to the *how* of behavior, not the *what*. Presumably, each of us brings a characteristic style to most situations. Voice, gestures, posture, and movements vary little from one context to the next. One reason for this consistency is that the way responses are delivered (style) is typically a background variable, usually out of the awareness of the person or others who might observe it. A related reason is that most of the impact of behavior on others derives from the content of the response, not its style. Having less impact, it is usually not noticed by others or shaped by environmental contingencies. One acquires a regional speech accent, for example, merely by imitating the speech of others in the area, and talks this particular way in virtually all situations. Typically, the particular manner in which a response is delivered is so well learned a habit that it is run off automatically. Some stylistic behavior derives from physique, heavy persons tending to lumber, for example. Thus style is an automatic, background aspect of behavior, sometimes the result of anatomy, barely noticed by others, and not especially affected by the specifics of environmental contexts. It follows that stylistic traits—being animated, eloquent, or clumsy, for example—are likely to be especially consistent.

Self

A constant across situations is oneself. It follows that any trait involving the self, especially self-reactions, is likely to be stable and resistant to the impact of situational variables. Thus the global trait of self-esteem involves a generalized sense of self-worth that is an intrinsic part of each of us. When confronted with failure on tasks that might relate to one's intelligence, for example, persons high in self-esteem tend not to become upset, cope well with the negative outcomes, are ready for new challenges, and their self-esteem remains high (Brockner, 1979). Persons low in self-esteem are devastated by such failure, wish only to avoid any possible repetition of the challenge, and use the fact of failing to confirm their low opinion of themselves.

However, a person high in self-esteem might acknowledge a lack of ability in any particular endeavor, say, athletics, music, or mathematics; and a person low in self-esteem might acknowledge doing well in these endeavors. Do these facts suggest inconsistency of self-esteem? No, they reflect only the confidence persons have about engaging in particular tasks, and confidence about a particular task does not define the trait of self-esteem. This trait consists of a *global* evaluation of oneself, an evaluation that is not merely the algebraic sum of all the potential sources of self-esteem. Even if global self-esteem were simply a sum of abilities, one's underlying feeling of self-value would color how the facts were interpreted. Recall that those high in self-esteem, when confronted with a lack of ability, dismiss it by regarding it as unimportant; they know that they are worthwhile. Those low in self-esteem tend to disregard any evidence of superior ability and focus on their inabilities, regarding them as confirming that they are not worthwhile. In brief, global self-esteem is expected to be one of the most consistent personality traits.

There are two grounds for believing that the trait of private self-consciousness would be consistent. First, it is a self-related trait, and any trait involving the self is expected to be consistent. Second, it is a covert trait, unobserved by others. As such, it is not under the control of social or nonsocial determinants and therefore is not as susceptible to the situational demands or influences that would render the trait inconsistent.

Private self-consciousness also acts as a moderator variable, enhancing the correlation between self-reports and other measures of behavior. Those who are high in this trait tend to examine their emotions, motives, history, and their own personality tendencies, which means that their self-reports should tend to be veridical. Recall that Scheier, Buss, and Buss (1978) divided subjects into top and bottom thirds on the basis of the private self-consciousness scale, and the aggressiveness factor of the hostility inventory (Buss & Durkee, 1957) was administered. The trait of aggressiveness was correlated with behavioral aggression as measured by the aggression machine. For those low in private self-consciousness, the correlation between trait aggressiveness and behavioral aggression was .09, but for the Highs the correlation was .66. Clearly, those high in private self-consciousness offered a veridical self-report, whereas the Lows did not.

Wymer and Penner (1985) had subjects rate themselves on bipolar adjectives describing extraversion, agreeableness, conscientiousness, and emotional stability. Three friends also rated the subjects for these adjectives, and the friends' ratings were pooled. For those high in private self-consciousness, the self-ratings were in closer agreement with the ratings of their friends than was true for those low in private self-consciousness. These two studies are a small sample of the research, discussed in Chapter 10, which has verified the hypothesis that persons high in private self-consciousness know themselves better than the Lows. Consequently, their self-reports are more accurate, which makes it more likely that these self-reports will correlate with other trait measures.

Some people go beyond merely focusing attention on the private aspects of themselves to processing self-related information and organizing it into integrated concepts, called *self-schemata* (Markus, 1977). Perhaps the traits of such people are more consistent, but there are two troublesome issues. First, such people are likely to be high in private self-consciousness, and it must be demonstrated that self-schemata add any variance when private self-consciousness is controlled. Second, Markus identified self-schematic subjects as those who were either high or low in the trait of independence; those in the middle range were labeled *aschematic*. We already know that people at the extremes of a trait distribution tend to be consistent. Thus if self-schemata are to be regarded as relevant to consistency, the concept

TABLE 12.2   Variables Affecting Consistency

Method

Self-reported	Subjects reporting more consistency are more consistent
Ranking and rating	Ranking yields more consistency

General variables

Observability	Traits checked against the knowledge of peers are more consistent when the traits are more observable
Relevance	Traits subjects regard as important tend to be more consistent
Extremes of dimension	Those at the extremes of trait dimensions tend to be more consistent

Traits

Inheritance	Inherited traits are more consistent
Stylistic traits	Stylistic traits are more consistent than content traits
Self-related traits	Self-related traits are more consistent than other traits

will have to be separated from the issue of extremes, and any impact of private self-consciousness would have to be partialled out.

This section on self-related traits concludes the discussion of the variables that affect consistency of personality. These variables are summarized in Table 12.2. Notice that the way researchers investigate personality—through self-reports and rankings rather than ratings—affects whether consistency is an outcome of their research. Observability and relevance are also important, but in my opinion, consistency of personality is most likely to be found in people who occupy the extremes of trait dimensions. Inherited personality dispositions surely are more consistent than those that are acquired through experience. Finally, self-related personality tendencies appear to be more consistent than other traits.

$Chapter$ 13

Classification

Kinds of Classification

Do we need to classify in order to organize the field of personality? Given the welter of personality dispositions, the answer to this question must be yes. Two major kinds of classification have been used: conceptual and empirical (Buss & Finn, 1987).

Conceptual Classification

One way of sorting out the diverse aspects of personality is simply to make a list. Calling them needs, Murray (1938) contrived a list of twenty personality traits:

Abasement	Harmavoidance
Achievement	Infavoidance
Affiliation	Nurturance
Aggression	Order
Autonomy	Play
Counteraction	Rejection
Defendance	Sentience
Deference	Sex
Dominance	Succorance
Exhibition	Understanding

Notice that some pairs are bipolar opposites, for example, dominance and abasement; and some are complementary, for example, nurturance (helping) and succorance (wanting help). This list was later the basis of a personality inventory, the Personality Research Form (PRF; Jackson 1984). A factor analysis of these traits in an earlier version of the PRF yielded three higher-order factors: social leadership, autonomy, and impulse expression-and-control (Lei & Skiner, 1982). Thus, in addition to organizing the field of personality, Murray's list eventually led to an empirical, three-factor classification.

A list is a first step in attempting to organize personality, but it cannot be considered a map of personality, because it does not organize the personality dispositions. The next step, then, is to organize the traits in some way. An early example is Jung's (1923) eightfold classification. He conceived two attitudes as the major orientations to personality: extraversion and introversion. These concepts are slightly different in Jung's conception than in their use by most psychologists. For Jung, extraversion was the tendency to turn outward toward the world, whereas introversion was the tendency to turn inward toward the self. These two tendencies were crosscut with four functions: thinking, feeling, sensing, and intuiting. The result was an eightfold (two by four) classification. The system was further organized by placing pairs in opposition: extraversion opposed by introversion, thinking by feeling, and sensing by intuiting.

Does Jung's typology hold up empirically? After conducting six studies, Stricker and Ross (1964) concluded, "These studies, with one or two exceptions, offer little support for the structural properties attributed to the typology" (p. 68). Later studies reported similar negative findings (McCrae & Costa, 1989a). Jung's typology does not survive empirical test, though introversion-extraversion remains an important part of current classifications of personality.

Another approach is to start with areas or spheres of behavior and crosscut them with dimensions of behavior. Guilford (1959) divided personality-relevant behavior into general, emotional, and social spheres, and crosscut them with five dimensions, the result being a set of organized bipolar traits (traits defined by two opposite poles). Thus for the active versus passive dimension the bipolar trait in the general sphere is impulsiveness versus deliberateness; in the emotional sphere it is nervousness versus composure; and in the social sphere it is social initiative versus passivity. His other dimensions are positive versus negative, responsive versus unresponsive, controlled versus uncontrolled, and objective versus egocentric. The advantage of this classification is that it contains personality traits that have already been studied and organizes them into conceptually meaningful classes. Its disadvantage is that, like most purely rational classifications, it has not been verified empirically.

There is a hierarchical classification of personality that extends into intelligence, values, and motor performance (Royce & Powell, 1981). One part of the classification, dealing with what the authors call the affective system, is relevant here (Royce & McDermott, 1977). The lowest level consists of twenty traits, some familiar ones being gregariousness, dominance, and fearfulness. The next, more inclusive level consists of seven larger traits, such as anxiety, excitability, and social inhibition. And the highest, most inclusive segment in the hierarchy consists of three supertraits called emotional stability, emotional independence, and introversion-extraversion.

A hierarchy offers a more complex and detailed classification than one that has just a single level—Jung's eightfold scheme, for example. A hierarchy is complex in linking lower levels to higher levels, offering a finer-grained understanding of personality. In addition, researchers may investigate personality at any of the several levels of the hierarchy, though as we saw in the last chapter the middle level of individual traits is typically optimal in breadth.

Empirical Classification

To understand the personality classifications that dominate the field today, we need to delve into their history, which began in the 1930s with the application of factor analysis to self-report questionnaires and adjectives.

Guilford, Cattell, and Eysenck

J. P. Guilford (Guilford & Guilford, 1934) was the first to use factor analysis for this purpose. He factor analyzed a questionnaire designed to measure introversion-extraversion. Four factors emerged: social introversion-extraversion, emotional sensitiveness, impulsiveness, and interest in self.

After improvements in factor analysis by Thurstone (1934), Guilford and Guilford (1936) reanalyzed their data, coming up with these factors: social introversion, emotionality, dominance, rhathymia (happy-go-lucky), and thinking introversion. Cattell (1943) factor analyzed self-reports of thirty-five clusters of adjectives, which yielded twelve factors. With some of the names altered to make them more familiar, the bipolar factors are: friendly-hostile, intelligent-unintelligent, stable-emotional, hypersensitive-phlegmatic, dominant-submissive, bold-shy, mature-immature, warm-cold, anxious-unanxious, impulsive-conscientious, cultured-boorish, and trusting-suspicious.

Subsequently, the original twelve factors were modified, and four new factors were added to make a total of sixteen (Cattell & Eber, 1961). These were further factor analyzed, yielding eight higher-order factors (Gorsuch & Cattell, 1967). This result is not surprising, for a reading of the above factors suggests some overlap—between dominant-submissive and bold-shy, for example.

Perhaps the most influential classifier has been Eysenck (1947), who proposed three factors. The first is extraversion, which originally consisted of these traits: sociability, impulsivity, rhathymia (happy-go-lucky), ascendance (dominance), and activity.

The other two factors are neuroticism, which overlaps the temperament of emotionality, and psychoticism, a misleading label, as will be seen. The identity of these three factors shifted gradually to accommodate subsequent research, and the personality traits that currently define them are listed in Table 13.1.

Classification Using Adjectives

The dominant classification of personality traits today is a set of superfactors called the *Big 5*: extraversion, agreeableness, conscientiousness, emotional stability, and culture. This classification originated in factor analyses of adjectives. Thurstone (1934) presented raters with a list of sixty adjectives and asked them to think of a person they knew well and underline the adjectives that would describe the per-

TABLE 13.1   Personality Traits That Define Extraversion, Neuroticism, and Psychoticism

Extraversion	Neuroticism	Psychoticism
Active	Anxious	Aggressive
Assertive	Depressed	Antisocial
Carefree	Emotional	Cold
Dominant	Guilty	Creative
Lively	Irrational	Egocentric
Sensation seeking	Low in self-esteem	Impersonal
Sociable	Moody	Impulsive
Surgent	Shy	Tough-minded
Venturesome	Tense	Unempathic

son. A factor analysis yielded five clusters of adjectives, three of which are comparable to Big 5 factors:

1. *Friendly, congenial, broad-minded, generous;* these appear roughly equivalent to agreeableness
2. *Persevering, hardworking, systematic;* these appear roughly equivalent to conscientiousness
3. *Patient, calm, faithful, earnest;* these overlap the opposite pole of emotional stability, but it is a very rough fit
4. *Capable, frank, self-reliant, courageous;* there is no comparable Big 5 factor
5. *Self-important, sarcastic, haughty, grasping, cynical, quick-tempered;* there is no comparable Big 5 factor

A couple of years later Allport and Odbert (1936) listed thousands of adjectives. These were grouped into thirty-five clusters by Cattell (1943), as we saw earlier. Building on Cattell's work, Fiske (1949) discovered five factors that held consistently across self-ratings, peer ratings, and observers' ratings: confident self-expression, social adaptability, conformity, emotional control, and inquiring intellect. With slight variations in labels, this classification is the Big 5.

The next research, consisting of eight studies with adjectives, first appeared as a technical report in 1961 and was published three decades later (Tupes & Christal, 1992). Five factors recurred across all eight studies: surgency, agreeableness, dependability, emotional stability, and culture. Close reading of the research reveals overlap among the factors, especially between conscientiousness and culture. In addition, some of the adjectives loaded on more than one factor. Thus talkative and mild loaded on both surgency and agreeableness, and emotional maturity, cooperativeness, adaptability, and responsibility appeared on both the agreeableness and emotional stability factors.

Norman (1963) selected the adjectives with the highest loadings on the Tupes and Christal (1992) factors and had college men rate people they knew. Not surprisingly, he found the same five factors as Tupes and Christal. Again, there was overlap among the factors: Agreeableness correlated with conscientiousness, emotionality, and culture, the range being .31 to .55; culture correlated an average of .61 with conscientiousness. Thus four of the five factors are not independent, the exception being surgency (extraversion).

The Big 5

This tradition of using adjectives to yield a classification of personality has been continued by Goldberg and his colleagues (1981, 1990, 1993; Hofstee, De Raad, & Goldberg, 1992). One study analyzed fifty-seven bipolar adjective sets in self-reports and peer nominations (Peabody & Goldberg, 1989). There was strong agreement among the different data sets for the factors of surgency, agreeableness, and conscientiousness, and less agreement for emotional stability and culture. In addition, a sixth, minor factor was obtained, called values.

Another paper reported three studies that yielded essentially the same Big 5 factors (Goldberg, 1990). In this paper and others written by adherents of the Big 5 classification, there is appropriate attention to the fact that the same (or almost the same) five factors keep appearing. However, there is virtually no mention of the overlap among factors. For example, in Goldberg's (1990) research the adjective categories of adventure and energy load, as they should, on the surgency factor but also appear where presumably they should not, as part of conscientiousness (opposite pole) and emotional stability. The adjective category of warmth, which would seem to be the essence of agreeableness, does load on that factor, but it also appears as part of surgency, conscientiousness, and emotional stability. Similar overlaps have also been reported in other studies with adjectives, for example, McCrae & Costa (1985).

An approximation to the Big 5 was also obtained when teachers used adjectives to rate schoolchildren (Digman & Inouye, 1986). They found the usual five factors plus two minor ones with lower factor loadings. But again there was overlap for many of the adjectives. To cite one instance, assertive loads (appropriately) on surgency but also (negatively) on agreeableness.

Most published papers do not report sex differences in factorial structure, but a paper by Conley (1985) did. When his labels are translated into current usage, the women's factors were extraversion, agreeableness, conscientiousness, and emotional stability; culture did not appear. The men's factors were the same as the women's but with the addition of culture and attractiveness factors.

There is a questionnaire specifically designed to assess the Big 5. McCrae & Costa (1987) started with their NEO Inventory, which measured neuroticism (opposite pole of emotional stability), extraversion, and openness (highly similar to culture). They added scales of agreeableness and conscientiousness, and a factor analysis of items yielded the Big 5 factors (Costa, McCrae, & Dye, 1991). The particular components or facets of each factor are shown in Table 13.2.

During the last decade or so, research on the Big 5 has poured forth in ever-increasing volume, providing evidence of the Big 5's generality and value as a classification of personality. Adherents adduce four reasons for their belief that it represents the basic structure of personality: "(a) longitudinal and cross-observer studies demonstrate that all five factors are enduring dispositions that are manifest in patterns of behavior; (b) traits related to each of these factors are found in a variety of personality systems and in the natural language of trait description; (c) the factors are found in different age, sex, race, and language groups, although they may be somewhat differently expressed in different cultures, and (d) evidence of heritability suggests that all have some biological basis" (Costa & McCrae, 1992, p. 653).

The Big 5 is empirically based, deriving from modern quantitative techniques. One or another variant of the Big 5 is consistently found by different investigators, using different subjects and different research tools. As we shall see in the next chapter, the Big 5 also has implications for understanding abnormal behavior. For these reasons, it represents a great step forward in the search for the structure of personality, and for some psychologists it is the ultimate solution. But critics have pointed to problems with the Big 5. Its very predominance requires a closer look.

Which Big 5?

After asking this question, John (1989) assembled eight different versions of the Big 5 in a table and observed, "Although some general themes emerge from the factor

TABLE 13.2   **Components of the Big 5 Factors**

Extraversion	Agreeableness	Conscientiousness
Warmth	Trust	Competence
Gregariousness	Straightforwardness	Order
Assertiveness	Altruism	Dutifulness
Activity	Compliance	Achievement striving
Excitement seeking	Modesty	Self-discipline
Positive emotions	Tender-mindedness	Deliberation

Neuroticism	Openness
Anxiety	Fantasy
Hostility	Esthetics
Depression	Feelings
Self-consciousness	Actions
Impulsiveness	Ideas
Vulnerability	Values

names [in the table], the labels do vary substantially. The third factor, for example, has variously been interpreted as Conscientiousness, Dependability, Conformity, Prudence, Task Interest, and Will to Achieve. Factor V has been labelled Culture, Intellect, and Openness to experience. It appears as if each investigator has his or her 'own' Big Five" (p. 262).

One reason for the different classifications is that each researcher includes his or her own set of adjectives or personality scales. As a result, each reports five factors that are similar to others' Big 5s but different enough for a disinterested observer to wonder if they are really the same.

Even when the same adjectives are used, they are not necessarily assigned to the same factors. Thus warmth is placed in the extraversion factor by some investigators but in the agreeableness factor by others. Jealousy falls under the heading of agreeableness in one Big 5 classification but under the heading of emotional stability in another.

A related reason is that different researchers take slightly different perspectives on the five factors, tilting toward one or another of the personality traits that make up the factor and naming the factors differently. Thus the term *extraversion* implies social interest, social initiative (opposite pole of shyness), and enthusiasm. But the term *surgency* implies considerably more social impact, which emphasizes the contribution of the trait of dominance.

The fifth factor is especially problematic. If the emphasis is on the polished-crude dichotomy, the factor is called culture. If the emphasis is on the kind of abilities that intelligence tests assess, the factor is intellect. And if the emphasis is on imagination and creativity, the factor is openness. In one study these shifts were demonstrated empirically: "We showed how the selection of variables can determine the interpretation of Factor V, which we have labelled *Intellect*. If all the variables representing both expressive and controlled aspects of intelligence are excluded from the analyses . . . then one might obtain a factor that can be labelled *Culture*. On the other hand, if primary expressive aspects of intelligence are included, then one might obtain a factor that can be labelled *Openness*" (Peabody & Goldberg, 1989, p. 565).

Adherents of the Big 5 classification admit these problems but dismiss them as minor. Others regard them as too serious to be ignored: "The specific components of the five factors seem to vary as a function of the items included and the particular sample. Thus whereas there is a general resemblance in the factors that replicate from sample to sample, and investigator to investigator, the resemblance is more fraternal than identical. The five (plus or minus two) factors have yet to be defined by consensus with any degree of specificity" (Briggs, 1989, p. 248).

The problem may lie in a positive feature of the Big 5 classification: its considerable breadth, which makes it a candidate for the structure of personality. The breadth of the classification makes it likely that several different versions of five similar factors are likely to occur repeatedly. The presence of several variants forces us to consider which Big 5 represents the structure of personality. This issue begs for resolution, preferably by research.

How Many Factors?

Not all research with adjectives has yielded five factors, which raises the question of how many factors are needed. When Peabody (1984) compared his analysis of adjectives to the Big 5, he reported, "The first three unrotated factors here generally correspond to three of the Big Five factors: Agreeableness, Conscientiousness, and Surgency. . . . For the remaining two factors of the Big Five, Emotional Stability and Culture, no real trace can be found in the present results" (p. 397).

Several classifications of personality have fewer than five factors. The best known is Eysenck's (1947) previously mentioned trio of extraversion, neuroticism, and psychoticism. Extraversion and neuroticism, which have received most attention from researchers, may be part of the Big 5. Tellegen (1985) reported that three factors underlay his personality scales: negative emotionality (similar to neuroticism), positive emotionality, and constraint. The original NEO questionnaire of Costa and McCrae (Costa, McCrae, & Arenberg, 1980) consisted of only three factors: neuroticism, extraversion, and openness. And at the other end of the numerical dimension, there are Cattell's sixteen factors (Cattell & Eber, 1961).

So if we ask how many basic categories are needed to describe personality, the answer seems to be between three and sixteen. One study, however, by Zuckerman, Kuhlman, and Camac (1988) offers evidence that the choice may be somewhere between three and seven factors. They administered a battery of questionnaires that included the various traits subsumed by the Big 5, with the exception of culture. Statistical analysis of the respondents' answers yielded three different factor solutions: seven, five, or three factors (see Table 13.3).

In the seven-factor and five-factor solutions, activity and sociability are separate, but they coalesce to form an extraversion factor in the three-factor solution. Anger versus restraint, and neuroticism-anxiety, are separate in the seven-factor solution, but they coalesce to form negative emotionality in the five- and three-factor solutions. Autonomy versus conformity, impulsivity, and aggressive sensation seeking are separate in the seven-factor solution, but the first two come

TABLE 13.3   Three Different Factor Solutions

7 Factors	5 Factors	3 Factors
Activity	Activity	—
Sociability	Sociability	Extraversion
Anger vs. restraint Neuroticism-anxiety	Negative emotionality	Negative emotionality
Autonomy vs. conformity Impulsivity	Impulsivity	
		Impulsive sensation seeking
Aggressive sensation seeking	Aggressive sensation seeking	

together to form impulsivity in the five-factor solution. Then the impulsivity and aggressive sensation seeking factors of the five-factor solution coalesce to form the impulsive sensation seeking factor in the three-factor solution.

The three-factor solution strongly resembles Eysenck's (1947) triad of extraversion, neuroticism, and psychoticism, the latter having been revised to consist mainly of impulsivity (Eysenck & Eysenck, 1985). The five-factor solution contains two of the Big 5 factors: negative emotionality (opposite pole of emotional stability) and impulsivity (opposite pole of conscientiousness). Thus a factor analysis of personality, using standard questionnaires, did not yield the factors of the Big 5. It might be argued that if other questionnaires had been used, the Big 5 might have emerged. True, but if so, should the Big 5 be regarded as *the* basic structure of personality?

The Zuckerman et al. (1988) research used questionnaires, but adjectives have frequently been used. Digman and Takemoto-Chock (1981) analyzed eight previously collected sets of data on words describing personality, including the adjectives used by Tupes and Christal (1992) and Norman (1963). The factor solutions for the eight data sets varied from five factors to eight. This study and that of Zuckerman et al. (1988) suggest that as few as three overarching factors and as many as eight factors may define the structure of personality.

However, there may be reasons for choosing a larger number of traits. Consider how well personality questionnaires predict real-life outcomes such as pay, tenure, or supervisor's ratings. Mershon and Gorsuch (1988) compared the sixteen first-order factors of the 16PF personality test with the six second-order factors (Gorsuch & Cattell, 1967) with regard to how well they predicted these criteria. The larger number of factors offered better prediction: "Our major conclusion is that at least twice as much variance is generally accounted for when 16 personality factors are used than when using only 6" (Mershon and Gorsuch, p. 678).

The issue here is the *optimal level of analysis*, discussed in the last chapter under the heading of Breadth. How many overarching factors should there be? The answer depends on the goal of the researcher. If the aim is to encompass the wide range of personality tendencies with just a few categories, there should be just a few broad factors, somewhere between three and seven. If the aim is a more detailed understanding of personality and more precise prediction, a larger number of narrower factors would be preferable.

Included Traits

This book has dealt with a number of areas within personality, and for virtually all of them the individual differences have cohered into traits. Now we can ask where the various traits discussed here are located in the Big 5, with its terms placed in parentheses if they are different from mine.

The first factor, extraversion, includes sociability (gregariousness), activity, dominance, and shyness as the opposite pole of extraversion. The second factor, agreeableness, includes the prosocial traits of altruism and empathy (tender-mindedness) and perhaps aggressiveness at the opposite pole of agreeableness. The third factor, conscientiousness, representing the opposite pole of impulsivity, contains two components of impulsivity: self-discipline and reflection (deliberation). The fourth factor, neuroticism, includes anxiety, hostility, self-consciousness, and the lack of control component of impulsivity (impulsiveness). The fifth factor, openness, is not represented in this book, my reason being that it is too closely linked to both intelligence and social class.

What is omitted from the Big 5? One omission is identity, which is not a trait, individuals differing only in their sources of identity. Also missing is attachment, which may be too specific a topic, for it refers only to close relationships. Self-consciousness is listed as a facet of neuroticism by Costa et al. (1991), which means that it is really shyness (see Table 13.2). Private and public self-consciousness, which clearly do not belong under the heading of neuroticism, are omitted. And the trait of self-esteem is missing, perhaps because it would overlap extraversion (high self-esteem) and neuroticism (low self-esteem).

Blends

The self-esteem issue raises the question of *blends:* personality dispositions that may be placed on more than one factor. As we saw earlier, warmth belongs with both extraversion and agreeableness. And if the extraversion factor is tilted toward surgency, it includes dominance. Otherwise, dominance can be assigned to the opposite pole of agreeableness. Hostility also poses a problem for the Big 5. It is clearly related to both neuroticism and (low) agreeableness (Watson & Clark, 1992).

Another blend is shyness, which is a facet of neuroticism but would seem to be linked to introversion as well. Not surprisingly, shyness items correlate with measures of both introversion (opposite pole of extraversion) and neuroticism (Briggs, 1988). Correlational data suggest that shyness is a mixture of (low) sociability and emotionality: Cheek and Buss (1981) found that shyness correlated −.31 with sociability and .50 with fear, a major component of emotionality (neuroticism).

One reason for blends is the overlap among some of the factors, even though presumably they are orthogonal. Whether the Big 5 is that of Norman (1963) or of Costa and McCrae (1992), there is overlap among several of the factors (Johnson, 1993). Correlations among the factors tend not to be mentioned in published articles, but I obtained one set based on data from Botwin and Buss (1989). In their self-report data, extraversion (surgency) correlated .25 with openness, and agreeableness correlated .33 with both conscientiousness and emotional stability. In the reports by significant others, extraversion again correlated with openness, this time .35; agreeableness correlated .50 with emotional stability and .30 with openness; and emotional stability correlated .33 with openness. Given these correlations, some blends are inevitable.

Understanding Traits within a Factor

The Big 5 classification packs together personality traits that cluster empirically but that for some purposes might be better kept separate. Consider three facets of the Big 5 factor of extraversion: gregariousness (sociability), assertiveness (dominance), and activity. Sociability and dominance refer specifically to interpersonal behavior, whereas activity is a general motive. Activity and sociability are temperaments, first occurring in infancy, whereas dominance starts later in the preschool era.

It is true of course that these three traits intercorrelate and occupy the same factorial space, but we need to delve into *how* they are linked. Dominant people tend to be sociable because dominant behavior necessarily occurs in the interpersonal arena. But there are sociable people who are not at all dominant. Similarly, other things being equal, sociable people tend to be active, their energy directed toward being with others. But many active people are unsociable, their energy directed toward solitary work and recreation. Dominant people tend to be active, for it is difficult to dominate without the energy to persist in gaining the upper hand. But many active people are not at all dominant. In brief, dominance may depend on the need to be with others (sociability) and having the energy to dominate (activity), but being active or sociable requires no dominance. And being active does not require that one be sociable.

Another example may be found in the fourth factor, neuroticism (opposite pole of emotional stability). It includes both anxiety and depression. It is true that some anxious people are depressed, and some depressed people are also anxious. But anxiety and depression are clearly different, and combining them in one factor ignores a distinction that clinicians know is important.

What about people who fall in the middle of the dimension of extraversion, the ambiverts who are neither extraverts nor introverts. Some of them might score average in sociability, dominance, and activity. Some of them might score moderately high in sociability and activity but low in dominance. Some might be low in sociability, average in dominance, and high in activity. Some might score average in dominance, high in sociability, and low in activity. Clearly, within this group of ambiverts there are distinctly different patterns. Thus two ambiverts might be mismatched for sociability or activity, but this information would be lost if all we know is their extraversion scores,

The point is that placing these three traits under the heading of extraversion conceals differences among them that are revealed when the traits are examined individually. What is true for the extraversion factor holds as well for agreeableness and conscientiousness, and for emotional stability, and to a lesser extent for openness (intellect). What the Big 5 gains in inclusiveness it loses in specificity: the details that offer a more complete understanding of personality.

Next, consider sex differences. There is no sex difference in the Big 5 factor of extraversion, but there are sex differences in the individual facets. Thus men are slightly more active than women and somewhat more dominant, but women are slightly more sociable than men. And, as we saw in Chapter 4, men's sociability tends to be directed mainly toward groups, but women's sociability is directed mainly toward one-on-one interaction. Of course, all an investigator need do is examine the individual facets of a superfactor to discover these sex differences. But if it is necessary to move to the level of individual traits, why do we need the superfactors?

Top and Bottom Halves of Trait Dimensions

To explore beneath the surface why traits cluster together in superfactors, let us divide each trait dimension into those high versus those low in each trait—respectively, the top and bottom halves. The following examples include traits in the Big 5 and some that are not.

Dominance is correlated with sociability. People who are high in dominance necessarily prefer to be with others (high sociability), for dominance is an entirely social motive. But those who are low in dominance do not necessarily avoid others, which means that they may be either high or low in sociability. The relationship between the two traits may be attributed largely to the top half of the dominance dimension.

Dominance also correlates in the thirties with self-esteem. People who are dominant are likely to be high in self-esteem, else they would not be sufficiently confident to strive for the higher interpersonal status. However, those who are low in dominance may have high or low self-esteem, for, as we saw in Chapter 8, there are many sources of self-esteem other than dominance. Thus the positive relationship between these two traits may be attributed largely to the top half of the dominance dimension.

Self-esteem and shyness are strongly (negatively) correlated. People who are low in self-esteem tend to be shy. Lacking in self-worth, they expect others to find them unappealing and, as a result, expect to be ignored or rejected. But those who are high in self-esteem may be high or low in shyness. If they are shy and therefore derive little esteem from social contacts, there are other sources of self-esteem, and people with high self-esteem are adept at compensating for events that threaten self-esteem. This time, the relationship between the two traits may be attributed largely to the bottom half of a dimension (self-esteem).

Then there is the positive correlation between private and public self-consciousness. Some people rarely or never focus attention on themselves, either their private or their public aspects, which means that they occupy the bottom half of both the private and the public self-consciousness dimensions. What about those who are high in both traits? They clearly are preoccupied with all aspects of themselves, and such obsessive fascination with oneself is infrequent in the population. Thus most of those who are high in one kind of self-consciousness are not necessarily high in the other. It follows that the positive correlation between private and public self-consciousness may be attributed to those in the bottom half of both traits.

Notice that these analyses of dimensions occur at the level of traits and could not be attempted with superfactors, which consist of combinations of traits. Indeed, the issue of dimensionality cannot arise at the level of superfactors. Of course we might use the individual facets (traits) of the superfactors. One problem is that some traits are not included in the superfactors—self-esteem, for instance. But most relevant traits are included. The Big 5 supertrait of extraversion contains the facets of gregariousness and assertiveness, which are equivalent, respectively, to the sociability and dominance traits just discussed. Again, if it is necessary to use individual facets, why bother with superfactors?

Interpersonal Circumplexes

More than forty years ago psychologists started to arrange social behaviors in a circle, those nearer being more closely related and those farther being more distantly related (Freedman, Leary, Ossorio, & Coffey, 1951). Leary (1957) and his colleagues used two dimensions as the bipolar axes around which interpersonal traits might be aligned. The first axis was dominance-submission. The second was called love-hate, defined this way: for love, the terms were *affiliate, approve,* and *praise,* and for hate, the terms were *disaffiliate, disapprove,* and *criticize.* Therefore, this second bipolar axis might be better characterized as sociable versus aggressive, or, to make contact with a Big 5 supertrait, agreeable versus disagreeable.

The underlying assumption of all circumplexes is that the two axes are orthogonal, in the optimal case having a zero correlation. Diagrammatically, they are represented at a right angle to each other (see Figure 13.1). Once the two axes are established, blends of the two dimensions can be located around a circle. Thus sociable plus dominant equals extraverted, whereas unsociable plus submissive equals introverted. And unsociable plus dominant equals manipulative, whereas sociable plus submissive equals trusting (in the sense of being innocent).

The placement of particular traits around the circle should be done empirically. When Lorr and McNair (1965) computed the appropriate correlations, sociability correlated .00 with submissiveness (complete independence) but .38 with dominance. This correlation between dominance and sociability means that the hypothetical interpersonal circle in Figure 13.1 does not check out empirically. The Lorr and McNair correlations suggested a reasonable ordering of interpersonal traits around a circle, but there were other problems. For example, dominance correlated .38 with submissiveness, when the correlation should have been .00.

It remained for Wiggins (1979) to offer a circumplex of interpersonal traits that could be proved empirically. He extracted two orthogonal factors that he called status (power, dominance) and love (solidarity, affiliation). Then, using these two factors as axes, he aligned sixteen personality traits (eight pairs) on a circle.

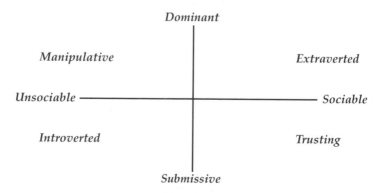

FIGURE 13.1   A Hypothetical Interpersonal Circumplex

Starting from the top of the circle and proceeding around it, they were ambitious-dominant, gregarious-extraverted, warm-agreeable, unassuming-ingenuous, lazy-submissive, aloof-introverted, cold-quarrelsome, and arrogant-calculating. Each of the sixteen terms was the aggregate of a set of adjectives. For example, *submissive* was defined by this list: *self-doubting, self-effacing, timid, meek, unbold, unaggressive, forceless,* and *unauthoritative*. These adjectives add low self-esteem and shyness to submissiveness, thereby rendering the overall term (*submissive*) less precise. Perhaps in response to this issue, Wiggins (Wiggins, Phillips, & Trapnell, 1989) altered the vertical axis to assured-dominant versus unassured-submissive to convey the self-esteem and shyness aspects of this dimension.

But these are minor issues, for this circumplex accurately locates interpersonal traits in a compelling manner. Nearby traits are positively related, those at a right angle are unrelated, and those opposite to one another are negatively related and therefore complementary—gregarious-extraverted versus aloof-introverted, for example. A subsequent interpersonal circumplex essentially verified that of Wiggins (1979) with a slight change of the axes to dominant-submissive and friendly-hostile (Kiesler, 1983). And later, Wiggins and Broughton (1985) linked their interpersonal circumplex to Murray's (1938) well-known list of needs.

A circumplex offers two distinct advantages (Wiggins, 1979). First, it specifies in quantitative terms where particular traits should be located within the circle, which makes it possible to empirically test the assumption of two particular dimensions or axes. Second, gaps in the circle are revealed, places where there appear to be no traits, spurring researchers to find the missing traits or explain why they are not there.

The Interpersonal Circumplex and the Big 5

If the two axes of the interpersonal circumplex seem familiar, it is because they overlap two of the Big 5 factors. As Trapnell and Wiggins (1990) pointed out, "The interpersonal circumplex and the five-factor model of personality originated in different research traditions and were developed in relative isolation from each other. The recent recognition that the interpersonal dimensions of dominance and nurturance correspond closely to the Big Five factors of surgency/extraversion and agreeableness provides an occasion for close integration of the two traditions" (p. 788).

The circumplex axis of nurturance fits well with the Big 5 factor of agreeableness, which includes altruism, compliance, and tender-mindedness (see Table 13.2). But the circumplex axis of dominance is not quite the same as the Big 5 factor of extraversion. In the Wiggins and Trapnell (1990) circumplex, gregarious-extraverted is a blend of the dominance and nurturance axes (see their fig. 1 on p. 782).

To determine how an interpersonal circumplex fits in with the Big 5, McCrae and Costa (1989b) combined interpersonal adjectives with self-reports and spouse reports on their NEO-PI inventory of the Big 5 and factor analyzed the correlation matrix. These circumplex trait pairs loaded on either the extraversion or the agreeableness factor (see Table 13.4).

TABLE 13.4   Circumplex Traits Loading on the First Two Big 5 Factors

Extraversion	Agreeableness
Assured-dominant	Assured-dominant
Coldhearted-quarrelsome	Coldhearted-quarrelsome
Warm-agreeable	Warm-agreeable
Aloof-introverted	Arrogant-calculating
Unassured-submissive	Unassuming-ingenuous
Gregarious-extraverted	

McCrae and Costa (1989b) concluded that the axes of the interpersonal circumplex were defined by the extraversion and agreeableness factors of the Big 5. But notice that the first three pairs of interpersonal traits appear on *both* extraversion and agreeableness. Assured-dominant, coldhearted-quarrelsome, and warm-agreeable clearly are blends of the extraversion and agreeableness factors.

In discussing the issue of circumplex and factorial models, the latter of which McCrae and Costa (1989b) called dimensional models, they wrote, "Whether a circumplex or dimensional model should be applied to a particular area is not a matter of faithfully reproducing the ways in which traits occur in nature. Psychologists choose the traits they wish to study, and they measure traits with scales that are themselves developed often to fit one or another model. A proponent of simple structure may discard items that do not load clearly on a single factor; an advocate of circumplex structure may seek precisely such items" (p. 587).

The implications of this statement are important. The Big 5 factors represent a structure of personality that is partly determined by the scales or adjectives that researchers select. Similarly, the interpersonal circumplexes represent a structure of the interpersonal domain of personality that is partly determined by the scales or adjectives that researchers select. To the extent that adjectives or scales relevant to personality are discarded or omitted, these classifications cannot be complete representations of the structure of personality.

The McCrae and Costa (1989b) research also highlights the issue of blends. Saucier (1992), assuming that there are other blends within the Big 5, set out to find where they were. He discovered that most of the blends were located within a three-dimensional space defined by three of the Big 5 factors: extraversion, agreeableness, and emotional stability: "Evidence suggests that circular models for affective and interpersonal traits are not preferred by coincidence. Rather, these domains may have a latent continuous or circumplex character, yielding a comparatively poor fit to simple structure" (Saucier, 1992, p. 1032). He proceeded to demonstrate circumplexes by pairing the three factors with the blends. For example, when extraversion was paired with agreeableness to form the two axes of a circumplex, one of the blends was a combination of these adjectives: *humble, obliging,* and *unaggressive.* And when the axes were extraversion and neuroticism (opposite pole of emotional stability), one blend consisted of these adjectives: *dramatic, flir-tatious,* and *tempestuous.*

Using a different approach, Hofstee, de Raad, and Goldberg (1992) used each of the Big 5 factors as a dimension or axis and then constructed ten circumplexes of adjectives by using two axes at a time. Thus the horizontal axis of one circumplex was defined by flamboyant versus quiet (extraversion) and the vertical axis by kind versus unsympathetic (agreeableness). This method produced a number of blends. The following are some examples:

Extraversion plus agreeableness produced *friendly.*
Extraversion plus conscientiousness produced *ambitious.*
Agreeableness plus emotional stability produced *unselfish.*
Agreeableness plus intellect produced *tactful.*
Conscientiousness plus emotional stability produced *concise.*
Conscientiousness plus intellect produced *sophisticated.*

A follow-up study also reported many blends: "What are we to make of the fact that (with the exception of Extraversion) most of the scales used by FFM [five-factor model] researchers are defined by blends rather than factor-pure terms? We suggest that it may be due to what Hofstee et al. (1992) called the 'natural promiscuity' of factors, that certain factors cannot help but couple with each other, producing many hybrid offspring" (Johnson & Ostendorf, 1993, p. 573). Thus the overlap among Big 5 factors, mentioned earlier in the section Blends, appears to be an essential prop-erty of this classification. One unfortunate consequence is that there are bound to be several interpretations of the factors. Clearly, then, it is premature for anyone to declare that the Big 5 classification represents *the* structure of personality.

Three Axes
Recall that in a circumplex, closely related traits are placed next to each other, unre-lated traits are placed at a right angle to each other (dominance and love), and strongly negatively related traits are at the opposite poles of the circle (dominance and submission). Are two dimensions sufficient? Peabody and Goldberg (1989) analyzed seven different sets of personality data, and factor analyses yielded three large factors that held up across all seven data sets. They reported,

It is clear that the loadings on the three large factors come closer to a circular pattern. The highest loadings are surrounded in both directions by those that progressively decrease; moreover, such a progression applies to the same sequence of scales for each of the three factors. This suggests a circular type of relation among the scales associated with these factors. . . . Is there any way to represent the circular relations for all three factors at the same time? (p. 556)

Their solution was to rotate the factors to three dimensions: general evaluation (desirable versus undesirable traits), loose-tight, and assertive-unassertive. This procedure led to two circumplexes, each defined by two axes: loose-tight and assertive-unassertive. One circumplex contained only adjectives denoting desirable personality traits. Thus an opposite pair on the assertiveness-nonassertiveness axis is bold versus modest, and an opposite pair on the loose versus tight axis is cheerful versus serious. The second circumplex contained only adjectives denoting undesirable personality traits. Thus an opposite pair on the assertiveness-unassertiveness axis is conceited-unassured, and an opposite pair on the loose-tight axis is frivolous-grim.

These two circumplexes then were linked by the third dimension: evaluation. Examples of adjectives that are polar opposites when the evaluation (desirable-undesirable) and loose-tight dimensions were the axes are spontaneous-inhibited and flexible-inflexible. Examples of polar opposites when the evaluation and assertiveness-unassertiveness dimensions are the axes are bold-timid and peaceful-quarrelsome.

Bipolar and Unipolar Dimensions

Let us return to two-dimensional circumplexes and focus on the dominance-submission axis, which is not only an axis but a trait dimension (see Chapter 7). Dominance-submission is an example of a *bipolar dimension*. It may be split into halves with the following adjectives, which were scaled for intensity by clinical psychologists (Buss & Gerjuoy, 1957):

dominance	*submissiveness*
dictatorial	assenting
high-handed	compliant
forceful	deferent
assertive	servile

At the top of the dimension is *dictatorial*, and each successive adjective in the left-hand column represents less intense dominance. Just below the adjective *assertive* would be the midpoint of the bipolar dimension, but there is no available adjective for zero dominance without connoting submissiveness. The lower half of the dimension contains adjectives of increasing submissiveness in the right-hand column, the endpoint being *servile*.

The trait of activity is an example of a *unipolar dimension*: a great deal of energy at the top of the dimension, dropping off to moderate energy in the middle, and decreasing to an extremely low amount of energy at the bottom of the dimension. Another example is aggression, which ranges from extremely intense or frequent attacking behavior to no aggressive behavior at all. The trait of aggression is unusual in that the bottom of the dimension is represented by a zero point: no aggression at all. The bottom end of most unipolar traits—activity, sociability, and self-esteem, for example—involve at least some behavior.

These examples illustrate the relationship between unipolar and bipolar dimensions. A unipolar dimension, by definition, has only one pole: the upper end, which represents the peak of the trait. The bottom of the dimension consists of either very little or no behavior (aggression) or just a little behavior (sociability).

The bottom of a bipolar dimension involves just as much behavior as the top. To take a geographic example, picture the earth's sphere, with the frigid Arctic at the North Pole and the cold diminishing steadily until the equator is reached. Continuing south, the cold increases in intensity until the frigid Antarctic is reached at the South Pole.

Similarly, a bipolar trait dimension, by definition, has two opposite poles, each representing the extreme of the trait (dominance-submission). The low point of behavior is in the middle of the dimension. Thus a bipolar dimension may be regarded as a combination of two unipolar dimensions that are connected back-to-back so that their lowest ends touch each other.

The Bases of Bipolarity

One extreme of a bipolar trait dimension is expected to be strongly negatively correlated to the opposite extreme, for any other relationship would make no sense. Thus extreme dominance is expected to have a high negative correlation with extreme submissiveness, and of course it does. Does it follow that a high negative correlation necessarily signifies the presence of a bipolar dimension? No, because the top and bottom of a unipolar dimension are negatively correlated: high and low activity, for example. So there must be conceptual bases for bipolarity that involve dichotomous behavioral tendencies.

The most important conceptual basis may be *bidirectional behavior*. Thus behavior may be directed toward the self (selfishness) or toward others (altruism). In the selfishness-altruism dimension, as behavior becomes less selfish, a midpoint in the dimension is reached, where behavior is neither selfish nor prosocial. Then at the other half of the dimension, behavior becomes increasingly prosocial, reaching a peak of altruism at the opposite pole. Another example of self-directed versus other-directed behavior is the masochism-aggression dichotomy.

Behavior may involve a tendency to move toward others (friendly) or away from others (aloof). Behavior may involve positive feelings toward others (friendly or trusting) or negative feelings toward others (hostile or suspicious). Instrumental social behavior may be directed toward others (friendly) or against them (competitive). There may be empathic feelings toward others and going easy on them (tender-mindedness) or having no empathic feelings toward others and being hard on them (tough-mindedness).

Another basis of bipolarity is whether behavior is expressed or inhibited. Examples are impulsive-overcontrolled and exhibitionistic-shy. Finally, behavior may be represented metaphorically by the up-down dichotomy: joyous versus depressed.

Thus conceptually there are three major bases of bipolarity: the direction of behavior (self versus other), inhibited versus expressive, and up versus down. These dichotomies and examples of them are summarized in Table 13.5.

TABLE 13.5   Conceptual Bases of Bipolarity

Self versus other

> Self-directed versus other-directed
> > Selfish-altruistic
> > Masochistic-aggressive
> Toward versus away from others
> > Friendly-aloof
> For versus against others
> > Friendly-hostile
> > Cooperative-competitive
> > Trusting-suspicious
> > Tender-minded–tough-minded

Inhibited versus expressive

> > Overcontrolled-impulsive
> > Shy-exhibitionistic

Up versus down

> Status: dominant-submissive
> Affect: joyous-depressed

Bipolarity and the Big 5

Three of the Big 5 factors appear to be bipolar, though not all the traits that make them up (facets) are bipolar (see Table 13.2). Bidirectionality appears in two of the facets of extraversion. Both warm-cold and friendly-gregarious involve moving toward people or away from them. The factor of agreeableness has three bipolar facets. Trust-distrust is an example of being for or against others; altruistic-selfish is an example of behavior directed toward others or toward the self; and tender-minded-tough-minded illustrates a cognitive basis of bipolarity not previously mentioned (and difficult to characterize). The factor of conscientiousness has two facets, impulsive-deliberate and disciplined-undisciplined, which are bipolar on the basis of the expressive-inhibited dichotomy.

Classes and Dimensions

In Chapter 5, Attachment, a classification of children had three categories or classes: secure, ambivalent, and avoidant. But two dimensions were seen to underly these classes of attachment: seeking proximity and anxiety. Similarly, in this chapter, the major classification of personality traits has five classes or superfactors. But interpersonal behavior has been ordered into a circumplex consisting of two axes or dimensions, and even the Big 5 traits are susceptible to dimensionalizing. Thus the alternative means of classification are by classes and by dimensions.

The assignment of personality dispositions to a class rests on two assumptions: that the traits cohere and that their class is qualitatively different from other classes of traits. Another way of stating the second assumption is to say that there is a discontinuity between each class of traits and every other one. Problems arise when there is evidence of continuity. For the Big 5, continuity may be seen in the correlations among some of the superfactors and in the blends: traits that fall into more than one class or superfactor.

How serious are these problems? After all, the Big 5 empirically imposes order on diverse personality tendencies, and this classification has been linked with diverse phenomena in personality. So we can focus on its obvious advantages or on its problems. Evaluating it then becomes a matter of deciding whether the glass is half full or half empty.

When traits are ordered empirically into a circumplex, they are aligned simultaneously along two dimensions, differing quantitatively along these dimensions. The underlying assumption is one of continuity. There is an additional assumption in circumplexes: bipolarity of the two crucial dimensions and of the traits and their opposites around the circumplex. However, some interpersonal traits are not bipolar. Sociability, for example, refers to a stronger or weaker need to be with others; there is no opposite pole. And beyond interpersonal traits, dispositions such as activity and anxiety are unipolar.

In addition, two dimensions may not be sufficient for interpersonal behavior and certainly not for the broader domain of personality. Do these problems negate the advantages of the interpersonal circumplex? Probably not, but they do tell us about its limitations.

As these comments suggest, both classes and dimensions have much to offer in the classification of personality, but each has its problems. Instead of deciding which one to use, we should us both, for they complement one another. When we examine their assumptions, we are left to contemplate which aspects of personality are best regarded as continuous and which are best regarded as discontinuous. As we shall see in the next chapter, a similar issue arises: Which abnormal disorders appear to be continuous with personality dispositions, and which are not?

Chapter **14**

Personality and Abnormality

This chapter extrapolates what we know about personality into the realm of abnormal behavior. An immediate issue is continuity over time. Abnormality tends to develop over years or even decades, and in this time sequence personality may play one of two roles. Personality may be *prodromal* to abnormal behavior, meaning that the abnormal behavior is so slight as to be undetected as such and therefore regarded as nothing more than a personality tendency. However, over time it becomes worse in a manner analogous to mildly elevated blood pressure eventually leading to serious cardiovascular problems.

Alternatively, personality may establish the conditions for abnormal behavior to develop gradually, the personality tendencies being maladaptive and therefore gradually leading to abnormal behavior. The personality dispositions may make the person especially generally vulnerable to succumbing to the difficulties that often attend everyday living, or they may render the person susceptible to a specific disorder. Particular personality traits may themselves be maladaptive, leading to specific psychological symptoms.

These two roles assume a causal continuity between personality and abnormality. However, the other possibility is discontinuity: the personality dispositions merely accompany the abnormal behavior. Everyone has personality dispositions, but they are not necessarily a cause of abnormal behavior. The focus here is narrow: not on all abnormality but only that for which personality is relevant.

Hardiness and Vulnerability

Consider the calamities that might visit any of us during the course of life: physical abuse, death of a loved one, divorce, wasting disease, disability, or even the loss of a job followed by chronic unemployment. Any of these stresses might cause a variety of psychological abnormalities. Yet, some people survive disasters without being bowled over by them. During the Battle of Britain, when bombs rained on the country every night, the population feared for their lives and spent sleepless nights in bomb shelters. Many people became chronically anxious or suffered debilitating depression, but others came through with no lasting psychological scars.

In brief, some people are *vulnerable*, succumbing to the impact of stress and developing acute or chronic psychological disorders. Others are *hardy*, resisting the impact of negative events and remaining well adjusted. The term *hardiness* was coined by Kobasa (1979), who studied stress in relation to general health and disease. Hardiness involves two ways of dealing with stress. First, it may serve as a buffer against stress, minimizing its impact. For example, a heavily muscled man can better withstand blows to the body (buffering). Second, it may lead to better means of coping with the problems brought on by stress. Thus a woman who has exercised regularly may recover from a heart attack because she has alternative coronary arteries to compensate for those that are blocked (coping).

These examples and most research on hardiness deal with physical health; for reviews and critiques on hardiness and physical health, see Funk and Houston (1987) and Hull, Van Treuren, and Virnelli (1987). Our concern here is with psychological abnormality, and the focus is even narrower: on personality dispositions leading to hardiness or vulnerability. Vulnerability, of course, is the mirror image of hardiness. Vulnerable people are more susceptible to the impact of stress and have difficulty dealing with the problems caused by stress.

What follows is a discussion of the contribution of each of the personality dispositions discussed in Chapters 3–11, with an exception. Prosocial behavior and asocial or antisocial behavior appear to be unrelated to hardiness and vulnerability. Also, shyness appears to bear the same relationship to hardiness and vulnerability as fear (anxiety) regardless of whether the shyness is anxious or self-conscious. Therefore, what is written about the temperament of emotionality applies equally to shyness.

Temperaments

Emotionality

The temperament of emotionality, as will be seen later, considerably overlaps a factor called *negative emotionality*, which correlates with a variety of psychological disorders (Watson, Clark, & Carey, 1988). These correlations suggest that emotionality tends to make people vulnerable to abnormality.

Recall that emotionality differentiates into fear and anger. Anger will be discussed shortly under the heading of aggression. Here, we deal with fear (anxiety).

Anxious people high in fear, by definition, react more intensely to threats, disappointments, and other negative events. Not only are they unable to resist such stressors (no buffering), but they are especially vulnerable to them. Anxious people are sensitive to threatening stimuli and condition quickly, generalizing their fears to an ever-widening spectrum of environmental conditions.

The various components of the anxiety reaction make it difficult to cope with stress. In the affective realm, the terror that many people experience denies them the opportunity to use realistic means of dealing with the situation. The instrumental component of avoidance shields the person from the threat at the expense of developing coping responses. And the cognitive component of worry and imagining worst-case scenarios only further incubates anxiety.

Those low in anxiety are buffered from threat because their reaction to it is milder and less frequent (by definition). When on a ship, for example, if the vessel seems to be in trouble, they are unlikely to panic and instead trust the captain and crew to handle the situation. Any fear that does ensue is mild enough to allow them to cope. They tend to remain sufficiently calm to put on a life jacket and to remember where to assemble if the ship must be evacuated. They may try to help other passengers, this instrumental activity being useful in keeping them occupied and not reflecting about dire consequences. As a result of the buffering and coping, the stressful experience is likely to leave behind no residual maladjustment.

Activity

Activity is neither a sensitizer to stress nor a buffer except when there is a mismatch. Thus if a person low in activity is stuck in a job that requires a frantic pace, say, working on a newspaper or television show with daily deadlines, the excessively fast tempo is likely to be stressful. Or if a person high in activity is stuck in a restrictive environment that allows little movement, say, at a computer all day long or in a crowded jail cell, the confinement would surely be stressful.

In the case of most stressors, low activity makes it hard to cope, for there may not be enough energy to struggle with the problem. Other things being equal, people low in activity tend to let events take their course, depressively accepting their fate or passively allowing others to solve the problem.

Those high in activity cannot just sit there and bemoan their fate. They are likely to try something, anything to deal with the negative events that befall them. These are the people who, confined to a wheelchair, insist on continuing their jobs, fight for better access for people who are disabled, and enter wheelchair marathon races. They are less likely to develop psychological problems.

Sociability

Again, sociability is neither a sensitizer nor a buffer against stress unless there is a mismatch, and then only for highly sociable persons. If they are isolated from others, as in some rural or forest settings or in wintry northern climates, they may suffer from great loneliness. If they cannot communicate with others by radio or telephone, their insular existence may well lead to depression.

When others are available, though, sociability enhances coping. Those who prefer to be with others are likely to turn to them in time of need. Knowing that you can depend on others induces calm and an optimism that problems might be solved. And sociable people, because they chronically seek out others, tend to have support groups—church, a vocational group, or a club—which can sustain them. There may be a sex difference also. Even sociable men, if they have been socialized to be independent and self-sufficient, may be reluctant to ask others for help. Women are more likely to seek help and possess the close friends who might deliver it. This sex difference may explain why divorce or widowhood has more devastating long-term effects on men than on women.

Impulsivity

The high end of the impulsivity dimension is neither a sensitizer nor a buffer against stress. The low end, represented by obsessiveness, makes people vulnerable to stress, for they may dwell excessively on their problem. They may extrapolate too much from any present bad situation and assume that everything is going downhill. Or, like those high in anxiety, they may focus so intensely on problems that the problems seem worse than they really are.

The low end of the impulsivity dimension also poses problems for coping with stress. Those who are too deliberate tend to spend so much time planning or thinking about obstacles that they never get around to acting. Chronically hesitant to act, they may be even more inhibited when confronted with a negative life event.

Those at the high end of the dimension at least try to do something about their problems, but their reactions may turn out to be foolhardy. Such people tend to act without sufficient prior thought, without weighing alternatives or risks. Though they do try to cope, their responses to stress may be so rash as to worsen the problem rather than solve it. Clearly, the optimal place to be is in the middle of the impulsivity dimension: enough motivation to take action but enough anticipatory thought to make the action a good way to cope with stress.

Social Dispositions

Attachment

Secure attachment is a buffer against stress, for secure people tend to be stable and not easily thrown off by the inevitable negative events of everyday living. Insecurely attached people expect to be let down by others and are especially affected by rejection or divorce. They are likely to misinterpret the death of a loved one as abandonment.

With respect to coping, it is necessary to divide insecure individuals into the types outlined by Bartholomew (1990). Ambivalent people tend to be low in self-esteem, which means that they are pessimistic about any attempts to deal with stress. Unsure of others' affection, they may resist being helped and therefore may have to cope with stress alone. Fearful people are also low in self-esteem and expect little or no help from others. They tend to feel sorry for themselves and, being afraid, tend to avoid dealing with the problems that confront them. Detached people, who have "solved" the problem of intimacy by not getting close to anyone, depend solely on themselves. They may deal adequately with nonsocial stress, for their self-esteem is all right. But they have difficulty coping with interpersonal stress—for example, difficulties with a spouse or children. And secure people, other things being equal, are expected to cope well with stress, for they are not easily thrown off balance and know that they can rely on others for help.

Aggression

The key component in vulnerability to stress is hostility, for minor disagreements are amplified and given a life of their own. Hostile people, being resentful and suspicious, tend to magnify any of the interpersonal negatives that occur in everyday living. They are sure that they are not getting their fair share, believe that others have it in for them, or assume that others are shunning them when there is no such intent. In brief, even neutral situations tend to be interpreted as negative, such that hostile people see the world as a hostile place. Living in such a world is bound to be stressful.

With respect to coping, all three components come into play. Hostile people are so nasty toward others that they cannot compromise when it is necessary, and interpersonal difficulties remain unsolved. Angry people tend to lose control quickly and say or do things in the heat of rage that worsen any interpersonal problems. Or they may become so furious because of their own blunders that they cannot engage in the calmer behavior that would rectify the mistakes. Aggressive people are so ready to abuse others verbally or physically that they intensify any stress that already exists. And aggression rarely copes with the problems of everyday living.

Dominance

Dominant people are confident that they will come out on top of most interpersonal conflicts and therefore are not threatened by them. By the same token, submissive people know they will wind up losing interpersonal conflicts, so they are more strongly affected by them. Thus dominance buffers against stress, and submissiveness sensitizes.

With respect to coping, dominant people are expected to struggle with their problems. If competition is at issue, they persist in competing. If leadership is at issue, they tend to assert it. And they are willing to boss others around to solve their own problems. There may be a social cost of the actions of dominant people, for their behavior is stressful to those being dominated.

Submissive people have trouble coping with problems because, by definition, they cannot assert themselves with others. They back off from competition and settle for being followers. Thus they are likely to be passive and perhaps dependent in the face of the everyday stresses of life.

Self

Self-Esteem

Recall from Chapter 8 that people low in self-esteem are devastated by failure or rejection. Lacking self-worth, they are easily threatened and tend to blame themselves for misfortunes. Of all the personality dispositions, low self-esteem renders people most vulnerable to stress.

If people low in self-esteem unrealistically depreciate themselves, the opposite bias appears to hold for those high in self-esteem. Taylor and Brown (1988) listed three illusions that foster mental health: an unrealistically positive view of the self, exaggerated perception of personal control over events, and excessive optimism about the future. These illusions characterize people high in self-esteem, who are thereby buffered against stress.

With respect to coping, those high in self-esteem try harder after failure, continue to set high goals or at least reasonable goals, and are optimistic about succeeding. These tendencies are precisely what are needed to cope with stress.

Those low in self-esteem are self-protective, setting low goals and doing poorly after failure, and generally avoiding challenges. So when a negative event requires rising to the occasion, they lack the needed psychological resources and consequently cope poorly with stress.

Identity

Recall the two major kinds of identity: social and personal. When social identity is lacking, there is a feeling of not belonging or of lacking a place in the larger scheme of things. Such rootlessness is often accompanied by existential anxiety. When personal identity is lacking, there is a lack of individuality, that feeling of being a special, unique person. The result is often a feeling of being a pawn of fate, tossed by the winds of misfortune. Thus when either kind of identity is weak and especially when both kinds are lacking, there is likely to be vulnerability to stress and a related inability to cope.

The opposite also holds: Those with a strong identity are likely to be hardy. Having a social identity means that you have roots in a heritage and a place in the universe. Having a personal identity means that you feel special, a master of your fate. These sources of identity offer a stability that is not easily shaken by the occasional catastrophes of everyday living and a better chance of coping with them.

Self-Consciousness

Only private self-consciousness is relevant to reactions to stress, specifically, only the high end of the dimension. Those high in this trait, as we saw in Chapter 10, react more intensely to all affects. Of special relevance here, they become especially distressed by the negative events of daily life: Recall that of recovered alcoholics who had bad experiences, only those high in private self-consciousness tended to go back to drinking. After reviewing evidence of the role of private self-consciousness in clinical disorders, Ingram (1990) concluded, "Chronically high levels of self-focused attention may serve as a vulnerability factor by placing individuals at risk for the onset or prolonged maintenance of dysfunction" (p. 162).

However, the low end of the dimension, low private self-consciousness, does not provide a buffer against stress, nor does it affect coping with stress. And beyond the impact of high private self-consciousness on vulnerability, it appears to have no further impact on the ability to cope with stress.

The contributions of personality dispositions to vulnerability or hardiness are summarized in Table 14.1.

TABLE 14.1   Contributions of Personality Dispositions to Vulnerability and Hardiness

Personality dispositions	Vulnerability	Hardiness
Temperaments		
Emotionality and fear	High	Low
Activity	Mismatch	—
Sociability	Low	High
Impulsivity	High or low	Average
Social dispositions		
Attachment	Insecure	Secure
Aggression	High	—
Dominance	Submissive	Dominant
Self		
Self-esteem	Low	High
Identity	Weak	Strong
Private self-consciousness	High	—
Shyness	High	Low

Personality Traits and Specific Disorders

Personality Disorders

"Personality traits are enduring patterns of perceiving, relating to, and thinking about the environment and oneself, and are exhibited over a wide range of important social and personal contexts. It is only when *personality traits* are inflexible and maladaptive and cause either significant functional impairment or subjective distress that they constitute *Personality Disorders*" (American Psychiatric Association, 1987, p. 335). This quotation raises two questions.

First, which of the personality dispositions covered in this book are linked to personality disorders? This question will be answered shortly. Second, what is it about a personality trait that might render it inflexible and maladaptive? The answer may lie in personality dimensions. Other things being equal, the extremes of a personality dimension tend to involve inflexible behavior, virtually by definition. Thus a highly sociable person has a strong need to be with others, and an unsociable person has a strong need to be alone. But, as we saw above, extreme unsociability may be maladaptive, while extreme sociability appears to be adaptive. Thus in linking personality traits with personality disorders, we need to examine the extremes of any given personality dimension and determine whether they are maladaptive.

The personality disorders have been grouped into three clusters. Cluster A includes oddness and eccentricity (one member of this group, schizotypal personality disorder, is defined solely by mental peculiarities and has no linkage to personality traits; therefore it will not be discussed). Cluster B includes emotional or erratic behavior. Cluster C includes anxiety or maladaptive attempts to cope with anxiety.

Cluster A

Paranoid.   The symptoms of this disorder are jealousy, expecting to be harmed physically or psychologically, and being sensitive to slights. If these symptoms seem familiar it is because they overlap the behaviors that define hostility. Recall that the hostility factor of the aggression questionnaire (Buss & Perry, 1992) includes resentment and suspicion. This factor includes these items: "I am sometimes eaten up with jealousy" and "I am suspicious of overly friendly strangers."

There is a questionnaire that should be used to diagnose paranoid personality disorder, the paranoid scale of Fenigstein and Vanable (1992). This scale correlated in the high thirties with public self-consciousness. Evidently, people at the high end of public self-consciousness dimension are so preoccupied with themselves as social objects that they can drift into paranoid fears.

Schizoid.   People so diagnosed are called loners. They have no real friends and no motivation to develop friendships. They are entirely unresponsive to social rewards and punishments, and in their dealings with others they seem cold and aloof. This is a description of those at the extreme low end of the sociability dimension. Recall that unsociable people are only weakly motivated to be with others, would just as soon be off by themselves, are generally not susceptible to social rewards, and, being unresponsive to others, are seen to lack warmth.

It might be thought that schizoids are shy, but that is not true. They are neither fearful nor self-conscious when with others, instead being indifferent to others' behavior.

Cluster B

Antisocial.   The antisocial category, as its name suggests, includes behavior directed against others: lying, stealing, vandalism, and acts of cruelty, all these without remorse. Additional symptoms are an erratic work history, inconsistency of behavior, irresponsibility, and a lack of planning. Antisocial people are also irritable and aggressive, sometimes to the point of abusing spouses or children. This is a picture of people who were once called psychopaths, a term that is too descriptive to give up.

Psychopathic behavior appears to derive from the extremes of three personality dimensions. One is the bottom end of the prosocial dimension, which is marked by selfishness, self-centeredness, and an absence of empathy. Lacking any prosocial tendencies, psychopaths behave toward others as if people were objects that can be abused and discarded.

The second relevant personality trait is impulsivity. Recall the three components of this trait: lack of control over emotions and motives, lack of discipline (impatient and inconsistent), and lack of reflection (acting rashly and without forethought). Being impulsive, psychopaths indulge in their selfish whims without stopping to reflect on the consequences to others or even to themselves.

The third relevant personality trait is aggression. Psychopaths tend to assault others, belabor them with curses and threats, become enraged easily, and dislike others. These three components of aggression, when combined with impulsivity and the absence of prosocial behavior, produce behavior that society inevitably must punish.

Borderline.   This category is a mixture of symptoms, perhaps reflecting the fact that the diagnostic classification emerged from committees of clinicians ("A camel is a horse designed by a committee"). There is a disturbance of identity, examples of which are unstable gender identity and a feeling of emptiness. There are unstable relationships, these people desperately seeking others but fearing abandonment. And there is marked self-harming impulsiveness, for example, binge eating, shopping sprees, and gambling.

The personality trait of impulsivity is obviously an issue here. So is insecure attachment, especially the fearful and ambivalent varieties. Recall that such people are either intensely anxious about being rejected (fearful) or continually preoccupied with problems in relationships (ambivalent). The third relevant area of personality is identity. This includes not only a problem with gender identity but also feelings of rootlessness and lack of individuality. Not knowing who they are or being able to establish meaning in their lives, borderlines are bound to feel empty.

Histrionic.   People so labeled are flashy, stagy, and excessively demonstrative in speech and exaggerated emotions. They must be the center of attention or they pout. Self-centered, they continually seek praise, reassurance, or at least approval from others.

They combine the immature end of three personality dimensions. They are impulsive in being unable to control their emotions, shallow though they be. They represent the extreme, opposite end of the shyness dimension, that is, exhibitionism. And they are located at the egocentric, selfish end of the prosocial dimension. In these respects they are so childlike as to be described, metaphorically, as fixated at the show-and-tell stage of childhood.

Narcissistic.   This adjective derives from the legend of Narcissus, who fell in love with his image as reflected in a pool of water. Like the legendary man, such people have an exalted sense of their self-worth and grandiose ideas about their place in the larger scheme of things. Their focus is entirely on themselves, and they use others as "mirrors" of their own beauty or ability. Seeing themselves as special, they are envious of others' success or renown.

Their egocentricity places them at the extreme opposite end of the prosocial dimension. And their conceit places them at the extreme of self-esteem. If we ask how such a pattern might have developed, the answer may lie in the core-periphery theory of self-esteem (see Chapter 8). Presumably, parents' unconditional love continued well past infancy, and as children, narcissists were treated as especially talented and lovable. Simply by imitating how parents and others treated them, such children might easily become entirely self-centered and believe that they are entitled to special treatment. Once this set of attitudes was in place, it would be difficult to dislodge. Thereafter, any criticism would be met with hostility and dismissed as the product of envy.

Clinicians report that some of their clients with narcissistic personality disorder are superficially conceited, but this apparently excessive self-esteem is a defensive maneuver. It conceals a truly low level of self-esteem. However, these people are the ones who seek help, surely a minority of narcissists. The majority, to whom the above explanation is directed, believe that they are better adjusted than most people and would never seek help.

Avoidant. The reference here is specifically to social avoidance. This disorder is marked by social distress, fear of being evaluated by others, and inability to withstand criticism. Avoidants tend to refrain from social contacts and jobs that involve interaction with others. They are especially susceptible to embarrassment and are concerned that they will show it by blushing. If the pattern seems familiar, it is a telling description of both anxious and self-conscious shyness. In addition, avoidants tend to be low in self-esteem, which is hardly surprising, given its strong correlation with shyness.

Dependent. People with this disorder seem helpless in the face of life's difficulties and require others to offer aid and tell them what to do. If help and direction are not forthcoming, they ask for it. Lacking confidence, they need a strong leader, either in a group or in a family, to guide them. They tend to cling to others and fear being abandoned and left to their own devices, for, like young children, they seem unable to fend for themselves.

The most salient trait is the submissiveness end of the dominance dimension. Low self-esteem is also relevant. The pattern is completed by insecure attachment, particularly the ambivalent type.

Obsessive-Compulsive. People with this disorder are fussy and overcontrolled. They have trouble expressing emotions, are preoccupied with rules and trivial matters, and cautious in their everyday behavior. They are excessively concerned about making mistakes and therefore make such elaborate plans that they sometimes do not get around to acting on them.

This description locates such people precisely at the opposite end of the impulsivity dimension, for they display all three components of this trait. They excessively inhibit their motives and emotions, remain stuck in one activity when they should move on to another, and deliberate at such length as to remind one of Hamlet.

Passive-Aggressive.   When confronted with dominant others, one may welcome the direction and leadership, as do those with dependent personality disorder. Or one may rebel covertly and spitefully, as do those who are passive-aggressive. They do not openly flout authority but undermine it by delay, subtle resistance, and deliberate forgetfulness. When asked or ordered to do something, they sulk like a disobedient child.

As the name implies, a relevant trait is aggression, specifically, the indirect aggression that is difficult to punish. Gossiping, backbiting, and sabotaging are the preferred behaviors. The affective and cognitive components of aggression are also present. Such people are easily irritated, and they bear grudges against what they see as ill-treatment by superiors. But even more important is the negativism that is one reaction to dominance. Passive-aggressives will not openly oppose others but indirectly display their resistance by roundabout means, saying, in effect, "I won't."

Other Disorders

Anxiety disorders of various kinds require no particular comment, for they obviously involve the high end of the fear dimension, a component of emotionality. Social phobia is a more specific anxiety, one that is limited to social contexts "in which the person is exposed to possible scrutiny by others and fears that he or she may do something or act in a way that will be humiliating or embarrassing" (APA, 1987, p. 241). This description may be familiar, for it echoes that of extreme shyness (see Chapter 11). Social phobia includes both self-conscious shyness (embarrassment) and anxious shyness (fear and avoidance).

One of the more intriguing abnormalities is multiple personality disorder, which is characterized by the presence of at least two different behavioral patterns, social relationships, and names. Some people are aware of more than one "self"; others are unaware.

The personality aspects of this disorder involve identity. In Chapter 9 we saw that most of us have a strong feeling of continuity: being the same person as ten years ago and being the same person who behaves differently in different situations. Consider a recently graduated woman teacher with no prior experience in teaching. On the first day of a large class she may feel as though she is acting a part in a play, for the teacher role is not yet part of her. Imagine also that she is introverted but is called on to be extraverted in front of an auditorium full of students. Though she behaves differently in class (extraverted) than outside of class (introverted), she knows that she is the same person. Gradually she becomes more familiar with the teacher role and integrates her classroom behavior into the rest of her sense of self. But what if she could not integrate these two different patterns of behavior? Then she would have two personalities, that is, a discontinuity in identity. No one knows why a small percentage of people develop multiple personalities. However, most such clients report having been abused as children. Child abuse may play a role, though we must bear in mind that many people who have been abused as children never develop multiple personalities. Whatever its origin, this disorder represents a fractured identity.

Problems of identity are also involved in transsexual disorder. This disorder is exhibited by biological men who are uncomfortable with the masculine role and feel more like women. Their counterparts are women who psychologically are male. Recall the gender identity questionnaire (Finn, 1988), which assesses precisely this kind of maladaptation (see Table 9.2 in Chapter 9).

An abnormality observed mainly in children is attention-deficit hyperactivity disorder (ADHD). It is marked by fidgetiness, restlessness, impatience, lack of attention, inability to concentrate, and accident-proneness. These tendencies sound suspiciously like two of the temperaments. One is impulsivity, and all three components are involved: failing to inhibit action or resist temptation (control), easily distracted and impatient (discipline), and acting rashly (reflection). The other temperament is activity; recall that those extremely high in this trait are always on the go. Metaphorically, those with ADHD have a powerful engine (activity) but weak brakes (impulsivity).

Continuity

Continuity between a personality disposition and abnormal behavior is present when the disorder represents the extreme, maladjusted end of the personality dimension. The disorders that are continuous with personality dispositions are shown in Table 14.2.

Appearing first is paranoid personality disorder, which is regarded as continuous with two personality dimensions. The first is the hostility dimension, the low or average segments of which involve no maladjustment. But as hostility intensifies toward the high end of the dimension, it shades into paranoid behavior. Similarly, the high end of the public self-consciousness dimension shades into suspiciousness so extreme as to be abnormal. Thus paranoid personality disorder is continu-

TABLE 14.2   Continuity of Disorders and Dispositions

Disorder	Disposition
Personality disorders	
Paranoid	Hostile, high in public self-consciousness
Antisocial	Aggressive, egocentric, impulsive
Borderline	Insecurely attached, impulsive
Histrionic	Exhibitionistic, impulsive, egocentric
Narcissistic	Egocentric, extremely high in self-esteem
Avoidant	Shy, low in self-esteem
Dependent	Submissive, low in self-esteem, insecurely attached
Passive-aggressive	Negativistic, hostile
Other disorders	
Anxiety	Emotional (fearful)
Social phobia	Shy

ous with these two personality dimensions. Simply said, paranoid personality disorder *is* the combined extremes of hostility and public self-consciousness.

The rest of the personality disorders and their associated personality dispositions listed in the table have already been discussed. In each instance the disorder presumably represents the endpoint of two or three personality dimensions. Some personality dimensions are listed with more than one personality disorder, notably, impulsivity, egocentricity, and self-esteem. Thus these personality dispositions are not specific to any single personality disorder. Rather, they are regarded as continuous with any particular disorder when in combination with at least one other personality disposition. Thus avoidants are low in self-esteem, but the more crucial dimension here is shyness. Dependents are low in self-esteem, but the more crucial dimensions are submissiveness and insecurity of attachment.

At the bottom of Table 14.2 are the two abnormal conditions and their associated personality dispositions. Anxiety disorders represent the extreme endpoint of the dimension of the fear component of the temperament of emotionality. And social phobia is clearly an instance of extreme shyness. Notice that shyness is crucial in both avoidant personality disorder and social phobia. This dual role of shyness suggests that the two abnormal conditions overlap, with social phobia perhaps being merely the more intense form of avoidant personality disorder.

Partial Continuity

The four disorders listed in Table 14.3 are examples of partial continuity, a concept that will become clear as these disorders are discussed. Schizoid personality disorder may be regarded, in part, as the extreme low end of the dimension of sociability. However, this disorder also includes flattening of affect, such persons rarely being elated, depressed, or angry. This absence of affect is an important feature in the diagnosis of this abnormality; thus schizoid personality disorder is not solely the extreme low end of sociability. It falls under the heading of disorders that are partially continuous with personality dispositions.

Similarly, obsessive-compulsives are located at the bottom end of the impulsivity dimension (deliberateness). But they are also excessively moralistic, judg-

TABLE 14.3   Partial Continuity of Dispositions and Disorders

Disorder	Disposition
Personality disorders	
Schizoid	Unsociable
Obsessive-compulsive	Low impulsive (deliberate)
Other disorders	
Multiple personality	Fractured identity
Attention-deficit hyperactivity	Extremely impulsive, active

mental, inflexible, and stubborn. Thus (low) impulsivity does not entirely capture the disorder, which means that this personality disposition is only partially continuous with the disorder.

Multiple personality disorder is obviously an example of fractured identity, but the dissociation typically extends beyond identity. In most cases there is at least some amnesia, and at least one of the personalities tends to be maladjusted. Thus saying that this disorder represents an extreme discontinuity of identity is only part of the story.

Attention-deficit hyperactivity disorder (ADHD) is clearly a combination of extreme impulsivity and activity. But some of the children so diagnosed have symptoms of minimal brain dysfunction. Recently a gene has been discovered the malfunction of which appears to account for some of the cases of ADHD.

This situation may be analogous to that seen when the distribution of intelligence is examined. There is a bump on the curve at the bottom end of the otherwise normally distributed scores. The excess of low IQs is due to individuals with brain damage. Thus the group of people with low intelligence consists of two kinds: those with brain damage and those with normal brains who merely occupy the bottom of the IQ distribution.

Perhaps a similar situation exists for ADHD. Some of the children with this disorder might have slightly dysfunctional brains, perhaps caused by an inherited enzyme problem. Others with normal brains might be inordinately impulsive and active. This distinction raises an intriguing issue about the drugs that help only some of those with ADHD. The drugs might not work at all with those at the high end of the impulsivity and activity dimensions but work well for those with the brain dysfunction.

Mood Disorders

Mood disorders constitute a special case in their relation to personality traits: The traits accompany the disorders and worsen them. Personality traits are included when these disorders are diagnosed, but the traits are secondary, and abnormality of mood is primary. Only the extremes of (unipolar) depression and mania are discussed here, and the focus is on diagnosis, with causality ignored.

Depression

As its name suggests, this disorder involves recurrent, enduring episodes of a complete loss of pleasure, in which the world looks dim and uninteresting. Suicidal thoughts are prevalent, and suicidal attempts pose a danger. People with this disorder typically have little energy and move slowly and not often. Their feelings of worthlessness are profound, and they cannot escape obsessively mulling over their predicament, their dark mood casting a pall over all thought.

This description includes or suggests several personality traits, the first two of which are obvious. Depressives clearly are extremely low in self-esteem and activity. They are high in private self-consciousness, continually turning the focus of attention inward toward their psychological insides (see Ingram, 1990). In analogue research with college students, a popular depression questionnaire correlated in the twenties and thirties with the private self-consciousness scale (Ingram & Smith, 1984; Smith & Greenberg, 1981). Samples of clinically depressed patients would probably yield higher correlations.

Depression is also marked by an absence of *positive affect*. This term has been defined by a set of adjectives that has emerged from factor analyses of affectively toned terms (Watson, Clark, & Tellegen, 1988): *active, alert, attentive, determined, enthusiastic, excited, inspired, interested, proud,* and *strong*. The other factor, called *negative affect*, is defined by these adjectives: *afraid, ashamed, distressed, guilty, hostile, irritable, jittery, nervous, scared,* and *upset*. Notice that except for *ashamed* and *guilty*, the terms describing negative affect come close to describing the temperament of emotionality and its two differentiated traits, fear and anger.

In a study of psychiatric inpatients and outpatients, negative affectivity "was broadly correlated with symptoms and diagnoses of both anxiety and depression, confirming earlier findings that it is an important general correlate of psychiatric disorder" (Watson, Clark, & Carey, 1988, p. 351). Positive affect was negatively correlated with symptoms and diagnoses of depression. Thus depression includes both the presence of negative affect and the absence of positive affect, the latter distinguishing it from anxiety and other psychological disorders.

Positive affect correlates strongly .64 with activity, .49 with ascendance (social assertiveness), and .27 with sociability (Watson & Clark, in press). These three traits are regarded by these authors as major components in extraversion. We know that depressives are low in activity, are anything but ascendant, and tend to withdraw from others and from the world in general. It follows that they should be low in extraversion. Accordingly, a review of the literature led to the conclusion that introversion characterizes the premorbid personality of depressives (Akiskal, Hirschfeld, & Yerevanian, 1983).

A longitudinal study of adolescents yielded interesting links between personality and depression (Block, Gjerde, & Block, 1991). Subjects self-described as depressed at eighteen years of age had been observed when they were fourteen years old. The depressed girls earlier felt a lack of meaning in life, were concerned with personal adequacy, thought in unusual ways, and tended to be privately self-conscious. The depressed boys earlier were hostile toward others, distrustful, self-indulgent, power oriented, and negativistic. Evidently, potentially depressed girls turn inward and deprecate themselves, a pattern associated with low self-esteem (see Chapter 8). Potentially depressed boys, however, display a pattern not associated with low self-esteem: they are rebellious and self-indulgent.

Mania

Mania occupies the opposite pole from depression, and self-esteem is elevated. Manics have an elevated, expansive mood, for their confidence that they can accomplish anything reaches the level of grandiosity. They cannot stop talking and are unceasingly active. They are busy planning ambitious projects and attempting to carry them out. Their attention is focused entirely on the outside world, never on themselves.

TABLE 14.4   Personality Traits That Accompany Mood Disorders

Personality trait	Depression	Mania
Activity	Low	High
Self-Esteem	Low	High
Positive affect	Low	High
Private self-consciousness	High	Low
Extraversion-introversion	Introversion	Extraversion

Thus their symptoms are mirror images of those of depressives. Similarly, the personality traits that accompany mania and are part of its diagnosis are polar opposites of the personality traits of depressives. These traits are hyperactivity, enormous self-esteem, extremely high positive affect (see the above list of adjectives denoting positive affect), and low private self-consciousness. A review of the literature also found manics to be flaming extraverts (Akiskal et al., 1983). These various personality traits, together with those of depressives, are summarized in Table 14.4.

A Dynamic Approach to Personality Disorders

Millon played a major role in originating the personality disorder a part of the DSM III-R (APA, 1987). To account for these disorders with a dynamic personality approach, he outlined a theory with these assumptions (Millon, 1990):

1. People vary in the degree to which they seek pleasure versus avoid pain. They also differ in how sensitive they are to pain, which refers to psychological distress, especially anxiety.
2. People vary according to whether they focus on the self or others in seeking rewards and minimizing pain, as well as whether they regard the self and others positively or negatively.
3. People vary in modes of adaptation, of which there are three: active, passive, and dysfunctional.

Millon's approach to personality is dynamic in that it assumes threat, conflict, and psychological means (adaptation modes) of dealing with them. I have simplified his complex theory and divided the schemes into four sets.

Pleasure-Pain and Adaptation Modes

In the first set, Millon (1990) crosscut pleasure-pain with three adaptation modes: passive, active, and dysfunctional. These modes were used to explain schizoid, avoidant, and schizotypal personality disorders.

With respect to pleasure and pain, schizoids are entirely passive. They feel neither pleasure nor pain. They experience neither enjoyment nor discomfort and, as a result, display little or no affect.

Avoidants have little capacity for pleasure but are extraordinarily sensitive to pain and active when threatened with it. Like those who have been conditioned in a traumatic avoidance paradigm, they stay far away from anything associated with pain, especially social contact.

Schizotypals have a dysfunctional adaptation mode. They experience little or no pleasure and have trouble differentiating between active and passive modes of adaptation. "Depending on whether their pattern is basically more active or more passive, there will be either an anxious wariness and hypersensitivity or an emotional flattening and deficiency of affect" (Millon, 1990, p. 126).

Self-Other and Adaptation Modes

In these three schemes, self-other is crosscut with adaptation modes.

Self Plus, Other Minus

Those with narcissistic personality disorder are the prime example of this category. They rely completely on themselves to maximize pleasure, engaging in self-reward, whether or not anyone else rewards them. Not needing help from others, their adaptation mode is entirely passive. And they minimize pain by denying they ever fail or might have faults.

Antisocials also expect no rewards from anyone else, but their adaptation mode is active, and it takes two forms. First, they extract rewards from others and from society in general by means of aggression or cheating. Second, they seek to harm others for real or imagined pain that has been inflicted on them.

The adaptation mode of paranoids is dysfunctional in what Millon (1990) calls "a confused mix of *pain*-sensitivity and *self*-assertion" (p. 129). Unlike antisocials, who openly aggress against others, paranoids are more cognitive, developing hostile feelings and prejudices against a world they see as threatening and potentially painful.

Conflicted

Obsessive-compulsives tend to conform superficially, which masks an intense desire to rebel. Their conflict is between obtaining pleasure by rebelling and avoiding pain by knuckling under. The result is a chronic state of ambivalence, usually *not* accompanied by action, for their basic adaptation mode is passive.

Passive-aggressives also are conflicted, but their adaptation mode is active. Therefore, their ambivalence tilts toward action, and they rebel against those whom they see as more powerful, expressing their independence by stubbornness and negativism.

Personality Classification and Personality Disorders

The Big 5

The Big 5 superfactors have been related to the personality disorders by two separate teams of investigators (Costa & McCrae, 1990; Wiggins & Pincus, 1989). Both used the self-reports of normal subjects, and there were only slight variations in the measures of personality and personality disorders. For simplicity, I have converted their quantitative data (factor loadings or correlations) into the Big 5 labels. The Big 5 superfactors that describe each personality disorder are shown in Table 14.5. The table is divided into two main sections. In the top section both sets of researchers arrived at the same findings. In the bottom section there was partial overlap, and I shall mention here only those traits found in both studies.

Schizoids tend to be introverted, and histrionics extraverted. Avoidants are introverted and neurotic. Passive-aggressives are neurotic and not conscientious. Borderlines are neurotic. Antisocials are not agreeable. Narcissists are extraverted and not neurotic. Obsessive-compulsives are neurotic. Paranoids are not agreeable. Dependents are neurotic.

Concerning the last row in the table, there is no agreement between the studies on the personality traits of schizotypes, which is not surprising in light of my not listing any personality traits for them earlier. For all the other personality disorders, the two studies agree completely or partially, which is a testament to the value of the Big 5 in its application to personality disorders. One might wish there

TABLE 14.5   Personality Disorders and Big 5 Factors

	Big 5 factor	
Personality disorder	Wiggins & Pincus (1989)	Costa & McCrae (1990)
Studies completely overlap		
Schizoid	Introverted	Introverted
Histrionic	Extraverted	Extraverted
Avoidant	Introverted, neurotic	Introverted, neurotic
Passive-aggressive	Neurotic, not conscientious	Neurotic, not conscientious
Borderline	Neurotic	Neurotic
Studies partially overlap		
Antisocial	Not agreeable, extraverted, not neurotic	Not agreeable, not conscientious
Narcissistic	Extraverted, not neurotic, not agreeable	Extraverted, not neurotic
Obsessive-compulsive	Neurotic, conscientious	Neurotic
Paranoid	Not agreeable	Not agreeable, neurotic
Dependent	Neurotic, agreeable	Neurotic, introverted
No overlap		
Schizotypal	Open	Neurotic, introverted

were closer agreement for six of the personality disorders, but perhaps this convergence is as good as might be expected when the methods and quantitative analyses of the two studies are different.

Table 14.5 conveys one more set of facts: the superfactors that predominate among the personality disorders. For Wiggins and Pincus (1989) extraversion (or its opposite pole, introversion) appears five times, and neuroticism appears seven times out of a total of nineteen superfactors mentioned. For Costa and McCrae (1990) extraversion appears six times, and neuroticism appears eight times out of a total of eighteen superfactors mentioned. These numbers tell us that most of the personality disorders fall under the headings of extraversion and neuroticism. The other superfactors may be useful, though, to differentiate among diagnostic categories. Thus both passive-aggressives and borderlines are neurotic, but passive-aggressives are also not conscientious.

The Interpersonal Circumplex

The Wiggins (1979) circumplex has been used in several studies of personality and abnormal behavior on the assumption that the two are continuous: "The Interpersonal Circle is a conceptual representation of the domain of interpersonal behavior that depicts interpersonal variables as vectors in a two-dimensional circular space formed by the coordinates of dominance and love. Within that circular space, the vectors that emanate from the center of the circle are interpreted as continua of intensity ranging from the moderate and generally adaptive to the extreme and often maladaptive" (Wiggins, Phillips, & Trapnell, 1989, p. 303). Vector length refers to how extreme any segment of the circle is: for example, the aloof-introverted segment. These researchers correlated vector length with a self-report of mental health and found significant correlations, ranging from .41 to .69, for five segments of the circle. For these segments at least, there is continuity between personality and abnormality.

Wiggins and Pincus (1989) used the MMPI and adjective checklists as self-report measures of the personality disorders, and there were also adjective checklists that yielded placement of subjects within the interpersonal circle. This method led to the location of five personality disorders within the two-dimensional space of the circle. Pincus and Wiggins (1990) followed up with similar research, and the combined results are presented in Table 14.6.

It is instructive to compare the self-report findings in Table 14.6 with my conceptual application of personality traits to the personality disorders. The latter, constructed on the basis of the descriptions in the DSM III-R and before examining the research literature, may be found in Table 14.2. Schizoids, whom I characterize as extremely unsociable, are located in the aloof-introverted segment of the interpersonal circle. Avoidants, whom I suggest are shy and low in self-esteem, are located between in the aloof-introverted and unassured-submissive segments, which matches my description. Antisocials, whom I say are egocentric, impulsive, and aggressive, are located in the coldhearted segment. Histrionics, whom I describe in trait terms as impulsive, egocentric, and exhibitionistic, are located in

TABLE 14.6   **Personality Disorders and the Interpersonal Circumplex**

Personality disorder	Segment of the circle
Schizoid	Aloof-introverted
Avoidant	Aloof-introverted, unassured-submissive
Antisocial	Coldhearted
Histrionic	Gregarious-extraverted
Narcissistic	Arrogant-calculating
Paranoid	Coldhearted, arrogant-calculating
Dependent	Unassured-submissive, unassuming-ingenuous

the gregarious-extraverted segment. Narcissists, whom I see as egocentric and conceited, are located in the arrogant-calculating segment. Paranoids, whom I describe as hostile and high in public self-consciousness, are located between the coldhearted and arrogant-calculating segments. And dependents, whom I see as submissive, low in self-esteem, and insecurely attached, are located between the unassured-submissive and unassuming-ingenuous segments.

In both studies, but especially in Pincus and Wiggins (1990), a problem arose. When the MMPI was used to assess personality disorders, it yielded different locations within the circle for the personality disorders than did the use of adjective checklists. Clearly, we need to classify the personality disorders better if they are to be linked with personality traits or located within the interpersonal circle.

The problem may not lie in the method, however, but in the nature of the classification of the personality disorders. As we saw in the last chapter, a major problem with categorical classification is the issue of blends. Categorical classification assumes discontinuity among the categories, but blends deny discontinuity and instead suggest continuity. A decade ago, this prescient conclusion was offered:

> Dimensional models have the advantage of providing more flexible, specific, and comprehensive information, whereas categorical systems tend to be procrustean, lose information, and result in many classificatory dilemmas when patients fall at the boundaries of the categories. . . . In the absence of any clear boundaries between a normal, adaptive personality trait and a maladaptive, inflexible trait, or between the different constellations of maladaptive traits, a dimensional model is more consistent with the current research than a categorical model. (Widiger & Frances, 1985, p. 619)

Psychotherapy

Some psychotherapies focus exclusively on symptoms, whereas others are directed toward long-standing ways of dealing with problems. Regardless of differences in approach, however, therapists cannot ignore clients' personality. The relevance for psychotherapy of each of the dispositions discussed in the book will be treated in turn.

Temperaments

Emotionality

Emotionality, it will be recalled, differentiates into fear (discussed here) and anger (to be discussed shortly). Anxiety is such a frequent problem of clients that its importance for psychotherapy needs no further emphasis. But what some therapists may neglect are its various components: instrumental, affective, cognitive, and expressive. Some clients report intense anxiety, which they bottle up and do not reveal to others. They need to be encouraged to open up and reveal their feelings. Others are cognitively so sensitized to the least threats that they misinterpret neutral situations. Many people with panic attacks focus abnormally on normal bodily reactions and misinterpret them as signs of intense fear. Some phobic clients have "mastered" their fears by complete avoidance, and this instrumental component needs to be the focus of therapeutic attention. Therapists should also be aware that some components of anxiety may start improving, while others lag behind and need continued attention.

Activity

The low extreme of activity poses a problem for psychologists who are dealing with depressives, who tend to sit around and think black thoughts. In inpatient settings, they need to be forced to work or play (increased activity), which has two benefits. It keeps them occupied, preventing them from turning inward toward their dark feelings. And they may discover a rewarding activity, which would lighten their mood.

Sociability

Sociability is not an issue for psychotherapy unless there is a mismatch. The mismatch may occur in marriage, with the couple occupying opposite extremes of the sociability dimension. Both partners will need to be seen in therapy to attempt accommodation. Or the mismatch may occur between a person and a job. If attempts to deal with the work situation are impossible or are unsuccessful, the solution may lie in another line of work.

Impulsivity

Impulsivity and activity are the crucial issues in attention-deficit hyperactivity disorder. It may be difficult to achieve self-control of activity in youngsters. A likely alternative is to channel the excessive energy, ensuring that before school or during recess the youngster is given oppportunities to run around until tired. The problem of distractibility, the discipline component of impulsivity, requires training on focusing (here, as elsewhere in this section, I do not discuss drug therapy).

   The opposite end of the impulsivity dimension, obsessiveness, involves two related problems: excessive cognitions and insufficient action. For some clients, the focus must be on the cognitive side: the frequency of bothersome obsessions. For others, the focus must be on the instrumental side: their inability to make decisions, stalling so long before acting that opportunies are lost. It bears repeating that we need to attend specifically to which component of the problem is foremost, when treating maladjustment, and not just the overall problem.

Social Behavior

Attachment

People with problems of attachment are likely to seek therapy. Recall that those with an ambivalent attachment style desperately seek approval but are unsure whether they will receive it. They are likely to latch onto the therapist and beg for praise and affection. The therapist will need to keep reminding such clients of the professional nature of the relationship. Many sessions will be needed to establish the roots of the ambivalence and implications for current relationships. These clients are preoccupied with problems in relationships, and they must learn not to obsess about them and get on with making them work.

Those with a fearful attachment style are lonely and pessimistic about finding someone to love. They need to feel better about themselves, else they can never believe that anyone would find them worthwhile. Presumably, the negative feelings derive from parental rejection, which may have to be explored during the course of psychotherapy. But the basic problem is a lack of self-esteem, an issue that will be discussed shortly.

People with a detached attachment style rarely seek therapy, for they have made their peace with the absence of intimate relationships, and their self-esteem is good. The only time they might seek help is when there is a mismatch either in marriage or on the job. In marriage, the spouse might want a closer relationship, something that a detached person finds difficult. On the job, the detached person might be required to work closely with others, again a difficult task. Such mismatches pose a dilemma for the therapist. Should the detached client start dealing with close relationships, which might cause considerable distress? Or should the client realize that he or she cannot change the enduring pattern of detachment and may have to settle for environmental change, either in marriage or job?

Psychoanalytic and the neopsychoanalytic therapies that emphasize self and object relations may be appropriate for people with insecure attachment. In such therapies, the client develops a strong bond with the therapist, which Freudians call the *transference neurosis*. This bond is highly similar to a child-parent attachment, which means that it may serve as a way of dealing therapeutically with insecure attachment.

Aggression

If the presenting problem is aggression, the therapy depends on which component is at issue. If it is the instrumental component, verbal or physical attack on others, the client will almost certainly be a child or adolescent, and, typically, a male. An immediate goal of therapy is to distinguish between verbal attacks and physical aggression, the former allowed in therapy and the latter not. Then therapy will need to focus on pinpointing the rewards for aggressing, and teaching nonaggressive means of attaining them. It may not be too late for the client to discover the negative consequences of aggression to both the aggressor and the victim. And since the current environment usually encourages aggression or at least tolerates it, some environmental change may be needed.

If the major component is anger or hostility, the roots of the affect and cognitions need to be explored. Some clients are so inhibited that they bottle up these feelings and must find means of expressing them in socially acceptable ways. Others need to control their frequent temper outbursts or their verbalized hatred of others. Therapists walk a fine line between encouraging ventilation of feelings and allowing excessive emotional outbursts.

Dominance-Submission

Dominant people do not ask for therapy, but submissive people do. The preferred treatment, popularized in the last few decades, is assertiveness training. The clients, usually women, are taught first with the therapist and then in everyday situations to state opinions openly and firmly without attacking others. They learn the distinction between independence and rebellious negativism, and they slowly practice coping with others' attempts at domination. Finally, they are shown that their newfound assertiveness may pose problems for relationships in which they were previously submissive.

Self

Self-Esteem

Low self-esteem is pervasive among those who seek help, and, typically, there is a weak core and an unstable periphery of self-esteem. The core is unlikely to change, so the focus must be on the periphery. In Chapter 8, I discussed the various ways that those high and those low in self-esteem deal with everyday problems. That material is appropriate here.

The therapist might start with the question of whether a glass is half empty or half full. Those low in self-esteem, being pessimists, insist that it is half empty. They must be made aware that saying it is half full is just as realistic and much more satisfying. Everyone has good qualities and faults. They should concentrate on the glass being half full (one's good points), not half empty (one's faults).

A related issue involves comparison. Clients may already know about downward comparison. If so, they should be encouraged to continue focusing on those less fortunate than themselves, which can boost self-esteem. When they are confronted with a sibling or spouse whose performance is superior, they should practice self-esteem maintenance (Tesser, 1980). One option is to reduce the relevance of the particular performance; the other (less palatable) is to distance themselves from the sibling or spouse, at least temporarily. Either option nullifies any potential loss of self-esteem and, better yet, allows the client to bask in reflected glory (see Chapter 8).

Then there is the impact of mood on self-esteem. Clients should learn not to generalize about themselves when their mood is low, waiting instead until their mood is lighter before indulging in self-examination. Generalization is also a problem in reacting to failure: Those low in self-esteem assume that they are just no good at anything. They must be shown that after failure there are alternatives. One is to try harder; the other is abandoning the struggle, seeking other goals, and not looking back. At the same time, they can minimize the potential for failing by sticking to what they are good at.

Sooner or later, all of us suffer rejection, but to those low in self-esteem, it is devastating. They need to copy the mechanisms of those high in self-esteem. One is to deny that it is your fault or to assume that most of it is not your fault. Another is to understand, realistically, that mismatches in personality do occur, and no one is at fault.

As any therapist knows, none of these goals is easily accomplished, for clients with low self-esteem tend to have self-defeating ways of dealing with problems. Telling them to boost their self-esteem is like telling a person who is overweight to eat less. But when therapists deal with detailed and concrete issues like those just suggested, their clients often benefit.

Identity

The problem may be a weakness of personal identity, an issue that has come into prominence as many women struggle for equality. The sources of identity for many women have been social roles and relationships, to the detriment of a feeling of being special and even unique. And as women search for identity, men may be subsequently confused, as well.

In therapy the focus must be on the sources of personal identity. The client, often a woman, needs to be reminded of her special appearance, behavioral style, and character, features open to observation by others. Perhaps even more, she needs to concentrate on the private aspects of herself: bodily sensations, feelings, daydreams, particular memories, and gender identity (those features of womanhood that separate women from men).

Of course the problem may be an insufficiency of social identity, which often surfaces as existential anxiety. This issue may be especially poignant during what has been called the mid-life crisis, when individuals ponder the meaning of life. Typically, such people have accomplished some of their personal goals but have drifted away from religion, extended family, and, generally, their roots. They need to be reminded of these roots: family, ethnicity, and religion, all reference groups we are born into or which we spawn. Then there are the voluntary associations: fraternity or sorority, college alumni, special club (Elks or Shriners), and vocation.

All these various sources of social identity have existed before we are born and will continue after we die, so our membership means that we are part of something that is not mortal. To the extent that we can identify with these reference groups, death loses its sting. Perhaps the most crucial source of identity for most people is religion, whether or not religious identity is accompanied by a belief in life after death. Most clients suffering from existential identity have sufficient social sources available, though they might not be investing enough of themselves in these sources. They need to focus on them, participate in them, and perhaps even lose themselves in these larger identities, thereby defeating existential anxiety.

Self-Consciousness

High private self-consciousness may be maladaptive in that clients may obsess about all their problems. We saw earlier in this chapter the role of this kind of self-consciousness in depression and in Chapter 10 its role in alcoholism. Clients who excessively turn inward in this way may need to learn how to distract themselves by turning their attention outward toward the world.

High private self-consciousness is helpful in an uncovering therapy such as psychoanalysis. Clients who have thought long and hard about themselves are better able to recall events of childhood, better able to recall intense affects, and, generally, better able to disclose the important events of their lives. By the same token, those low in private self-consciousness are not good candidates for an uncovering therapy because they are unaccustomed to examining themselves. Before such a therapy makes any headway, these clients would need to be taught to introspect, not an easy task after decades of not doing so.

Shyness

Public self-consciousness was not mentioned just now because it is dealt with here under the heading of self-conscious shyness. Clients with this problem are easily embarrassed or feel uncomfortable when conspicuous. They might learn the stopgap technique of directing others' attention elsewhere, which at least temporarily allows the clients to relax and cope better in interpersonal situations. In the long run, however, they need to habituate to being the center of attention or being teased whenever that occurs. The appropriate therapy appears to be systematic desensitization involving gradually increasing conspicuousness and tolerance of teasing.

Anxious shyness is a more serious problem, sometimes intensifying to the extreme of social phobia. It requires the therapy used in any other kind of anxiety, with the complication that the fear is interpersonal. These shy clients expect rejection, for they tend to be low in self-esteem. Therefore, the therapy may require dealing with both self-esteem and social avoidance. Furthermore, it bears repeating that therapists must be aware of the instrumental, affective, and cognitive components of anxiety. Dealing with only one component may be insufficient. Finally, the social phobia may be just one aspect of a broader, more generalized anxiety, which means that nonsocial sources of fear may also need treatment.

References

Abramovitch, R., & Grusec, J. E. (1978). Peer imitation in a natural setting. *Child Development, 49,* 60–65.

Ackerson, L. (1943). Inferiority attitudes and their correlations among children examined in a behavior clinic. *Journal of Genetic Psychology, 62,* 85–96.

Adorno, T. W., Frenkel-Brunswik, E., Levinson, D. J., & Sanford, R. N. (1950). *The authoritarian personality.* New York: Harper & Row.

Agatstein, F. C., & Buchanan, D. B. (1984). Public and private self-consciousness and the recall of self-relevant information. *Personality and Social Psychology Bulletin, 10,* 314–325.

Ahlgren, A., & Johnson, D. W. (1979). Sex differences in cooperative and competitive attitudes from the 2nd through the 12th grades. *Developmental Psychology, 15,* 45–49.

Ainsworth, M. D. S. (1967). *Infancy in Uganda.* Baltimore: Johns Hopkins.

Ainsworth, M. D. S., Bell, S., & Stayton, D. (1971). Individual differences in strange situation behavior in one-year-olds. In H. R. Schaffer (Ed.), *The origins of human social relations.* London: Academic.

Ainsworth, M. D. S., Blehar, M. C., Waters, E., & Wall, S. (1978). *Patterns of attachment: A psychological study of the strange situation.* Hillsdale, NJ: Erlbaum.

Ainsworth, M. D. S., & Bowlby, J. (1991). An ethological approach to personality development. *American Psychologist, 46,* 333–341.

Akiskal, H. S., Hirschfeld, R. M. A., & Yerevanian, B. I. (1983). The relationship of personality to affective disorders. *Archives of General Psychiatry, 40,* 801–810.

Alexander, K. L., & Entwistle, D. S. (1988). Achievement in the first 2 years of school: Patterns and processes. *Monographs of the Society for Research in Child Development, 53* (1, Serial No. 218).

Allport, G. W. (1961). *Pattern and growth in personality.* New York: Holt, Rinehart & Winston.

Allport, G. W., & Odbert, H. S. (1936). Trait names: A psycho-lexical study. *Psychological Monographs, 47* (1, Whole No. 211).

Allport, G. W., & Ross, J. M. (1967). Personal religious orientation and prejudice. *Journal of Personality and Social Psychology, 5,* 432–443.

American Psychiatric Association. (1987). *Diagnostic and statistical manual of mental disorders* (3rd ed., rev.). Washington, DC: Author.

Amsterdam, B. (1972). Mirror self-image reactions before the age of two. *Developmental Psychology, 5,* 297–305.

Angyal, A. (1951). A theoretical model for personality study. *Journal of Personality, 20,* 131–142.

Apsler, R. (1975), Effects of embarrassment on behavior toward others. *Journal of Personality and Social Psychology, 32,* 145–153.

Archer, J. (1991). The influence of testosterone on human aggression. *British Journal of Psychology, 82,* 1–28.

Argyle, M. (1969). *Social interaction.* New York: Atherton.

Arkin, R. M. (1981). Self-presentational styles. In

J. T. Tedeschi (ed.), *Impression management theory and social psychological research* (pp. 311–333). New York: Academic.

Arkin, R. M., & Grove, T. (1990). Shyness, sociability and patterns of everyday affiliation. *Journal of Social and Personal Relationships, 7,* 273–281.

Aronfreed, J., & Reber, A. (1965). Internalized behavior suppression and the timing of social punishment. *Journal of Personality and Social Psychology, 1,* 3–16.

Aronson, E., & Mills, J. (1959). The effect of severity of initiation on liking for a group. *Journal of Abnormal and Social Psychology, 59,* 177–181.

Asendorpf, J. B. (1987). Videotape reconstruction of emotions and cognitions related to shyness. *Journal of Personality and Social Psychology, 53,* 542–549.

Asendorpf, J. B. (1989). Shyness as a final common pathway for two kinds of inhibition. *Journal of Personality and Social Psychology, 57,* 481–492.

Asendorpf, J. B. (1990). Development of inhibition during childhood: Evidence for situational specificity and a two-factor model. *Developmental Psychology, 26,* 721–730.

Asendorpf, J. B. (1991). Development of inhibited children's coping with unfamiliarity. *Child Development, 62,* 1460–1474.

Asendorpf, J. B. (1992). A Brunswikian approach to trait continuity: Application to shyness. *Journal of Personality, 60,* 53–77.

Asendorpf, J. B., & Meier, G. H. (1993). Personality effects on children's speech in everyday life: Sociability-mediated exposure and shyness-mediated reactivity to social situations. *Journal of Personality and Social Psychology, 64,* 1072–1083.

Aspinwall, L. G., & Taylor, S. E. (1993). Effects of social comparison direction, threat, and self-esteem on affect, self-evaluation, and expected success. *Journal of Personality and Social Psychology, 64,* 708–722.

Ax, A. (1953). The physiological differentiation between fear and anger in humans. *Psychosomatic Medicine, 15,* 433–442.

Bailey, M. J., & Pillard, R. C. (1991). A genetic study of male sexual orientation. *Archives of General Psychiatry, 48,* 1089–1096.

Bakan, D. (1966). *The duality of human existence: Isolation and communion in western man.* Boston: Beacon.

Baldwin, J. M. (1894). Bashfulness in children. *Educational Review, 8,* 434–441.

Bandura, A. (1965). Influence of models' reinforcement contingencies on the acquisition of imitative responses. *Journal of Personality and Social Psychology, 1,* 589–595.

Bandura, A. (1986). *Social foundations of thought and action.* Englewood Cliffs, NJ: Prentice-Hall.

Bandura, A., Ross, D., & Ross, A. D. (1963). Imitation of film-mediated aggressive models. *Journal of Abnormal and Social Psychology, 66,* 3–11.

Barefoot, J. C., Peterson, B. L., Dahlstrom, W. G., Siegler, I. C., Anderson, N. B., & Williams, R. B. (1991). Patterns of hostility and implications for health: Correlates of Cook-Medley scores in a national survey. *Health Psychology, 10,* 18–24.

Barkley, R. A. (1977). The effect of methylphenidate on various types of activity level and attention in hyperactive children. *Journal of Abnormal Child Psychology, 5,* 351–369.

Barnett, M. A., Howard, J. A., King, L. M., & Dino, G. A. (1980). Antecedents of empathy: Retrospective accounts of early socialization. *Personality and Social Psychology Bulletin, 6,* 361–365.

Barratt, E. S. (1965). Factor analysis of some psychometric measures of impulsiveness and anxiety. *Psychological Reports, 16,* 547–554.

Bartholomew, K. (1990). Avoidance of intimacy: An attachment perspective. *Journal of Social and Personal Relationships, 7,* 147–178.

Bartholomew, K., & Horowitz, L. M. (1991). Attachment styles among young adults. *Journal of Personality and Social Psychology, 61,* 226–244.

Bates, J. E. (1980). The concept of difficult temperament. *Merrill-Palmer Quarterly, 26,* 299–319.

Bates, J. E., Maslin, C. A., & Frankel, K. A. (1985). Attachment, security, mother-child interaction, and temperament as predictors of behavior-problem ratings at age three years. In I. Bretherton & E. Waters (Eds.), Growing points of attachment theory and research. *Monographs of the Society for Research In Child Development, 50,* 167–193.

Batson, C. D. (1976). Religion as prosocial: Agent or double agent? *Journal for the Scientific Study of Religion, 15,* 29–45.

Batson, C. D. (1987). Prosocial motivation: Is it ever truly altruistic? In L. Berkowitz (Ed.), *Advances in experimental social psychology* (vol. 20, pp. 65–122). New York: Academic.

Batson, C. D. (1991). *The altruism question: Toward a social-psychological answer.* Hillsdale, NJ: Erlbaum.

Batson, C. D., Batson, J. G., Griffitt, C. A., Barrientos, S., Brandt, J. R., Sprengelmeyer, P., & Bayley, M. J. (1989). Negative-state relief and the empathy-altruism hypothesis. *Journal of Personality and Social Psychology, 56,* 922–933.

Batson, C. D., Bolen, M. H., Cross, J. A., & Neuringer-Benefiel, H. E. (1986). Where is the altruism in the altruistic personality? *Journal of Personality and Social Psychology, 50,* 212–220.

Batson, C. D., Duncan, B. D., Ackerman, P., Buckley, T., & Birch, K. (1981). Is empathic emotion a source of altruistic motivation? *Journal of Personality and Social Psychology, 40,* 290–302.

Batson, C. D., Dyck, J. L., Brandt, J. R., Batson, J. G., Powell, A. L., McMaster, M. R., & Griffitt, C. (1988). Five studies testing two egoistic alternatives to the empathy-altruism hypothesis. *Journal of Personality and Social Psychology, 55,* 52–57.

Batson, C. D., Fultz, J., & Schoenrade, P. A. (1987). Distress and empathy: Two qualitatively distinct vicarious emotions with different motivational consequences. *Journal of Personality, 55,* 19–39.

Batson, C. D., & Gray, R. A. (1981). Religious orientation and helping behavior: Responding to one's own or to the victim's needs? *Journal of Personality and Social Psychology, 40,* 511–520.

Batson, C. D., Oleson, K. C., Weeks, J. L., Healy, S. P., Reeves, P. J., Jennings, P., & Brown, T. (1989). Religious prosocial motivation: Is it altruistic or egoistic? *Journal of Personality and Social Psychology, 57,* 873–884.

Batson, C. D., & Shaw, L. L. (1991). Evidence for altruism: Toward a pluralism of prosocial motives. *Psychological Inquiry, 2,* 107–122.

Battle, E., & Lacey, B. (1972). A context for hyperactivity over time. *Child Development, 43,* 757–773.

Baumeister, R. F. (1982). Self-esteem, self-presentation, and future interaction: A dilemma of reputation. *Journal of Personality, 50,* 29–46.

Baumeister, R. F. (1987). How the self became a problem: A psychological review of historical research. *Journal of Personality and Social Psychology, 52,* 163–176.

Baumeister, R. F., Heathertom, T. F., & Tice, D. M. (1993). When ego threats lead to self-regulation failure: Negative consequences of high self-esteem. *Journal of Personality and Social Psychology, 64,* 141–156.

Baumeister, R. F., & Tice, D. M. (1985). Self-esteem and responses to success and failure: Subsequent performance and intrinsic motivation. *Journal of Personality, 53,* 450–467.

Baumeister, R. F., Tice, D. M., & Hutton, D. G. (1989). Self-presentational motivations and personality differences in self-esteem. *Journal of Personality, 57,* 547–579.

Baumrind, D. (1971). Current patterns of parental authority. *Developmental Psychology Monographs, 4,* (1, Part 2).

Bell, R. Q. (1968). A reinterpretation of the direction of effects in studies of socialization. *Psychological Review, 75,* 81–95.

Bell, R. Q., & Harper, L. V. (1977). *Child effects on adults.* Hillsdale, NJ: Erlbaum.

Bem, D. J., & Allen, A. (1974). On predicting some of the people some of the time: The search for cross-situational consistencies in behavior. *Psychological Review, 81,* 506–520.

Berkowitz, L., & Rawlings, E. (1963). Effects of film violence on inhibitions against subsequent aggression. *Journal of Abnormal and Social Psychology, 66,* 405–412.

Berman, M., Gladue, B., & Taylor, S. (1993). The effects of hormones, Type A behavior pattern, and provocation on aggression in men. *Motivation and Emotion 17,* 125–138.

Bernstein, W. M., & Davis, M. H. (1982). Perspective-taking, self-consciousness, and accuracy in person perception. *Basic and Applied Social Psychology, 3,* 1–19.

Berscheid, E., & Walster, E. (1978). *Interpersonal attraction* (2nd ed.). Reading, MA: Addison-Wesley.

Bertenthal, B. I., & Fischer, K. W. (1978). Development of self-recognition in the infant. *Developmental Psychology, 14,* 44–50.

Berzonsky, M.D. (1992). Identity style and coping strategies. *Journal of Personality, 60,* 771–788.

Black, S. L., & Bevan, S. (1992). At the movies with Buss and Durkee: A natural experiment on film violence. *Aggressive Behavior, 18,* 37–45.

Blehar, M. C., Lieberman, A. F., & Ainsworth, M. D. S. (1977). Early face-to-face interaction and its relation to later infant-mother attachment. *Child Development, 48,* 182–194.

Block, J. H., & Block, J. (1979). The role of ego-control and ego-resiliency in the organization of behavior. In W. A. Collins (Ed.), *Minnesota Symposia on Child Psychology, 13.* Hillsdale, NJ: Erlbaum.

Block, J. J., Gjerde, P. F., & Block, J. H. (1991). Personality antecedents of depressive tendencies in 18-year-olds: A prospective study. *Journal of Personality and Social Psychology, 60,* 726–738.

Block, J., & Robins, R. W. (1993). A longitudinal study of consistency and change in self-esteem from early adolescence to early adulthood. *Child Development, 64,* 909–923.

Boldizar, J. P., Perry, D. G., & Perry, L. C. (1989). Outcome values and aggression. *Child Development, 60,* 571–579.

Botwin, M. D., & Buss, D. M. (1989). Structure of act-report data: Is the five-factor model of personality recaptured? *Journal of Personality and Social Psychology, 56,* 988–1001.

Bouchard, C., Tremblay, A., Leblanc, C., Lortie, G., Savard, R., & Theriault, G. (1983). A method to assess energy expenditure in children and adults. *American Journal of Clinical Nutrition, 37,* 461–467.

Bowlby, J. (1958). The nature of the child's tie to its mother. *International Journal of Psychoanalysis, 39,* 350–373.

Bowlby, J. (1967). Foreword. In M. D. S. Ainsworth, *Infancy in Uganda.* Baltimore: Johns Hopkins.

Bowlby, J. (1969). *Attachment and loss: Vol. 1. Attachment.* New York: Basic Books.

Bowlby, J. (1973). *Attachment and loss: Vol. 2. Separation.* New York: Basic Books.

Brennan, K. A., Shaver, P. R., & Tobey, A. E. (1991). Attachment styles, gender and parental problem drinking. *Journal of Social and Personal Relationships, 8,* 451–466.

Brewer, M. B. (1991). The social self: On being the same and different at the same time. *Personality and Social Psychology Bulletin, 17,* 475–482.

Bridges, K. M. B. (1931). *The social and emotional development of the preschool child.* London: Kegan Paul.

Bridges, K. M. B. (1932). Emotional development in early infancy. *Child Development, 2,* 324–341.

Briggs, S. R. (1988). Shyness: Introversion or neuroticism? *Journal of Research in Personality, 22,* 290–307.

Briggs, S. R. (1989). The optimal level of measurement of personality constructs. In D. M. Buss & N. Cantor (Eds.), *Personality psychology: Recent trends and emerging directions* (pp. 246–260). New York: Springer-Verlag.

Britt, T. W. (1993). Metatraits: Evidence relevant to the validity of the construct and its implications. *Journal of Personality and Social Psychology, 65,* 554–562.

Broberg, A., Lamb, M. E., & Hwang, P. (1990). Inhibition: Its stability and correlates in 16- to 40-month-old children. *Child Development, 61,* 1153–1163.

Brockner, J. (1979). Self-esteem, self-consciousness, and task performance: Replications, extensions, and possible explanations. *Journal of Personality and Social Psychology, 37,* 447–461.

Brockner, J., Derr, W. R., & Laing, W. N. (1987). Self-esteem and reactions to negative feedback: Toward greater generality. *Journal of Research in Personality, 21,* 318–333.

Brockner, J., & Lloyd, K. (1986). Self-esteem and likability: Separating fact from fantasy. *Journal of Research in Personality, 20,* 496–508.

Bronson, G. (1970). Fear of social novelty: Developmental patterns in males and females. *Developmental Psychology, 2,* 33–40.

Brown, J. D., & Mankowski, T. A. (1993). Self-esteem, mood, and self-evaluation: Changes in mood and the way you see you. *Journal of Personality and Social Psychology, 64,* 421–430.

Brown, J. D., & Smart, S. A. (1991). The self and social conduct: Linking self-presentations to social conduct. *Journal of Personality and Social Psychology, 60,* 368–375.

Bruch, M. A., Giordano, S., & Pearl, L. (1986). Differences between fearful and self-conscious shy subtypes in background and adjustment. *Journal of Research in Personality, 20,* 172–186.

Bruch, M. A., Gorsky, J. M., Collins, T. M., & Berger, P. A. (1989). Shyness and sociability reexamined: A multicomponent analysis. *Journal of Personality and Social Psychology, 57,* 904–915.

Buck, R., Parke, R. D., & Buck, M. (1970). Differences in the cardiac response to the environment in two types of stressful situations. *Psychonomic Science, 18,* 95–96.

Buss, A. H. (1961). *The psychology of aggression.* New York: Wiley.

Buss, A. H. (1962). Two anxiety factors in psychiatric patients. *Journal of Abnormal and Social Psychology, 65,* 426–427.

Buss, A. H. (1966a). The effect of harm on subsequent aggression. *Journal of Experimental Research in Personality, 1,* 249–255.

Buss, A. H. (1966b). Instrumentality of aggression, feedback, and frustration as determinants of physical aggression. *Journal of Personality and Social Psychology, 3,* 153–162.

Buss, A. H. (1971). Aggression pays. In J. Singer (Ed.), *The control of aggression and violence: Cognitive and physiological.* New York: Academic.

Buss, A. H. (1978). *Psychology—Behavior in Perspective.* New York: Wiley.

Buss, A. H. (1980). *Self-consciousness and social anxiety.* San Francisco: Freeman.

Buss, A. H. (1983). Social rewards and personality. *Journal of Personality and Social Psychology, 44,* 553–563.

Buss, A. H. (1985). Two kinds of shyness. In R. Schwarzer (Ed.), *Self-related cognitions in anxiety and motivation* (pp. 65–75). Hillsdale, NJ: Erlbaum.

Buss, A. H. (1986a). *Social behavior and personality.* Hillsdale, NJ: Erlbaum.

Buss, A. H. (1986b). A theory of shyness. In W. H. Jones, J. M. Cheek, & S. R. Briggs (Eds.), *Shyness* (pp. 39–46). New York: Plenum.

Buss, A. H. (1988). *Personality: Evolutionary heritage and human distinctiveness.* Hillsdale, NJ: Erlbaum.

Buss, A. H. (1992). [Ranking of group identification]. Unpublished data, University of Texas, Austin.

Buss, A. H., & Durkee, A. (1957). An inventory to assess different kinds of hostility. *Journal of Consulting Psychology, 21,* 343–348.

Buss, A. H., & Finn, S. E. (1987). Classification of personality traits. *Journal of Personality and Social Psychology, 52,* 432–444.

Buss, A. H., & Gerjuoy, H. (1957). The scaling of terms used to describe personality. *Journal of Consulting Psychology, 21,* 366–371.

Buss, A. H., Iscoe, I., & Buss, E. (1979). The development of embarrassment. *Journal of Psychology, 103,* 227–230.

Buss, A. H., & Perry, M. (1991). [Sources of self-esteem in men and women]. Unpublished data, University of Texas, Austin.

Buss, A. H., & Perry, M. (1992). The Aggression Questionnaire. *Journal of Personality and Social Psychology, 63,* 452–459.

Buss, A. H., & Plomin, R. (1975). *A temperament theory of personality development.* New York: Wiley-Interscience.

Buss, A. H., & Plomin, R. (1984). *Temperament: Early developing personality traits.* Hillsdale, NJ: Erlbaum.

Buss, A. H., Plomin, R., & Willerman L. (1973). The inheritance of temperaments. *Journal of Personality, 41,* 513–524.

Buss, A. H, & Portnoy, N. W. (1967). Pain tolerance and group identification. *Journal of Personality and Social Psychology, 6,* 106–108.

Buss, D. M. (1981). Sex differences in the evaluation and performance of dominant acts. *Journal of Personality and Social Psychology, 40,* 147–154.

Buss, D. M., Block, J. H., & Block, J. (1980). Preschool activity level: Personality correlates and developmental implications. *Child Development, 51,* 401–408.

Buss, D. M., & Craik, K. H. (1980). The frequency concept of disposition: Dominance and prototypically dominant acts. *Journal of Personality and Social Psychology, 48,* 379–392.

Buss, D. M., & Craik, K. H. (1983). The act frequency approach to personality. *Psychological Review, 90,* 105–126.

Buss, D. M., Larsen, R. J., Westen, D., & Semmelroth, J. (1992). Sex differences in jealousy: Evolution, physiology, and psychology. *Psychological Science, 3,* 251–255.

Buss, L. (1978). Does overpraise cause embarrassment? Unpublished research, University of Texas, Austin.

Bylsma, W. H., Luhtanen, R., & Rothbard, J. (1992). *Attachment style differences in domain-specific and global self-esteem.* Paper presented at the meetings of the Eastern Psychological Association, New York.

Byrne, D. (1961). The repression-sensitization scale: Rationale, reliability, and validity. *Journal of Personality, 29,* 334–349.

Byrne, D. (1972). *The attraction paradigm.* New York: Academic.

Byrne, D., Ervin, C. R., & Lamberth, J. (1970). Continuity between the experimental study of attraction and real-life computer dating. *Journal of Personality and Social Psychology, 16,* 157–165.

Campbell, H. (1896). Morbid shyness. *British Medical Journal, 2,* 805–807.

Campbell, J. D., & Fairey, P. J. (1985). Effects of self-esteem, hypothetical explanations, and verbalizations of future performance. *Journal of Personality and Social Psychology, 48,* 1097–1111.

Cannon, W. B. (1929). *Bodily changes in pain, hunger, fear, and rage.* New York: Appleton.

Canter, S. (1973). In G. Claridge, S. Canter, & W. I. Hume, (Eds.), *Personality difference and biological variations.* New York: Pergamon.

Carbonell, J. L. (1984). Sex roles and leadership revisited. *Journal of Applied Psychology, 69,* 44–49.

Carducci, B. J., & Webber, A. W. (1979). Shyness as a determinant of interpersonal distance. *Psychological Reports, 44,* 1075–1078.

Carlo, G., Eisenberg, N., Troyer, D., Switzer, G., & Speer, A. L. (1991). The altruistic personality: In what contexts is it apparent? *Journal of Personality and Social Psychology, 61,* 450–458.

Carpenter, C. J., & Huston-Stein, A. (1980). Activity structure and sex-typed behavior in preschool children. *Child Development, 51,* 862–872.

Carson, R. C. (1969). *Interaction concepts of personality.* Chicago: Aldine.

Carver, C. S. (1975). Physical aggression as a function of objective self-awareness and attitudes toward punishment. *Journal of Experimental Social Psychology, 11,* 410–519.

Carver, C. S. (1977). Self-awareness, perception of threat, and the expression of reactance through attitude change. *Journal of Personality, 45,* 501–512.

Carver, C. S., & Ganellin, R. J. (1983). Depression and components of self-punitiveness. *Journal of Abnormal Psychology, 92,* 330–337.

Carver, C. S., & Scheier, M. F. (1978). Self-focusing effects of dispositional self-consciousness, mirror presence, and audience presence. *Journal of Personality and Social Psychology, 36,* 324–332.

Carver, C. S., & Scheier, M. F. (1981a). *Attention and self-regulation: A control theory approach to human behavior.* New York: Springer-Verlag.

Carver, C. S., & Scheier, M. F. (1981b). Self-consciousness and reactance. *Journal of Research in Personality, 15,* 16–29.

Caspi, A., Elder, G. H., Jr., & Bem, D. J. (1988). Moving away from the world: Life-course patterns of shy children. *Developmental Psychology, 24,* 824–831.

Caspi, A., & Moffitt, T. E. (1991). Individual differences are accentuated during periods of social change: The sample case of girls at puberty. *Journal of Personality and Social Psychology, 61,* 157–168.

Cattell, R. B. (1943). The description of personality: Basic traits resolved into clusters. *Journal of Abnormal and Social Psychology, 38,* 476–506.

Cattell, R. B., & Eber, H. W. (1961). *The Sixteen Personality Factor Questionnaire* (3rd ed.). Champaign, IL: Institute for Personality Ability and Testing.

Chaplin, W. F. (1991). The next generation of moderator research in personality psychology. *Journal of Personality, 59,* 143–178.

Chaplin, W. F., & Goldberg, L. R. (1985). A failure to replicate the Bem and Allen study of individual differences in cross-situational consistency. *Journal of Personality and Social Psychology, 47,* 1074–1090.

Cheek, J. M. (1982). Aggregation, moderator variables, and the validity of personality tests: A peer-rating study. *Journal of Personality and Social Psychology, 43,* 1254–1269.

Cheek, J. M., & Briggs, S. R. (1982). Self-consciousness and aspects of identity. *Journal of Research in Personality, 16,* 401–408.

Cheek, J. M., & Buss, A. H. (1981). Shyness and sociability. *Journal of Personality and Social Psychology, 41*, 330–339.

Cheek, J. M., Carpentieri, A. M., Smith, T. G., Rierdan, J., & Koff, E. (1986). Adolescent shyness. In W. H. Jones, J. M. Cheek, & S. R. Briggs (Eds.), *Shyness* (pp. 105–115). New York: Plenum.

Cheek, J. M., & Melchior, L. A. (1990). Shyness, self-esteem, and self-consciousness. In H. Leitenberg (Ed.), *Handbook of social and evaluation anxiety* (pp. 47–82). New York: Plenum.

Chlopan, B. E., McClain, M. L., Carbonnell, J. L., & Hagen, R. L. (1985). Empathy: Review of available measures. *Journal of Personality and Social Psychology, 48*, 635–653.

Cialdini, R. B., Baumann, D. J., & Kenrick, D. T. (1981). Insights from sadness: A three-step model of the development of altruism as hedonism. *Developmental Review, 1*, 207–223.

Cialdini, R. B., Borden, R. J., Thorne, A., Walker, M. R., Freeman, S., & Sloan, L. R. (1976). Basking in reflected glory: Three (football) field studies. *Journal of Personality and Social Psychology, 34*, 366–375.

Cialdini, R. B., Darby, B. L., & Vincent, J. E. (1973). Transgression and altruism: A case for hedonism. *Journal of Experimental Social Psychology, 9*, 502–516.

Cialdini, R. B., & Kenrick, D. T. (1976). Altruism as hedonism: A social development perspective on the relationship of negative mood state and helping. *Journal of Personality and Social Psychology, 34*, 907–914.

Cialdini, R. B., Schaller, M., Houlihan, D., Arps, K., & Fulz, J. (1987). Empathy-based helping: Is it selflessly or selfishly motivated? *Journal of Personality and Social Psychology, 52*, 749–758.

Cicone, M. V., & Ruble, D. M. (1978). Beliefs about males. *Journal of Social Issues, 34*, 5–16.

Clarke-Stewart, K. A., Umeh, B. J., Snow, M. E., & Pederson, J. A. (1980). Development and prediction of children's sociability from 1 to 2½ years. *Developmental Psychology, 16*, 290–302.

Clary, E. G., & Miller, J. (1986). Socialization and situational influences on sustained altruism. *Child Development, 57*, 1358–1369.

Cline, W. B., Croft, R. G., & Courrier, S. (1973). Desensitization of children to violence. *Journal of Personality and Social Psychology, 27*, 450–458.

Cohen, D. J., Dibble, E., & Grawe, J. M. (1977). Fathers' and mothers' perceptions of children's personality. *Archives of General Psychiatry, 34*, 480–487.

Collan, D. P., & Buss, A. H. (1991). *Individual differences in motivation for privacy.* Unpublished manuscript, University of Texas, Austin.

Collins, N. L., & Read, S. J. (1990). Adult attachment, working models, and relationship quality in dating couples. *Journal of Personality and Social Psychology, 58*, 644–663.

Colman, N. M., & Oliver, K. R. (1978). Reactions to flattery as a function of self-esteem: Self-enhancement and cognitive consistency theories. *British Journal of Social and Clinical Psychology, 17*, 25–29.

Compte, I. A. (1851). *System of positive policy* (Vol. 1). London: Longmans, Green. (Republished 1875)

Comrey, A. L. (1965). Scales for measuring compulsion, hostility, neuroticism, and shyness. *Psychological Reports, 16*, 697–700.

Conley, J. J. (1985). Longitudinal stability of personality traits: A multitrait-multimethod, multioccasion analysis. *Journal of Personality and Social Psychology, 49*, 1266–1282.

Cooley, C. H. (1902). *Human nature and the social order.* New York: Charles Scribner's Sons.

Coopersmith, S. (1967). *The antecedents of self-esteem.* San Francisco: Freeman.

Costa, P. T., Jr., & McCrae, R. R. (1984). Personality as a life-long determinant of well-being. In C. Z. Malatesta & C. E. Izard (Eds.), *Emotion in adult development* (pp. 141–157). Beverly Hills: Sage.

Costa, P. T., Jr., & McCrae, R. R. (1990). Personality disorders and the five-factor model of personality. *Journal of Personality Disorders, 4*, 362–371.

Costa, P. T., Jr., McCrae, R. R. (1992). Four ways five factors are basic. *Personality and Individual Differences, 13*, 653–665.

Costa, P. T., Jr., McCrae, R. R., & Arenberg, D. (1980). Enduring dispositions in adult males. *Journal of Personality and Social Psychology, 38*, 793–800.

Costa, P. T., Jr., McCrae, R. R., & Dye, D. A. (1991).

Facet scales for Agreeableness and Conscientiousness: A revision of the NEO Personality Inventory. *Personality and Individual Differences, 12,* 887–898.

Crockenberg, S. (1981). Infant irritability, mother responsiveness, and social support influences on the security of infant-mother attachment. *Child Development, 52,* 857–865.

Cronbach, L. J. (1957). The two disciplines of scientific psychology. *American Psychologist, 12,* 671–684.

Dabbs, J. M., Frady, R. L., Carr, T. S., & Besch, N. F. (1987). Saliva testosterone and criminal violence in young prison inmates. *Psychosomatic Medicine, 49,* 174–182.

Darwin, C. R. (1873). *The expression of emotions in man and animals.* New York: Appleton (Philosophical Library, 1955).

Davies, M. F. (1984). Conceptual and empirical comparisons between self-consciousness and field-dependence-independence. *Perceptual and Motor Skills, 58,* 543–549.

Davis, D., Kasmer, J., & Holtgraves, T. (1982). *The relationship of private and public self-consciousness to the weights of attitudes and subjective norms as predictors of behavioral intentions.* Unpublished manuscript, University of Nevada, Reno.

Davis, M. H. (1983). Measuring individual differences in empathy. *Journal of Personality and Social Psychology, 44,* 113–126.

Deluty, R. H. (1985). Consistency of assertive, aggressive, and submissive behavior for children. *Journal of Personality and Social Psychology, 49,* 1054–1065.

Diamond, S. (1957). *Personality and temperament.* New York: Harper.

Dibble, E., & Cohen, D. J. (1974). Companion instruments for measuring children's competence and parental style. *Archives of General Psychiatry, 30,* 805–815.

Diener, E., & Larsen, R. J. (1984). Temporal stability and cross-situational consistency of affective, behavioral, and cognitive responses. *Journal of Personality and Social Psychology, 47,* 871–883.

Digman, J. M., & Inouye, J. (1986). Further specification of the five robust factors of personality. *Journal of Personality and Social Psychology, 50,* 116–123.

Digman, J. M., & Takemoto-Chock, N. K. (1981). Factors in the natural language of personality: Re-analysis, comparison, and interpretation of six major studies. *Multivariate Behavioral Research, 16,* 149–170.

DiPietro, J. A. (1981). Rough and tumble play: A function of gender. *Developmental Psychology, 17,* 50–58.

DiTommasso, E., & Spinner, B. (1993). The development and validation of the social and emotional loneliness scale for adults (SELSA). *Personality and Individual Differences, 14,* 127–134.

Dodge, K. A. (1983). Behavioral antecedents of peer social status. *Child Development, 54,* 1386–1399.

Dodge, K. A., & Somberg, D. R. (1987). Hostile attributional biases are exacerbated under conditions of threats to the self. *Child Development, 58,* 213–224.

Donahue, E. M., Robins, R. W., Roberts, B. W., & John, O. P. (1993). The divided self: Concurrent and longitudinal effects of psychological adjustment and social roles on self-concept differentiation. *Journal of Personality and Social Psychology, 64,* 834–846.

Dovidio, J. F., Allen, J. L., & Schoeder, D. A. (1990). Specificity of empathy-induced helping: Evidence of altruistic motivation. *Journal of Personality and Social Psychology, 59,* 249–260.

Dubin, E. R., & Dubin, R. (1963). The authority inception period in socialization. *Child Development, 34,* 885–898.

Duggan, E. S., & Brennan, K. A. (1994). Social avoidance and its relation to Bartholomew's adult attachment typology. *Journal of Social and Personal Relationships, 11.*

Duval, S., & Wicklund, R. A. (1972). *A theory of objective self-awareness.* New York: Academic.

Dweck, C. S., Davidson, W., Nelson. S., & Enna, B. (1978). Sex differences in learned helplessness: II The contingencies of evaluative feedback in the classroom and III. An experimental analysis. *Developmental Psychology, 14,* 268–276.

Dweck, C. S., & Leggett, E. L. (1988). A social-cognitive approach to motivation and personality. *Psychological Review, 95*, 256–273.

Dworkin, R. H., Burke, B. W., Maher, B. A., & Gottesman, I. I. (1976). A longitudinal study of the genetics of personality. *Journal of Personality and Social Psychology, 34*, 510–518.

Eagley, A. H. (1983). Gender and social influence. *American Psychologist, 38*, 971–981.

Eagly, A. H., & Crowley, M. (1986). Gender and helping behavior: A meta-analytic review. *Psychological Bulletin, 100*, 283–308.

Eagly, A. H., & Karau, S. J. (1991). Gender and the emergence of leaders: A meta-analysis. *Journal of Personality and Social Psychology, 60*, 685–710.

Eagley, A. H., & Steffen, V. J. (1986). Gender and aggressive behavior: A meta-analytic review of social psychological literature. *Psychological Bulletin, 100*, 309–330.

Easterbrooks, M. A., & Lamb, M. E. (1979). The relationship between quality of mother-infant attachment and infant competence in initial encounters with peers. *Child Development, 50*, 380–387.

Eaton, W. O. (1983). Measuring activity level with actometers: Reliability, validity, and arm length. *Child Development, 54*, 720–726.

Eaton. W. O., & Enns, L. R. (1986). Sex differences in human motor activity level. *Psychological Bulletin, 100*, 19–28.

Eaves, L. J., & Eysenck, H. J. (1975). The nature of extraversion: A genetical analysis. *Journal of Personality and Social Psychology, 32*, 102–112.

Edelmann, R. J. (1987). *The psychology of embarrassment*. London: Wiley.

Egeland, B., & Farber, E. (1984). Infant-mother attachment: Factors related to its development and changes over time. *Child Development, 55*, 753–771.

Ehlers, C. L., Rickler, K., & Hovey, J. E. (1980). A possible relationship between plasma testosterone and aggressive behavior in a female outpatient population. In M. Girges & L. G. Kiloh (Eds.) *Limbic epilepsy and the discontrol syndrome* (pp. 183–194). New York: Elsevier.

Ehrhardt, A. A. (1985). Gender differences: A biosocial perspective. In T. B. Sonderegger (Ed.), *Nebraska symposium on motivation, 1985.*

(pp. 39–57). Lincoln, NE: University of Nebraska.

Ehrhardt, A. A., Epstein, R., & Money, J. (1968). Fetal androgens and female gender identity in the early treatment of androgenital syndrome. *Johns Hopkins Medical Journal, 122*, 160–167.

Eisenberg, N., Fabes, R. A., Miller, P. A., Fulz, J., Shell, R., Mathy, R. M., & Reno, R. R. (1989). Relation of sympathy and personal distress to prosocial behavior: A multimethod study. *Journal of Personality and Social Psychology, 57*, 55–66.

Eisenberg, N., Fabes, R. A., Schaller, M., Miller, P., Carlo, G., Poulin, R., Shea, C., & Shell, R. (1991). Personality and socialization: Correlates of vicarious emotional responding. *Journal of Personality and Social Psychology, 61*, 459–470.

Eisenberg, N., & Giallanza, S. (1984). The relation of mode of prosocial behavior and other proprietary behaviors to dominance. *Child Study Journal, 14*, 115–121.

Eisenberg, N., & Lennon, R. (1983). Sex differences in empathy and related capacities. *Psychological Bulletin, 94*, 100–131.

Eisenberg, N., Lennon, R., & Roth, K. (1983). Prosocial development: A longitudinal study. *Developmental Psychology, 19*, 846–855.

Eisenberg, N., & Miller, P. A. (1987). The relationship of empathy to prosocial behavior. *Psychological Bulletin, 101*, 91–119.

Eisenberg, N., Miller, P. A., Shell, R., McNalley, S., & Shea, C. (1991). Prosocial development in adolescence: A longitudinal study. *Developmental Psychology, 27*, 849–857.

Eisenberg, N., Shell, R., Pasternack, J., Lennon, R., Beller, R., & Mathy, R. M. (1987). Prosocial development in middle childhood: A longitudinal study. *Developmental Psychology, 23*, 712–718.

Eisenberg-Berg, N., & Mussen, P. (1978). Empathy and moral development in adolescence. *Developmental Psychology, 14*, 185–186.

Ekman, P., & Friesen, W. V. (1971). Constants across cultures in the face and emotion. *Journal of Personality and Social Psychology, 17*, 124–129.

Ekman, P., Friesen, W. V., O'Sullivan, M., Chan. A., Diacoyanni-Tarlatzis, I., Krause, R., Le-Compte, W. A., Pitcairn, T., Ricci-Bitti, P. E.,

Scherer, K., & Tomita, M. (1987). Universals and cultural differences in judgements of facial expressions of emotion. *Journal of Personality and Social Psychology, 53*, 712–717.

Elizur, A. (1949). Content analysis of the Rorschach with regard to anxiety and hostility. *Journal of Projective Techniques, 13*, 247–284.

Elliott, E. S., & Dweck, C. S. (1988). Goals: An approach to motivation and achievement. *Journal of Personality and Social Psychology, 54*, 5–12.

Ellis, L. (1986). Evidence of neuroandrogenic etiology of sex roles from a combined analysis of human, nonhuman primate, and nonprimate mammalian studies. *Personality and Individual Differences, 7*, 519–552.

Ellis, R. J., & Holmes, J. G. (1982). Focus of attention and self-evaluation in social interaction. *Journal of Personality and Social Psychology, 43*, 67–77.

Ember, C. R. (1973). Feminine task assignment and the social behavior of boys. *Ethos, 1*, 424–439.

Emde, R. N., Plomin, R., Robinson, J., Corley, R., DeFries, J., Reznick, J. S., Campos, J., Kagan, J., & Zahn-Waxler, C. (1992). Temperament, emotion, and cognition at fourteen months: The MacArthur longitudinal twin study. *Child Development, 63*, 1437–1455.

Emmons, R. A., Diener, E., & Larsen, R. J. (1986). Choice and avoidance of everyday situations and affect congruence: Two models of reciprocal interaction. *Journal of Personality and Social Psychology, 51*, 815–826.

Endler, N. S., & Magnusson, D. (1976). *Interactional psychology and personality*. New York: Wiley.

Epstein, S. (1986). Does aggregation produce spuriously high estimates of behavior stability? *Journal of Personality and Social Psychology, 50*, 1199–1210.

Erikson, E. K. (1950). *Childhood and society*. New York: Norton.

Erikson, E. K. (1968). *Identity youth and crisis*. New York: Norton.

Erkut, S., Jaquette, D. S., & Staub, E. (1981). Moral judgment-situation interaction as a basis for predicting prosocial behavior. *Journal of Personality, 29*, 288–298.

Eron, L. D. (1982). Parent-child interaction, television violence, and aggression in children. *American Psychologist, 37*, 197–211.

Eron, L. D. (1987). The development of aggressive behavior from the perspective of a developing behaviorism. *American Psychologist, 42*, 435–442.

Eron, L. D., Walder, L. O., & Lefkowitz, M. M. (1971). *Learning of aggression in children*. Boston: Little, Brown.

Exline, R. V. (1971). Visual interaction: The glances of power and preference. In U. J. Arnold & M. M. Page (Eds.), *Nebraska symposium on motivation* (pp. 163–206). Lincoln, NE: University of Nebraska.

Exner, J. E. (1986). *The Rorschach: A comprehensive system. Vol. 1. Basic foundations*. (2nd ed.). New York: Wiley-Interscience.

Eysenck, H. J. (1947). *Dimensions of personality*. London: Routledge & Kegan Paul.

Eysenck, H. J. (1953). *The structure of human personality*. London: Routledge & Kegan Paul.

Eysenck, H. J., & Eysenck, M. W. (1985). *Personality and individual differences: A natural science approach*. New York: Plenum.

Eysenck, S. B. G., & Eysenck, H. J. (1963). On the dual nature of extraversion. *British Journal of Social and Clinical Psychology, 2*, 46–55.

Eysenck, S. B. G., & Eysenck, H. J. (1977). The place of impulsiveness in a dimensional system of personality description. *British Journal of Clinical and Social Psychology, 16*, 57–68.

Fabes, R. A., & Eisenberg, N. (1992). Young children's coping with interpersonal anger. *Child Development, 63*, 116–128.

Falconer, D. S. (1960). *Quantitative genetics*. New York: Ronald.

Farrell, A. D., Mariotto, M. J., Conger, A. J., Curran, J. P., & Wallander, J. L. (1979). Self-ratings and judges' ratings of heterosexual social anxiety and skill: A generalizability study. *Journal of Consulting and Clinical Psychology, 47*, 164–175.

Feeney, J. A., & Noller, P. (1990). Attachment style as a predictor of adult romantic relationships. *Journal of Personality and Social Psychology, 58*, 281–291.

Feeney, J. A., & Noller, P. (1991). Attachment style and verbal descriptions of romantic partners. *Journal of Social and Personal Relationships, 8*, 187–215.

Feiring, C., & Lewis, M. (1980). Temperament: Sex differences and stability in vigor, activity, and persistence in the first three years of life. *Journal of Genetic Psychology, 126,* 65–75.

Feldman, K. A., & Newcomb, T. M. (1969). *The impact of college on students.* San Francisco: Jossey-Bass.

Fenigstein, A. (1979). Self-consciousness, self-attention, and social interaction. *Journal of Personality and Social Psychology, 37,* 75–86.

Fenigstein, A. (1984). Self-consciousness and the overperception of the self as a target. *Journal of Personality and Social Psychology, 47,* 860–870.

Fenigstein, A., Scheier, M. F., & Buss, A. H. (1975). Public and private self-consciousness: Assessment and theory. *Journal of Consulting and Clinical Psychology, 43,* 522–527.

Fenigstein, A., & Vanable, P. A. (1992). Paranoia and self-consciousness. *Journal of Personality and Social Psychology, 62,* 129–138.

Ferster, C. B., & Skinner, B. F. (1957). *Schedules of reinforcement.* New York: Appleton-Century-Crofts.

Feshbach, N. D., & Roe, K. (1968). Empathy in six- and seven-year-olds. *Child Development, 39,* 133–145.

Festinger, L. (1954). A theory of social comparison processes. *Human Relations, 7,* 117–140.

Finn, S. (1988). The structure of masculinity-femininity self-ratings. Unpublished research, University of Texas, Austin.

Fischer, W. F. (1963). Sharing in preschool children as a function of amount and type of reinforcement. *Genetic Psychology Monographs, 68,* 215–245.

Fish, M., & Crockenberg, S. S. (1981). Correlates and antecedents of nine-month infant behavior and mother-infant interaction. *Infant Behavior and Development, 4,* 69–81.

Fiske, D. W. (1949). Consistency of the factorial structures of personality ratings from different sources. *Journal of Abnormal and Social Psychology, 44,* 329–334.

Flavell, J. (1968). *The development of role-taking and communications skills in children.* New York: Wiley.

Fleischer, R. A., & Chertkoff, J. M. (1986). Effects of dominance and sex on leader selection in dyadic work groups. *Journal of Personality and Social Psychology, 50,* 94–99.

Fleming, J. S., & Courtney, H. E. (1984). Dimensionality of self-esteem: II. Hierarchical facet model for revised measurement scales. *Journal of Personality and Social Psychology, 46,* 404–421.

Fleming, J. S., & Watts, W. A. (1980). The dimensionality of self-esteem: Some results for a college sample. *Journal of Personality and Social Psychology, 39,* 921–929.

Fox, N. A. (1989). The psychophysiological correlates of emotional reactivity during the first year of life. *Developmental Psychology, 25,* 364–372.

Fox, N. A., Kimmerly, N. L., & Schafer, W. D. (1991). Attachment to mother/attachment to father: A meta-analysis. *Child Development, 62,* 210–225.

Franzoi, S. L. (1983). Self-concept differences as a function of private self-consciousness and social anxiety. *Journal of Research in Personality, 17,* 275–287.

Freedman, D. G. (1971). An evolutionary approach to research on the life cycle. *Human Development, 14,* 97–99.

Freedman, M. B., Leary, T. F., Ossorio, A. G., & Coffey, H. S. (1951). The interpersonal dimension of personality. *Journal of Personality, 20,* 143–161.

Friedrich, L. K., & Stein, A. H. (1973). Aggressive and prosocial television programs and the natural behavior of preschool children. *Monographs of the Society for Child Development, 38* (Serial No. 151), 1–64.

Froming, W. J., Allen, L., & Jensen, R. (1985). Altruism, role-taking and self-awareness. *Child Development, 56,* 1223–1228.

Froming, W. J., & Carver, C. S. (1981). Divergent influences of private and public self-consciousness in a compliance paradigm. *Journal of Research in Personality, 15,* 159–171.

Fromm, E. (1941). *Escape from freedom.* New York: Rinehart.

Frone, M. R., & McFarlin, D. B. (1989). Chronic occupational stressors, self-focused attention, and well-being: Testing a cybernetic model of stress. *Journal of Applied Psychology, 74,* 876–883.

Fultz, J., Batson, C. D., Fortenbach, V. A., McCarthy,

P. M., & Varney, L. L. (1986). Social evaluation and the empathy-altruism hypothesis. *Journal of Personality and Social Psychology, 50,* 761–769.

Fultz, J., Schaller, M., & Cialdini, R. B. (1988). Three related but distinct vicarious affective responses to another's suffering. *Personality and Social Psychology Bulletin, 14,* 312–325.

Funder, D. C., & Colvin, R. (1991). Explorations in behavioral consistency: Properties of persons, situations, and behaviors. *Journal of Personality and Social Psychology, 60,* 773–794.

Funder, D. W., & Ozer, D. J. (1983). Behavior as a function of the situation. *Journal of Personality and Social Psychology, 44,* 107–112.

Funk, S. C., & Houston, B. K. (1987). A critical analysis of the hardiness scale's validity and utility. *Journal of Personality and Social Psychology, 53,* 572–578.

Gallaher, P. (1992). Individual differences in nonverbal behavior: Dimensions of style. *Journal of Personality and Social Psychology, 63,* 133–145.

Gallaher, P., & Buss, A. H. (1987). *Components of dominance.* Unpublished manuscript, University of Texas, Austin.

Gallup, G. G., Jr. (1970). Chimpanzees: Self-recognition. *Science, 167,* 86–87.

Gallup, G. G., Jr. (1977). Self-recognition in primates: A comparative approach to the bidirectional properties of consciousness. *American Psychologist, 32,* 329–338.

Garcia, S., Stinson, L., Ickes, W., Bissonette, V., & Briggs, S. R. (1991). Shyness and physical attractiveness in mixed-sex dyads. *Journal of Personality and Social Psychology, 61,* 35–49.

Garside, R. F. (1975). Dimensions of temperament in infants and school children. *Journal of Child Psychology and Psychiatry, 16,* 219–231.

Geen, R. G. (1968). Effects of frustration, attack, and prior training in aggressiveness upon aggressive behavior. *Journal of Personality and Social Psychology, 9,* 316–321.

Geen, R. G. (1981). Behavioral and physiological reactions to observed violence: Effects of prior exposure to aggressive stimuli. *Journal of Personality and Social Psychology, 40,* 868–875.

Gellert, E. (1961). Stability and fluctuation in the power relationships of young children. *Journal of Abnormal and Social Psychology, 62,* 8–15.

George, C., & Main, M. (1979). Social interactions of young abused childen: Approach, avoidance, and aggression. *Child Development, 50,* 306–318.

Ghodsian-Carpey, J., & Baker, L. A. (1987). Genetic and environmental influences on aggression. *Aggressive Behavior, 13,* 173–186.

Gibbons, F. X., Carver, C. S., Scheier, M. F., & Hormuth, S. E. (1979). Self-focused attention and the placebo effect: Fooling some of the people some of the time. *Journal of Experimental Social Psychology, 15,* 263–274.

Gibbons, F. X., & Gerrard, M. (1989). Effects of upward and downward social comparison on mood states. *Journal of Social and Clinical Psychology 8,* 14–31.

Gibbons, F. X., & McCoy, S. B. (1991). Self-esteem, similarity, and reactions to active versus passive downward comparison. *Journal of Personality and Social Psychology, 60,* 414–424.

Gibbons, F. X., Smith, T. W., Ingram, R. E., Pearce, K., Brehm, S. S., & Schroeder, D. J. (1985). Self-awareness and self-confrontation: Effects of self-focused attention on members of a clinical population. *Journal of Personality and Social Pscyhology, 48,* 662–675.

Gifford, R., & Gallagher, T. M. B. (1985). Sociability: Personality, social context, and physical setting. *Journal of Personality and Social Psychology, 48,* 1015–1023.

Goldberg, L. R. (1981). Language and individual differences: The search for universals in personality lexicons. In L. Wheeler (Ed.), *Review of Personality and Social Psychology,* (Vol. 2, pp. 141–165). Beverly Hills: Sage.

Goldberg, L. R. (1990). An alternative "description of personality": The Big-Five factor structure. *Journal of Personality and Social Psychology, 59,* 1216–1229.

Goldberg, L. R. (1993). The structure of phenotypic personality traits. *American Psychologist, 48,* 26–34.

Goodall, J. (1986). *The chimpanzees of Gombe.* Cambridge, MA: Harvard University.

Goodenough, F. L. (1930). Interrelationships in the behavior of young children. *Child Development, 1,* 29–47.

Gormly, J. (1983). Predicting behavior from personality trait scores. *Personality and Social Psychology Bulletin, 9,* 267–270.

Gormly, J., & Champagne, B. (1974). *Validity in personality trait ratings: A multicriteria approach.* Paper presented at the meetings of the Eastern Psychological Association, New York.

Gorsuch, R. L., & Cattell, R. B. (1967). Second stratum personality factors defined in the questionnaire realm by the 16PF. *Multivariate Behavioral Research, 2,* 211–214.

Gough, H. G. (1956). *California Psychological Inventory.* Palo Alto, CA: Consulting Psychologists Press.

Goy, R. W. (1978). Development of play and mounting behavior in female rhesus monkeys virilized prenatally with esters of testosterone or dihydrotestosterone. In D. J. Chivers & J. Herberts (Eds.), *Recent advances in primatology* (Vol. 1). New York: Academic.

Goy, R. W., & McEwen, B. S. (1980). *Sex differentiation of the brain.* Cambridge, MA: MIT.

Green, R. (1985). Gender identity in childhood and later orientation: Follow-up of 78 males. *American Journal of Psychiatry, 142,* 339–341.

Greenberg, J. (1983). Self-image versus impression-management in adherence to distributive justice standards. *Journal of Personality and Social Psychology, 44,* 5–19.

Greenberg, J., Solomon, S., Pyszczynski, T., Rosenblatt, A., Burling, J., Lyon, D., Simon, L., & Pinel, E. (1992). Why do people need self-esteem? Converging evidence that self-esteem serves an anxiety-buffering function. *Journal of Personality and Social Psychology, 63,* 913–922.

Greenberg, M. T., & Marvin, R. S. (1982). Reactions of preschool children to an adult stranger: A behavioral systems approach. *Child Development, 53,* 481–490.

Gross, E., & Stone, G. P. (1964). Embarrassment and the analysis of role requirements. *American Journal of Sociology, 70,* 1–15.

Grossman, K. E. (1990). The wider concept of attachment in cross-cultural research. *Human Development, 33,* 31–47.

Guilford, J. P. (1940). *An inventory of factors STDCR.* Beverly Hills: Sheridan Supply Co.

Guilford, J. P. (1959). *Personality.* New York: McGraw-Hill.

Guilford, J. P., & Guilford, R. B. (1934). An analysis of the factors in a typical test of introversion-extraversion. *Journal of Abnormal and Personality Psychology, 28,* 377–399.

Guilford, J. P., & Guilford, R. B. (1936). Personality factors S, E, and M and their measurement. *Journal of Psychology, 2,* 109–127.

Haas, R. G. (1984). Perspective taking and self-awareness: Drawing an *E* on your forehead. *Journal of Personality and Social Psychology, 46,* 788–798.

Haimes, E. (1987). "Now I know who I really am" : Identity change and redefinitions of the self in adoption. In T. Honess & K. Yardley (Eds.), *Self and identity* (pp. 359–371). London: Routledge & Kegan Paul.

Halberstadt, A. G., & Saitta, M. B. (1987). Gender nonverbal behavior and perceived dominance: A test of the theory. *Journal of Personality and Social Psychology, 53,* 257–272.

Hall, E. T. (1966). *The hidden dimension.* Garden City, NY: Doubleday.

Halverson, C. F., Jr., & Post-Gordon, J. C. (1983). *The measurement of open-field activity in children: A critical analysis.* Unpublished paper, University of Georgia.

Hamilton, D. (1971). A comparative study of five methods of assessing self-esteem, dominance, and dogmatism. *Educational and Psychology Measurement, 31,* 441–452.

Hamilton, W. D. (1964). The genetical evolution of social behavior. *Journal of Theoretical Biology, 7,* 1–52.

Hampton, R. O. (1927). Shyness. *Journal of Neurology and Psychopathology, 8,* 124–131.

Harlow, H. (1949). The formation of learning sets. *Psychological Review, 56,* 51–65.

Harlow, H. F., & Harlow, M. (1962). Social deprivation in monkeys. *Scientific American, 207,* 136–146.

Harlow, H. F., & Zimmerman, R. R. (1959). The development of affectional patterns in the infant monkey. *Science, 130,* 421–422.

Harris, D. B. (1957). A scale for measuring attitudes of social responsibility in children. *Journal of Abnormal and Social Psychology, 55,* 322–326.

Harrison, R. (1941). Personal tempo and the interrelationship of voluntary and maximal rates of movement. *Journal of General Psychology, 24,* 343–379.

Hart, D., Maloney, J., & Damon, W. (1987). The meaning and development of identity. In T. Honess & K. Yardley (Eds.), *Self and identity* (pp. 121–133). London: Routledge & Kegan Paul.

Harter, S. (1982). The Perceived Competence Scale for Children. *Child Development, 53,* 87–97.

Hazan, C., & Hutt, M. J. (1991). *From parents to peers: Transitions in attachment.* Unpublished manuscript, Cornell University.

Hazan, C., & Shaver, P. (1987). Romantic love conceptualized as an attachment process. *Journal of Personality and Social Psychology, 52,* 511–524.

Hazan, C., & Shaver, P. (1990). Love and work: An attachment-theoretical perspective. *Journal of Personality and Social Psychology, 59,* 270–280.

Hetherington, M. E., & Brackbill, Y. (1963). Etiology and covariation of obstinacy, orderliness, and parsimony in young children. *Child Development, 34,* 919–943.

Hirt, E. R., Zillman, D., Erickson, G. A., & Kennedy, C. (1992). Costs and benefits of allegiance: Changes in fans' self-ascribed competencies and team victory versus defeat. *Journal of Personality and Social Psychology, 63,* 724–738.

Hodgson, R., & Rachman, S. (1974). Desynchrony in measures of fear. *Behaviour Research and Therapy, 12,* 313–326.

Hoffman, M. L. (1977). Sex differences in empathy and related behaviors. *Psychological Bulletin, 40,* 712–722.

Hoffman, M. L. (1981). Is altruism part of human nature? *Journal of Personality and Social Psychology, 40,* 121–137.

Hofstee, W. K. B., de Raad, B., & Goldberg, L. R. (1992). Integration of the Big Five and circumplex approaches to trait structure. *Journal of Personality and Social Psychology, 63,* 146–163.

Hoge, D. R., & McCarthy, J. D. (1984). Influence of individual and group identity salience in the global self-esteem of youth. *Journal of Personality and Social Psychology, 47,* 403–414.

Holden, G. W. (1983). Avoiding conflict: Mothers as tacticians in the supermarket. *Child Development, 54,* 223–240.

Holter, H. (1970). *Sex roles and social structure.* Oslo: Universitetforlaget.

Horn, J. M., Plomin, R., & Rosenman, R. (1976). Heritability of personality traits in adult male twins. *Behavior Genetics, 6,* 17–30.

Huesmann, L. R., Eron, L. D., Klein, R., Brice, P., & Fischer, P. (1983). Mitigating the imitation of aggressive behavior by changing children's attitudes about media violence. *Journal of Personality and Social Psychology, 44,* 899–910.

Huesmann, L. R., Eron, L. D., Lefkowitz, M. M., & Walder, L. O. (1984). The stability of aggression over time and generations. *Child Development, 55,* 746–775.

Hull, J. G. (1981). A self-awareness model of the causes and effects of alcohol consumption. *Journal of Abnormal Psychology, 90,* 586–600.

Hull, J. G., Levinson, R. W., Young, R. D., & Sher, K. J. (1983). Self-awareness-reducing effects of alcohol consumption. *Journal of Personality and Social Psychology, 44,* 461–473.

Hull, J. G., Van Treuren, R. R., & Virnelli, S. (1987). Hardiness and health: A critique and alternative approach. *Journal of Personality and Social Psychology, 53,* 518–530.

Hull, J. G., & Young, R. D. (1983). Self-consciousness, self-esteem, success-failure as determinants of alcohol consumption in male social drinkers. *Journal of Personality and Social Psychology, 4,* 1097–1109.

Hull, J. G., Young, R. D., & Jouriles, E. (1986). Applications of the self-awareness model of alcohol consumption: Predicting patterns of use and abuse. *Journal of Personality and Social Psychology, 51,* 790–796.

Humphreys, A. P., & Smith, P. K. (1987). Rough and tumble, friendship, and dominance in school children: Evidence for continuity and change with age. *Child Development, 58,* 201–212.

Hutt, C. (1972). *Males and females.* Middlesex, England: Penguin.

Ingram, R. (1990). Self-focused attention in clinical disorders: Review and a conceptual model. *Psychological Bulletin, 107,* 156–176.

Ingram, R., & Smith, T. W. (1984). Depression and internal versus external focus of attention. *Cognitive Therapy and Research, 8,* 139–152.

Isabella, R. A., & Belsky, J. (1991). Interactional

synchrony and the origin of infant-mother attachment: A replication study. *Child Development, 62,* 373–382.

Izard, C. E., Porges, S. W., Simons, R. F., Haynes, O. M., Hyde, C., Parisi, M., & Cohen, B. (1991). Infant cardiac activity: Developmental changes and relations with attachment. *Developmental Psychology, 27,* 432–439.

Jackson, D. N. (1974). *Personality Research Form* (Rev. ed.). Port Huron, MI: Research Psychologists Press.

Jackson, D. N. (1984). *Personality Research Form Manual* (3rd ed.). Port Huron, MI: Research Psychologists Press.

James, W. (1890). *Principles of psychology.* New York: Holt.

Jensen, A. R. (1956). Aggression in fantasy and overt behavior. *Psychological Monographs, 71* (Whole No. 445).

John, O. P. (1989). Towards a taxonomy of personality descriptors. In D. M. Buss & N. Cantor (Eds.), *Personality psychology: Recent trends and emerging directions* (pp. 261–271). New York: Springer-Verlag.

Johnson, J. A. (1993). *Toward a consensual definition of the Big Five.* Paper presented at the meetings of the Eastern Psychological Association, Arlington, VA.

Johnson, J. A., & Ostendorf, F. (1993). Clarification of the five-factor model with the abridged Big Five dimensional circumplex. *Journal of Personality and Social Psychology, 65,* 563–576.

Jones, E. E., & Berglas, S. C. (1978). Control of attributions about the self through self-handicapping strategies: The appeal of alcohol and the role of underachievement. *Journal of Personality and Social Psychology, 4,* 200–206.

Jones, W. H., Briggs, S. R., & Smith, T. G. (1986). Shyness: Conceptualization and measurement. *Journal of Personality and Social Psychology, 51,* 629–639.

Josephs, R. A., Larrick, R. P., Steele, C. M., & Nisbett, R. E. (1992). Protecting the self from the negative consequences of risky decisions. *Journal of Personality and Social Psychology, 62,* 26–37.

Josephs, R. A., Markus, H. R., & Tafarodi, R. W. (1992). Gender and self-esteem. *Journal of Personality and Social Psychology, 63,* 391–402.

Josselson, R. (1988). The embedded self: I and thou revisited. In D. K. Lapsley & F. C. Power (Eds.), *Self-ego, and identity* (pp. 91–106). New York: Springer-Verlag.

Jung, C. G. (1923). *Psychological types.* London: Routledge & Kegan Paul.

Jung, C. G. (1933). *Psychological types.* New York: Harcourt.

Kagan, J. (1966). Developmental studies in reflection and analysis. In A. Kidd & J. Rivoire (Eds.), *Perceptual development in children.* New York: International Universities.

Kagan, J. (1971). *Change and continuity in infancy.* New York: Wiley.

Kagan, J., Reznick, J. S., Clarke, C., Snidman, N., & Garcia-Coll, C. (1984). Behavioral inhibition to the unfamiliar. *Child Development, 55,* 2212–2225.

Kagan, J., Reznick, J. S., & Snidman, N. (1987). The physiology and psychology of behavioral inhibition in children. *Child Development, 58,* 1459–1473.

Kagan, J., Reznick, J. S., Snidman, N., Gibbons, J., & Johnson, M. O. (1988). Childhood derivatives of inhibition and lack of inhibition to the unfamiliar. *Child Development, 59,* 1580–1589.

Kahle, L. R., Kulka, R. A., & Klingel, D. M. (1980). Low adolescent self-esteem leads to multiple interpersonal problems: A test of social adaptation theory. *Journal of Personality and Social Psychology, 39,* 496–502.

Kane, P. (1955). *Availability of hostile fantasy related to overt behavior.* Unpublished doctoral dissertation, University of Chicago.

Kenrick, D. T., Baumann, D. J., & Cialdini, R. B. (1976). A step in the socialization of altruism as hedonism: Effects of negative mood on children's generosity under public and private conditions. *Journal of Personality and Social Psychology, 37,* 747–755.

Kernis, M. H., Brockner, J., & Frankel, B. S. (1989). Self-esteem and reactions to failure: The mediating role of overgeneralization. *Journal of Personality and Social Psychology, 57,* 707–714.

Kernis, M. H., & Reis, H. T. (1984). Self-consciousness, self-awareness, and justice in reward allocation. *Journal of Personality, 52,* 58–70.

Kiesler, D. J. (1983). The 1982 Interpersonal Circle:

A taxonomy for complementarity in human transactions. *Psychological Review, 90,* 185–214.

Kingsbury, S. J. (1978). Self-esteem of victim and intent of third-party aggression in the reduction of hostile aggression. *Motivation and Emotion, 2,* 177–190.

Klesges, R. C., & McGinley, H. (1982). The interactive effects of typical and maximal measures on private and public self-consciousness. *Journal of Personality Assessment, 46,* 44–49.

Knudson, K. H. M., & Kagan, S. (1982). Differential development of empathy and prosocial behavior. *Journal of Genetic Psychology, 140,* 249–251.

Kobak, R. R., & Hazan, C. (1991). Attachment in marriage: Effects of security and accuracy of working models. *Journal of Personality and Social Psychology, 60,* 861–869.

Kobasa, S. C. (1979). Stressful life events, personality, and hardiness: An inquiry into hardiness. *Journal of Personality and Social Psychology 37,* 1–11.

Kochanska, G. (1991). Patterns of inhibition to the unfamiliar in children of normal and affectively ill mothers. *Child Development, 62,* 250–263.

Kochanska, G., & Radke-Yarrow, M. (1992). Inhibition in toddlerhood and the dynamics of the child's interaction with an unfamiliar peer age five. *Child Development, 63,* 325–335.

Koestner, R., Franz, C., & Weinberger, J. (1990). The family origins of empathic concern: A 26-year longitudinal study. *Journal of Personality and Social Psychology, 58,* 709–717.

Kohlberg, L. (1969). Stage and sequence: The cognitive-developmental approach to socialization. In D. A. Goslin (Ed.), *Handbook of socialization theory and research* (pp. 347–380). Chicago: Rand-McNally.

Korner, A. F., Hutchinson, C. A., Koperski, J. A., Kraemer, H. C., & Schneider, P. A. (1981). Stability of individual differences in neonatal motor and crying patterns. *Child Development, 52,* 83–90.

Krebs, D. L. (1975). Empathy and altruism. *Journal of Personality and Social Psychology, 32,* 1134–1136.

Kreuz, L. E., & Rose, R.M. (1972). Assessment of aggressive behavior and plasma testosterone in a young criminal population. *Psychosomatic Medicine, 34,* 321–332.

Krueger, R. F., & Caspi, A. (1993). Personality, arousal, and pleasure: A test of competing models of interpersonal attraction. *Personality and Individual Differences, 14,* 105–111.

Lang, P. J., & Lazovik, D. (1963). Experimental desensitization of a phobia. *Journal of Abnormal and Social Psychology, 66,* 519–525.

Langlois, J. H., & Downs, A. C. (1979). Peer relations as a function of physical attractiveness: The eye of the holder or behavioral reality? *Child Development, 50,* 409–418.

Langlois, J. H., Roggman, L. A., Casey, R. J., Rieser-Danner, L. A., & Jenkins, V. Y. (1987). Infant preferences for attractive faces: Remnants of a stereotype. *Developmental Psychology, 23,* 363–369.

Leary, T. (1957). *The interpersonal diagnosis of personality.* New York: Ronald.

Lei, H., & Skinner, H. A. (1982). What difference does language make? Structural analysis of the Personality Research Form. *Multivariate Behavioral Research, 5,* 209–216.

Lennon, R., Eisenberg, N., & Carroll, J. (1986). The relations between nonverbal indices of empathy and preschoolers' prosocial behavior. *Journal of Applied Developmental Psychology, 3,* 219–224.

Lewinsky, H. (1941). The nature of shyness. *British Journal of Psychology, 32,* 105–113.

Lewis, C. C. (1981). The effect of firm parental control: A reinterpretation of findings. *Psychological Bulletin, 90,* 547–563.

Lewis, M., & Feiring, C. (1989). Infant, mother, and infant-mother interaction and subsequent attachment. *Child Development, 60,* 831–837.

Lewis, M., Sullivan, M. W., Stanger, C., & Weiss, M. (1989). Self-development and self-conscious emotions. *Child Development, 60,* 146–156.

Lipton, E. L., & Steinschneider, A. (1964). Studies on the psychophysiology of infancy. *Merrill-Palmer Quarterly, 10,* 102–117.

Loehlin, J. C., & Nichols, R. C. (1976). *Heredity, environment, and personality.* Austin: University of Texas.

London, H., Schubert, D., & Washburn, D. (1972).

Increase of autonomic arousal by boredom. *Journal of Abnormal Psychology, 80,* 29–36.

London, P. (1970). The rescuers: Motivational hypotheses about Christians who saved Jews from the Nazis. In J. Macauley & L. Berkowitz (Eds.), *Altruism and helping behavior* (pp. 241–250). New York: Academic.

Lorr, M., & McNair, D. M. (1965). Expansion of the interpersonal behavior circle. *Journal of Personality and Social Psychology, 2,* 823–830.

Lorr, M., & More, W. W. (1980). Four dimensions of assertiveness. *Multivariate Personality Research, 15,* 127–138.

Lykken, D. T. (1982). Research with twins: The concept of emergenesis. *Psychophysiology, 19,* 361–373.

Lykken, D. T., McGue, M., Tellegen, A., & Bouchard, T. J. (1992). Emergenesis: Genetic traits that may not run in families. *American Psychologist, 27,* 1565–1577.

Maccoby, E. E., & Jacklin, C. N. (1974). *The psychology of sex differences.* Stanford: Stanford University.

Magnusson, D. (1971). An analysis of situational dimensions. *Perceptual and Motor Skills, 32,* 851–867.

Magnusson, D., & Hefler, B. (1969). The generality of behavioral data: III. Generalization potential as a function of the number of observation instances. *Multivariate Behavioral Research, 4,* 29–42.

Main, M., & Cassidy, J. (1988). Categories of response to reunion with the parent at age 6: Predictable from infant attachment classifications and stable over a 1-month period. *Developmental Psychology, 24,* 415–426.

Main, M., Kaplan, N., & Cassidy, J. (1985). Security in infancy, childhood, and adulthood: A move toward the level of representation. In I. Bretherton & E. Waters (Eds.), Growing points in attachment theory and research. *Monographs of the Society for Research on Child Development, 50,* 66–106.

Major, B., Carrington, P. L., & Carnevale, P. J. D. (1984). Physical attractiveness and self-esteem: Attributions for praise from an other-sex evaluator. *Personality and Social Psychology Bulletin, 10,* 43–50.

Maracek, J., & Mettee, D. R. (1972). Avoidance of continued success as a function of self-esteem, level of esteem certainty, and responsibility for success. *Journal of Personality and Social Psychology, 22,* 98–107.

Marcia, J. (1966). Development and validation of ego identity status. *Journal of Personality and Social Psychology, 35,* 551–558.

Marcia, J. (1987). The identity status approach to the study of ego development. In T. Honess & K. Yardley (Eds.), *Self and identity* (pp. 161–171). London: Routledge & Kegan Paul.

Markus, H. (1977). Self-schemata and processing information about the self. *Journal of Personality and Social Psychology, 35,* 63–78.

Marsh, H. W. (1986). Global self-esteem: Its relation to specific facets of the self-concept and their importance. *Journal of Personality and Social Psychology, 51,* 1224–1236.

Maslow, A. H. (1936). The role of dominance in the social and sexual behavior of infra-human primates. *Journal of Genetic Psychology, 48,* 261–277.

Maslow, A. H. (1937). Dominance feeling, behavior and status. *Psychological Review, 44,* 404–429.

Mason, W. A. (1970). Motivational factors in psychosocial development. In U. J. Arnold & M. M. Page (Eds.), *Nebraska Symposium on Motivation* (pp. 35–62). Lincoln, NE: University of Nebraska Press.

Matheny, A. P. (1980). Bayley's Infant Behavior Record: Behavioral components and twin analyses. *Child Development,* 51, 1157–1167.

Matheny, A. P., Jr. (1989). Children's behavioral inhibition over age and across situations: Genetic similarity for a trait during change. *Journal of Personality, 57,* 215–235.

Matheny, A. P., Wilson, R. S., & Dolan, A. B. (1976). Relation between twins' similarity of appearance and behavioral similarity: Testing an assumption. *Behavior Genetics, 6,* 343–352.

Mathes, E. W., & Kahn, A. (1975). Physical attractiveness, happiness, neuroticism, and self-esteem. *Journal of Psychology, 90,* 27–30.

Matthews, K. A., Batson, C. D., Horn, J., & Rosenman, R. H. (1981). "Principles in his natures which interest him in the fortunes of others . . .": The heritability of empathic concern. *Journal of Personality, 49,* 237–247.

Mavissakian, M., & Michelson, L. (1982). Psychophysiological pattern of change in the treatment of agoraphobia. *Behaviour Research and Therapy, 20,* 347–356.

McClelland, D. C. (1975). *Power: The inner experience.* New York: Irvington.

McCord, J. (1979). Some childrearing antecedents of criminal behavior. *Journal of Personality and Social Psychology, 37,* 1477–1486.

McCrae, R. R., & Costa, P. T., Jr. (1985). Updating Norman's "Adequate Taxonomy": Intelligence and personality dimensions in natural language and in questionnaires. *Journal of Personality and Social Psychology, 49,* 710–721.

McCrae, R. R., & Costa, P. T., Jr. (1987). Validation of the five-factor model across instruments and observers. *Journal of Personality and Social Psychology, 52,* 81–90.

McCrae, R. R., & Costa, P. T., Jr. (1989a). Reinterpreting the Myers-Briggs Type Indicator from the perspective of the Five-Factor model of personality. *Journal of Personality, 57,* 17–40.

McCrae, R. R., & Costa, P. T., Jr. (1989b). The structure of interpersonal traits: Wiggins' circumplex and the five-factor model. *Journal of Personality and Social Psychology, 56,* 586–595.

McCrae, R. R., & Costa, P. T., Jr. (1990). *Personality in adulthood.* New York: Guilford.

McDougall, W. (1908). *Introduction to social psychology.* London: Methuen.

McFarlin, D. B., & Blascovitch, J. (1981). Effects of self-esteem and performance feedback on future affective preferences and cognitive expectations. *Journal of Personality and Social Psychology, 40,* 521–531.

McGowan, J., & Gormly, J. (1976). Validation of personality traits: A multicriteria approach. *Journal of Personality and Social Psychology, 34,* 791–795.

McGue, M., Bacon, S., & Lykken, D. T. (1993). Personality stability and change in early adulthood: A behavior genetic analysis. *Developmental Psychology, 29,* 96–109.

McGuire, W. J., McGuire, C. W., Child, P., & Fujioka, T. (1978). Salience of ethnicity in the spontaneous self-concept as a function of one's own ethnic distinctiveness in the social environment. *Journal of Personality and Social Psychology, 36,* 511–520.

McKillop, K. J., Berzonsky, M. D., & Schlenker, B. R. (1992). The impact of self-presentations on self-beliefs: Effects of social identity and self-presentational context. *Journal of Personality, 60,* 789–808.

McNally, R. J. (1987). Preparedness and phobias. *Psychological Bulletin, 101,* 283–303.

Mead, G. H. (1934). *Mind, self and society.* Chicago: University of Chicago.

Megargee, E. I. (1969). The influence of sex roles in the manifestation of leadership. *Journal of Applied Psychology, 53,* 377–382.

Mehrabian, A., & Epstein, N. (1972). A measure of emotional empathy. *Journal of Personality, 40,* 525–543.

Meleshko, K. G. A., & Alden, L. E. (1993). Anxiety and self-disclosure: Toward a motivational model. *Journal of Personality and Social Psychology, 64,* 1000–1009.

Mengelsdorf, S., Gunnar, M., Kestenbaum, R., Lang, S., & Andrews, D. (1990). Infant proneness-to-distress temperament, maternal personality, and mother-infant attachment: Associations and goodness of fit. *Child Development, 61,* 820–831.

Mershon, B., & Gorsuch, R. L. (1988). Number of factors in the personality sphere: Does the increase in factors increase predictability of real-life criteria? *Journal of Personality and Social Psychology, 55,* 675–680.

Messer, S. B. (1976). Reflection-Impulsivity: A review. *Psychological Bulletin, 83,* 1026–1052.

Meyer, J. P., & Pepper, S. (1977). Need compatibility and marital adjustment in young married couples. *Journal of Personality and Social Psychology, 35,* 331–342.

Meyer-Bahlburg, H. F. L., Nat, R., Sharma, M., & Edwards, J. A. (1974). Aggressiveness and testosterone measure in man. *Psychosomatic Medicine, 36,* 269–274.

Mikulincer, M., Florian, V., & Weller, A. (1993). Attachment styles, coping strategies, and posttraumatic psychological distress: The impact of the Gulf War in Israel. *Journal of Personality and Social Psychology, 64,* 817–826.

Mikulincer, M., & Nachshon, O. (1991). Attachment styles and patterns of self-disclosure. *Journal of Personality and Social Psychology, 61,* 321–331.

Miller, L. C., & Cox, C. L. (1982). For appearances' sake: Public self-consciousness and makeup use. *Personality and Social Psychology Bulletin, 8,* 748–751.

Miller, R. S. (1991). *Empathic embarrassment: Situational and personal determinants of reactions to the embarrassment of another.* Unpublished manuscript, Houston State University, Huntsville, TX.

Miller, R. S. (1992). The nature and severity of self-reported embarrassing circumstances. *Personality and Social Psychology Bulletin, 18,* 190–198.

Millon, T. (1990). *Toward a new personology: An evolutionary model.* New York: Wiley.

Mineka, S., Davidson, M., Cook, M., & Keir, R. (1984). Observational conditioning of snake fear in rhesus monkeys. *Journal of Abnormal Psychology, 93,* 355–372.

Mischel, W. (1961). Preference for delayed reinforcement and social responsibility. *Journal of Abnormal and Social Psychology, 62,* 1–7.

Mischel, W. (1968). *Personality and assessment.* New York: Wiley.

Mischel, W. (1974). Processes in delay of gratification. In L. Berkowitz (Ed.), *Advances in experimental social psychology* (Vol. 7). New York: Academic.

Mischel, W., Ebbesen, E., & Zeiss, A. (1973). Selective attention to the self: Situational and dispositional determinants. *Journal of Personality and Social Psychology, 27,* 129–142.

Modigliani, A. (1968). Embarrassment and embarrassibility. *Sociometry, 3,* 313–326.

Moskowitz, D. S., & Schwarz, J. C. (1982). Validity comparison of behavior counts and ratings by knowledgeable informants. *Journal of Personality and Social Psychology, 42,* 518–528.

Mueller, J. H. (1982). Self-awareness and access to material rated as self-descriptive or nondescriptive. *Bulletin of the Psychonomic Society, 19,* 323–326.

Mullen, B., & Suls, J. (1982). "Know thyself": Stressful life changes and the ameliorative effect of private self-consciousness. *Journal of Experimental Social Psychology, 18,* 43–55.

Murray, H. A. (1938). *Explorations in personality.* New York: Oxford University.

Nasby, W. (1989). Private and public self-consciousness and articulation of the self-schema.

Journal of Personality and Social Psychology, 56, 117–123.

Norman, W. T. (1963). Toward an adequate taxonomy of personality attributes: Replicated factor structure in peer nomination personality ratings. *Journal of Abnormal and Social Psychology, 66,* 574–583.

Nyquist, L. V., & Spence, J. T. (1986). The effects of dispositional dominance and sex role expectations on leadership behaviors. *Journal of Personality and Social Psychology, 50,* 87–93.

O'Brien, M., & Huston, A. C. (1985). Activity level and sex-stereotyped toy choice in toddler boys and girls. *Journal of Genetic Psychology, 146,* 527–533.

Ohman, A. (1986). Face the beast and fear the face: Animal and social fears as prototypes of evolutionary analyses of emotions. *Psychophysiology, 23,* 123–145.

Olweus, D. (1978). *Aggression in the schools: Bullies and whipping boys.* Washington, D.C.: Hemisphere.

Olweus, D. (1979). Stability of aggressive reaction patterns in males: A review. *Psychological Bulletin, 86,* 852–875.

Olweus, D. (1980). Familial and temperamental determinants of aggressive behavior in adolescent boys: A causal analysis. *Developmental Psychology, 16,* 644–660.

Olweus, D. (1984). Aggressors and their victims: Bullying at school. In N. Frude & H. Gault (Eds.), *Disruptive behavior in the schools* (pp. 57–76). Washington, D.C.: Hemisphere.

Olweus, D., Mattson, A., Schalling, D., & Loow, H. (1980). Testosterone, aggression, physical and personality dimensions in normal adolescent males. *Psychosomatic Medicine, 42,* 253–269.

Omark, D. R., & Edelman, M. S. (1976). The development of attention structures in young children. In M. R. A. Chance & R. R. Larsen (Eds.), *The structure of social attention.* London: Wiley.

Ozer, D. (1986). *Consistency in personality.* New York: Springer-Verlag.

Parrott, W. G., & Smith, R. H. (1993). Distinguishing the experiences of envy and jealousy. *Journal of Personality and Social Psychology, 64,* 906–920.

Parten, M. B. (1933). Leadership among pre-school

children. *Journal of Abnormal and Social Psychology, 27,* 430–440.

Patterson, G. R. (1986). Performance models for aggressive boys. *American Psychologist, 41,* 432–444.

Patterson, G. R., Littman, R. A., & Bricker, W. (1967). Assertive behavior in children. *Monographs of the Society for Research in Child Development, 32,* (5, No. 113).

Paunonen, S. V. (1989). Consensus in personality judgments: Moderating effects of target-rater acquaintanceship and behavior observability. *Journal of Personality and Social Psychology, 56,* 823–833.

Pavlov, I. P. (1927). *Conditioned reflexes: An investigation of the physiological activity of the cerebral cortex* (G. V. Anrep, trans. and ed.). Oxford: Oxford University.

Peabody, D. (1984). Personality dimensions through trait inferences. *Journal of Personality and Social Psychology, 46,* 384–403.

Peabody, D., & Goldberg, L. R. (1989). Some determinants of factor structures from personality-trait descriptors. *Journal of Personality and Social Psychology, 57,* 552–567.

Pederson, D. R., Moran, G., Sitko, C., Campbell, K., Ghesquire, K., & Acton, H. (1990). Maternal sensitivity and the security of infant-mother attachment: A Q-sort study. *Child Development, 61,* 1974–1983.

Pederson, F. A., & Bell, R. Q. (1970). Sex differences in preschool children without histories of complications of pregnancy and delivery. *Developmental Psychology, 3,* 10–15.

Pedersen, N. L., Plomin, R., McClearn, G. E., & Friberg, L. (1988). Neuroticism, extraversion, and related traits in adult twins. *Journal of Personality and Social Psychology, 55,* 950–957.

Peevers, B. H. (1987). The self as observer of the self: A developmental analysis of the subjective self. In T. Honess & K. Yardley (Eds.), *Self and identity* (pp. 147–158). London: Routledge & Kegan Paul.

Pelham, B. W., & Swann, W. B., Jr. (1989). From self-conceptions to self-worth: On the sources and structure of global self-esteem. *Journal of Personality and Social Psychology, 57,* 672–680.

Perry, D. G., Kusel, S. J., & Perry, L. C. (1988). Victims of peer aggression. *Developmental Psychology, 24,* 807–814.

Perry, D. G., Perry, L. C., & Rasmussen, P. (1986). Cognitive social learning mediators of aggression. *Child Development, 57,* 700–711.

Perry, M., & Buss, A. H. (1990). [Trait and situational aspects of shyness]. Unpublished research, University of Texas, Austin.

Phinney, J. S. (1990). Ethnic identity in adolescents and adults: A review of research. *Psychological Bulletin, 108,* 499–514.

Piaget, J. (1962). *Play, dreams and imitation in childhood.* New York: Norton.

Pilkington, C. J., Tesser, A., & Stephens, D. (1991). Complementarity in romantic relationships: A self-evaluation maintenance perspective. *Journal of Social and Personal Relationships, 8,* 481–504.

Pincus, A. L., & Wiggins, J. S. (1990). Interpersonal problems and conceptions of personality disorders. *Journal of Personality Disorders, 4,* 342–352.

Pistole, M. C. (1989). Attachment and adult romantic relationships: Style of conflict resolution and relationship satisfaction. *Journal of Social and Personal Relationships, 6,* 505–510.

Plomin, R. (1974). *A temperament theory of personality development.* Unpublished doctoral dissertation, University of Texas, Austin.

Plomin, R., & Daniels, D. (1986). Genetics and shyness. In W. H. Jones, J. M. Cheek, & S. R. Briggs (Eds.), *Shyness* (pp. 63–80). New York: Plenum.

Plomin, R., & Daniels, D. (1987). Why are children in the same family so different from one another? *Behavioral and Brain Sciences, 10,* 1–60.

Plomin, R., DeFries, J. C., & Loehlin, J. C. (1977). Genotype-environment interaction and correlation in the analysis of human behavior. *Psychological Bulletin, 84,* 309–322.

Plomin, R., DeFries, J. C., & McClearn, G. E. (1980). *Behavior genetics: A primer.* San Francisco: Freeman.

Plomin, R., & Rowe, D. C. (1977). A twin study of temperament in young children. *The Journal of Psychology, 97,* 107–113.

Plomin, R., & Rowe, D. C. (1979). Genetic and

environmental etiology of social behavior in infancy. *Developmental Psychology, 15*, 62–72.

Pollak, S., & Gilligan, C. (1982). Images of violence in Thematic Apperception Test stories. *Journal of Personality and Social Psychology, 42*, 159–167.

Porterfield, A. L., Mayer, F. S., Dougherty, K. G., Kredich, K. G., Kronberg, M. M., Marsee, K. M., & Okazaki, Y. (1988). Private self-consciousness, canned laughter, and responses to humorous stimuli. *Journal of Research in Personality, 22*, 409–423.

Porteus, S. D. (1950). *The Porteus Maze Test of Intelligence.* Palo Alto, CA: Pacific Books.

Povinelli, D. J. (1993). Reconstructing the evolution of mind. *American Psychologist, 48*, 493–509.

Prince, M. (1906). *The dissociation of a personality.* New York: Longmans, Green.

Pryor, J. B., Gibbons, F. X., Wicklund, R. A., Fazio, R. H., & Hood, R. (1977). Self-focused attention and self-report validity. *Journal of Personality, 45*, 513–527.

Radke-Yarrow, M., Zahn-Waxler, C., & Chapman, M. (1983). Children's prosocial dispositions and behavior. In P. H. Mussen (Ed.), *Handbook of child psychology* (pp. 469–546). New York: Wiley.

Raskin, R., Novacek, J., & Hogan, R. (1991). Narcissistic self-esteem management. *Journal of Personality and Social Psychology, 60*, 911–918.

Ray, J. J. (1981). Authoritarianism, dominance, and assertiveness. *Journal of Personality Assessment, 45*, 390–397.

Reis, H. T., Senchak, M., & Solomon, B. (1985). Sex differences in the intimacy of social interaction: Further examination of potential explanations. *Journal of Personality and Social Psychology, 48*, 1204–1217.

Rethlingshafer, D. (1942). Relationship of tests of persistence to other measures of continuance of activities. *Journal of Abnormal and Social Psychology, 37*, 71–82.

Riesman, D. (1950). *The lonely crowd.* New Haven: Yale University.

Rogers, C. R. (1951). *Client-centered therapy.* Boston: Houghton Mifflin.

Rogoff, B., Sellers, J., Perrotta, S., Fox, N., & White, S. (1975). Age of assignment of roles and responsibilities in children. *Human Development, 18*, 353–369.

Rohner, R. P. (1976). Sex difference in aggression: Phylogenetic and enculturation perspectives. *Ethos, 4*, 57–72.

Romer, D., Gruder, C. L., & Lizzadro, T. (1986). A person-situation approach to altruistic behavior. *Journal of Personality and Social Psychology, 51*, 1001–1012.

Rose, R. J., Miller, J. Z., & Cardwell, G. F. (1981). Twin family studies of common fears and phobias. In L. Gedda, P. Parisi, & W. E. Nance (Eds.), *Twin research 3: Intelligence, personality, and development.* New York: A. R. Liss.

Rosen, G. M., & Ross, A. O. (1968). Relationship of body image to self-concept. *Journal of Consulting and Clinical Psychology, 32*, 100.

Rosenberg, M. (1965). *Society and the adolescent self-image.* Princeton: Princeton University.

Rowe, D. C., & Plomin, R. (1981). The importance of nonshared (E1) environmental influences in behavioral development. *Developmental Psychology, 17*, 517–531.

Royce, J. R., & McDermott, J. (1977). A multidimensional system dynamics model of affects, *Motivation and Emotion, 1*, 193–224.

Royce, J. R., & Powell, A. (1981). An overview of a multi-factor system theory of personality and individual differences: I. The factor and system models and the hierarchical factor structure of individuality. *The Journal of Personality and Social Psychology, 41*, 818–829.

Rubin, Z. (1970). Measurement of romantic love. *Journal of Personality and Social Psychology, 16*, 265–273.

Rushton, J. P., Chrisjohn, R. D., & Fekken, G. C. (1981). The altruistic personality and the self-report altruism scale. *Personality and Individual Differences, 2*, 293–302.

Rushton, J. P., Fulker, D. W., Neale, M. C., Nias, D. K. B., & Eysenck, H. J. (1986). Altruism and aggression: The heritability of individual differences. *Journal of Personality and Social Psychology, 50*, 1192–1198.

Russell, D., Peplau, L. A., & Cutrona, C. E. (1980). The revised UCLA loneliness scale: Concurrent and discriminant validity. *Journal of Personality and Social Psychology, 39*, 472–480.

Sadalla, E. K., Kenrick, D. T., & Vershure, B. (1987). Dominance and heterosexual attraction. *Journal of Personality and Social Psychology, 52,* 730–738.

Sagi, K. A. (1990). Attachment theory and research from a cross-cultural perspective. *Human Development, 33,* 10–22.

Sampson, E. E. (1988). The debate on individualism: Indigenous psychologies of the individual and their role in personal and social functioning. *American Psychologist, 43,* 15–22.

Sattler, J. M. (1965). A theoretical, developmental, and clinical investigation of embarrassment. *Clinical Psychology Monographs, 71,* 15–79.

Saucier, G. (1992). Benchmarks: Integrating affective and interpersonal circles with the big-five personality factors. *Journal of Personality and Social Psychology, 62,* 1025–1035.

Saudino, K. J., & Eaton, W. O. (1991). Infant temperament and genetics: An objective twin study of motor activity level. *Child Development, 62,* 1167–1174.

Savin-Williams, R. C. (1976). An ethological study of dominance formation and maintenance. *Child Development, 47,* 972–979.

Savin-Williams, R. C. (1979). Dominance hierarchies in groups of early adolescents. *Child Development, 50,* 923–935.

Savin-Williams, R. C. (1980a). Dominance and submission among early adolescent boys. In D. R. Omark, E. F. Strayer, & D. G. Freedman (Eds.), *Dominance relations: An ethological view of human conflict and social interaction* (pp. 217–229). New York: Garland.

Savin-Williams, R. C. (1980b). Social interactions of adolescent females in natural groups. In H. C. Foote, A. J. Chapman, & J. R. Smith (Eds.), *Friendship and social relations in children.* London: Wiley.

Scarr, S. (1966). Genetic factors in activity and motivation. *Child Development, 37,* 663–673.

Scarr, S. (1969). Social introversion as a heritable response. *Child Development, 40,* 823–832.

Scarr, S., & Carter-Saltzman, L. (1979). Twin method: Defense of a critical assumption. *Behavior Genetics, 9,* 527–542.

Scarr, S., & Grajek, S. (1982). Similarities and differences among siblings. In M. E. Lamb & B. Sutton-Smith (Eds.), *Sibling relationships: Their nature and significance across the lifespan* (pp. 357–381). Hillsdale, NJ: Erlbaum.

Scarr, S., & McCartney, K. (1983). How people make their own environments: A theory of genotype-environment correlations. *Child Development, 54,* 424–435.

Schachter, J. (1957). Pain, fear, and anger in hypertensives and normotensives. *Psychosomatic Medicine, 19,* 17–19.

Schachter, S. (1959). *The psychology of affiliation.* Stanford: Stanford University.

Schaefer, E., & Bayley, N. (1963). Maternal behavior, child behavior, and their intercorrelations from infancy through adolescence. *Monographs of the Society for Child Development, 28* (Whole No. 87).

Schaffer, H. R., & Emerson, P. E. (1964). The development of social attachment in infancy. *Society for Research in Child Development Monographs, 29* (No. 3).

Scheibel, M. E., & Scheibel, A. B. (1964). Some neural substrates of postnatal development. In M. L. Hoffman (Ed.), *Review of child development research.* New York: Russell Sage Foundation.

Scheier, M. F. (1976). Self-awareness, self-consciousness, and angry aggression. *Journal of Personality, 44,* 627–644.

Scheier, M. F. (1980). Effects of public and private self-consciousness on the public expression of personal beliefs. *Journal of Personality and Social Psychology, 39,* 514–521.

Scheier, M. F., Buss, A. H., & Buss, D. M. (1978). Self-consciousness, self-report of aggressiveness, and aggression. *Journal of Research in Personality, 12,* 133–140.

Scheier, M. F., & Carver, C. S. (1977). Self-focused attention and the experience of emotion: Attraction, repulsion, elation, and depression. *Journal of Personality and Social Psychology, 35,* 624–636.

Scheier, M. F., & Carver, C. S. (1980). Public and private self-attention, resistance to change, and dissonance reduction. *Journal of Personality and Social Psychology, 39,* 390–405.

Scheier, M. F., & Carver, C. S. (1985). Optimism, coping, and health: Assessment and implications of generalized outcome expectancies. *Health Psychology, 4,* 219–247.

Scheier, M. F., Carver, C. S., & Gibbons, F. X. (1979). Self-directed attention, awareness of bodily states, and suggestibility. *Journal of Personality and Social Psychology, 37*, 1576–1588.

Scheier, M. F., Carver, C. S., & Gibbons, F. X. (1981). Self-focused attention and reactions to fear. *Journal of Research in Personality, 15*, 1–15.

Scheier, M. F., Fenigstein, A., & Buss, A. H. (1974). Self-awareness and physical aggression. *Journal of Experimental Social Psychology, 10*, 264–282.

Schlenker, B. R., & Leary, M. R. (1982). Social anxiety and self-presentation: A conceptualization and a model. *Psychological Bulletin, 92*, 641–669.

Schlenker, B. R., & Weigold, M. F. (1990). Self-consciousness and self-presentation: Being autonomous and appearing autonomous. *Journal of Personality and Social Psychology, 59*, 820–828.

Schlenker, B. R., Weigold, M. F., & Hallam, J. R. (1990). Self-serving attributions in social contexts: Effects of self-esteem and social pressure. *Journal of Personality and Social Psychology, 58*, 855–863.

Schneider, K. S., & Rothbaum, F. (1993). Quality of parental caregiving and security of attachment. *Developmental Psychology, 29*, 358–367.

Schoenfeldt, L. F. (1968). The hereditary components of the Project Talent two-day test battery. *Measurement and Evaluation in Guidance, 1*, 130–140.

Schulman, A. H., Kaplowitz, C. (1977). Mirror-image response during the first two years of life. *Developmental Psychology, 10*, 133–142.

Schulman, J. L., & Reisman, J. M. (1959). An objective measure of hyperactivity. *American Journal of Mental Deficiency, 64*, 455–456.

Schwartz, S. H. (1975). The justice of need and the activation of humanitarian norms. *Journal of Social Issues, 31*, 111–136.

Sedikides, C. (1993). Assessment, enhancement, and verification determinants of the self-evaluation process. *Journal of Personality and Social Psychology, 65*, 317–338.

Seligman, M. E. P. (1970). On the generality of the laws of learning. *Psychological Review, 77*, 406–418.

Seligman, M. E. P. (1971). Phobias and preparedness. *Behaviour Therapy, 2*, 307–320.

Senchak, M., & Leonard, K. E. (1992). Attachment styles and marital adjustment among newlywed couples. *Journal of Social and Personal Relationships, 9*, 51–64.

Shantz, D. W. (1986). Conflict, aggression, and peer status. *Child Development, 57*, 1322–1332.

Shapiro, E. G. (1975). Effect of expectations of future interaction on reward allocation in dyads: Equity or equality. *Journal of Personality and Social Psychology, 31*, 873–880.

Shaver, P. R., & Brennan, K. A. (1992). Attachment styles and the "Big Five" personality traits: Their connections with each other and with romantic relationship outcomes. *Personality and Social Psychology Bulletin, 18*, 536–545.

Shipley, T. E., & Veroff, J. (1952). A projective measure of need for affiliation. *Journal of Experimental Psychology, 43*, 349–356.

Shrauger, J. S. (1975). Responses to evaluation as a function of initial self-perceptions. *Psychological Bulletin, 82*, 581–596.

Siegler, I. C., Zonderman, A. B., Barefoot, J. C., Williams, R. B., Jr., Costa, P. T., Jr., & McCrae, R. R. (1990). Predicting personality in adulthood from MMPI scores: Implications for follow-up studies in psychosomatic medicine. *Psychosomatic Medicine, 52*, 644–652.

Simmons, R. G. (1987). Self-esteem in adolescence. In T. Honess & K. Yardley (Eds.), *Self and Identity* (pp. 172–192). London: Routledge & Kegan Paul.

Simner, M. L. (1971). Newborn's response to the cry of another infant. *Developmental Psychology, 5*, 136–150.

Simpson, J. A. (1990). Influence of attachment styles on romantic relationships. *Journal of Personality and Social Psychology, 57*, 971–980.

Simpson, J. A., Rholes, W. S., & Nelligan, J. S. (1992). Support seeking and support giving within couples in an anxiety-provoking situation: The role of attachment styles. *Journal of Personality and Social Psychology, 62*, 434–446.

Sizemore, C. C., & Pittillo, E. (1977). *I'm Eve.* New York: Jove/HBC.

Sjostedt, E. M. (1955). *A study of the personality variables related to assaultive and acquisitive crimes.*

Unpublished doctoral dissertation, Purdue University.

Smith, A. (1976). *The theory of moral sentiments*. Indianapolis, IN: Liberty Classics. (Original work published 1759)

Smith, C., & Lloyd, B. (1978). Maternal behavior and perceived sex of infants: Revisited. *Child Development, 49*, 1263–1265.

Smith, J. D., & Shaffer, D. R. (1986). Self-consciousness, self-reported altruism, and helping behavior. *Social Behavior and Personality, 14*, 215–220.

Smith, P. K., & Sloboda, J. (1986). Individual consistency in infant-stranger encounters. *British Journal of Developmental Psychology, 4*, 83–91.

Smith, T. W. (1986). The polls: Gender attitudes toward violence. *Public Opinion Quarterly, 48*, 384–396.

Smith, T. W., & Greenberg, J. (1981). Depression and self-focused attention. *Motivation and Emotion, 5*, 323–331.

Smith, T. W., Ingram, R. E., & Roth, D. L. (1985). Self-focused attention and depression: Self-evaluation, affect, and life stress. *Motivation and Emotion, 9*, 381–389.

Smith, T. W., McGonigle, M., Turner, C. W., Ford, M. H., Slattery, M. L. (1991). Cynical hostility in adult male twins. *Psychosomatic Medicine, 53*, 684–692.

Snodgrass, S. E., & Rosenthal, R. (1984). Females in charge: Effect of sex of subordinate and romantic attachment status upon self-ratings of dominance. *Journal of Personality, 52*, 355–371.

Solomon, R. L., Kamen, L. J., & Wynne, L. C. (1953). Traumatic avoidance learning: The outcomes of several extinction procedures with dogs. *Journal of Abnormal and Social Psychology, 48*, 281–302.

Sorrentino, R., & Short, J. A. C. (1977). The case of the mysterious moderates: Why motives sometimes fail to predict behavior. *Journal of Personality and Social Psychology, 35*, 478–484.

Spence, J. T., & Helmreich, R. L. (1983). Achievement-related motives and behavior. In J. T. Spence (Ed.), *Achievement and achievement motives: Psychological and sociological approaches* (pp. 10–74). New York: Freeman.

Sroufe, L. A. (1979). Socioemotional development.

In J. D. Osofsky (Ed.), *Handbook of infant development*. New York: Wiley.

Sroufe, L. A. (1985). Attachment classification from the perspective of infant-caregiver relationships and infant temperament. *Child Development, 56*, 1–14.

Sroufe, L. A., Fox, N. E., & Pancake, V. R. (1983). Attachment and dependency in developmental perspective. *Child Development, 54*, 1615–1627.

Staub, E. (1978). *Positive social behavior and morality* (Vol. 1). New York: Academy.

Staub, E. (1979). *Positive social behavior and morality* (Vol. 2). New York: Academy.

Stone, H. (1956). The TAT aggressive content scale. *Journal of Projective Techniques, 20*, 445–442.

Stotland, E., Mathews, K. E., Sherman, S. E., Hanson, R. O., & Richardson, B. E. (1978). *Empathy, fantasy, and helping*. Beverly Hills: Sage.

Strayer, F. F., & Strayer, J. (1976). An ethological analysis of social agonism and dominance relations among preschool children. *Child Development, 47*, 980–989.

Strelau, J. (1983). *Temperament, personality, activity*. London: Academic.

Stricker, L. J., & Ross, J. (1964). An assessment of some structural properties of the Jungian personality typology. *Journal of Abnormal and Social Psychology, 68*, 62–71.

Susman, E. J., Inoff-Germaine, G., Nottelman, E. D., Loriaux, E. D., Cutler, G. B., Jr., & Chrousos, G. P. (1987). Hormones, emotional dispositions, and aggressive attributes in young adolescents. *Child Development, 58*, 1114–1134.

Swann, W. B., Jr. (1984). Quest for accuracy in person perception: A matter of pragmatics. *Psychological Review, 91*, 457–477.

Swann, W. B., Jr. (1987). Identity negotiation: Where two roads meet. *Journal of Personality and Social Psychology, 53*, 1038–1051.

Swann, W. B., Jr., Griffin, J. J., Jr., Predmore, S. C., & Gaines, B. (1987). The cognitive-affective crossfire: When self-consistency confronts self-enhancement. *Journal of Personality and Social Psychology, 52*, 881–889.

Swann, W. B., Jr., Stein-Seroussi, A., & Gieseler, R. (1992). Why people self-verify. *Journal of Personality and Social Psychology, 62*, 392–401.

Swann, W. B., Jr., Stein-Seroussi, A., & McNulty, S. E. (1992). Outcasts in a white-lie society: The enigmatic worlds of people with negative self-conceptions. *Journal of Personality and Social Psychology, 62*, 618–624.

Takahashi, K. (1990). Are the key assumptions of the "Strange Situation" procedure universal? *Human Development, 33*, 23–30.

Taylor, S. E., & Brown, J. (1988). Illusion and well-being: Some social psychological contributions to a theory of mental health. *Psychological Bulletin, 103*, 193–210.

Tellegen, A. (1985). Structures of mood and personality and their relevance to assessing anxiety, with an emphasis on self-report. In A. H. Tuma & J. D. Maser (Eds.), *Anxiety and the anxiety disorders* (pp. 681–706). Hillsdale, NJ: Erlbaum.

Tellegen, A., & Atkinson, G. (1974). Openness to absorbing and self-altering experiences ("absorption"), a trait related to hypnotic susceptibility. *Journal of Abnormal Psychology, 16*, 268–277.

Tellegen, A., Lykken, D. T., Bouchard, T. J., Wilcox, K. J., Segal, N. L., & Rich, S. (1988). Personality similarity in twins reared apart and together. *Journal of Personality and Social Psychology, 54*, 1031–1039.

Tennen, H., & Herzberger, S. (1987). Depression, self-esteem, and the absence of self-protective attributional biases. *Journal of Personality and Social Psychology, 52*, 72–80.

Tennov, D. (1979). *Love and limerence.* New York: Stein & Day.

Tesser, A. (1980). Self-esteem and family dynamics. *Journal of Personality and Social Psychology, 39*, 77–91.

Tesser, A. (1991). Emotions in social comparison and reflection processes. In J. Suls & T. A. Wills (Eds.), *Social comparison: Contemporary theory and research* (pp. 115–145). Hillsdale, NJ: Erlbaum.

Tesser, A., & Campbell, J. (1983). Self-evaluation maintenance and the perception of friends and strangers. *Journal of Personality, 50*, 261–279.

Tesser, A., Millar, M., & Moore, J. (1988). Some affective consequences of social comparison and reflection processes: The pain and plea-sure of being close. *Journal of Personality and Social Psychology, 54*, 49–61.

Thigpen, C. H., & Cleckley, H. (1954). A case of multiple personality. *Journal of Abnormal and Social Psychology, 49*, 135–151.

Thomas, A., Chess, S., & Birch, H. (1968). *Temperament and behavior disorders in children.* New York: New York University.

Thomas, A., Chess, S., Birch, H. G., Hertzig, M., & Korn, S. (1963). *Behavioral individuality in early childhood.* New York: New York University.

Thomas, M. H., Horton, R. W., Lippincott, E. C., & Drabman, R. S. (1977). Desensitization to portrayals of real-life aggression as a function of exposure to televised violence. *Journal of Personality and Social Psychology, 35*, 450–458.

Thompson, R. A., Connell, J. P., & Bridges, L. J. (1988). Temperament, emotion, and social interactive behavior in the strange situation. *Child Development, 59*, 1102–1110.

Thorne, A. (1987). The press of personality: A study of conversations between introverts and extraverts. *Journal of Personality and Social Psychology, 53*, 718–726.

Thornton, G. R. (1939). Factor analysis of tests designed to measure persistence. *Psychological Monographs, 1* (Whole No. 229).

Thurstone, L. L. (1934). The vectors of the mind. *Psychological Review, 41*, 1–32.

Tice, D. M. (1991). Esteem protection or enhancement? Self-handicapping motives and attributions differ by trait self-esteem. *Journal of Personality and Social Psychology, 60*, 711–725.

Titchener, E. (1909). *Elementary psychology of the thought processes.* New York: Macmillan.

Tobey, E. L., & Tunnell, G. (1981). Predicting our impressions on others: Effects of public self-consciousness and acting, a self-monitoring subscale. *Personality and Social Psychology Bulletin, 7*, 661–669.

Toi, M., & Batson, C. D. (1982). More evidence that empathy is a source of altruistic motivation. *Journal of Personality and Social Psychology, 43*, 281–292.

Torgersen, A. M., & Kringlen, E. (1978). Genetic aspects of temperamental differences in twins. *Journal of the American Academy of Child Psychiatry, 17*, 433–444.

Trapnell, P. D., & Wiggins, J. (1990). Extension of

the interpersonal adjective scales to include the Big Five dimensions of personality. *Journal of Personality and Social Psychology, 59,* 781–790.

Triandis, H. (1989). The self and social behavior in differing cultural contexts. *Psychological Review, 96,* 506–520.

Trimble, D. E. (1993). *Meta-analysis of altruism and intrinsic and extrinsic religiousness.* Paper presented at the meetings of the Eastern Psychological Association, Arlington, VA.

Trivers, R. L. (1971). The evolution of reciprocal altruism. *The Quarterly Review of Biology, 46,* 35–57.

Troy, M., & Sroufe, L. A. (1987). Victimization among preschoolers: Role of attachment. *Journal of the American Academy of Child and Adolescent Psychiatry, 26,* 166–172.

Tryon, C. McC. (1939). Evaluation of adolescent personality by adolescents. *Monographs of the Society for Research in Child Development, 4* (No. 4).

Tryon, W. W. (1984). Principles and methods of mechanically measuring motor activity. *Behavioral Assessment, 6,* 129–139.

Tupes, E. C., & Christal, R. E. (1992). Recurrent personality factors based on trait ratings. *Journal of Personality, 60,* 225–251.

Turner, R. G. (1978a). Consistency, self-consciousness, and the predictive validity of typical and maximal measures. *Journal of Research in Personality, 12,* 117–132.

Turner, R. G. (1978b). Effects of differential request procedures and self-consciousness on trait attributions. *Journal of Research in Personality, 12,* 431–438.

Turner, R. G. (1978c). Self-consciousness and speed of processing self-relevant information. *Personality and Social Psychology Bulletin, 4,* 456–460.

Turner, R. G. (1980). Self-consciousness and memory for trait names. *Personality and Social Psychology Bulletin, 6,* 273–277.

Turner, R. G., Gilliland, L., & Klein, H. M. (1981). Self-consciousness, evaluation of physical characteristics, and physical attractiveness. *Journal of Research in Personality, 15,* 182–190.

Turner, R. H. (1975). Is there a quest for identity? *The Sociological Quarterly, 16,* 148–161.

Turner, R. H. (1976). The real self: From institution to impulse. *American Journal of Sociology, 81,* 989–1016.

Ugurel-Semin, R. (1952). Moral behavior and moral judgment of children. *Journal of Abnormal and Social Psychology, 47,* 463–474.

Vandell, D. L., Owen, M. T., Wilson, K. S., & Henderson, V. K. (1988). Social development in infant twins: Peer and mother-child relationships. *Child Development, 59,* 168–177.

Vaughn B. E., Stevernson-Hinde, J., Waters, E., Kotsaftis, A., Lefever, G. B., Shouldice, A., Trudel, M., & Belsky, J. (1992). Attachment security and temperament in infancy and early childhood: Some conceptual clarifications. *Developmental Psychology, 28,* 463–473.

Veroff, J. (1957). Development and validation of a projective measure of power motivation. *Journal of Abnormal and Social Psychology, 54,* 1–8.

Walters, R. H., & Brown, M. (1963). Studies of reinforcement of aggression: III. Transfer of responses to an interpersonal situation. *Child Development, 34,* 563–571.

Watson, D., & Clark, L. A. (1992). On traits and temperament: General and specific factors of emotional experience and their relation to the five-factor model. *Journal of Personality 60,* 441–476.

Watson, D., Clark, L. A. (in press). Extraversion and its positive emotional core. In S. Briggs, R. Hogan, & W. Jones (Eds.), *Handbook of personality psychology.* San Diego: Academic.

Watson, D., Clark, L. A., & Carey, G. (1988). Positive and negative affectivity and their relation to anxiety and depressive disorders. *Journal of Abnormal Psychology, 97,* 346–353.

Watson, D., Clark, L. A., & Tellegen, A. (1988). Development and validation of brief measures of positive and negative affect. *Journal of Personality and Social Psychology, 54,* 1063–1070.

Watson, D., & Friend, R. (1969). Measurement of social-evaluative anxiety. *Journal of Clinical and Consulting Psychology, 33,* 448–457.

Weiner, B., & Kukla, A. (1970). An attributional analysis of achievement motivation. *Journal of Personality and Social Psychology, 15,* 1–20.

Weisenfield, A. R., Whitman, P. B., & Malatesta, C. Z. (1984). Individual differences among adult women in sensitivity to infants: Evidence for support of an empathy concept. *Journal of Personality and Social Psychology, 46,* 118–124.

Weisfeld, G. E., Omark, D. R., & Cronin, C. L. (1980). A longitudinal and cross-sectional study of dominance in boys. In D. R. Omark, E. F. Strayer, & D. G. Freedman (Eds.), *Dominance relations: An ethological view of human conflict and social interaction* (pp. 205–216). New York: Garland.

Weiss, R. S. (1973). *Loneliness: The experience of emotional and social isolation.* Cambridge, MA: MIT.

Wellems, R. W., Malina, R. M. M., & Buss, A. H. (1990). Activity as a temperamental trait: Relationship to physique and energy expenditure in young adults. In G. Beunen, J. Ghesquire, T. Reybrouchk, & A. L. Claessens (Eds.), *Children and exercise* (pp. 170–176). Stuttgart, Germany: Ferdinand Enke Verlag.

Wells, L. E., & Marwell, G. (1976). *Self-esteem: Its conceptualization and measurement.* Beverly Hills: Sage.

Werry, J. S., & Sprague, R. L. (1970). Hyperactivity. In C. G. Costello (Ed.), *Symptoms of psychopathology: A handbook.* New York: Wiley.

Wheeler, L., & Miyake, K. (1992). Social comparison in everyday life. *Journal of Personality and Social Psychology, 62,* 760–773.

White, R. W. (1959). Motivation reconsidered: The concept of competence. *Psychological Review, 66,* 297–333.

Whiting, B., & Edwards, C. P. (1973). A cross-cultural analysis of sex differences in the behavior of children aged 3 through 11. *Journal of Social Psychology, 91,* 171–188.

Widiger, T. A., & Frances, A. (1985). The DSM-III personality disorders: Perspectives from psychology. *Archives of General Psychiatry, 42,* 615–623.

Wiegman, O., Kuttschreuter, M., & Baarda, B. (1992). A longitudinal study of the effects of television viewing on aggression and prosocial behavior. *British Journal of Social Psychology 31,* 147–164.

Wiggins, J. (1979). A psychological taxonomy of trait-descriptive terms: The interpersonal domain. *Journal of Personality and Social Psychology, 37,* 395–412.

Wiggins, J., & Broughton, R. (1985). The Interpersonal Circle: A structural model for the integration of personality research. In R. Hogan & W. H. Jones (Eds.), *Perspectives in personality: Theory, measurement and interpersonal dynamics* (vol. 1, pp. 1–47). Greenwich, CT: JAI.

Wiggins, J., Phillips, N., & Trapnell, P. (1989). Circular reasoning about interpersonal behavior: Evidence concerning some untested assumptions underlying diagnostic classification. *Journal of Personality and Social Psychology, 56,* 296–305.

Wiggins, J. S., & Pincus, A. L. (1989). Conceptions of personality disorders and dimensions of personality. *Psychological Assessment, 1,* 305–316.

Williams, H. M. (1935). A factor analysis of Berne's "Social behavior patterns in young children." *Journal of Experimental Education, 4,* 142–146.

Wills, T. A. (1981). Downward comparison principles in social psychology. *Psychological Bulletin, 90,* 245–271.

Wilson, E. O. (1975). *Sociobiology: The new synthesis.* Cambridge, MA: Harvard University.

Wilson, E. O. (1978). *On human nature.* Cambridge, MA: Harvard University.

Winter, D. G. (1973). *The power motive.* New York: Free.

Witkin, H. A., Dyk, R. B., Faterson, H. F., Goodenough, D. R., & Karp, S. (1962). *Psychological differentiation.* New York: Wiley.

Wolpe. J., & Lang, P. J. (1964). A Fear Survey Schedule for use in behaviour therapy. *Behaviour Research and Therapy, 2,* 27–30.

Wong, M. M., & Csikszentmihalyi, M. (1991). Affiliation motivation and daily experience: Some issues on gender differences. *Journal of Personality and Social Psychology, 60,* 154–164.

Woodall, K. L., & Matthews, K. A. (1993). Changes in and stability of hostile characteristics: Results from a 4-year longitudinal study of children. *Journal of Personality and Social Psychology, 64,* 491–499.

Wrong, D. H. (1979). *Power.* New York: Harper & Row.

Wylie, R. (1974, 1979). *The self-concept.* Vols. 1 and 2. Lincoln, NE: University of Nebraska Press.

Wymer, W. E., & Penner, L. A. (1985). Moderator variables and different types of predictability: Do you have a match? *Journal of Personality and Social Psychology, 49,* 1002–1015.

Yerkes, R. M. (1943). *Chimpanzees.* New Haven: Yale University.

Youngblade, L. M., & Belsky, J. (1992). Parent-child antecedents of 5-year-olds' close friendships: A longitudinal analysis. *Developmental Psychology, 28,* 700–713.

Zajonc, R. B. (1965). Social facilitation. *Science, 149,* 269–274.

Zeldin, R. S., Small, S. A., & Savin-Williams, R. C. (1982). Prosocial interactions in two mixed-sex adolescent groups. *Child Development, 53,* 1192–1198.

Zimbardo, P. G. (1977). *Shyness.* Reading MA: Addison-Wesley.

Zuckerman, M. (1975). Belief in a just world and altruism. *Journal of Personality and Social Psychology. 31,* 972–976.

Zuckerman, M., Bernieri, F., Koestner, R., & Rosenthal, R. (1989). To predict some of the people some of the time: In search of moderators. *Journal of Personality and Social Psychology, 57,* 279–293.

Zuckerman, M., Koestner, R., DeBoy, T., Garcia, T., Maresca, B. C., & Sartoris, J. M. (1988). To predict some of the people some of the time: A reexamination of the moderator approach in personality theory. *Journal of Personality and Social Psychology, 54,* 1006–1019.

Zuckerman, M., Kuhlman, D. M., & Camac, C. (1988). What lies beyond E and N? Factor analyses of scales believed to measure basic dimensions of personality. *Journal of Personality and Social Psychology, 54,* 96–107.

Name Index

Subject Index